In search of belonging

Reflections by transracially adopted people

In search of belonging

Reflections by transracially adopted people

Edited by Perlita Harris

BAAF
ADOPTION
& FOSTERING

Published by
British Association for Adoption
& Fostering
BAAF
Saffron House
6–10 Kirby Street
London EC1N 8TS
www.baaf.org.uk

Charity registration 275689

British Library Cataloguing in Publication Data
A catalogue record for this book is available from the British Library

ISBN 1 903699 77 0

Editorial project management by Miranda Davies
Photographs (cover) provided by Laura Fish, Li-Da Kruger, Bella Frey and Perlita Harris

Designed by Andrew Haig & Associates
Typeset by Avon DataSet Ltd, Bidford on Avon, Warwickshire
Printed in Great Britain by Creative Print and Design, Harmondsworth

To my mother, Phulwati,
with love and remembrance

Contents

Note about the editor

PERLITA HARRIS is a transracially adopted adult who "reunited" with her *Papaji* and paternal extended family in 1983, and later with her younger maternal siblings and maternal extended family. She is a qualified social worker who specialised in adoption support prior to undertaking a PhD in Social Work at the University of Warwick. She is currently a lecturer at the University of Bristol, School for Policy Studies, where she teaches on the qualifying and post-qualifying courses in social work. Perlita has written several journal articles on users' views and experiences of adoption support; *In Search of Belonging* is her first book. She may be reached at Perlita.Harris@bristol.ac.uk.

Acknowledgements

Thanks to all the adoption support services, black community groups, service-user groups, social workers, writing networks, friends and acquaintances who helped to publicise the call for submissions.

I have been privileged to have contact with over 70 transracially adopted people during the making of this book. A huge thanks goes to all the contributors for whom writing or being interviewed sometimes brought to the surface immense sorrow, pain and unresolved questions, as well as the opportunity to express happiness, hope, and thoughts and experiences that had previously gone unsaid. Thank you for your generosity of spirit and for your strength in sharing your life stories, reflections and hopes for the future.

A very special thank you goes to Laura Corballis who, in her own time, facilitated a writing group for transracially adopted people in Bristol, and offered editorial support in the early stages, as well as encouragement and friendship. I am grateful to Deborah Weymont, Jade Laing and Bunge Adedeji for hosting meetings of the writing group – meetings where writing skills were developed, tears shed and laughter abounded as we reflected on our experiences of being raised in a white family, contact with our birth families and where we are today. Those people who participated in the writing group but chose not to write for the anthology also played an important part.

I am particularly appreciative of Laura Fish, Bella Frey and Li-Da Kruger for allowing their photographs to appear on the front cover.

Further thanks go to Shaila Shah at BAAF, for recognising the value of this collection and for locating the poet and novelist, Jackie Kay; Jo Francis for transcribing some of the interviews; and Shaila Shah and Miranda Davies for their feedback on the manuscript. A very special thank you goes to Professor Audrey Mullender for kindly agreeing to review the manuscript and for doing so with such attention to detail, thoughtfulness and care. I am indebted to her.

For writing the Foreword I must thank the poet, Lemn Sissay, whose poetry continues to inspire so many transracially adopted and fostered people.

Finally, this book is for all transracially adopted young people and adults – today, tomorrow and in years to come. I hope that reading these words will bring comfort, strength and reassurance that you are not alone. Breaking the silence that surrounds our experiences, from our own perspectives, is vital, as is sharing our stories of happiness, hope, struggle, healing and survival with each other. Between these pages we have achieved this and demonstrated that not only are we are the authors of our own experience, but we are an exceptional group: resilient, talented and resourceful.

Perlita Harris
March 2006

Foreword

Secrets are the stones that sink the boat.
Take them out. Look at them. Throw them out and float.
(Lemn Sissay, *Something Dark*, BBC Radio 3, 2005)

Never has a book so eloquently honestly and truthfully shown the experience of transracial adoption for what it is. No story in this book is the same. Each experience is different. There's no agenda. And once you have taken solace that each experience is different, then maybe you can see that what binds them together is a unique and moving experience.

There is no elephant in the room. If we all ignore it then we can all be safe in the knowledge that it isn't there. Here are some ways of making the elephant disappear. If we can all chant the following: 'Love is all we need' or 'We are colour blind, we see no elephants' or 'We are all the same under the skin' or, more bizarrely, 'We all have red blood'. The list is endless. All together now: 'THERE IS NO ELEPHANT IN THE ROOM.' Whether sitting alone in the front room, watching the TV or eating dinner with their family, for the transracially adopted child, it's still there. It is following the child, not *them*, and the child knows it.

The search for my own birth family has been the narrative of my adult life. It has taken me from the Lilliputian villages of Lancashire to the Simeon mountains of Ethiopia via Gambia, Senegal and New York. It has taken me twenty years.

Birth families, as a rule, treat a new arrival atrociously. They may not mean to but they do. Often most of the birth family members have no idea about the child. A ferocious tremor rushes through the birth family, as uncles and aunts check dates and themselves. The past explodes and a dust fills the room as stories fall open mid-air for all to see; secrets and lies are all over the place. All because a child who grew into an adult simply asked, 'Are you my birth mother?' and 'Who is my birth father?'

For the transracially adopted child, the search is precipitated by a lifelong knowledge that they are not the same as the people around them. They know this because everyone tells them so. Meanwhile the same child's adopted parents are beside themselves with worry for the child they love. Have they gone in search of something better? The adoptive parents are dealing with feelings of rejection, anger, love and possibly loss. But isn't a transracially adopted child searching for their birth parents a reflection of how well they have been brought up – how strong they are? On top of all this, the transracially adopted child has to deal with a birth parent who may not speak their language, a birth parent who is from a different part of the world.

Is it too extreme to think that we were experiments? Experiments in racial harmony and love-transplant surgery. We are the only ones who can tell all about the laboratory conditions and the effect that those conditions had on us. That sounds cold and I am not sure that any one of the participants in this book would agree with such a clinical metaphor. But the metaphor remains. I guarantee that most parents who adopted transracially had no experience of others who had done the same. These are the conditions of the experiment. I can also guarantee that most children who were transracially adopted were transplanted into an alien environment. There's the laboratory.

When you pick up this book forget for a moment all the research about transracial adoption. Forget all the arguments for and against. Forget all the seminars and the action groups. Forget all the conferences where professionals get together and discuss transracial adoption. Forget all the transracial adoption websites.

Instead of politicising the issue, instead of projecting or formulating a view, instead of taking a stance, instead of reverting to one side or the other . . . Instead of all this, take a deep breath and listen to the solitary voices of men, women and children in this book. Some of the contributors have never, *ever* spoken about their transracial adoption – until here, until now. This is not just a piece of social research. It is so much more. You are about to embark on what was, for me, an experience of enlightenment and joy, sadness and tears. This book is long overdue.

Lemn Sissay
March 2006

Introduction

Creating this book

It took time to find transracial adoptees who might be interested in coming together to create this book. The project was publicised over roughly eight months, from April to November 2004. UK statutory and voluntary adoption agencies, BAAF, regional adoption support services, social workers, transracial adoptee friends, intercountry adoptive parent groups, Race Equality Councils, black community and arts groups, and writing groups were all targeted, as were intercountry adoptee organisations in other countries. Friends, relatives and acquaintances also helped to spread the word. In addition, postings were placed on adoption-related websites, including those of BAAF and Adoption UK; on the Adoption News Service and Adoption Umbrella listservs; in various publications, among them the *New Nation*, *Adoption Today*, *Writers' News*, and in newsletters of the National Organisation for the Counselling of Adoptees and Parents (NORCAP), Bristol Race Equality Council and the Asian Arts Agency.

Responses came through word of mouth (often from people with no recent contact with any adoption services), contact with adoption support agencies and through the BAAF and other websites. Over 70 transracially adopted adults got in touch, 56 of whom went on to contribute to this book. Forty-five were born in England, Scotland, Wales or Ireland. Eleven are transnational adoptees from Cambodia, El Salvador, Hong Kong, Indonesia, Kenya, Korea, Singapore and Sri Lanka. In addition, a piece of writing previously published by BAAF has been included, bringing the total number of contributors to 57.

It was inevitable that not everyone who responded to publicity would contribute to the collection, often due to the complex feelings and thoughts that writing brought to the surface: emotions and experiences that were too difficult and painful to think and write about. For other potential contributors, the timing of the call to write was simply too difficult, competing with other demands in their lives.

Contact with several people in Bristol led to the formation of a writing group. Facilitated by a white non-adoptee experienced in editing community-based creative writing publications, the group met on six occasions over three months in 2004. Eight adults took part, six of whom have contributed to this edited collection.

In the summer of 2004, after hearing from a teenage transnational adoptee, I decided to see if there were other children and young people who might like to participate.

Letters were sent via Adoption UK to a number of transracial adoptive families. One child responded, while contact with a local authority social worker led to an interview with another. Where a contribution has been written by a child, his or her age is given.

In addition, ten adults were interviewed (either in person or over the telephone) and their experiences written up. Each was encouraged to take an active role in the editing process, and, as with the written submissions, all had the final say on the version that went forward to publication. The pieces of writing based on interviews come from (in published order): Jade, Rachel, Marie-Jamila Skilton, Ros Gihan Williams, Leyton, Laura Fish, Elinor Young, Sharon Beazer, Chris Atkins, Ima Jackson and Michael Caines. Two other contributions – by Fay Hallsworth and Wushan – combine written work and conversations with the editor.

Significantly, a number (14) of contributors have chosen to write under a pseudonym, their first name or their initials. This may reflect both the continuing stigma of adoption and a desire to maintain some privacy in their own personal and professional lives and in the lives of their adoptive and/or birth relatives. One person was concerned not to be recognised by her adoptive father. Where the names of family members have been changed, this has been indicated.

Fundamental to the creation of this book has been a belief that every transracially adopted person has important things to say about their experience and the capacity to write or tell their life story of adoption, even if some need support to do so. Thus, the anthology has taken an inclusive approach. Every transracial adoptee who responded before the deadline to the call for submissions was invited to contribute. Crucially, every submission was welcomed, irrespective of any views they expressed about the practice of transracial or transnational adoption. As editor, I tried to change only minimally the work of the author, instead working with him or her to maximise readability and clarity. Sadly, one of the contributors is now deceased so this was not possible but hers is a powerful voice that should be heard. Some submissions have not been included (in order to keep the book to a reasonable length), but only where the same writer and/or artist has one or more other pieces included.

The experiences described within these pages are wide ranging and cover adoptive placements made over half a century (1950–2000) by a range of adoption agencies. Primarily, they are the perspectives of transracially adopted adults, the majority of

3

whom joined their adoptive family in the 1960s and 1970s. Contributors range in age from six to 56 years. They encompass those who were placed with their adoptive family in infancy and others placed as older children following a period in residential care, foster care and/or social services intervention. Some people were raised in rural areas and others in towns and cities. They include adoptees who evaluate their adoption experience positively, negatively and, as with many people, a complex mixture of the two. Most people lived with their adoptive family throughout the remainder of their childhood while a few placements disrupted, resulting in reception into care and placement in foster care, a children's home or an approved school, or becoming homeless. A small but significant number of contributors are known to have experienced physical, sexual and/or emotional abuse within their adoptive family and/or residential care, although few write about this. Some but not all have contact with others of a similar cultural heritage and/or have visited their country of origin or heritage. There are those who are searching for birth family members and others who have not; some who now have ongoing contact and others where a search has resulted in no contact, or in learning that the sought-after relative is deceased. There are those who struggle in their lives on an emotional level, while many have achieved some equilibrium.

While the collection is as comprehensive as possible, there remain a number of gaps in the perspectives presented. These include: the experiences of disabled adoptees who had an impairment at the time of placement with their adoptive family; Vietnamese adoptees from the "baby airlift" of 1975; and writers who explicitly address issues related to being lesbian, gay, or bi-sexual, such as the process of "coming out" to birth family members. Despite these limitations, this collection breaks new ground: it is the first time in the UK that the experiences and life stories of transracial adoptees, as told in their own words, artwork and photographs, have been brought together in one book.

Setting the context

The contributors to this collection tell their stories against a backdrop of the debate over the practice of transracial adoption (the placement of black children in white families) that raged during the 1980s and into the early1990s in the UK, and which more recently has become merely a quiet murmur. Their telling of their life stories and their interpretations of their respective childhood and adulthood experiences are inevitably influenced by this wider discourse. It is, therefore, important that we acknowledge the larger picture.

Over the last fifty years there has been a shift from adoption practice viewing black children as "unadoptable" or "hard to place" (Small, 1982; Rowe, 1991), to adoption agencies in the mid-late 1960s demonstrating that these children are adoptable and establishing transracial adoption as a practice. Further, recruitment initiatives in the 1970s and 1980s showed unequivocally that black adoptive homes can be found for black children (Soul Kids, 1977; Brunton and Welch, 1983; Schroeder *et al*, 1985; James, 1986; Small, 1986) and a critique emerged that viewed agency failure and institutional racism as the main causes of the shortfall of black families (Kirton, 2000).

From the early 1980s, a number of challenges have been made against transracial adoption: that white families are ill-equipped to prepare black children (including those with one white parent) for the racism they will experience in society (as they have not experienced racism themselves), unable to provide them with coping skills for dealing with racism or to enable them to develop a positive black racial identity; and that a "positive black identity" is vital for self-esteem. More recently the charge of "political correctness" has been levied against social services departments that have sought to place black children with families of a similar "race", culture, religion and language, the crucial matter being seen as "love", which many white families can provide.

However, the Government takes a clear position – 'it is unacceptable for a child to be denied loving adoptive parents solely on the grounds that the child and the adopters do not share the same racial background' (LAC 98(20)) – and transracial adoption remains a placement option for black children. Contrary to popular opinion, such adoptions have never stopped. Black children continue to constitute a significant proportion of looked after children awaiting adoption. The 2003 Annual Report from the Adoption Register for England and Wales (a Register of children waiting adoption and approved adoptive parents) shows that 22 per cent of all children on the Register were black, with black children with a white parent strongly over-represented (Frazer and Selwyn, 2005).

Transnational adoption (the adoption of children from another country) in the UK has a different history, with numbers steadily increasing since the early 1990s. Just over 300 children enter England and Wales for adoption each year. Between 1 January and 31 December 2004, 333 applications were received for children entering England and Wales for the purpose of adoption. Originating from 32 countries, the largest numbers came from China (166), Russia (40), India (26), Cambodia (18),

Guatemala (16), USA (13) and Thailand (11) (personal communication with Public Communications Office).

In recent years, there has been an increasing interest in service-user knowledge(s) (knowledge based on people's first-hand experience) and the recognition that service users are experts. The late 1970s and 1980s saw the emergence of service users' own organisations, each with their own perspectives and demands for different, better and more responsive services (Beresford and Croft, 1997). Although there are differences within and between these user movements, they all demand the right to "speak for themselves", to participate in debates and decisions affecting them, both in their own movements and in society (Croft and Beresford, 1998). Transracially adopted adults are one group of service users who have come together to speak about their experiences, to form their own organisations, to make demands regarding adoption and adoption support services and, for some, to challenge the practices of transracial and transnational adoption. They have also begun to write about their experiences both in the UK and in other countries. Thus, this edited collection needs to be seen as coming from part of a larger user movement of transracially adopted adults that spans not only the UK but right across the world.

Whose truth?

> *Marginalized bodies are constantly silenced and rendered invisible not simply through the failure to take issues of race and social oppression seriously but through the constant negation of multiple lived experiences and alternative knowledges.* (Dei and Calliste, 2000, p 11)

When it comes to the writing and artwork of transracially adopted people, we should remember that 'alternative knowledges' do matter. Material produced by transracial adoptees is a form of service-user knowledge. It is knowledge based on direct personal and collective experience of adoption policy, family placement and adoption support services, and the specific practices of transracial and transnational adoption.

Yet, claims to knowledge are often deeply contested and this is clearly the case regarding transracial and transnational adoption. In the public discourse around this topic, crucial questions arise: who is allowed to speak and how is what they say received? Arguably, this discourse is dominated by the voices of liberal academics, white adoptive parents (and prospective adopters) of black children, legislators, government and advocates of transnational and transracial adoption. Rarely do we hear the voices of transracial and transnational adoptees. We need to ask ourselves: are we ready to listen?

The words of transracial adoptees may become 'targets of criticism, co-option and silencing' (Collins, 2004, p 3). Knowledge and power are interrelated and it is not easy to create the space to raise the issues and concerns of transracially adopted young people and adults using paradigms (and literary forms) that differ from those promoted by more powerful groups. Many of the experiences described within these pages do just that. They challenge any preconceptions that love is enough, "race" does not matter, white families should unquestionably be allowed to adopt black children, black children will be better off in a white family rather than a black family, or that transnational adoption is a benevolent act that creates "a happy ever after" for a child who might otherwise be without a family, in institutional care or dead. Instead, this collection turns these notions on their head and grapples with the lived experience of transracial and transnational adoption, the day-to-day complexities people experience in living with this throughout their life.

As a result, some readers may find many of the perspectives and experiences described within these pages both challenging and disturbing. They may be tempted to deny the impact of racism, loss and physical and cultural dislocation, to render these experiences invisible and these voices silent, due to a need to hold on to whatever feels safer for them. They may be tempted to dismiss the validity of what people are saying, perhaps by arguing that this group is not representative of transracial adoptees, that they typify only those who are "unhappy" or who have had "difficulties" and have used adoption support services; or by assuming that they have been selected on the basis of their views, or that adoption practice is substantially different now so that these experiences have little relevance for social work and social care today. We should question all of these assumptions, beginning with 'the idea that how "representative" they are affects the validity of what they say' (Beresford and Campbell, 1994, p 319). We should bear in mind that the publicity was wide ranging, with all submissions welcomed; that many of the contributors have not made any use of adoption support services; and that, while adoption placement and adoption support services have developed significantly over the past few decades, this does not mean that there are no lessons to be learned from the experience of those placed in the past, lessons that can inform current family placement work and the development of adoption support services. Indeed, it is only by listening to transnational and transracial adoptees and reflecting on their experiences that we will develop adoption support provision that is tailored to their specific needs and those of their relatives by birth and adoption.

Not surprisingly, many contributors have been influenced by the paradigms of those powerful individuals and groups whose writing and voices on transracial adoption have dominated public debate, and this is reflected in some of the writings that follow. Thus, themes of gratitude and loyalty to adoptive parents are expressed alongside the view that 'if it was not for my adoptive parents I wouldn't have been adopted'. The latter, while it may be true, is not the whole story. Many transracial adoptees (as with the general public) have not asked why there weren't attempts to recruit and assess black adoptive families at the time their placement was made, to question the politics behind transracial and transnational adoption, or to wonder whether there might be viable alternatives to their continued practices.

It is important that transracially adopted people claim space and visibility. People who are oppressed 'resist by defining their reality, naming their history, and telling their story' (Bernard *et al*, 2000, pp 68–9). This is what the contributors to this book are doing: defining their life experience as transracially adopted people, telling their her/history and their life stories:

> *Telling our stories through our own voices enables us to claim space and visibility. Sharing these stories in . . . scholarship allows for others to develop an understanding of the struggles, barriers, and challenges we face . . . We are also able to then analyse the gifts and strengths that we embody, and through this we hope to make a difference to others in struggle.* (Bernard *et al*, 2000, p 70)

Our life stories are at times painful and seemingly riddled with loss and grief. At other times, they are filled with the wonders of family life (whether through adoption, birth, partnership or becoming a parent) and new friendships, with cultural and geographical reconnection, search and reunion, happiness and hope. They also reveal the damaging impact of racism, disappointments and frustration, emotional distress, the complexities of managing contact with birth relatives after reunion, and the reality of living *always* with the experience of transracial adoption.

Sharing our experiences through these stories is an act of empowerment (Collins, 1991), as it offers us an opportunity to think and speak for ourselves about our experience of adoption. It is also 'an act of resistance' (hooks, 1989, p 8) as we seek to define our own experiences, often breaking from the culturally imposed norm of the "acceptable" face of the transracial adoptee: forever grateful and loyal to his/her adoptive parents, unwilling to "betray" them by questioning the practices of transracial and transnational adoption or by voicing our experiences of racism, cultural dislocation and alienation. These accounts, poems and artwork largely seek to break that culturally imposed silence. In doing so, they reveal immense pain and grief. We are not seeking to criticise our adoptive parents for adopting us – they did what they thought was best – or to deny the love and care that most of us have received from our adoptive families. However, this book conveys a clear message: being transracially adopted is a complex, challenging, and at times very difficult and painful, lifelong experience.

The impact of writing

For each contributor, being part of the creation of this book held a special meaning, in varying ways. Here are extracts from emails from two contributors:

> *Well, firstly I found to write my story on paper and [to] send it to someone, and actually realise what has happened to me in my life has been very powerful to me. I can talk about it, but actually to write it down made me feel so many emotions that I guess I had tucked away for so long. It has been really good for my own personal development.*

> *I also wanted other transracial adoptees to maybe realise that some of the emotions that they have experienced have a similar thread to mine, so there is a connection and they are not alone. What I have realised about myself is [that] the core pain for me is the feeling of [being] not quite good enough. My mother had given me up, so was I not good enough for her? Of course my logical adult mind tells me this was not so, but, unconsciously, I wonder how many adoptees hold this, and then go on a path of doing, doing, doing – always trying to succeed to prove to themselves that they are good enough, because this is certainly something that I do.* (Katrina)

> *When I was initially approached about writing a contribution for this anthology, I had no hesitation in agreeing. It seemed a wonderful opportunity to share some of my life experiences for the first time. As the months passed, I felt more able to write in greater depth and openness. The processes of articulating the deep senses of pain, rejection, loss and hope have at times been painful. Indeed, the pieces I have written have exposed some of the most private and intimate details of my existence as a transracial adoptee. Yet the processes of writing have certainly been very cathartic.*

> *Having the chance to contribute to this groundbreaking book has also helped me understand, and accept, that whilst there are a range of diverse challenges that transracial adoptees face, we do share some unique commonalities . . . [including] our struggles in coming to terms with our identities, against a backdrop of societal prejudices and institutional racisms.* (David Gilbert)

It soon became evident that many contributors were isolated from other transracially adopted adults, perhaps having only met one or two (if any) during their lifetime. For some, I was the first transracially adopted person with whom they had really talked about their experience. And so, within these pages, you will find thoughts and experiences that may have previously gone unspoken. The process of writing has been healing for some, allowing the creation of meaning and a coherent narrative about their life; it has enabled people to value their own lived experience of transracial adoption, and to feel that transracial and transnational adoptees and others are interested in hearing about their lives and that they can share their learning and experiences.

The structure of this collection

The book is divided into eight main sections. I have deliberately chosen not to introduce individual items as each piece of artwork, photograph or writing speaks more powerfully for itself. The sections take us from the initial separation and loss through childhood, reconnection with culture and country of origin or heritage, through to searching for birth family members, life stories and learning to live with transracial adoption. There are over-arching themes in each section and cross-cutting themes that readers may want to look out for. I have tried to select pieces that illustrate a variety of issues – a diversity of experiences and a range in terms of where people are on their respective journey, including the sense that they have made of it.

Each new section opens with an image of artwork or a photograph. Then follow pieces of writing, often including poetry and oral testimony, although the composition of each section varies. Some are longer than others, reflecting the topics that contributors chose to write or speak about. Interestingly, more adoptees focused on loss, search, reunion and life stories in their submissions than, for example, on childhood or healing. Perhaps people tend to write about the areas of their life that they are trying to make sense of or work through at that particular time. Some pieces of writing and poetry were written many years ago, others specifically for this collection.

A number of people have contributed several pieces of writing and/or artwork. Thus, where there is more than one contribution from the same author, you will often see a discernible movement in their thinking and emotional expression. Sometimes, what you will read is raw and painful, and then the author has moved on. On other occasions, do not be fooled into thinking that you are hearing from the same person. You may not be. Instead, there may be similarities in the experiences being told by different people. However, it is important that we hear about these experiences again and again. For example, that we be informed about the impact of racism, the extent of emotional distress and the importance of cultural reconnection. Several pieces of writing have been published elsewhere since being submitted to this collection. Finally, this is not a book to read in one sitting, from beginning to end. It is an anthology to dip into and then take time out for thoughtful reflection.

The first section, 'Separation and loss', focuses on the initial separation from and loss of our mothers, other multiple losses, and the consequent cultural and geographical dislocation. These include the loss of fathers, siblings, country of origin or heritage, history, family resemblance, ancestry, language and culture. The pain and grief associated with these losses are revealed. Contributors also write about loss and grief connected to the ill-health of an adoptive father and the death of an adoptive mother.

Section 2, 'Childhood', opens with several pieces of writing by transracially adopted children, including one by a young woman who has contact with her birth family. This is followed by adult memories and reflections on childhood, and includes experiences of fostering and residential care in addition to transracial adoption. Issues addressed include lack of physical resemblance to the adoptive family, relationships with (adoptive) mothers and fathers, isolation, racism, loss of history and ancestry, cultural disconnection, hair care, physical and emotional abuse, and placement disruption. The section conveys a clear message that "race" certainly does matter: that even when adoptive parents and other community members may not acknowledge the impact of living with a family that looks dissimilar and the impact of racism, the transracially adopted child is only too aware of this.

The third section shifts attention to the question of identity, encapsulated in the phrase, 'Who am I?'. This is a question that many transracial adoptees struggle with and answer in different ways at different stages in their life. Contributions address allegiance with British culture and Britain, the importance of names, lack of history, coping with questions from others, internalised racism, self-hate, body image, emotional distress, the failure of psychiatric services to meet specific needs, becoming a mother, and rejection and abandonment issues. Some of the poems here are a little more obscure in their writing, with two people addressing themselves through images of the "dream sister" and "the other woman": the non-adopted self. The section closes with several pieces offering messages for adoptive parents.

Section 4, 'Reconnection', focuses on making links with one's cultural, historical and geographical heritage. It shows some different forms that reclaiming culture and country might take, and the range of meanings that transracial adoptees may attach to this, including the search for birth family. Experiences described include buying one's first sari and *shalwar kameez*, visiting country of origin or heritage (Cambodia, Hong Kong, Korea, Sri Lanka, China, Kenya) as an adult, through to the personal impact of the Tsunami in Sri Lanka. It demonstrates the importance transracial adoptees attribute to reconnecting in some way to their lost heritage.

Section 5, 'Search and reunion', looks at adult experiences of searching for family members and, where contact has been established, the developing relationship(s). Often, people talk about their childhood experiences first, in order to contextualise their respective searches. The section brings together accounts of searches for and contact with mothers, fathers, siblings and extended family. Although none addresses learning that the sought-after relative is deceased, this can be found elsewhere in the book (see Louise McCoy). This section highlights: the emotional impact of searching and establishing contact, particularly heightened feelings of loss and grief; difficulties in searching with only limited information; the possibility of discovering information that may cause distress (such as conception through rape or a refusal of contact); the complexities of post-reunion contact and the negotiation of these relationships. The themes of roots, identity and belonging run throughout these accounts. In addition, several clear messages emerge. First, searching, for transracial adoptees, is often strongly linked to a quest for racial and cultural identity. Second, finding the sought-after person (whatever the outcome) is only the beginning of the journey and never the end. Third, the search for family is, in fact, a search for self and what we learn about ourselves along the journey is as important, if not more important, than the actual outcome. Fourth, despite establishing contact, many transracial adoptees still feel like a cultural (and sometimes linguistic) outsider within their birth family, an experience that may be accentuated for transnational adoptees. Fifth, personal and professional support during the search and immediate post-contact period is very important.

We should remember that, through the experience of pain, there is also healing (Bernard *et al*, 2000) and the capacity to learn to theorise (hooks, 1989) about our experiences. Thus, many of the pieces of writing in Sections 6 and 7, 'Life stories' and 'Living with transracial adoption', address learning to live with the complexity of transracial adoption – drawing out some ways of healing from the pain of living with transracial adoption that have worked for contributors. Within the 'Life stories' section, more experiences of childhood, search and reunion, healing and living with transracial adoption can be found. The latter includes both positive and self-destructive strategies: psychotherapy, counselling, creative writing, peer support and alcohol and drug misuse. In Section 8, ways of healing and living with adoption that contributors describe include art, religion, searching for one's birth family, learning about one's cultural heritage, making links with community of origin, and connecting with other transracial and transnational adoptees. A theme that emerges is of people finding their own solutions or coping mechanisms at different times in their lives. The material should not be read as identifying instant solutions or as illustrating the correct way to search or to live with transracial adoption. Instead, it is important that we read it and look for the journeys people make; that we recognise that it is never easy and there is no end point or final destination. We can gain an understanding of the complexity of the process and the support that is necessary along the way, whilst recognising that there is not one kind of support. Instead, there are many kinds of support that people may benefit from. The authors offer hope and demonstrate that it is possible to move on from feeling acute pain and grief, to gaining a more grounded sense of self, a sense of being rooted within oneself and a sense of belonging. Perhaps the strongest message is the profound difference and strength that comes from meeting and talking with other transracial adoptees, thereby normalising our experiences, and opening up the opportunity to learn from and support one another. Reading about the life experiences of other transracial and transnational adoptees and meeting others is very special, as no therapy or religion can offer that shared experience. Meeting the authors and artists through these pages will be very special too.

Although the material has been organised thematically, themes overlap and are interconnected in a complex myriad of ways. For example, one cannot fully comprehend search or reunion and post-reunion experiences and relationships without an understanding of what may have been lost: mother, father, siblings, extended family, resemblance, personal history, family history, shared family experience, country of origin/heritage, culture, language, religion/ spirituality, community, ancestry, nationality, personal and family health history – the list goes on. Thus, the themes of loss, grief, dislocation, alienation and reconnection run throughout the book. A sense of belonging also pervades these pages: belonging to adoptive family, birth family, own family, community of origin/heritage, country of origin/heritage, and to communities of transracial and transnational adoptees.

Section 8 provides the contributors' details including childhood or adult photographs of many. This is followed by a selection of useful resources for transracial and transnational adoptees. A more detailed list, including many resources of interest to practitioners and family members by adoption and birth can be found at www.baaf.org.uk

Finally, I hope that we have created a resource for ourselves and for other transracial and transnational adoptees that will also be of great interest to adoptive parents, birth family members, social workers, social work students, psychotherapists, counsellors, and mental health and other professionals.

References

Beresford P and Campbell J (1994) 'Disabled people, service users, user involvement and representation', *Disability and Society* 9:3, pp 315–25

Bernard C, Thomas Bernard W, Epko C, Enang J, Joseph B and Wane N (2000) '"She who learns teaches": othermothering in the academy', *Journal of the Association for Research on Mothering* 2:2, pp 66–84

Brunton L and Welch M (1983) 'White agency, black community', *Adoption & Fostering* 7:2, pp 16–18

Collins P H (1991) *Black Feminist Thought: Knowledge, consciousness, and the politics of empowerment*, New York and London: Routledge

Collins P H (2004) *Black Sexual Politics: African Americans, gender and the new racism*, New York and London: Routledge

Croft S and Beresford P (1998) 'Postmodernity and the future of welfare: whose critiques, whose social policy?', in Carter J (ed) *Postmodernity and the Fragmentation of Welfare*, London: Routledge

Dei S J S and Calliste A (2000) 'Mapping the terrain: power, knowledge and anti-racism education', in Dei S J S and Calliste A (eds), *Power, Knowledge and Anti-Racism Education: A critical reader*, Halifax: Fernwood Publishing

Frazer L and Selwyn J (2005) 'Why are we waiting? The demography of adoption for children of black, Asian and black mixed parentage in England', *Child & Family Social Work* 10, pp 135–47

hooks b (1989) *Talking Back: Thinking feminist, thinking black*, Toronto: Between the Lines

James M (1986) 'Finding and working with families of Caribbean origin', in Coombe V and Little A (eds) *Race and Social Work: A guide to training*, London: Tavistock Publications

Kirton D (2000) *'Race', Ethnicity and Adoption*, Buckingham: Open University Press

Rowe J (1991) 'An historical perspective on adoption and the role of the voluntary agencies', in Fratter J, Rowe J, Sapsford D and Thoburn J (eds) *Permanent Family Placement: A decade of experience*, London: BAAF

Schroeder H, Lightfoot D and Rees S (1985) 'Black applicants to Ealing recruitment campaign', *Adoption & Fostering* 9:2, pp 50–53

Small J (1986) 'Transracial placements: conflicts and contradictions', in Ahmed S, Cheetham J and Small J (eds) *Social Work with Black Children and their Families*, London: Batsford/BAAF

Small J (1982) 'New black families', *Adoption & Fostering* 6:3, pp 35–39

Soul Kids (1977) *Report of the Steering Group of the Soul Kids Campaign: London 1975–1976*, London: BAAF

1

Separation and loss

Indecision

by DYLAN CLEMENTS

*(Sandstone) Exhibited in 1999 at The Art Garden,
Bristol and Woodlands Christian Centre, Bristol*

Severed

MICHELLE ANDERSON

The
Cutting
Of the
Cord
r-e-l-e-a-s-e-d
you . . .   *from me . . .*
I had NO WORDS
to plead my case
mother stay
no one can take your place

Acknowledgement: 'Severed' by Michelle Anderson was first published in the *ATRAP Newsletter*, Issue No. 4, December 2000.

Black holes – mapping the absence

DEBORAH WEYMONT

I remember being abandoned. It is etched deep inside my body. It is a wholly sensory memory. Something is wrong. It feels cold (the absence of warmth). It feels like nothing (the absence of something). It is the sound of my own cries. It is the sound of the silence that follows (no one is listening). It tastes like shit (bottled milk). It smells like shit. It hurts like hell. It feels lonely. It looks like I'm on my own.

It is a pre-verbal memory.
I told no one about it.
I had no words, so I could not tell anyone about it.

Imagine that!

I imagine it as a black hole.

Small eyes

BELLA FREY

A ballooned belly full of a turning emptiness
an uncomfortable heat
forced burning saline drops from small eyes.

Small eyes displayed the illusion
of strength and defiance
silently pleaded for a different outcome.

Small eyes desperate for a chance to remain on land
where ancestors walked
and where histories would remain traceable in the soil.

Those eyes, too full to expose desires
to remain rooted
and too stubborn to identify hidden sadness and loss.

Behind those small eyes, a betrayal and isolation
a permanent difference
daily identified by those whose land became "mother".

Small eyes, desperate to be opened by the brightness
of a morning calm
in their mother's land, immersed in their likeness.

Transcripts of a transracial adoption

MICHAEL CANDON

Here follow excerpts (word verbatim) from the transcripts of my adoption records that I received in 1995, when I was 26, while tracing my birth mother. These records are all that I have of the first 22 months of my life – they are sacred to me and fill a void. Stored with them is a photo of me and another baby boy with an "x" marking the baby my adoptive parents wanted to adopt.

Context

12. Details of child movements between birth and placement – with all relevant dates:

Born 23.7.67 Dulwich Hospital
    31.7.67 Received into care (sec 1 CA 1945)
               Placed temporarily with foster mother.
    4.9.67 To St Mary's Nursery, Parrock Rd,
               Gravesend, Kent.
    2.4.69 To adopters

24. Nationality (of mother): British

28. Race: Northern Ireland (Belfast)

42. Can the husband be contacted directly? Unwilling to discuss child.

44. Reasons mother gives for wishing child to be adopted: Unable to make home for child as husband antagonistic to his existence. Mother also cannot reconcile herself to the child's mixed blood. Husband refused to have mother back in house unless child placed for adoption.

52. What is the adoption agency's present contact with the mother?
Occasional visits but care is taken not to visit too

frequently because mother's husband does not wish to know any more about child.

Child's father

66. Name: Milton Eliot
67. Address: Present address unknown
68. May he be contacted directly? Now seems to have moved away.
70. Occupation: Bus driver
71. Nationality: British
72. Race: West Indian (his father West Indian, mother Dutch)
73. Age: 36
75. Does he acknowledge paternity? Does not know of child's existence.

Report on home visit

I visited Mrs Collins in hospital, a quiet and neat woman. She has decided to have the baby adopted, as she is unable to take him home.

Observations by medical officer of health

12.3.69 From information obtained it would appear that this child is suitable for adoption.

Officers' reports

Mrs Cathleen Collins
1, Gautrey Road

23.7.67
Mrs B phoned, this mother has 4 children and her 5th child, a boy born at Dulwich hosp 23.7.67, is not her husband's child and is half coloured.

31.7.67
Saw Mrs Collins in hosp. She was due for discharge today

but we have been unable to find a vacancy.

Because the child is not her husband's he will have nothing to do with her and she says that when she returns home he plans to make a separation order. Their R/C priest has been round to see Mrs Collins but she is still adamant. Mrs Collins has had no recent contact with Mr Eliot, the putative father although he knows the child was expected.

The father is W. Indian but the baby is a bonny very fair skinned child with dead straight hair.

1.8.67
Baby taken to foster mother Mrs Ball, 27 Brookhill Road, SE18

3.8.67
Miss Ralph phoned re: Mrs Ball and the milk books. Evidently she is very keen to adopt this baby but is unaware that he is half cast.

7.8.67
Saw Mrs Collins - she is not feeling very well. She has been unable to get the registration of birth. She said things between her husband and her had proved better and he hadn't left as was thought. I discussed the religious aspect of an adoption should Mrs Ball really feel she wanted to apply to be considered as adopter, but the colour problem has not been discussed and Mrs Collins said she would come on Thurs to discuss the matter fully.

9.8.67
Called on Mrs Collins to discuss the religious aspect. Since my last visit she has had time to carefully consider the religious aspect of the future for her child and feels certain that she has no objection to the child being adopted by parents of another faith. She feels that the SCCS [Southwark Catholic Children's Society] have neglected

her as no one has visited her since she left hosp and
therefore has no further interest in the child. I told her
I would see Fr C tomorrow re the future for the child.

16.8.67
Fr C willing to try to provide R/C adopters. It is
difficult at this stage to tell what colouring Michael will
have but when I spoke with Miss Ralf she said his eyes and
hair were very dark although his skin was still quite fair.
Mrs Collins phoned. She is unable to make up her mind and I
suggested she speak to her priest. She wondered if she
might be excommunicated if she allowed her baby to be
adopted by non Catholics. Mrs Ball is now incapable of
keeping Michael any longer because of health reasons –
letter attached.

1.9.67
Wrote to Mrs Ball telling her plans for removal.

4.9.67
Removed Michael who is a very bonny and still very fair
baby. Took him to St Mary's at Gravesend – a lovely nursery
beautifully organised.

5.9.67
Mrs Collins phoned to find out how things were.

19.9.67
Wrote to Mrs Collins to tell her baby had settled in well.
He has a mild tummy upset and is under doctor observation.
Visited Michael at St Mary's. He is a beautiful, very alert
strong child and is doing very well. He is still very light
of complexion and has straight dark hair.

1.2.68
No sign of adopters yet.

Summary to October 1968
Michael is a very good looking boy, with scarcely any trace
of coloured features, etc. He is a friendly child. Was
walking at 11 months. Is not talking yet.

24.10.68
SCCS rang. They have adopter for Michael. Want to adopt 2ch
of whom M is the older. SCCS have decided little girl
should go first 'as there will be no problems with her'. If
there was possibility of any trouble at all they would not
place M.

May 1969
The adopters are Mr and Mrs C. Mr C is dark skinned and
Michael resembles him; placed temporarily they now wish to
adopt him.

Summary

Michael Candon born to an Irish mother and West Indian father, a result of an extra-marital affair. Unwanted by mother and deemed "suitable for adoption". My adoptive parents convinced themselves and I that I was theirs of the same blood. Indeed they 'chose me cause I looked like daddy'. But the bullies in school could see it; the aunts, the cousins and everyone else could see it. More importantly – I knew it. I knew I was different, my skin colour and body shape, and my facial features were different. A friend would say 'a hint of a tint' in winter and l would stay out of the sun in the summer.

As for a lot of adopted people, I do not know the full names and the roles that some of the above people played in my adoption. All of them influenced and controlled my fate as an infant and continue to do so every day of my life. The language and remarks speak for themselves and the times in which they were written, and hopefully are a sign of how things have changed.

Still waiting for you

SUE JARDINE

Patiently I waited – so well behaved
Told to be good, not to cry, or scream in anguish
At the possibility you would never return to me.
How could I be expected to comprehend that?
Enough to be born into the world
Too much to be abandoned in it

Still I wait – holding on to the thought,
That you might come for me
Gather me in your arms and reclaim me.
So unbelievably naive after all these years.
How could it be that you know where I am?
Or even exist to think such thoughts

Almost beyond endurance – the waiting
But I have no choice
Forced to breathe in a foreign country
Taken away from my source
How I wish for death, to drown in the pain –
But my survival instinct demands life

The strain of waiting – I can no longer bear
Of having perhaps to finally acknowledge,
That you won't be coming for me after all.
Acknowledge the harsh reality –
That I have no mother, have no father.
Will never look at them and see my self – my human mirror.

Yet, how can I accept that I have no roots?
Make sense of why this has happened to me.
Brought to an alien place
So far from my beginnings –
Where I have to reach out to others
That they might feel comfortable with me

Me – who envies the lives of others so much,
That I am frozen, I am the observer.
Unable to take part, for fear,
Fear of destruction that I may cause
In trying to fill the emptiness within me –
A hunger that cannot be satisfied.

How I wish for simplicity of thought
Not simplicity of background.
I, who am the adopted one, the foundling –
Found, yet completely lost to my self.
I know, I have it all, so lucky
But can't you see I am crippled?

Must not move from here, cannot end my waiting
Afraid I might miss you when you come for me.

Dear Mother

MAYA

Dear Mother,

Today I doubt myself. It is something that comes and goes. Some days I am full of self-doubt, other days it is not so daunting. I know where these feelings come from; they are connected to my early experience of loss, separation, fear, confusion, rejection and loneliness.

Maybe, I am exaggerating these feelings but, when they surface, they are clear to me, and it is a scary place to be, vulnerable and on the edge.

What is the role of a mother? To love and cherish her child and to be there for her; to do what is right for her; to do the best thing. Is it not called unconditional love?

No one knew how things would turn out. You were willing to gamble my life and to wait and see because you knew what was best for me. I know you will have suffered and thought about me; how I longed to know how you felt about me. You used to visit me in the children's home, but why did you not stay with me? When I was four years old, you told me that I was going to live with another family, but you were my mother. How confused I was; it made no sense. No one explained anything to me and the feelings inside me were overwhelming. No doubt you gave careful consideration to me and to what I needed and should have: love and stability. You hoped that I would get this and away you went.

Regards,

Your secret daughter

Why do I still love you?

CARLY STACEY (age 16)

She may have loved me,
But she abandoned me,
Scarred me for life,
Worse than the scar
Made with a knife.

Why does she treat me like this?
Does she think it's her I never miss?
On my mind, every minute, every day,
What is she doing?
Or is she still alive today?

I don't know how I can
feel this,
But why did she do this?
Because of her, I now cannot
trust others,
rely on others,
Find it hard to be let down,
rejected.
Wish I had a say then, wonder
if my thoughts would have been respected?

I hate when peeps say,
'I hate my mum!'
It's only then,
if they really knew, how lucky
they actually are.

It's only then, if they realised,
they should understand what it means
to know YOUR OWN mother and father,
and not to be left in the dark.

Not to take them for granted,
because if they are suddenly out of
your life, it's their name
that'll be chanted . . .

'Mum! Mum! I wish you
were here!! For you I will
always shed a tear.'

But, as for us, a big part of
our lives missing.
For some,
never found.

Those are the times we
appreciate close ones for
being here, and wish like hell
that those who are close
to us at heart were around.

So we could cry tears of joy
No necessary doubtful
ideas we'd employ
Living each day to the full,
Telling them both, 'Mother,
Father, I love you.'

Dear Mum

LOUISE McCOY

Dear Mum,

This is your story; this is for you. This is what I dreamt. My aim is to fit together some of the pieces of shattered glass. It will never be complete. I have put this together from what my biological sister told me when I eventually met her. The social services files have also contributed.

But aside from your blood that's in me, this illusion of a story is just about all I have of you.

In 1954 you took a risk, travelling from Ireland to England to escape. You faced British racist reality: "No Blacks, No Irish". Once again you felt isolated and alone, just like back in Ireland where you had had to fit into someone else's family, a family that was not your own. I wonder who and where your mother was, and why you had been separated from her and your family. I do not know what situation had put you into this family of strangers, and whether anyone acknowledged your loss and your grief at being separated from your biological connections and family history. Genetic access is taken for granted and yet so easily misunderstood. It was here you missed out on the basic fundamentals of being a secure, self-loved human being that would provide you with the building blocks of life. Block one security; block two self-love; block three identity.

The Catholic nuns played a role in your upbringing although this part is blurred. Recently information on how the nuns treated children in their care has come to light. I think I prefer this area of cloud, as it feels more comfortable. We now know all the strategies that they used when dealing with children. The nuns were also involved in organising my adoption. How they love to withhold information. The courts still refuse to release my Guardian ad Litem report, saying that it is confidential. How these laws are still used to control the amount of information we can find out about our identity. History can repeat itself.

In England, the only people who invited you in for coffee were black people, the social circle who accepted you. They too felt alone here. Your low self-esteem and a limited idea of who you really were meant that you stayed within your comfort zone of menial jobs. Afraid of change, you could not plunge into the supervisor's role to upgrade your status at work: lack of block two. I remain in the same job, knowing it's not benefiting me in any way yet too afraid to step out of my comfort zone. Lacking confidence in my abilities. History can repeat itself.

You too would have experienced issues of identity and feelings of loss. I wonder if they became more evident as you encountered milestones in your life. I missed you at my graduation. It was obvious in my family that I was not one of the biological family. Everyone in my family is white and I am mixed race. That obvious observation stimulates interest and interest stimulates questions. Not equipped to disclose personal information to my fellow students, I boycotted my graduation ceremony. Not only did I not allow my adoptive parents to go, I didn't allow myself to go either.

Establishing one's identity is a major task in life. Not resembling the family who brought you up may have stimulated intense feelings of loneliness. At family reunions I still feel this loneliness of wondering what I really have in common with the rest of the family. My daughter, a darker product of myself, feels this too: 'Why am I the only brown child in our family, Mummy?' I explain the situation again. History can repeat itself.

The search for personal identity is complicated because of the mystery of genetic background. Transracially adopted people have to search harder for their identity.

This determination to search led me to my biological sister, Mum, your eldest daughter. She too is mixed race like me, only she grew up with you. So all those pre-conceptions about you abandoning me because I was black have now gone. Mum, I understand your situation more now. Single parenting in the millennium is hard enough and single parenting in the sixties doesn't bear thinking about. I too have woken up in the mornings wanting to give up parental responsibility. History can repeat itself.

My only regret is that I did not have the opportunity to meet you. Cancer took you away when I was 18 years old. If I had met you I would have held you and told you, that it's OK, Mum, I understand, you are forgiven. Instead I hold your picture, a piece of my identity, a piece of shattered glass.

One thing I have learnt is that the more information I have found about you, the deeper my understanding. The deeper the understanding, the more determined I am to ensure that history repeats itself only if you allow it to.

xxxxxxxxxx

Empathy and love,

Your daughter

I shall never hear you whisper

PERLITA HARRIS

I shall never hear you whisper, *Tum meri jaan hai*
    (You are my life)
I shall never hear you say, *Mujhe tum pyaar hai*
    (I love you)
I shall never hear you call me, *Meri beti*
    (My daughter)
I shall never hear you tell me, *Tum khubsurat aur haushyar ladki hun*
    (You are a beautiful intelligent girl)
I shall never feel your hug and kisses again

Nor you mine.

Nor shall I whisper to you, *Aap meri jaan hai*
    (You are my life)
Nor gaze at your beauty with recognition in my eyes
Nor hold your hand in mine and say, *Aap meri Maji hai*
    (You are my mother)
Nor show you that, *Mujhe aap se pyaar hai*
    (I love you)

Don't erase your memories of me
Cutting me dead while I grow up
Don't forget me, *aapki beti*
    (your daughter)
For I shall never forget you

Koi goria
(Some white people)
rubbed your memory from my mind
Another stole my dreams one night
Koi baat nahin
        (Never mind)
For, *kal*
        (yesterday or tomorrow)
my memories will return

In my memories
Phir milenge
(We will meet again)

I was down to see Perlita on last Friday. She is becoming a beautiful intelligent girl and grown up a lot. She recognised me well and liked to be hugged and kissed all the time. I can't rub off her memory out of my mind. I was very upset when I left her.

Therefore I have decided not to visit her anymore. My plans are definite to leave this country in Dec. '69.

(Extract from a letter by my mother, dated 16 September 1969)

Thoughts . . . in no particular order

CAROL MOY

Today I have again woken up and realised just how alone I am.

I am a black woman. Currently 41 years old and for the most part I am satisfied, nay happy with my life. I have the most amazing son. He's 12 and such a credit to himself, me and everyone who has the pleasure to know him. But, still, I feel so alone.

I was born in Norwich in 1963. My birth mother, a nurse from Trinidad, felt unable to keep me so I was placed with a white UK family in Suffolk. At the age of three-and-a-half I was legally adopted. My memories of my childhood are that it was a fabulously happy, healthy and carefree time. My family, and to all intents and purposes they are my family, could not have been better to, for or with me. Although visually and biologically I am not a member of their family, I never felt anything but loved, accepted and as much a part of the family as those my mother had given birth to. Now, sadly all that is behind me. In the past few days I have had to say goodbye to my mother and accept that things have changed.

This is a strange time for me. I'm now officially not just an adult, but a Grown Up. There's no longer that comfort, that safety net of knowing that, whatever I do, wherever I am, whatever I might need, Mum is always there. Strange how it's only now I feel in freefall, so out of control. (Strange because Mum suffered with dementia for the last 18 months of her life.) I'll admit I wasn't the best daughter in Mum's last few months. I didn't visit as much as I could. I can't remember the last time I phoned, and I was always busy being useful or supportive somewhere else. But I always knew Mum was there. And always would be there even if I didn't set eyes on her for months.

So why do I now feel so alone? It's not that I don't believe she's looking down on me and watching, caring, protecting, worrying from afar. It's more than that. Now I have to admit that the only person I *know* I have a legitimate connection with is my son. I'm sure my brothers and sisters will all be there for me for as long as possible but things move on. Relationships change and now we are all heads of our own households and all that that entails. Now there is no specific reason for looking up the family tree. Now the focus has to be on the future. The tree no longer has solid roots. Now there is nothing to hold onto. I just have to remember the solid foundation I once had, and stay true to the love and guidance that has brought me safely this far.

So what's this got to do with being adopted? Well, nothing and everything. Now I can go in search of my birth mother. This past couple of weeks has made me totally clear that I am in no way trying to replace Mum or find someone or something that's been missing from my life up until now. No, all I'm looking for is a holiday in a far away place with some nice names. It's not about finding out, it's about getting closure and tying up those last few loose ends. I'm happy with who I am. I am alone but I am strong and I have been blessed to have known so much love and support up until now.

Loss and grief

JADE

Background

My dad was diagnosed with Alzheimer's two years ago. I want to make the most of him while he's still mentally and physically able, although his memory is deteriorating. He could have a reasonable quality of life over the next five or more years, we don't know really. Through going to group therapy over the last five years, I've been thinking a lot about my issues, and one of them is being half-Iranian and not having any link to Iranian culture – the loss and the grief I feel about that. I want to find my birth father and I feel guilty about that, especially now my dad's slipping away very slowly. I feel really sad, as my dad has been a good father to me. I'm going to miss him. It's not that I need to find another father, but I want to know who my birth father is and about my Iranian ancestry.

My dad

My dad is from the north east, from a working-class family. He's very down to earth, with a good sense of humour. As a child, he was great fun to have as a dad. I have two older brothers as well. Being a Baptist minister, my dad was very reliable and caring. He encouraged me a lot when I was growing up, particularly when I had trouble learning to read and write. He used to get me to read out loud, and gave me a confidence about my reading and writing. He is very warm, affectionate, and dependable.

The Alzheimer's has been a very gradual thing. It's only become apparent that his memory is failing him over the last couple of years. He's become quieter. He's struggling with it, quite frustrated that he doesn't remember things, and desperately trying to keep his brain active. My parents live in the north east. I'm going to see them this weekend and I am trying to make more of an effort to see them, despite the distance. Each time I visit, I see a small change in his condition. When I first moved to Bristol, they were in Clevedon, just nearby. But since my dad retired, they have moved back up north where they have a good friendship and support network.

My dad has given me my adoption papers. He understands that it's important for me to know where I come from and whom I'm related to. He had an unusual family background. Maybe that experience made him aware of the importance of knowing one's family history and having a stable family life.

My birth father

My birth father was 24 when I was born in 1967, and he was studying engineering at Exeter Technical College. His family was from Tehran, both his parents were doctors, as far as I know, and the family owned an engineering business. His family were of the B'hai World Faith. His parents left Tehran and moved to Italy in the early to mid-sixties. He was my birth mother, Hélène's, boyfriend for about a year and a half. She is English and I believe I was conceived in Exeter. When he'd finished his studies, he went to visit his parents and she went with him. It was after that visit that she discovered that she was pregnant with me. She told him and he wanted to marry her, but I think she felt, at 19, she wasn't ready. She couldn't imagine being married and living in another country. I don't think he would have been able to stay in this country unless they got married. All that my adoption papers say about him is: 'He has two brothers and a sister. He is five foot and six inches tall, of slim build, with dark hair and dark eyes. He enjoys football, reading and ten-pin bowling.'

So my birth father knows that I was born and given up for adoption. He kept in touch with Hélène for a while after my birth, but the relationship fizzled out. When I first traced Hélène, she gave me a gold coin with the head of the Shah on it that he had given to her. That's the only material possession I have of his. Apparently it's part of a set. His name is Shervin Manoucheri but I don't even know the correct pronunciation. Someone said his last name was a "good name" whatever that means. Maybe he came from a rich family if he was studying abroad. Hélène says that I look more like him than her.

Looking for my birth father

I've been thinking about trying to find my birth father for the last three years, but haven't got very far at all. I paid £100 to the International Social Services. They tried tracing in Italy and getting information from the Iranian Embassy, but to no avail. I need more information to do a proper search. There's no record of him in Italy, and he's not registered in this country. Without a passport number or date of birth, it is very difficult to trace him. If he's still alive he'd be 63 now. I don't know his parents' names so I can't look for them. I've made some small steps forward, but it tends to be two steps forward and one step back. It's painful. I think my birth father would want to hear from me. At times, it's all very overwhelming.

What am I hoping to find? I'm hoping for peace of mind about who I am and where I come from, and not to always feel like I'm not a whole person. All my life I've had that, since I was about ten, when we moved to the north east from London, which was quite a culture shock. That's when I had to face the fact that I am a different colour, mixed race and not related to my family. So began an intensely painful period in my life. People would stare at me – I was the only mixed race girl in my school – and I had never experienced racism and prejudice before. I started feeling self-hate, anger, pity, confusion and self-doubt. The pain had to come out, starting with painkillers, then laxatives, cigarettes and, finally, by cutting the skin on my wrists with keys and my own nails. Suicidal feelings soon followed.

All my life people have asked questions about where I am from, and when I say I'm half Iranian they assume I can speak Farsi and that I know something about the culture. Or they assume it's too cold here for me or that I might go home to another country for Christmas. But this is where I was born and brought up and my culture is English.

It saddens me and makes me angry that I've not had that knowledge and cultural connection. Although I've had a very stable family upbringing, my parents couldn't tell me anything about my ancestry. They just didn't think that it was important. Sometimes I get very angry, confused and emotional. Doing group therapy, I've been able to get in touch with my feelings more clearly and understand myself better.

I always have to explain myself, as my background is confusing to other people. Yet, I get tired of explaining. I say, 'My birth mother' and people ask, 'Is that your first mother or your adoptive mother?' Sometimes I'd like my family background to be a bit more simple.

I've met my birth mother, Hélène, her twin sister, and my half-brother and half-sister. Tracing Hélène resolved quite a few issues for me. Knowing someone that I'm related to has added to my sense of self and my inner security. But I still feel lacking in a lot of ways because I look Iranian. Occasionally I meet people who are of mixed parentage and have their feet firmly in both cultural worlds. I envy people who have that.

My relationship with my birth mother

I've got two mothers now, one that mothered me, and I have my birth mother who didn't mother me, but with whom I do now have a relationship. We are similar in character and temperament, although I don't need her to be my mother. I feel I can be myself in her presence, be exactly how I would be around my friends. She just accepts me as I am.

I don't feel an emotional connection in a daughterly way towards her but I feel affection, and she feels the same. She's not your average mother, not a motherly mother, even to her own children and not very sentimental. She doesn't always remember her other children's birthdays, although when I first made contact with her she made a real effort, as I'd receive a birthday card a week late. I understand that's what she's like.

Hélène married three years after I was adopted and her husband was insecure about the previous relationship that she'd had. He asked her to get rid of letters, photographs, anything to do with my father. If he hadn't been so jealous maybe she would have kept things like that, which I could have seen now – last known address, that sort of thing. I think my birth father went back to Tehran but that may have been temporary. People have asked me if I'd visit Tehran, but why would I go there? I don't have any connections there, I'd feel like an alien. I would have to cover up and act like women do in that country, which would be totally unfamiliar to me. I would visit if I knew somebody in Tehran.

My mum

My mum really wanted a daughter and that is one of the reasons why my parents decided to adopt me. She had already given birth to two sons. I can remember my mum's loud 70s clothes and how she did the housework in lime green crimplene flares. She was a very well-organised mother who provided for her children materially and emotionally. I felt very well cared for. She was a firm but fair parent, warm, caring and loving, and I have a strong emotional attachment to her. My mum can also be very opinionated and set in her ways, often disapproving of other views. She is conventional and adheres to traditional Christian family values. This has given me a strong foundation, even though I might hold different views today. We accept and love each other. I feel secure in her love and I know that she wants me to have a happy life.

When I first spoke to my mum about wanting to find Hélène, she felt quite threatened and spoke honestly with me about her feelings. I reassured her that I was not looking to replace her, to find another mum; that she is my mum who mothered me and nothing could take that away. I needed to connect with my genetic background. My mum has met Hélène on several occasions and understands why I need to search for my father.

Racism

I once lived with a friend I got on really well with. Then one day she said, 'I'm just going down the Paki shop.' It was like she'd slapped me in the face. From the age of ten in the north east, I was the only mixed-race kid in my school and I got a lot of questions, a lot of staring, and a certain amount of racism and taunting, because I stood out like a sore thumb. People used to call me "Paki", "Sambo", "nigger" and "half caste". So, when she said that it was like a poke in the eye. She couldn't understand why I was hurt by her words and thought they were derogatory and abusive. She thought I was being over-sensitive.

Knowledge about Iran

I sometimes wish my parents had made an effort to tell me something about Iran when I was a child. I didn't know where Iran was on a map until I was an adult and did a project in art college about identity and needed to look at Persia. I have a friend who's Turkish and who is part of an organisation called, "A Thousand and One Nights", which puts on cultural nights with music and dance. I went to one at Persian New Year. It was weird, to be in a room surrounded by people who looked like me. I had mixed emotions – happiness to be in the company of Iranian people, sad to feel that I could not really connect, and uncertainty about how to be. I'd never had the experience of being in a room with people who look like me before. I felt very uncomfortable, almost like I had gate-crashed a family party. I didn't feel I had anything in common apart from my Iranian looks and, yet, I really wanted to connect with them.

Messages for adoptive parents

It's really important for people who are adopted, particularly transracial adoptees, to know where they come from. Through working at "Our Place", a centre for adopted children and families, I've met families who've adopted from overseas. At a conference, I was talking to a woman whose son is from South America. He was having problems. She was a lovely caring woman, although naïve about the issues he would have to face. Afterwards, I invited her back here for a chat with me and two of my transracially adopted friends. It was really good for her, and for us. She really wanted to find out what she could do to help her son feel more secure in himself, which was great. She was making an effort to understand our point of view, in order to help him. It turned out that she knew something about her son's parents that she hadn't told him. We encouraged her to tell him and tried to help her to understand how he might feel knowing that information.

I believe that knowledge about adoption should be shared openly, from as early an age as possible. My parents told me from a very young age that I was adopted, which I think is the right thing to do. I met someone who only found out at college that she was adopted; it undermined her self-esteem and sense of identity. She found it very, very difficult. Of course, if you look totally different to your adoptive parents, as many transracial adoptees do, you are likely to know you are adopted.

Messages for other transracially adopted people

I found it really valuable, and good for my psyche, to know other transracially adopted people, to actually have a relationship with other people who have had similar upbringings. This has only happened in the last ten years and I wish I'd known other transracially adopted people when I was younger. Knowing that I'm not alone, and having others to share my feelings, thoughts and disappointments with people who understand is important. My family are supportive and empathetic, but I don't need sympathy or empathy – I want people to understand me.

I also go to group therapy, which has been very helpful. I'm the only transracially adopted person in the group, but there are similarities with other members around abandonment, loss, and grief. Being able to talk openly and share feelings, fears and issues has been really good for my growth and development, laying to rest my ghosts, and increasing my understanding of myself. Now I know why I get upset over things that most people wouldn't. A simple question, 'Where do you come from?', is loaded for me. I never know whether to respond with my life history or to say, 'I live in Bristol. Where are you from?' But other transracially adopted people understand this. I didn't know anyone who was transracially adopted until I started going to group therapy, but one of the other people knew someone who was. Since then my contact with other transracial adoptees has snowballed and it's been wonderful.

Letter to you

ANNA JAI LEI RIBKA

I've never even met you, nor do I know your name
We may be total opposites but p'haps may look the same
We've never shared a birthday, even though our dates are one
The only thing we match on, is the birth country we're from

Some would say it's such a shame that we grew up apart
But I can say you've always had a place within my heart
I'd love to write and tell you about how life is for me
Of all the things I've seen and done and all that's yet to be

I'd love to know where you are now and if you miss me so
But maybe you don't know I'm here; perhaps you just don't know
I wonder what you love and if you'll walk the extra mile
I wonder what will make you cry and what will make you smile

I've grown up a city chick with shops and crowds galore
A far-flung place from Solo, where I started out before
But you don't have to worry, as I am very safe and sound
I'm happy, loved & gorgeous but with both feet on the ground!!

Somewhere out there you're far away, not knowing who I am
Just maybe we're not meant to fit together in life's plan
But if our paths should one day cross, I hope that we can be
The best of friends and close at heart, true twins, just you and me

For now I wish you well and hope that all is fine and good
And that you have a happy life, just as you truly should
So joy and love and laughter, I hope that life will bring
This letter is for you, my one but unbeknown dear twin

2

Childhood

Untitled

PERLITA HARRIS (at age 6)

My mummy is white and my daddy is white and Wendy is white and Ian is white and Peter is white and I am brown and I have black hair.

From left to right: Perlita, Ian, Wendy and Peter

My family

LUKE HOWARD (age 6)

I came with problems – they helped me solve them
I came with my memories – they listened to them
I have my differences – they liked them
I brought my love – they shared theirs with me

Untitled

LUKE HOWARD (age 6)

My mum and dad have lots of children. When I came to be adopted I was not ill then. When I got ill I thought they might be sad and wish they had got a boy with no bad bones. I never thought before being black was sad for them. I know I am good with just how I am. Everyone is different not just me, Daddy says so.

Being different

RACHEL (age 10)

I like being adopted. Just because you don't know who your mother and father is, doesn't mean you have to think you're different to everybody.

My background

In the family that adopted me, there's René,[1] my older sister and there's Mum, Bow the dog, and there's Mum's mum. There's René's father, David, who is like a dad to me but is not my dad. Then there are lots of cousins, aunts and uncles.

René will be 15 in December. I'm 10 and I'll be 11 in December. I was born in 1993, in Luton, in a hospital. I lived with my own mum mostly, and each weekend I would see my nan – she lived next door. I don't remember living with my mum. I lived with my mum and my brother, Brad-Lee. I can't remember how long I lived there. Then I went to live with Cathy, my foster carer, when I was three-and-a-half. In foster care it was quite fun. Cathy has two adopted sons, and they just think that life has to be fun for children while they're in foster care, so we had a good time. I came here to my adoptive family when I was seven-and-a-half.

My brothers

Brad-Lee and Sam, my brothers, they didn't come with me. Brad-Lee is 15 and Sam is about 10; he was born in 1994. Brad-Lee went to other places. The first place he went to was a bad place; he didn't like it. Then he moved to another place and he didn't like it there. Then he changed to a really nice house. But he messed up by going out with the wrong friends. Now he's wishing he never did that stuff because he's in a children's home.

I have contact with Brad-Lee when I go to my nan's. Nan said I might be able to see him before I go away for Christmas. His voice has changed into a man's voice and he's very tall. I really like it when we can chat. Sometimes he turns up late at my

---

[1] Names of people have been changed throughout.

nan's house. Last time I saw him, he didn't call or anything, he just came. He came here once too. I like seeing him. He teaches me about so many things he's done wrong. He looks back and says, 'Oh, I did that wrong, I'm not going to do that wrong ever again'. He says, 'I'm going to look back when I'm 22 and say, "I'll never do that again".' He's changed his mind about how I'm his little sister, his baby sister, and instead he treats me like I'm a more grown-up sister. It's like I'm showing him how to follow the right footsteps.

Mum made up this thing called "the washing machine", where you have different emotions so, when he is upset I teach it to him. I tell him you have bad, happy and sad moods all together, like a washing machine in your tummy, and you're hiding it, and you can't keep it in for long. I tell him to tell his social worker, because he has one, and since he's been doing that he's been feeling a lot better.

He says that there are two directions to go, he's just learnt the left way, and I've learnt the right way. So I say, 'Instead of going left, you might as well go right.' I say, 'If you want to go to the right, you have to stop thinking about everything bad you do.' He's made massive changes.

Brad-Lee and I see each other and we phone. I've sent Brad-Lee a picture of when I was at school with my hair in plaits, and I wrote to him and I gave him a Christmas card.

I'm writing to Sam as well and he writes to me. We send pictures. He's in London; he's adopted. He's adopted by a white family, but he's a browny-white, a middle-brown. He writes to me more than I write to him! I'll send him a card for Christmas.

Who do I look like? I look like Brad-Lee mostly, and my attitude is more like Brad-Lee in a kind of way. My eyes are the same, and we have the same habit of biting our nails. I don't know if I'm like Sam, his eyes look the same in the photograph. I last saw him in photos. I've never seen him in real life.

Being adopted

When I came here, I was a bit scared at first but, then, when I actually got to know mum and René, I felt they wouldn't do anything like smacking or hitting because they don't believe in that. René's brown too. It's nice being with someone else who's brown. When I first met her I was like, 'Oh thank God, I'm not the only one who's brown.' I found it easy getting on with her. In foster care, I was worried I'd go somewhere where I was the only brown person.

René's been great, she's not like a normal horrible sister. When I first came here, I was scared about whether I'd chosen the wrong people, the wrong family. But René and I have loads of fun together. We tickle each other and we dress up, sing, dance and play tricks on each other. She helps me with my homework, hair and clothes, and gives me advice. Sometimes we argue but Mum says that's normal for sisters.

The adoption court hearing

When I was adopted, my mum came into the school and they surprised her by celebrating my adoption. I was given that Tigger when I got adopted. I went to the court when I got adopted, the judge was there in old-fashioned clothes, like a wig and coat. It was so funny because when I looked at the judge he'd got the old-fashioned wig on, and I couldn't stop laughing. He said, 'Do you know what your name is?', and I said my name. I changed my name when I was adopted, that was my choice.

Racism at school

At school, I've had one person say that I'm a nigger, but the rest thought it was really stupid. People don't call me things; I've got quite a lot of friends. When I'm in trouble, or in a fight, my friends say, 'No, you'll have to get past us before you can fight her.' The fight was about them talking about the colour of my skin behind my back. So, because I stick up for everybody, because I don't like anybody hurting my friends, my friends think, 'She stands up for us so we should stand up for her.' The boy who wanted to fight, he has hardly any friends. I did tell Mum but my friends had already helped sort it out. If I respect them then they'll respect me. The boy was so amazed, because he has hardly any friends and I had loads of people sticking up for me.

Another girl, she had her mother in for the whole day, as she was in detention for two weeks. Our Head Teacher said if he hears anybody else talking about my brown skin, he'll have their parents in for the whole day. The girl sent me a letter saying she's really sorry and she won't do it again, and if she does, then the Head Teacher said that she'll be suspended for five days, because he won't put up with it. There are three other brown children at school.

My birth family

In my birth family, I have contact with Nan too, and my two aunties. I've seen them about four times each year. I go and visit them at their house. We hardly ever see them any more. My auntie doesn't look after her kids well, she's got four and finds it hard to cope with them. They are older than me. It's so much fun to see them.

My nan takes me out everywhere. Last time we went on this walk, we had a step monitor, we went to the sea and walked up the pier, and then all the way back to the town where she lives. I stay overnight for a week as she lives a long way away. Sometimes Mum will take me half the way, then swap over with my nan. I like visiting Nan. She's quite small. She's honest and gives the right opinions. I don't think I could have a better nan. My granddad needs another hip operation. He knows a lot more mathematics and how to work mechanical things.

My birth mum and father

I don't have any contact with my birth mum; I don't have a clue where she is. I think she's in heaven. My nan said she might be in Canada, but I don't know. I've just got a feeling; I've felt it for a long time. Brad-Lee and I think she's in heaven. We talk about it, and decide on things together, and show our feelings to each other. My birth mum doesn't keep in contact with Nan, she hasn't heard from her in ages. I last saw her when I was three, and in the picture in my life story book. My feelings are all kind of mixed up when I talk with Brad-Lee.

Some people are adopted, and they've been adopted because their mum can't handle them, and they left when they were older. Most of them know their mum. I think most children know who their birth mum is but I feel different because I don't. I don't think about my birth mum much; I've got a lot more things to think about.

I don't know my birth father. My birth mum went out with millions and millions of people, none of us know which one's our father. When people ask who my parents are, I just have to say, 'I don't know my real mum'. They say it's sad, and they keep it a secret. They think it's weird because it's not normal for them. I just tell them, 'I don't know who my dad is,' and there's no point in asking questions if you don't know. It doesn't annoy me or make me feel sad, it doesn't make me feel anything. I find it quite boring when people ask these questions. And then I just make up something. I say, 'I come from Morocco,' and then that I come from Jamaica, and then they say, 'You said you came from Morocco!'

One girl asked if I've ever seen my other brother, and I said, 'I haven't seen him, only in pictures.' So she went away and she did a draft copy of a book of all the questions people were asking me, and took it to the Headmaster. People were reading it and found it really interesting.

Sometimes it feels as if there are no other adopted children at school, although there are three. I have met some other children and adults who are adopted. It would be OK to meet someone else who is adopted, to talk about it, to seem like I'm not the only person in the world who's adopted. So many people must be, but sometimes it feels like I don't know anyone. It's hard being the only one because I have different things in my mind, but I don't want to think about them. It's funny because if you didn't know that somebody else was adopted and didn't know about anyone else who was adopted, then you wouldn't know there were other people like that in the world. I thought I was the only one. It's strange.

I talk to the teachers and about four friends and they always cheer me up. One boy, he makes up these things that are so funny. He can cheer me up if nobody else can. I talk to my mum and can ask her questions. I don't talk about adoption to anybody really.

I was in the newspaper on Adoption Day, and this person saw it, and they asked, 'What's it like being adopted?' And I said, 'It doesn't matter if you're adopted, you don't have to hate someone just because they're adopted.' It's like, 'You might as well ask me everything, because I'm the only person who's adopted.' So they ask me everything. They do understand what adoption is. In Year Five the teacher taught them everything about adoption. She took me up as a demonstration. I found it really fun. I only don't find it fun if people are being horrible.

Advice for other adopted children

Just to say that it doesn't mean that you're the opposite to everybody because you're adopted. You're special in one way; you may not be special in other ways. I've got dyslexia, which I find really hard, and I'm adopted, and everything else is the same. But everybody's special because they have different personalities. And one person might know science, and another person might know art, and they can help you.

Everybody says I'm special because I'm adopted, but I say that everybody's special in some way.

Feeling safe and secure

It's nice being in a family you know is going to take responsibility for you. I feel safe and secure, and that's good. Then I can relax. I know I'm not going to get adopted again. They want to keep me, and I can be safe and secure here. That's what I really like. On a good day, I'd describe my relationship with Mum as the best of all my relationships.

In a foster family you know it's not forever. It feels like you're there for your whole life, and then the social worker rings you up and says they've found someone to adopt you, and you thought you were going to be there forever. It feels good to just be adopted and be here. But at the time, I didn't want to go. Even though I wanted to stay with my foster family, you have to let it go.

It's not that different being adopted. Sometimes it doesn't feel like being adopted anyway, like Mum is my real parent. Like I've always been here. It's nice. I've never regretted being adopted. I don't think I've ever said that before. It seems like my social worker and I found the right people.

Past

FAY HALLSWORTH

I was brought up by my birth mother and her family in the Welsh Valleys. My father was of West Indian origin. I've only just found out his name. I haven't started to try to find him yet or his family. At the moment I am satisfied with a name after all these years. My three sons want to find out about their grandfather but my mother, who is now 80 years of age, will not speak about him. It's as if he never existed. She's always said that as long as you have a good mother, you don't need a father. Until my mum passes on, I will not try to find him.

When I was ten years old, my mother married and I was adopted by my stepfather. He was a lovely man and, although he passed away seven years ago, I still miss him. I didn't realise I was black and wasn't white like my mother until I went to school. I've never mixed with a black community. There were no black people in the Valleys and I was even afraid of the Indian gentleman who came around selling his wares from a suitcase. Today, although I'm not white, I feel white.

Here is a poem, *Past*, that I wrote 32 years ago. In it I try to describe how it felt being brought up by a white family in the Valleys.

When I was three I was so happy
Then I became four and found I had no Daddy
Soon I was five and started school
Then I found out children can be so cruel
I just couldn't understand why
I had two arms, two legs, two eyes
and was of sound mind.

There wasn't anything wrong physically
as my Mother explained.
It was just that they were fair of face
and God made me the colour of my Dad's race.

As I've grown older I can't live it down
The fact remains I'm still brown.
I still get scared to pass small faces
I remember their cruel words
and the times I cried.
But now I forgive them and hold
my head high and just pass them by.

Steps beyond

ANGIE

Leaving behind little in the way of love and human attachment at the age of three-and-a-half, I was encountering my sixth move. On a "trial" basis I was fostered in to a family of five boys, one girl, two parents and a pedigree dog. In my world, stability had been nothing more than a distant foreign word. Yet I wasn't stupid; I had a plan. I had subconsciously worked out a comfortable survival strategy. Do not open your heart to others, particularly women, and if by any chance you slip up, proceed with great caution.

In the early months of my arrival, disturbed and inconsolable, I screamed out my emotional pains in the interiors of my new family's home. My expressive vocal tools were gradually smothered out of existence in the garden until I quietened down. So my natural instinctive form of deep emotional release became subconsciously locked in whatever body parts would reluctantly hold them. By the age of nine, the trial was over and I was legally bound to the family through adoption.

I wasn't adopted by any old family for I lived in a big house complete with a garden. The garden stretched around the house and was supported by trees bearing fruit, a number of sunflowers, a rose bed and two swings. Every spring time, the two pink blossom trees at either side of the front gate melted my heart. The fresh fragrant smells with the vibrant coloured petals annually adorned the driveway.

Inside the house, I had a favourite room known as the Captain's Cabin. It was a tiny room shaped in the form of its name. The round window overlooking the blossom trees assisted in confirming this notion. I did not immediately occupy this space but none the less it was to become mine. On the surface of things I appeared to have everything that any adopted child would wish for.

But I could see that I was not like other parents' children, with the same skin tones and physical features. In fact, I seemed to be on my own in that department. Even the same-race adopted children, like my sister, had the same skin tones as their adoptive parents.

If I were to calculate the cultural diversity in my local community, the number one springs to mind. I visualise six cardinal arrows fixedly pointing in the direction of myself. My uniformed body amplifying my personal history was to make me the inquisitive subject of the community. I secretly feared and desired to meet other outsiders like me. Male or female was of no concern just as long as they were wearing the same type skin and tight dark hair.

There is little that I remember about the emotionally and physically alienating feelings that engulfed me when I was a child. I have learnt that children are not fuelled with the vocal ammunition or authority to freely journey through their emotions. Nor are they equipped to deal with the pains that embed themselves in the shadowy corners of the body. An overly energetic bundle of life, I swiftly avoided any contact with these deeper emotions. However, I had a recurring dream that echoed the emotional struggles I experienced as a transracial adoptee. Whilst I had little insight into the meaning of the dream, I was forced to confront the density of my feelings. Ordinarily these feelings could not externally be displayed without a cost to my survival. The dream takes place in the house of my adoptive family, where we lived for eleven years.

We have just arrived in our new home; that is, my adoptive parents, five brothers and one sister. In this dream-state world everything is familiar and compatible with that of the external world in which I live and breathe. The house is filled with boxes ready for unpacking and the front room, which all seven of us children are occupying, has become the living room. Finding an instrument of vision to occupy us, we are left to watch the television whilst Mum and Dad are busily unpacking. The television has been placed on a removal box to be the centre piece of our attentions. As we are bundled together on the settee the Saturday matinee comes on. I am positioned at the end nearest the door and have a sense of not belonging. I am distracted and show little interest in the movie. Whilst the other children are fixated on the television, I suddenly leave the room unnoticed. Moving without thought to direction and with a sense of purpose, I head towards the thick, dark green carpeted stairs. As I ascend the stairs, they gradually change form, becoming the steps of a castle. Undaunted by this, I continue to journey up the stairs that are supported by big grey blocks of stone. I arrive at the top of the stairs and enter a room resembling that of a castle tower. In front of me I see a large black cauldron and standing next to the cauldron is a skeleton. Its brown stained frame hints at the age of this skinless figure.

The skeleton is stirring the pot with a wooden spoon and places a number of objects in the pot. At first I am overcome with fear, but the skeleton, reassuring me, wins my trust.

Showing me warmth and love, we become the closest of friends. We have great fun playing together and I can feel the deep connection between us. I am joyous in the company of my new friend. Together we place things in the pot and the skeleton stirs the mixture. We are having a great time when the skeleton suddenly falls in the cauldron and disappears. The separation is quick, intense and immediate and I hold no power to change the situation. It feels like our connection has been sliced in half with a quick clean swipe of a knife leaving no traces of blood. I am drowning in a pit of sorrow. I have lost my friend and I don't know how to get my friend back. On waking from the dream I am left with an overwhelming feeling of loss and abandonment.

Although I stopped having the dream, over the years it occasionally played on my mind. In the dream my family situation amplified my feelings of being an outsider. The feeling is heightened through not quite fitting into society's "normal" cultural rules of family identity. Our genetic make-up symbolically serves as a marker that legitimises our connection to a particular family group.

As a child I had no connection with my immediate family or people who culturally or symbolically represent that side of me. The skeleton represents my ancestral heritage and, along with the skeleton, the castle is a symbol of the passage of time. The objects that are being stirred into the cauldron are my genetic make up. I desired to connect with my family identity and cultural heritage. This is a significant part of who I am. The skeleton falling into the pot is symbolic not only of the loss of my ancestral heritage but the loss of part of my personal history and self.

I did not fully understand the dynamics of the dream until I was a mature woman in my late twenties. As a teenager, I was confused about who I was and where I came from. Some of my so-called friends told me, 'You're not black, you're one of us.' As I got older and ventured into the black community, I was either told that I was black or not black enough. Some African people perceived me as being black whilst others saw me as being white. Some white English people questioned my colouring, rudely demanding to know if I was black or white. When I described myself as being black, my mother accused me of denying being white. My mother did not understand the concept of being black and at that time I struggled to explain what I meant by black.

For years I wished I had been aborted. But I now know that life is a learning process and people will forever label each other, forgetting that we are all genetically the same. We are all struggling for power in one form or another, some more than others. We want to belong, we want to be part of a group. It helps to validate our identity. But not everyone wants you to be in their group as they see it as a threat to their cultural identity and position in society. I think that one of the hardest battles in life is not to be swayed by other people's opinions but to be who you are to the best of your ability. I am a unique human being of Italian, Canadian, American, African and possibly Latin American descent. As a transracial adoptee, I am no longer ashamed or confused about who I am. We live in a world in which we are forever being labelled. Depending on our external and personal belief systems, labels can carry very negative or positive connotations. We can change the negatives into positives or vice versa. We can form sub-groups that challenge the majorities, but we never get away from the entrapment of labels. As a result of my experience, I have begun to slowly realise that I am part of a much richer world that goes beyond labels. I recognise that I am a multi-coloured rainbow of life.

Healing balm

MICHELLE ANDERSON

My birth and birth parents

As far as I know and according to my birth certificate, I was born Michelle Leechee, at Homerton hospital in Hackney, London on April 24th, 1965. I found this discovery somewhat unsettling because, for most of my life, I had considered myself a real south Londoner. Born and bred as it were. If you have ever lived in London you will know that a tangible divide seems to exist between one side of the river and the other. And so, to have such a strong allegiance with one side, when all the time, birth-place-wise at any rate, I actually "belonged" to the other side, more or less sums up how most of my past is: snippets of misinformation that never quite add up, that are never totally accurate.

The name of my father is not recorded on my birth certificate. I remember how incredibly disappointed I was when, after all the rigmarole, I finally received an original copy of my birth certificate. I had very naively, stupidly even, believed that I would finally find out my father's name. When it wasn't there I was in an angry funk for days, bulldozing my way through work and taking out my anger on any unsuspecting and innocent person. I seem to have a lot of anger simmering in me, and it has a way of erupting at the most inopportune moments and usually against my better judgment and will.

To this day I am not certain what my father is called. However, I do know that he was Sudanese and that he came to study medicine in London in the 1960s. This might all be untrue because my sources, as you can imagine, are shaky. Like all the tiny snippets that I have about my past, I have held on to this "fact" tightly. Believing that my father was a doctor in part helped me believe that I was capable of being educated and going to university. It certainly wasn't the expectation of many of the disillusioned teachers I encountered in my run-down inner London schools of the 1970s and 1980s, with the exception of a very few.

The name of my birth mother *is* recorded on my birth certificate. However, this was no fantastic revelation as I had always known her name as far back as I could remember. She was a name with no face, but long silky black hair. My adoptive family always talked about her long silky hair. That was another reason for me to resent her because my hair was and still is wild and bushy and, though reasonably long, far from silky. Only black girls know what they suffer with their hair!

By the time I had got hold of my birth certificate I had actually tracked my birth mother down and, in characteristic angry fashion, had rejected her way before she could even begin to reject me again. But it was never really my birth mother that I had wanted because my adoptive mother had mostly filled her place. It was always my father that I longed to find because no man as yet has replaced him for me.

My adoptive parents

The relationship I had with my adoptive father was distant; he had the capacity to make me seethe with anger and resentment. He was prone to bouts of violence and plate throwing. Nobody in our family ever sat and had family discussions. If you wanted something, you shouted about it; if you were upset, you shouted. Being volatile and Mediterranean seemed to go hand in hand. Yet this was the man who had literally allowed his wife to take me in off the streets. He was also someone who had experienced being in a German prison camp. Is it any wonder, then, that emotionally he was not the most forthcoming of men? I could never initiate a real conversation with my adoptive father. In all the years that I lived in his house I don't remember one real conversation about anything that really mattered. My role in the house was to make sure his bed was made (he didn't sleep in the same room as my adoptive mother – their relationship seemed to have soured years before and they co-existed in their sexless, loveless marriage), to set out the table for when he came in – we rarely ate as a family – and to make myself scarce.

In my whole life I never felt accepted or close to my adoptive father but on the night that he lay dying I dreamed of him and, later on, I found out that, the very hour that he died, I had uncharacteristically awoken disturbed from my dreams. This first lack of bonding with a father figure appears to have impacted on the men I have allowed into my life subsequently – men that I can barely communicate with or men who are emotionally aloof. I am desperate to break away from this cycle.

My adoptive parents, and particularly my adoptive mum, were always vague about the circumstances of how I came to be in their "possession". She over-compensated for the fact that I was not one of her real children by protecting me to the point of smothering me. She protected me so much that, when I finally did meet the world head on, I was truly naive and unprepared.

One early incident I can recall was when my next door neighbour, a Jamaican girl a few years older than I was at the time – I being about seven – decided to inform me with glee, spite and malice that I was adopted and that the family I lived with were *not* really my family. The only explanation for her malevolence was that she had recently lost her own mother and no doubt felt that she shouldn't be alone in her suffering. Perhaps, in some way, my life appeared idyllic to her.

It always baffled me as to how I came to be adopted by a Turkish family in London. It seems that I wasn't properly adopted until I was maybe seven or eight years old. There is no one who can verify these details. I lived with my Turkish family in some sort of informal arrangement until I was at least at primary school. I have vague memories of going to some sort of court and being asked questions about whether or not I wanted to remain with the only people I had ever known as family! I don't think that would have been the moment to have struck out for independence but I suppose they felt they were doing the right thing by consulting me. It makes me think of myself almost like an abandoned pet taken in by a kind family. It is truly bizarre that I could just be left with them and it didn't seem to matter enough to anybody to find out about my circumstances. But, then again, who was really going to care about an abandoned illegitimate black baby in the 1960s?

I loved my adoptive mother because she loved me unconditionally; even in my teens when I made her life hell. She saw the world through rose-tinted glasses and was the sort of person who saw good in everyone. She would always reason with me, even when I was being belligerent, an unfortunate character trait which, however, may be one of the reasons I haven't gone completely over the edge.

I grew to love words because she loved words. She was a talker, a joke teller, and a lover of life; a gossip and a storyteller. Her words were often my healing balm. When I exhibited my characteristic trait of impatience she would say, '*Saburli ol*', be patient, be patient. When things didn't work out it was because of *kismet*.

She was a matriarch, in some senses keeping the family together; she was a pillar of her particular community and well respected. The ramshackle house in which we lived in Camberwell was always a hive of activity with the comings and goings of nearby neighbours and more distant friends. I was always helping my adoptive mother with kneading dough for her varied fried delicacies or stirring batter for her cakes and sweetmeats.

My adoptive mother was a general busybody in the nicest sense. If someone was ill, she would cook food for him or her or visit them. If someone's daughter was coming up to marriageable age, she would offer her tuppence worth on the subject and involve herself in finding a potential husband. She claimed to have fortune-telling skills and the ability to read the dregs of Turkish coffee. If she saw a mouse (in the coffee cup) this would indicate that something would be lost. If she saw a brown envelope it might indicate that you would get good news or even sometimes bad news (no doubt depending on who you were). If you were a single woman, she always saw rings indicating that you would soon be getting engaged. Whenever she read my coffee cup she would see money, fortune and love. Sadly, most of this seems to have alluded me, but I know she meant well.

We spent hours in the kitchen together kneading the *bulgur* for *kofte*, one of her specialties that her friends and neighbours would come to savour. *Bulgur kofte* is a bulgur wheat kneaded into a dough-like texture, filled with savoury minced-meat made with parsley and onions and deep-fried. I still have her *tepsi* hanging in my living room to this day; it is older than me and a reminder of the many happy hours I spent in our small, pokey, ill-equipped kitchen in Camberwell helping my adoptive mother to cook her specialities.

My big brother's best friend's brother

MARIE-JAMILA GILLHAM

When I was nine I had my own bedroom with pink curtains and a duvet to match.
When I was nine I lived in a house with my mum, my dad and my three brothers.
When I was nine, life was simple.

The doorbell rang and, as usual, I ran to the top of the stairs to peep through the banister to see who it was. I knew that I would have to be still and quiet because, really, it was past my bedtime.

I used to find out everything from the top of those stairs. Listening to my mum chatting to my grandmother about her day, or hearing who was going out with who from my brothers. I could work out what was happening to everyone from there. Although, at nine years old, two plus two generally made five!

Dad opened the door and I heard the familiar sound of my big brother's best friend. This time there was another voice; one that sounded like his but different. It was his brother. My big brother's friend's brother was visiting too.

As they came up, I made my presence known. I loved to see and meet new people. My big brother's friend said, 'Hello,' as usual but his brother looked at me in such a way that it made me freeze to the very spot where I stood. It wasn't the usual, 'You're an irritating little girl and I must treat you with the disdain that you deserve.' This was a look of hate, disgust and repulsion. It filled me with apprehension.

I asked my brother, the one that's like me, why he had given such a look. 'They don't like people like us. We steal their women and take their jobs,' he informed me. I didn't want a job, I was only nine and, as for women, what would I want one of them for? I didn't peep through the banisters any more after that.

When I was nine I had my own bedroom with pink curtains and a duvet to match.
When I was nine I lived in a house with my mum, my dad and my three brothers.
When I was nine, life was simple.

'Brown girl in the ring'

NICOLE McKENZIE

'Oh yes, that's a lovely shade of brown, n*gg*r brown we call it.' Two words launched out of that casual remark and winded me like a physical blow to the chest.

The noise in the crowded shop became a distant throng, as n*gg*r brown rang in my ears, ricocheting about in my mind like a stray bullet. Time seemed to stand still, waiting for my reaction. Had anyone else heard? There did seem to be a few glances our way. Were they wondering if their ears had deceived them too, thinking that she can't have said that, not when she was clearly talking to a black person?

Her oblivious ignorance did nothing to lessen the blow, in fact, it just intensified it. This moment like a convulsion forced the other memories to mind, memories that usually lay dormant.

"N*gg*r brown", was a new one to me. I had never heard the expression before. How had I managed to avoid it up until now?

The last time my mother had uttered the "N" word in my presence, I had tried to excuse it and console myself that it was a generational thing. That was despite the fact that it was being gaily recited to my unsuspecting daughter, during a rendition of that notorious nursery rhyme that haunted my own childhood, 'Eenie Meenie Minee Mo'. It had made my stomach turn, seething with resentment and anger. Then, as now, I said nothing, I had been too shocked. On that occasion I had not been alone; my siblings, who were present, jumped in to scold her and try and tactfully explain that it was no longer considered an acceptable rhyme, particularly not for a child of black heritage. I've often wondered what my siblings thought about times like this, if they ever considered the effect these experiences had on my life. Did they ever feel anger towards her and pity towards me? But they never broached the subject, never asked if I was alright. I guess they were too embarrassed. My foster sister was the only one who ever put her neck on the line for me. Once, when we were kids on a camping holiday down south, she took on a group of white youths who were throwing stones at me to the tune of 'Brown girl in the ring'. God, how I hate Boney M. What on earth were they thinking of?

When I came out of my state of shock, I didn't know what to do. Deep inside I wanted to lash out and hurt her. I wanted to utter the most offensive thing I could think of about her whole being, but there was no equivalent! This woman could give the Duke of Edinburgh and Enoch Powell a run for their money. Why did I have to put up with this?

I wanted to scream at her and for everyone to hear so that she felt some kind of shame or public humiliation. I wanted to burst into tears and run away, but I didn't. Instead I took control of my feelings as I had always done and waited for the right moment to explain to my own mother that this was considered to be extremely offensive and racist language. Thank God she had never said anything like this to a black person who wasn't obliged to be so forgiving.

Whilst I stood dead in my tracks, my mother bought the dress which contained a lovely shade of brown, for me to wear to my brother's wedding. I was in such a daze I couldn't offer any resistance, and it ended up in a charity shop, because I couldn't bring myself to look at it let alone wear the damn thing. It's a shame really, it was a nice dress. Now someone else wears it, blissfully unaware of the incident surrounding its purchase.

That was just one comment and one situation. I could tell you of several more like: 'Just remember you are three-quarters white,' or 'You could do with a few white faces on your walls'. The worst experience for me, though, was the day my beautiful Afro hair fell to the floor of a white hairdresser's. This scalping exposed a layer of scabs on my scalp that I could do nothing to disguise. At 12 years of age, and having just started secondary school, where black faces were few and far between, this was hell on earth. I was utterly devastated. I felt like Samson, the little confidence I did have eradicated in one fell swoop of the scissors. You can imagine the ridicule that I faced at school. I still can't even bear to look at photographs of myself from that time of my life. After this catastrophe my mother decided to take advice on black hairdressers. It's a pity she hadn't thought of that before, to grow Afro hair back to that length was going to take years. My mother only managed the one trip with me to the black hairdresser. She felt far too uncomfortable to put herself through that experience more than once. She didn't understand that was a daily occurrence for me but, hey, it's not like I wasn't still the odd one out in there too!

My adolescence was bound to culminate in disaster. It is a difficult enough time for anyone, in terms of establishing one's identity. I was completely lost. White lads didn't seem interested in me and I suddenly found myself overwhelmed by attention from black guys. So, in my quest to be accepted into the black community, I sacrificed myself to the first black guy that came along: one who proceeded to terrorise me, my family and friends. I became pregnant during my teens and things spiralled into another form of hell on earth, but for my daughter, who summoned up a strength and determination in me that transformed our lives. I removed us from that oppressive and abusive situation and we have never looked back since. We found a new home and new friends. I went on to study at university and I am now happily married. I wonder if you can guess what racial group my husband belongs to?

How different my daughter's experience of life has been. She is now a teenager and stands tall and proud. White children look up to her and are envious of her braided hair. She is in the centre of the ring for very different reasons. She doesn't realise how lucky she is!

My daughter knows the troubled times I have been through and I think she admires me for my achievements all the same. She also loves her grandparents dearly, as she should, despite her knowledge of their ignorance. I don't like my mother, but I do love her. I would hate anyone to think that I am not grateful for my upbringing in white, middle-class society, for many of its good qualities and good times. Indeed, looking back, things could have been a whole lot worse. I guess my mother's only fault was thinking that my colour didn't matter, that it is only skin deep. I'm not sure what world she lives in, but it isn't mine.

My story

DYLAN CLEMENTS

I was born on 24 May 1969 at St Brenda's Maternity Hospital, Bristol. I was given the name Darrel John Clements. My mother, Lynn Clements, was 21 and had become pregnant by a 41-year-old married Jamaican man. From that moment, her life fell into turmoil. During the 1960s, it was unacceptable for a white woman to even be in a relationship with, let alone have a child by, a black man. She was given an ultimatum: give up the baby or leave home.

My mother decided to keep me and was asked to leave home. She turned to St John's Mother and Baby Home for help and support. St John's was a national charity, which offered unmarried mothers a place to live prior to having a baby; the infant would then be placed into foster care or found adoptive parents. A month before my birth, my mother was given a short-term residence in St John's. She was unemployed and had nowhere permanent to live with me.

On 31 July 1969, I was taken from my mother and placed in foster care with a family named Hagley, for reasons I would only find out about years later. According to the records, my mother needed time to find work and somewhere where she could live with me. It was decided that foster care would be in my best interest.

The Hagleys, my new foster parents

My first memory could have been when I was six months old, or even older. I was sleeping in my cot and was awoken by the buzzing of a bee or a fly. The buzzing was monotonous and unrelenting, and the room in which I awoke was warm and clammy. It must have been midday or afternoon. I was aware of light filtering through the drawn curtains and a stuffy ambience within the room. It was a rude awakening from my first conscious slumber, to a sense of fear and insecurity. Anxiety overcame me and I started crying. I guess I needed the attention or affirmation of a significant other, someone with the ability to reassure and comfort me. The reason this memory has stayed with me for so long is due in part to the fact that no one came to my assistance. I was alone and must have cried myself to sleep.

My memories of Mrs Hagley are of a woman of warmth and softness. I do not remember her voice ever being raised. She was a gentle being and my primary carer: she fed and clothed me and comforted me when I was overwhelmed by my emotions. Mr Hagley is an enigma; in fact I have very few memories of his presence, yet he must have existed because I have photos and documentary evidence to verify it.

The visit

The second memory engraved into my consciousness is the day when Mrs Hagley said, in a soft and tentative voice, 'Darrel, there is someone here to see you.' A young woman approached the front room where I had been playing, 'Darrel, this is your mother.' These words initially had no bearing for me. They were devoid of meaning. Although I was old enough to glean and interpret non-verbal cues and construe vague nuances in speech, it was only when the young, attractive, dark-haired woman approached me that I was able to understand the deeper significance of what had been said to me. She came across as shy and lacking in confidence but possessed gentle features. Initial words must have been exchanged between Mrs Hagley and my mother, before she was granted permission to cross the unseen boundary separating mother and son.

My mother was not overbearing. I was given time and space to approach her. Reluctantly I crossed the threshold, and a physical bond was reconsecrated after months of separation. When Mrs Hagley had left the room, my mother was able to articulate her truest feelings: 'I love you so much . . . you mean everything to me . . . soon I will come back for you and we will be together again.' This could have been written by a Hollywood script writer or, conversely, a self-constructed fantasy, but this short dialogue always remained within the confines of my memory. The above statement was repeated again and again, in the way that a Buddhist prayer mantra is repeated to reinforce meaning, significance and intention. I have never forgotten her loving mantra, her eternal poem.

This is an early memory. I could not have been older than two and this is the last time I ever saw my mother. It makes this memory amongst the most poignant of all. For years, I was never certain whether it was real, or whether I had constructed it for the purpose of filling in the blank spaces and ultimately creating an ideal fantasy in which a mother disclosed her true love for a son. In my mid-twenties, I conducted a lengthy and thorough search pertaining to my history; no stone was left unturned. I gathered every document I could get my hands on and, to my joy, I discovered that my mother had actually visited me in my foster home, hence my memories were in fact credible.

My mother's words are eternal blessings; these words were all she had to offer. She had no home in which she could care for me, she had lost all remnants of a supportive family and would tragically die within a year of our encounter. She died aged 23.

Rhubarb and sugar

Eating rhubarb, even to this day, triggers in me a primitive memory. My foster parents had a biological son, a year or so older than myself. Bizarrely, I do not recall his name. The few photographs I have of this time depict a young, fair-haired boy. He possessed a nonchalant personality and I have no recollections of him ever smiling.

This memory is of a conversation between my foster brother and myself. We were both sitting in the back yard of the house. It was a bright and hot day. We sat on the floor with a jam jar containing strands of raw rhubarb and a separate bowl of sugar was set between us. I had never seen rhubarb before. It wasn't until my brother demonstrated, that I understood the significance of these objects. He grabbed a stick of rhubarb from his jar, stuck the tip in his mouth, and next, without biting or chewing, dipped it in the bowl of white stuff. The final destination of rhubarb and sugar was disclosed, and the whole combo was vigorously consumed, and the same process re-enacted.

During a pause in the ingestion of rhubarb, my brother exclaimed, 'They're going to get rid of you.' Although I was only four, from my brother's brief but harsh utterance, I immediately understood the gravity of his covert disclosure. It was also apparent that he did not share my discomfort concerning my newfound status of short-term tenant. I can only presume that he had overheard my foster parents discussing my impending removal from their lives and home. This created in me a feeling of absolute fear and horror.

The next chronological memory confirms that my brother's disclosure was genuine. I was swept from my feet and placed on my foster mother's lap in a tight embrace. Normally, being in this woman's arms was one of the most comforting experiences.

Although I do not remember exactly word for word what was said to me, I do remember the core phrases used in her declaration: 'Darrell you know that we love you very much. We have to go away and we won't be coming back. Although we really want you to come with us, I'm afraid we can't take you. You will be really well looked after. We will always love you.'

From my foster mother's intonation rather than the meaning of her words, I realised that my life as I knew it hung in the balance. Insecurity had been implanted deep within me. I was unable to contend against the combined wills of my foster parents. If my struggle for acceptance had been purely waged against my foster mother, maybe I could have won and remained as part of the family. I believe that, in this case, though, my foster father wielded the ultimate power.

The removal

The most difficult memory occurs in the hallway of my foster parents' home, the grand finale of three turbulent years. The hallway was narrow and solely served the function of exiting or entering the home. The front door was fitted with a small pane of frosted glass. The doorbell was rung only once, a sign that my mysterious visitor was expected. I was dressed in my finest outfit, a child's three-piece suit. I was in my foster father's arms; my foster mother was slightly further away from the front door. I was aware of the shadowy outline of a figure standing motionless on the other side of the door. My foster father opened the door with me still clinging to him. A grey looking man wearing a grey suit appeared before us.

My nemesis had arrived, the bearer of bad tidings, the middle man, the errand boy or the reluctant third party. What he was was irrelevant, but what he did was profound. The man never crossed the threshold of the home. I was passed to the grey man in one efficient and purposeful movement, reminiscent of how an auction steward would move a precious antique onto a podium for sale; with no thought to my impending fate but simply relieved to relinquish responsibility.

As I was being passed towards the grey man, my foster mother became overcome with grief. What happened next shook my foundations: a deep resonating cry exploded from her. It was only when she cried out in grief and loss that I realised the finality of my predicament; her cry mirrored my sense of hopelessness. I never saw the Hagleys again.

The social services report stated:

> *At that time Mr and Mrs Hagley's family consisted of their five-year-old son and Darrell, and it was thought that they were unable to have more children of their own. However, in February 1971, Mrs Hagley gave birth to a daughter and another daughter arrived in September 1972. With the addition of these two children of their own Mr and Mrs Hagley's attitude towards Darrell seemed to change. Because of his colour they say they had experienced difficulty with relatives and neighbours and, in addition, Mrs Hagley was unable to give Darrell the time he was used to with the result that he became rather clinging and attention-seeking. He had always been a very affectionate and demonstrative child and had strong feelings of rivalry towards the younger children in the foster home, although he was never aggressive towards them. Marital disharmony following the birth of the youngest daughter made the home situation very tense and Darrell became the scapegoat, culminating in his removal from the foster home at Mr and Mrs Hagley's request on the 3rd June 1973.* (Gloucestershire Social Services report, 1975)

This shed light onto the circumstances of my removal from the Hagleys' home, but it left many questions unanswered. The document is blunt and unsentimental, as official documents tend to be. If the Hagleys were around today, they could well disagree with the official version of events. I am surprised that I had two younger sisters, as I have no memory of them.

The orphanage

My first encounter was with a young woman who, for a brief moment, became infatuated with me. The young woman picked me up and exclaimed to the other staff, 'Isn't he beautiful . . . his skin is lovely, he is so cute.' I guess in those days a mixed-race child was still a novelty, but her feelings for me were probably sincere. I remember feeling slightly embarrassed by the attention. I sucked on my thumb and with the other hand twirled my hair around my forefinger and thumb. This amused the young woman and my helplessness was bared for all to see.

My memories of this lowest point in my life are fragmented and vague. The only record of my year there states:

Darrell was then placed at Walton House, Tewkesbury, Gloucestershire, a residential nursery, where the insecurity he had experienced during his last few months in his foster home was aggravated and he became withdrawn and unhappy.

My memories of being in the nursery are mainly of spending vast amounts of time on my own. For any four-year-old this could be disastrous, and only years later did I discover the full extent of what being neglected means. I have fragmented memories of being alone in a stark room on many occasions. Although alone, I would converse with a presence within the room. There was something with me and I felt comforted by its being there. I was at the most vulnerable point in my life and was alone but not alone.

Even to this day, I have an over-developed familiarity with being alone. It is a state that appears to belong to me, and it can be strangely comforting to exist in a space devoid of other people. I sometimes feel that I am still trapped in that small room in the nursery. My isolation in those formative years has imprinted indelibly in my head a feeling of suspended animation. That year produced in me a state of arrested development, so I always see myself as being a year younger than my actual age, the year spent in the nursery does not count.

Adoption

On 11 November 1973, a family called Braddick expressed an interest in me, and I spent a number of introductory weekends with them. After spending the Christmas of 1973 with the Braddicks, I apparently refused to go back to the nursery. This was a turning point and, on 25 September 1974, the Braddicks formally adopted me.

The Braddicks were a liberal, middle-class couple. Bill Braddick was 24 and Kate was 29. Kate had a daughter from a previous marriage, Samantha, two years older than myself.

My adoptive parents decided to re-name me; the story goes that when they asked me what I wanted to be called, I replied that I wanted to be called Bill. This caused some amusement and it was explained that I could not be called Bill because that was my new father's name. They asked me if I wanted to be called Dyl – short for Dylan and sounding very much like Bill. I agreed.

Bob Dylan was one of Bill's musical icons, and we share the same birthday, 24 May.

I was also given a new middle name, Gabriel. Years later, I discovered that the word Gabriel is Hebrew and means "Man of God". This has always amused me because my adoptive parents had no particular religious convictions, and Kate always exhibited hostility towards Christianity. I realise that the naming of a child is hugely significant and, being a person of faith, I realise that God's divine will may have prevailed and decreed the granting of a Hebrew name.

At first I was cautious of the Braddicks, my faith in family units having been severely tested. The transition was helped by having a new sister and, in a short time, Samantha and I became best friends. Kate, during this period in my life, was a competent and loving mother. She appeared to enjoy having a new son, and relished the challenge of bringing up this mysterious child.

We spent a lot of time as a family going on walks and doing constructive, life-affirming things. Bill was a rock for me: he was a fair, joyful and enthusiastic man. I vividly remember his laughter and feeling comforted by it. We spent a lot of time visiting other families, going on boat trips, walks in the country, swimming, picnics, exciting journeys, making things, building camps, visiting relatives, etc. There was so much stimulation; for the first time in my life I understood what it meant to be a member of a family and I flourished. Love became tangible.

I feel my life only really started after the Braddicks adopted me. It is as if I had awoken from a bad dream, and now I could really begin to live. Even so, I knew from experience that things could change at any moment. I attempted to suppress these insecurities by testing my new parents. I had to know that the Braddicks were in for the long haul and that they would not abandon me.

The next four years were to be the happiest of my childhood, maybe just enough to give me a feeling of belonging. Maybe my faith in the family had been salvaged and resurrected. However, there was always an uncomfortable reminder that I did not entirely belong to the Braddicks; because I was brown and they were white, it made me conscious of being different to everyone else, never quite legitimate.

The broken vase

I was never as competent in the art of deception as my sister. If challenged when something was mysteriously broken, I would doggedly reply, 'It wasn't me,' even though it was. I was petrified of the consequences of owning up and taking the rap.

However much Kate tried to persuade me of the merits of being honest, I could not imagine being forgiven. Kate often called me a pathological liar. She believed that my deception was based on an unwillingness to face the truth, but it was actually fear of abandonment if I admitted to the truth.

All good things come to an end

Most of my childhood with the Braddicks was spent in a nomadic existence: Kate was a costume designer, which meant regular moves from one theatre to another. I never spent more than three years in any one school. In the early days of my adoption Bill was househusband, while Kate was the primary breadwinner.

Bill was a competent carer and I have fond memories of the time we spent together. In Norridge, Norfolk, we moved into a bungalow. Our new house was substantially smaller than our former, three-storey city dwelling. I was impressed by a garden that appeared to go on forever. The new garden was oblong, and possessed a number of features worthy of any adventurous child's attentions. For me it was a personal laboratory of fun, a place where I was free from the prying and interfering attentions of adults. It was a place where I was able to develop a degree of independence and freedom.

The summers of 1975 and 1976 were exceptionally hot and long, and Samantha and I spent hours playing in the garden and bonding as brother and sister. We became very close, relying on each other for entertainment and companionship.

On the move again

After a couple years, we were once again on the move, this time back to Bristol. I do not know what prompted my parents to move back. I believe this is when cracks started to appear in their marriage.

Moving meant making new friends and adjusting to a new school. Our new house was a Victorian terrace in the middle-class suburb of Westbury Park, with a much smaller garden than the one we had left behind. However, there was a network of alleys connecting the back gardens, which became an extended playground in which friendships developed with local children. It was here that Bill taught Sam and I to ride bikes.

At school I was a slow learner and was usually placed in the remedial groups, which came with the stigma of being "thick", being constantly ridiculed by others and excluded by the majority of other pupils. I was finally diagnosed with dyslexia but this did little to protect me from ridicule and exclusion. Teaching methods in the 70s and 80s usually consisted of public humiliation and ridicule; within the classroom my confidence became fragile, to the extent that I made a conscious effort to give up on formal learning. I spent a large amount of time day-dreaming and fantasising. My play revolved around war and fighting. It also consisted of contradictions. I used to love constructing three-dimensional forms out of Lego, but also enjoyed destroying things, including plants, flowers, toys, clothes, small insects – in fact almost anything I could get my hands on.

The divorce

One day I awoke to discover that Bill was leaving us. Kate had a letter from Bill saying he would not be coming back. I was absolutely devastated. I realised I would no longer have anyone to fight my corner and would be exposed to Kate's bias. My trust and respect for her began to evaporate. Kate's gentle approach was replaced by hostility, fear and neurosis. It was at that point I became a scapegoat for Kate's fury. On many occasions she beat me. With hindsight I realise that I was being punished for Bill's absence from her life; maybe she thought that in punishing me she would somehow be getting back at Bill.

For years I was in denial that my adoptive mother actually physically and emotionally abused me. It took a long time for me to come to terms with this.

Kate experimented with a number of short-term relationships until Peter Bowls became her permanent partner. Pete was a 30-year-old Londoner who had lived in Bristol for a number of years and was a builder. He was in many ways the antithesis of Kate – informal and relaxed, whereas she was formal and rather staid. I made an instant connection with Pete; he had a natural aptitude for communication and entranced me with his wide and varied knowledge of many interesting subjects. I probably learnt more from Pete than I did in formal education. Not long after Pete moved in with us, Kate became pregnant.

Boarding school

Due to tensions in the household and my inability to progress within the state education system, Bill and Kate had decided that it would be in my best interest to be sent to a specialist public school.

Bill had broken the news during a restaurant meal. The boarding school option was spun to make me believe the plan was a brilliant idea. I am sure that Bill's intention was genuine, and eventually I was persuaded to comply. In some ways, I became genuinely excited about starting a new school but I have always been suspicious of Kate's motives for sending me to boarding school, I think it was simply a convenient way of removing me from her life under the guise of meeting my educational needs. Whichever way you look at this, the basic fact is that the spirit of my adoption was broken. To adopt a child at five and then to send that child back into an institution at nine is a gross betrayal of the principles of adoption. Regulation of adoption then was minimal if not non-existent. When a child was adopted the state no longer had any interest in the welfare of the adoptee. It amuses me that the RSPCA have educated the nation with the campaign slogan "A dog is for life, not just for Christmas". It should have been "An adoptee is for life, not just for Christmas".

So I was packed off to Edington boarding school, a public school designed to meet the needs of dyslexic children. Classes were smaller and most of the teachers were specialists. Self-discipline and personal responsibility were encouraged; the school was resourced to a high standard and the facilities were excellent. Every minute was structured and planned. This routine was reassuring and brought an element of stability back into my life. My teachers were patient, competent, and exhibited empathy, which I had not experienced in the state education system. The downside was the use of corporal chastisement; on three occasions I experienced the ferocity of the headmaster's stick. Yet, I never begrudged the headmaster, Mr Trump, who was a fair, fun and kind-hearted man and genuinely wanted to help us.

Mr Trump and his wife (the matron) detested Kate for not visiting me. Each time I was not visited it caused me great pain and heartbreak. Words cannot describe the feelings that come with abandonment. On one holiday weekend I was the only pupil not to go home, and stayed with Mr and Mrs Trump. They were extremely kind to me and allowed me stay up late and eat as much ice cream as was humanly possible. Over the weekend I overheard them expressing their disbelief at Kate's neglectful treatment of me.

With hindsight, I am grateful that, throughout the traumas of my childhood, there were always a number of inherently good and compassionate people around. Without their support, I may well have turned out with worse traits and possibly abandoned notions of goodness and traded them for hate and rage. I have absolutely no idea why Kate acted in the way that she did. I find it hard to believe that she would have consciously engineered making those moments at Edington a misery for me. I think it is more a case of "out of sight, out of mind". After two-and-a-half years I was pulled out of the school and returned to live with Kate.

Kate loses the plot

When we moved to Cornwall in the early 80s, Kate's divorce from Bill was almost complete and there were two additional members of the family: my mother's recent partner Pete and their daughter Tamarisk or Tam for short.

Pete was a pleasant individual and genuinely seemed to enjoy interacting with me and I think was aware of my strong character and sense of individuality, traits we both shared. Pete had a profound love of the arts and became my mentor in many areas of creativity. While others doubted my abilities and talents, Pete was genuinely supportive and did not indulge in Kate's practice of deprecating my academic ability. I was fascinated by Pete's eccentric behaviour and his rebellious nature; he didn't appear to care about how others perceived him. In Pete, I found a male role model.

When we moved to Cornwall, a drastic change occurred in Kate's character. She made things very difficult for me and it was hard to relax in her presence. If I was watching TV, she would start hoovering and cleaning; this became the trademark of her obsessive behaviour. Her verbal assaults became ritualised and her behaviour became increasingly manic. I was regularly ill with coughs and colds, probably exacerbated by constant feelings of insecurity. Kate's verbal, physical and emotional abuse eventually reached a crescendo. She woke me, prodding me in the chest, and began ranting that I was the one to blame for the breakdown of her relationship with Pete. Her eyes were filled with hatred and venom. The penny had finally dropped and I realised at the age of 13 that Kate had lost the plot, and that, maybe, just maybe, she and not myself was the real cause of the problem, whatever that might be. This revelation gave me strength and I was determined not to become a victim of her cruel and callous behaviour.

Kate was often alarmingly superficial and disloyal. One Christmas, a puppy was bought for Tam. After a couple of months, it became a hassle and was dumped. This fate was shared by many of our pets during my childhood: when the novelty had worn off, they were usually disposed of, seemingly without much care or concern. The same fate would befall me. Kate's cruelty appeared to have no boundaries at this time; she was capable of doing anything to achieve her objectives.

The verbal threats started when I was 13. At first, they were subtle and veiled, but eventually turned into a declaration of total war. I believe that Kate had planned for many months a way in which she could get rid of me legitimately. She had to somehow convince the social services that I was a liability and could no longer live with her.

Kate wrote a letter to the social services and then read it out in front of me. The letter pleaded with them to take me into care. By this point, I had become numb to her emotional assaults. During the last couple of months, Kate would not speak to me for days on end; when she did, it was communication in monosyllables. It could not have been made clearer to me that my presence was no longer required.

I was given very little notice that I would be leaving to take up residence in a children's home, 150 miles away in south Cornwall. After months of threats, it still came as a shock to hear that I was being kicked out. The sense of betrayal was immense. However, even to the last moment, my abandonment was spun as a very good thing for everyone. No matter what anyone said, in my heart I knew that Kate was about to betray me. I realised that my adoption was a sham, the certificate was not worth the paper it was written on. I was now going to share the fate of the unwanted pets.

Pete accompanied Kate and me on my final journey to Endsleigh House. When I first heard the name it worried me, reeking of an institution, and the first syllable, End, represented the end of any notion that I belonged to a family. I realised very quickly that those things that I had taken for granted were now going to be permanently removed. What was once personal would now become impersonal; everything would be turned on its head. My life as I had known it was finished; I would now lead a public existence under the close and constant scrutiny of the supervising residential staff.

As we drove up the short drive to the house, I noticed an austere Victorian building before me; the façade of the house was in the style of Victorian gothic. The house was gloomy and foreboding; it would be fair to say that this was the archetypal House of Evil. The house did not have a welcoming vibration and my heart sunk when the reality began to sink in that this was to be my home.

3

Who am I?

What do you see? *Miranda Wilkinson*
The transracial adopters' shopping list *Shakti*

Self-portrait with attachment disorder

by DEBORAH WEYMONT

*Exhibited in '. . . living with loss . . .' by Deborah Weymont
at Our Place, Bristol, 22–26 March 2004*

England forever!?

BELLA FREY

I wake, being informed by the great BBC,
I rise, in anticipation, of a hot cup of tea.
My breakfast consists of marmalade on toast,
And on Sunday, at two, it's the best British roast.
Yorkshire puds, gravy, beef on the bone,
England to me will forever be home.
My heart and my head have always been there,
Though people still point, pass comment and stare.
'How's life in China?' How the hell should I know?
Now get lost you creep, I'm not a freak show!
Korea gave me life, sent me on to the West,
I can't really blame anyone, they thought it was best.
Why is it so hard for people to see
That I'm part of England, and she's part of me?
My whole life has been here, I'm as English as you,
If my face matched my heart, it would be red, white and blue!

What's in a name?

MARIYAM MAULE

What's in a name?
The love of a mother, whose daughter is yet unborn,
Suspended in the chamber of life
Still to be revealed in all her beauty.

What's in a name?
The roots of a father
Land whose blood runs through you
As the Nile runs through the land of your birth.

A missing link in the chain of life
The clue that solves the puzzle
A name to remember, to be proud of
A name to greet you first thing in the morning
To say farewell at night.

What's in a name?
A sense of your history
Your birthright.
I ask the question again
What's in a name?
A name is everything
To me.

Who am I?

SHARON HARWOOD

Sharon . . . that has been my name.
For twenty-six years that's who I've become . . .
I was born in the year 1975, November 17th,
So I was told, made to believe.
South Korea, Pusan, shanty town, as it's known,
My birth place, my first home.
Korean by race, by face,
But Korean at heart it's hard to place . . .
Twenty-six years I've not been that girl,
who once was Korean, with a surname, a father, a citizen place.
For without a father, a surname, there is no place,
for me.

Twenty-six years ago I became BRITISH property,
Like many others, just a simple novelty!
Clear the fear, drawn upon my palette,
Tears stinging my cheeks as the exchange, from him to them . . .
as they took me to what was to become my new den!
Lucky for me they were loving and kind
and always knew what played on my mind.
'Are they my new family just for now or forever?'
They didn't need to answer, ever.
Because I knew that they loved me.

So . . . twenty-eight years later, I'm living the British way,
In all that I do and most of what I say!
I have two beautiful children that I love so much,
But a chord on my heart it does touch,

For when they were born and I looked in their eyes,
I'm sure they could hear my silent cries . . .
How can a MOTHER give up her child?
And now that I near the thirty mark,
I have that question still to ask.

I'm torn into pieces to know what to do,
Should I stay as I am, or look for you?
You being the person that left me . . .
on the doorstep of a stranger to hold my destiny.
All those years ago, you just left.
Did you just keep on walking, or did you watch?
Did you see the stranger take me in?
How did you know that the stranger would look after me?
Or didn't it matter, just as long as you were rid?
WHO THE FUCK AM I?

I want to know my name at least.
My birthday, is it the same?
Was I really born in a shanty hut fit for rats,
Or was I a princess, with gold lace and diamond hats?
Is my size three shoe the same as you?
And my tanned peasant skin, the tale within,
Eldest daughter, only slaughter,
Or just the draw of the straw,
Better luck next time!!

I've been beating myself up, these past few years,
Wondering who brought me into this world I live in,
But is it you I need to find?
For who am I?
Only you know where I get my looks, my height and shoe size,
But not even you know who I am,

and for that I'm kinda sad . . .
Sad that I wasn't given the choice to stay or go,
and that I didn't know.
I must have been standing alone for so long.
At eighteen months I'm supposed to be strong!
I must have cried as you walked away,
cried and staring, in dismay.
As you walked, ran, away from me forever,
WE were supposed to be TOGETHER!!
How am I supposed to move on and forgive,
when I don't really know why my story is this?

If I looked for you, what would I find?
How would I feel, staring you in the eyes?
Or would I simply be blind?
What could you say to take away
the loneliness I have had all this time?
Would we embrace, like families lost at war
Or are the wounds still very sore?
Would we cry in each other's arms
Or stand frozen in alarm?
What would be the first words said
Or can you read the words in my head?
For if you could, it would simply be . . .
WHO AM I? PLEASE TELL ME!
And set me free . . .

Free from the hurt and the loneliness that I
carry in my heart, my soul, my eyes.
For you owe me this at least –
One love, one peace!

So where are you from?

So where are you from?

The question was inevitable yet I was always unprepared, disappointed. For most people this question would appear simply to be part of the course of a social conversation. I felt as if I were being interrogated, as though on trial for crimes of a constantly changing nature. I was being judged. I had to justify my existence, prove that despite having foreign features I was actually "white".

I grew up in a small rural market town. I was sent to "good" schools. I received much love and attention from my white adoptive parents. I used to cry a lot. I was told I was "sensitive".

Like most kids I craved the approval and acceptance of my peers, but they seemed so different to me. They seemed to know something secret. Although I had been told from an early age that I was adopted, that my African father and English mother could not look after me so I have been specially chosen, I did not really understand the full implications of being an "off the peg" baby. I remember going to a party organised by the adoption agency and being interviewed by a Radio 4 journalist on what it was like to be adopted. 'It means that I was specially picked out by mummy and daddy.' I was asked if I knew why I was a different colour to mummy and daddy. 'Because I have been in the sun too long,' I replied, much to the shock of my parents.

I wanted so much to look like the other kids in my class. In my eyes the main difference seemed to be my hair. The other boys I knew had brown hair, or blond hair, or red hair. Hair that moved as they moved. Hair that blew around in the wind into their eyes and mouths. Hair that they could hide behind. My hair was cut close to my scalp. My head looked like an egg. I felt exposed and alien. When I left home to go away to college I decided to see what would happen if I grew my hair, ironing out the crinkles with my travel iron. I no longer looked like an egg but I looked even more alien. I gave up playing with my hair and also gave up looking in mirrors. I removed every mirror in my flat. I stopped trying to look like anyone else. In fact I went out of my way to appear more alien. I wore odd clothes and listened to strange music. But despite this I was desperate for people to like me.

'So where are you from?'

'I'm from Buckingham. It is a small rural market town in the Home Counties.'

'Oh really! That sounds very nice . . . but where were you born?'

'In London, I think.'

'But I mean where are your parents from?'

'From Hampshire.'

'Oh really! I cannot help noticing that you have a bit of a tint.'

'Oh really! Where are you from?'

I finished my degree and moved to London. This was the first time I had early been near to black people. I was near but I was not close. They seemed to know a similar secret to the people back home in my small rural market town. I could see vague physical similarities between myself and these black people but I still felt very much like an alien. There were just more of us aliens.

'Hey, where are you from?'

'I'm adopted. I grew up in the country. My parents are white.'

I found myself a job. I found myself a partner. A white partner. I found myself with emotional and professional responsibilities. Three and a half years of juggling these responsibilities with my regular nervous breakdowns became a drag. I decided to find my *self*. Or more specifically, to find my natural parents.

As it turned out I did not have to do much searching. I contacted the adoption agency, which in turn was able to quickly contact my natural mother. She sent back a message saying she could not see what purpose would be served by my contacting here and as far as she was concerned the details of my father were something she wished to keep in here past. She was emphatic. The matter was closed.

Despite not getting the outcome I had wanted, I was comforted by the knowledge that someone had owned up to my existence. I had concrete proof that I was not from Mars. For the first time I actually felt I had something in common with the rest of the world. I found hope.

'Where are you from?'

'I'm black. My father is African and my mother is English. I'm also adopted. My adoptive parents are white.'

Last week I discovered that my partner's new car had been broken into.

'I'm so sorry about your car. I know how much it means to you.'

'I know. It is unfortunate, but I'm ninety-nine per cent sure the person who did it is your colour.'

I felt ashamed, angry, confused. My hope is gone.

'So Russell . . . where are you from? You look so exotic.'

'I'm not sure. But believe me, you don't want to go there.'

Acknowledgement: 'So where are you from?' was first published in Phillips R and McWilliam (eds), *After Adoption: Working with adoptive families*, London: BAAF, 1996.

Narcissus

JULIA AUSTIN

Love was never a rainbow
Love was white.
In mirrors lay my heart
Worn by recognition and rejection
Sweet dream sister
We two of a kind
I wanted to love you
But I couldn't reach you
And all my white lovers can't piece us together.

Fantasy, for Maura

E. STANHOPE

In another place, on another plane,
alongside now yet sight unseen,
I'm living a life with familiar actors
whose moves are known but have never been.

This other woman's reflection is equal,
yet moves with a grace that is taken for granted.
She knows who she is and where she has come from.
She belongs where she grew and stays where she's planted.

It's a dangerous game to think of her so,
because I'm related to her but curiously not.
She's more desirable than me and able to keep.
She's the original model that no one forgot.

And so, I will always be in her presence
but not in her shadow. I'm earning a place
where kinky hair and rootless roots
are enough.
I've learnt to love my face.

Fish outta water

MICHELLE ANDERSON

Here I am in the land of the Kiwis, both the feathered and *Pakeha* (European) variety. It is as beautiful as all the glossies say. New Zealand has everything going for it: "fresh new country", space, less pollution, less traffic, less noticeably crazy people, less people altogether! Yet, why do I feel such a fish out of water here? I don't think it's just about feeling displaced because I am a "foreigner abroad". I think it has more to do with being transracially adopted. Here's how . . .

New Zealanders, at least the ones I have met, are fairly family-orientated, very decent sorts. Sitting around someone's dinner table we held hands to say grace and the sentiment was genuine. New Zealanders, both *Pakeha* and Maori, have strong cultural, religious and family bonds. The Maori talk about the *Whanau, hapu, iwi* (levels of family and other relatedness) which extends beyond the immediate family members and encompasses the whole community. Having a family, being part of a community and love are seen as interlinked. Whilst Maori history in New Zealand spans over a thousand years and *Pakeha* history covers a far shorter span of time, the two histories have become inextricably interlinked. That is not to say there are no tensions here, because there are.

On a visit to Rotorua, a place of spiritual significance for Maori, where geysers throw out clouds of steam metres high into the air, where there is a constant smell of sulphur in the air, where mud puddles gurgle ominously, and where the Maori have learnt to use the strange quirks of nature – for instance, using the boiling volcanic water to cook with – my sense of not belonging was very much heightened. Our guide was keen to emphasise that Maori had a long and successful occupation of Aotearoa (New Zealand) prior to the arrival of the *Pakeha*; that the carvings on the *Marae* (the meeting house in the village) were done by his ancestors. For someone who can't even go as far back as my own father, this leaves a very hard lump in the throat!

Maori have their own oral traditions, songs and dances passed on communally. The village that we were visiting was due to close to tourists later on that day because someone had died and the whole community was due to turn up to observe the burial traditions. At this point, as a transracially adopted adult, I have to stop and ponder about the traditions that have been lost to me. When I pass on, I certainly won't have a "community" showing up to read the last rites. And what traditions can I hand on to my son? Certainly not centuries-old traditions to help ease the pain of death and to give explanations in comforting stories.

I can't be alone in thinking that, being transracially adopted, we have lost something: lost our languages, traditions, culture and, most importantly, the subtleties and nuances of these languages and cultures. We have lost something we never had which we may not have even valued had we had it and, yet, we continue to mourn. Am I alone in this grief?

New Zealand, a place of immense beauty, has brought out the saddest feelings in me. Sitting on a deserted beach, shimmering with black volcanic sand, knowing hardly anyone and with time on my hands, maybe I have too much time to think. London is busy, fragmented and stressful. Maybe London is a healthy context to find yourself in if you are transracially adopted. New Zealand has brought home to me that I never really belonged, that my Whanau is non-existent; that I walk this walk alone.

To be a foreigner and stand strong, one needs to have a certainty about oneself, a confidence that your foreignness marks you as foreign because you belong to some distinctive group or culture, speak some distinctive language to which you are "genetically" linked, have some sense of pride in being Chinese, Greek, Croatian. It doesn't matter as long as *you* know. But what essence and certainty does this transracially adopted, African-Caribbean-origin, brought-up-by-a-Turkish-family person have? Who knows? Certainly, not me.

Foreigners abroad have a way of finding each other. Here there are Chinese, Samoan, Tongan, Albanian, South African, Turkish and Sudanese communities (to name but a few). I had the urge on several occasions to pop into a Turkish café and say, 'Hi', to make a connection with a "community"; to say, 'I understand your language, I know about your food, I understand the subtleties of your culture, I can read your signs.' But, having to explain over and over again how I have come to gain this knowledge has become wearisome; pariah is a hard place to be. On one occasion, when I was attempting to "connect" again, we went to a "cultural" day – an event to promote the refugee service. I wanted to say to the people at the Sudanese stall, 'I too am of Sudanese extraction . . . maybe you're my cousin? From the same place?' That was until the Sudanese group started performing. Then I squirmed and shifted, and felt glad that I could not be readily connected as being connected. My westernised mind was ashamed by the unsophisticated display that was taking place on the stage. These people didn't know anything about what a "performance" to the westernised mind should consist of; that it had a beginning, middle and end; that people didn't get up and leave or join in the middle; that the sunglasses worn by one or two of the men seemed to be directly at odds with the traditional costumes; that there was a right time to take the cue to exit, before large numbers of the crowd started moving on! This wasn't a performance at the Africa Centre! I hated the organiser for not letting these people into some of the secrets, for exposing them in this way. I hated them for not realising that they were making a total spectacle of themselves and *mostly, I hated myself*, for not seeing through anything but westernised eyes.

I have realised my "Englishness" whilst aboard. This revelation in itself has been a shock. My Englishness sits uncomfortably with the skin without. With my colonised and colonial mentality, I have worried that the areas where the "natives" live may be less safe than where the *Pakehas* are. Certainly, they are noticeably poorer. I have tried not to believe the stories about Pacific Islanders. I have worried about my son's school, hoping that it is not composed predominantly of one group or another. I have been as guarded and aloof as a Victorian Englishwoman abroad; affronted when my Englishness is not recognised, elated when my "high status" British accent has received a positive response from *Pakeha* or Pacific Islander.

Deeply entrenched in me are feelings and beliefs that are abhorrent to me but that seem to form some core part of me. *I have been assimilated beautifully . . .* how about you? My links to the "motherland" have also placed me in several discomforting situations. On one occasion, I found myself singing World War Two songs with a group of ex-pats! I had been accepted into that particular circle because I, too, was from the homeland. I found this unnerving and bizarre. Would I have been welcomed so easily in the local British Legion club? And when, oh when, had Vera Lynn slipped into my unconscious mind to become part of a repertoire (I didn't even know I had), waiting to be regurgitated so easily? Surreal. A learning experience.

Acknowledgement: A version 'Fish outta water' was first published in the *ATRAP Newsletter*, Issue No. 3, September 2000.

More thoughts

CAROL MOY

I struggle to find the right words. How does anyone put into words what it is or feels like to be transracially adopted? As a phrase it has dominated pretty much my whole life but herein lies the difficulty. It's the only norm that I know. I can't compare it to being born or raised in any other type of family, as I don't know any other type of personal situation.

I seem to have spent the last forty years saying that I was adopted into a white family and expecting other people to be able to get their heads round what that must mean to a black woman like me and how they, as friends, family, loved ones, workmates, whatever, should appropriately react.

It's a hell of a thing to ask, especially when there can be no right or wrong answers. But I would say I'm lucky. Almost everyone I've ever known has reacted how I would want them to. Polite indifference touched with embarrassed curiosity.

I'm wondering if being in this slightly unusual situation could be why I have, at various points in my life, had problems regarding my self-image. As a developing teen I wasn't happy with my size – a curvy 10 to 12. I wanted to be flat and skinny like my white school friends. Later on in my teens I began to like myself when boys and then men took an interest in me.

I've had battles with my weight for most of my adult life, even though friends are envious of my curvy/athletic proportions. Maybe if I'd seen someone else in my family who looked like me I wouldn't have spent so much time trying to be someone or something I'm not. And maybe that's why I've always thought I would be happier, and more successful in my love life, if only I were thinner, shorter, blonder (ha!), younger, or some other physical type that I will never be.

In my skin

SUE JARDINE

In my skin,
I often wonder why it is
I'm in this skin –
The token Chinese of unknown origin.
I look around and see
Few people who look like me.

On my skin,
I bear a stamp:
"Made in Hong Kong".
That was a joke, or so they thought.
I tried to laugh too –
What else could I do?

In this skin,
I'm called a bloody foreigner
And told to go back home.
An easy target, by white and black.
Just a quiet Chinese
Whose stereotype is to please.

Beneath my skin,
I hide and shrink
Cannot fail to flinch
At the names and comments directed at me.
I try to be tough
But cannot say, 'Stop, enough!'

In my skin,
I so want to be you
With eyes so blue.
'Not fair,' I cry and continuously ask why
I'm treated this way –
No opportunity to have my say.

Behind my skin,
I cannot even begin
To express the loss,
The devastating cost of trying to fit in,
The need to belong.
How I wish it were gone.

Sad not mad

MARIYAM MAULE

Pack up my troubles
In my empty delusions
Loaded with confusions
Screwed-up paper dreams
Abandoned in life's rubbish bin
To me that is a sin
Disregarded, rejected as a social pariah
In abusive tones
Condemned as mad

Emotional distress and using psychiatric services

DARSHAN DAVIES

I have experienced emotional distress over a number of years. Part of my emotional distress is to do with being adopted.

As a child, when I was upset with my adoptive parents and unhappy, I would "wish" I was with my natural family and assume I would have a better life there. This wish developed into a preoccupation, which has been present throughout my life, wondering who my "real" mum was and so many other questions. Did she miss me? Did she love me? Why did she give me up? Did she want to find me? Did she think about me? Did I have any brothers and sisters? And so on. I would pass by Asian women in parts of Birmingham wondering if they were my mother.

In my teenage years, despite having all the things I needed and more – a good education at a costly boarding school, activities, hobbies, holidays, etc. – I felt an emptiness which was always with me, but especially when I was on my own. I started smoking and drinking at a young age, 13 or 14 years, and, following drinking and using cannabis, my depression became worse. It was a feeling of deep loneliness and sorrow that was with me and, although I could be the joker in the group or party, inside I felt lost.

Moving back home after boarding school, I didn't have any friends really and no structure, and my depression was deep. I drank to get away from my feelings. I also used cannabis, which didn't agree with me and severely upset my mental state. Following my breakdown in India, when I was 18, I tried suicide a few times and entered the psychiatric world. For the last 16 or 17 years I have been on different types of medication, for "manic depression", "schizo-affective disorder" and "nervous debility". I have had many hospital admissions and been an in-patient in psychiatric hospital too many times to mention. I am still struggling but keep on fighting.

When I have been "ill", many of these periods of emotional distress and confusion have resulted from issues of identity and colour, and not having come to terms with "black and white" and identity issues arising from being transracially adopted. Unfortunately, very little time or concern was given to these issues for many years by the professionals I saw. As a result, I was being treated with medication but not having a chance to look at my real concerns.

Within the psychiatric services there have been some very caring individuals who have given me support and time. However, I feel that for a long time I did not receive the appropriate resources to deal with my issues.

The social services department did eventually pay for me to see a counsellor, someone of the same origin as me. I did benefit from this counselling but the counsellor also had his own agenda, which made me decide to withdraw from his services. I feel that I was being encouraged to move away from white British culture and my family and friends, towards Indian culture. I also believe this counsellor had double standards and his own misgivings about white society, and played Indian and English against each other.

I am at a point now where I have only one choice and that is to succeed and to create a life that I can attain, a life that has what I want. I use the psychiatric services such as MIND to build my life (from nothing), and I still see my psychiatrist and psychologist. My psychologist definitely is a benefit in helping me to look at my beliefs and negative thoughts – to help me to progress and lead a more "normal" and positive life.

Adoption rap

JOHN-PAUL POULSON

Adoption – there wasn't any fucking option.
Whether it's right or wrong,
This poem isn't a song.
I was mixed race, my family they were white.
They made the choice to put up the fight, that's right.
We're all the same, you and me,
Let's face up to the reality.
Whether you're black or white, Muslim or Jew,
Racism just isn't for you
Shit, I grew up with it everyday.
'Golliwog', 'Nigger', that's what they'd say.
Being mixed race isn't a game. Well, I said before, we're all the same.
The reason for racism, there is no reason, let's not believe them.
It's hard to see why they do it. People, let's get through it.
Growing up was great for me, I was blessed with the best family.
Life was good, life was sweet. I learned to stand on my own two feet.
As you grow older, as you grow stronger, you'll see racism isn't our
reality.
Don't live in a world full of hate,
Let's show the fascists our lives are great.
About to start my own family,
Sabrina, JJ and me, let's teach our children a better way of life.
People, stand up and make a fight!

Mother, Mummy and me

MARIE-JAMILA GILLHAM

I wanted to write about my birth mother and my mother, and how they have both influenced me. I have found it incredibly hard to write and I don't think it's just because it has brought up adoption issues. It's because I had such a hard time having my own daughters. I had five miscarriages before I had my eldest daughter and she was very premature; I had to have medication all the way through, injections, and then she was nearly three months early. She was in an incubator for two months. My second daughter was born a month and a half early.

Being adopted, I felt that what my birth mother did was quite – not selfish but thinking of herself; slightly selfish because she had come over to study. I thought she just didn't want her mother to find out that she'd "sinned", because I knew that she came from a very strict Christian background. But at the beginning of this year I went to see a professional intermediary to initiate my tracing process and we went through my file which contained a lot of information about my adoption (not that that helps the tracing because it is still a headache). But we went through the file and the intermediary was saying things like, 'Oh, poor thing. This social worker would have told her this. The other social worker had told her that. The nurses were giving her this kind of grief in the hospital. The mother and baby home weren't being that supportive.' I was listening and thinking, 'My God, this woman, thirty years ago, was in a country she'd been in for about a year, she found herself pregnant, left an area where she had some acquaintances, moved up to Huddersfield' which, let's face it, thirty years ago wasn't as embracing as perhaps it is now. And, even now, it's not one big melting pot. And she was given a really hard time and, all of a sudden, my thinking about her changed from selfish to selfless. All I could think of was that I love my girls so much and, if I was in that situation, would I have the strength to give up (not abandon) this baby for her best interest? She must have felt absolutely horrific. Yet, all these years, I'd put how she felt out of my mind.

So every time I put pen to paper my emotions just flood out. After I'd been to the intermediary's office in London, I walked down towards King's Cross tube station, and I thought it must be raining because I could feel wetness around my face. I thought, 'People are looking at me a bit strangely' and it didn't occur to me that I was absolutely sobbing. I had no idea that that's how raw my pain was. I don't think

I could ever feel that kind of emotion again because it was so raw. I had to go and sit down and have a coffee and just calm down and relax, and then I phoned my mum.

Mum is always my mother. She has always been there through everything, every time. I couldn't have more respect for my parents. They are two of the most amazing people in the world, particularly my mum because she was the one who had to carry me about like a papoose when I was five weeks old, when I first came to stay with them, as I moaned and whinged because I was feeling abandoned. She was the one who I remember explaining various aspects of adoption to me. My dad did too, but Mum was more aware because of the work that she does. She had ways of explaining things to me so that I'd understand. I suppose because she does know me better than my dad does.

I didn't allow myself to get close to my dad until I was about 18. I just didn't trust men. The story in my head was that my birth mother had found herself pregnant – my birth father had just gone off and left her and so, potentially, all men would reject. My worst emotion is a feeling of rejection. When I was younger I had lots of boyfriends but it was always me jumping from one boyfriend to another because I didn't want to be the one who was dumped. This applied in friendships and in my relationship with my dad until he had a heart attack, when I was about 17 or 18. I went to visit him in hospital. All of a sudden, I saw him as someone that I really deeply cared about, whom I couldn't bear to lose. I realised that we do have a lot in common, my musical interests and my musical "talent". As a child I remember my Dad was always playing music with me. We sat and played music together. We used to listen to music together too.

I can always talk to my mum about anything to do with adoption because she is just open to it. Even if I phoned Mum at three o'clock in the morning and said, 'Mum, can we just have a chat about my birth mother or whatever?', she'd sit there for hours and listen to me because she knows how important it is to not feel like avenues are closed. I rely on her so much for my emotional stability.

I think she has regrets she didn't get to make a life story book and that we didn't have a life story book with photos of my birth mother, because the pictures of me as a baby show me to be very much like my birth mother, apparently. It would be really nice to see what my mother looked like and what I may look like in the future. My girls look like me to some extent. Even though my mum and I look completely different, we have some very similar facial features and mannerisms. Maybe that's changed since we've not lived together. Everybody says, 'I'm amazed that you don't look anything like your mum, but you do look like your mum, at times.' I find that bizarre. Mum and I used to chat for ages about nature and nurture. I think our experience has answered a lot of questions, yet left a load open.

My story is obviously about adoption and the selflessness of motherhood. My birth mother must have taken out a whole chunk of her heart to be able to let go of her child because, the minute you hold your child, it's just . . . She had me for three weeks; I can't imagine what letting a baby go would be like. And then my adoptive mother who took me on. I wasn't born of her and yet I don't feel any difference in the love that she shows to my brothers. I've never felt that, ever. That's an amazing thing to have been able to do. Thank you very much birth mother and Mum, you are fantastic, but it's a heck of a lot to live up to! These two women, the two most important women in my existence so far, could not have done more, as far I could see, if they tried.

Beautiful baby girls

When I was miscarrying a lot, and I know this is ridiculous, but it felt like I was being rejected again by my genetic relatives. Every time I went through that, I went through the same kind of abandonment issues I'd felt every time I'd been made too aware of my adoption status. It felt like I was being abandoned and pushed away. I was feeling, 'Oh my God, none of my biological family wants me.' It was just, 'Oh God, these babies don't even want to stay.' I was feeling very emotional and hormonal and so I did become quite irrational.

I think pregnancy is quite an irrational time. I absolutely adored being pregnant, even though I was sick and had to have injections every day. I adored it because there was a little person in me that was part of me. She was going to come out and be a person who was directly connected to me and that was just an amazing feeling. When she came, I just immediately loved her because she was part of me. Even though she did look like an alien, as she was so tiny, she did have my head shape and she was mine. She was part of me. It was just amazing. I was so proud. Even her hair looked like mine. I can't describe the feeling because it was just so strange. It's not a mirror and it's not a photo. This is a little person who's got her own little will and does what she wants to do and yet she does resemble me. And that's really strange because there's no one else that looks like me. I embraced her more because of that. It was the same when my second child was born. It was like, it's happened again, wow! So, there's two now, not just one that resembles me.

I'm very aware of how I am bringing up the girls because I don't want them to feel rejected or abandoned in any way because that's my worst nightmare, to put that on to my children. Of course they are going to have a completely different experience from me, because I was a little 'brown girl in the ring'. That's what my brothers used to say. We thought that was hilarious. Now it is a running joke that we cannot believe that we were singing, 'Brown girl in the ring'. My brother sent me a card for my 30th birthday of a little black girl on a swing with written inside, 'brown girl on a swing, tra la la la la'. It's a running joke. It's so beyond what is acceptable now, which is why we love it!

'There ain't no black in the Union Jack'[1]

I live in Stafford, which is a rural area. I could safely say that ten years ago, if I'd walked into a rural area or an area with lots of white people, I would be nervous and tense. I would feel paranoid and very uncomfortable. Now I know I have every right to be everywhere I want to be because this is my country too. Whereas before I felt that I was on a visa, I was a visitor. I wasn't quite resident but I lived here. I had so many issues.

I always had such a thing about being a good representative of black people because I felt, every time a white person looked at me, I was representing an entire race, which obviously is ludicrous. Everything that happened to me for so many years would be reflective of race in some way or another. And that was exhausting. My black (adopted) brother had a baby with his white girlfriend and they broke up and got back together and they did that on and off over years. I was so angry with him. I remember once just phoning him and saying, 'The last thing we need you . . . [it was a we thing] . . . The last thing we need you to do, is be a baby father and wander off backwards and forwards, and be that horrible negative stereotype. And you are being that stereotype and it makes me so angry that you are being that stereotype,' because I felt like it reflected on me. I think that a lot changed when I became an adult and saw the real world.

Angry is probably one of the ways that racism has left me: very angry over the years. That anger has mellowed with age. I used to be furious and take it out verbally on the people closest to me – my mum and dad. I felt they had a responsibility to ensure

[1] This sub-heading is taken from a book of the same title by Paul Gilroy (Routledge, 1987)

that I wouldn't be feeling like this. Of course, they didn't have a clue what was going on – no one did in those days. Mum and Dad faced a lot of my anger over the years. I'd say, 'Blood's thicker than water.' If I was told off for doing something to my brothers (which nine times out of ten would have been my fault), I didn't end up doing half the housework that they did because I'd say, 'I'm a girl and I'm black, you can't put me in that position.' I was very manipulative, very early, and knew what to do. It's not something I'm proud of, but an ability I've fine-tuned.

Skin like velvet, hair that shines

When I left home I moved in with two black girlfriends of mine in Walthamstow. They taught me how to do my hair. They taught me how to deal with my skin. As much as Mum had tried, and she had done a lot, there's nothing that's going to stay with you more than experience and understanding. My friends used to say, 'Well, why don't you do [this] with your hair or why don't you do [that]?' Or 'Your skin's . . . why don't you just do that?' Learning to care for my hair and skin was so important, as was learning about different styles. I remember having short-cropped blonde hair – Oh god, that was a disaster and another story! One thing I was always envious of was some of my white girlfriends – they'd have a different hair colour, a different haircut. My hair grows about a centimetre a decade. It's so slow growing, it's rubbish. Now I've had all kinds of hairstyles – braids, extensions, a hairpiece. It's so nice to be able to have that pampering, just to do something different with my hair that feels really positive, really good. It's a nice feeling at the moment.

Supper time

Living with my friends in Walthamstow was significant in terms of food, also. Mum, bless her, she's tried so hard to cook all different dishes. She's got these cookbooks that have been written by someone who has just thought, 'I'll do a Caribbean cook book'. Mum did try; she did jerk chicken and rice and peas, goat curry, and other Caribbean food. She also cooked Asian food and all different types of food because she wanted us to be open-minded and aware of different flavours. Learning how various friends vary in their use of food and the range of foods – that was really interesting and something I've kept with me. When I come down to London I go to Walthamstow market and buy food and hair products.

There's nothing wrong with transracial adoption is there?

How my views on transracial adoption have changed. They've changed from: 'There's nothing wrong with transracial adoption whatsoever. As long as the baby is loved, that's what it's all about' and 'It doesn't make any difference whatsoever' to thinking: Cock and shit, of course it does! It's about all those stares. I consider myself to be particularly well adjusted and very lucky to have parents who've been able to explain things to me – who've brought me up (oh yes, Chingford wasn't the best place but we were on the edge of Walthamstow).

I think transracial adoption was a lazy solution to a big problem, which was lots of black children in the care system and they wanted to do something. They had lots of white couples who wanted to adopt babies. The only babies they were allowed were black or disabled children, and so that was a way of appeasing people. But it's not just about colour. It's about having cultural links, and links to heritage and understanding. Things as simple as hair and skin care, because it's very different. Transracial adoption makes it just that little bit harder to settle into a family because you have an obvious difference. I just think it was laziness. I know Mum works for Barnardo's and she is placing children with families where there is as close a parental match as possible; that's what they are trying to do. I think that's fantastic. Yes, it takes a bit more time but I don't care – it's a child's life, it's the rest of someone's life.

Obviously, I wouldn't change my family for the world but I would have preferred to not have to do the bloody story about 'I was adopted and blah blah blah' every time my brothers or my parents came and met people. What I would have loved to be able to do was say, 'This is my mum, this is my dad'; end of story, no more explanation. My adoption is nobody's business but something that's very personal to me; that privacy was taken away from me.

If I open up like that, people feel my adoption is something they can ask me about, but it's something I don't want to talk about. At the moment the big thing is, 'How's the tracing going?' I want to be able to say, 'You know, I was having a nice relaxing meal with you until you asked me that. Could you not ask me about that right now? I might have just had a phone call saying we're at loggerheads, it could be a really hard time.' I just don't want to talk about it all the time.

Transracial adoption is something I would definitely, definitely not recommend. I am very against it. I don't think it's fair at all, on anybody, parents and children alike.

False family

KYM COOPER

Surrounded by love,
Smothered by love,
Gratitude for being rescued,
We love you to death,
How much do you love us?
Why do you never tell us that you love us?

We rescued you from a home
We took you in as our own
Why do you treat us in this manner?

You tortured me
Took away my soul
My inner being,
My self-esteem,
My sense of belonging,
My ability to bond,
My pride to stand tall,

I am powerless with no control,

I can no longer pretend,
I hide behind a mask,
You'll never see the real me.

How can you?
I don't even know who I am,
I'm not really yours,

I can no longer pretend,
I was never really yours in the first place.
I mourn the loss of my mother,
I suffer in silence.

In the still of the night
You may hear the real emotion behind my smile.
I cry myself to sleep wishing I could love myself
Wishing I could be like normal families
Who bond and feel real love.

I'm shattered by fear
Fear of rejection,
Fear of always feeling alone,
Fear of the unknown.

Who am I?
How was I created?
Whose eyes do I have?
Whose limbs are long like mine?

Will this sadness ever leave me?
Your love will not heal my wounds.

Warning to adoptive parents

LIZ SIBTHORPE

Why didn't someone warn you
That disappointments would come?
Adopting children cannot insure
Against the loneliness of old age
Or creeping disability.

We all face an uncertain future.
No one can promise what we want –
Independence or constant companionship.
Each of us is born an individual,
Not easily moulded by another's will.

We brought with us
Fragments of culture and family traits
So different from your own.
You can't own another being.
Even a slave's spirit is free.

You can't force another to love you.
Only offer freedom to choose
To accept or reject your love.
If you had loosened our chains,
We may have loved you.

What will you tell your adopted child?

LIZ SIBTHORPE

Will you tell them
That you couldn't bear
To be without children?
That it didn't go with your image
Of caring liberal people?

That you needed
To be like other families,
Checking the family calendar
For dental appointments missed,
And football matches to be watched?

It's unlikely that you'll admit
To a selfish desire
To possess a child,
Or a fear of growing old
Without grandchildren.

It's not likely that you'll say,
'You weren't what we hoped for.
You're older, blacker,
Less able, challenging
And different.'

It's almost impossible
That you'll say,
'We made a mistake.
You will never be like us.
You don't have to try.
Just be yourself.'

What do you see?

MIRANDA WILKINSON

What do you see when you look at me:
A baby born to be taken away,
There and then, on that very day?

What do you see when you look at me:
A toddler who brought joy to a man and woman
Who thought they couldn't have a child of their own?

What do you see when you look at me:
The child with the face that does not fit,
Who looks like her parents not one little bit?

What do you see when you look at me:
A girl who has learnt to accept confused stares,
And pretend it's OK and that she does not care?

What do you see when you look at me:
A teen who's adept at explaining the reality
To those with one view of what constitutes "family"?

What do you see when you look at me:
Do you see a young lady with dark brown skin
Who has tried all her life to simply fit in?

What do you see when you look at me:
A mother troubled as she cradles her baby,
Feeling hurt and confused,
Thinking, 'How could she leave me?'

What do you see when you look at me:
A woman who, through everything, knows
That, although there have been many highs, many lows,
If her white middle-class parents had not adopted
A little black baby on whom they have doted,
Her life would have likely been far more tragic?
Never to have known that wonderful magic
That only comes with unconditional love,
That can take the smooth as well as the rough.
Thank God my parents chose to adopt me.
Without them, I truly don't know where I'd be.

The transracial adopters' shopping list

SHAKTI

Thinking of adopting transracially? Make sure you buy all the essential items for your child. Set your child up for life!

The "must have" items are:

1. One healthy dose of self-hatred
2. Two spoonfuls of gratitude
3. A cupful of desire to look just like you!
   (If your child is under five years of age, please buy a scrubbing brush, soap and bleach.)
4. A mirror ready with reflection of a girl/boy with blue eyes and long blonde hair
5. TV images of starving black children and poverty to boost your "rescue" rating
6. A crowd of school bullies (also known as "friends"), preferably violent
7. A local British National Party candidate/follower to instil fear
8. A home in a rural community called, "Whitesville bordering fields green"
9. English culture pills – take one a day to keep black culture away!
10. A tree, of the "family" variety, complete with your ancestors
11. An injection of internalised racism
12. A phobia about black people
13. A handful of shame mixed in with self-blame
14. A cocktail of confusion
15. Plenty of loyalty
16. A cat called "Rejection"
    (When she has kittens, please name them "Primal wound",

"Trauma", "No Trust", "Appropriation", "Acculturation" and "Displacement")

17. A "Happy Abandonment" card
18. Some erased memories
19. A shipment of loss (Special Delivery only)
20. A crate of loneliness
21. A childhood of isolation
22. Pain that has no name
23. Silent grief
24. Bucketfuls of tears
25. The CD "After all we've done for you!" by "Love is Enough"
26. A measure of guilt
27. A T-shirt with the words, '16 today. Who am I? Where do I belong?' embossed across the chest
28. A bottle of suicidal feelings (may be bitter to swallow)
29. An appointment with a psychiatrist/psychotherapist
30. A lifetime of racism
31. A ricochet of resilience

And, last but not least, one black child!

4

Reconnection

Belonging: a search for identity

LI-DA KRUGER

Li-Da Kruger at Genocide Museum, Tuol Sleng, Cambodia (taken by Jonathan Perugia)

'Can you hear me Father Christmas? I want a blonde wig!' shouted the little girl as she crouched down, head stuck up the chimney, her eyes wide with anticipation as she dreamt of being an English princess. I remember that Christmas so clearly because Santa granted me my wish. It was weeks before my parents managed to prise away from me what had become a mass of blonde knots atop my naturally jet black hair – typical for a Cambodian but not the Cotswolds.

I grew up as the adopted daughter of the British restaurateur and businesswoman, Prue Leith, and her writer-husband, Rayne Kruger. They already had their own son, Daniel. I was lucky and could not have asked for more. Throughout my childhood I was blissfully happy, my parents loved me and I had a privileged education.

I felt all the more fortunate because I knew what my life would have been like if I had not been evacuated from Cambodia. But the few images of Cambodia I had were of towering piles of skulls and stories of genocide. It was no wonder I grew up wracked with guilt about having "survived" – guilt that I knew was irrational.

By 14 years old, I had begun to take a real interest in my past. I felt terrible when I found I couldn't picture my birth parents, let alone grieve for them. I assumed they were dead. I couldn't get past the glossy, cinematic images of paddy fields and pointy Vietnamese hats. After all, I had never met a Cambodian. I knew I had to go back to Cambodia and discover what had really happened to my birth parents. It was not that I had been told lies, but all knowledge of my early life was encapsulated in what my adoptive parents had been told at the time by the people who handed me over, who themselves were only passing on what they had been told. So how much of my story was a myth?

I wanted to claim the story for myself before it was too late. My adoptive parents were totally supportive and had diligently collected what they could of my past for this very reason. Although they had wanted to tell me more about Cambodia, most of the information was about the Khmer Rouge history. Having thought I had no real clues, it was only in my twenties, when I was sorting through a file that my father had forgotten about over the years, that I discovered a few strong leads. My Cambodian birth certificate and contract for adoption revealed the names of my birth parents, the officials who released me and the area of Phem Penh where I was from.

Working in the TV industry, I finally had the opportunity to realise my dream. I had decided to document my search, to place Cambodia on the map, in the hope that other people could learn something from my story. On 7th December 2001, twenty-six years after I had been airlifted out of Cambodia, I flew out of London to Phnom Penh. I was about to embark on what would probably be the biggest journey of my life and to make a documentary in search of the truth: the truth about my past, the truth about my country's past, and the truth about what is going on in Cambodia today.

I was born in Cambodia in 1974, at the height of a terrible civil war. Government forces loyal to the King and supported by the Americans were losing to the communist guerrillas who called themselves the Khmer Rouge. I had grown up with the story that my birth mother had been killed by a rocket blast, which were frequent occurrences. Apparently my father, a government soldier fleeing the Khmer Rouge, left me at the international orphanage in the capital. He had been fatally wounded and never saw me again. I was eleven months old. Meanwhile, foreigners were being evacuated en masse. An American called Meyer Burstein, who had been working in Cambodia, wanted to adopt a baby for himself and his English wife. Before he left, he asked a French woman called Yvette Pierpaoli, who was connected to the orphanage, to help find him a baby. Incredibly, I was that baby. In April 1975, the Americans withdrew their troops. And it was at this very moment that Pierpaoli managed to organise exit papers, just in time to fly me out on the last American helicopter. Three days later, the murderous Khmer Rouge marched triumphantly into the capital to win the war. Starting from what they called Year Zero, they emptied the entire urban population into the countryside under the pretext that the Americans would start bombing again. Cambodia's Killing Fields had begun. Hundreds of thousand of Cambodians are still missing today, their fate unknown, my birth parents among them.

The path from Cambodia to Gloucestershire was incredibly random. The American took me back to England. But within two weeks, his wife died. I was not yet legally adopted and, as a single man, Burstein was unable to adopt me. A Parisian friend offered to take me. But, on my arrival in Paris, due to personal complications, she had to give me up. Burstein put his English house up for sale. Friends of my adoptive parents happened to be looking round it and he told them about me. My soon-to-be adoptive mother flew to Paris and immediately fell in love with me and tried to smuggle me into Britain. She was rumbled by immigration, but with help from the British Consul was allowed to keep me, and went through the normal adoption procedures. I was not yet two years old.

Now, at 29, considering the amount of trauma that surrounded me at such a young age, my friends cannot believe why I'm not an emotional wreck. But apparently, when I first arrived in London, I would cower beneath my mother's skirts when I heard loud noises. Unable to use a knife and fork, I grabbed some chopsticks and masterfully ate my way through a bowl of spaghetti bolognese. My mother still laughs about the day I was introduced to her mother, who had been opposed to my adoption. Mum wanted me to look immaculate, so worked out exactly the time it would take to feed and bath us first. What she hadn't counted on was that I was a greedy little child and fell asleep, mouth stuffed full of sausage, clutching more sausages in each hand. This is how my grandmother met me. Somehow that clinched it; she was bewitched.

On my return to make the film of my search, like any visitor, my initial impression of Cambodia was seductive. The people are a mixture of incredibly friendly and highly traditional. For the first time, I melded into a crowd unnoticed. However, I did feel ashamed that I couldn't speak the Khmer language. To my surprise, all the Cambodians I met welcomed me "home" and offered me advice. The purpose of my visit brought the harsh realities quickly to light.

I started my search by making a missing persons advertisement for television, radio and newspaper. As a result, eight families responded. Suddenly everything was put into perspective when I realised that all these people, who were genuinely looking for lost relatives, represented a whole country. The difficulty for me, and all Cambodians searching, is that the Khmer Rouge were not only responsible for the deaths of nearly two million people, but they also destroyed almost everything, including written records, from the past. Yet, like the Nazis, the Khmer Rouge kept meticulous records of their own actions, torturing and killing.

To begin with, coming from such a cosy life in England, I was afraid to question people about their experiences of war and loss. They accepted me immediately as one of them but it only became easier when I started to connect more with my dual identity and feel part of a shared history. And I couldn't have done this without the support of the small team of Cambodian friends that I made during my visit, who were brutally honest and wonderfully supportive. So, when my search took me to places such as the notorious Killing Fields and genocide museum, I felt I had a right to be there and was not simply following the tourist trail of atrocities.

After nearly thirty years of civil war, Cambodia is a mess. My two-and-a-half month search in Cambodia was bitter sweet. I truly enjoyed discovering my new-found culture but was deeply affected by the daily revelations and sad truths. Despite an apparent democracy, political killings, corruption and a strong culture of impunity are still rife. People are afraid to voice opinions due to a history of being terrorised. I felt humbled by these people who had survived what seemed to me the impossible. I was amazed that any kind of society was able to function at all.

Li-Da with Buntha, one of the potential birth mothers

I had set out to find out whether my parents were dead or alive and what it actually meant to me to have Cambodian blood in my veins. I'm not sure that, in the end, the information I gathered was the whole truth of what happened to my parents – almost certainly less information than I started out with. But what I did discover was that one mother's pain of losing a child speaks for all mothers. And if I had met a birth parent, how much would it change my life? In the end, my experiences reinforced my feelings of Englishness. However much I want to be Cambodian, I cannot. As I discovered, it is not only about having a shared trauma, it's also about language, values and culture. But now I have access to a huge Cambodian network across the world. Some day, I will continue to search for clues about my birth parents, but what is more important now for me is to continue my relationships with the Cambodian families I met and learn more about their lives. Ongoing, is working out a way in which I can put back into Cambodia some of the luck I have been blessed with.

While my actual search has come to a temporary end, I have since become a Trustee of a small but highly impressive British-based NGO called the Nginn Karet Foundation for Cambodia (NKFC), which sponsors a number of economic and educational projects in Cambodian villages. But the least expected outcome of my search, and the best possible one for me, is the response from people who have watched the film, saying that they have either learned something from my journey or have had similar experiences.

Though I did not find my Cambodian birth family, I have absolutely no regrets. To undertake a search is a highly personal decision, which is not right for everyone. So my advice to anyone wanting to search for their birth parents is to go for it, but to be careful of one's expectations and to be absolutely open to all outcomes. I think the hardest part for me was dealing with not what I didn't find out, but what I discovered on my journey.

Acknowledgements: 'From Pol Pot to Prue Leith' by Li-Da Kruger, a version of which was published in the *Sunday Times*, 7 September 2003.

Belonging is the film of my search. It received its first public showing to a capacity audience at the Other Cinema in London's West End, November 2002. Several international film festivals have screened *Belonging* and a shortened version of 40 minutes attracted over one million viewers when it was shown in a Sunday lunchtime slot in September 2003. For details of how to purchase a DVD, please refer to the Resource List.

The heart of humankind

MARIYAM MAULE

In the beginning it was one
The world, with no borders, definition or difference
With the heart-shaped land mass in the centre
Afrika

Afrika
The heart of humankind
Giving the means of life to the world
Circulating the essence
For humankind's will to live in harmony
The nucleus of humanity
A legacy of peace, love and understanding

Afrika
Mother of humankind
Tenderly watching over the sons and daughters of man
The cradle of civilisation

Then, an almighty earthquake shook the earth
Splitting the heart of humankind
Into many separate veins running through continents
A shift of consciousness occurred
Causing pain, anguish and great suffering
The heart was displaced, fractured
Usurped by the mind

An exodus flowed outwardly
Blood ties broken

The loving union divided
Signalling a schism
Creating nation states and partition

The hair now torn from the roots
Of the nourisher
The umbilical cord disconnected from humankind
The children separated from the birth mother

O, rainbow citizens of the world
Look to the beginning
Look to the roots
Look to the self

Afrika
Mother Afrika
Her heart never stops beating
Yearning for all her children to return home

The sari shop

SUZANNA

The shop front was a little comical. A few old-fashioned tailors' dummies in the window, inane smiles on their faces, blonde locks, clumsy eye-shadow, light beige rubber shaped into elegant wrists and hands . . . details I would never have noticed had the dummies not been exhibiting saris. Yards of vibrant, luscious fabrics transforming suburbia into Asia.

I was ready to launch myself as my self. I wanted to put behind me the bland truth of my white upbringing. My family was as colourless as these saris were colourful. The valiant hours reading books about Sri Lanka had enabled me to proudly inform others of her traditions and people as if I had lived there all my life. So now it was time to dress the part.

It was unlike any other clothing store I had been to. The air was thick with the smell of sandalwood, racks burst with colour, every corner of the room was displaying some kind of two-for-one deal. The melange of chatter was mixed with the tinkling of cheap, tinny bangles as the women rooted through piles of fabrics, checking the workmanship of the seams.

'What are you looking for?' Beside me was a 20-something-year-old, idyllic from her *bindi* to her toes. Her appearance was so right. Could I ever look that convincing? 'What are you looking for?' she repeated. I didn't tell her that I was looking for a sense of belonging.

'A sari,' I responded, 'with all the trimmings.'

'Going to an Indian wedding, are you?' she asked with an encouraging tone, eyeing me up and down. I was accustomed to people not acknowledging Asian looks in me – my eyes are green, my skin is more sun-tanned than anything, my hair is a dull shade of brown, but for once it was important that I be taken as authentic. 'Actually, I am half-Asian,' I mumbled, and added, 'I have been transferred here with my job and my favourite sari got lost in the move.' I wasn't going to let this woman trump me.

We looked at each other for a couple of seconds, while my lie sank in. She led me through rolls of materials, stacks of curly-toed slippers and piles of silk trousers to the back of the shop. She had explanations for fabric thickness, the pros and cons of silk, and the reason for the price differences. At last it was time to grapple with yards of unfamiliar cloth, silk trousers and tight sari blouses in the changing room. As if they had seen me coming, there were picture diagrams stuck to the wall. I started enveloping myself in Sri Lanka, fold by fold.

In the privacy of that changing room, faced with my reflection, I felt my eyes welling up with tears. Honestly, the sari looked good. My light eyes didn't look so light, the cloth was perfectly draped and my skin surely didn't look too unlike the lady's in the picture diagram on the wall. But still the tears started rolling. For the first time in my life, I was wearing the culture of a man I had never met. My father. All of a sudden, I missed him. I wanted to know if I looked like him; I wanted to know if I looked Sri Lankan; I wanted to know *his* opinions on the fabric thickness, not the young woman's; I needed to know him. The resentment at having been adopted away from all of this was suddenly so massive. I needed to belong to something more exotic than the white middle class. CaucAsia, let me in!

I bought the sari – yards of emerald green with a silver border, tiny elephants embroidered in the detail. I bought jangly belts, sari blouses, silk trousers for underneath, bangles, toe rings, a little card with *bindi* stickers on and a *shalwar kameez*. 'That's what all young Asians are wearing these days,' my assistant was happy to tell me. Why not, then? How easy it seemed to be to purchase a piece of culture.

Wearing these items for the first time would not be easy, I realised. After all, I couldn't speak any Asian language, nor did I have anything more than the clothes to play the part. Genes seemed useless. My cultural knowledge was limited to the content of websites and books. However, dressed in my sari at a party a couple of weeks later, I realised that nobody questioned my choice of clothing. Enveloped in those folds of Sri Lanka, I had found myself.

A journey to Hong Kong

SUE JARDINE

Heathrow airport. The sign for Terminal 4 came into view and, immediately, I experienced a physical reaction. I was about to embark on a journey. It was a journey for which I had been preparing for quite some time.

I was about to visit Hong Kong, my birth place, for the first time since my adoption as a baby thirty years ago. The country was unknown to me and I was a stranger to it and its people. I also knew that I would not be greeted by my birth parents or long-lost relatives. My fantasies of reunion would remain unrealised.

I had, however, come to the point where the need to see my birth place overruled my feelings of loss. I wanted to see where I had spent the first year and a half of my life. I wanted to reclaim it as part of my identity, to at least have photographs of the orphanage and of what "might have been" had I not been adopted and sent to live with an English family in the UK. My decision to visit Hong Kong had been long in the making for a number of reasons:

My assimilation into my adoptive family meant that I had a new life, far removed from my origins. Although I knew I was different to my family and friends, I held on to the belief that I was the same as them.

It was too painful to acknowledge that I had been relinquished by my birth parents.

From a young age, I was under the impression that there was nothing in Hong Kong for me. I knew that I was adopted and that I had been found without any identification on me, so tracing my birth parents was not something I had ever considered.

The need to find out more about myself only surfaced in adulthood. Before then, it never occurred to me that my adoptive status would have such a strong impact on how I perceived my sense of self. It became increasingly difficult for me to deny my difference. My difference was of interest to people, but I did not have the answers to their questions. I had grown up without any sense of my origins and without family and relatives with whom I could compare my features. At times, I felt quite alienated from people around me. Gradually, I came to realise my feelings were associated with the losses I had experienced as a baby.

Even though my interest in Hong Kong was getting stronger, I thought it would be impossible to go back. I did not think that I would be able to cope emotionally. I knew it would make me feel completely inadequate and vulnerable. Not only would I be confronted with the pain of never knowing my birth parents, but I have had very little contact with Chinese people, and I was a Chinese person who could not speak her mother tongue.

I was also wary of Hong Kong being a colony of the UK. It was my birth place, but I wanted to experience a connection with Chinese people. To that end I decided that I would visit China after Hong Kong. Another reason why I was reluctant to visit Hong Kong was that I did not want to upset my adoptive parents. I had strong guilt feelings about being disloyal to them because they have given me so much.

However, despite my fears, I also knew it was a journey that I had to take, whatever the outcomes.

Looking around the airport lounge, I saw more Chinese-looking people than I had for a long time. I observed a family with their young daughter and wondered at how circumstances can be so different.

I boarded the plane and, as it moved slowly but steadily towards the runway, I could feel my emotions rising again, at what was to come . . .

The first impressions I got of Hong Kong were quite deceptive because it was not until the plane turned to the runway that I gained any real sense of the number of buildings that make up its distinctive skyline. We flew low amongst the high-rise flats and blocks. The roads were so close that it was possible to see the Chinese characters on street signs.

It suddenly struck me that, in one of the streets amongst all this concrete, I was born. It was quite awesome to have arrived.

Prior to arranging my trip to Hong Kong, I had visited International Social Services and, through them, I discovered that I had lived in two orphanages before my adoption. It was arranged that I would visit one of the orphanages because the other had been knocked down. I had already been told that my files in Hong Kong did not hold any information additional to that I had already seen in the UK, so my hopes of finding out more about the circumstances around my birth were not going to be fulfilled.

I felt very anxious at meeting the social worker from Hong Kong International Social Services because there was much I wanted to ask her, but I knew she did not have the information. Initially, I was a bit confused about where we were going. I thought we needed to take the underground to the New Territories. I knew that at one time I had been in Fanling, an area in the New Territories, so I assumed that was where the other orphanage was as well.

We walked amongst the high-rise and street noise of central Hong Kong for a short period of time. Then, across the busy road from us, I caught sight of trees and the walls of the orphanage. As we got closer, the entrance came into view. It had a traditional Chinese-style roof and a sign with the words 'Po Leung Kuk' written in Chinese characters and in English.

The orphanage had been established since 1882 and was still taking in babies and children. We toured the buildings and saw the colourful rooms where children took their lessons in one half, and in the other, the beds where they slept. Looking into the older girls' rooms, I could see their desks adorned with glossy photographs from magazines, and a radio was playing Chinese "pop" music.

Of most impact on me was the babies' room where there were ten or so cots. A baby turned round to look at us as we entered. Eyes deep dark pools. A girl. Born 21.11.94. I tried to concentrate on what I was being told about how the nursery was run but I was drawn to those eyes. As I moved round the room my thoughts focused on the babies, hoping they would give me clues as to what it would have been like for me when I was living there. It seemed to me that my head was empty and full at the same time. There were many questions I wanted to ask, but in order to keep my emotions at bay I tried to remove all thoughts from my mind.

It was enough at that time to know that I had made a connection with my origins.

However, after the visit to Po Leung Kuk I felt very much that it was not enough. I wanted more information. I still do not know who my birth parents are, where I was born, or under what circumstances. The likelihood is that I will never know and that is a loss that is always with me.

Acknowledgement: A previous version of 'A journey to Hong Kong' was first published in the *Post-Adoption Centre Newsletter*, January 1996.

Eleven hours!

SHARON HARWOOD

Eleven hours. Just the number in my mind rang alarm bells that couldn't stop banging inside my brain. Eleven hours away from home. Eleven hours before I put my feet upon the soil that brought me life. Eleven hours until I said hello to my "motherland".

Isn't that how it's supposed to go? Or somewhere along the lines of: excitement, anticipation, longing, wanting to be back home? Well, sadly for me, that's not how it went.

When I first learnt that I had the opportunity to go "back home" to Korea I was excited, but I was also very nervous. I wanted to see the land that had always been portrayed as beautiful, calming and out of this world, but the reality is it's not my home. When I first arrived in Korea, I was very sad. That's the only way I can describe how I felt at that time. I felt homesick for England, and my son and my family. There were so many Koreans! I instantly felt as though my face didn't fit, like I was an English girl in a foreign country. It was as if the whole world was watching my every move. But even more scary than that, I knew that I could be related to any one of those people but not know whom.

People smiled and made sure that we were more than catered for. In fact, their hospitality couldn't be faulted. Yet, at the back of my mind, I couldn't help wondering if inside they were laughing at us. For here we all were, with English friends and family by our sides, speaking and looking English! We smoked in public, we held our partners' hands in public and we didn't rush off to the loo every time we wanted to blow our nose. And we had a big tour bus with 'Welcome Korean adoptees to your motherland' plastered all over it. I felt like a monkey in a cage, only I was performing for the audience. In fact, I went out of my way to prove how un-Korean I was. Why? Because I felt betrayed by my country and my so-called natural family. This was my home, my country, yet I've spent all but two years of my life in England. For the first two days of my visit I hated Korea. As far as I was concerned, the only good thing it had going for it was the food, which, by the way, was out of this world.

The group of people I went to Korea with were, in the main, "first timers" too. That made me feel so much better, knowing I wasn't the only one going through this scary journey. It made it so much easier to confront my fears. Throughout our time there, we laughed, we cried and we experienced emotions not even we knew we had. I'd like to think that somehow we helped each other. We became one big family returning to the "motherland" and this didn't seem so bad.

The more I walked around this beautiful Korea, the more I grew to love her and her people. I am so glad I had the chance to go back home and experience the emotions that I did, because now I love my country more than words can describe. Although I am very much an English girl, there's a whole lot of Korean in me. It wasn't until I went back that I realised who I am inside. So the irony is, yes, I'm still angry and bitter for being taken from my country, but I'm also grateful that I could, and can, return.

I will never be the Korean woman Koreans would expect of me, but I am still Korean, and that's something no one can take from me.

Sri Lanka: a part of me

ROS GIHAN WILLIAMS

I was born in Sri Lanka in 1973, in a place called Gampaha, a small town just outside the capital, Colombo. I was abandoned there, on the street, a year after I had been born. A lorry driver found me in the early hours of the morning and took me to the police station. From there, I was taken to the children's ward at the local hospital. Although I wasn't sick, fortunately they took pity on me and admitted me. Because of the circumstances, my story appeared in an English-language newspaper, *The Colombo Times*, on 17 May 1974. My adoptive mother, who was living in Sri Lanka at the time, saw the article and came to see me. I made an impression on her and she decided to adopt me. I stayed in Sri Lanka for six months before coming to Britain.

I grew up in predominantly white areas and went to schools where I was amongst a handful of children from minority ethnic backgrounds. Even though my adoptive mum is Chinese, race was seldom discussed at home. I grew up hoping that everyone saw me as white. I suffered name-calling at school. I tried, and succeeded, in tuning it out but in doing so managed to tune myself out, crushing my spirit in the process. I became very introverted and shy. Racism was not a daily occurrence but when it happened, it was brutally hurtful and it was hard for me not to internalise the negativity at a deep level. A lot of my energy was taken up completely denying any kind of Asian-ness or otherness about myself. Fantasies of blonde hair and blue eyes abounded in my head and resulted in me purchasing skin-lightening cream as a teenager.

Fortunately I was forced to change my "race-less" stance when I came to London to go to university and encountered people from all over the world. I'm still a long way from feeling grounded and secure with my racial identity but I'm further along the path now. Becoming a member of the Association for Transracially Adopted and Fostered People (ATRAP) was really important. Suddenly, I was meeting people who had been through similar situations to me and I realised that I wasn't as freakishly unique or isolated as I had once thought.

The traumatic transition of leaving university and the breakdown of a long-term unhealthy relationship stirred something in me and I realised that I no longer wanted to go through life shut down emotionally. Counselling led to the unearthing of some very deeply buried issues. When the college year ended, so did the counselling. I felt that I had been literally left with huge amounts of emotion and trauma just hanging out of me. The experience of being abandoned had left a legacy of huge insecurity and emotional problems which I had not been able to understand or deal with. I knew I had reached a point in my life where I had to sort my head out for myself.

I started to see a therapist who used psychosynthesis which was enormously helpful. Whereas with the counselling, at the end of the hour I would feel really bad, dissected in a way, with psychosynthesis, I would leave each session feeling almost invincible. I felt I was being put back together, as opposed to being taken apart. The majority of my twenties has been just learning to be this new, much more grounded, assimilated person. Therapy had altered how I encountered the world – how I interacted with people, family issues, relationships, operating from a place of security rather than a place of trauma.

As I write, I am one week away from my first visit to Sri Lanka. It's thirty years since I left there as a baby. I'm going there to visit the place I was taken to as an abandoned baby and to make a film about the situation of orphans after the civil war. I always knew that I needed and would go back to Sri Lanka when the time was right. I waited and waited, knowing that this was something I shouldn't force myself to do. At one point I was beginning to worry that I would never be ready! Then, suddenly this summer, I thought, 'I'm going to Sri Lanka this year.'

Once I had made the decision, things started to fall into place. Now the tickets are booked and there's no turning back. At the moment I'm lurching from elation to despair. How will I be received by people? What will Sri Lanka be like? A lot of adoptees are able to trace their birth parents; because of my abandonment it's unlikely I'll be able to do this. Will I find what I'm searching for? What am I actually searching for? I suppose a sense of peace, a sense of identity, a sense of what it is to be truly Sri Lankan. So that I feel it from the inside out, rather than just looking Sri Lankan from the outside with nothing to back it up inside.

Doorstep children

ROS GIHAN WILLIAMS

Proposal for a documentary film
Script and directing: Ros Gihan Williams
Length: 50 min
Format: DVCAM

Outline

A dusty road in Sri Lanka. Lorries pass by:

Voice over: 'It was Tuesday 17 May 1974 that the photograph of a tough little creature, aged about one, appeared on the front page of the single double spread that was *The Colombo Times*. She had been found, abandoned, by a lorry driver in the early hours of the morning and was taken to Gampaha Hospital.'

We see a news clipping and photo of the baby.

Ros Gihan Williams was left on the roadside when she was a year old. She doesn't know what happened to her during her first year of life or why she was abandoned. She only knows that she was found and taken to a local orphanage, from where she was adopted.

Colombo, the capital of Sri Lanka, is a frightening, intriguing cacophony of sights and sounds. Situated on the beautiful Indian Ocean, it is completely cut off from the shoreline by its chaotic urban sprawl. Ros is overwhelmed by the noise, the poverty and the rootless families. This is the first time she has returned to Sri Lanka and she is desperate to discover how she fits into this picture. Will she be embraced or spat out again?

21 October 2004

Jetlagged and deprived of sleep, we're up at 5 am to make the seven-hour journey from Colombo down to Still Waters Children's Home in Tangal on the south coast.

Ros Gihan Williams in Galle, Sri Lanka, November 2004

We drive along the coastal road. The scenery is stunning. Alluring beaches and calm sparkling seas – picture-book perfect.

Twenty children live at Still Waters. They range in age from four to 14. They greet me and my camera operator, Caitlin, with a traditional Sri Lankan ceremony – garlands and all. The home is set in 14 acres of beautiful land quite close to the sea.

In the evening the children gather in the main building and Fred, the founder of the home, asks me to talk to them about who I am and why I'm here. As I speak, I feel a bond with the children but also almost a crash survivor's guilt – I was once in the same situation as them but was lucky enough to be adopted and brought up in the West.

25 October 2004

Another early start as we catch an internal flight up to Jafna in the north of the island. This is where the main bulk of fighting occurred during the civil war and the area is under Tamil control. Many children have been orphaned as a result of the conflict.

We're taken to an orphanage where about 40 boys live. The place is in stark contrast to the comfort and family atmosphere of Still Waters. The boys sleep on bare wooden bunks, some without sheets or pillows. They follow a strict regime, each day consisting of work and prayer. It's Dickensian and depressing to be here.

Jafna is a poor area; the place has been rocked to its knees by war but things are looking up. There are many projects that concentrate on rehabilitating victims and which are regenerating the area. I leave feeling optimistic.

28 October 2004

The end of the trip – my journey to the hospital where I was taken as a baby. I'm not sure how I'll react when I get there – floods of tears or worse? But upon seeing the ward, my feelings are more of elation. It's incredible to see this place which I've heard my adoptive family talk about but have no memory of. Later on, I sit on the road where I was abandoned. I feel like I've found some sort of peace within myself, some closure. When I was a baby, I had no choice about being here. Now, as an adult, I can come here, experience the place and walk away when I choose – it's very empowering.

November 2004

Back in London, I think about my trip and Sri Lanka. It's been amazing to see the country of my birth. And to see how the island has recovered from the bloodshed of the twenty-year civil war that killed over 60,000 people. Peace has been maintained. Tourism is starting to flourish. The future looks bright.

26 December 2004

Boxing Day. A relative of my husband tells me that there's been an earthquake in Asia, which has affected Sri Lanka. We turn on the news channel . . .

The news unfolds over the next week with sickly inevitability. Latest figures report that over 30,000 have died. Whole coastal villages have been decimated. One man who is interviewed on the evening news has lost 145 people in his extended family. Many others are the sole survivors in their families, having lost partners and all their children.

January 2005

Never has a world disaster touched me so deeply. I seem to be grieving not for a particular person but for a country. I want to go back to see what has happened. Perhaps this documentary can raise awareness of the situation and plight of the children who have been orphaned. Government statistics put the number of children who have lost their parents at over 600. How will the country cope with this situation? Already there are reports of orphaned children being snatched from refugee camps by grieving parents who have lost their own children. Horrifically, some children have been abducted by Western paedophiles. The government has been forced to stop all adoptions until further notice.

My plan is to go back when the world's news crews have left and the West will start to wrongly assume that everything is back to normal. Aid has poured into Sri Lanka from around the world, how will this be spent to alleviate the orphans' situation?

The relief agencies have galvanised themselves. UNICEF is endeavouring to set up a programme to match orphans with grieving families and a Sri Lankan organisation called Sarvodaya has pledged to take in and provide for all children aged 11 and below who have been orphaned by the disaster.

Going back will be difficult and heart wrenching. But hopefully I can find a way to be part of the rebuilding and healing of my country of origin.

May you live in interesting times

JEANNETTE LOAKMAN

Rubber-moulded plastic seats – bright yellow, green and red in rows like the packets of assorted peppers on the supermarket grocery table. Huge sheets of windows with poorly painted thin iron frames. Beijing departure lounge, a piece of 1966 held in time. I was born in 1966.

The toddlers crouching quietly around the white, fat legs of their new families were probably born in 1992. All girls. I'm a girl.

So restrained, so strained. Their hesitation in being taken away – a salvation or a solution?

Sixteen proud, plump Québécois parents prepping their frightened tots with little toys and soothing words, "rescuing" them to go to their loving homes and superior standards of living.

> *Rock-a-bye Baby on the tree-top! – Oh! It's a baby! – Ching-Chong!*
> *Slanty Eyes! – What a beautiful girl, Chinese girls are so sweet – You're*
> *SO tall! Christ you're huge for a Chinese – WM seeks petite, demure,*
> *Asian for discreet sexpot adventures – You went to Waterloo? Civil*
> *engineering, what a surprise!*

*   *   *

They call people like me "Bananas" – yellow on the outside, white on the inside. It's an Asian insult: I betray the race. I think of myself more as an egg: white trying to grow my yolk.

It was no surprise to learn I was adopted. I mean, I just had to look in my mum's mirror. It was OK when I was small; most comments went straight over my head. 'Where did you find her?', 'Was it easy to adopt?', 'How much did it cost?' What the adults feigned not to notice, the odd schoolmate would slam in my face, so much so, I thought my flat nose really was from being shoved into posts and running into doors bawling my eyes out. I developed a steely wall around me and lusted over supernatural powers like the blonde in *The Champions* and superior kicking skills like the other blonde in the *New Avengers*. I worked on both diligently at teatime over the sandwiches and pork pie. 'Ah! Gwasshopper!' – I hated that show.

Things started developing around puberty. There was a new show on TV, *The Water Margin: Tales of a thousand and one heroes* with Lang Shan Po – the secret hiding place of folk heroes who defended the poor Chinese farmers, merchants and honest lords from the evil Emperor. They fought, joked, wore great outfits and everyone looked the same. There was even a bunch of neat women, from the Emperor's haughty and scheming young concubine, to the dashing sword-wielding horsewoman secretly in love with one of the hero leaders. Thank you, Hong Kong TV and BBC2. Then there was *Enter the Dragon*. Thank you Bruce Lee and the Odeon Cinema Group (and for your ice-cream). Then there was Moira Stewart the newsreader. (She was black and not East Asian, but I was prepared to overlook the colour of her skin.) Thank you (at last) BBC1.

I gained new respect: Kung Fu was cool. People treated me with extra special caution lest I sent them flying into a heap in the corner. When I entered the pub, that quiet pause, a dull lull in the local gossip of conversation, was because I was to be feared. I was Bruce Lee's little sister or, perhaps, I was one of the girls defending Roger Moore in *The Man with the Golden Gun*. Or, perhaps . . . er . . . I dunno.

All those sandwiches and pork pies suddenly moved from around my waist to around my bust and I grew a bit. Adolescence – alienation – alteration. I actually started fancying boys, but the problem was, they didn't fancy me. From the Young Farmers Club to the Fen Tigers: Lords of the London Overspill, they fancied Page 3 look-alikes, *Charlie's Angels* and the twigs in *Vogue*. How can they aspire to fancy someone they were not conditioned to desire?

Adolescence passed painfully slowly. Thirteen. Fourteen. Fifteen.

* * *

'Flight 16 to Montreal via Tokyo is ready for boarding. Will those passengers with small children or who require assistance, please board first.' The nascent mamas shovel their newly beloveds cooingly into their arms and shepherd them expediently towards the exit. Clothed in Gap, Osh Kosh and La Baie, they are already sealed in the first layers of their new identities ready to be reborn from Shanghai to Sherbrooke, from Lushan to Lac St Jean.

A pained reflection of myself imprints itself on the Chinese flight attendant waiting outside by the bus to the plane. The American Airlines uniform fights to mould her slender build into a sleek billboard image. The new blue court shoes clasp her feet, her hamstrings now locked and plumped. This is her great leap forward; screw Maoism, give me the poster.

* * *

Seventeen. I wasn't fashionable until David Bowie sang 'China girl'.

* * *

The flight attendant smiles and tries to bow, hoping she looks acceptable. The Chinese businessmen push and scramble onto the bus while their grey suits scream 'Careful! My seams might go!', their black slip-on shoes and white piping socks a clash of mod. Everyone's ruddy face gleeful at leaving East Asia, excited to be going to the land of Disney. Montreal – Orlando – Canada – the States? Who cares? Everything's going to be all white.

The Québécois mothers and fathers and eighteen children watch stunned.

Suddenly, the baby in the Osh Kosh breaks their silence as she dumps a big one in her knickers.

* * *

Attention at last! . . . A boyfriend!

If Lee Majors was sizzling prime steak speared with lashings of Lurpak butter, I was supping from a tepid can of mushy peas; but Geoffrey, bless his cotton socks, was definitely male. And bonus points: white. (Well, they were all white where I lived!)

I had a man! And what a man. You could almost smell the Y chromosome all over him! He was smashing even for his amazing spotty skin and his "squash gait" which made him prance like a Lipanzer doing dressage. He was charming, well dressed and very affectionate. We'd walk arm in arm, hand in hand everywhere, and I was dead chuffed. Look, I'm a *Cosmo* girl now. I've got one of these – *un homme*!

'Your nose. It's cute.'
'Oh.'
'I've always loved your features – I think Orientals are so beautiful. You don't realise it, but even the way you move, it's different. Lighter.'
'*Oh?*'
'Why don't you grow your hair long? It's beautiful. I love stroking your hair – it's so shiny and black.'
'*Oh!*'
I purred with flattered delight. At last, someone who appreciated me!

'David's going back to Hong Kong this summer. I've asked him to get you something.'
'*For me?*'
'For both of us!'
'*Uh oh.*'

It seemed harmless enough; I was given a couple of gifts: a pair of chopsticks and a traditional Chinese dress – a *chong-san*. I stuck the chopsticks in the bun of my lengthening mane and wore the dress. Geoffrey suggested heels, bright red lipstick and dark kohl eyeliner. Then we went out to the Szechuen Garden to thank David.

The next morning we broke up.

'China girl' left the Top Ten and *Absolute Beginners* was a flop at the box office. Look, I really am a *Cosmo* girl now!

*   *   *

Except for the couple sporting diaper pins in their mouths, all the new families were on board the bus to the plane. The mothers coocooed their daughters into a gentle, smiling group, whilst the fathers soberly corralled their new families into a corner, the men's faces a wall of stone shields to ward off the shrieks of delight from the businessmen who had just discovered the pamphlet on the joys of duty-free shopping. The piteous looks of disapproval on one of the fathers' faces reminded me of the crushed expressions of tourists at Tiananmen Square upon finding the largest KFC fast-food counter in the world.

'How could they build it?', were the cries. 'Don't lose your culture!' were the admonishments. 'Keep China Chinese!', was the message. 'Keep China quaint!' it said to me. Occidental companies sell the world on Coca-Cola, McDonalds and Nike promoting their "right way of life"; first-world governments spend millions on tearing down the slums to create wonderful new country-homogenous habitats; and yet, when a second- or third-world country tries to emulate them, the cry is, 'No! You'll spoil your beauty – keep your culture.' A wonderful sentiment, but when that beauty is concrete tenements and a culture that considers a baby girl "disposable", that sentiment seems arrogant.

Lurching forward, the bus juddered over to the patient, white, wide-body jet that sat winking on the runway. My reflection in the window shook as the vehicle backfired, belching a cloud of exhaust over the ready-to-please flight attendant.

The tannoy barked the next seat rows for Flight 16. My turn now. I haul my tattered backpack over my shoulder and plod to the lounge door to await the next plane bus. The flight attendant doesn't even try to smile at me. I'm not Chinese to her and I'm not "Big Nose" either. 'Banana,' she thinks. 'Egg,' I want to tell her, 'with a big yolk.'

* * *

We moved from Slough to Toronto when I was 20. Dad got a new and better job, and I switched to Waterloo University. I watched with other Canadian-Chinese as the Democracy movement in China was crushed. The others talked of betrayal, economics and political action. I was happy to find Connie Chung.

Two-and-a-half years later, the Gulf war took over people's consciousness and Connie Chung was let go by ABC. That's when I decided I'd really better find my own icon, and where better than the "Motherland" – China.

When I arrived in Beijing two months ago, I was totally unprepared. Just the year before, my only contact with Chinese culture had been the dinner specials for two at the Jade Garden: hot and sour soup, spring rolls, General Tao chicken, *bok choy* in oyster sauce and a bowl of rice. I had mastered the chopsticks and even forced myself to drink the bitter brown tea they served at lunchtime. I struggled with the nine tones in Cantonese, then the four in Mandarin, to discover my only linguistic talent was pointing at *dim sum* baskets and asking, '*Lay hie mut yere?*' (What is that?).

The shock on arrival was tremendous. I remember standing on the 40 hectares of concrete called Tiananmen Square, unable to fathom which alien landscape I had landed on. No bloodstains on the pavements, the army and families ambling lackadaisically across the square. Chinese tourists hamming to the photographer, having their pictures taken in front of the Imperial Gate, the massive portrait of Mao in the distance. Bicycles everywhere! Smog layered over the slabs of government meeting halls, and not a patch of green to be seen. This was not my China.

After my shock at the industrial grey metropolis of Beijing, I retreated to Shanghai and Hangzhow. By the second week, I got used to the air pollution from the silk factories, the hustling in the streets by haggard women who were probably all of 30 years old and the instant inflation as I walked into a market. It still wasn't my dream – it was their reality, and if there's one characteristic about the Chinese I found out, it is that they're realistic:

Why are you here? Why be one in two billion? You think you're going to find your roots? Why come back to a place like this? We're poor. No food, no soft beds. Culture? Go to the cinema. The Imperial Palace is like Disneyland – you want Disneyland? Why aren't you married yet? What are you eating? Have some KFC.

To be Chinese is a state of mind. I feel my yolk grow, and I splash out on Beijing Duck. Confucious said, 'To eat is heaven.'

Even after two months of slogging my way around Eastern China, I'm not mistaken for anything other than occidental. At best, they think I'm BBC or CBC, British-born or Canadian-born Chinese. At worst, they think I'm Japanese. My face means nothing to them. My features aren't what is on my face – it's my clothes, my behaviour, my money. I really am white on the outside.

'32A. Please, down the aisle on your right.' The nicely dressed Japanese flight attendant gives me her Mickey Mouse smile and I return the customary "Hello Kitty" one back. The clean, sanitised seat with pillow and blanket in hermetically sealed packages greets my tired body. At the door closes, I pull out the in-flight magazine. The Tokyo Film Festival is starting and the major movie from Hong Kong is a gritty drama starring Gong Li, the lead in many of China's rich historical films. I read the review: 'Mary, a wife brought from Beijing to Hong Kong, finds herself caught between her traditional upbringing and the more liberal Western standards. The film mirrors the anxiety of the Chinese as they merge with the West, symbolised in the city of Hong Kong.'

The plane starts its roll down the runway. I catch my reflection again, this time in the seat window, the airport building completing the tableau. I realise that I am further ahead than 'Mary from Beijing', as are the 18 other little transplants with me on the flight. We are already on our way to being part of China's future, and as the jet lifts off I resolve to make sure that my egg becomes a rooster.

As the pressure in the cabin rises, a piteous bawl comes from the row behind me, starting a cacophony of sobs and yells. The sound of a pack of pacifiers being ripped open explodes in my right ear and I can tell that this plane ride, as well as the future, will be one of those "interesting times".

A–Z of Kenya

KAGEHA JERUTO MARSHALL

A is for Africa – continent of my birth, a place I have not been for a long time

B is for black British – how I have always thought of myself

C is for Courage – my feelings of uncertainty made it difficult to plan such a journey

D is for Destiny – my personal circumstances brought me back to where I originally came from

E is for Experience – finding out about Kenyan people, culture and customs by visiting the country

F is for Family – being accepted as a member of a group, even though I had been away for so many years

G is for Growth – learning from what I have achieved this year and moving on as a person

H is for Happiness – happy in the knowledge of finding out about my "roots"

I is for Identity – I know who I am and where I come from

J is for Journey – there are miles and miles between England and Kenya

K is for Kenya – my travels were from Lake Victoria to the Indian Ocean

L is for Life – accepting the life that I have and the growth of a new life in Kenya

M is for Memories – remembering the friendly, warm welcome I received in Kenya

N is for the Nandi Hills – in the shadow of Nandi Rock, the area I come from

O is for One – at one with myself, at one with my family

P is for Peace – that I experienced when I made contact with my family and feel now

Q is for Quakers – who supported me before and during my personal journey, and who continue to support me

R is for Relatives – I learned I have so many

S is for Smile – I remember a lot of smiling faces

T is for Tribe – I belong to the Kalenjin and Luhya tribes

U is for Umbrella – I felt an umbrella of warmth enveloping me when I met my Kenyan extended family

V is for Village – set amongst huge green rocks in lush green vegetation with red walled houses; the area where I would have lived

W is for Welcome – it was with open arms by everyone

X – marks the spot on the map of the world where I come from in Africa

Y is for Yellow maize – drying in the sun and yellow bananas growing high in the trees

Z is for the Zigzag road – the journey I took to reach my family's village in Kenya and the route I hope to follow again in the future

Shalwar kameez

DEBORAH WEYMONT

Today I am going to reclaim a piece of land that was stolen from me at birth. I am going to annexe an unoccupied territory. I am going to give back to myself, a 'corner of a foreign field that was forever England'. Today I am going to Rajani's "House of Silk" on Stapleton Road. I am going to buy myself a *shalwar kameez*.

I am possessed of a sense of my own dispossession. I am on foot. I am walking to this place because I live near it. But it wasn't always so. Every day for seven years, I had to travel twenty miles on the school bus, through the rolling green patchwork hills of Devon just to get to school; a school with 1,500 children and only one other brown-skinned face.

It wasn't easy growing up so far from civilisation. I started grammar school the same year that Enoch Powell delivered his 'Rivers of Blood' sermon. Overnight, this speech made Devon a more dangerous place to live. School became a little less safe. Each morning, when I got on the school bus I was greeted by the whooping taunts and hollers of the boys from the council houses. They would put their hands over their mouths and speak like Little Plum (um) from the . . . um Beano um . . . to mock my assumed first American origins . . . um.

In class my biology, my history, my geography and my religious education were all subsumed under the dominant social Darwinist discourse on race, sex and Empire. In biology we learned that hybrids are infertile and that cross-breeds and mongrels weaken (rather than strengthen) the gene pool. "Paki" and "half-caste" were terms of everyday abuse tolerated by teachers. In history the seeds of racialised sexuality were sown in textbooks that fell open at well-thumbed pages depicting Columbus or Cook or Cabot fully clothed next to half-naked "natives". In the geography room, the colour pink polluted the four corners of the globe and when "Miss" explained that South Africa and Australia liked to 'keep their countries for the white people' this seemed a good enough explanation for why there were no "brown" countries. And even in religious education, Christianity was presented to us as a salve to civilise the savages, justifying British imperial ambition rather than an ethical way of life. Where I come from, the rest of the world is a dangerous, seething mass of fornicating, heathen infidels.

Happily, the quaint customs and superstitions of the indigenous peoples of the British Isles are largely extinct in the cosmopolitan, multi-cultural urban landscape that I now inhabit. The history and geography books have been re-written. For example, did you know that in 1488 a petty Portuguese nobleman called Vasco da Gama rounded the Cape of Good Hope and reached India? And did you know that while most of Europe languished in the shadow of the dark ages, he found there, a sophisticated network of trade, communication and social administration that had been in existence for thousands of years? This event, along with Christopher Columbus's so-called "discovery" of America, marked a turning point in history: an economic and social upturn for Europe, the start of centuries of decline for most of the rest of the world. But this information was written in invisible ink. It was hidden between the lines of my school textbooks. And I could have saved a fortune in therapists' fees if someone had told me it is political and cultural analysis, not psychoanalysis, that is needed to make sense of it all. The personal is indeed political.

*   *   *

Anyway, that's a long time ago. This is Bristol 1999, and I am walking the pavements of this great city looking for something to wear to welcome the new millennium. I am 'on a mission' (as they say in these parts) to find an outfit for the party season.

I know, because I've seen it and smelt it, that there are times when you can walk the streets of this city and blood actually oozes up from the cracks between the paving stones. Each stone slab of pavement along the City Road is the headstone of a slave grave, laid horizontal in remembrance of the people who really built this city. The names Adeyimi, Tembeke, Menelik long worn away by the English rain, heavy-soled shoes and forgetting.

But today there is no sign of that particular diaspora. Instead, the dry cold wind reminds me of inhospitable mountain corridors and the dusty desert plateaux of the old silk routes. I am an archaeologist. I am digging an interior landscape in the kingdom of Gandhara. I am walking in the footsteps of the three wise men. I am connecting the micro to the macro.

I am trying to remember the noise of the markets and the bustle of business drummed up inside the walls of ancient cities (glimpses of which emerge from time to time beneath the shifting sands of the Talikaman desert). I am imagining the glamour and the energy of the nomadic caravans as they entered remote towns and cities linking East to West with goods to sell or barter: terracotta knick-knacks, lacquered bamboo and fine porcelain from China; malachite and silver jewellery, wooden and ivory artefacts from Africa; stitched leather and woollen garments from Mongolia; bronze bells, bowls and gongs and richly woven rugs from Persia; incense, drugs and spices; tinctures and oils infused with herbs and the obscure body parts of exotic animals. The collision and fusion of Christianity, Jewish Gnosticism, Zoroastrianism, Hinduism and Buddhism. Women with dark skin falling in love with men with pale skin. The exchange of goods, ideas and body fluids.

Somewhere leftfield emerges an image of myself walking the well-trodden path of young women, to be fitted out with clothes for festivals and weddings.

But this is a romantic fabrication! The old silk routes are actually much further north than Bangladesh. They start at Changan, head up the Gansu corridor towards Dunhuang, and then skirt the Talikaman desert, north and south. They are separated from the Indian sub-continent by the highest mountains in the world: the Himalayan, Karakorum and Kunlun ranges. While some traders did get through, it would have been through icy passes five thousand metres high. So, while the old silk routes did link East with West in a fertile and fruitful exchange of goods, ideas and genes, it was actually their transformation into the (safer) shipping routes of the East India Company from the 16th century onwards that first linked England with India. And it was along these well-navigated paths that my father (a Bangladeshi merchant sailor) travelled to this country in the 1950s.

* * *

Anyway, I can't pretend that India's history is mine. In truth, I am better connected to Luther and the madness of the Medieval European Church than to the minarets and mosques of the silk routes (land or sea). I am actually more English than anyone I know.

My father was an Anglican vicar, my mother (like me) a vicar's daughter. And it was the Bible, not the Qu'ran, and the *Daily Mail*, not Sanskrit Scrolls, and the gentle Exmoor landscape, not the drama of the Himalayas, that shaped my identity.

I am comfortable with chintz and the proportions of Georgian architecture. On Sunday afternoons I like to bake scones, and I know that tea tastes better drunk from bone china cups. I can make cucumber sandwiches to die for: the secret is to slice the cucumber and leave it in a little vinegar while you spread the bread with fresh farm butter. Drain the cucumber slices before you place them between slices of bread. For best results, eat them whilst seated on weathered wrought-iron garden furniture in the shade of a fig tree (brought back from the Empire).

I also understand how Victorian values and Edwardian sensibilities both underpin and frame the English male and female psyches. I see through the whitewash of our duty to "love thy neighbour as thyself" and I can "read" the minute calibrations of class and status that threaten to suffocate us all.

This is how it is. Mince pies and a schooner of sherry for the carol singers on Christmas Eve at the front door. Cheap china mugs of tea for the grave diggers at the back door, and the same for the Irish (and Catholic) "men of the road". Gilt-edged porcelain cups with saucers for the archdeacon or the bishop served from the trolley in the library in the morning, or the withdrawing room in the afternoon. The willow-pattern set (with matching sugar bowl and milk jug) for parish council meetings, the church wardens, flower arrangers and visits from families planning christenings, weddings and funerals. A tea cosy was fine, and sitting in the kitchen with the more familiar, regular, church-going guests (particularly in winter) was sometimes OK.

After all this consideration of front door, back door, kitchen, drawing room, library, it was a shock to answer the door one day to the exorcist (definitely a library guest) and have him follow me into the kitchen where I had gone to find Mother. He was the vicar of a neighbouring group of parishes and there were stories about him that had touched my imagination. He had an unmistakeable presence. He was six feet four and always wore a black, calf-length cape over his cassock. Unlike my father, he always wore the clothes of his profession, thus denoting himself as "high" rather than "low" church. Occasionally, he even wore a deep red cassock rather than the regulation black. My father was a little disapproving of his 'swagger'; mother found him 'really rather charming'.

Mother was hanging clothes to dry in front of a wood-burning Rayburn. He greeted her warmly as Kathleen, enquiring as to the whereabouts of my father, Geoffrey. I found this very exciting. No one apart from family ever called my parents by their first names.

My father was out, but my mother always knew his affairs and without any niceties enquired of the well-being of the young woman from the village she knew he had come about. Her name was Joyce and she had been 'sent to Digby' (the local asylum). I knew about this from talk on the school bus. David Kingdom (one of my tormentors) had seen and heard it all because he lived in the adjoining council house. Apparently, she had been 'carted off to the loony bin' in the early hours of the morning, after being found walking drunk and naked in the lane that ran between the graveyard and the rectory (my home).

The Church of England has only a handful of exorcists and it keeps very quiet about them because of associations with witch-burning and Catholicism. I later discovered that this man, a regular visitor to our house, did some ground-breaking work, both within asylums and the church, with women with mental health issues. While I knew nothing of the detail of his ideas, I had a sense of their substance even then. He seemed to know and understand more than most of us.

The exorcist and my mother seated themselves at the kitchen table with mugs of tea from the family teapot. They seemed to have forgotten me. I went quietly out of the back door of the kitchen into the scullery to listen. The scullery itself had a back door into the stable yard where coal and wood were stored, so I knew I could make a quick exit if need be. This was where the gravediggers drank their tea.

There was a tone and an urgency and informality to their discussion that I found intoxicating. For a start, neither of them seemed to notice that they were drinking tea in the wrong cups, poured from the wrong pot in the wrong room! The exorcist brought drama and uncertainty to the world but that day, he also planted the seed of something new in my head, when he lowered his voice to tell my mother:
'It all goes back to the time when she had to give her babies up for adoption.'

Standing silent in the scullery, something shifted inside me and I understood myself a little better.

I have ridden with the Devon & Somerset foxhounds. I never had a curry until I was 20. Red wine in my home was to do with the blood of Jesus and the debate around transubstantiation. Garlic was something you could use to ward off evil. Where I come from, the year turns upon the twin axes of the first Easter uprising and harvest supper. From the first spring lamb to the first loaf of the first ground flour at Lamastide; from ploughed field to seed sown; from baling to hedging and fencing and ditching, we walked in tandem with the seasons and the needs of the land. The social calendar was signposted along the same route. Summer fêtes, weddings, christenings and funerals, cider making, badger baiting, grave digging, rabbit shooting, flower arranging, choir practice, bonfire building, carol singing and a glass of sherry at the Boxing Day meet.

From Advent to the Epiphany, from Ash Wednesday to Maundy Thursday, from Mothering Sunday to Good Friday, from Palm Sunday to Easter, to the beating of the bounds on Rogation Sunday, to Whitsun and the Pentecost, from Ascension Day to All Souls Day, I am indissolubly connected to the rhythms and customs of the English countryside and the Anglican Church.

Where I come from, "partition" was the triptych tapestry screen (depicting grouse, pheasant and partridge) that the three kings stood behind in church nativity plays. And so it was that I was a little unsure of the territory I was about to enter.

* * *

I open the door to the "House of Silk". I look like I know who I am and I know what I'm doing. I am a global citizen. I am a trader in the world market. I am standing at the crossroads of the old trading routes once charted by the East India Company. I am crossing continents and centuries. I stand astride the world. I have one foot in Chittagong and the other foot in Chigwell.

There are no other customers. My anxiety barometer wavers. Perhaps all good Bengalis right now are saying prayers. I am engulfed in colour and texture. There are rolls of fabric propped floor to ceiling against two walls. The floor space is crammed with rails full of garments on hangers. Reds (tomato, chilli and paprika), yellows (saffron, mustard, ginger and lemon), blues (indigo, turquoise, sky and ocean) and all the colours in between. Some of the paler fabrics and more gorgeously embroidered items are encased in clear plastic to protect them.

To my left are several deeply shelved and tall, narrow units stacked high with folded fabric. These are in fact lengths of silk and polyester and they have been stacked and graded according to tone and hue. The pinks alone take up several shelves (baby, peach, papaya, princess, cerise and salmon). There at least twenty shades of carefully graded brown.

Even though I look a bit like the people in this shop, I am not anonymous. I can't just walk in and browse. I am clearly (my clothes, my haircut) both of and not of. I hesitate. I have eye contact with a man to my right and there is a woman a little further away. She bows her head towards me and smiles, 'And what are you looking for please?' It would be difficult to explain right now the elusiveness of it all. How I'm looking for somewhere to belong. How I'm trying to get all the different bits of myself talking to each other and how I want to integrate my personal and political selves. So, I just say, 'I want to buy a *shalwar kameez.*'

'Yes, yes, come this way please,' she gestures for me to follow her. The man to my right says nothing. He looks away from me through his thick glasses at some fabric laid out beside a sewing machine. He has a tape measure around his neck and his face is still. I think maybe I have embarrassed him, or maybe he's just concentrating (the barometer swings gently up).

The woman leads me to the back of the shop. She is wearing low-heeled yellow patent leather sandals, a soft brown sari and a cream headscarf. Her hair and nails are well groomed and my eyes are drawn to her hands by the jewellery glistening on her wrists and fingers. There is another older woman (also sari-clad) at the back of the shop who comes forward now to help.

The two women have a brief exchange in an Indian language that (of course) I do not understand. The older one smiles at me and begins rapidly leafing through the hangers on the rail in front of her. She pauses occasionally to unhook one. First she chooses something blue and holds it up with a nod towards me. Emboldened (I think) by my silence and what (I think) she reads as approval in my body language, she continues along the rail making selections, each one more unsuitable than the last. I am frozen by fear and the apparently insurmountable communication gap opening up between us. I don't like any of these outfits and, for all I know, they may cost thousands of pounds. They look like the sort of thing minor royalty might wear to a wedding feast.

I focus on her hands. They are elegant, beautifully manicured and old. She is wearing clear nail varnish and several rings. Her skin is thin and marked with age. It seems to be stretched over the bones. She seems particularly pleased with a choice of cream with gold-edged cuffs and hem. She holds it up and gestures to ascertain my response.

'Yes, yes ?' she queries. I hesitate. The cream garment is encased in clear plastic so I can't really see it. But what I can see looks tacky and tasteless. I wave my hand in the negative. 'No, no . . . it's not a wedding.' I laugh nervously . . . 'It's for a party.'

To my relief, she smiles and returns the garment to the rail. But I know she doesn't understand that, at the sort of party I go to, everyone wears black and, if they're not wearing black, then they would have a postmodern rationale for it. She is still smiling and nodding her head. 'Of course, of course . . .' She again speaks to her colleague (who it occurs to me is probably also her daughter) in her first language. She is also flicking the tops of hangers looking for something.

Without consulting me, the two women continue with their selection. Then each of them, with one arm loaded, proceed to hold the chosen garment up for inspection (still on its hanger) roughly checking for size and fit and some other weird criteria, of which I, of course, know nothing.

I shake my head at some of the more outlandish offerings. They both look a little puzzled. Clearly, they do not know quite what to do with me. Each outfit seems to me to be more garish, more tasteless and outrageous than the one before. Mustard, maroon, cerise, tangerine, lime green (for God's sake!) . . . I have to act fast.

I join in the selection process and force them to begin organising a "yes" pile and a "no" pile. I'm sure they are as puzzled by my selection criteria as I am by theirs; but they join in willingly saying 'yes, yes, yes' or, 'no, no, no', thus placing an unnecessary importance on the decision-making process. My criteria is now reduced to, 'Would I wear this with a bag over my head?' or, 'Would I die rather than wear this?' I resign myself to wearing a bag over my head for the start of the new millennium and comfort myself with the thought that Kofi Annan would be proud that we found a way to sort out our cultural differences without UN intervention. The "no" pile is now bigger than the "yes" pile and it is time to try some on.

The younger of the two women swiftly gathers up the "yes" pile and moves behind where we are standing. She pulls one of two curtains aside and tells me to 'Come this way please.' I understand. I nod and reach out for the pile of clothes hanging over her arm. But she holds onto them and gestures for me to go into the cubicle. She hands me just one garment and then pulls the curtain behind me.

There is no mirror in the changing area. My heart sinks. I am going to have to show them. I am going to have to look at myself in the mirror out there, with them looking at me looking at myself in the mirror. I am feeling deeply uncomfortable and foolish. How could I have ever imagined that this might be a useful place to stop on my journey to myself? What vanity or false confidence gave me the idea that I might be welcome in this shrine to female coquetry, which has had some sort of triple bypass on 70s feminism, 80s minimalism and 90s cool? Clearly they were both going to stand there and wait and watch. We are going to choose my outfit through a process of consensus rather than individual choice.

I try it on. It's too tight and it's garish. I've not worn anything made of embroidered purple satin since I last took acid back in 1974. I pull the curtain to one side and peep out my head. She looks pleased, 'All right my dear. Shall we have a look now then?'

My heart sinks. 'No . . . it's too small. Let me try another on,' I say bravely. I reach out and grasp another hanger, which she relinquishes a little reluctantly. I'm not playing this particular game according to the rules. We all know it. I go back into the cramped cubicle and huff and puff my way out of this piece of fashion suicide. I then struggle into an equally uncool concoction of sea-green polyester and cotton. At least it fits. I step out from behind the curtain and pull a face that I hope conveys the awfulness of it all. She responds with a smile and turns to a narrow case of shelves stacked with scarves standing adjacent to the changing cubicle. 'Here,' she says, and throws a pea-green length of chiffon silk around my neck. It falls effortlessly over my shoulder and gracefully embraces my neck. 'Very nice, very nice,' she fusses slightly.

I'd never imagine that pea green and sea green could blend other than as vomit from a novice sailor, but I was surprised to look in the mirror and notice that she had managed to pick a colour that simultaneously complemented, blended and contrasted at the level of tone and texture and hue with the deep sea green of the *shalwar* (or is it *kameez*?) top. I catch the eye of the older woman who is standing beside the mirror at the end of a rail of tightly packed garments. I can only see her top half but she is nodding and smiling and seems happy about this choice.

I am a little seduced by the colours but, unfortunately, the top has a sequin studded and lace macramé-edged yoke and cuffs. There is a superficial trashiness to it which I'm sure will one day be "owned" by really cool retro-bhangra-loving-fifth-generation non-Punjabi speaking professional "Indians" living in Hampstead. In 1999 I just look ridiculous.

I look down to where polished nails should be peeping through strappy gold sandals and see my scuffed Doctor Marten shoes. I sigh inside. I haven't got it in me. I'm a failure. I'm never going to be an "Asian babe". I don't know how to extricate myself from this situation. I look up. The younger woman reaches forward and begins fussing with little details of position upon my shoulders and hem. She brushes imaginary dust from my back. She pulls gently on my short hair as if willing it to be long.

She steps back to admire her efforts. I feel sea-sick. I look past her and over her shoulder, and see what I came to buy . . . but she interrupts me. 'Oh, my dear, this is very fashionable now.' She holds up a third pantomime outfit ready for me to take to the changing cubicle. She is smiling but her voice is bright and brittle. Again, I have to act fast.

'That's it!' I say and point up and behind her. 'There! That's what I want . . .' I hesitate. 'Is that a *shalwar kameez*?'

High above her head, on the opposite wall is the most gorgeous, "must have" understated garment I had ever seen: an androgynous slate-grey tunic with a little upright Nehru collar and four small buttons to fasten the neck opening. It is hanging, as it should be worn, over cuffed trousers made of the same fabric. The colour is like shadow worked up with the side of a thick stick of graphite. It is probably a linen silk mix. I feel comfortable. This, I know, is fashion as it should be, transformatory – something that expresses the intersection of your individual "self" with society and lets you say, 'This is me. Now! Look!' It was perfect.

'Ah,' the younger woman smiles anxiously and looks across to her colleague, as if for help. The older woman nods faintly. 'This one . . . well . . .' she gestures meaninglessly.

By what I imagine might be some sort of ancient Ayurvedic system of yogi-auto-suggestion she brings my eyes back to focus on the rail of brightly coloured clothes in front of us. My back is turning away from the more sober colours that seem to dominate the other side of the shop. Eventually she manages to get out what has been so difficult for her to say: 'But those are for the gentlemen.' Her head is tipped slightly to one side and she has a sort of pleading expression on her face. She is clearly deeply embarrassed. (I'm not sure but I think she was actually wringing her hands at this point.)

I have a choice. I can put my hands in the air and say, 'OK . . . I'm an imposter . . . I don't belong here . . . I'm a fraud . . . I'm not really Indian . . . I'm not even female . . . I'm a transracial transsexual . . . my skin is brown but inside I'm actually white . . . I'm a transgendered, Bounty bar hermaphrodite with a false tan . . . (I'm so sorry) . . .' Or . . . I could do this. I pull them into the postmodern, post-colonial, Buddha of the absurd Suburbia, *White Teeth*, *Brick Lane*, beat-mixed musical underground "places where the races meet".

I smile and put my hands out as if despairing of myself. 'I'm sorry.' I shake my head in mock self-disbelief. 'I know, I know . . . Allah won't like it . . .'

We all hold our breath. I continue. 'But that is what I want . . . it's really cool . . . it's perfect . . . I'm sorry.' I turn my palms up in a gesture of supplicatory appeasement (learned while watching aforementioned exorcist say the Lord's Prayer).

We've all started breathing again. I am escorted across the crowded shop floor, to the invisible line demarcating female from male. The two women start to laugh. I hear them speaking and laughing at the same time. A man I hadn't noticed before appears from behind some rolls of fabric. The man hears what they are saying. I hear the word 'Allah' and what are now almost shrieks of laughter. The man looks at me and smiles and then he laughs. I look behind me at the man with the tape measure around his neck. He holds my gaze briefly and then he starts smiling too. The other man leans close towards me . . . his eyes are twinkling. 'So, you will not be going to heaven for this party, then?' There is more laughter behind me.

'Look,' I say lightly. 'I just came to buy something to wear . . . and that's the one I like.' I shrug as if to say, 'I'm sorry I can't help it.'

'Ah! Yes,' he laughs . . . and then more carefully, 'The customer is always right!'

'Especially if he's a man!' I quip, and catch the eye of the younger woman. She laughs again. We are all laughing now. And standing there in this shiny sea-green costume, for one moment the cold grey swell of the Atlantic feels warmed, ebb and flow, by the clear blue waters of the Indian Ocean. The British Isles have been annexed by the Maldives; and I am not alone.

It's not quite over but the anxiety barometer has dropped low. I have to be measured by the man with the tape measure. Inside leg, outside leg, hips, waist, bust, neck and arms. All done respectfully and fluently, the information transcribed to a handwritten ledger on his counter. I have to choose a fabric and am guided in my choice by the second man, who seems completely at ease chatting to a woman about fabric and the effect of washing soap on silk and the benefits of hand-washing. I choose a silk-linen mix in "hairdresser black". It costs just £18 for the fabric plus £40 for the tailoring. Fifty-eight pounds for a perfect fitted garment which I collect three days before the eve of the next millennium. I buy some stars and sequins from a stall in St Nicholas's market and stitch them on the hem and trouser cuffs. I buy a length of polyester sparkling glitz (from the hippy shop on the Gloucester Road), throw it around my neck and prepare to party.

December 31st 1999 and we dance into the bright and shiny dawn of the new millennium. I look beautiful in my *shalwar kameez* and I am beautiful.

Walking home, around eight o'clock in the morning of January 1st 2000, I find myself looking over the Ashley Vale allotments and I think about this. All over the world, people have been dancing on the turning earth to welcome in the new millennium. Some have sat in secluded places or on hills with views to meditate upon the meaning of it all. Others have crowded into streets, squares and other public places, and bars and cellars and the sitting rooms of strangers and the kitchens of friends to embrace change and bear witness to our lives. All over the world, people have risen at dawn for the call to prayer and bells have rung out in holy places from Chittagong to Chigwell, from Brick Lane to Bristol, and from Barnstaple to Bangladesh. I close my eyes. I call up my people and I listen to the wisdom of the ancestors. Sshh!

I can hear an ancient thrum, a neural imprint, sound of drum, a universal hum, my mother's heartbeat, a gentle pulse upon the street beneath my dance-tired feet. It is a sound that surrounds. And I am proud to be coming home to this world I call my own.

5

Search and reunion

African masks *Jackie Kay*
Pathan and *puri* *Veronica Dewan*

'An only child with siblings'

KAREN MOIR

Birth Family – Hong Kong 1966
(Karen Moir)

This is the first time that I've ever written about my experiences of being an adoptee. Throughout my life, friends and colleagues have, from time to time, engaged me in lengthy discussions about the issues of being adopted. Writing them down, however, allows people I don't know the opportunity to read them and perhaps make some links with their own experiences.

What does being a sibling mean?

I always imagined having a brother or sister to be a mixture of a play companion as a child, someone to share school experiences and someone to angst over adolescence with. In short, someone who has a shared common history. I grew up as an only child within my adoptive family. I had the usual imaginary friend as well as a small circle of childhood "best friends". Some of these friends I am still in contact with, and some friends that I have had for many years have become almost "sister-like" in my eyes.

However, I also knew that somewhere in the world (namely Hong Kong) I had four older sisters (two sets of twins). I had no names or ages, just one black and white photograph of them with my birth parents before I left for England.

It's a strange feeling to know you have blood relatives in another part of the world. You don't know them; you have no idea what they look like, what their characteristics are like, or whether they have any knowledge of your existence.

As a child, when asked, 'Do you have brothers or sisters?', I would often have to make a quick mental decision as to whether I wanted to elaborate on the fact that I had four older sisters but knew very little else about them, or opt for the quick easy answer of, 'No, I am an only child.' I believe that adopted children often have to make these conscious decisions as to the level of information they divulge about themselves. These dilemmas are influenced by what information they have, how open and comfortable they are with their adoption, the level of support given by their adoptive parents and, of course, who they are talking to.

As I grew older and issues of identity became stronger, I began to wonder how different things might have been if I had stayed with my family in Hong Kong or if I had been adopted with one or more of my siblings. Although somewhat disillusioned by family life due to the divorce of my adoptive parents, I think that I still had an urge to be part of an identifiable family; a family with common roots, familial bonds and "blood thicker than water". I began to realise that, in fact, I had used close friends as substitutes for the usual sibling relationships.

At the age of 25, I finally made my 'journey of a lifetime' across the world to meet my birth family. I was filled with huge excitement but at the same time immeasurable anxiety. This was matched only by my family's complete unconditional welcoming of me back into their lives. At the risk of using religious metaphors, my family described my visit as nothing short of a miracle. The baby that had left the family had returned to look for them, having achieved all the educational achievements they could have hoped for. As for me, as others have expressed before me, it completed the incomplete jigsaw of my beginning.

Let me not mislead you into thinking that the visit was without difficulties. As much as it answered questions for me, it also raised other thoughts and feelings that I continue to work through. Communication itself can be difficult for transracially adopted people if there is no common language with their birth family. Using others to interpret for you can inhibit the nature of the emotional response at times like these. However, my journey also brought into my life a younger sister whom I had been unaware of and it is largely thanks to her knowledge of English that members of our family and I were able to communicate our feelings during this visit and relive some of our shared history.

The emotional bond that I feel towards my sisters was a completely new experience. I began to find out about who they were, and find common links as well as physical resemblance and similarities. Watching the rest of the family interact with each other and, in particular, the strong relationships between my sisters left me both very proud to be part of this family but also quite envious. They had the shared childhood history and strength of cultural identity that I believe I have always sought but struggled to make sense of. Because of their experiences, these aspects of their lives will be taken for granted, whilst mine are so different and, therefore, take some thought and conscious effort.

Eight years on and three visits later, I am still in contact with them all. Although physical distance prevents regular contact, the links have been made. I now accept my part within this new family but also acknowledge my different experiences. I cannot turn back the clock, or live in a "what if . . ." world. So, for now, I am comfortable being an only child with five siblings.

A journey without end

DAVID GILBERT

As I neared the end of my journey on a Boeing 747, 30,000 feet above the sea and within an hour of Logan airport (Boston, USA), I reflected on the long and meandering pathway that had taken me to this point.

Roughly 18 months earlier, on my thirtieth birthday, I had sat alone, tears rolling down my cheeks, bewildered at the range of emotions tearing through my heart. For the first time I had had a very clear desire to trace my birth parents. I knew this was essential for my own well-being, and I hoped it might complete a circle in my life. A journey had begun.

The following day, I scoured the internet for adoption agencies, visited my local library and contacted the National Organisation for Counselling of Adoptees and Parents (NORCAP). The next significant stage was meeting with a social worker prior to being able to access my adoption records. The meeting reaffirmed that it was going to be a long and challenging process. The next time I met the social worker I was allowed to see my adoption records, my heart raced and my stomach was twisted in tight knots. I discovered, to my dismay, that my entire background was presented on less than a third of a piece of A4 paper. (It later emerged, furthermore, that many of the details were wholly inaccurate!) Importantly, I did discover the names of my parents, their occupations at the time of my adoption, their countries of origin and their last recorded addresses. Perhaps most significantly, there were two items of correspondence from my mother. One letter thanked a social worker for all her help and support, and expressed gratitude for posting a picture of me to her; the second was a postcard from my mother saying that she was happy about the new opportunities in the USA. I asked the social worker if I could have a copy of each of these. Slightly disgruntled at my request, she hurriedly photocopied them. In her haste, she had not folded the treasury tags back far enough and so large pieces of the copied letter were missing. When I asked if I could have a full copy, she replied that I had seen the original and what more did I want? This summed up her approach to my situation and me. She seemed devoid of any sensitivity or understanding about what these disclosures represented for me and why I would naturally want treasured copies of what my mother had written. To me these were not merely words on a page, they were pieces of concrete evidence about my life. Something that, up until that point, I knew *nothing* about.

My father's details were far sketchier. I had always known he was a doctor, just as I knew my mother was a nurse. The greatest insight into him came from two contrasting sources. First, a scruffily hand-written letter without an address or date, confirming that he agreed to my mother having me adopted. Second, I discovered that he was from the Yemen. (Up until that point, I was unsure of his country of origin. My adoptive parents had only been told he was from the Middle East.) I left the meeting in emotional turmoil. After 30 years, I was discovering missing pieces of the puzzle of my life.

For the next seven months, I systematically searched databases in libraries and wrote to adoption organisations in England, Scotland, Ireland and the USA. I kept detailed records of every telephone call, filed every piece of evidence and recorded any other information that might be of some use in tracing my parents.

The journey to discover whether my parents were still alive, and if so, where they lived, proved to be remarkably short by comparison to those of some adopted people who have searched for their natural parents. Within seven months, I had discovered which country my father lived and worked in. I wrote a letter to him posing as a former colleague of his from London. I followed the letter up twice before receiving a letter from a hospital administrator saying the doctor had no recollection of me. I wrote again, now sure he was at this particular hospital, this time repeating the same claims but mentioning in passing the name of my mother and enclosing a duplicate photograph of himself, taken in London. (The photograph remains the one piece of visual evidence I have of him.) Within days, I received a telephone call from him. It was very late at night, his voice whispering and clearly full of anxiety. He had realised who I was from the most recent letter. He was concerned as to what I wanted from him. I explained that the only thing I wanted was to talk to him and perhaps meet sometime. He promised that, on an annual visit to England, he would call me and we would meet. I was filled with joy and excitement. The telephone call lasted no more than three or four minutes. I did not hear from him again until a further 15 months had passed. This was after my mother had written to him, asking him to call me. The call was once again very brief but, significantly, he told me important information about his family. He explained he would be visiting England again. Still, I held onto the hope that he would fulfil his promise. He never did and I have not spoken to him since. I wrote letters asking him to confirm whether he would be making contact again or whether he wanted to cease our tenuous communication. If it was the latter, at least then I could begin to reconcile that chapter of my life. I never received any acknowledgement of any of my carefully worded letters; I have never received another phone call. Yet that journey of coming to terms with my identity continues along a rocky and unpredictable path. I remain the son of a Yemeni doctor; I have dark skin, brown eyes and jet-black hair to remind me of outward components of my ethnic heritage. Yet I still have not fully come to terms with his lack of interest in me.

As Logan Airport came into view, the previous eleven months streamed through my mind. I was within minutes of meeting my birth mother for the first time. I had discovered where she lived two months after I had traced my father. Through a combination of hard work, good fortune and considerable help from a librarian in the Midlands, I traced her brother. I posed as a son of a former colleague of my mother's and asked my mother's brother for his sister's address and telephone number. He provided me with these without hesitation. I contacted the NORCAP intermediary service. I spoke at length with a volunteer intermediary, who offered me tremendous support, guidance and warned me of all the possible eventualities. Later that week I received an unexpected telephone call from "Michael", who said that he had just spoken to my mother and she wanted me to telephone her immediately. I trembled with anticipation. It was hard to believe that I was going to be in contact with the woman who had given birth to me, who had cared for me in hospital for nine days, a woman I had only been able to dream about.

When I heard her voice, I was immediately struck by her strong American accent. Was this really her? We talked and talked and talked. That night I sat up all night and wrote her pages and pages of a long, emotional letter. At midday the following day, I received a call from her and we talked endlessly, almost trying to catch up on 30 years of separation. During the following months, we continually wrote letters and spoke at length on the telephone. She was able to explain her relationship with my father and that he had proposed to her. Yet she felt that she could not fit in with his traditional Muslim culture in the Middle East. She confided in me that she had only ever told her husband (whom she had married some ten years after my birth) and a close nursing friend of hers in England that she had given birth to a baby in 1962. No one else in her world knew of my existence and she was adamant that she did not wish anyone else to find out about her secret child whom she had given up for adoption.

My journey was coming to an end. As I collected my baggage at the airport I searched for her face in the crowd. She had sent pictures of herself spanning the last 30 years, but still I was unsure how she would look in the flesh. We eventually found each other amongst the crowds. We hugged tightly. She was tiny but not frail. We exchanged a few words and set off to the car park hand in hand. At that moment in time, it felt that we had only been separated for a week or two and I was returning home as usual, to my mother. For the first time in my life I felt secure. There is no rational explanation for the emotions she and I felt, but it genuinely seemed as if we had only been apart for a matter of days rather than 31 years. We talked and talked during the fortnight that I was there. For the first time I could see someone I resembled. By hugging her or holding her hand like a young child, I could touch some tangible evidence of my mother: a mother I had never known; a mother I had only dreamt about; a mother who had been absent during my most formative years; a mother who had not known of the trials and tribulations of my life. Yet so much of what she told about herself helped put so many things in my life into perspective. At last, I knew that physical and psychological difficulties were in some respects genetic. I felt a sense of reassurance in knowing that, rather than health professionals or my adoptive parents pathologising me as an individual suffering from x or y, so much more could be explained by hereditary characteristics. I was no longer the "odd one out". My journey seemed to have ended and the missing pieces of the jigsaw appeared to have been discovered.

The initial optimism and ecstatic joy of finding my mom matured yet, more significantly, the relationship has partly disintegrated. I have met with my mother on three subsequent occasions, once more in the States, the following year, and on two five-hour visits to my home whilst she was in England visiting relatives. Her insistence that no one should know of my existence has led her to become obsessively secretive. I am no longer permitted to write, despite the fact she had initially used a PO Box number. I can only receive phone calls from her. I am not allowed to call her at home or at work. She has refused to seek counselling. At times, she has unexpectedly protested to me that she is neither my actual mother, nor a grandmother to my children. The former is difficult for her to deny in my eyes, but I have certainly never given her any indication that she should be involved with my two children. Indeed, she even refuses to receive any pictures of them. The relationship is unequal: she dictates if and when we make contact. She has expressed the unlikelihood of us meeting again. We do talk once a fortnight, but I realise I shall probably never see her again.

As I arrived at Logan airport, I had no idea where my journey would take me. I do feel desperately disappointed by both of my natural parents for very different reasons. Perhaps my expectations have been unrealistic. My father has let me down because he has refused to acknowledge my existence, apart from two cursory telephone calls. My mother has withdrawn into a shell of secrecy and denial. I wonder if either of them realises the turmoil and torment they have put me through over the years. Would that knowledge change their responses and actions towards me? I doubt it. Both appear frightened, confused and perhaps selfish about the consequences of their past lives.

For my part, I now feel a tremendous responsibility, undying love and fierce protection towards my own two young children. Yet I wake up each day and see my brown body. For me, my brown body symbolises the sense of dislocation I feel about my identity. I feel an individual on the margins. In some respects, I am as far away on my journey as I was prior to my thirtieth birthday; in other respects, I am just on a different journey. I love my mom. I am undecided about my father. I think of them both every day, even several times a day, without fail.

A journey without end.

In the name of Allah, the Merciful

DAVID GILBERT

Dear *Walid*,[1]

AS-SALAAM-ALAIKUM

I am writing this letter in the hope that it reaches you safely. I do not know whether you are still working at the same address. I am writing again, knowing that, even if this does come into your hands, I am very unlikely to hear from you. Nevertheless, I am determined as, however much you try to forget or ignore me, you are still very much in my thoughts. Indeed, not a day goes by without me thinking about you.

We spoke so briefly all those years ago (eleven years to be precise) and you promised to be in touch and arrange a time when we could meet. Yet as each day, as each month, as each year has passed, I have not received any acknowledgement from you. Not a telephone call, not a letter, not an email. Nothing. I want you to know that, despite the loving support of my wife and enduring encouragement from a close friend, my life feels dislocated and in a state of permanent isolation and bewilderment. Why? Because you deny my existence and refuse to acknowledge me in the most fundamental terms.

What sort of man are you? My mother, Ann, spoke of you with warmth and affection. She talked of your sensitivity, your intelligence and your sense of humour. Yet I have seen none of these things. You have turned your back on me. You have disowned me. If only you knew the mental anguish you have put me through. My mental state has always been fragile and long-term physical complications are exacerbated by the permanent anguish you have put me through.

In my adoption file, I discovered another side to you. To me, you are a man who wrote on a scrappy and torn piece of paper that, 'I have no objection to having the baby adopted.' Apart from the picture of you, which Ann gave to me, that is the only piece of concrete evidence I have of you. How do you think that makes me feel? The

---

[1] *Walid* is Arabic and emphasises biological fatherhood, or a way of expressing a high degree of respect. In this case, the former definition is applied.

"letter" (I hesitate to give it such credence) obviously took a mere few seconds to scribble, and yet the outcome for 'the baby' has been profound. Do you know how I still ache with the pain of my adoption? Do you have any idea how much I yearn to piece together the jigsaw of my life? Are you/were you so heartless not to take more time and thought about the consequences of your relationship with Ann? Was I a mistake who had to be disposed of quickly and quietly, so as not to interfere with your ambitions and social standing? Perhaps I should be grateful I was not aborted.

You claim to be a practising Muslim. In the Holy Qur'an, the Most Merciful prophet (peace be upon Him) teaches of the responsibility of parents to their children. I may not have been planned, I was clearly not wanted by you, but is there nothing inside of you that feels anything towards me? You have talked of fear and intolerance in your own community, but what of my fears, my distress, my alienation in my community? Are you so self-interested that you cannot bring yourself to understand that I too have needs that need to be comforted?

I have had several periods of very serious, deep depression that have required considerable support, patience and empathy. Each time I see a new psychiatrist or therapist, the same issues repeatedly resurface. The same questions asked, the same irreconcilable difficulties seem to remain: my absent father, my distraught and confused mother (a woman who has had to hang on to a false perception of who you really are, for the sake of her own sanity). As a professional, you have dedicated your entire life to seeking to make people well. Surely your Hippocratic Oath also extends to your family members. Could you not bring yourself to stretch out and offer a healing hand of comfort to your own flesh and blood?

Why did you lie about staying in touch? I have only spoken to you twice and those were such very brief conversations. All that seemed to concern you was what my motives were. Did you think I was after money? You misjudge me and do me a great disservice, *Walid*. I have no such desires.

I now have a family and two small wonderful children. I am incredibly proud of my children and nothing in the world would stop me wanting to nurture and protect them. Equally, I want you to be proud of me.

Do you ever wonder about me? I have a first-class honours degree, a Master's and a PhD. I feel a deep affinity with the Islamic faith, though I am not a Muslim. I have in the recent past, worked tirelessly with a local Muslim community in trying to get them better opportunities and improved services for their education, personal protection and a sense of belonging in an overtly hostile environment. Not that I have done great deeds. Nor am I particularly special or conceited, but I am unique. I want you to have pride in who I am, because, for better or for worse, *I am* your son. Nothing in the world will ever change that.

The only thing I want is for you to pick up the telephone and talk to me. To reassure me that you do acknowledge my existence, and perhaps even acknowledge how distressed our endless separation makes me feel. Please reflect on what I have said. Is it not now time for us to reconcile our differences? Let us not let life pass by without grasping the opportunities that are here.

God, the Almighty, the Creator, the Protector, the Eternal have mercy on me. I pray in the name of Allah, that you will answer my prayers and guide *Walid* to act in the way which would bring You pleasure.

If I hear from you *Walid*, I know that Allah, the Merciful, has guided you.

From your son – now and forever

Becoming British Asian

AMINA CLARK

My beginning

The best place to begin this story is to explain how I came to be born in London. My birth mother is Hindu and was born near Mumbai in India, but her family migrated to Africa to improve her father's career when she was a teenager. She wanted to escape the small South Asian community, and persuaded her father to let her study computing in London as girls could not study 'A' levels locally. My birth father is Catholic, from Goa, and also came to London to study computing. As a child, I believed I was adopted because my birth father wouldn't marry my birth mother, and that Indian communities do not accept unmarried mothers. My search as an adult revealed a more painful truth. Although I knew these details, until I searched for my birth family I did not claim ownership of my history and, for me, my history started from the day I was adopted.

My birth mother arranged my adoption through social services before I was born. My (adoptive) parents have told me that, after months of excruciating parent support meetings, they were overjoyed to visit me at the foster home. They were told that they could take me home once they had chosen my new name. My parents appreciated my Indian name, which meant "forgive" in Sanskrit but, as the spelling seemed complex, they dropped a letter and unknowingly changed the meaning to "a light" or "flame" and this suited my position as their long-awaited first child. It also transformed it into a typically Muslim name. This confuses people when I explain that I was born Hindu and Catholic, but raised in a non-practising Christian and Jewish family. Names are important to many South Asians as they indicate your religion and family background. My unusual name that is both South Asian 'Amina' and typically English 'Clark' encompasses the discordant identity that defines me.

It also raises questions from people. Each time I give my name when introducing myself, paying by credit card or displaying my staff identity badge while working with the public, I am likely to be questioned on my whole adoption story. I prefer not to satisfy people's curiosity because their uncensored opinions can be upsetting. I don't want to hear strangers' pity, disapproval or horror stories on the devastating global violence between Catholics, Christians, Jews, Hindus and Muslims; or their views on the faults or elevated status of English people willing to adopt. I don't want to discuss transracial adoption, racism, ethnic identity, family values and illegitimate pregnancies, or subject myself to their disdain at my lack of knowledge of Indian cultures and languages. My reservation about disclosing personal information makes me appear cold towards new people.

My childhood

My (adoptive) mum and dad had travelled in India by van on 'the hippy trail' so they were delighted to be offered an Indian child. They are artistic, unconventional and left wing, and settled in London because they felt different to their families. My grandparents on my mum's side are very traditional and middle class. They live in a farmhouse in the country and enjoy pheasant shooting. At four in the afternoon, we eat a sliver of fruitcake and sip tea out of Duchess bone china cups and saucers with silver teaspoons, in the drawing room by the log fire. On my dad's side, I remember my nana wearing a pink-checked housecoat and fluffy slippers with a permanent cigarette stuck to her lip telling us, 'Children should be seen and not heard,' but she taught us card games and sneaked us dolly mixtures from a large tin by her polyester TV chair. Back in the 1950s, Nana used to disapprove of Grandad inviting black Caribbean men home for tea when they all finished work at the factory, yet they fuelled my dad's passion for jazz.

My mum was a childminder and a social work student, and my dad had just started his career as a freelance cartoonist. We lived in the basement of a big red Victorian terraced house in central London, with an "extended family" of two other couples and an assortment of lodgers and lovers living on the floors above. I remember placing pots of raisins in the garden for the midsummer evening fairies, and my dad playing his trumpet along to jazz records in the steamy kitchen, while a pungent curry bubbled on the cooker. On the ground floor, a student nurse told me of her visit to Nigeria to find her father and, upstairs, another couple showed me intricate Balinese shadow puppets. There was a mysterious photo dark room that we were forbidden to open, and I spied on and gossiped about budding relationships. Up on the second floor daily yoga practice took place, along with breakfast-table political networking over dense bricks of organic brown bread and fairly-traded coffee. My favourite room was the attic, with its hammock and rope ladder to the roof on which to practice my acrobatics. Our household was a colourful stream of parties and community activism. My early years consisted of accompanying my family on demonstrations and community centre launches. We marched in support of the miners, and I wielded my pushchair laden with banners, balloons and badges. We danced at the Notting Hill Carnival to Calypso music in gravity-defying sparkling costumes. I played barefoot outside camper vans at music festivals while adults took illicit substances, and we protested against nuclear weapons at Greenham Common with feisty women and their children.

My parents were open about my adoption and this helped satisfy other people's curiosity when they compared me to my white family. My friends fantasised to me about my "real" mother becoming rich and famous and coming back to get me. I was not interested in their fantasies of money; in my life, our "family" was built on shared experiences and caring for each other. Then, against the odds, my mum gave birth to my sister when I was four years old. Our parents have always treated us equally as their children, but I have always felt different to my sister because I was transracially adopted. My white, heterosexual sister born into her natural family was rarely questioned on her identity and made friends easily. As a teenager, she tried on my grandmother's wedding dress and it fitted her tall, slim figure like a glove. She fantasised about getting married in the village church where her ancestors are buried. I never felt the church was part of my history, and neither the white wedding dress nor the idea of a church wedding fitted me. I have had to question every aspect of my identity, my religion, my right to be British, a history to claim, the meaning of ethnic identity and race, the importance of genetics, the meaning of family, how to form relationships, and my place amongst peers divided by ethnicity and class. I take time to trust people enough to form new friendships. As a child, I felt inferior next to my sister's self-assured confidence and sense of belonging.

My parents separated soon after my sister was born and Mum moved upstairs into the attic. I had not been raised in a nuclear family so little changed. Our parents both cared for us and maintained a friendship with each other. My dad loved to cook and working from home meant he was always around. He would never allow us to miss breakfast and, one day when I forgot my sandwiches, he delivered them to my school. My mum used to record tapes of herself reading our bedtime stories to help us sleep, and we would take our bikes on the train for rides in the country together. At school, I appeared well adjusted and academically successful, but appearances can be deceptive.

Despite attending a multicultural primary school, I was still confused about my ethnic identity. I used to walk to school with two friends who lived with their white single mothers and had African fathers. In the playground children asked if we were "half-caste". I thought this meant that you have a white mum and we all did, so I agreed. I gained popularity as the children in my school were mainly of Caribbean origin and they assumed that my dad was black.

When new children arrived at the school having fled from Bangladesh, it became clear that I looked South Asian like them. I lost popularity and we South Asians all played together. I couldn't speak Sylheti and they had not learnt much English yet, so I felt lonely.

One day my Bangladeshi friend invited me to her home. Her smiling mum came to greet us, her sari framing her worn face. She offered me a stainless steel plate of rice and vegetables and started chatting to me in Sylheti, but I could not understand. I knew she expected me to know how to behave because I looked like her, but I didn't. Panicking, I bolted away in tears, leaving her standing there holding the plate. I went home and told my dad and he tried to help me. The next day he and my sister came with me up the dark, urine-stained stairwell of the notoriously rough council estate. My friend lived with her seven brothers, plus six adults in a three-bedroomed flat. They took turns to sleep, depending on who was working nights in the Indian restaurant. They had two huge sparse sofas and little other furniture. My friend's mum prepared a loaf of cheap sliced bread. I remember the tinkle of her glass bangles as she warmed the soft white slices, pressing them round a smooth black pan with her fingers. My dad looked too big on their sofa and my eager little sister looked like she was on a day-trip to see Bangladesh. I pitied their poor family who had employed servants "back home". The sickly sweet, rancid smell of their coconut hair oil stuck in my nostrils and it was a source of bullying at school that I wanted to disassociate myself from. I felt painfully different to them, yet being there I felt different to my dad and sister as well. Ethnic identity is not just looking the same or knowing about cultural festivals and languages. It is also about lifestyles rooted in class and immigration histories, and the different opportunities that are available because of our experiences. I did not have an Indian family to share an immigration history with. As I have said, my history began with my adoption.

My mum and her boyfriend eventually bought a spacious semi-detached house with open fireplaces, a lush garden, a piano and a cat. At secondary school, I had private tutoring to catch up with the privileged education of my white peers. To avoid discussing my identity at school, I kept busy with books, dance classes, choir, music lessons, wind band and orchestra practice. I was often the only South Asian and I hadn't realised that these activities would distance me from other South Asian people in later life. The only stories I had heard about minority ethnic people were about starvation and floods, and these influenced my internalised racist assumptions about my birth family and my own feelings of low self-esteem. For a while, I would only wear second-hand clothes because I didn't feel like other children and believed I should feel grateful for any money spent on me.

Dad stayed at our old house, which also became a home for the foster and step-children of my mum's best friend, Shelly,[1] who was like my aunt. Christmas celebrations were arranged so that we five children were together on alternate years. We marked our heights, names and ages on a strip of wallpaper by the fridge to see who was the tallest. My childhood was unconventional but these shared experiences with other children in my life made me feel secure at home in London.

Although I love my grandparents, visiting them in the countryside was often a painful experience as I was put on the spot by ignorant comments. I still remember when a famous white singer appeared on TV with her mixed-parentage baby. Grandpa sniggered, 'She must have slept with a nigger!' My mum responded, 'What, like your grandaughter?' He quickly replied, 'Oh no, not her, I don't mean her.' Another time, at Christmas, we were all seated at the grand mahogany dining table and my cousin wondered how they sold unbroken shelled Brazil nuts. He continued, 'They must have a load of Pakis to shell them.' The whole table went silent and everyone looked uncomfortably at me. I was about eight, I was not sure what "Paki" meant, or whether I ought to be offended as I wasn't from Pakistan. Another cousin sympathised with his brother by saying, 'I feel sorry for you mate,' realising that his language had been inappropriate. I knew that they only felt embarrassed because I was there, making me feel that it was my presence that was wrong, not their language. The same cousin was born in Africa when my uncle worked for the then ruling British government. He was married in the ancestral church and became a pheasant-shooting farmer. He fits into the family history in a way I never will and, even today, I feel uncomfortable around him.

Searching for my birth family

My search for my birth family was intermittent. Going travelling in India as my parents had done was a childhood ambition and I decided to do voluntary work there during my gap year before university. It suddenly occurred to me that I could

[1] Names of people have been changed throughout.

pass my birth mother on a street in India without knowing it was her. So, before I left, I applied for my birth certificate from the Family Records Centre. I went with a group of excited teenage friends to the address my birth mother had had when she registered my birth, to ask the occupants if they had any information about her. No one was in and I was leaving the next day for India. In my fear of being successful, I had subconsciously left it too late.

Arriving in India was exhilarating. Madras was hot and smelly; jostling crowds of brightly clad people negotiated squelchy black mud in flip-flops; beggars brandished bandaged limb stubs and motorcycle rickshaws beeped ceaselessly at cows adorned with jasmine, resting in the congested roads. I felt different to the other English travellers who, due to their white skin, struggled with the heat, were harassed for wearing revealing holiday clothes and were targeted by touts. They viewed all Indian people with suspicion and reacted to their situation with patronising superiority. I found this embarrassing so I escaped being associated with them by identifying as Indian.

By protesting at their ignorant comments, I was forced to reconsider my own negative stereotypes about Indian people. I had imagined my birth mother having a forced marriage to a violent husband to preserve the family honour and her family being poor and hungry, waiting for Oxfam deliveries in a dusty, dry or flooded country. In the family I stayed with, the Indian women I met were intelligent and independent, and the men respected them. I worked alongside disabled people on a lush organic farm with gently rustling coconut palms, papaya trees and eucalyptus groves, doe-eyed water buffalos and shimmering lime paddy fields. People seemed content herding their buffalo, carrying spindly bundles of firewood on their heads, and spinning cotton, and we sang songs and joked every day. They ran accessible community talks on subjects such as women and Ghandiism, and promoted sustainable farming. I learned more from them than I could ever have offered as a volunteer.

Returning to London, I felt depressed trying to adjust to my old life. At this point I approached my first counsellor through my GP. He attempted to start a debate about a possible internal conflict between my restrictive Indian parents' values and growing up in Britain as an independent woman. I didn't tell him I was transracially adopted through all four sessions until I left.

I continued my search in my second year at university as I had the necessary distance from my family. I felt I needed some connection with my Indian family to claim the identity "Indian", otherwise it was just my appearance, not my heritage. I applied to read my adoption file and it arrived on my 21st birthday. I was strangely tearful and vulnerable all week and felt sure that my friends had abandoned me. They hadn't, but thinking about my adoption brought back emotions and fears from a time before I could speak. The white social work student who offered the statutory counselling while I read my file was another voyeur curious to see the results of a social experiment in transracial adoption that is my life. I felt responsible for educating her on the complexities of ethnic identity and had a need to list my experiences of racism within my family to justify my ambivalence about transracial adoption. What I really needed was a safe space to explore my own unanswered identity questions and confusion, without the complexities of the unequal dynamic between us.

My adoption file is a fascinating collection of notes from the obstetrician about standard measurements at my birth and notes by the social worker about my birth mother, my adoptive family and my foster carer. There was a letter to the social worker in unfamiliar handwriting from my birth mother lying next to a similar letter in the familiar handwriting of my mum. It was overwhelming to see the story of my birth and transfer between these two important women in my life. It was a very emotional experience, and my file still holds these powerful emotions between the lines of the sparse details enclosed.

Slowly, I started to build a picture of the circumstances surrounding my birth. According to the social worker's notes, my birth mother completed her course at a polytechnic that was more tolerant of pregnant women. She was made homeless and became a childminder for a Mrs Burton-Jones. I contacted Mrs Burton-Jones and she informed me that my birth mother had spoken English without an accent and worn fashionable boots. I found this a frustrating analysis that told me little about her personality. Or perhaps Mrs Burton-Jones was trying to protect me from the harsh reality that my birth mother faced. On her overseas student visa she could not claim any money to keep me, and her stay and employment in the UK were restricted. She did not think the South Asian community in Africa would accept her back and her parents were funding her.

Some (including my birth mother) have suggested that I should feel angry towards her for not trying harder to keep me. I cannot blame any woman in that situation for the difficult decisions she took care to make. I think restrictive family values and immigration policies are more to blame. I am sad about being separated from my mother as a child, but anger does not help us to have a relationship as adults.

After I was adopted, my birth mother rented a room with a Mrs Brown, very near to where my mum now lives. I decided to visit the house. Following the advice in the Searching For Family Connections booklet from NORCAP, I pretended my birth mother was an old college friend of my mum and that I wanted a forwarding address to send some old photos to her. Obviously the other adopted people using this search strategy were not young South Asians, calling on wary Londoners in an area of high crime and racial tension. Mr Brown denied everything, then looked around suspiciously (I presumed for my criminal gang waiting to rob his house) and slammed the door in my face. Afterwards, I wrote a truthful letter explaining my adoption story and the next day I had a phone call from Mrs Brown telling me about my birth mother's fashionable boots, her wonderful flawless English accent and that she had chainsmoked in her room until she left.

I cherished the information I gathered in case I never traced my birth mother. Mrs Brown also wanted to know everything about my search and knew nothing about my birth. I felt I owed her something, but I did not want to betray my birth mother. I felt guilty discussing my search with my family and friends, but I needed to share my excitement about my successes. My birth mother is no longer a young woman, but uncovering her past allowed my adoptive family to view her as a forlorn girl in need of rescue which relieved their guilt about adopting another woman's child. The closer I got to finding her, the more I realised she was a real person whose privacy deserves respect.

I found no forwarding address after Mrs Brown. My birth mother could have stayed in England, returned to Africa or even gone to India. If she had married, then her last name would have changed. The internet had just become available at university and, as she was a computing student, I guessed her email address might be registered somewhere. I tried searching for her first name and ended up with a list of about 12 people in India, Russia and America. I was planning a clever letter that would identify the correct one, but my search was delayed by coping with my identity struggles.

Finding my voice

I was studying anthropology and postcolonial theory as part of my degree. I started to become fearful in every class as students and tutors assumed I had cultural knowledge based on my Indian appearance. I didn't want to disclose my adoption story in case minority ethnic students assumed I identified as white. One such South Asian student had derogatorily called me a "coconut", "brown on the outside and white on the inside". I found it hard to position myself in the arguments. In another class, I began to have panic attacks triggered by the word "primitive" which appeared on every page of the required reading on Levi Strauss. It still baffles me that it was considered important to read an historical text by a European anthropologist explaining that "primitive" (non-European) people are capable of intellectual thought. I thought we should read books written by intellectuals of African, Caribbean, Asian, South American, Middle Eastern and Aboriginal descent instead. There were none on the syllabus and, as I was isolated, no one validated my frustration. I felt afraid to join the South Asian Society in case I was asked difficult questions about my family background.

That year, I made the mistake of attending a family holiday to post-apartheid South Africa. We stayed with my stepfather's white Jewish family who rang a little bell for the black maid to serve dinner. Electric barbed-wire fencing and armed guards defended the huge house with its swimming pool and tennis courts. My sister wanted to play golf on the golf course, watered daily. Our comforts contrasted with the house of the black maid. She was grateful that Nelson Mandela had brought a single water pump to the overcrowded township where her children lived three hours away. There were no black people in the idyllic tourist areas we visited, despite white people being a minority in the country as a whole. Hypersensitive to feeling unwelcome because of my skin colour, I became mentally exhausted by the constant discomfort. My panic attacks grew more persistent. My family ignored my dilemmas as apartheid was over, after all. I stopped speaking to my parents because I felt so angry about being adopted by a white family, the historical power differences between us and my lack of a proud Indian heritage as a resource to draw strength from in the face of racist rejection. I felt that transracial adoption was another example of European cultural imperialism, white supremacy and exploitation of other cultures.

Back at university, I survived on long walks by the sea and yoga. The active physical relaxation slowed my spiralling thoughts. Then I discovered a smooth bald patch on my head the size of a golf ball, hidden by hair. This shocked me into drastic action to make myself better. I strongly believe that physical and emotional health are linked, despite my doctor telling me there was no real explanation. I joined an ethnically diverse black women's group and they offered me support against racism without judging my cultural knowledge. In fact, once I stopped being nervous and listened, I found that many of them also had complex histories. I forced myself to overcome my fear and attended a club for South Asians where I identified a few new friends who equally negotiated complicated families. I commuted to London to a therapy group for transracially adopted people that was both supportive and difficult because my feelings about transracial adoption were validated, yet compounded the experiences of others in the group into an exhausting rage. At the same time, it is some of these friends with whom I have felt closest and have shared the greatest and most accepting support over many years.

During my panic attacks, I also used the white university counsellor. When I tried to explain how frustrated and angry I felt about my course reading list and the isolation I was experiencing, she responded defensively, 'Why do you want everyone else to think the same as you?' I told her I did not expect other people to think like me, but wanted them to stop being oppressive towards me. It reminds me of when I was on holiday with my sister and a boy told me, 'Britain was better before all the blacks came,' looking menacingly at me, making it clear I was not welcome. My sister told me it was just "a difference of opinion" and continued to befriend him, disregarding the hurt I felt and the unequal power dynamic between us. Later, the same boy confessed that his father had committed suicide when he could not find work and support his family. I realised the boy was really hurt about losing his father and had misdirected the blame onto black people (and me) migrating for employment and taking "his father's job", undermining this man's masculinity and ultimately causing his death. Understanding that racists are usually defending their own hurt or their own assumed position of relative privilege has helped me understand that I am not to blame, and strengthened my resolve to challenge racism as someone equally entitled to be British. By meeting people who shared similar experiences and in finding a voice to challenge those around me, my panic and anxiety attacks ended and I resumed tentative contact with my family. Thankfully my hair grew back again too!

Reunion

Almost a year later, I searched the microfiche copy of the marriage register at my local library and was surprised to discover that my birth mother had married in London six years after I was born. When I applied for a copy of her marriage certificate, I noticed she had lied about her age when I was adopted. The certificate was signed by her and witnessed by her father. It was so strange to hold that piece of paper containing her signature without her knowledge. It made her seem more like a real person. To my surprise, my birth mother's married name matched one of the names from my internet search a year before. She ran her own business in the USA and I found the website; I even found books she had written in my university library.

When I returned home, my "aunt" Shelly was terminally ill with cancer. She encouraged me to contact my birth mother before it was too late. I made contact through a post-adoption counsellor and together we wrote a letter and sent it out into the unknown.

She soon got in touch and her response was warm but cautious. The same week that I made contact, her mother had visited her for the first time after a 15-year disagreement. To prevent another family feud, my birth mother wanted to keep our weekly email exchange a secret. She had been only 17 when I was born, and it was in her second email that she told me about the rape. I felt upset and angry and wished I could crawl out of my skin because it felt dirty. Curious friends kept asking about my birth father and I hated being reminded. These feelings slowly passed as I remembered I was not a bad person. My birth mother made it clear that it was not my fault, but I have no inclination to find my birth father. Knowing the truth helped me to understand her ambivalence about meeting me.

The only counsellor who really helped me begin to heal was an Asian woman whom I saw privately, who did not judge me for my cultural knowledge and acknowledged my pain and anger without being threatened by my "opinions". In that safe space, I was able to explore my feelings about ethnicity, race and class and to realise the important elements of my relationship, both with my adoptive family and my birth family. I realised that my feelings of grief following Shelly's death were linked with the loss of my birth mother. As a result of my progress, I started the first long-term romantic relationship that felt equal and in which I was not taken advantage of. I also made arrangements to meet my birth mother.

We arranged to meet in New York, where she worked. Even though I know people there, I rented a holiday apartment with a friend so I would not need to be a polite guest while I was so emotionally vulnerable. We met in a smart restaurant serving oversized American portions. She arrived from work wearing a sharp black skirt suit, heels and carrying a briefcase. Her straight black hair was cut in a stylish bob and she looked young and professional. I didn't know if we should hug. We brushed arms awkwardly, then sat and stared at the menu. It swam around before me, while I wondered if it was rude to stare. I still hadn't had a really good look at her. The waitress was hovering with irritation to take our order, unaware of the importance of this event. In her assertive New York accent, my birth mother told her to come back later. My birth mother's hands look exactly like mine and our build is similar. She is direct and to the point, feminist, ambitious and very modern. This was a surprise to me after trying to attain traits I perceived as typically Indian, but it meant we had more in common.

It made me question what it meant to be Indian. My Indian mother seemed very American and had grown up in Africa. I wondered what specific essential Indian characteristics she had that I felt I needed to be able to call myself Indian. Living in a country where my ethnicity is assumed based on how I look is different to the experience of Indians who have lived in India, so who is an authentic Indian? At what point in our generations of migration do we stop being Indian? I think ethnic identity is a feeling, a sense of belonging. Put simplistically, my birth mother can feel Indian because she knows that her ancestors are from India. Meeting my birth mother enabled me to feel a sense of connection with India because she represents the missing link to my Indian family history.

I think my birth mother found seeing me very hard as it reminded her of a difficult time in her life that she had tried to forget and she became tearful. I was hurt that she had tried to forget about me, and she seemed unhappy that I had traced her. When we parted, she was reluctant to continue contact and it was difficult to leave her and walk away back to the station in the drizzling rain.

My counsellor was invaluable in helping me when I returned. I had to take a week off work just to sit and cry for the years of loss brought up by that one meeting. Yet lots of people wanted to ask me all about my trip and experience the glory of a family reunited forever. I couldn't provide their happy ending, and staying in my room seemed an easier option than weeping in public over the emotional journey that had been successful just for a single meeting. I had not expected more, even though I knew I secretly wanted it. In fact, my birth mother was brave enough to continue emailing and steadily our relationship has grown over time, although never to a banner-waving or party-throwing happy ending like you see on TV.

We met again recently because she was diagnosed with cancer. (Shelly was right to encourage me to make contact.) Our time together was more relaxed this time, despite the unspoken possibility that we might never see each other again. Taking a friend with me eased the tension and we talked and laughed about normal things and tried fancy cocktails. My birth mother seemed able to be more caring towards me and accepted some gifts that I had bought for my siblings, whom I have never met. Being a secret from them is upsetting but childhoods are delicate, and with patience we will meet in time.

Reflections

My life struggle has been harder because I was transracially adopted rather than social services investing the resources into recruiting an Indian family to adopt me. Imagine the mental weight and responsibility involved in trying to negotiate issues of racism and ethnic identity alone, as a child, against your own ignorant extended family who love you. Even established academics writing about race and ethnicity cannot agree on how these issues should be defined. I am thankful and feel that I was adopted by very competent parents, but adoption is rarely a selfless act and adoptive parents also benefit. There is an unequal relationship between white adopters and minority ethnic adoptees, as we are led to believe that we should be grateful for being adopted because of the cultural and financial capital we gain in learning to behave white in a white dominated society. Having observed that many minority ethnic people would like to adopt, I am amazed that transracial adoptions still happen. I am now a strong person, but this is a result of the years of hard work I have put in, and the unconditional love and support my family offered me throughout my search. Other adopted children could be spared some of these struggles with suitable placements. I have resolved that, whatever blame I have attributed to different people, the way forward for me is to assert my voice and to ensure I create choices about my future in spite of life's challenges.

My birth mother's health has been good so far since she was cleared of cancer, but I will also have to have regular health checks as I am at risk. That is the undeniable part of our relatedness. My adoptive dad survived a heart attack and we have both changed our diet, so both nature and nurture play their part. Before I met my birth mother, I found it hard to trust anyone enough to maintain intimate relationships. Now I have become less angry and have a better relationship with my family and my partner. Meeting my birth mother has given me the missing link to my Indian heritage, and made me understand that cultural values can never be an absolute measure of ethnic authenticity since culture is constantly changing and variable. I have embraced a British Asian identity, in the realisation that my complex adoption experience and lack of cultural knowledge is part of my immigration journey to the British Indian I have become.

Belonging

NICK PENDRY

I find it difficult to think about my self, my identity, who I am, where I fit and where or to what I might belong. I am a black Indian man, who doesn't speak Hindi, Urdu or Gujarati, and I sometimes feel like a cultural impostor when I try to embrace my Indian-ness. I can relate to the white British norms and values that represent middle England. I understand what these norms and values might mean, and I feel, begrudgingly at times, a part of white Britain, but this is a white Britain that I feel doesn't want me and to which I will always be an outsider. The pain and hurt of rejection that I feel as the baby who wasn't wanted by my mother is compounded by the pain of feeling that I don't truly belong to any culture or race, at least not that the culture or race to which I might feel connected will warmly embrace me and treat me as one of their own.

When I was a child growing up in a white British family, I noticed I was different. This was no big deal at the time. I had an English name and I only saw that I had brown skin when I looked in the mirror. If I didn't look, I didn't notice, and then I might as well have been white. I laughed at school when the Indian kid in my class was teased for smelling of curry. When I moved schools and my history teacher abused me for being "ethnic", I didn't really understand. When my friends started to call me "Paki", I began to understand. When two men in a van stopped me on the way home from school and spat in my face, I understood more. When I saw graffiti abusing me for being "a disgusting Paki", I understood. I was different, not white, not like them. But who could I turn to? Not my parents: they had adopted me, given me a home, been good to me, and besides I didn't think they'd really understand, but then I didn't give them the chance. Not my friends: they were all white, wouldn't understand, and most were in on the joke anyway. No, I kept it to myself, and just wished I was white.

In adolescence I was desperate to find out more about where I might belong. I wrote to *Jim'll Fix It* asking him to fix it for me to find my biological mother. I wrote to charities concerned with adoption asking them for help. I got nowhere. When I turned 18, I went to the adoption agency that handled my adoption. I remember just staring at the paperwork in my file. I read words I didn't understand. I saw names I had never seen before. I tried to speak to a social worker about how I was feeling, but I couldn't even begin to talk about how I felt, or even feel the feelings myself. I blocked things out, tried not to think any more about what it all meant and went off to university.

It was only in my university years that I felt the beginnings of a sense of pride in my self and my emerging sense of racial identity. I was taught by an Indian Professor, and it was the first time I had someone who looked like me that I could really look up to and strive to be like. I discovered Indian politics and history, which had previously been hidden from me while I was taught the history of being white and British. I made friends with people who shared my racial identity and I began to eat Indian food. I was finding out about me, about who I was and where I might belong. I decided that as soon as I could, I would travel to East Africa and find my biological mother.

I planned my trip carefully. I was going to visit the town where her family lived and where she conceived me. I was going to see where I might have grown up had things been different. The one thing I didn't plan for was that she might now be living in England. The search for her that I had started when I was 18, and which I thought would only be completed when I travelled to Kenya and knocked on her front door, came to an end just months before my flight was due to leave. She was living in the UK after all. I was shocked, I was numb. We were encouraged by the social worker to exchange letters and photos before we met. I still have that photo, kept safe in my wallet, and every time I look at it I can still feel what I felt when I first took it out of the envelope and traced my hand over her face. She looks like me. I had never known what it was like to see someone who looks like me. We have the same nose, the same eyes, we're the same, we're from the same place. I can still hardly come to terms with it. And so we met. I can't remember the talk, the food, the weather; I can only remember tears and confusion. She has children, my brother and sister; why did she keep them and not me? Why didn't she want me? I still torture myself with these questions. I think maybe they're such a part of me that I'd feel naked without them.

I travelled to Kenya anyway. I visited the places that I wanted to see. I stayed for some weeks with my biological mother's parents, and with her sister and family. Only her mother and her sister knew who I was. I learnt then what it was to be a secret. I also got a glimpse of what might have been. The food I might have eaten, the language I might have spoken, the religion I might have followed and the places I would have seen. These all seemed so alien to me at the time. I wanted to belong, but I just knew that I didn't.

The idea of belonging has permeated every part of my life since then. My relationship with my biological mother has developed. It's been difficult, up and down, and at times I've wanted just to break all contact with her, but I feel held by a sense of wanting to belong, although I still feel that I don't. I'm still a secret. My brother and sister still know nothing of me. It's not the same with all the family. I have felt welcomed by my aunts and cousins. I feel a part of their family, but I don't share a family history or a language with them, I still feel like I don't really belong. I mean my name's an English one and only yesterday somebody asked me whether I had Europeanised it as it didn't seem to fit with who I am.

I am now married with a baby son. At last I feel like I belong to a family. I can be me, with all my identity confusion and cultural contradictions. But when I go outside, I still feel it. Parts of white Britain still look at me like I'm a piece of shit at the bottom of their shoe. And some South Asians still don't really see me as a proper Asian, a real Indian. Do I wish things had been different? Of course, don't we all? I feel like my self has been stolen and given back to me in a different form, and no one really understands what that's like. But I like who I am. It's taken me my life but I can now look in the mirror and feel proud of my self, my skin colour and my family. I would not be in this position were it not for my adoptive family and my biological family. I belong to me and my wife and child now, and that's enough. Perhaps that's all I can hope for.

Acknowledgement: 'Belonging' by Nick Pendry was first published in *Context*, the magazine for family therapy, April 2005.

Gifts to birth mother

MICHELLE ANDERSON

For Christmas,
I send you
a wreath of mistletoe, kissed with tears.

For Mother's Day,
I send you
a puzzled gaze
and velvet petals to strew your path.

For Easter,
I send you
thirty pieces of silver
and a smile loaned from Judas.

For my birthday,
I send you
rusted nails
to stir your wounds.

For your birthday,
I send you
handfuls of despair
wrapped in slithers of brown skin.

For my son's birthday,
I send you
a rainbow smile
and hope its radiance undoes our wrongs.

Acknowledgement: 'Gifts to birth mother' by Michelle Anderson was first published in the *ATRAP Newsletter*, Issue No. 4, December 2000.

Tattie 'n' chapatti

JENNY MOHINDRA

I always knew that I tanned well. It sort of fitted in with my Caucasian family in that I was like my dad since he tanned and my mum was like my brother in that they both had much fairer skin. My dad had dark hair and so did I, and my mum had brown hair and so did my brother. I think that's where the physical similarities between me and my family ended. I think that I just assumed that, because they were white, well so was I. I'd always known that I was adopted and had been born in Edinburgh, so I assumed my mother was Scottish. I'd also been told that she was quite young, not married and that my birth father had been quite a lot older than her and had not wanted to get married just for the sake of the child. This had not been a solid enough reason for marriage according to him and according to what I had been told. That's about all that I knew and, as this was a closed adoption, I didn't expect to find out any more information although I did ask my mum and dad from time to time, as I was growing up, if they knew anything else about my origins.

I grew up in several different countries and I spent part of my childhood in Nairobi, which was a wonderful opportunity for me to experience living in a developing country. I had moved from England to Kenya and from a predominantly white community to a predominantly black population. There was also a large Indian community living there and, although the schools were mainly attended by white children, I also mixed with some Indian children at both my primary and secondary schools. I can recall being in a school play at my primary school and having to wear a sari on stage as my costume for my character. None of the other children recognised me as they thought that I looked like one of the Indian girls. Another memory that I have of being in Nairobi was being at secondary school and looking at one of my school friends who happened to be Indian. She had my arms exactly. When I say that she had my arms, I mean that her arms looked exactly like mine – same shape, bone structure, almost the same colour since I was fairly tanned from living in a sunny climate. I can distinctly recall looking at her arms and looking at mine, noticing the similarities but thinking 'but she's Indian' and then thinking nothing of it.

People always used to ask me where I was from because of my appearance, to which I would answer that I was Scottish by birth but I was adopted and therefore didn't really know what my origins were. I certainly didn't sound Scottish and didn't look it either but I clung on to the knowledge of knowing that I'd been born there to try and establish some form of knowing where I came from. It wasn't until I was 29 that I decided to search for my birth mother. This saw me obtaining my original birth certificate, which showed my name at birth as well as my birth mother's full name. My certificate also shows my birth father's name. This was a handwritten document that was barely legible to me and, although I couldn't make out exactly what my father's name was, I saw that it was a very Indian sounding name. Naresh Kumar were hardly the first names of a white Caucasian male. I chose not to think much about this at the time as I still thought that I was white. After all, my adoptive surname is Swedish but my family are not of Swedish descent so, in my mind, it was no guarantee that an Indian name meant Indian blood. I lived then with the possibility that I had Indian blood in me but it didn't really sink in until about a year later. It took that long, from receiving my original birth certificate to making the decision to look for my birth mother. I had grown up always having some level of curiosity about my mother but never my father. Even with this recent find about my father (which I pretty much chose not to acknowledge), I still maintained the higher level of curiosity towards my birth mother. So I made the necessary steps to obtain documentation from the adoption agency in Edinburgh which turned out to be a very easy process for me. I'd known that my adoption had not been a religious matter and so it was just a case of making a phone call to one agency and explaining who I was, to which I received a reply of, 'Oh yes, we have your details on file. We'll send them out to you.'

The day was a Friday, late in October, when the envelope arrived. I'd been checking the letter box ever since I'd made the phone call to the adoption agency and knew exactly what the plain brown A4 envelope was when I saw it. There was no one home as I sat on the floor in my bedroom, opened the envelope and started to read about my adoption and about my self.

The biggest shock for me that day was to discover that I am half Indian, my father having been born in Delhi. The next biggest shock was to learn that my adoptive parents had known when they adopted me that I was mixed race and that they had never told me. Another bombshell was that my birth parents had gone on to get married after having given me up and that I also had a full-blooded brother. There was a lot to take in that day.

Emotions ran between being hurt and angry with my adoptive parents for not having told me of their knowledge, to feeling exhilarated at finally knowing my origins, to feeling an enormous sense of grief for having lost my birth mother. That grief was a completely new emotion for me. In fact, I feel like I have only learned how to feel emotions from that day. I'd never been one to express much emotion and was certainly not one to cry at the movies – one of about two exceptions had been whilst watching Mike Leigh's *Secrets and Lies*. Having said that, though, I always used to feel a wave of sadness if I saw a baby or toddler crying, especially if it was not in someone's arms. I simply could not look at the scene and had to literally look away. Both scenarios have now changed. I can cry at the movies and can watch a toddler crying without feeling that uncontrollable sadness within myself.

The new knowledge of my half-Indian-ness found me looking at every Indian person that I saw, wondering if they could tell that I was like them. I also felt extremely ignorant of this culture that I could now embrace as being part of me, and proceeded to embark on a steep learning curve in terms of all things Indian. Having lived in Nairobi for five-and-a-half years I had had a glimpse into Indian culture, as there is a large Indian community there, but I was still very ignorant of this society. For about a year or so I took on anything Indian I could get my hands on, which meant going to the local Diwali fair, reading books by Indian authors, seeing Indian movies, talking to Indian people with a new interest, even going into local Indian shops and looking at the goods on display. It was an exciting time and I did embrace the fact that I had discovered a new part of me.

Looking back, I think that the period of accelerated learning about Indian culture and perhaps my increased level of excitement lasted for about a year or so. It gave me something to cling to for a while, to make me feel a sense of belonging to this culture. Now, some four years later, I don't feel exactly the same way. I am half Indian but I don't feel it. I feel like, now, I have to explain my limited knowledge of the culture by saying that it's been a fairly recent discovery for me. Most people are understanding of this, or at least they don't show otherwise, although there are those who just can't accept the fact that I assumed I was white. It doesn't really matter what other people think. I know who I am. I know what makes me tan so well. I can say proudly that I'm half Scottish and half Indian and that my nationality is British and Australian and that I was raised by white, English parents and that I now have two sets of parents and siblings and that my surname was Swedish but I am not! It always makes for an interesting conversation when someone asks me where I'm from and I now have the choice as to how much I wish to disclose. That choice is mine to make, now that I have the knowledge which was not there for most of my life.

As well as embarking a steep learning curve in terms of all things Indian, I also started reading about adoption issues on the internet and in books. This led me to find an adoption support group for intercountry adoptees (ICASN – the Intercountry Adoption Support Network based in Sydney). I read some articles from the website and ended up contacting the founder of the organisation. This, in turn, led to some social meetings with other adoptees. I have come across many adoptees in my lifetime, some of whom I have shared adoption experiences with, but to meet a group of adoptees on my own, with the common thread that brought us together being the fact that we were not only adopted but adopted into countries or cultures different to our birth was a wonderful experience. No matter how much I have read about all things related to adoption, I have found the most healing experience to be talking to other adoptees. I sat in a restaurant with a group of strangers from ICASN and spoke about such personal details with the greatest of ease. It's a beautiful thing to be able to have that level of understanding: the unspoken words that just aren't required.

I recently moved to London, partly to be closer to my birth family and to be able to get to know them without being in the pressured situation of whirlwind holiday visits from Australia. So far, so good! I am enjoying spending time with them and feel that I am gaining a much closer relationship than would have been possible from the other side of the world. According to an adoption seminar that I attended, it usually takes about seven years to get to know one's birth mother so I still have a few years to go! I still find it strange, almost surreal sometimes to look at my "new" parents and believe that they are mine. Would I change a thing about the discovery process though? Not at all!

I'll keep trying

LEYTON

My background

I was born in Neath General Hospital in 1974. My biological mother, Inez Williams, is from Port Talbot, as is my whole birth family. I have the letters and typed background information that the adoption agency sent to my parents. Together, they give a brief summary of the circumstances and how I came to be available for adoption. Basically, my biological mother was married to Stanley, had two grown-up children and was in her 40s when she had me. She had fallen pregnant by another man at a time when she and her husband were having problems.

My mother worked in a dry cleaner's and a man who went there kept asking her out. One night, she had had a big argument with her husband and was walking home in the rain when a car drew up beside her. It was my birth father. He offered her a lift and they had intercourse in the car that night. When I was born, nine months later, she could not pass me off as her husband's child as she had hoped. Her husband was adamant that he was not going to have me. In the 1970s it was a scandal to have an affair, let alone with a black man. When I was born, her daughter came to the hospital. They decided that I should be left in the hospital and then adopted. They told the neighbour and her son that I had died.

It was when I was 28 that I read my parents' papers and accessed my adoption file. I was devastated to learn that I had had a different name at birth, Craig Williams. As far as I had known, I was a nameless child in an orphanage. I didn't think I had a name before. I was also quite shocked to find out how close I lived to my birth family. It is only about a 15-minute drive from Port Talbot to the village where I was raised.

My adoption

My (adoptive) mother had lost four children. She could not carry girls due to a genetic condition. The last child she had was born premature and she died, and so my parents decided to adopt. That is how I came to be adopted. I think I was two months old when I was adopted from the nursery in Neath.

I grew up in the valleys, in a very small village in West Glamorgan, South Wales, called Resolven. I was literally the only black person in the village. Although my older brother is adopted, he is white.

I knew from a very young age that I was adopted. I soon realised that I was not a biological child of my parents because of my colour. I was bullied and teased, which I found difficult. I was called names, such as, "golliwog". Sometimes I was teased by other children for being adopted, as was my brother.

My mother had quite dark skin and very long, dark, straight hair. People used to think that she was Indian. My father had very light skin. My parents told me about an incident in a holiday park when someone said to my mother, 'Oh, you've been a very, very naughty girl, haven't you?' My father went bezerk.

I had a happy childhood. I was very close to my mother, although not to my father. I just did not really get on with him, nor my brother. My brother and I were miles apart in terms of hobbies and interests and had completely different friends. We are not really that close to this day.

Searching for my biological father

I lost both my (adoptive) parents in the year 2000. My mother had a heart attack and my father stopped taking his medication for his heart condition because he did not want to go on without her. I lost them both very suddenly. I always said I would never try and trace my biological parents. It is only since they died that I have felt able to do so.

I really want to find my biological father. I traced all the black people in Port Talbot when I was searching for him. One man put me in touch with a black society who tried to help me. I tried for months to find out who my father is but kept hitting a brick wall.

I also searched for my birth mother to see what she could tell me about my father. My birth mother is getting older and I do not want to risk her dying. The After Adoption worker wrote a letter to my birth mother, who took it to her daughter and asked her to telephone for her. She did not tell her husband about the letter. According to my birth mother's daughter, my mother was distraught. She referred to me by my birth name, and told the worker that her father was very ill and that, perhaps, if her father died, her mother might be prepared to say a bit more. She said that my father went back to the Caribbean and that was all she knew about him. The After Adoption worker made it clear that I did not want to impose on their lives or to know them. I do not want anything to do with them; I just want to know about my biological father.

I do not even have a name for him or know which island in the Caribbean he was from. Unfortunately, no one in the black society could remember any black man who was working in Port Talbot in 1974. I wonder whether my father worked locally in the steel industry and saw that my mother was pregnant. Perhaps he was young and irresponsible and did not want to know. Surely my birth mother must have a name for him? I think that my biological father would be inquisitive about me because, after all, I am his child. I think that he has a right to know that he has a son.

It is possible that my birth mother is afraid that any contact with me will open a whole can of worms. When I was born and her husband realised that she had had an affair with a black man, he would have been gunning for my father, so perhaps he drove my father away? I know from my adoption file that my birth mother's husband threatened to throw me in the canal when I was born. He was so angry that he would not talk to the social worker. I am wondering whether she was forced to give me up. She would obviously have been grieving for me.

Once I spoke to an elderly woman in the area where my biological mother lives. I explained the situation to her and asked if she could speak to my biological mother, but she said that my mother's husband died four years ago and that she was in her 60s. This contradicts everything I know. My biological mother's daughter told the worker last year that the husband was very ill. So, did she lie? Have they just woven a whole web of lies? Or could the elderly woman have been talking about a different person with the same name? Perhaps the daughter is scared that she will be left out of pocket with the inheritance.

I just need a name for my biological father. If I traced him and he did not want to know me, I would leave it. I would like to know my heritage and if I look like his side of the family. I am a dark-skinned person and must have half-brothers and half-sisters. I have always wanted to meet someone who looks like me.

People assume that I have black parents. They are so nosey. I usually say my mother is white and my father is West Indian. That is all I say. Sometimes it is really hard.

I am Welsh, but I am proud of being black as well. I am comfortable with who I am and I am accepted in Wales. I do not have contact with any other black people. To trace my biological father, I just need his name or to know where he was working at the time. It is so hard scavenging around for crumbs of information and trying to piece things together, but I am not ready to give up yet.

A black fish in a white sea

LAURA FISH

Laura with her cousins

I spent almost a year abroad when I was 21. I travelled through Egypt, Sudan, India and Nepal. Maintaining a relationship with such huge areas of the planet is an emotionally exhausting way to be, but being so far away from home helped me to put the past into some kind of perspective.

My natural mother came to London from Guyana in 1959. She was 20 when she gave birth to me in January 1964. At the age of nine months I was adopted into a white, middle-class English family. When I used to ask why I'd been adopted and my two older brothers hadn't, my parents would comfort me by saying that I was special in that I had been chosen by them all. I won't go into all the reasons my parents give for adopting me; they did what they thought was the right thing.

My parents believe that everyone is equal and that colour doesn't matter. This was the rule at home but the moment I stepped outside the warmth of my family, colour seemed to matter terribly. In fact, to my great surprise, it was the first thing that everyone noticed about me. Occasionally, the outside world penetrated into my family. Friends of my parents would come and visit, and I would be briefly introduced as Laura. After about an hour, the visitors would invariably say, 'So where's the daughter we've heard so much about?'

People used to (and still do!) pat my head, feel my hair, and comment on how well I speak English. I was continually the object of curiosity and interrogation. "Do you love your parents? They're not your *real* family. Do you want to find your *real* mother?" My adopted parents were the first thing I could remember and, with their help, I was convinced, rightly or wrongly, that I wanted, needed nothing else; although my mother says that, as a child, I always seemed to be desperately in search of something and it worried her terribly.

I grew up in the New Forest, near Lymington, where there is a considerable number of militant, white ex-Southern Africans. I rarely met black people and was taught that they were Aborigines who wore grass skirts, ate each other and beat drums all day in the sun. I knew nothing about black history and was terrified when Timmy and Tao, a Nigerian couple my father knew from when he was at university, came to stay. Tao would immediately set to work on my hair. She would grab me, hold me firmly between her knees, fill my hair with pungent creams and oils, and comb it and pull it until it was finely plaited into little squares. My head hurt for days and I dreaded her return.

My school friends, like my parents, suffered from the disease of white liberals who claim to be "colour-blind", although many of my friends had fascist parents. The father of one of my best friends was in the National Front, two good friends of mine said that their parents would not let me into their house and a boy I had a crush on at an early age said that, although he was very fond of me, he couldn't go out with me because I was black. During my late adolescence, boys would ask me out all the time – I was thrilled, naturally – but found that the relationships never lasted longer that the first night in bed. One poor friend had to explain to me that they only wanted to see what black birds were like. My ignorance makes me sick to this day.

As a child, I accepted racism quite calmly. I had known it from day one and nobody explained what was happening or why it happened. One of my older brothers did exceptionally well academically and I used to watch him being teased at school for his achievements. He had no real friends and I gained strength from his weakness and resolved never to let people get me down, never to show the pain, no matter how severe. So I rarely reacted when attacked or abused. I do remember kicking a sixth-form boy in the balls when I was in my first term at secondary school. He and his friends always called me "Nigger" and, although I didn't understand it, the insult hurt so bad that I kicked out uncontrollably. To my bad luck, the deputy headmistress saw me and I was dragged into her office to explain. She shouted at me, condemning me as a rebel and saying it was my fault they called me "Nigger". There was no one to turn to, no sympathy, no understanding and no point in reacting.

As I grew into my teens and my body began to take on some shape, I found my clothes didn't fit me as they did my girlfriends. Jeans didn't hug, my legs seemed too short and my bottom seemed to stick out too far. I thought I must be deformed. (That reminds me of the ballet teacher I had who continually told me to "tuck my bottom in". No matter how hard I tried, it always stuck out. She said that if I couldn't keep my bottom in, then I'd never be a ballerina). My skin was always dry, itchy and flaky and my hair became the bane of my life. My girlfriends were busily saving up for the latest hair dryers, curling tongs, hair sprays and dyes, while my mother and I washed my hair with washing-up liquid and set to work on it with a European comb once a week. I went through a phase of always wearing a head scarf in the summer, and my coat hood up with the chin straps drawn tight to prevent over-curious people from pulling it down, in the winter.

Despite all this, I was a happy child and my parents were continually providing me with interesting things to do.

Now that I live in a more multiracial society, I am learning about so many of the things that were denied to me as a child and yet were essential to aid me in coping with living in a predominantly white country.

I refuse to condemn my parents; they always did what they believed was best. My father in his well meaning way would say, 'I don't see people as black and white, I just see people.' But black is what I am and I sometimes wonder whether he *sees* me at all. The more I meet black people and realise I can share something special with them and regain some sort of identity, the more I become aware of the racist traits of the people I was once so close to, although in a life of travel and learning, as it becomes harder to find white people I can really relate to, I realise that this is often a symptom of their ignorance and not my blackness.

Letter to my self

LAURA FISH

Dear Laura,

You may think that in finding our birth parents you will come to the end of a
journey. I am writing to let you know that it's really only the beginning, and when
you find our parents, that's when the journey truly starts.

I have realised through my experience of search and reunion over 20 years that your
quest may be less difficult, less painful, if you take something to accompany you on
the journey. Perhaps a travel companion – a lover, a friend; or something familiar – a
favourite book, a picture, a poem. If you can't take a person or an object, take
something physical and tangible, perhaps even the wind. There is so much to
discover that you have no idea about, that you may feel more lost arriving at your
destination than you did when setting off. Take something with you so that, when
you reach the beginning that you'd hoped would be the end, you don't lose sight of
the start and everything that has happened on the way.

While searching, if you experience a sense of loss of self – feelings of not fitting in
anywhere, not knowing where you belong – when you find our birth parents the
sense of loss will be compounded. Not only will there be the loss of hope, people
you had hoped could understand you, there will be the loss of places you had
considered homelands – England and Jamaica. You will soon feel an alien in each.

Remember, when you find both of our birth parents you won't find what you've been
searching for. And it is only when you find our parents that you will really discover
what it is you have lost.

If the loss feeling was the size of a pea when you started searching, when you find
our parents it will rise up before you like Mount Everest. Arriving in Jamaica you
will see a beautiful lush green island. A paradise. Bright crimson flowers climb the
stone walls of our father's palatial house. The house itself overlooks a bay of warm
golden sand. The blue Caribbean sea sparkles with stars in the sunshine. A gentle
wind with a fragrance of honey blows in from the ocean. You will feel that this is
part of you. That you belong. But you will soon learn that you don't belong in

Jamaica. And this island will never be home to you. Although you may say you belong, although you'll blend in, think you fit, although people won't stare at you as they did when you were a child in Hampshire, this feeling of belonging is an illusion. There's a big part of you that doesn't fit anywhere, for we have lost our past. Over time, an overwhelming sense of loss will be all that feels familiar to you.

Our birth parents will have expectations of you that you can't meet. You, similarly, will have expectations of them that they can't meet. The idea of having people who resemble you, or whom you resemble, after having no one who resembles you may, initially, be comforting. But when you first find our father, it will cause so great a shock that you'll be unable to speak for at least two days. You won't be able to take your eyes from his. To you, those eyes are bewitching: deep dark brown pools reaching back into past generations of our family. You may feel the floor dissolve beneath your feet, because everything you thought you knew about yourself appears no longer true.

You will need support as the realisation gradually dawns that this new-found family is not "yours", despite your desire to belong to it. But is there anyone in this family who possesses the insights to offer the support you need?

You will sit in our birth father's enormous silver-grey Mercedes, directly behind him in the back seat, watching his eyes in the mirror. Our father's reflection will resemble your own: broad nosed, full-lipped, the shade of skin matches yours exactly. And his eyes will glance at the mirror too. His reasons for doing this will be ambiguous. When you visit Jamaica he welcomes you, and for that you are eternally grateful. But, as with your adoptive parents, does it matter to him whether you live or die? In 15 years, he'll phone you twice and send one postcard. Realising this, you'll feel sick with sadness. This is the first lesson in how our birth parents' understanding of life is painfully different from ours.

So, while it's probably impossible not to have expectations, remember, the chances are that you won't find what you are looking for. Indeed, you may find everything you aren't looking for.

In looking for our parents, it is most likely that you will discover how incomplete people's lives and histories can be. Instead of gaps being filled, you will discover gaping craters. You may have viewed our past as a puzzle, and thought that by gaining information about our birth parents you can gather pieces of this puzzle together to form a picture of our past. In fact, you'll come to realise the pieces don't fit together; the picture will be permanently incomplete. Pieces are missing years later. Answers can't always be found. In time you will see life as a collection of haphazard events, an incomplete mosaic, a montage or abstract collage, rather than a puzzle where everything fits neatly in its place.

Living with knowing little about our history, and then finding our birth parents and discovering that you know even less, you will spend several years engaged in historical research in and about Jamaica, trying to find out more about ourselves and our family through doctoral study and research. By immersing yourself in the pain and the loss of hope, you may begin to see a path through it.

Writing will become a way for you to express feelings and the concerns in which you believe. Writing will be a way of working out what you don't understand. It's only once you've written that you'll realise that much of what you want to say concerns people who live in an ongoing state of mistaken identity. Writing is lonely. But then the experience of being transracially adopted is also lonely – and you'll always have to live with that. When looking for our birth parents, you will be looking for somewhere you can feel safe, where racism doesn't exist, where it is OK to be black. And a woman. OK to be you.

When you were younger, your beliefs were similar to those of our adoptive parents: you denied racism existed. But racism used to eat you up inside. You will grow to challenge racism and challenging racism will grow to become part of your life. You have carried a lot of anger that you aren't aware of and which you haven't developed mechanisms for dealing with because our adoptive parents ignored our feelings, pretending they didn't exist. As a parent you will want to help your son to feel good about who he is. You will discover that your views of yourself and of the outside world are linked, and that through challenging the outside world you can feel more positive about yourself.

When you go to Australia you will work with Aboriginal people who, due to previous government policies, have been removed from their birth parents. Some of these Aboriginal people will have traced their origins. It will be a hugely valuable experience for you to find these people to share with. The experience will affect you deeply, leave a lasting impression, and shed light on the two issues that are behind your first novel. Firstly, our history. You will discover other black swans. Black swans are not only birds native to Western Australia, they are Aboriginal people who originate from the Black Swan tribe. The black swan will become a powerful symbol for you. Relationships will build between you and Aboriginal people who, like you, have felt like an ugly duckling, growing up without their culture, not looking like the people who raised them, feeling isolated, rejected. The second issue will be the situation of the Aboriginal people you meet. Some have fought for and bought back their land, to discover the only way they can pay off loans incurred by doing this is to work cattle on the land – a paradoxical situation because the cattle's hard hooves destroy the fragile land. This exquisitely painful and poignant issue is, in part, at the heart of your work and helps fire your desire to write the book.

In time, through writing, you will feel more whole as a person, more confident. Having a son and feeling needed, feeling loved, you will have a reason to get up in the mornings. Love. Love is what you have lacked for years.

A few years after writing 'Black fish in a white sea' you will be married, and then working your way up in the BBC. You will not expect that, 20 years later, you will end up a single parent, teaching and studying at university. But you will feel a lot more fulfilled spiritually with a lot less materially. Material achievements will become less important to you, feeling more whole spiritually will mean more. Continually digging down into our past will be where the losses and riches lie. When you wrote that article, 'Black fish in a white sea', you thought you could put everything in boxes, and that life could be tidied; that you could revisit the past, then move on.

When embarking upon the search for both of our birth parents you begin to try to prepare yourself for a situation that's impossible to prepare for. How will you come to terms with the past through a mother and father who are your blood relations but who don't know you at all, and don't know each other? There are things you can do to further strengthen yourself, to try to manage a pretty unmanageable situation. Remember, whatever our birth parents do, whatever our adoptive parents do, and however they respond, you are not responsible. It is not because of you that they behave as they do: it's the only way they know how to be.

I hope that, by telling you in this letter what I've come to learn, you will be less hurt.

Remember, there are experiences in life for which one cannot prepare oneself.

Remember, you must learn not to expect anything from our parents.

Remember, you are entering a very complex situation: you have to keep letting go although you'll discover you don't know how to let go of something you've never really had.

Lots of people will give advice or ask questions: 'Oh, you must want to know who your real parents are;' 'You must stay in touch with your adoptive parents.' Whatever you do, try to find that place within yourself that feels safe.

Remember, children are free spirits, as are parents. Listen to your inner voice, yourself. Listen to yourself because you do have knowledge and wisdom of how to nurture strength in the most barren of situations. Maybe the inner voice is what you can take with you on this journey.

In reality, the journey never ends.

Love,

Your self

Acknowledgement: 'A black fish in a white sea' by Laura Fish was first published in *Libertarian Education: A magazine for the liberation of learning*, December 1987. For further details please see: http://www.libed.org.uk

Great expectations, great disappointments

KATE HOOKINGS

My background

I was three months old when I was adopted. The reason was that my mum had me when she was about 17, and she was kicked out because she was pregnant. Her parents didn't know I was going to be black. When I was born I looked white, although I had a Mongolian blue spot. So when my mum last saw me, when I was three months old, I looked white. My mum was English and my dad was Nigerian. He was studying building at a college, and they met at a party and had a one-night stand. At least, that's the nice version that I've heard. The not so nice story is that she was raped. I overheard friends saying that she was raped when I was a teenager.

I have always remembered this, in case I wanted to meet her, to know the truth. She may never want to meet me because it would be going back into a nightmare, sort of thing. I try and imagine things aren't always going to be rosy, and to think of reasons why they may be bad in the future. As long as I've got that in my head, then disappointments will be easier to cope with. If it turns out better, then that's a bonus.

My foster carer

I was born in 1981, in Salisbury in Wiltshire. I was in foster care in Trowbridge with Molly for three months. When I used to go round there with my mum now, Jenny, each and every visit Molly would take photographs of me, lots of photographs. When I was 17, I went back to see Molly. At the time, I was looking for my birth mum and she took photographs of me again. Every child she has fostered, she has a portfolio of, but she could never find mine. It made me think, where has it gone, and why does she still take photos of me? I thought she might still be in contact with my birth mum, but she would not tell me. When I asked questions she seemed to hurry me out of the house, and she was never like that before.

What was also strange is she told me she couldn't remember things that were massively important, that no one would forget. Yet, she can remember that when she was ill in bed on a cold wet day, my mum came and talked to her in bed. So my mum used to come and visit me. She could remember that, but she couldn't remember what colour her hair was. I think she's continued to have contact with my mum right up until now. If she has, then my birth mum can't want to meet me, because she would have known from Molly that I was looking for her.

My adoptive family

I grew up in Swindon. John, my brother, is seven years older than me and he was not adopted. Then there's my mum, Jenny, and Martin, but he's not my dad any more. It was a horrible childhood because of Martin. I didn't really have friends. Everything was bad. School was horrible; the teachers were racist. I had to have the racial people go to the school. I was running away from home because of Martin; he used to beat me and my mum up. Mum was really scared of him.

School

At school, I got suspended and expelled lots of times because I'm black. It was just down to stupid things, like you weren't allowed to wear black boots at school, but everybody did, so I did, then I'd get in trouble. People would wear their ties the other way round because it was the fashion. The teachers would grab hold of my tie and talk to me like I was a baby, 'Now this is how you put on a tie.' Every year, a black person would leave the school. Two black people left the year before me, they had lots of trouble, and then I was the last one to go.

My mum went to the Head Teacher to complain about the racism, and he went absolutely mad that she could suggest such a thing. A few weeks later, they had black people performing in assembly, like to cover their backs, and even one of the teachers said to my friend, 'the coloured people have been dipped in the coffee too long'. There was so much racism. It took its toll in the end and I couldn't deal with it. I never had a "chip on my shoulder" about my colour, but the teachers and children were making me seem like I was the problem. I ended up getting suspended and expelled all the time. And if they had me back they wanted me on school report, which I refused, because that was for naughty kids and I wasn't naughty. This happened at senior school. I must have only been there 18 months, but I still passed all my exams. I left school at 16.

Going back into care

I was 12 when I went back into foster care. I was running away from home because of Martin's violence. Mum couldn't tell the truth, she was too scared. On one of the first occasions I ran away, I was picked up in town, really late. I told the police why I was running away, and they said I needed to press charges, or something along those lines. And I said, 'I can't, because of my mum.' The police said I was a liar because I wouldn't press charges, yet surely they could see it was true. I had cuts on my knees.

I was in and out of foster care; at one time, they threatened to send me to the same secure unit as Bolger's killers because Martin said I was mad, though I wasn't. We were having social services meetings all the time. One time I walked out of my foster home while they were having a meeting and I started getting mad at Martin's car. At that age it was all too much to cope with, and the foster carers were horrible

I'd go home and Martin would pretend to have a heart attack and have ambulances and police cars there, and then blame it all on me. He didn't want me at home and said I was a problem child. From the first time that he leant across the table and smacked me in the mouth, it just got worse. From when I was about five or seven, I can remember Martin beating my mum up upstairs. He didn't want me; he never wanted to adopt. His mum was racist; she always used to talk about 'the horrible blackie down the road'.

My brother and Martin beat me up once, and they phoned the police and said it was me. The police came and handcuffed me, in front of everybody. I was put in a cell. As soon as I left the cell, I went into foster care. Some nights I ran away from foster care and had nowhere to sleep. I'd phone my mum and say I was sleeping in a phone box. I was scared and crying. She was crying back to me, saying, 'There's nothing I can do, there's nothing I can do.' A few days later, Martin phoned someone and said he wanted me to come home. So I went home and knocked on the front door. He chucked my suitcase at me, took my bracelet off me and said, 'There you go, now you're definitely out.' Mum was at the top of the stairs crying. A lot of worse things happened, but I don't remember everything any more.

I used to get angry but I've calmed down a lot now. Mum used to say I was cold. She believes all the beatings made me like that, but I don't think so. It did for a bit, make me cold, I didn't care about anybody or anything and was angry all the time, but I'm not anymore. I haven't seen Martin for six years. I suppose I have got a bit of anger left, because, if I saw him, I'd want to kill him. But I wouldn't do it. If he died tomorrow, I'd be happy. Some people find that hard to believe, or think it's sick, but those are my feelings.

Turning my life around

I'm 23 now. I don't really know why my life changed. I went to live with Emma's mum, my friend from school. But then my mum and Martin split up, when I was 15 or 16, so I went home for a couple of years. Then Mum got a boyfriend and now she is married to him.

I used to be into drugs and stay in places with prostitution. I never did prostitution, but it was there. I've seen people my age who've killed themselves with drugs and I know that could have been me. Now I couldn't even smoke cannabis, I would never touch drugs. The reason why, I don't know. I think I've grown up, got more responsible. But how I did it, I can't really explain. Emma's my partner and I'm secure now. We've been living together for almost four years. I'm living somewhere where I want to live, with all the little things that people take for granted. Like all my teeth went bad back then, but now I'm having three proper meals a day. I'm living a normal life. When I look back I know I was insecure. My mum's OK now, and everything's building back up around me.

Unfortunately, most people around me didn't help because they couldn't understand. All I could do was get on with my life. The only person who helped was my social worker. Basically I had a choice, to live like a tramp or not, so I just sorted myself out. When I went home, when I was 16, things got better from there. It was just me and my mum, so that was nice. Then my group of friends changed, I got a job, things like that. I just got up and changed.

Advice for other transracial adoptees

Be strong. Think of tomorrow. Things are going to get better, but you have to make it happen. People can't help you because they don't always understand. You understand yourself, and deep down know when things are going wrong. Just pick yourself up because, if you don't, you'll always stay down.

Social work

I'd like to be a social worker but, being sensible, I'm not going to do it because I'd have to not work, and go to college and university, which I can't afford to do. You can do it here now, part time, in four years, at the campus, but again you have to earn money at the same time, and you have to pay for university too.

I've just recently had dealings with social services for something else. Swindon is a nought per cent rating social services; they're rubbish. When I had a social worker, sometimes I'd get different ones assigned to me because Sarah wasn't allowed to be my social worker at the time, depending on her job. They'd say, 'We dress like this to make you feel comfortable,' and I'd say, 'You look like a hippy, you're not making me feel comfortable.' My mum had a lot of trouble with them too; they sit there and read you advice that they've read out of a textbook. They've had a happy little life, they've got no kids themselves, and they don't know what they're talking about because they've not been through it. I think I'd be better as a social worker because I've been there. To understand what someone's talking about is a big help. Just to have the support of someone knowing what you're going through. Understanding gives people help, makes a big difference.

Accessing my adoption records

When I was 18 I decided I wanted to see my records because I was looking for my birth mum. I sent off all the forms and got the booklet back. But I am still waiting to see my adoption file. I don't think there'll be much in the file. It's just that I want to carry on and search; to have some closure. I want to know the reasons for my adoption, whether she was from an army family. I want to know if what I've been told is true. I'm not looking to find out anything new.

Advice for adoptive parents and social workers

Listen to people and try to understand them more, whether that's about attending more courses or reading more. Remember you're dealing with people's lives, it's not just a job, it is people's lives. Think carefully before you say things, especially to adopted teenagers.

For adoptive parents, again, listen to the children, the teenagers. I know teenagers go through bad times, but try and listen to them and understand them – which is difficult, I suppose, because no one really understands teenagers!

Even though teenagers probably don't want to talk to anyone, it would be nice for them to have someone to talk to, a trusted adult. I think adopted teenagers should always have a social worker, the same one, who is there to help the parents and the child.

I haven't met any other adopted people, apart from you. It wouldn't have been useful to me. Basically, if you're having a really bad upbringing as an adoptee, and then you meet someone who's having everything, it wouldn't help. For some people it might help, meeting other adoptees.

Postscript

Since being interviewed for this book, I have seen my adoption records and met my mum. I met her on 23 January 2005. I have seven younger brothers and sisters aged between nine and 21 years. It turns out she had not stayed in contact with Molly. However, my social worker, Sarah, who I trusted and was so close to, had always known where my mum was but did not tell me. I spoke to her about this, as she knew that I wanted to find my mum. She says it was her manager's decision. Social services have been involved with all the children. At the moment, three are living at home with my mum and one is in foster care. She has struggled to parent them well and I don't think she is doing very well with the youngest three. For the past five years, I have wanted to find her. Perhaps it would have made a difference if I could have been there for my brothers and sisters. They always knew about me. The situation I've found is not what I expected at all. My mum hasn't rejected me, which is good, but it is more that I am rejecting her. At least I now know where she is and can decide for myself how much contact I want with her.

My mum told me that my father raped her. She has given me his first and second name but I can't find anyone with that surname. I even wrote to the Nigerian Embassy to see if I have the correct spelling for his name. I don't know how old he was when she met him. He may have returned to live in Nigeria, I don't know. I contacted NORCAP and was referred to the South West Adoption Network, but it is help with searching that I need, not counselling support.

My feelings about adoption have changed since finding my mum. Sometimes I think you should stick with what you know. The grass isn't always greener on the other side, as I have found out, and now I have to live with that and I wish I didn't have to.

Rebuilding the foundations

ELINOR YOUNG

Background to my adoption

I was born in Bradford in 1977. Both my parents are Pakistani Muslim, from Peshawar. I am the fifth of seven children and was the only child to be adopted. I have two older brothers, two older sisters and two younger sisters. I lived with my birth family for six months and then was in and out of hospital for the next 18 months, going backwards and forwards between hospital and my birth parents. My mother was suffering from post-natal depression at the time, but she received no help. I was placed on the child protection register for neglect and social services decided to remove me from my family and to place me in foster care. When I was about two I joined my white foster family who were living just outside Leeds. I was fostered until I was nine, when they adopted me. As my birth parents were protesting against the adoption, the case went to the High Court. I think I had contact with my family until we moved to Sussex when I was five. After that, social services stopped all contact.

My childhood

During my childhood, I was unaware of any differences and only experienced the occasional comment. I led a very protected life. I did not think about race and identity or anything like that. I was just being a child. It was not until I was at sixth-form college, when I had a lot more people questioning my identity, that I started thinking about who I am. This questioning continued at university. People would ask me why my culture did not match my Asian appearance. The Asian and African-Caribbean students would ask why, if I knew I was Pakistani, I hadn't done anything about this. I knew what people were saying but I did not see how my life could have been any different. I was dumbstruck. I did join the African-Caribbean and Asian society, but it was like nothing I had experienced before. I remember being called "a coconut" there and I left quickly.

Contact with my birth family

From the age of 16 onwards I have received a birthday card each year from my birth family. They always knew my home address in Sussex as I had been fostered before being adopted. When I was 16, my brother came down to my secondary school and tried to abduct me. My birth family wanted to claim me back, believing that I was fostered and could now return to live with them. They did not understand that I was adopted. They had always thought that I would return to them when I was 16 years old. As a result, my adoptive parents said that my birth family could not have any contact with me, other than by letter. Then, when I was 16 or 17, I started to have contact with my sister who is a year younger than me.

I contacted the Post-Adoption Centre in London when I was 19, asking to see someone about my birth family. I received some counselling sessions from a black counsellor. As I had a permanent home in East Sussex (which subscribes to the Post-Adoption Centre), I was able to receive six free counselling sessions. I then attended the Post-Adoption Centre group for transracial adoptees. I found the group quite liberating. Going to the group almost blew me away; it was the realisation that I was not on my own. Growing up, I was so isolated and thought that I was the only one, but I was not. The groups were very useful. They made me identify issues and areas I hadn't thought about and probably wouldn't have without that help. People say that, once you open a can of worms, you can't put the lid back on again and that is what going to the Post-Adoption Centre did for me. Through the groups, I met an Indian transracial adoptee who has become a good friend of mine and a number of other transracial adoptees.

When I was 20, I met two of my sisters at Victoria Station in London for the first time after all those years: one sister who is younger than me and one who is older. They had been sending me photographs and writing me letters. That first meeting was quite strange. It was like friends telling me about their life. Seeing people who look like me was very nice and, at the same time, quite freaky. My younger sister is a mirror image of me.

In 1999, when I was 21, I went to Bradford to meet my parents. It was the summer and I stayed with a friend in Blackpool. I told my adoptive parents I wanted to meet my parents. What is really scary is that my adoptive parents met me in Bradford to go and meet my birth family. I wanted to include my adoptive parents in the reunion. My adoptive mother is a counsellor and psychotherapist who has worked in the adoption area. My adoptive parents both agreed that that's what they wanted. I was so "not with it" that I got off the train at the wrong station, two stops early at Halifax. That's what shock did to me. When I arrived at Bradford my parents were waiting for me. We went to see my birth family and met everyone. It was most odd, my birth parents and adoptive parents meeting, because they had spent such a long time in rivalry towards each other, fighting the adoption through the courts. So my birth parents inviting them into their home was very humbling. My birth parents speak Urdu so to facilitate communication we had an interpreter, provided by social services. I wanted more time with my birth family, but without my adoptive parents being there. Having my parents there was the right thing to do, but I really wanted to see what it would be like without them.

Over the last five years I have had mainly letter contact with my birth family. Other events in my life have tended to take priority, such as going to India at the end of 1999 (which was a disaster), returning to university to train to become a teacher in September 2000, and starting to work as a teacher in London in 2001. Then, in 2002, when I moved to south London with my flatmate (another transracial adoptee), I decided that I was going to see my birth family more regularly. I had only seen my sister once since that first meeting in Victoria. That summer I visited my family. I stayed in bed and breakfast for one night and then with my sister (the one I had been in contact with, as this is what my family wanted) for a few days. I saw my family and spent time getting to know my brothers and sisters.

What was the visit like? It was surreal. I enjoyed getting to know them. It was amazing because my family looks like me and shares my traits. I realised that I can't escape from this, however much I might try to deny that we are related. I look like my mother and even more like my father. My face is very much like my father's. I am physically petite like my mother and my hands are like hers. I am more like my mother than I would like to think, to be honest. In terms of personality, I'm like my mother, which is hard for me as I grew up not liking her. In some ways we are very much alike. We are both on-lookers or observers, watching what is going on. The more crowded it is, the more I observe and I've noticed the same with my mother. Stubbornness is a big thing that we share, too. It's all the little things I see reflected in my birth family. So contact has changed the way I view my mother. Realising that I am like this woman whether or not I like it; accepting that I look like her, although I've tried to pretend I don't. I can't dislike this woman, my mother, because she is a part of me.

Since then I have made successive visits each school holiday. In October 2003, one of my adoptive parents was ill. I didn't go to visit my birth family until summer 2004; I guess it was split loyalties and feelings of guilt if I had gone. I thought it best to restrict contact with my birth family to telephone calls. Later in the year, I started to visit again.

During this time, I bought my own flat in London and I gained independence. My birth family was keen for me to live in Bradford. It would be easy to live near one family (birth or adoptive), but it was important for my identity for me to live in a multicultural area located somewhere between the north and south of England. Also, it was important for me to live where I had already made myself an independent base, in terms of defining all parts of my identity. I have made my flat very much my home. I don't hide anything about my background or deny my adoption, so inviting people around is interesting. I have photographs of my adoptive family and my birth family on display, and books about adoption and by Asian women. It has almost been like an unveiling of who I am without denying any part of me. It was a very big step to take.

In August 2004, I visited my birth family for four days. My birth parents were in Pakistan at the time. It was like visiting friends. I didn't feel under any pressure to behave a certain way. For the first time, I stayed in the family house where my youngest sister, my brother and sister-in-law and their baby live. Then I visited again just last weekend. This time my mother was there and my dad was in Pakistan. She was very, very respectful of my space. I feel uncomfortable around large groups of people, even if I am closely related to them. She was very thoughtful in how she organised the weekend, spacing out the visits by family members. I even stayed in the same room as my mother, as my nieces and nephew decided to stay over. It was quite weird staying in such close proximity to my mother as we had never really been alone. I always felt more comfortable when one or two others were with us.

There was a lot of pressure, though, as it was Ramadan. The first day my family politely made me food. Then I fasted for one day, out of respect, which pleased my mum. Fasting and learning about Islam was an eye opener for me. My family say 'You were born a Muslim,' but I say 'I didn't grow up a Muslim.' My sister repeatedly asked me if I will become a Muslim (as she does each time I visit). I said to her, 'I don't think I will. Will that stop me being your sister?' She said, 'No.' It's too much for me to change my lifestyle. It was lovely seeing my brothers and sisters and being with my family. The religious dimension and my relationship with my mother are more difficult, but my nieces and nephews are wonderful because they lighten the whole situation.

The emotional impact of search and reunion

I'm a singer and during the search and reunion process I had great difficulty performing without all my emotions coming to the surface. Everything is interlinked. In singing, you have to show emotion without it spilling over. Throughout the reunion my boundaries spilled over because of all the innate and intense emotion. I was overcome by my lack of control. I realised that what I had always done before was to put on a mask before I went out. But now, I was constantly looking in the mirror to see how much of a mask I had on. My mask kind of cracked for two years. In the end, I learned self-protection. As I built myself from within, the control came back.

It was necessary to go back and spend time with my family, to build relationships with them and accept their culture, and then to acknowledge how much a part of me they were and what the other parts of me are. I went to counselling to rebuild my sense of identity. Stupidly, I had built my identity on abandoning the first few years of my life. The foundations of my identity were a bit rocky, like a hammock with holes in it. It was necessary for me to fill in the holes in the hammock (the gaps in my identity from my birth family) to make my sense of identity more secure. You can't abandon your past; you have to go back to basics and rebuild. Previously, I thought I had my identity and that denying those early years and connection to my birth family would not matter. When I went into counselling, I realised that my constant agitation and fear and moving jobs and flats was me running away and not confronting what I needed to address – my adoption.

Advice for other transracially adopted people

I think fear stops many people from embarking on searching or establishing contact with their birth family. I would say it is better to know than to not know. It's better to know who you are, where you come from; to accept and acknowledge this. Before, I denied the whole adoption thing, but there is a need to know, a yearning to know. I made a conscious effort to find out about my birth family by the time I had reached 30. I didn't want to wait until I was married with children to be blown away by this. I was quite sure what I wanted and when I wanted it. One of the hardest things is carrying people with you, people you've known all this time; making them aware that there are other parts of you. I had this big question about people who knew me. I wondered, do they really know me? I don't believe you can know someone just by knowing a fragment of their life. I've always valued my friendships on the basis of who I truly am.

Who am I?

Who am I? I'm an Asian woman with a British background and an Asian birth family. I am aware of my culture, although I don't fulfil it. I have made a decision not to make the culture a huge part of my life. I speak very little Urdu but I can say the odd thing, which my birth family finds very funny. My mum speaks a little English and my brothers and sisters speak English, so we are able to communicate. I do wear *shalwar kameez* when I visit them. Eating with my hands was new to me, and home-cooked food is nothing like restaurant food. My first attempt at making chapattis was quite interesting. They weren't round enough.

Importantly, I now know who I am and where I'm from. I'm aware of people's expectations of me. I'm strong in who I want to be and I am aware (whereas before I wasn't aware of anything). It's about knowing, it's a choice. I know who I could be if I chose to, and what I could have been like if I had grown up within my birth family. I respect my birth family but chose to live my life differently. I want to be able to achieve this balance in my life.

A unique experience

SHARON BEAZER

My adoption

I grew up in a small village in Wiltshire called Broughton Gifford. It's a very rural area and we lived next door to a farm. I lived here from five weeks of age until I was 17 years old.

My parents had four of their own children, and they adopted me. I come in the middle with a brother and sister either side of me. In many ways it was pretty idyllic, because I look back and school holidays were spent playing in nearby fields and orchards, and maybe helping a farmer to bale hay – things like that. We played a lot with each other and generally amused ourselves. It was a fairly sheltered upbringing.

My mother was born in Jamaica and came to England when she was about 16. I was born in Swindon, in Wiltshire, not too far away. For the first five weeks of my life I believe I lived with my mother and sister, staying with an aunt of my mother's. My mother already had a one-year-old daughter when she fell pregnant with me. She herself was one of several children who were all still living at home and so it was difficult for her to stay at home with my sister and me, due to lack of space. When I arrived she went to live with an aunt, and I think that's where I was for the first five weeks.

The plan had definitely not always been adoption. The plan was that I would be fostered on a temporary basis and my mother would sort out some accommodation. Then she would come and get me, and my mother, my sister and I would live together, but it didn't quite work out like that. My adoptive parents, my mother in particular, were very keen to adopt. I think, to be honest, in those days, because she was married and my birth mother wasn't, and she is white, the authorities were just much more in favour of my mother adopting me, so that was how it was.

I wasn't actually adopted until I was about 16. Because I was fostered, I still had visits from the social worker. At some stage, he basically encouraged my mother to drop wanting to adopt me, and to wait until I was old enough to decide whether I wanted to be adopted, which is what happened. When I was younger it was a bit back and forth, my birth mother would say, 'Right, I'm coming to get her,' so my mum would say, 'Right, I'm going to adopt her,' and it was a bit like that for the early years of my life. So, my social worker said, 'Look, just wait until she's older,' so that's what happened. I remember my social worker being there one evening and it was all a bit bizarre, and he said, 'You can get adopted now if you want to.' It wasn't the best decision, but that's what happened.

I only remember seeing my birth mother once, but I saw her on probably two or three other occasions. I think the other visits were aborted. The visit I do remember was when my adoptive father came to take me out of school when I was about five, and I went home and met my birth mother.

My experience of adoption

My experience was a mixture of things. For me, the decision to be adopted was a bit rushed and a bit pressurised. I felt that I was beholden to my adoptive mother to just go through with the process, whereas, if it had just been down to me, I wasn't really that bothered about being adopted. But I felt that I owed my mother something, and I knew it meant a lot to her, so I went through with it. It was just such a simple process. I remember having a morning off school and going to court, and it was just, like, 'Do you want to do this?', 'Yes', and that was it. Your name's changed and that's it.

I think it just makes for a really unique experience, having grown up in the way that I did. When you're in it you just think, 'Oh this is life then, I don't know anything different.' But then you grow up and hear other people's stories and think, 'Well, that was quite different, quite a different experience to a lot of people!' Obviously, things have changed again since I made contact with my family and found out more about them. I think that's all I can say: a unique experience.

Racism

As a child, I didn't really experience a lot of racism: none at primary school. When I moved to secondary school, there were definitely some problems but nothing too bad. Obviously, I was different – I was the only black kid there – but I think I developed strategies to cope with it. I was very good at mimicking people and making people laugh, and I used that before anyone had a chance to pick on me. But there was always someone to stick up for me and fight my corner, or I could fight my corner, so it wasn't a big issue really. I've spoken to friends who have grown up where they were black in an all-white community, and they've been chased down the streets with people throwing sticks and stones and bottles at them, but I never experienced anything like that. The racism was much more subtle, more along the lines of people saying, 'Well, you're not like them,' and me saying, 'Who do you mean by them?'

Contacting my birth family

I remember I was out with this guy who had been adopted or long-term fostered, and he was appalled that I hadn't tried to find my family. It really got me thinking because, up until that point, I had been saying, 'Well, I'm really not bothered.' It was quite easy. I basically contacted the man who had been my last social worker; he'd been with me up until the age of about 16. He was still working in the same place, so it was quite easy to contact him. He actually offered to act as a go-between; he contacted my mother to say that I was interested in meeting up, which was a bit of a lie actually, because I wasn't that interested in meeting my mother! The only person I wanted to meet was my sister because we had the same parents. So, anyway, he contacted my mother and got an address for my sister who lives in London. I was living in London, so I contacted her first, and then needless to say the rest of the family followed, and I met everyone else. I was 24 then. I remember phoning my sister and saying, 'Are you sitting down?' She didn't know who I was but I thought this was going to be a shock! We were living really close to each other and probably had been for a while, probably passed each other on the street and didn't know. It wasn't as big a shock as it could have been, as she did know about me.

When I was in my teens, my then social worker paid me a visit one evening; he had come to talk about my adoption but he also presented me with a picture of this sister. I can only presume that he had been in touch with my birth family before the visit. Anyway he said that my sister wanted to get in touch and gave me the photograph. This completely threw me and, at that time, I said, 'Thanks but no thanks,' and handed back the picture.

I arranged to meet with my sister soon after our initial phone call and then, shortly after that, I met my mother and some of my siblings when they came to London. Meeting my family really showed the cultural differences between us; I had been brought up in the countryside and, during that time, had barely seen any other black people.

After a couple of meetings with my sister, I felt a real affinity with her even though we've had completely different experiences. Physically, there is a strong resemblance and we have the same mannerisms; we've even been known to turn up in almost identical outfits, which was uncanny at the time – it definitely feels as if there is a connection between us. However, with the rest of my family it's quite a different story; I don't *feel* related to them, which has been awkward at times.

Post-reunion relationships

My relationship with my birth mother has been far from natural and at times has felt really strained. I found it hard to accept that she was my mother. I didn't feel that we had anything in common. Also, we were coming to the reunion from very different angles. I think from my mother's point of view she was just so pleased to see me after such a long time – it was simple, her daughter was back in her life. I, on the other hand, didn't feel like that, I already had a mother; I didn't need another one and I wasn't able, and never will be able, to fulfil the role that she would like me to take. I guess that is where the difficulties lie. I don't think that we will ever be particularly close but, in a way, we've found some sort of rhythm to our relationship.

My sister and I have a very good relationship in many ways. I feel as if I have always known her; there seems to be an unspoken understanding between us. I know it sounds strange but she feels like a real sister. As I got to know her, it was amazing for me to see how much we have in common. Sometimes I've even thought, maybe there's something my mother's not saying, maybe we are twins! We have very similar tastes and the same sense of humour.

I remember my sister once said she went through the phone book when I was a child and found my adoptive family name and was on the verge of calling but didn't. I think it was hard for her.

Every time I visit my family, I suppose it brings the same sort of things up: a slight sense of loss. That's the only way I can describe it. Loss of years, I suppose, of shared experiences, just loss of knowledge that we have about each other because, of course, there are so many gaps. When you grow up with brothers and sisters, there are just so many things you know about each other. Now there are things we assume that we know about each other but we actually don't and, of course, you can't get that back. It's like memory loss. You can feel you know as much as you can, but there'll always be those areas where maybe you weren't there, and you can never fill that person in.

It affects me like, we can be in a group, we can be laughing and joking or whatever, and then there'll be a moment when I kind of sense and acknowledge there was something that wasn't actually shared by me, but maybe they might assume I know the person they're talking about. They wouldn't assume I would know a recalled situation, because obviously I wasn't there, but it's when they talk about somebody I obviously don't know, and I can't join in that conversation.

When I have left them, I often feel quite sad. I remember there was one time when one of my sisters was living in London and all of my siblings came to London and we all met up. It was probably one of the only times we've done that. I remember saying goodbye to them at Oxford Circus, and it was so weird because they were all going back to Gloucester and I was staying in London. They were on one side of the ticket barrier and I was on the other, and I was waving them off. I thought, 'Yes, what you can see here, the physical situation, this describes how I feel.' There's this barrier between us, even though I've made the contact and made the effort. I suppose each meeting is tinged with some feeling of sadness or loss. I think it's definitely got better; the feeling used to be quite traumatic and I would have an almost physical reaction, but now it's more diluted.

Culture

When I met my family I suppose I was a bit different, I was a bit more uptight about things. The truth of the matter is that I'm never going to be like them because I've never had their experiences. I just think I've accepted that this is who I am. These are my experiences and what I've learnt, and this is what I've learnt in addition, about my culture. And that's great. In many respects it's great because growing up there was nothing, absolutely nothing where I could learn about my culture. I always knew I was black. I never wanted to be white. I felt I had quite a strong identity, although I had very little knowledge. Obviously, having met my family, it's cemented a bit of who I am: these are my parents and grandparents, they are Jamaican. That was nice because I'd never had that. I'd always been surrounded by white people. Everybody's white, all my relatives are white, and there was nothing at all to give me any sense of cultural identity. That didn't come until much later. I am glad that I know my family and, it may sound weird, but for me it is still a bit of a novelty, in a good way, having a black family.

I have gradually got to know some other Caribbean people. It wasn't immediate. When I moved to London I was working as a nanny and I met a mixed-race girl who was working as a nanny and we became great friends. Through her, and a couple of other people, I would meet the odd black person but not huge numbers. It was when I joined a church that I met more black people with African or Caribbean origins. In a way I didn't know how to relate to other black people. I didn't move to London until I was 17, and it was quite strange to me to see so many black people. I thought that people would be instantly friendly to me, but that wasn't always the case, especially when I opened my mouth! Coming to London was a bit of a shock. I didn't know anything, I was really green. But I was determined to leave the country because I felt that I couldn't stay there. It's definitely been a good move and I'm still here.

Support services

What is interesting is the ongoing feelings and thoughts, in terms of being transracially adopted. A lot of years have passed since I've traced my family. In many ways, it all feels quite complete and whole now. When I was looking to find my family, there was quite a lot of literature about people who were searching and there were organisations, and that was really helpful. But there's not a lot about when you've found them. Because that's quite intense: you meet with your family and, even if you thought it was a good idea at the time, there are just so many things that come out of it. I was relatively lucky that my mother was interested in meeting me, and so were my siblings, and my father who lives in Canada. It could have been quite different, so I think I have been incredibly lucky. But despite this, there are so many issues.

Of course, you're just turning up in someone's family and it has repercussions in their family. Even if things do go well, it's still hard work and you just have to count the costs – whether you're willing to take on board all that comes with it – and there's a lot that comes with tracing your family, there's a lot emotionally. You might meet your family and think, 'I've had a look, now I want to leave it,' but it doesn't work like that because it's also about them.

The thing I have felt in the years since I found my family is the need for a body where you could meet other transracially adopted adults, that could put you in touch with each other. Because it is such a unique experience and because we're human we make assumptions about people. We look at someone who's black or Asian and we assume we know something about their life. Yet, if you have been transracially adopted you've probably had some really interesting experiences, and I think it would be great if people could be put in contact with one another. Not even necessarily to go over and over your childhood but because, as an adult, you'll be a different kind of person to the one you would have been had you grown up with your family, and just to talk about life in general. I think that would be great.

I did contact the Post-Adoption Centre, in the past, particularly when I was going to try and find my father. I went along for a few sessions to have some counselling. I thought it would be a good idea to go through what might happen because, even though I was very gung-ho and let's just do it, I hadn't really thought about the eventualities. It was brilliant, and so good to talk to somebody about it. Then, recently, I did contact them to see if there was some kind of body for transracially adopted adults.

Searching for my birth father

I searched for my birth father quite recently, four years ago. I had never been interested in my father whatsoever. I just thought he was useless, had abandoned my sister and I, and didn't want to know. Then, one day, I literally woke up and just thought, 'I have to know who my father is.' Again, it was quite easy, amazingly. I knew that he wasn't in this country, but I didn't know if he was in the States or Canada. I didn't even know what his name was. I contacted quite a few people and they all told me something different, though they could remember him. So, I contacted my mother and she gave me his correct name, and I got a Canadian directory. His name is not that common, so there were only eleven in the Toronto area, and I just phoned them one by one. My mother had actually seen him; she has relatives in Toronto and she'd stayed with them. While there, she'd been in a cab and literally looked out of the window and seen my father on the street – quite bizarre. So she knew he was there.

I called these numbers and, eventually, one of them was my father's brother, my uncle. Then I went over to Toronto and I met up with him. I was staying with a friend of a friend in Toronto. They came with me, kind of to make it a more safe. I met with him one evening. My uncle wasn't in great contact with my father, they didn't speak a lot and he didn't really know where he was living, but he had an idea where he was working, so he agreed to take me there. We literally turned up there one day. This was a huge shock for my father. I was sitting in the car and my father came out to the car, and my uncle obviously hadn't really said who he was bringing him to meet. So my uncle opened the car door and my father was, like, 'So who's this, a new girlfriend?' I thought, 'You're going to get a shock in a minute!' I said, 'I'm Lynne's daughter,' and by saying that he knew who I was. We had a very shocked, short meeting, and then he had to get back to work. We made a vague arrangement that I would try and see him again at work in a few days, so we did that. I contacted him and I went to his work.

It was so different from when I met my mother. I didn't feel anything after I'd met my mother; she could have been anybody, which probably sounds a bit cold. But when I met my father it was completely different; he was absolutely my father. I think, physically, there's quite a resemblance. I just felt this flood of warmth for this guy who I'd never met before, which I didn't really understand. We chatted for a couple of hours and then we kept in touch by letter. I only had his work address because although his wife knew about me, I don't know how keen she was about me being in touch. So we did that for a couple of years, but then he was made redundant and I didn't have a contact address for him. But only this year, I called his old place of work and spoke to someone who had worked with him, and they gave me his home phone number, so I called him there. I chatted to him at home, which was nice, and so we're kind of back in touch after a gap of a year. He was pleased to hear from me. Even though we hadn't kept in contact, I felt confident to do that and felt that it would be OK, which it was.

It could have been absolutely disastrous because my father was already married before I was born. He's still with the same woman and he has a daughter who's probably the same age as me, who I haven't met. I'm not that bothered to meet her. I've met a lot of family. There's a limit. You have to give a lot of yourself and you have to decide when, and how much, you're going to give yourself. I have another half-sibling as well. When we are in contact it's good. I'm glad I did it. I may try and see my father, because I'm going to the States later this year. I think I'll contact him and say he could meet me halfway. I don't think I'll make a huge effort to go up to Canada if he's not that keen. I'm going to be in Boston, not a million miles away, so we could meet.

I haven't been to Jamaica, I would like to go at some stage. My maternal grandparents are both dead. I don't know about my paternal grandparents. My father, from what I can remember, wasn't really in contact with anyone in his family – something happened somewhere. He wasn't even in contact with his own brother.

Managing relationships with my birth and adoptive family

My relationship with my adoptive parents definitely was a bit challenging when I did this. I contacted them and said I was going to trace my family, and that didn't go down too well. I think because my mother had put up quite a fight to keep me she felt quite threatened. As a result, I don't really discuss either family with the other. Whenever I have, it always gets a bit out of hand. I think they easily become critical of each other. Even my sister is quite resentful of my adoptive parents, my mother in particular. Like my mother stole me from them. On the other hand, she thinks my (birth) mother should have fought harder to keep me.

I've often wondered, what would I do if I got married? I'd have to go to Vegas or something, because I couldn't have them both there, it would be a nightmare! My adoptive mother just gets incredibly emotional; I can't even go there. I know some people are able to have quite a grown-up relationship with their adoptive parents, but I suppose it's quite natural for there to be some resentment or difficulty. Also, my birth family is fairly resentful of the authorities. I just keep them all separate. Things are on a fairly even keel, really.

I was talking to someone the other day and was saying that my loyalties lie with my adoptive family, because they are my family. I was in a situation a couple of years ago: my sister-in-law was diagnosed with cancer in one family and a grandfather died in the other family, and his funeral clashed with a phone call saying, 'Your sister-in-law's cancer has spread to her brain. Come home.' I didn't even think twice about it, it was my birth grandfather and I didn't really know him. If I'd been around, I would have gone. My birth family accept that's how things are, and it's always going to be like that. I will make time to see them and visit, but it's when I'm able, or ready, or wish to.

When I initially contacted my family, I felt really obliged to see a lot of them and it was too much, having two families, so I pulled back and see them less now and on my terms. My birth family's quite big, so there's always a christening or a blessing, or this or that. It's nice that I get invited, but nine times out of ten I don't go. It's not that I don't want to, but I just have other things on. From their point of view it probably doesn't feel all that great, but it's what I can cope with or I'd have to call a halt to it altogether. It means that I get to see them and they get to see me. I know about their lives, although I'm not heavily involved. Sometimes a huge amount of time will go by, but we always manage to pick up where we left off. I think my mother finds it the hardest; the siblings are fine with it. As adults now, we're mates more than anything. My mother, she would like something more, but I'm not able to give it.

People just take it for granted, looking like someone and having a similar body build. With respect to my adoptive family, everything's different. I was a very different build and shape to my siblings. When I met my father, I looked at his hands and saw that they were just like mine and my sisters. It's just a tiny thing but it's huge when you've never had it.

When I go to Gloucester now and I visit my family, if I'm in a different place to my sister, people think I'm her. They come up to me and say, 'Hi Pat,' and I say, 'No, I'm not Pat.' We're not identical but we're similar enough. She has young children, and the smallest ones will call me "Mum", while the older ones just stare at me, and say, 'You look like Mummy.' Getting mistaken for her is nice because I look like someone, although it's strange and I'm still a little bit taken aback when it happens. It's funny, we have very similar taste in clothes too. I remember once, we hadn't seen each other for a couple of years and we met in London. We had practically the same coat and trousers on. Even recently, when I went to her fortieth birthday party, we had both chosen black dresses with a huge silver buckle on. If I ever wanted to know what to buy her as a present, I'll just buy her what I'd like.

I often think that it might have been nice to grow up with that, but maybe we would have been bitter rivals instead. I suppose the good thing is, because we didn't grow up with each other, we are glad to know each other now. I remember once, we were about to get into an argument, and then both just thought, forget it, because life is short and, when you haven't had your life together, then it's even shorter. We try not to make too many assumptions about each other or get into petty arguments.

My birth family fear that they might do or say something that would push me away, and they'd never see me again. One of my sisters said there's the fear they could lose me again. I don't always have an understanding of that or know how they perceive me. When things occur to highlight that they really do want me in their life, I'm always a bit surprised. I'm always, 'Oh do you?' I'm not treated the same as the others, they are much more careful with me. My relationship with them isn't as unconditional. It's weird because it's like there's room in that for me to do anything I want.

Finding myself

LIZ SIBTHORPE

I was 42 years old before I really saw my face.

Of course I was able to recognise myself in photos long before that day, but I looked and didn't see.

I knew that I was tall, slim and had olive brown skin that changed with the seasons: healthy brown in summer and fading to beige in the depths of winter. I knew I had almost black hair, curled so tightly that only a broad-toothed comb could tame it. I hadn't ever looked at the shape of my mouth, nose or ears. There was no reason to do so, because I had no one to compare myself with. I had never heard the words, 'You do look like your mother' or, 'You've got your father's nose.' In fact, very little was said about my birth parents. I had been told that my mother had blue eyes and fair hair and that my father was black and probably African.

The one aspect of my face I did know well was the colour of my eyes. They were grey-green and flecked with amber, and I felt that they were my best feature. I had heard adults say that I had beautiful eyes. Often I detected a relief in their voice that they had found something to compliment, some aspect of me that passed for white. Even my adoptive parent was audibly pleased when winter arrived and my skin paled so that I blended in with all the other children in the neighbourhood. When I was a teenager she told me that I would stand a better chance of getting a job if I went for interviews in the winter when it wasn't so obvious that I was of mixed race.

I grew up feeling embarrassed about our unusual family. I didn't want to be part of my adoptive parent's family, but I didn't know where else I belonged. I loved my siblings but we were six individuals with little in common apart from adoption. I was drawn to black American literature and the history of apartheid in South Africa. I read about the slave trade long before I learned that it was part of my own history. I was angry: I hated colonial white nations and yet I had a white brother and sister whom I loved and I was partly white. My interest in black culture was not encouraged. Its music was too loud and secular for her. She was unashamedly prejudiced against Africans in general, whom she considered had a tendency to be lazy and dirty, and she believed that all Indians were hot-tempered. Every spark of individuality that didn't fit in with her middle-class, middle England background was seen as a defect to be corrected rather than a gift to be nurtured.

Becoming an adult, graduating and taking up primary school teaching didn't solve the question of who I was. I had dreamed of finding my mother since I was a small child but, until 1976, I didn't have the legal right to trace my birth family. Even then, I didn't know how to do it. My adoptive parent didn't want me to trace my mother and was sure that there was no way I could find out who my father was. She had letters and papers that held information on my birth mother but she refused to let me see them. It wasn't until I was in my mid-thirties that I took up the challenge of tracing my birth parents and it took another few years before I made face-to-face contact with a cousin, the daughter of my one of my father's brothers.

On a cold wet day in February of 1991, I stepped nervously from the train at Plymouth. Anxious questions tumbled round my mind: Would she be there? How would I pick her out in a crowd? Would she recognise me from the photo? I spotted Prudence immediately and, in that instant, I saw myself.

Her hair, not quite as dark as mine, was loosely curled; her eyes were brown and she was several inches shorter than me, but I saw myself in her. Throughout the day, I was caught up in the excitement of family likenesses: the angle at which we held our heads, the slightly pointed facial features, lobed ears and strong eyebrows. Her mouth was wide and her voice sounded soft, like mine. She had the same thin build, and movement that I recognised as mine. I hardly knew if the long brown arm that stretched out across the table for the salt was hers or mine.

I still found it hard to describe my facial features, but I knew that I looked like someone else. I had a face and I was part of a birth family.

For ten years we exchanged letters, and my aunt and cousin wrote down our family history and sent me photos of my father, his parents and his brothers and sister. I was content. Then, one day, my aunt phoned me with stunning news. She had met my half-sister again and told her about me. I gasped audibly. I knew I had an older brother and sister but my aunt hadn't seen them for over thirty years. They could have been anywhere in the world or even dead. Neither Sheila nor John knew of my existence. Sheila's shock was quickly replaced with excitement and eagerness to know more about me. A few days later, we talked on the phone and began to share our life histories and it wasn't long before we met.

It's harder to see a family likeness between me and my brother and sister than it was with my cousin Prudence. Our similarities are more obvious in our personalities than in our facial features. Despite the vast differences in our upbringing and life experiences we have forged a bond that is as strong as if I'd been born into their family. We share a father, we are family, and at last I know who I am.

Dearest Gogo

KAGEHA JERUTO MARSHALL

Dearest Gogo

May I call you Gogo, the Kalenjin word for grandmother? Do let me know which you prefer.

I am writing to you to try to put into words my feelings about meeting you for the first time. I can hardly believe that I am your oldest grandchild. Nothing could have prepared me for what I experienced last summer. For 34 years, I have been the only African child adopted into an English Quaker family. I have had very little knowledge about my past.

Although I knew my mother had died soon after my birth, I discovered only last year that my father Matayo was alive and living in a remote village in western Kenya. Imagine my surprise to learn not only that he had remarried, but that I have seven half-sisters and four half-brothers!

On the day of our meeting, I was so nervous. I did not know what to expect. Previously, relatives and friends in England warned me about the dangers of visiting an isolated area. 'Beware of the tribal elders . . . Be warned – they will demand a high bride price . . . Didn't you know that a black American woman tried to do the same thing two years ago? She was seized and circumcised against her will . . . The area you want to visit could be too risky.'

I was prepared to encounter suspicion, coolness, even hostility. I was petrified. But something inside pressed me on.

A missionary friend who had known me as an infant kindly offered to take me, my husband and two children back to the village I originated from. We got lost several times as there was no road. We passed in the shadows of the towering Nandi Rock, which tribes used for human sacrifices only thirty years ago. Our journey was temporarily interrupted when crowds of women and children streamed on to our path, carrying food and clothing to the young men in the forest. Unbeknown to us, this was the year of the male circumcision which took place every five years.

After two hours, I was glad to get out of our vehicle and walk the final part of the journey. It had been a long, hot and dusty drive. We walked down into the valley and up the other side. The hillside was covered in maize swaying in the heat. When I looked up into the sunlight, I saw two women running towards me, arms outstretched. I know now that they were Damaizy, my father's second wife, and her first-born child, Wangeri. Their faces were lit by the sunshine and their smiles and hugs made me feel instantly welcome. We walked back to the home compound, a clearing with two separate mud-walled houses, and although my father was not at home at that time, I met you.

Grandmother, your blindness means your family were your eyes. We could not speak the same language but your tears as you kissed my fingers humbled me. You held me. I heard you sing. I heard you laugh. We all danced. You fed us. My children, your great-grandchildren, played with their Kalenjin cousins among the lush green vegetation.

For a time, I imagined I was a young Kalenjin girl helping to take care of the cattle with the older children. We roamed the Nandi Hills looking for new pastures. We guarded that which would be our children's with the passing years – cattle, land, family.

Suddenly, I feel proud of who I am and where I come from. I feel privileged to be the centre of such celebration. I hope we will meet again. We can walk together in the Nandi Hills and you will whisper, 'Let the vision of Kenya grow within you.'

Thank you for accepting me into your life. Your oldest Kalenjin grand-daughter has at last returned.

Acknowledgement: 'Dearest Gogo' by Kageha Jeruto Marshall was first published in 1998 in *Origins: Personal stories of crossing the seas to settle in Britain*, The Kuumba Project, Bristol.

A white African dress

JACKIE KAY

Yesterday, as I thought about what my father wore
That Sunday in Abuja when we first met,
A huge heron lit up my path through the woods,
Far from the river bank where the bird
Usually stood, grave as a prayer.

It flew ahead of me away from the water –
Its huge wings hesitating like a heavy heart –
Through gold leaves fluttering from the bright trees.
He was dressed all in white, my father:
A long white African dress, ornate like lace,

Repeating its pattern in intricate stitching,
The bright white lit up his black face.
My father chanted and ranted and prayed at my feet,
creating wings with his hands, 'Oh God Almighty'.
My hands, clasped tightly, nursed on my lap.

He clutched a Bible and waved it about
As he sang and danced around the hotel room,
Until the Holy Book opened its paper aeroplane wings
And my father flew off, his white dress trailing
Like smoke in the sky, all the lovely stitches dropping,

Dropping, like silver threads on the dark red land.

The wood father

JACKIE KAY

His hands were bark, his hair was leaves,
He stood tall and dark amongst the trees.
His arms waved in the wind, 'Hello', 'Goodbye';
Words fluttered like birds from his eaves.

I couldn't tell if he loved me or not –
His eyes were darker than his barking hands –
Nor if he wanted to meet again
In the dark forest, in the old red land.

His daughters, his sons, he would not name
Or speak of them or anything they had done.
And when the rain fell down in the rainy season,
He got up and moved across the forest floor

Like a tree from Shakespeare; dragging his roots
All the way from Abuja to Enugu,
In the dead of night into the red of dawn.
Before he left, he gave me a name – Umeoja;

And I didn't point a twig or a finger.

Things fall apart

JACKIE KAY

My birth father lifted his hands above his head
And put the white mask of God on his handsome face.

A born-again man now, gone were the old tribal ways,
The ancestral village – African chief's nonsense, he says.

I could see his eyes behind the hard alabaster.
A father, no more real, still less real – not Wole Soyinka.

Less flesh than dark earth; less blood than red dust.
Less bone than Kano camels; less like me than Chinua Achebe.

Christianity had scrubbed his black face with a hard brush.
'You are my past sin, let us deliberate on new birth.'

The sun slips and slides, and finally sinks
Into the swimming pool in Nico hotel, Abuja; lonely pinks.

I knock back my dry spritzer, take in the songs
Of African birds. I think he had my hands, my father.

African masks

JACKIE KAY

ONE, FERTILITY MASK

Make me a baby Father – I saw you help the Sister here.
Make a baby before the end of the rainy season.
Hold my belly, here; talk my baby into coming.
Let me sing my baby a sweet song till morning.

You have a good face; your eyes see my longing.
Give me a boy who will see through holes in his chest.
I will dress him in a fibre dress and feed him my spirit.
When the bird eats the millet, it will fall down and die.

The fire will light itself and the bird will cook slowly.
Four trees will grow in the place I fall with child.
Feed me some sheep's liver; I will give it to my baby.
Open the earth for me; give the moon eyes to see me.

Father, don't let me lose my way; hear me.
The leopard pursues its prey. Morning breaks a day.
Give me a baby father before I break my heart.
Let me be with child, Father, before I am torn apart.

TWO, MEDICINE MAN

My father puts on his healing mask,
Smells of cardamom and eucalyptus
Rise from the carved wood.
'Heal me! Heal me!' I say softly.

He jumps up and kneels at my feet.
I can see his eyes through the mask.
He cooks words in a clay pot,
rubs them roughly into my forehead.
He shakes my head back and forth.
'You can walk through fire, you won't be burnt.
You can be tossed into the angry seas,
You won't drown. Don't even bother with
your hotel safe. You are protected.'
His hand covers my face. I can't breathe.
He takes off his healing mask and replaces
with the father mask. 'Those were the beer-
drinking days. All the women loved me.'
A bird, a beautiful bird, lands on the table
And flies off. My father eats his hot pepper soup.
'All the women loved me. All the women loved me.
I played in a band. Scotland was lovely fun.
None of my children are dullards.
You are evidence of my past sin.
You have my genes.' One mask is on the table.
The waitress clears it up with the empty plates.
My father flies off. I say the words over again:
I can walk through fire. I won't get burnt.
I can get tossed into angry seas.
I won't drown. All the women love me.

THREE, RUBBER GIRL

I am made from the sticky resin of the rubber tree.
The spider that called me bastard child stuck to me.
I have a beautiful long neck, lovely large breasts.
When you insult me, I hold you tighter.

When you say I am the illegitimate child of low parents,
I kiss your cheeks, rub your back, whisper sweet things.
There is nothing you can do to me.
I am made from the sticky resin of the rubber tree.
All the men stick to me. I hold them tightly.

FOUR, AKWEKE

And oh what a glorious sight –
the water people that night!
I was the first to witness
The man slide into a woman's dress.
I saw the wild dancing –
Grinding, swaying, twirling,
Even the water was whirling
in the muddy flat land.
Oh they were lifting hands in the air
Shaking the hips, feet bare,
They were dancing in the dark.
I saw a pregnant woman with a penis
Hidden behind her back. The whites of my eyes
Were shining. The stars were singing.
The moon was a big drum in the sky.
The birds were singing like Ali Farka Toure.
Women with big headdress,
the wind billowing their costume dress,
moved their bellies to the music.
Down by the water, even the boats were
changing – before my eyes – boats
Into fish, then birds. Oh my.
Nobody looking at all surprised.
I am the first on earth to see.

I have seen people change before my eyes.
I have seen women change into men.
I have seen men change into women.
I have seen all this under the African skies.

Acknowledgement: 'A white African dress', 'The wood father', 'Things fall apart' and 'African masks' were first published in Kay J, *Life Mask*, Newcastle Upon Tyne: Bloodaxe Books, 2005.

Pathan and *puri*

VERONICA DEWAN

This is an extract from a work in progress, about my experiences of meeting my biological father and his family.

1989, Southampton Row, London

'Look up – higher, near the roof, leaning out from the fourth floor window, surely you can see her? Now she's waving, she's beckoning us. Yes, that's her, that's my Indian grandmother.' Dave follows my gaze. 'So you found her, finally.' 'Not only have I found her but she cooks my favourite *puri* and potato curry.'

My Indian grandmother is here for one month. It is her annual visit to Jatender, her son, a solicitor who lives alone and, while she is here, sleeps alone. At the start of each visit, he is full of hope and promises to turn over a new leaf, to abstain from alcohol, tobacco and not to gamble. It is his mother's discipline that will help him to wake early each morning and go to the office, the firm of solicitors where he is consultant and I am his PA. I should start at 9 a.m., but I'm usually ten or 15 minutes late. He is confident he will arrive there before me. For two days, he makes the effort and is irritated by my tardiness. 'Can't you ever arrive on time?' Then, 'It's been two days of hell', as he slams down another file on the desk. 'I'm like a prisoner in my own home.'

Two weeks have passed and now he waits until his mother is asleep before slipping out to the casino in Russell Square, eventually stumbling home around five in the morning and sleeping all day.

My grandmother says I can call her *Baaji*, like her other grandchildren do. This tiny woman in her eighties with angina and arthritis, her eyesight impaired by cataracts, gives me huge warm hugs and almost pulls my cheeks off my face to kiss me. I met her for the first time in 1986. I was with my Asian partner who had trained me to show deference to my elders by touching their feet but, as I stooped down, *Baaji* grabbed my arms and pulled me up. 'No dear, no. I not like it, no more.'

We are on the fourth floor of Cranfield House. I lead Dave from the lift through the front door of number 26. It opens into a cramped hallway, humming with traffic sounds from the street below. A shaft of light from the living room illuminates *Baaji* as she steps from the kitchen, and I am suddenly flushed with excitement as I'm about to introduce my Indian grandmother to a dear friend. Her tiny hand pumps his as she peers up over his ribcage. She speaks a little English but understands a lot; it is her sixth language after Pashtu, Punjabi, Urdu, Hindi and Sanskrit.

Before I can say their names, my father, in indigo and white-striped dressing gown, bursts from the bedroom, his eyes thunderous. 'How dare you bring strange men home without my permission.' Lurching forward, his hand is raised to strike my cheek, but *Baaji* wedges herself between us and barks at him in Punjabi. I hover at her shoulder as she pummels his tassle-belted pot belly and propels him back into the bedroom. She slams the door shut, slumps back against it and sighs. With a jolt, as though waking from deep sleep, she glances down, adjusts her powder blue silk sari at the pleats, flips her expression like a coin and swishes forward, extending her hand once more. My voice is taut and unfamiliar as I introduce them, 'Dr David, meet Dr Satyavati.'

'Aah, so happy to meet dear friend of Veronica, please forgive Jatender, my son, he not well, all today, yesterday, and before. Please dear, take your guest to sit and drink. Soon we eat.' She seems to melt back into the kitchen while Dave kneels, struggling to undo his shoe-laces, finally placing black brogues next to my red mules on the shoe rack behind the door.

We are in the living room and, since *Baaji*'s arrival two weeks ago, no trace or trail of ash or new burns on the carpet, no drink stains on the table. I pour Dave a large scotch, adding cubes from the ice bucket, freshly filled. I should let go of the tumbler, but instead I take a huge gulp from his glass. 'Welcome to my family.' I fumble to fill a fresh tumbler with Teachers. He takes the bottle from me.

Why did I have to walk through Queen Square on my way to Southampton Row? I was on my way to see *Baaji*. She wanted to speak to me urgently; I was to go straight there after work; I had to help her persuade Jatender to get out of bed. I was preoccupied; another shit day at the office; secretaries pouring over tabloid reports about a murderer who allegedly killed his adoptive parents for their money. 'God, how can you ever trust these people?', 'And after all they did for him!' 'They might look sweet when they're babies but they turn into monsters sooner or later.'

I had avoided seeing friends since I started to work for Jatender. I no longer knew if my past ever really existed and I didn't know how to explain the present. I felt foolish. Having chosen to search for my biological parents, I had waded in too far, was out of my depth, and now had to deal with an increasingly confused and fragmented identity. Yet, here before me was a dear friend. As I stepped into Cosmos Place, we collided, Dave about to go into the Queen's Larder for a quiet pint.

'My grandmother is preparing fresh *puri* with potato curry at this very moment.' I knew when he heard the word "*puri*", I would get his attention. It was my old school friend Dawn, and Dave, her partner, who introduced me to *puri* at Diwana restaurant in Drummond Street, who took me shopping for fresh ginger and coriander, and showed me the essential ingredients to make a great curry. *Puri*? Near here?'

I tried to present a happy *puri* story. 'My grandmother, she's visiting from India, and I know you love *puri*, why don't you come with me?'

Suddenly, the past stepped into the present as we turned the corner into Southampton Row, in dapples of shade and light, and, weaving through the crowds of happy tourists jostling with grumpy office workers, I spotted my grandmother leaning at the kitchen window four floors up, to the right of the Bedford Hotel. I tried to get her attention as taxis, buses, cars and bikes streamed past. It would be at least another decade before the arrival of bicycle rickshaws.

'Please wave; you're so tall, she'll notice your blonde hair.' Dave, who was normally quite reserved, had gathered such enthusiasm that his white-sleeved waves attracted bus passengers who waved back and, by now, my grandmother had seen us and her hands were wings beckoning us both to fly above the traffic to join her.

I couldn't begin to tell you what was real and what was imagined, so little made sense. Like, in 1985, when Jatender's lover rang my grandmother in New Delhi in the middle of the night to tell her about 'the imposter in polyester', a woman who was pretending to be his daughter, a fraudster after his money. It was the very first time *Baaji* had heard of my existence. I would have to admit to you about the yellow and white *shalwar kameez* I bought in Southall, a bad choice when set against accusations flowing from one who wears only silk and cashmere and gold.

'I'm sorry about . . . about your drink.'

'I would have done the same.'
'You're not the stranger.'

In 1982, I had just returned from my first trip to India where I had gone in search of
Jatender. I was given an address in New Delhi that another friend, Alastair, had
found for me in the records at Middle Temple. Jatender originally came to London
on a Nehru Scholarship to study law and, after being called to the Bar in 1962, he
had returned to India. But I didn't find him in New Delhi; he had come back to live
in London. I had become ill in India with suspected typhoid and, on arriving back in
England, I was whisked into an Isolation Unit for seven days.

'Remember the Hospital for Tropical Diseases?' Dave chuckles. 'How could I forget?
Dawn was phoning the lab, disguising her identity, monitoring the results of your
bowel movements!' Dave and Dawn visited me every evening after work while I was
in captivity; they would change into sterile white suits, masks, caps . . . It was surreal.

Dave interrupts his sip, carefully guiding the tumbler down on to the square,
smoked-glass coffee table, his eyes scanning the bookcases stuffed with law books,
the silk wall hangings, floor to ceiling windows and french doors leading to the
narrow balcony overlooking the garden.

'My father . . .' I pause as a violent snore from the next room rocks the wall behind
us. Luckily, the snore subsides and the wall sighs with relief. 'Finally, you meet the
man I've been searching for all my life.'
'Umm, yes. But would this be the moment you finally notice that most of us have
been trying to get away from our families all our lives?'
'God, I'm glad you're here.' He has borne witness to the crumbling of all my
certainties.

Dave empties his glass, stretches his arms along the black leather sofa, one of two
bulky shapes in the L-shaped room, and glances across to the dining table with its
stern brass legs, dining chairs with matching frames and padded blue, leaf-patterned
seats. His eyes rest on the photograph hanging in a silver frame on the wall behind
the table.

'That's my grandfather, Dr Tegpal Chand Dewan. He's dead now.'
'You didn't meet him?'
I shake my head. 'It's the drink. It got his father, now it's got his son.'

'Is Jatender not having treatment?'
'He says he doesn't have a problem.'

It's the moment for Dave to get up and pour himself another scotch and one for me.
He presses the tumbler into my hand. I want to knock it back in one but I set it
down. 'I can't. If Jatender comes in and sees me drinking whisky he'll hit the roof.
It's a respect thing. I mustn't smoke or drink in front of elders. That's why he's out
all night. But he keeps a supply of Teachers and Benson & Hedges under the bed. I
top them up for him.'

'So you're colluding with him.'
'Am I?'

I hear the kitchen door open and a burst of cumin fills the air. *Baaji* needs me to
bring the dishes through. I stand up. 'Dave, you once lent me *A Short Walk in the
Hindu Kush* by Eric Newby.' Dave nods. 'Did you give it back?'
'Yes, of course I did.'
'It's just that my grandmother was born in North West Frontier Province.'
He looks up. 'You're not a Pathan are you?'
'I don't know.'
'My God, if I'd known you were a Pathan . . .'
'What about it?'
'Tell me more.'

Baaji is at the door. 'Please come. Your guest, my dear, he has drink?'
'Yes, he's fine. It's OK.' *Baaji* pats the flat yellow disks into shape in her palms, then
throws them one by one into the pan of hot oil and immediately they are
transformed into golden puffs of *puri*, the shape of flying saucers. She places them
on a stainless steel platter while I spoon the fragrant potato curry from the saucepan
into a deep white serving dish. I take the dishes to the table set for two.

Baaji comes through to replenish our plates and claps in delight at the sight of Dave
tearing the bread and squishing potato into the pocket he has made between fingers
and thumb. He always eats Indian food with his hands; tried to teach me but I've
never perfected the art. I'm too clumsy.
'Doctor David, you most welcome to come to Delhi, stay in my house for some
time?'
'Thank you, I would love to come one day, but will you not join us now?'

'No, today I am cook, in kitchen. I like very much to cook for my son, my grandchildren, and for dear friend of Veronica.'
'Dave likes to cook curries too, *Baaji*.'

Baaji clasps her hands together. 'Then next time, in Delhi, Dr David you cook my kitchen.' I know that won't happen. Even if Dave were to visit her, *Baaji*'s cook would never allow a guest in the kitchen. I tried it once when I was there, and it was definitely out of bounds.

A roar from the bedroom becomes a regular rumble; Jatender is still asleep. I clear the dishes from the table and take them to the kitchen. *Baaji* leans on the windowsill, the space even more crowded now by the evening traffic heading for Covent Garden and the South Bank. I touch her shoulder and she's wiping her eyes and puts on her glasses and turns towards me. 'Veronica, you try understand him, you talk to him. He sick man, but he will listen, forgive him the past. Please dear. Please come for him in the morning, take him to office.'

'I can't do that.' She doesn't know I go home each night, knock myself out with wine to get to sleep, that I've run out of excuses for his absences, that I've started taking anti-depressants, that I spend half the day in the office loo, shaking and throwing up.

'You can. You Dewan, you strong woman.' I have no strength, all wrung out, nothing to give. 'You strong like your *Baaji*. I understand you. My mother died as I was born. We are not alone. Remember the ancestors. You warrior, you fighter, you Pathan.'

My grandmother's hands that have wrested thousands of foetuses from the brief sanctuary of the womb are clamped on my shoulders, hands so small yet so strong, her steel gaze fixed on my flooding eyes. 'Please, Veronica, be strong woman, don't cry, don't cry.'

I visited *Baaji* once more that summer; she was exhausted and in a lot of pain. I massaged her feet. When she returned to India, I was heading for a breakdown. I took two weeks off work and Dave and his new partner generously scooped me up and took me with them on holiday to France. When I returned from the trip, I immediately resigned as Jatender's PA. He was bathed in sunshine outside the Bedford Hotel. 'But I had such hopes for us, Dewan and Daughter. I promise you, Veronica, I will stop drinking, but only you can help me now.'

'I can't do this, you have to help yourself, go to AA.' Then I went home, got drunk and so sick I couldn't get out of bed for two weeks. That autumn, I commenced my law degree.

I received a letter from my dear friend, Indu Jain, in New Delhi, dated 14 January 1990:

As promised, I have been to Dr Satyavati's home with best wishes for a New Year. She was up and alert, but in pain. She has a tumour in her liver, a suspected cancer for which she will be soon operated. It was very cold in Delhi last week, hence her operation was postponed. It's sad that you had to cut off from your father. Your grandmother was full of praises for you. I don't know how true they were, but she was happy amidst her three sons and daughter looking after her.

December 1986, New Delhi

My only visit to the family home in Ring Road. I am staying with my friends, the Jains. *Baaji* sends a driver to collect me, insists I stay with her instead. I am introduced to immediate and extended family members as Dr Satyavati's grandson's godsister. The moment I arrive, she leads me into the living room, locks the door and presses a burgundy pouch into my hand. The pouch contains a pair of delicate pendant earrings, each earring composed of two gold circles – one large, one small – inlaid with a central pearl and outer circle of tiny seed pearls. Then she pulls me onto her lap and feeds me yoghurt with honey.

Baaji died in the Spring of 1990. Jatender died the following summer. Their ashes are scattered in the Ganges at Haridwar.

6

Life stories

Black hole No. 17,438, 24 February 2004

DEBORAH WEYMONT

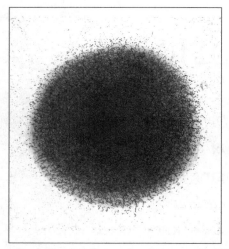

Exhibited in '. . . living with loss . . .' by Deborah Weymont at Our Place, Bristol, 22–26 March 2004

I was born on April 3rd 1956. My Mother breastfed me for seven weeks and six days. On May 28th 1956 I was placed in a children's home. In the words of another care survivor, 'It felt like I had been thrown out of this world.' Sometimes it feels like I have spent the last 47 years, 38 weeks and six days trying to get back in.

This etching represents the number of days that I have been living with that loss. There is a comfort in the mathematical certainty of dates and of counting days. It is a way of placing order on chaos. It is a way of making sense of the world.

Black sheep

KYM COOPER

'Brown girl in the ring'

For as long as I can remember, I have always felt different from the other members of my family, both in my physical and spiritual being. My parents were always honest about my adoption and, from an early age, I asked questions about why I was a different colour to them. At home, as an infant, I distinctly remember being in a warm and loving environment; yet, when I entered the outside world I received cold and hostile responses from the community around me. My natural mother gave birth to me at the age of 14, so I was placed in a children's home as a baby. I have no memory of her, except I do remember crying for her sometimes in the middle of the night. I was fostered during my infant years by a married couple who already had an adopted young boy.

They eventually adopted me, at five years old, and a huge family celebration took place in our household. I can remember being a playful, sociable and happy child until I went to nursery school. At home, I enjoyed playing games with my brother and loved the security of my new parents. I never wanted for anything and enjoyed many family holidays abroad. The area I grew up in was on the outskirts of Birmingham, in a leafy suburb; within a short distance you could walk to the countryside. There were plenty of farms and parks around to play in.

When I started nursery school, I clearly remember the hostile attitude of my playmates. None of them ever wanted to hold my hand in 'Ring a ring o' roses' and I remember them holding my cardigan sleeve rather than holding my hand. Some children were quite curious about my physical differences and would touch my Afro hair and comment that it was like touching cotton wool. Other children in the street on the way home would ask if I was from Australia or Africa, and would quite literally just stare at me as I walked past them. At times, I used to feel like a bit of a freak show with all the unwanted attention I received.

It did not take long for the children to start saying what they saw and calling me "Blackie". The boys in the school were particularly cruel and would constantly taunt me about my appearance. Unsurprisingly, I was never the girl chased during Kiss

Chase! Over time, this affected my self-esteem and I became withdrawn and isolated. I did not want to play with the other children and I sank into a deep depression. Although the bullying got worse, the teachers did very little to put things right or punish the perpetrators.

My parents tried their best, but they had difficulties relating to just how painful these comments were and how traumatic school was. To me it was living hell. They told me to ignore it. Even my own brother would sometimes comment on my "wide nose" and tease me that it was too big. I absorbed Western beauty ideals, which are geared towards long blonde hair and blue eyes. The most popular girls at school had these attributes; the Hollywood stars reflected this, and even my Barbie doll sported this look too. I was, however, lucky that a friend of the family brought me a black baby doll that I cherished and from whom I became inseparable.

Far from having long blonde hair, I had short nappy Afro hair and often got mistaken for a boy. I would wrap a towel around my head and pretend that I had long blonde hair like the girl in the *Timotei* advert. I would pray to God every night that I could be white and fit in with my family. I quite literally used to avoid looking in the mirror because I could not stand what I saw staring back at me. I hated that it was me who stood out in pictures. People would always ask for explanations about our family set-up. I cannot put into words the type of crippling emotional pain that I felt in my childhood that led me to several suicide attempts. I took pills and tried to strangle myself with one of my dolls' dresses.

When it came to bullying, on occasions my parents did intervene and go to the school and speak to the teachers, and they confronted the mum of the boy who called me "Nigger". I did not understand what it meant at the time, and innocently asked my parents why I was called that. My older brother also stuck up for me several times. My mum did eventually take me to black hairdressers in an inner-city area, to have my hair plaited in extensions with beads on the end. I could see the fear in her face as we walked through a black neighbourhood, and I remember her squeezing my hand tightly.

I was lucky in that respect, that a few times a year my hair looked nice. My mum always dressed me up in lovely clothes and made me feel feminine. My hair was such a big issue, though, as it was always the springboard for conflict. Having it combed was so painful as the comb tore through my tight curls. Taking the braids out was unbearable; my mum did not know how to take cane rows out, so she literally tore them out with her hands. I felt like I was being punished for my physical differences and, understandably, I developed a loathing for my hair.

The only black people I saw on television were either African "savages" in films, entertainers, or criminals in the news. I couldn't comprehend the relationship between Africa and me, as I felt English. Academically, at school I was bottom of the class at everything. I could not concentrate, I was in a constant state of confusion and I was too scared to put my hand up in class. Teachers had very low expectations of me and steered me towards sports. My dad would talk fondly about black athletes and encourage me to represent Britain one day.

Teenage rebellion

The transition from cute little black girl into threatening black youth became evident as I entered adolescence. The hostile environment that I had experienced at previous schools manifested itself further at secondary school. My first day there was intimidating as I walked to school past the local shops and pupils shouted, 'What's this, an invasion?' I walked up the hill, shaking with fear, towards the school gates and heard taunts of racial abuse. The school gates were plastered with graffiti images of swastikas and National Front logos. These first impressions were just a taste of what was to come.

My school overlooked a rough white council estate, which was also home to the local headquarters of the BNP (British National Party). A large number of boys at the school were either related to or associated with local bigots who despised anyone who was not *purely* white. There was even a girl I can remember who was white but just had a tinge of olive in her complexion and dark hair. She forever had to prove her "whiteness" to them. When the bells rang for breaktime, instead of feeling relieved my heart sank with fear of what would unfold next. I would walk down the corridor and skinheads with green bomber jackets and army boots would spit at me. If I accidentally brushed past them in class, they would act like I was contaminated with a deadly disease as it repulsed them that a black person had come into contact with them. I remember they would say I resembled a gorilla and tell me to go back to the jungle where I belonged. I had absolutely no ammunition to defend myself with; I could only hang my head in shame. Kids were just starting to form romantic relationships, and I did not enter into that equation.

Thankfully, in my second year at school, a new girl started who was Indian. We instantly bonded and kind of rescued each other. We became best friends for many years and, although she could not teach me directly about black culture, she did introduce me to various black music styles, which was a significant change from heavy metal! I learned a great deal from her, simply by having a friend to relate to who was not white, but was also someone with a rich culture to be proud of.

The year 1995 saw the arrival of a significant number of black pupils in the year below. There were about ten altogether, which in our school was very visible. I was scared of them and, being totally honest, I was an honorary white who felt superior to them. One of them asked me if my jerry curls were natural and I lied and said they were, in a snooty manner. She took a dislike to me from then on and all her friends bullied me for being a "coconut". Now I had to deal with being too black for whites and too white for black people. I was totally torn and my schoolwork suffered. I was bottom of the class at everything and this gave the bullies even more ammunition: "Thick nigger". When I complained to the school and my parents, I was told that I was exaggerating and that I should get on with my work. People would say that I blamed everything on my colour. I used to feel like I was going insane, as the racism was crystal clear to me.

At home, my mother was forever complaining that the perm activator in my hair was getting on the sofa and causing stains. She forbade me to sit on the sofas in the lounge so I spent a lot of time alone in my bedroom. This made me feel like even more of an outsider and deepened my self-hatred. My white brother was academically gifted and he got into grammar school. I could barely multiply or spell. Lack of understanding towards racism alienated me more. There was a common assumption within the community that black people are a threat.

The arguments spiralled and the emotional despair exploded. At 13, I completely changed into a rebellious monster and acted out my inner turmoil, answering the bullies back and being cheeky towards teachers. I figured, if you can't beat them join them, and ended up being lap dog to the in-crowd that I had previously been excluded from. I went from being a quiet good girl, to unwittingly playing into their stereotypes. I was challenged to a fight by one of the black bullies and I finally accepted. After losing the fight, I was suspended from school and in deep trouble at home. I ran away from home several times and put my parents through hell. They threatened to send me back to the children's home.

I began drinking alcohol and losing control. One of my teachers told me that I was not doing myself any favours, being black, and that I was behaving ungratefully after my adoptive parents adopted me. There was one positive teacher who spotted my talent for English and tried to nurture it. He told me he had black friends and stuck up for me when I was bullied whilst the other teachers turned a blind eye. My mother eventually came into school to see the headteacher about the bullying and he said to her, 'What do you expect? If a Chinese pupil walks down the corridor they will say "Chink"!' My mum was speechless, and to me the headteacher's attitude confirmed the institutionalised racism breeding through the school.

I desperately wanted to be considered as attractive so, at 14, one of my friends introduced me to a girl who could plait hair extensions. I picked it up very quickly and never took them out. Gradually I began getting contradictory compliments, like 'You're beautiful . . . for a black girl.'

I eventually left school with no GCSEs and limited prospects. After hearing the black girls at school speaking in patois, I developed a curiosity about my own culture.

Universal opening

During that summer, I spent a weekend at my friend's flat following an argument with my parents. Whilst I was sleeping, in the middle of the night, a bright golden aura of light surrounded the room. I looked up fully conscious and saw the silhouette of a person like a religious painting. The person had feathered wings made up of tiny individual feathers. The entity alarmed me, as I did not believe in ghosts and I'm not religious. I eventually told someone, who explained it could be my guardian angel. From that moment on in my life, things seemed to gradually change for the better.

After leaving school, I enrolled in a local college to re-sit my GCSEs. At the college there were plenty of black people but I was intimidated by them and felt conscious of my accent. I asked my mum about patois and she said that the only black language she knew of was 'Ya Mon!'. My dad reinforced this ignorance by explaining that black people did not have a culture. I knew this was not true because, if my best friend had an Indian culture, then black people must have one too.

I soon gained a reputation at college as being a coconut and the majority of the black students there resented me. I had plenty of other friends that I got on well with but again, they were all white and I was forever pulling them up on their racist assumptions. I was always accused of being too sensitive and they believed that they could define what is considered as racist, even though it was my race on the receiving end! I became friends with an African girl who was also transracially adopted, and we became thick as thieves. Later, I discovered black hair and beauty magazines and slowly began to learn the basics of Afro hair care. I was hooked on the Naomi-style human hair weaves, which I modelled on images in the media. My hair simply fuelled further hostility from black students, who said I wanted to be white. The good thing about me discovering the hair and beauty magazines though, was that they featured aspiring black professionals who represented to me positive role models. *Pride* magazine always had a section on black history too.

Although I did not pass all of my GCSE re-takes, I was determined throughout my studies to succeed and get into university. Despite the comments from teachers that university was an unlikely option, I proved them wrong and another college accepted me with my qualifications. After two years studying there, I gained sufficient qualifications to get a university place, but before I left a teacher suggested to me that I should have a dyslexia assessment.

At university, there were quite a few black girls who, on first impressions, I assumed would not accept me. After a few nights out and parties at the Student Union, though, we became friends. We covered modules on "Race and Empire". I learned about colonialism and began to understand where the racial myths came from and how it benefited white people to keep them alive today. I became fully accustomed to R 'n' B music and got my first taste of Caribbean food. There were times when I would be in the toilets feeling devastated that I had missed out on all of this earlier. I was terrified of it being found out that I was not "properly" black. I went to so many parties and drank so much that, unfortunately, I did not get the grades to get into the second year. On my twenty-first birthday, I had a party and we hired Caribbean cooks for canapés. For my birthday present, I went on holiday with one of the girls to Brooklyn, New York. Her uncle was a doctor over there and it was my first taste of living with a black family. It was great, and Brooklyn was rich with black culture.

On my return to England, I was accepted onto a place at a university in Manchester. I made a conscious decision to work very hard. I was diagnosed as dyslexic and all the appropriate support was given. I moved into an inner-city area that was predominantly black. I found this quite a culture shock and felt like an outsider. In the evenings I went and studied black history at one of the universities. We covered slavery, Pan-Africanism and the early black presence in the UK.

Slowly I began to become enlightened and, as if by fate, one day, whilst working at a bar in the city centre, there was a private function upstairs for an organisation called After Adoption. I asked one of the organisers for more information and confided in her about my experience. She was a beautiful Asian lady and admitted to me that she was also transracially adopted. She informed me of a support group being set up. Months later, I began attending and we discussed at great length the complex issues surrounding loss and separation and our experiences of growing up. I found this counselling priceless and I honestly don't think I could have got through that point in my life without it. For the first time ever, I could relate to black people who had been through exactly the same experience, and I realised that I was not alone.

Emancipation

In my final year at university, I began a print journalism module where you had to write a local interest story. I approached the Manchester Caribbean Carnival and arranged an interview with the carnival director. The office is based in the notorious Moss Side area and as I walked through, I was terrified of getting shot! I feel ashamed reflecting on this now, as I know better. Those stories in the media do have a powerful effect on your perceptions.

When I entered the office, the carnival director greeted me and encouraged me to use my article for their magazine. I found that being given this opportunity enabled me to be judged on my personality and how I could contribute my creative skills, instead of by my skin colour. Writing for the carnival magazine forced me to communicate with diverse characters in the black community that I would normally feel threatened by. There was a Rastafarian poet whose thick Jamaican accent I had difficulty understanding. There were Caribbean descendants of different generations and various islands who came to the office to socialise and organise events. By sitting amongst them, I absorbed so much cultural information that is far too complex to put into words. I met so many lively characters as well as serious academics and professionals. It made me realise there is not just one type of mystical blackness to be measured up against. Black people are as diverse as any other group.

I felt that the black community welcomed me with open arms and I embraced them. I accepted a job as a researcher on a black radio station, which gave me the opportunity to understand and get to know black people better. I slowly began to discover that, among Caribbeans, there are small but significant cultural differences depending on which island you are from. I was given the opportunity to meet workshop leaders, writers, dancers, DJs, costume makers, troop leaders and carnival committee members. One of the workshop leaders I met was teaching Egyptian symbol writing and he taught me that the Egyptians were actually black. He told me where to buy black history books from an Afrocentric perspective. The ironic thing was that he was transracially adopted too.

It was a relief to finally understand the concept of carnival and all the colourful carnival characters. I had never participated in a carnival before and could not wait to experience my first one. Through my work at the radio station, I met many new friends whom I will always cherish. I finally found belonging and acceptance. I became close friends with one of the DJs I worked alongside and we went to the carnival together. The day was a roaring success and I felt so much pride in black people. I now felt half way towards being a fully-fledged, fully conscious black woman and deep down I knew I had only touched the surface, as there would be plenty more to come! Later on in the summer, I went to Notting Hill carnival for the first time. I also discovered I had graduated in TV and Radio with a 2:1 degree.

Motherland

December 2003 saw my very first visit to the Caribbean Islands. A Caribbean friend asked if I wanted to stay with her for three weeks over Christmas. It was a dream come true. This would be my first proper taste of real Caribbean living as an islander with my people.

When we stepped off the plane, I immediately felt like I was coming home. We landed in Antigua and had to get a ferry to Monseratt. I could smell fresh sea air and had an overwhelming sense of delight when I saw the palm trees swaying. I raced down the stairs of the plane screaming in excitement and other passengers looked at me puzzled. I didn't care, as my spirit had been set free. I recall embracing the hot climate as we stepped into a taxi. Bashmant music was booming on the radio and we sped past countless black people! There were traditional Caribbean houses, authentic shops and Rastafarians chilling as we drove along a dusty road. The cooling Caribbean climate brushed past me, along with an intense feeling of belonging. I was finally in the majority and it took me so long to adjust. There were banks, courts, museums and schools, all run by black people.

The next day, my friend woke me up to show me the beautiful view of her island from our balcony. Monseratt is described as the Emerald of the Caribbean and I could see why. Clear blue skies were reflected in the glistening sea. The golden energy of the sun moved slowly towards the clear ocean, leaving an illuminated trail across the water. I was hypnotised by the dancing waves, effortlessly creating ripples in the marine. The Atlantic skyline was endless as the ocean surrounded us on this tropical island. I could hear chickens and goats on the farm next door. The island is mountainous, full of luscious greenery and vibrant flowers. A sense of calmness soothed me; I felt closer to nature and truly in Paradise. We both realised that, for three weeks, we were outside of the rat race and it would be blissful.

During my holiday, I had relaxed weekends out in island bars and nightclubs. Gradually, I gained confidence dancing to soca music. My friend introduced me to her family and we had special moments cooking for everyone. At times I did find it hard to understand patois, as it's spoken much thicker than in England. I had to ask people to slow down! My friend taught me various recipes and introduced me to her loved ones. I saw some beautiful scenery, including a volcano area. Our house was overlooked by a tall and steep forest on a mountain that we ended up climbing. Spending Christmas in the Caribbean was unique and very special. We spent our last week in St Kitts with her uncle, which was enchanting too as I experienced carnival in the Caribbean for the first time. I was so fortunate to get a glimpse of three different islands.

On New Year's day, we ate a traditional Caribbean festival meal. Plates were filled with plantain, pulses, banana fritters, grilled fish, goat meat, green banana and rice and peas. I could not fasten up my trousers, let alone go "on de road" to follow the procession! Eventually we caught up with the celebrations and it was one of the best days of my whole life. The costumes were breathtaking, full of imagination and oozing with carnival glamour. There were amazing entertainers and dancers. Me not being one of them I attempted to mimic moves, but my hips just were not accustomed to winding! Many of the little girls put me to shame, with slick rhythmic moves, although my Western eyes did find some of the gyrating a little too erotic for girls so young. The atmosphere was so uplifting and you did not need to drink alcohol to feel intoxicated with joy. A sea of faces and colours danced across the streets, following the floats, as the music embellished the spirit of the island. My first taste of the Caribbean went way beyond my expectations and fulfilled all my dreams.

It isn't like on *Surprise, Surprise*!

For as long as I can remember, I always had an awareness that I wanted to trace my natural family. Whilst growing up, I was often gripped by the reunions shown on the television show *Surprise, Surprise*. The programme triggered fantasies about what my reunion could be like. Once I left university, I decided to pursue my search. I was lucky to have a friend in London and a professional adoption adviser to show me how to begin. After many failed attempts at putting advertisements in newspapers, a lady I approached in Handsworth knew my aunty and passed my number on to her.

On a dark October night, I was at home and the phone rang. My flatmate passed over the phone. A voice said, 'Hello, is that Kym? Are you related to me? Are you my sister's daughter?' I replied, 'Yes'. We were both delighted and she explained that my birth mother would be pleased I made contact. She told me a little about my family and explained that she would pass my number on to her sister.

I took a relaxing bath to calm down. I walked into my bedroom and I had loads of missed calls. I retrieved the messages and heard a voice saying, 'Hi Kym, it's your mum.' I felt instantly disappointed and astounded that she had the audacity to say, 'It's your mum' . . . after 24 years! It freaked me out, a total stranger saying that. I called back and she explained that everyone knew about me and that I have a huge family. It was a lot to take in, with all the names and locations they inhabited throughout the UK. To my amazement she said that I had a brother and, before I had a chance to grasp this, she passed him over. It was an overwhelming surprise.

She asked me what I looked like and if I was fair like her. She said she felt proud that I had a degree and thought I must be clever. I asked if dyslexia ran in the family and she replied, 'You didn't get that from our side, but your uncle is a bit slow!' I bit my tongue in disbelief. The surrealism of the events unfolding consumed me. I was both excited and scared, relieved that she did not reject me. I had to lay down the rule that I would not refer to her as "Mum", out of respect for my adoptive mother. As she relaxed into conversation, she persistently probed me to answer personal questions which I found a little intrusive from a stranger. Eventually, we arranged a meeting in London. She mentioned that she had tried to find me but did not know my surname. Until this night, my family had always been a dark, mystical illusion.

When I reached London, my eyes rapidly searched around the coach station for her and my heart raced. A plump lady walked towards me with bright blue eye make-up and pink lipstick. She asked if I was Kym and I said, 'Yes'. She gave me a big hug and said she thought I was beautiful. I know this should have touched me but I froze. The woman I had fantasised about for years as being this aspiring professional black woman whom I would look up to was relatively ordinary. Throughout the day, she tried desperately hard to liken us but I felt we could not be more different. My middle-class eyes quickly detected the obvious social differences. At her house she showed me family photos and I remained distant, with fake smiles. The whole day was unreal and a great deal to take in. She told me that she had not kept any photos of me as a baby. She also spared me no details about attempting to have me aborted and refused to tell me my father's name. She expressed little tact and I simply could not relate to her life experiences. She is a born-again Christian and had religious pictures all over her walls. I felt horrified when people said that we looked alike, as all those self-image issues of ugliness came flooding back to haunt me.

In the last few hours of the visit, I met my brother whom I warmed towards. When it was time to go back she accompanied me to the coach station, which I reluctantly agreed to. I knew straight away that it was not going to be a fairy tale. She is a nice woman who tried desperately hard. Unfortunately it's difficult to force loving feelings towards a stranger who abandoned you as a child.

Over a year later, I am still finding excuses not to see her. I have met up with my uncle, two aunties and Gran. I clicked with my cousins too. After writing a few letters to my birth mother, I found myself cross-examining her story on the circumstances surrounding my adoption. Many of her explanations contradict what my parents and the authorities say. I found on the phone that she was judgemental about my lifestyle and could not comprehend my lifestyle choices, belief system and aspirations. She believes that I should settle down and have children. I still have plenty of living to do and aim to pursue a career and to travel around the world.

When different life experiences come into play, mixed with family values, culture and social class, it is hard to find common ground. Shows like *Surprise, Surprise* help to create a myth that reunited families instantly bond, fall in love and live happily ever after. There is no guarantee that I will ever click with my birth mother, but at least now I know my roots and, to me, that is priceless. In the meantime, I am enjoying forming bonds with other birth relatives and building bridges with my adoptive family.

I do not regret my reunion as I now feel complete and fulfilled. I still do not fully relate to or identify with all black people, and some still don't accept me. I feel I've progressed leaps and bounds forward, though, whilst remaining true to myself. I refuse to be pigeon-holed into other people's expectations of me by conforming to lifestyle choices that clash with my upbringing and belief system. I am proud to be black, although black is not all that I am. My recipe for happiness comes from mixing an assortment of the best aspects from both cultural flavours to create a harmony from within.

Not quite belonging

TM

I was adopted at 14. I first went into care when I was about two. We (my older brothers and I) went back and forth a few times and I last saw "the birth mother" when I was about six. Whilst I was in care I was placed with two families – both white – and the second time was with the mother who later adopted my older brothers and me. I've been with her since I was three; I was adopted at 14 because my mum waited until we were all old enough to be asked.

I'm black; "the birth mother" is Jamaican. I've always lived around black people and see myself as one of them, but I don't feel like I'm a member of Britain's black community. This is who I am. I'm English by birth and, if push came to shove, I would refer to myself as being British but never as English. When it comes to international sporting events, I always support Jamaica or the West Indies but never England or team GB. Yet I don't see myself as Jamaican either.

Being born in this country doesn't necessarily make me feel like I belong or am part of this country. I do have a favourite version of the British national anthem though! "The Queen" can be found on Jimi Hendrix's *In the West* album. I do know that this duality is part of the immigrant experience in this country; it's just that mine might be more extreme than most. I feel that I live between two cultures but don't belong to either outright, but I know that you can "be black" in a million different ways and that there is no set formula. And that's why I celebrate being black and British by enjoying a version of the national anthem being played by a black American. It's recognisable and virtually the same song, but obviously very different at the same time.

I've always lived in south-east London, born in one borough thirty years ago and living in the neighbouring one ever since. In my adoptive family, I'm the youngest of three children and I've lived with my biological brothers all my life. But, in my original biological family, I'm actually the middle child or one of the middle children. In five years "the birth mother" gave birth to six children – three sets of twins – four boys and two girls! I'm the girl; my older brothers are a year-and-a-half older than me; my twin died when we were about nine weeks old. My younger brother is three-and-a-half years younger than me, his twin died in an accident when they were six. So the younger two went to one family and us older ones to another – I've always known my younger brothers – our families have always lived close to each other – but that relationship is not as close as my younger brother imagines it to be.

Ethnic diversity has always been a part of who I am. In school, we were never the only black or ethnic minority kids, but were probably the only ones who had a white parent to whom they were not biologically related. Between the ages of three and 11, my peers weren't really interested in this or the topic of "blackness"; these problems came later when I was at secondary school.

In nursery school, it wasn't an issue at all. At that age I knew I was different but that was because my home life seemed to be a bit more hectic than everyone else's. It wasn't until infant and junior school that the questions started and, the older I got, the more direct they tended to be – and not always from people I knew. My way of dealing with these questions was always to answer honestly and state the obvious. It was never a subject I talked to school friends about: they knew I had a white mum and that was that. The people who tended to ask were usually friends of my classmates or people I did sports with – not close friends. This intrusion often took place in the playground or on the way home from school. I was asked who that white woman was and I would answer that she was my mum. I would then be asked why my mum was white and I would answer because she was born like that. It wasn't the answer they were looking for but they soon realised that this was the only one they'd be getting.

It wasn't until secondary school that being black became more of an issue and having a white parent was only part of the problem. The further I got into the school system, the more racial divisions became an everyday thing, and they came from those least expected. The biggest problems existed amongst the black students. It wasn't a black and white issue but an "us against them" situation between the Caribbeans and the Africans. Being of Caribbean origin, I witnessed and experienced first hand the prejudice that existed within this group. When I see and hear it nowadays it disappoints but doesn't surprise me, but at the time I was confused by what was going on. As a child, I was taught about white racism and how to deal with it, but prejudice between black people came as a total surprise. At the heart of this conflict was what it meant to be black. According to the Caribbeans, if you were an African you just weren't black enough! They thought that the Africans believed they were superior because they hadn't been burdened with the legacy of slavery. They thought that Africans wanted to be white because they tended to apply themselves more at school; doing well at school was seen as a white thing. The Africans, on the other hand, didn't think we were that black either; to them we didn't have much interest in working hard, blamed our shortcomings on being black and then accused those around us of racism. To the Caribbeans, the Africans became coconuts – brown on the outside, white on the inside – and any Caribbeans who did well at school and enjoyed being there were coconuts too! For the Africans, they couldn't understand how underachieving at school would be of any benefit to black people.

There was a racial hierarchy to deal with amongst the Caribbeans, too. The Jamaicans saw themselves as the best, those with parents from Barbados were second and the Trinidadians came in third. Those whose parents came from smaller islands were seen as not being worthy of calling themselves Caribbean.

I kept my home life out of school as much as I possibly could. During the five years I spent at secondary school I brought no friends home. Parents' evening was the worst time for me. Whilst other students found it stressful because they hadn't done so well, I found it difficult for other reasons. The other pupils would stare, teachers looked surprised and I was thoroughly annoyed by the whole thing! I knew that the next day at school I would be subjected to questions from some of my peers. Not only that, but I also had to deal with the fact that I hadn't done well at school yet again, though peer group pressure meant that any sort of academic achievement wasn't high on my list. I could never discuss this with anyone though: I couldn't exactly say that it's not the black thing to do, it's not cool to work, and that a lot of the other black students would give me a hard time for doing so. Parents' evening the following year was a stress-free affair though: I highlighted the names of the teachers that needed to be seen and sent my mum around on her own.

I had strange experiences with some of the teachers, too; they didn't know what do with me, whether or not to treat me like the other underachieving black students. I managed to get way with doing very little schoolwork for five years and didn't find myself in a lot of trouble for this. Black friends thought it was because my mum was white, but it was because I mastered the art of doing just enough work to satisfy teachers and not so much that I would alienate myself from my friends. I always thought I had a good time at secondary school, but looking back it was a total nightmare.

In your teens, the opinions of your friends are extremely important and I think going through those motions and conforming to particular stereotypes was very important for me at the time. I don't think that way now and don't need those around me – black or white – to reinforce who I am or tell me who I should be.

The older I've got, the fewer black friends I've had. It's not deliberate – at university and the places I've worked, there haven't been that many. I just tend to make friends with people I have things in common with; skin colour is often the last thing on my mind in this respect. In the world of work I've found, though, that when you are one of the few black people in the company you tend to acknowledge the other black people around you. I'm obviously used to being around white people, but I don't really like to be the only black face. But I am more comfortable being around whites; I suspect black people might be able to suss that I'm a bit of fraud. So I don't mind if I don't have that much to do with black people on a personal level, but it's very important that I live in a place where I see people who look like me on a regular basis.

I do think that white families should be allowed to foster and adopt children from different ethnicities. More importantly, every effort should be made to place them with the best family within their own ethnic group first. But, saying that, I do think it has been a positive experience for my older brothers and me. We went into care for our own safety and it so happened that the best parent we eventually ended up with was white. Stability (amongst other things) was extremely important for us and moving from family to family wouldn't have been a positive experience. We were just lucky that we were placed together and with someone who saw that positive black awareness was as important as providing a loving family.

I can't say the same for my younger brother though. His family thought and still think that love is more important than anything else. The result is that his view of himself as a black man, and how black people should be, is a distorted one. His parents are white, his older brother is white, and he has two younger sisters: one is black (origins from Barbados) and the other is Chinese. You identify with those around you and, if you can't find what you're looking for, you go elsewhere. And he's chosen particular areas of black American culture. His parents and siblings have never really shown any interest in racial awareness or aspects of cultural diversity, with the general opinion being that, whether your family is from Jamaica or Barbados, it's pretty much the same thing – it's all the Caribbean after all!

So, when placing children with families, ethnic and racial awareness has to be an important factor. It's all about making sure that potential parents and carers have the right access to as much information as possible. I don't think I can emphasise how important I think this is; it's equally important as providing a loving family.

But I don't feel any sense of loss when comparing my life to other black people; exactly the opposite, in fact. It doesn't bother me any more that I don't really like hot spicy food or have problems understanding strong Caribbean accents. I know there's more to being black than just these things and, because I know that, I try to take full advantage of this pretty unique and unusual situation.

Foundling

WUSHAN

About 11 am, first-floor staircase landing, 71–73 Ma Tau Chung Road, Hunghom, Kowloon, near Kai Tak airport, Hong Kong: a baby was abandoned by someone. She was unknown to the authorities. That baby was me. I became a foundling.

The date my loneliness began was 11 October 1965. My estimated date of birth was 11 May 1965. I was found by the police and taken to a reception centre. The records describe me as being about one foot six inches tall, with thin short hair and a flat nose. I had been breastfed shortly before I was found, and I was clean and healthy. There was no form of identification on me. The authorities tried to trace my family through the television, radio and newspapers. No one came forward. As I don't remember those events, I can't tell anyone what my family was like. I became a nothing, a no one, left empty, confused and scared. The superintendent at the reception centre gave me the name, Wushan. As my family had not come forward by the end of 1965, I was moved to an orphanage, Po Leung Kuk. I have no memories of living in Hong Kong.

*   *   *

My first memories are as if I was plonked on this planet at about four years old. I was living in Staffordshire, England, at the time, with my adoptive parents. I had had a fall in the garden and cut my head open. I remember looking at the rabbits crossing the garden, and then of being in hospital where I received stitches.

As a child, I heard voices and noises that no one else claimed to hear. I talked to my voices but my parents told me I would be taken away if I talked to myself. I didn't tell them I was hearing voices. I thought this happened to everyone.

During my childhood, I also lived in Cyprus for three years and travelled to Switzerland, Italy, Venice, Crete, Malta, Lake Como and the Black Forest. I liked travelling as I would meet different kinds of people and see different places. These were happy times in my life.

At school, I never had any proper friends. I've always been alone and solitary. I've lived in many places, which has meant that I always changed schools. People were not nice to me at school. I was bullied because I am Chinese. I find it hard to concentrate and always have done. I now know this to be hallucinations, confusion, fear, seeing and hearing things. At home I was given a negative self-image and poor self-confidence by a white, comfortably off, conservative couple: my adoptive parents.

When I asked my parents where I came from, they said I should be proud of being Chinese. They also lied to me, saying that my parents were dead. I didn't believe them. I would wait outside shops, looking at anyone that might be Chinese in the hope that my family would find me and take me home. I knew that no one could prove to me that my parents were dead. When I asked who my parents were and what they were like, I was told that my adoptive parents didn't know. I reasoned that, if they were dead, people would at least know who they were.

I've been suicidal since I was 14 years old because I couldn't find my family and didn't get on with my adoptive family at all. I also moved school when I was 14; the curriculum was different and I couldn't catch up. My parents still expected me to do well. I had left my friends behind at my old school and making new friends wasn't easy. My adoptive parents only added to my anguish. No one cared. No one expected me to be myself, they just wanted to mould me into something no one could be. I was put down and called not normal. I was called selfish too. Everything was conditional, including their love. They made all the decisions and, at the same time, said I should be thinking for myself but, when I did, they said I was in the wrong. There were so many battles. My adoption didn't work out. I am against children being adopted if, when there are problems, no one is there to support them or help their parents.

Although my adoption didn't work out, I stayed in touch with my adoptive nana right up until she died. She loved me a great deal. She stuck by me, even though she knew that I didn't want to see her son and daughter-in-law. She always remembered my birthday and welcomed me to her home. She could understand why I didn't get on with my parents. My nana gave me a photograph of myself as a baby that was taken in Hong Kong, when I was living with my parents.

I was under the psychiatric system by my early twenties. Here I was described as being of low intelligence, but I was not stupid. As my mental health deteriorated, I got care (or was it scare?) in the community. Over the years, I have become involved in the psychiatric survivors' movement. I have written about the mental health system in several service-user newsletters and magazines.

Most people are kind to me; they don't understand what has happened to me. I don't know what to say when they ask about my origins. They say, 'Where are your family?' or 'Where do they live?' Some people think that I come from a family that has a take away or restaurant. I just tell them I don't know where I come from. I am not racist but I do not know any Chinese people very well. I can only read, write and speak English and I am a British citizen. I don't know how to speak Cantonese or Mandarin. It's more embarrassing to meet Chinese people than it is to meet English people. Once, a Chinese man introduced himself to me in Cantonese or Mandarin but I couldn't understand. I had to tell him that I only speak English and he smiled and then spoke to me in English. But I was embarrassed. There was nowhere to learn Cantonese or Mandarin where I lived and there still isn't.

I have no hope of finding my true, real, natural family. I recognise that they saved me. It was a big sacrifice that they made, leaving me to be found. I don't know why they did it. I do know that, when I was found, I was well fed and healthy. They didn't harm me. I know they did their best for me, wanted me to have a better life, and probably didn't want to leave me. I could not hate them. Even though we are virtual strangers, my mummy has always been on my mind.

Today my life is much better. I am starting to accept hearing voices and seeing and hearing things. I'm on better medication. I've stopped punishing myself because I've learned who I am. I have started to accept that after all these years I am unlikely to find out any new information. In the past, I contacted International Social Service over and over again but now I realise that there is nothing more they can tell me, and that there are no leads. I am better off not being in contact with my adoptive parents. My pets love me unconditionally. My millions of voices talk to me nicely. I believe my voices are my birth family and that they have been talking to me all my life; that they've been sent to speak to me because I'm on my own.

I also have skills that I use to distract the nasty voices. I distract them by watching television, going for a walk, listening to music or going on the computer. By using these skills, the voices start to talk about the things I want to talk about. The voices are my thoughts. If other adoptees in my position can find their own coping skills, it will help them.

I have studied a bit about what Chinese people are like, and I have learned so much from my experience. I try to think positively and to focus on the future and not dwell on the past. Somebody once told me you can't change the past and they were right. I can't go back to Hong Kong, go back in time to the date I was left on the staircase, and stop my family from leaving me there.

I have reclaimed the name, Wushan. No first name, no family name, just Wushan.

I rely on race memory. I'm a stitch made in a sweat factory. I am Wushan. I am the only me. I am.

From Kowloon tiger to Chinese cockney

CHRIS ATKINS

My background

I was born in Hong Kong, on or around 18 December 1962. I say "around" because
when I was found I was estimated to be a week old. I was found abandoned in
Kowloon on the steps of a tenement building on Christmas day and was taken to a
police station and then to a hospital. The following day I was transferred to a
children's home in the New Territories where I stayed for almost a year. Then I was
brought over to the UK for adoption. I was initially fostered and then adopted by
my parents. We were flown over and fostered, pending social worker reports and a
court hearing. It's interesting to think what might have happened if the adoption
hadn't gone ahead.

I came to the UK at the end of 1963 and grew up in Hillingdon, west London. My
adoptive family are great. My mother is Cockney born and bred, born within the
sound of Bow Bells. My father was born in Harrow. I have a younger brother who is
adopted. He's two years younger and, although he's of white and Asian heritage, he
looks white. I have a younger sister by six years who is my parents' birth child. So
there were three of us.

Childhood

My childhood within my family was fine and I wouldn't want anybody to think
otherwise. However, my childhood experiences outside my family were not so good.
It was a different era and London wasn't the multicultural, eclectic place that it is
today. I grew up in a white area and went to an all-white school. I was the only non-
white person in my primary and secondary school and I quickly became known
amongst teaching staff as the only "Chinese Cockney".

How can I put this nicely? It felt a fairly lonely existence. I was bombarded with
racism and was told in no uncertain terms that I was different. I got called names –
"chinky" and that type of thing – and spent many playtimes alone. I wasn't the kid
who went to everybody's house after school because no one invited me. My life
consisted of going to school and then going home. I suspect my mother felt awful for

me but I didn't talk to her about it as I knew there was nothing she could do and I didn't want to worry her. I grew used to being alone.

Before I went to school I would not be parted from my adoptive mother even for the shortest time. Despite this, on the first day at school I was fine. However, from the second day, when it dawned on me where I was going, I started kicking, screaming and protesting, to the point where my mum had to pick me up and carry me into the playground where a teacher would be waiting. They would physically restrain me while my mum would run out of the playground. On occasions I would kick myself free and follow her up the road. I found out this lasted for years. My one abiding memory of that time is that I felt very alone and very frightened. I suppose abandoned comes back into my mind. I had been just left in this sea of people whom I didn't know, who didn't appear to want to know me and it was just too much for me to cope with.

Towards the end of my primary school years, I hooked up with a group of girls who, in various ways, were also different: one was overweight, another had parents who had split up. It was kind of the oddball-type mix. When I went to secondary school I was back in the same position of not knowing anybody and not having the confidence to make friends. It wasn't until my fifth and final year, that I developed what you would call a best friend, who was the person you went behind the shed and smoked with, or wandered home at lunchtime with to sneak a biscuit from the biscuit tin. It wasn't until I left home that my mother told me that she was worried because I hadn't made the type of lasting friendships that children tend to make through school.

My childhood contains little pockets of enjoyment. The times I really enjoyed myself were when I was with my family and when I was on my own. The feeling I always had when with other people was a fear of being rejected or a fear that, when somebody else came along whom they preferred, I would be left on the sidelines. This did happen a few times, although that's just part and parcel of being a child. But for me it took on a different dimension.

Leaving home

I left school when I was 16 and went to college in Watford, which I enjoyed as that was the first time I'd mixed with a more multicultural peer group. There were people there who were black, Asian, Italian. I felt that I was no different from them. From there, I worked for a short time as a lifeguard. Then, one day, I saw an advert for working for what was the Spastics Society, now Scope. I don't know why but I applied to become a live-in staff member. It was in a "home" in the middle of nowhere, in Buckinghamshire. I went along for the interview. By the time I had travelled home, the interviewer had telephoned to offer me the job, and my mother had answered the phone. I hadn't told her I was going for this job. I said, 'Oh yeah, there's something I've been meaning to tell you. I think we'd better have a chat.' About a month later, I'd left home and was living in. I can remember the day I moved in. I was too scared to leave the room I'd been allocated to go to the dining room. I was just paralysed with fear, thinking, 'What have I done? What am I doing here?' But I stayed there for nearly three years.

Working with a group of people who were ostracised from society because of how they looked, who were hidden away in the middle of nowhere "out of sight, out of mind", gave me a different perspective. My preoccupation with my own appearance seemed self-centred and rather inconsiderate by comparison with the social, political, economic and historical isolation experienced by disabled people. All of those with whom I was working maintained a sense of dignity, pride and self-respect. In turn, I also was accepted for who I was and my confidence started to grow. There was a connection there that I didn't really recognise nor understand. I started to feel more comfortable with myself. They accepted me for who I was and they changed the way I saw myself. I recognise they gave me the confidence to actually go on and start to accept myself. This is who I am and I'm not going to change. Until that point, I always wished that I could change. When I looked in the mirror, I didn't want to be who I saw, physically or otherwise. There was no way I ever wanted to look in that mirror and look at what was staring back at me. When I was a child, the way to get accepted was to look like everyone else who, in my world, was white. If somebody had said, 'Sell your soul to the devil and tomorrow morning you will wake up white,' I'd have done that. When I look back, it is sad, which is the understatement of the century. It's like self-hate; it's most certainly internalised racism.

Not belonging

For years I used to tell people I'm no different from them. Now I've got to the stage that I think, 'No, I am different and I'm also different from the Chinese community.' I no longer fit into an indigenous Chinese community, any more than I fit into a white community. As I got older, I began to read the look on people's faces and realised they're not going to accept me.

I wasn't born here and I didn't come here by my own volition. Although my life's here, my husband's here, my family are here, I still have this psychological and emotional feeling that I grew up abroad. If I was to be transported back to Hong Kong, though, I'd feel just as much abroad there. But that's fine. I don't belong to anywhere in particular. Some people might think that's sad, but I think 'Why should I be tied down to one place?' I can't think of anywhere in the world where I would want to spend the rest of my life. I think that's partly why I find it easy to move around.

Where I am today

What has helped me to get to where I am today? Denial! When did I first meet a Chinese person? I don't really remember, but it was probably in a Chinese takeaway! I did probably meet other Chinese people, but when they presented me with chopsticks at the dinner table, I had no idea what to do with them. This was a general joke at the time. I would have been in my thirties when I first met another adopted Chinese person to sit down and talk to. We'd been introduced through some research on intercountry adoption, so it wasn't like meeting another Chinese person from an indigenous Chinese community in the UK. I was meeting somebody who was in much the same position I was in. I am friends now with a Chinese couple. Part of me is slightly envious of the connection they have to Hong Kong and China because that's not something I'll ever experience. They go back every Christmas and spend a month there to reconnect with their community, their family and their heritage. I don't feel that I can do that. I've been to Hong Kong, but I don't have the same connection anymore. I do have this fantasy that, when I die, I will be cremated, with my ashes scattered over the South China Sea or in Hong Kong harbour. I also get pangs of envy when I look at Asian families and black people, and recognise the connection they have. They understand where they come from and have knowledge of their roots and heritage. I only recognise it momentarily and am only jealous for a moment. I feel it when I see other people, even white, who have a self-confidence about their family, their culture, where they come from, all of which I don't have. I think that would be nice. But I don't dwell on it too long because circumstances can't be changed.

Visiting Hong Kong

I first went to Hong Kong in 1991, before I'd met another transracial adoptee.

I've been to Hong Kong twice now. It was something I promised myself I'd do once I'd graduated and had money and I also promised my mother that she would come with me. So I was accompanied by my mother, my sister and my partner. As far as I was concerned I was going for a holiday. It did have a slight significance in that it was Hong Kong but it didn't have the kind of significance prior to going that other people think it should have done. Unknown to me, though, my mother had arranged with International Social Service (ISS) to have the children's home in which I'd been placed reopened. National Children's Home (the adoption agency) and International Social Service were very concerned because this was a surprise for me. It's a bit like Section 51 counselling today and somebody saying, 'I've got a surprise for you. Ta-da! There's your birth family!'

When we arrived, the social worker from ISS in Hong Kong was due to meet my mother at the airport. However, we were diverted out of China airspace because of a hijacking and had to land at Bangkok, refuel and fly on. So, unknown to me, sitting there in my own little world on the flight, my mother and my partner were panicking and giving each other little glances because they knew the social worker was waiting at the airport. The third night we were there, my mother said they'd meet me up at the bar. It was a beautiful hotel and the bar overlooked Hong Kong harbour. In the bar she said, 'I've got something to tell you.' Of course, when your mum says that you think somebody's died or dying so when she said, 'We've arranged for the children's home to be opened,' it was something of a relief, really! At first I was like, OK, because it just hadn't occurred to me, and then it sunk in.

The next day, we went to ISS to meet the social worker and made our way by train out to the New Territories to go to the children's home. It had been closed and the children decanted as they were due to demolish it to build flats. The children's home itself had been relocated to Kowloon. I wish I had the opportunity to go back now as I have gained a deeper understanding of what this meant. I have some very treasured photos of the children's home and of the day we spent there. When I visited, it took a big "leap of faith" and a lot of imagination to achieve any sense of belonging. What cemented it for me was, a number of years later, meeting somebody whose uncle three generations back had worked as a superintendent at the children's home and he had hordes of photographs. My sister managed to find a photo of me as a baby in this children's home. There's something about a photo that gives you a sense of history (albeit only a little). That's the only photo I have that says, 'You were here.' I've got a photograph of the children's home now that's blown up and framed. It's a trigger point for questions from my children now.

The reunion

A reunion was organised in 2000 by a woman who was adopted from Hong Kong. I was contacted by ISS to ask if I would be interested. There was publicity in the *Daily Mirror* and various magazines, to get more people to come forward. Hong Kong television heard about the story and sent a crew over. They came and did some filming in my house, following me around for a while. The film was broadcast back in Hong Kong. They said many people who'd had babies adopted in the UK didn't know what had happened to their children. About 300 children were adopted from Hong Kong in the 1960s. About a third came to the reunion. There were also a lot of family and interested parties. You kind of grow up, if you're in my situation, thinking you're the only one, and then you realise, 'Oh look, there's more of us out there.' It was a good day.

My second visit to Hong Kong

I went back just before my first daughter was born in 1995. That second time, I was really quite touched. On leaving Hong Kong, I really, really didn't want to go. I can remember crying on the coach. If somebody had said at the time, 'I'll switch tickets with you,' I'd have stayed. I just wanted to be there. I remember going to Stanley Market one day, with my family. In this country, apart from Chinatown or London, I'm pretty identifiable. I live in Hertfordshire. If I'm meeting people and they're new, I say, 'Just look for the Chinese one who emerges out of the station.' So we were in Hong Kong and Stanley Market and thought we'd have a wander and meet in half an hour. As usual, I was slightly late, and was 10 or 15 feet from where they were stood. I expected them to see me. They were looking, and then it dawned on me that they couldn't see me. I'm Chinese and everybody else was Chinese. It was only when I walked forward and waved that they recognised me. They said, 'We couldn't see you, don't walk away from us because you look like everybody else.' It was a complete turn of the tables.

Being there, I realised I'm not actually part of Hong Kong culture. Although I was born in Hong Kong I don't know my heritage, so I can't say that I have any sense of "belonging" when I think of Hong Kong. However, it's the only place I've got and on a superficial but positive note, I had a really great haircut there! As you'd expect, it's the only place I've found where they know how to cut Chinese people's hair, whereas in the UK people seem a bit frightened by it. There are other little things, like I can get clothes that fit me and I don't have to turn up jeans as they don't manufacture clothes for people with a leg length similar to that of Claudia Schiffer. I enjoy going over there. I want to go back and take my girls because it's part of their history, their heritage. Since I was last there, I have discovered where I was found and it would be nice to go to see where this was.

Being a social worker

From Scope, it was a very slippery slope into social work really. I have ended up working in adoption although I've not worked in assessment. I made a conscious decision not to work in an area of adoption that involved going out to assess potential adopters because I think my personal experiences and history could expose me to allegations of bias, especially if it involved intercountry adoption. I've always had a passion for post-adoption support. I think it's crucial. It frustrates me no end that a large part of support for adoptive families finishes when a child is placed. This is where the hard work for those families begins. There should be a seamless transition from assessment, placement and on to appropriate adoption support. I'm very fortunate that I can work for After Adoption. I like being able to provide support to people.

I would never profess to being an expert about adoption, but my own experience does give me an added depth of understanding that I probably wouldn't have otherwise. For some reason, people connect with that. I choose whether or not to tell people. Sometimes I will disclose my own circumstances; some people they need to know that the person they're talking to has personal experience of adoption. In my work, I'm totally non-judgemental whether I'm talking to birth parents, adoptive parents or adopted people. I always held the belief that, 'There but for the grace of God, go I.' Who knows what my life could have been like?

Are there disadvantages working in adoption? No, not as such. However, I'm quite acutely aware that I can be misheard and misinterpreted with allegations of, 'Well, you clearly don't believe in intercountry adoption.' People only do that because they know I'm adopted and they attack me personally. Also, I do have my moments when I am slightly tired; I do need to have my switch-off time when I stop thinking about adoption. I try to keep a perspective that, whilst adoption is part of my life, it's not all of my life.

I do reflect on my own circumstances regarding reunion. At work, we help people through reunions. That touches on areas, for me, like loss. I know I will never get the opportunity to do that. Whether or not I would take that opportunity is a different matter. Mostly, I think I've managed to deny and totally put that type of idea to rest, because what is the point? I enjoy my work immensely. I'm very passionate about the issues. I suppose that passion comes from having done it myself, and going through years and years of nobody talking to me about adoption and always saying, 'Well, aren't you lucky? Aren't your parents wonderful people?!' My parents are wonderful people, I agree wholeheartedly, but there is an "and" after that; the story does continue.

Gratitude

I still don't discuss much about my adoption experiences with my parents. They're now in their seventies and eighties. Neither of them has had an easy life and I truly believe that they did everything they could to help and protect me (as parents should), given the limited knowledge and understanding of adoption and its impact (both domestic and intercountry) at that time. I feel they deserve to live the rest of their lives as stress-free as possible. I was sent a copy of the film that was made by Hong Kong television and I had it for months and months before I showed it to my mother. She knew that I had it and every time she came over she would ask about it. I'd give some feeble excuse, like, 'Oh, I'll get it in a minute,' and then completely divert her attention. It was complete and utter cowardice on my part. Eventually I had to show the film to her. I knew what her reaction would be as I'd been pretty honest in it, explaining how I felt and what I'd gone through, much of which I had never told my parents. I had to sit down beforehand and warn my mum. I said, 'Look there's some stuff in here that I've never told you.' As soon as I started to speak on the film, she started to cry, which of course triggered me into "rescue mode". So, I'm sat there saying, 'It's OK, really, it wasn't really that bad.' We've never spoken about it since. I guess I would still go into "rescue mode", because I don't want to see my seventy-something-year-old mother thinking she did something wrong, or didn't protect her child. My parents did everything that they could have done at the time. And that's all you can ask.

Becoming a mother

The other thing that changed my perspective was having children. When my daughter was born, I can remember afterwards wondering what this connection was; it was bizarre. I can remember people saying, 'She doesn't look much like you, does she? She looks like your husband.' I was quite hurt by that but appalled that I should feel hurt. It did resurrect insecurities about my appearance, the lack of connection and the denial in me about what I look like. It brought up that buried, internalised, racist stuff.

I'd never had that genetic connection before and it took me months to work out what was going on. I never told anyone how I felt when they said, 'She doesn't look much like you'. Both my daughters (I know all parents say this) are beautiful. Because my husband is white, they're Eurasian. They've both got long dark hair and olive-coloured skin that tans to the most beautiful colour. Our eldest daughter is tall and slim and her legs reach up to her neck! Both my girls are everything that I wasn't at that age and everything that I want them to be: confident, outgoing, etc. Having children brings its own challenges regarding racism and how we deal with that. Becoming a parent has put a completely different dimension on how I deal with my own history. I can no longer deny it because it's not just me now.

Growing awareness

So many years I spent in a racial, cultural wilderness, wondering what was going on, kind of being there but not being there. I wonder what might have happened had I wised up a bit quicker. I suppose I've done it later, rather than never. The trip to Hong Kong was the beginning for me. Then there was the researcher who was the first person to ask me what it felt like being an intercountry adoptee. It was the first time that I didn't say, 'Oh, I'm fine, I'm no different to anybody else'. Something had moved me from that position to acknowledging and being comfortable with the differences I feel and live with. Going back to Hong Kong started triggering the realisation that I no longer "fit in" there. Growing up I'd felt very different to everybody else and I formed fantasies about where I would fit in in Hong Kong. That was where I came from, where I had been taken from, that's where I would feel safe and secure. When I went over there, I looked like everybody but my genetic needs were not met because only my birth family can meet those. I started to think about it. Sometimes I'd consider, 'Wasn't life simpler when I didn't think about it?' There weren't all these "ifs" and "buts", but I am glad I've moved on.

Meeting other transracially adopted people

For years, I wondered if it was true that nobody but me feels like this. Am I being ungrateful and should I feel very lucky because who wants to grow up in an orphanage? Then, when I met another transracially adopted person who said, 'I feel like that too,' my feelings were validated. Meeting another transracially adopted person was really, really good – very cathartic in some ways. I was able to express how I felt without having to justify my feelings and without anyone being hurt or offended. We were able to share experiences safely.

For many years, I felt unable to voice my feelings about being adopted and growing up within a white family in a predominantly white community. All too often, when you explain yourself and it sounds anywhere near negative about adoption, intercountry adoption or transracial adoption, what you're met with is, 'Oh, life could have been so much worse for you' and, 'You shouldn't feel like that.' Yes, I know life could have been much worse for me, which is why I also battle with the dilemma of balancing feelings of gratitude and being honest. I don't need anyone to tell me. Their response shuts you up, because what you are saying is really not what they want to hear; they don't want to know what the experience is really like. What they want to hear is you sitting there going, 'Well my life is great, it could have been a lot worse, I could have ended up face down in Hong Kong harbour, I could have ended up in prostitution, all sorts.' Well, of course I could. Couldn't we all, given different terms of our lives? Even if I hadn't been adopted and maybe if I'd been born here who knows?

I can remember going down the town where I grew up and, on numerous occasions, people would stop my mother and say, 'Where did you get her from?' If my mum was feeling facetious, she'd say, 'Oh, I've got a bike'. In which case, they wouldn't know what to say. But, usually, she'd say, 'We adopted her from Hong Kong'. Then they would turn to me and say, 'Aren't you a lucky little girl?' Like I say, '*I know how lucky I am!*' But, yet again, I haven't been asked; I've been told I am lucky and my parents are wonderful.

Talking to other transracially adopted people, you get an affirmation of your feelings, and the experiences you've had. It is lovely. You're in a place where you can be as honest as you have ever been with another person, without them making a judgement about you. Now I am part of a small group of transracial intercountry adoptees that meets up three or four times a year, to go for a meal. We get together and talk about what's happened. We can go into Chinatown and have something to eat. We all recognise that these people look at us and think we're all Chinese (well, no, two of us are Indian) but we get talked to in Chinese. The waiters expect all of us to be able to turn round and answer back, which is OK. If I go with a group of white friends to Chinatown, I'm the one who gets spoken to in Cantonese and I become acutely embarrassed because I can't reply in the same language.

Rejection

I do have issues around rejection and I am very wary about being who I feel I am. I would like to be more confident around other people and worry less about how I appear to others but I haven't got that far yet. I'm still too wary of the potential for rejection. As part of a counselling course, I had to receive counselling. I couldn't find a black or Asian counsellor, so I found a white counsellor who knows a bit about adoption. The counselling helped, but I wasn't as open as I should have been. Maybe that was because she was white. I found it difficult to relax. Even with friends, I tend to hold back.

Again, the fear is around rejection. I'm concerned that I'll overwhelm, embarrass and, ultimately, disempower them with depressing stuff and then, quite understandably, they'll be scared off. I suppose it's about the effect and impact of my experiences, not just about adoption but also racism. I choose what people know and what they don't know. For example, it depends on the circumstances whether I'll let people know that I was born before Christmas and abandoned on Christmas Day. It's bad enough being abandoned, in some people's eyes, but being abandoned on Christmas Day, what a hard deal! Who does that to a child? I've got no answer and I can do without pity. I don't want pity from anybody, least of all the people I would like as friends.

Advice

What advice would I give to other transracial adoptees? To try and connect with as many other transracially adopted people as you can. It is a great, great help. Once you've done it, you'll think to yourself, 'Why didn't I do this before?' It's a bit like stoking that fire, when you're feeling, 'I'm tired of the constant battles and always having to explain, I'm tired of feeling like I'm the only one.' To meet other people who have this tacit understanding of how you feel, you feel together in your isolation, which sounds contradictory but you do. It somehow stokes that fire so you can go out and face the world for a bit longer, and a bit stronger. Make those connections, go out there and talk to people. Failing that, find somebody that you can connect with and talk to, whether or not they're a member of your family, friends, whoever, because it does help.

Never feeling settled

SIMON SIBLEY

I was adopted at the age of six weeks, back in 1975. I don't know much about my natural parents, but what I do know is that they were in no way able to keep me. They were approximately 16 to 17 years old when I arrived. I was not planned. They were not in a relationship and, at the time, did not have their own accommodation. My father is Jamaican. He came over to England in 1964. He was a mechanic and of average height, about 5' 8". My mother is English and 5' 3" tall. She spent most of her life in Little Hampton and London.

Six weeks after my birth, my natural mother, it seems, could not make up her mind. One day she wanted me adopted, the next she wanted to keep me. She kept my birth from her parents for as long as possible but, when they found out, they wanted to look after me. By this time, the ball was already rolling and I was placed with a middle-class family with one other black adopted child in white suburbia.

Many people may think this is a success story: "black child from poor family adopted into a loving family", with all the love and money I could ever want! But I remember the endless comments when people met my parents, questions about how they could be my parents, me being black and them being white. I know my adoptive mum was the butt of endless jokes when I was young. Obviously, people concluded that she must have had a black partner or two in the past. My parents are amazing, but I cannot look at them and know why I look the way I do. I cannot learn about any health problems that may affect me in the future. And most strangely of all, I have to tell anyone who meets them that they are my parents, as there is no obvious link between us.

The outcome of my upbringing is that, through no one's fault, certainly not my excellent adoptive family's, I have never felt settled. I am 29 years old now and have a family of my own, yet I still have issues with my identity. I feel I don't know where I come from and so don't really know where I am. It is now my goal to trace my natural parents for information, photos, anything that can help me with my identity, to help me to identify with myself more.

I need closure. I have hit stalemate and need to go back before I am able to go forward. I have questions I need answered. Then, I may be able to feel settled in myself.

Living with adoption takes up a lifetime

DAVID

I am 37 years old. My birth father is Jamaican and my birth mother is German. I was fostered twice before being transracially adopted at the age of three months. This is part of my life story and my experiences as an adopted male, now living in Manchester.

My experience of adoption as a child was, on the whole, a difficult one. I grew up in a white family who already had two children of their own. I was not brought up in a black environment and realised my difference at a very early age. No attempt was made to teach me anything about black people, history or culture, as this was of no importance to my adoptive family. Doesn't my race or history or cultural heritage matter to them? I will always question their reasons for adopting a black child.

I experienced racism at school. I was told I was adopted at infant school. I didn't know anything about why adoption happens and I was not told why I was adopted. I was just told that I was special. From then on, I did not like being adopted. I didn't know who I was or what made me feel different. My infant and primary school was all white and there was one other mixed race child at secondary school. I felt I couldn't seek help from my adoptive family or any of my teachers as they were all white and would not understand my true feelings about being in the minority.

Whilst growing up, I tried to trace my birth family and to gain access to my birth records. Looking in the telephone book and electoral registers, applying for my birth certificate were all things that I did. This was very emotional as I felt that my life was one big jigsaw and I had to fit the pieces together. Who was my mother? Where was she? What was my father's occupation? All of these questions needed to be answered in order for me to feel complete. These times were extremely emotional for me but I just had to know. After many years, I found some members of my natural family and contacted them. Unfortunately, I was rejected. This was very hard to take and left my questions still unanswered.

My adult relationships at this time were unsuccessful as emotions were running high and also my relationship with my adoptive family had broken down. I had very little support as I decided to deal with this on my own. Looking back, this was the wrong thing to do. The strain started to show. I felt depressed. For the next ten years I was in and out of psychiatric services. I was trying to piece together my life. I needed counselling and psychotherapy. My life was chosen for me, I was losing control and I needed support. Recently, the post-adoption services have helped me and they are important in order for me to heal.

Every year on my birthday and at Christmas I feel a great sense of loss, as these are the times that I really miss my natural family. I am reminded of my mother and father and all my relatives. I feel isolated, as I know that I cannot see them.

Throughout my adult life I have experienced racism on different levels from many different people in all walks of life. It is through integration with the black community that my situation has become easier and I have become stronger. I was living in fear of black people for a long time but now enjoy building links with members of the black community. I am currently attending a group for transracially adopted adults. I now feel extremely sensitive on the issues raised surrounding transracially adopted children and feel that this matter should be taken very seriously by all concerned. An adopted child's life has been chosen for him or her, sometimes in very painful circumstances. A person who has been placed in a family of a different racial background has real issues to face, not only as a small child but throughout their adult life.

My hope for the future lies with adoptive parents. Frequent contact should always be left open to all concerned for the well-being of the transracially adopted child. My hopes for the future lie with helping others to come to terms with their own situation, living with adoption and to be of any support I can. Services need to be accessed at all times as living with adoption takes up a lifetime.

How it feels to be adopted

JOHN-PAUL POULSON

When my mum fell pregnant she was not in a stable relationship with my dad. She chose for me to be fostered as soon as I was out of hospital. I was fostered into a family where Janet and John already had two children of their own, Ian and Ann. After a few years they had another child called James. Then, after about five years, they fostered two more girls, Michelle and Lisa. I still found it hard to relate to Michelle and Lisa even though they were in a similar situation to me.

When I was at school, everybody knew I was adopted. This was never an issue I got bullied for. Janet and John were always very kind to me. They used to make me feel happy by telling me that I was special because I had two mums and dads.

Just before I was adopted at the age of three, my mum stopped visiting. She did want me to stay with Janet and John. She would come over and bath me. Then, after that, she stopped for her own reasons.

When I was about five or six, I made soap at school and it was sent to my nana and, when I met her later, after all these years she had still kept them. My nana used to write to me, but I never replied as I was too young. I never thought that she would still be at the same address but she was.

When I became a teenager, at about 14 years old, my head was messed up. I was very confused, I didn't know who I really was and I found this hard to come to terms with. I began to rebel against Janet and John. I became very unreasonable, I didn't want to admit I was being unfair.

When I was 15, I left Janet and John's and lived in different hostels. Then I left for Newcastle in 2000. I wasn't sure what to do but I decided to leave and make a fresh start. I had a good job and I knew what I wanted. I wanted to find my parents.

I got in touch with someone from After Adoption. She helped me find my mum. A few months before I met her I was given my files, which contained letters from both my mum and Nana. We were going to meet at the worker's house. When I turned up, my mum answered the door and the first thing I said was, 'You're beautiful.' I suddenly felt relieved; I had found my mum and was closer to feeling complete. We spoke for a while, then I visited her in Wigan. I met my family and was content.

I haven't tried to find my dad yet but I will. For now, I am coming to terms with my new life. I have also now moved to Wigan to be nearer to my mum. We have a great relationship; she isn't just my mum but my friend.

Ireland – a great place to grow up

IMA JACKSON

My childhood

I was brought up in Northern Ireland. I was born in Belfast in 1964. I was in a Barnardo's home in Ballycastle for a few months and joined my adoptive family within three months of my birth. My family lived in Portstewart, which is a small seaside town. They already had four birth children aged eight, six, four and two, and then they had me. After me, they adopted two more mixed-race children. I have a brother who is two years younger than me. He came two years after me, and I have a sister who was four-and-a-half when she came. She is only six months older than me. My lovely, loving parents are extraordinary. They and my brothers and sisters took me in, protected me, loved me and I have been very happy in my life.

Portstewart was a great place to grow up. Our house is called "Coolmara", corner of the sea. We ate every day looking out over the sea. We were definitely an unusual family in the small seaside town where I lived. We were a visible family. We had a fantastic home. There was nothing between us and the sea, just a footpath, the sea and the rocks. It has always been very beautiful. There was a fantastic freedom. People used to come past and ask if it was a children's home. There were lots of people to play with although, in other ways, we kept pretty much to ourselves – playing wild chasing games, sliding down the grassy bank in cardboard boxes and swimming in the sea.

Becoming aware of difference

But there were moments when I realised how different I was. There were things that would happen. We were so visible that people would talk to us. My mum would say that I was quite happy and then, sometimes, something would happen. On one occasion, I was parading in my new swimsuit and the next day (when it wasn't new), I was still getting all this attention and I didn't like it at all. I was only about three or four years old and I became quite upset. My mum noticed this change.

There was racism but we were often viewed as a kind of novelty. People wanted to touch you, or people not wanting to touch you, such as in "Kiss Tig". It was a time of particularly strong links with Africa, famine and the missions. I remember people engaging with us as if we were Africans. I remember thinking, why do they think I am anything to do with that? Although I could clearly enjoy the attention, there were also times when I was growing up when I got a bit fed up of being the novelty. As I saw it, I lived there and I was born in Belfast. It was only when I left Ireland at 18 that I really realised what "real" racism was all about. I think we had in some ways a very sheltered childhood, very self-contained. Nobody would sort of mess with us too much because I had four brothers and two sisters. Not that anything actually happened, it was just quite a presence.

Recently, Ireland has had a lot of immigration and it is just completely different now down south. As a child, I'd rarely seen a black person apart from my brother and sister. I had seen black people on *Top of the Pops* and there were black soldiers in the British army whom occasionally we would see. My sister and I were completely intrigued and wanted to go up and talk to them. We would go up to them and say, 'You're really black'. We were totally fascinated.

Becoming political

When I left home I became a bit more aware of what it was to be black, what it was to be black in other parts of Britain, which were completely different from Northern Ireland. There was a very different type of feeling around it. I just found it really strange how people interacted with you. Before, in Ireland, we were generally seen as kind of nice/unusual but this was not nice and I did not know anything about it at all. It was quite interesting though a bit distressing. I completely identified with black people and got dreadlocks and became fascinated by it all. This interest in black British culture really started when I was about 18. I now work with overseas nurses and refugees, supporting them towards regaining their professional status and employment in the NHS. Back then, I was looking to meet other black people and to find out what their experiences were. Many of the black people I met had had hard inner-city lives, whereas I had had this middle-class, country life.

It was when I came away from Ireland that I realised that there was some serious stuff around. I went to stay with my sister in London and loved it. However, there were lots of London Irish and I would hear all the same stuff I had had in Ireland, 'You can't be Irish,' so I stopped mixing with Irish people in London. They couldn't accept that I was Irish. I got tired of it. I did not want to go through life explaining to the Irish that I was from Ireland.

My birth mother and birth father

When I was in London, I trained as a midwife. There were a lot of Nigerian midwives and they would say to me, 'You're Nigerian,' and I would say, 'How do you know that?' My birth father *is* Nigerian. He was in Ireland studying when he met my birth mother. My initial drive was to find my birth mother. My birth father did not know about the pregnancy or my birth. I met my birth mother a few years ago. She is Irish. She was fine. I was always worried I would not like her. I think she has been quite brave. No one in her family knows about me. I think it must have been hard for her in her life. My birth mother was quite shocked and reluctant to have any contact at first, but she came a long way in a short time and agreed to meet me. I asked her if she could bring some photographs to our meeting. Her brother-in-law had recently married a Nigerian woman and she brought photos of them. It was some recognition of my parentage. It was really good just to see who she was. I don't think we will have any more contact. I just wanted to see who she was.

The birth records were always a bit vague about my birth father. I had done some tracing and had obtained a photograph of him from his student days, at least the man that I thought was him. I asked my (birth) mother if this was my birth father and she said, 'Yes'. That was so good. It gave me his name and also confirmed that it was the right person. I did not really ask what he was like. She did tell me that she had gone out with him a couple of times and that they went out to dances. Even that was quite good to know, to know that at least she liked him. I was conceived in June and he left at the end of June to return to Nigeria. I have not yet been to Nigeria.

Becoming an adoptive parent

I always knew that I wanted to adopt. Basically, I felt that adoption works and that I have lived it. That this is something that can work for us as a family and that I have some insights into how it can work in our case. It is something that my husband and I had thought about, particularly adopting a mixed-race child. We already have one beautiful daughter. He and his family have been completely supportive as, of course, have mine. If we (my siblings and I) had not been adopted by my family, most likely we would not have been adopted. We have a lot of adoption in our family. I have a cousin who is mixed-race and adopted, another cousin who is adopted, a brother and his wife who have adopted two children, and cousins who have recently adopted.

Just before our adopted daughter joined us, I suddenly had a real fear that maybe what I felt was not what happened; that perhaps I had not been loved and I had just thought that I had been. When she joined us there was so much adjustment for my husband, our first daughter and me. She has been here one year now. I had these strange feelings and they were powerful. It felt quite risky and I was quite surprised by that. One year on, and it has completely changed. The feeling I have for our newest daughter, I know that that is the feeling that my parents had (and have) for me. I was worried about being able to love a child and bringing him or her into our family. I know that adoption can work. It is great. I am amazed at what happens.

Reflection

I am quite political and have always been aware of the politics around transracial adoption and whether a child should be adopted or not by a family of the same race. I feel really strongly that, although there are things that happened because I was adopted transracially, what I gained through adoption was fantastic. My mix was matched with part of me. I am part black and part white and they are white and that is it. When I started to realise that this is not necessarily how people see you, that there are lots of negative images of black people, and that life can be really hard for black people because they are black, I have simply depended on the love, strength and joy I have in my life, which has come from my family.

My mother is now 74 and my father is 76. They are still living in the same house in Portstewart that I grew up in. Last year, they had a really difficult year and it simply heightens my love for them and I savour our time together. I am going back to visit in a couple of days. I will be taking both my daughters with me. I love to take them over the rocks, out to the beach and show them how to slide down the hill in a cardboard box.

Dedicated to all my family.

My journey

KATRINA

I was brought up by a white couple in a small town in Dorset. My birth mother was white; it was my birth father who was Jamaican. Looking back, it was hard for me at that time as I was only the mixed-race child in the area. I have horrific memories of when I was a little girl, of my mum dragging me into school at the age of four. I was a clingy baby, and then went on to being a clingy young child. I am now aware that I had attachment issues, as I had had three different carers by the time I was three months old. My birth mother had me until I was two months old. I then went to a foster mum and then on to my adoptive mum.

My adoptive mother always told me how clingy I was growing up. I believe that she had absolutely no awareness of how being separated from my birth mother had affected me. This separation is stored in your subconscious and you carry this pain with you for the rest of your life. You can work through this pain and things can get easier but it never totally leaves you. As a child it was very hard, but through my own personal development as an adult life has become so much easier and happier.

Going to school was difficult for me with my attachment problems and, of course, being a different colour I was always in the firing range for racist names: "Blackie", "Sambo", "nigger", etc. This added to my pain, and so I took on a role by the age of eight. It was the role of the bully. I was a tall lanky girl and very fast on my feet. So what I used to do when I got called a name, was go and punch the child and run away. After a time, I got a reputation and then I got into having a gang around me. Not only was I mixed-race but I was also a tough cookie. This made things worse for me as people always wanted to challenge me, so I grew up at school always in trouble for fighting.

Where were my adoptive mother and father in all this? They had issues within themselves. They did not "do" feelings and emotions. My mother dealt with things by shouting and ranting. I do not remember being cuddled after the age of five and rarely was I cuddled before then. I was this very emotional mixed-race child who needed so much love but actually received hardly anything. I was always in conflict with myself, as I was brought up in a white society but had such a pull towards my black roots which were never discussed with me, ever. I was lost for a very long time.

I got through my younger years by survival techniques and shutting down my feelings. I left home at 16 after many arguments with my adoptive mother. She never seemed to understand me, and my father was a "yes" man, always in the background. I had two older sisters who thought I was just a pain in the backside. My saving grace was that we lived on a council estate and I had a really great friend called Pauline (and we remain great friends today). Also, there were other kids on our estate so I was never at home except for my meals, and then back out playing with the other kids to escape my family life.

I was also very different from my sisters. They never wanted to experience life like I did. They both settled by 17, engaged to be married. So I guess it was hard for my mum and dad, to have this child who wanted to go to discos at 13, who hung around with a crowd and had attitude. I was bloody angry with the world for not giving me what I really needed: love and understanding.

There was no conversation within my family about my adoption. It was like they never wanted to speak about it. I do remember one time, I think I was five, when I looked in the mirror and tried to scrub my skin so I could be white like all the other people in my family (just writing this makes me feel very sad).

Then, in my adult years, I went to Ibiza to work. I was a loose cannon, doing drugs, drinking a lot, sleeping with men, just desperately trying to get people to love me. Of course, my mother did not know what was going on. In fact, we hardly kept in contact then. I realise that I was suppressing my pain with the drugs and alcohol. I would not change anything, though, in my life, as I have been taught so many lessons. I had two wild seasons in Ibiza. I then met my partner, who I am with now. I was 22 and he was 19.

We went and lived in California for two-and-half-years, where it was party and drugs once again. A fantastic experience but, yet again, I was still in a lot of pain and bringing my baggage wherever I went. Not recognising how I was feeling; in fact, I did not feel anything for years, I was really so good at numbing everything out.

During all of this I did wonder what my birth mother was like, but I never did anything about it until I had my first child, a son. This experience blew my mind. It was like someone had turned a light on and all my emotions came alive. Becoming a parent has been one of the most fantastic experiences in my life. Things were turning over in my head and I was aware that I wanted to start the process of searching, but it was not the right time. I got very busy with motherhood and then had my darling daughter. Our son has brown skin and our daughter has pale skin with these amazing blue eyes. Your children can be so different in features, even when they are from the same mother and father.

The advice that I will give to anyone when they start looking for their birth mother or father is not to have expectations of what he or she will be like. This is not an easy thing to do. I had dreamt of this loving mother for so long and this is not what I found.

I had to tell my adoptive parents that I was going to search as I did not want them to find out from anyone else, for example, my children. This went down like a lead balloon. Once again, my mother shouted and ranted and told me never to speak about this ever again. My dad cried. I think he thought that I was going to leave him, now that I was searching for my birth mother. This was really difficult for me to get my head around. Why was my mother being so awkward? Now I know that she was in pain but as she does not know how to converse, it is hard for her.

I found my birth mother. It was as easy as getting my original birth certificate and ringing up international directory enquiries, as she lives in Canada. It was very emotional, meeting her for the first time. I flew to Canada to see her and got on with her initially. Looking back, I think she was putting her best foot forward. We talked about her family and how it was; we laughed and we cried. She told me about my father and how they had a one-night stand. I did not feel that I needed to know much about him at the time, as I was getting to know her. I felt the ten days went well and I felt she thought that too. I also met my two half-brothers. One seemed to be a troubled soul and the other one was an OK, together guy. I also went out with them when I was in Canada. Everything seemed to be going well.

Then, my birth mother came over to meet my family: my partner and the kids. It was the summer of 1998 and I saw a difference in her. She became critical of my parenting and she was very ungrateful for the things we did for her. I challenged her behaviour. She seemed to have no awareness of what she was doing. In the end, she was asked never to return to our house as I was so upset by her behaviour.

After she left, I went into a deep depression and took to my bed for two weeks. I went back on anti-depressants, and this is something that I have done many times. I wrote to her and told her how I felt. It was like I had to become her parent and she wanted me to do all these nice things for her to feel special, and of course this is what I wanted her to do so neither of our needs were met. I realise I had a big dream for her to be this wonderful loving mother to me, but how could she? She hardly knew me and, of course, she has her own issues. It is a minefield of emotions.

I then kept in touch occasionally. Sometimes it is good but, at the moment, I am angry and hurt by her as she has chosen to not tell me my father's name, so she has taken away my choice, and the issues carry on. I dropped all my expectations of her after a lot of work with a therapist. Also, I trained as a counsellor as I realised that there is not enough support in my area for transracially adopted adults. My training has helped me immensely in getting on with my life. The social services helped me a little in searching for my birth mother but, when I struggled with my emotions, I feel they found it hard to connect with me.

The one benefit that has come out of all this is my relationship with my brothers. We get on so well and we have a fantastic connection. For me, this is really nice as I feel I finally have people in my family that I have really connected with. In fact, one of my brothers has just stayed with us all, from New York. We had a great time and talked about our relationship with our mother, and it has clarified for me that they have the same issues with her. I was wondering if it was only me as, when she sees me, a lot of things must come up for her. I can understand how difficult this is for her and I have a lot of empathy, but she does not seem to have the same respect for me. I think that is all I want. The most important thing when it comes to searching for your birth family is to be very open-minded. It could go well or it might not go as you expect. There is a lot of emotion in this relationship.

I have done work with social services, meeting people who want to adopt and are starting the process, and told them about my experience. Not one of the couples in the group was interested in adopting mixed-race children. I think white people can adopt mixed-race children only if they are very aware that these children can be very challenging and that they need to link into the children's heritage. They will test their adoptive parents time and time again, as all they know is abandonment and they want to be certain that their adoptive parents will not leave them.

What I would like to say at the end of this story about my journey is that you always have a choice as to how you want your story to affect the rest of your life.

The colour of love

CLARE GORHAM

Wimbledon, like many suburban towns in the South East, had that typical, pleasant, white middle-class veneer that keeps all the house prices up nicely, thank you. That's where I grew up. There was definitely a silent, insidious emphasis on conformity in our street. Our family therefore broke all the rules, as neither convention nor normality entered into our equation at all.

My parents (who are both white) had nine children, of which four were adopted. I was adopted in 1968, the second mixed-race baby in the family. My father found my brother (also mixed-race) trying to "scrub the dirt off" when he was two years old and they felt he needed a visual ally, as all of his other six brothers and sisters were white.

We were all adopted from a Catholic organisation, modestly called "The Crusade of Rescue", which, in its so-called godliness, put black and mixed-race babies in the same ward as mentally and physically impaired babies. Our colour was clearly seen as a major cause of disability in those days.

Our family epitomised the 60s' "melting pot" ideology, that so many beleaguered, misinformed social workers and local authorities now vilify. It was, and still is, a fantastically unique family. We were all brought up with the same amount of reciprocal, indiscriminate and unyielding love. None of our individual heritages was really taken into consideration, nor were we particularly encouraged to find out about them: that seemed like a superfluous, even inane pursuit. Ours was a family unit which, despite the geographic diversity of its members (our individual countries of origin include Nigeria, Switzerland, Newfoundland, Lithuania, Belgium, England and Ireland), thrived on the same stuff as any other family. To concentrate on our different cultural heritages, as far as my parents were concerned, would be introducing rift by emphasising the "otherness" of the adopted children. Theirs was a quest for familial unity, which they achieved brilliantly.

I was aware that I was different from my sisters mainly because they'd feign jealousy over my skin colour. It was the 70s and the long-haired Biba look was in, and I was stuck with this misshapen Afro that had never been anywhere near any of the multitude of black hair-care products around (not exactly a big call for them in Wimbledon village). My vanity was compromised, but the sense of alienation rarely touched deeper than the cosmetic.

I went through school with racial impunity, mainly because I was oblivious to it. I hadn't been primed to expect it by my parents, nor given means to defend against it, therefore I wasn't aware of any racist allusions or innuendos made by the teachers or other pupils. My parents just loved me as their child, not as a colour that might be discriminated against.

We were all instilled with the same level of middle-class confidence and were all encouraged to reach the same goals; the prospects of racial hindrance simply didn't come into it. That was their only way of loving me/us: idyllic and colour blind.

However benign their intentions, though, this wasn't representative of society's view of me. Both the black and white community would see my colour first and I'd be instantly judged – be it positively, negatively or with indifference.

I was 19 before I really experienced my first dose of overt racism. The word "nigger" was barked in my face by a Teddy Boy who I'd been staring at in admiration. It took me a while to realise who he was talking about. A few months later, someone suggested hailing a cab for me because that's the only way I'd get one. The person was white and was amazed that it hadn't occurred to me before.

Things then began to escalate. I felt like I'd been living in this bubble-wrapped cocoon for 20 years, which had just been ripped off me; up until then, although hard to believe, I'd been seemingly impervious to racism.

I suddenly became aware of the implications of being black, having been blissfully ignorant all my life. I felt ill-equipped to deal with this sudden awareness and subsequent paranoia. I started to feel quite removed from my family. They had no idea what it was like to be called a nigger. How could they? What white person can? They could never have that intrinsic understanding of racism. Their vicarious empathy felt redundant.

I began to rake up stuff from the past, which confirmed my suspicions that, actually, I'd been surrounded by racism all my life – just never really responded to it. Why were teachers so surprised by my academic achievements compared to my abortive sporting attempts, for instance? Why had people assumed I'd be a good dancer? Some of the boys at school would jeeringly sing that jingle: 'Cadbury's take'em and they cover them in chocolate', and I was puzzled by it. How could I have been so blind, so unaware?

Throughout this necessary and turbulent period it was the indomitable and consistently deep love of my parents and family that encouraged me to work through it. That's what gave me my sense of self and the subsequent strength and confidence to cope. Love gives you the impetus to find your own identity, regardless of colour. It also equips you to deal with the universal pain of prejudice and rejection, as much as anyone can be equipped to deal with it.

Whilst I soon became aware that some white people see colour as the one defining characteristic of your whole being – and will treat you accordingly – I didn't realise that the same judgement, and subsequent dismissal, would be made about me by sectors of the black community. Certainly black people see degrees of blackness and, in some cases, the wrong shade of black: the lighter shade – my shade. I had no idea that this would become another source of prejudice. On the one hand, being mixed-race can, in theory, allow you access to all cultural areas by virtue of having a white parent (or whole family in my case!). But, on the other hand, you don't feel totally accepted by either the white or the black community.

Acknowledgement: This is a revised extract from an article, 'Colour of love' by Clare Gorham, published in *The Sunday Times* on 9 August 1998.

Things may have been different, but I just don't know

MICHAEL CAINES

My adoption has been beneficial to me, on the whole a lot more good than bad. I was born in Exeter in 1969 and, to my knowledge, by mother was a white British citizen from London and my father was from Jamaica. He had settled in London where he met my mother. My mother and father were not married, as mixed relationships were not the done thing. The relationship was not too good when she fell pregnant with me. Her family moved to the South West of England. My birth mother did not have much support from her family regarding her relationship with my father. I was born in hospital and then went with my mother to a mother and baby home where I think she stayed with me for three months. My mother and father also had a daughter, older than me. My father tried to get her fostered or adopted. I really don't know what happened to my sister, which is a shame, and I would like to do something about that.

Under the circumstances, my mother simply could not keep me and so she had to put me up for adoption. My adoptive parents were looking for a daughter to adopt and they stumbled across me. They took to my charm. Both are teachers and middle class. I was the youngest child in a family of six children. They had previously adopted a boy, and they had three daughters and a son from their marriage.

As I have grown up I have realised that society was as much to blame for my adoption as my parents were. Single mothers weren't accepted and so many women were forced to give up children against their will. I have a lot of sympathy for my mother. The "free love" of the 1960s resulted in a lot of children being born outside of marriage and there existed many church-led mother and baby homes that were driven by religion. When I saw a television programme on mother and baby homes, it really affected me: I feel that there is an abandoned generation.

My childhood

I was adopted into a great, loving family. My parents' other adopted son is also mixed-race, so I wasn't the only mixed-race child in the family, but there were no cultural aspects to our upbringing. From a very young age I knew that I was adopted. My mum talked with me about the circumstances of my adoption from early on. I attended a predominantly white school. Going to an almost all-white school wasn't a problem. I suffered the inevitable racism and ignorance, but it wasn't a daily occurrence. It just made me a tough child.

Living in a very close family, I was never made to feel at all different. My parents' attitude was that I should get a good education and get a good job. They said, 'You're not going to make it in the world if you don't *educate* yourself, not because you're black.' So I worked hard at reading and writing, including in the school holidays. I was very sporty and good at art. I never, at any time, felt that I would be dealt with any differently to the other children as I did not hear that rhetoric while I was growing up.

There are things about being adopted. First, it's obvious that you are adopted if your adoptive family are white. I couldn't hide the fact of my adoption. There are also things that I missed. For example, no one ever said, 'You've got your father's eyes or you look like your mother'. There was no reference point. It was the same at the doctor's: no family medical history. There's a lot of my life that's missing, that I just simply don't know. When I had my own child, the immediate thing that made a massive impact was people saying, 'He's just like you, he's got your eyes'.

However, I didn't grow up feeling I was missing out – the reality of culture is, if you don't have it, you don't know what you're missing. For all black people there is a sense of history that is missing. My father was not from Jamaica, his ancestors had been shipped there in the slave trade from Africa. I grew up accepting there's a whole side of my culture that is missing. I have grown up looking to black role models, such as music icons, and looking for black history to absorb. I didn't grow up missing what I didn't know and I didn't feel persecuted for being black in a white society.

Now I'm older, I look back and there is a compelling sense of passion for the past, for what we as black people have had to go through, as well as a sense of pride. As a child I felt proud to be black. If you start life as a slave, you also have a passion for being a proud man. If you engage socially within sports, people are much more accepting of you. I never felt short of confidence as a child.

Belonging and searching

I had a sense of belonging in my adoptive family. I received love and compassion in that family unit. Being adopted by a white family was a positive factor because it didn't give me an outlook that I was going to be different. My parents told me that people are ignorant and that it's their problem, not mine. If my family had not been loving my experience might have been different, but I have no sense of regret or remorse.

That's why I haven't searched for my birth parents. I don't feel I don't belong so that isn't a driving factor. But I do think I owe my son a sense of belonging by searching for my mother and father now, and tracing back to the Caribbean. I think that's important because, when one looks in the mirror, one sees a person and wants to know more about how that person came about. I want to give my son a sense of family history.

I have a genetic resemblance to my son. I'm sure there's someone out there who looks like me who could be my father. Having my own son, I now realise that my father and I probably look very similar. My mother and father probably wonder about me, too. Looking after me in a mother and baby home for three months must have had a psychological impact on my mother. Out of duty to my son, it would be interesting to see where my father is and where he is from. Plus, medically, I might need to know information about myself. Having a child brings to a head a lot of issues that I have buried, possibly because of the pain. The right for adopted people to have access to their birth parents is only correct. I now understand the huge burden of responsibility and obligation that a parent has towards a child.

Reflection

I think that there are two kinds of people: those who dwell on their circumstances and misfortunes, and those who are grateful for opportunities and get on with their life. I am the latter. I was born unlucky (being adopted is not a great start) and my first experience was of being rejected by circumstances. Back in 1969, it was not socially acceptable to be a single mother with a mixed-race child. Thankfully, this has changed now.

Transracial adoption is proof of where society needs to be, where there is no social difference, and I am not going to be a different person for having a white family.

There are difficult experiences growing up in a white family but, at the end of the day, it is a better start than a foster home or being in your own family if there is abuse or neglect. Children, however, should not be placed in a family of a different religion; the integrity of their religion should be maintained. I have benefited so much from adoption. England isn't the same country that it was, though there will always be people who want to oppress others through being a bully or a racist.

My success as an individual is partly driven by my own inner strength and belief in what I am about. I have been able to get through some difficult times through having a strong family behind me. My parents are immensely proud of my achievements and I'm immensely proud that my name is Caines; I'll never change that. I've called my son the name I was born with, Joseph. I owe it to myself to acknowledge that I do have birth parents.

Some issues I've faced from being adopted

DARSHAN DAVIES

My childhood

As a child, I was the same as any youngest brother is with his brothers and sisters – the fights, the fun. I viewed my adoptive parents as my parents. I grew up in a white middle-class family and community, and attending church each week was a central part of this. I did, however, feel embarrassed when my adoptive dad introduced me as his son because I was very aware that we were different colours. In my teenage years I was closer to my adoptive mother as my adoptive dad was working abroad for some of the time.

From an early age I knew that I was different, along with my brother who is also Indian and adopted. We were close when we were young. We stuck together. After junior school this began to change, which continued throughout our teens. Although I have tried to talk with him about being transracially adopted, my brother has never talked to me about it. I got on well with my sisters but, when I went to boarding school, I saw much less of them. When I was with my sisters and they introduced me as their brother, I could see the confusion on their friends' faces. Yet I had the feeling that I was alright because the rest of my family was white. I felt I belonged in my immediate adoptive family but, in my head, I felt that I was not living how I should be living, as I was living in a privileged and not a working-class family.

Words of racial abuse hurt, and I was picked on because of my physical difference. As a result, I always felt I was trying to be accepted, for example, when I was at infant school, junior school and after that, or else I was being rejected by people. I still feel like this today, although I am learning not to.

As a child, I did not want anything to do with Indians or Pakistanis and did not have any Indian friends. I felt embarrassed and took on racist perceptions of Asian people: "bud bud", "ding ding", "greasy Paki"; clothes, accent and head wobbling. My brother and I were the only two Indian children in the school and there were very few in the area. In my teens, there were a few Indians at school but I could not relate to them. In a way, I felt like I was false, a con – neither Indian nor white. Some of these Indians did not like or accept me anyway. An example of my sense of not belonging was, when I was young, if I was with one of my sisters in town, shopping or something, I thought that people would think that she was my girlfriend so I was alright, whereas, if I was on my own, I would feel self-conscious. When people said, 'You're one of us,' this made me feel like I belonged but, at the same time, part of me wanted my difference to be accepted and not ignored.

I would wonder what my birth mum looked like and any brothers and sisters that I might have. This was always on my mind until I finally met up with them. I still do not know what my birth dad looked like or anything about him. But, it was always my birth mum that preoccupied my mind.

Visiting India

When I was 18 years old I decided to go to India to "find my identity". I was trying to be like the other people from school who were visiting India in their year off. Before I left my home, I felt as if I was going somewhere, into something I would not be able to handle, and my worries grew stronger at Heathrow airport. I arrived in Delhi in the early hours of the morning, in darkness, to an unbelievable heat. I seemed to be in the middle of nowhere. Someone even tried to buy my watch and other items from me. I took a rickshaw from the airport to various hotels in search of somewhere to stay. I was very scared and I did not feel in control at all. I had no idea how to work out the difference in money and was worried that everyone was ripping me off. So I called a friend of my parents and he came to the hotel and tried to calm me down.

My anxiety increased over the next two days. I ended up having a complete nervous breakdown. Somehow I was put on a plane back to England where my dad picked me up. The only positive thing was the sound of music, the flute and other instruments, which I heard through my headphones on the plane. The music gave me something to focus on.

Burying the ghosts

About ten years later, I went back to India with my adoptive parents. By this time, I knew more about Indian culture, had some knowledge of India and had a stronger sense of my own identity. We went around the "Golden Triangle" in North India. All the hotels were pre-booked and a driver or guide took care of us at each destination. I felt safe being there with them; they were both experienced travellers. I enjoyed the beauty of the places we visited: the palaces, the history, the views and scenery, as well as the cows and their spiritual quality. It was a great way to bring new memories to mind and to leave behind the previous ones that haunted me.

I cannot imagine having the confidence or desire to go to India alone but at least I now feel more at peace about the country. I like to look at India as I would any other country, even though it is my country of heritage. I did not feel any particular affinity with her people, although I did recognise many aspects of beauty and richness.

My relationship with my adoptive family

After I had my breakdown, my relationship with my family changed. I had a lot of anger towards my adoptive parents and spent some time not staying in touch with them much or, at times, the rest of the family. I blamed my parents for my unhappiness and depression and was angry with my brother and sisters.

Over many years, during which I experienced a lot of depression, I was admitted to psychiatric hospital and talked and behaved in ways that were hurtful to my adoptive family. I am now living my life away from my adoptive family members who are based in different parts of England. My adoptive mum has supported me through my hospital admissions and I have felt very close to her because of this, often in a child-like way. My adoptive dad has also supported me, though in a different way. The rest of my family have been supportive over the years in whatever ways they could. There has been much heartache for everyone, I am sure.

Meeting my birth family

> *Every Asian woman*
> *I passed in the street*
> *I wondered if you were one of them*
> *And would we ever meet?*

Meeting my birth mother for the first time, I did not feel anything towards her. But at least I now knew why I looked the way I looked and could see the similarities between us. I had hoped in a fantasy way that meeting my birth mother and family would sort out my depression and unhappiness and that I would be part of a new ideal life. This is not what happened in reality.

I met other members of my birth family – half-brothers, a half-sister and a sister-in-law – all of whom made me very welcome and involved me in their lives. As an adult, from reading, I had already gained some understanding of different Indian philosophies, beliefs and culture. After spending time with my birth family, I had first-hand experience of their culture and was able to learn more. For example, I went to Indian weddings, listened to Indian music and attended religious and cultural festivals.

With time, however, I realised that I could not carry on being a part of my birth family's life as it was not my world and they had expectations of me that I found difficult. For example, they wanted me to visit regularly and play an active part in their lives. Really, they had their lives, which they were living, and I had made my own life and was like a passenger in theirs. I became aware that I would not be happy unless I sorted out or found my reality.

My step-dad (my birth mother's husband) was talking about arranged marriages and saying that this was what I needed. I knew that to marry would be a disaster. Gradually, I was becoming more involved and being expected to behave according to their Indian culture. Yet, I could not fully understand their culture and this was not what I wanted to do nor how I wanted to be. I did not like the control that my step-dad exercised over his family and I did not want this to extend to me. My birth mother tried to make me feel some joy towards her husband and said that he would look after me and get me on my feet. But, at the end of the day, I did not want to live a lie.

With my birth family, I was unable to understand or communicate in Punjabi, although I tried to learn to speak my mother tongue at night class along with other Sikh people. I could not appreciate the differences in ways of thinking, speaking, expression or humour. When I am with my birth family, I am in a vulnerable position. I have no control or say in what goes on around me – no voice and no opinion. I am present, but am not part of it. While I can appreciate the style and sound of Indian music and films, I do not understand what is being said or communicated. With the Sikh religion, I can sense the beauty and the richness but this is merely superficial, as is my understanding of the whole way of life, and of the family structure and roles. If another Punjabi-speaking person asks me for directions or speaks to me on the bus, I am unable to answer. All these experiences go hand in hand with the need to maintain my sense of identity and belonging, and my ability to feel proud about myself.

My meeting my birth mother and her family was difficult for my adoptive mum. I did not want to hurt her or make her and my dad feel rejected. But I know it did hurt my adoptive mum. I had a lot of feelings of guilt about talking to her about my birth family, yet, in an ironic way, I wanted to share my experiences with her. Our relationship felt strained after I got involved with my birth family.

I became close to one of my half-brothers and his family and they were very nice to me, but I have made a choice to go my own way for now. I have taken control of my life instead of other people influencing it so much. The positive side of establishing contact with my birth family has been the insight I have gained into a different way of life: Indian culture and values. I value the affirmation and creativity of my birth family's culture, the richness, diversity and celebration of life. There is a common identity and shared interests to talk about, such as events, politics and sport in India, and the impact of these on the community here. Yet I do not belong to Indian culture or to the Indian community, just as I do not belong completely in white English society either. I only belong with those people who know me and with whom I have developed some sort of relationship. However, I do feel more comfortable among white society than I do within the Indian or Asian communities.

Today

Now, I am just trying to get a life together for myself, a life where I can receive sufficient help and support from professionals and have friendships with people I know, so that I can build up my own life and feel able to cope. Plus, I want to keep my relationships with my adoptive family separate and on an adult level. My adoptive family is the family I am part of and who have been in my life. They will always be my family. Hopefully, though, one day I will have a family – a partner and children – of my own.

From darkness to light – a transracial adoption

RON McLAY

PART 1: My own personal Holocaust (2001)

Childhood

I was born at 10.40 am on 9 December 1961 in Ross Hospital, Paisley, Scotland. My 19-year-old white Scottish mother was married and already had one son by her husband when she arrived at the hospital to give birth to me. My appearance at birth as a "coloured" child was a shock both to her and her husband. Two of the social worker's entries in the "Statement of Case" read:

> *This baby was coloured. Apparently the mother had allegedly been assaulted by a Pakistani who had been staying in the same lodging house. This had never been reported to police and Mr T had only been informed when it was discovered that the baby was coloured. Due to the fact that the child is coloured the husband is prepared to allow his wife to return only on the condition that the baby does not accompany her. 'Maybe the baby won't be so dark as his skin doesn't seem so dark today'.*

And thus began my painful journey.

Named after my father and given the married surname of my mother, I was sent to Crosslet House, an orphanage, at five days of age. When I was five months old, I joined my white Scottish adoptive parents. My adoptive mother had been an assistant nurse at Crosslet House and, over a period of time, she had decided that she wished to adopt me. She would often tell me that she had had a choice of me and a little girl and she chose me because I was so beautiful. She told me that all the nurses loved me and that I was special.

When I was 18 months old, my adoptive mother gave birth to her first biological son. We then moved down to England when I was three. From this time up, until we migrated to Australia, I have no recollection of being different. My adoptive mother had apparently explained to me that I was adopted and she had taken me for a visit to Crosslet House to show me where I came from, but I was too young to remember this.

Just before I turned nine, we emigrated to Australia. On my very first day in school, racism discovered me. The other kids called me names (they thought that I was Aboriginal) and, after a few days, this included fights. I told my parents that the other kids didn't like me and were calling me names. I remember my dad telling me, 'Sticks and stones will break your bones but names will never hurt you', a mantra he repeated many times over the years.

In all my schooling over the next few years, I was either the only dark-skinned kid or one of very few. I cannot remember periods of time when I was not racially discriminated against in school. I had many fights and was spat on and called names like "wog", "black bastard", "Abo", "black Jew", "f*** wog" and "c***".

I listened to The Beatles a lot at this time, particularly their sadder songs. These songs echoed the sadness that pervaded my entire being. I played them again and again. I was not accepted by the other children unless they were also part of an ethnic minority, usually the Greek guys who let me hang around with them. I was in an ethnic minority of one, the smallest minority of all.

Deep down, I always longed to know where I came from. However, when anyone asked, I would say that it wasn't important and that I wasn't interested. I said this so often that I believed it. Every time I met someone new I relived the shame and pain of telling them I was Scottish. I would always get a look of disbelief and feel obliged to explain my origins as I knew them. This has continued to this very day.

My mother told me my father was Persian and that my name meant "Red Prince". I never felt Persian and wondered why I had been given up for adoption. To add to the pain of adoption, my adoptive maternal uncle sexually assaulted me. When I told my adoptive parents about this, they brushed it under the carpet. It was like racism – they didn't have the ability to cope with it.

One strange aspect of my experience is that my upbringing has endowed me with a "white man's mind". I think like a white man even though I am not. I am very sensitive to racism of any kind, but I have had the mind-bending experience of looking at people who have the same features as me and having racist thoughts about them. I would often joke with people that I'd always wished I was a white supremicist racist but was the wrong colour.

I was a lonely and rebellious teenager and I "acted out", especially with my mother.

At one stage she had a mental breakdown from the stress of our fights. I asked my adoptive mother recently why she had had the breakdown and she said that it was because my adoptive father had sided with me against her. He displayed a great deal of love towards me all my life, and I remember him trying to keep the peace. They argued about me frequently.

At 15, I tasted alcohol for the first time and got very drunk. I drank brandy straight out of the bottle and with only one intention: to get "out of it". I was to use alcohol and drugs for the next 24 years for that exact purpose: to escape my own mind.

Adulthood

When I finished high school I went to Israel for a year. It was here that I had my first physical relationship with a woman. Then began a pattern in my life: I would start a relationship and then begin acting crazy, deliberately saying or doing terrible things to provoke my partner. I could never understand why I did this. I was obsessed about being touched. I wanted my partners to cuddle me and be affectionate without ceasing.

Returning to Australia, I spent the next two years using drugs. I used any drug I could that would help me escape reality. After an unsuccessful relationship at the age of 22, I began a downward spiral of drinking and was on tablets for depression because of the break-up, telling myself, 'I have no reason to live.' I hated myself and wished that I'd never been born. One evening, I took a packet of tranquillisers, drank a lot of alcohol and used my scuba knife to cut my wrists. I woke up in hospital. They pumped my stomach out and put over 30 stitches in my wrists. I spent some time in a psychiatric ward and, when I left the ward, my dad whom I always loved a lot and who treated me as his favourite, nursed me back to health.

Looking back, in much of my adult life I have been self-destructive, drinking heavily and binge drinking, sabotaging relationships and friendships, being controlling and threatening in my relationships with women, and having affairs. I mistakenly equated sex with love. I have had two failed marriages and a daughter whom I have not always cared for as well as I should have. Often I have felt suicidal. Eventually, when I was 39 a friend took me to hospital and I was sent to a private hospital to be treated for alcoholism. It was here that I finally acknowledged that I was an alcoholic.

Racism

As an adult, racism has always been just a little distance away. I remember one day I was working on the railways at a North Shore station. I was working at the station one day as the Station Master and there was a girl working with me who was selling tickets. I asked her if she wanted a break and I took over. An elderly, well-dressed woman came up to the ticket window and asked for a return ticket. I started looking for it as I wasn't familiar with the lay-out. She looked past me to the girl sitting behind me and said, referring to me, 'I think that it's a disgrace that they let these Indonesians into the country when they can't even speak the language. The worst thing is that my husband fought against people like him in the war.'

One of my bosses on the railways called me 'the black pearl' in front of the other staff. I never complained but inside I was hurting. When I was studying in the Station Masters' school, there was a Lebanese guy who was being racially taunted by two Australians from the country. I stepped in and the situation became so violent that the lecturer had to let me and the Lebanese guy go early every day for the rest of the course so that the two Australian guys couldn't catch us and beat us up.

Reflection

I started to see a psychotherapist and my first words to him were: 'I have three issues in my life I need to learn to deal with and accept. One, transracial adoption. Two, racism and three, being sexually assaulted by my uncle. I am an alcoholic but I go to meetings to deal with my drinking. These three issues are triggers for my drinking.'

I now attend eight or so meetings a week, as part of an anonymous 12-step programme, and have found a wonderful church with real people. I still have problems with low self-esteem and self-doubt and wonder if anyone really likes me. I have started to explore my feelings about being adopted and even to express some very painful emotions. Today I cried when I was explaining some of the issues to my ex-wife. This is probably the first time I've cried when sober in many, many years. Recently, I have started reading books about adoption. Whilst reading the The *Primal Wound* by Nancy Verrier, I found myself in its pages again and again, which was an amazing experience. I have realised that my personality was a front which I had created to protect myself from further hurt. I hope that one day I can love normally.

Perhaps the hardest part of this adopted life has been the loneliness that it induces and the lack of people who understand or give credence to my experience. I did try several times in my life to explain my pain and never found an understanding person. I hope to remedy this with a network of transracial adoptees that I have joined. If anyone asked me now what I think of transracial adoption, I would say that it can be an unspeakably horrible and hellish experience: not belonging anywhere, not fitting in my family, looking different, being constantly reminded, not knowing my racial background, not being able to defend myself against racism, terrible, terrible loneliness, never-ending sadness, rejecting oneself. I wouldn't wish it on my worst enemy.

Meeting my birth mother

I have wondered about my mother and my father all my life. My mother always seemed more important to me than my father. However, I often told people who enquired that I wasn't interested in finding my mother. I alternated between hating her and fantasising about her. From time to time, I wondered about my father and I have said many times in my life that I'd like to find out about "the dark side of me". I used to call myself "the dark sheep of the family".

At 30, I learned the name of my mother and that I was given the birth name Lal Shah Taylor at birth. I was in Scotland for a few days with my (adoptive) paternal aunt in Bearsden, Glasgow, at the time. That Thursday, I told her that I wanted to find my mother. The next day I caught the train to Edinburgh and went to the General Register Office at New Register House. I paid the fee and began my search. I felt a great deal of excitement as I searched. My head was spinning with many thoughts. I found my mother's birth certificate and traced a beginning of a family tree. Then I found a marriage certificate for a cousin who had been married in Dundee. I found my cousin's phone number in the telephone book and, in a state of high excitement (I was shaking), I called the number.

My cousin's wife answered the phone and I explained who I was and that I wanted to contact my mother. She said that she had the phone number of my brother and that he would phone me. A few minutes later my half-brother, older by one year, called. He was very emotional and obviously knew about me. However, he was guarded when I asked him about my mother. I remember feeling very strange when I asked him about "our mother". He told me that no one in the family had spoken to her for four years because she was an alcoholic. He briefly described the difficult and abusive life he and my other half-siblings had had. He told me about my half-sister, my dead half-brother and my other half-brother.

I asked if there was any information that he could give me that would help me find my mother and he told me that she liked drinking at a particular pub in Glasgow and was often with a friend called John M. At around 6.30 p.m. I caught a taxi from Bearsden into Glasgow and went straight to the pub. I asked people in the pub but no one had heard of her or John. I then spent the evening going from pub to pub. The evening wore on and I started to get very despondent. I had to catch a train back to England the next day to make my flight back to Australia. At about one in the morning, I decided to give up and jumped in a taxi. The driver asked, 'You're not from around here – what are you doing?' I told him I was from Australia and that I was trying to find my mother. He asked me what my mother's name was and I told him. He didn't know her. Almost as an afterthought I asked him, 'Do you know John M?' He said, 'I know John.' I said to him, 'Can you please take me to John's place. I've got to go back to Australia tomorrow and I won't have another chance.'

He took me to John's place and I knocked on the door. John eventually came to the door and had clearly had a big night drinking. I told him my name and started to explain my story. He stopped me and said, 'I know all about you. Your mother has talked about nothing else for 20 years.' We talked for a few minutes and I asked him to take me to my mother's place. So we walked to another flat. It was about two in the morning. Ironically, the flat was about 50 metres from a school where I had stood several times with my aunt.

John knocked on the door and the landlord let us in. The landlord knocked on my mother's bedroom door where she was staying with her new husband. She came out in a nightgown and I held my hand out and said, 'Hello, I'm Ron McLay but you probably know me better as Lal Shah.' She started trembling and shaking and she fell down at my feet. She held my feet and started crying bitterly. She said, 'Please forgive me,' over and over again. Her tears were falling on my shoes. I remember feeling it was like a dream: that I was having an out-of-body experience and looking on. I do not remember having any feelings at all.

Her husband calmed her down and she and I sat down in the lounge. She held on to me very tightly and started to talk, saying that I had been stolen from her and that the matron at the hospital had forced her to give me up. She told me that she had never stopped thinking about me and that she once saw a boy she thought was me and had followed him.

I started asking her questions like, how did she meet my father? What was he like? She insisted that it was a one-night stand. I deliberately asked her about the adoption papers saying that she had been assaulted, and she said that it was not an assault. She told me that she had hoped the baby was her husband's and she was shocked when I was born. Two of her brothers had even beaten her up a few days after she went home from the hospital. Her husband then opened a bottle of whisky and we all started drinking.

I returned to my aunt's place and packed my bags. My aunt drove me back to see my mother. I spent some more time with her and took some photos. I remember being very excited to be with her. My mother was quite bitter when she talked of the hospital staff and she was also very angry talking about my adoptive parents, as though they had stolen me from her. She had mourned for me ever since I was taken away. It seemed to me that I could no longer blame her for giving me away.

Two years later, I returned to see my mother with my then wife and my daughter. She was very friendly. But, on the third day of visiting her, she had been drinking and she became very abusive and was saying quite nasty things about my adoptive mother and the hospital staff. I stayed in touch for a few years but then stopped writing. The last contact I had with my birth family was a communication from my brother to tell me that my mother and her husband had broken up.

As I look back at meeting my birth mother, I have no regrets that I undertook to search for her. I felt sympathy for her predicament but my feelings for her were not strong. I do want to re-establish contact with her if I can though. I think it is important that we have contact and I believe that I would get more out of the relationship now.

PART 2: Free as a bird (April 2004)

Becoming whole

Nearly three years have elapsed since I wrote my life story. Since then so much has happened. Great changes have occurred. I would now like to tell my journey from victim and victimhood to survivor, and then to integration and acceptance.

Apart from meeting my 12-step sponsor, the most significant things to happen include reading *The Primal Wound*. When I read it I turned each page and, as I read, I said to myself 'that's me, that's me'. It tells my story and explains so much about the adoption experience. I am currently reading Nancy's follow-up book called *Coming Home to Self*. It is a worthy successor. It challenges the adoptee to drop the victim attitude and to move on to greater things.

A couple of years ago I travelled to India. A number of profound events occurred whilst I was there. I went to an orphanage where there were about 30 orphans aged from one to 15 years old. They were all smiling but I could see the sadness in their eyes, the same sadness that has been in my eyes all my life. After a while, I was overcome with emotion and I cried and cried. The healing of my shame about my ethnicity began in India.

Once I was on the path of sobriety, I began to chase emotional sobriety: I wanted to be whole. I was very enthusiastic because I saw that it was possible that I could be well and that life could be wonderful and fulfilling. At first, I went to a psychotherapist and two psychologists. I wanted to explore my adoption issues and the sexual abuse issues. Let me recommend not seeing so many practitioners concurrently: it's very confusing! I also contacted the Post Adoption Resource Centre at Bondi (in Sydney) and was given the contact number of a woman who has become a dear friend. This woman had founded the organisation ICASN (Inter Country Adoption Support Network) and had organised a meeting of adoptees at a restaurant. I turned up at the restaurant and my journey of recovery from the wilderness of adoption and aloneness began in earnest. As I listened to her story, talked with and observed the other adoptees, I could see that I was no longer alone. I was 39 years old and had never ever spoken with a group of adoptees about adoption. Suddenly, I was surrounded by adoptees who were interested in my story.

Being a transracial adoptee has made the adoption experience a complex one. I have spent the years from age eight, when I first experienced racism at an Australian school, until last year feeling shame at being half Pakistani. However, on a recent trip to the UK, I went to a 12-step programme meeting in the Midlands and was sitting there when two Indians/Pakistanis walked in. The most amazing thing happened: I felt like I was no longer the only one! As I strolled around parts of Birmingham and Wolverhampton, I walked in areas where Indians and Pakistanis predominated. I felt like I was no longer the "odd man out". Another very interesting thing happened. I began to see how beautiful Indian and Pakistani women are. I undertake to eat Indian and Pakistani food when I have a chance, and I wear my *kurta* pyjamas when I eat at these restaurants.

I also felt shame that I was half Scottish, particularly when asked to explain my origins. I would say that I was born in Scotland and watch the look of disbelief appear on the face of the person I was speaking to. One of my natural uncles helped me to feel proud of my Scottish ancestry. I went on a tour of the highlands, including the home of my Scottish clan on the Isle of Skye, and found out that my ancestors were Vikings.

I have taken various actions along the way to further my recovery. These include embracing my origins by wearing a bracelet that has my Pakistani birth name, my Scottish clan name, the name the nurses used in the orphanage for me and my adoptive name. I have joined a committee that assists adoptees and adoptive parents. I participate in service work and 12-step work (visiting and talking with those still suffering from active alcoholism) and I also take opportunities to share my adoption story within the organisation. At a recent conference, three adoptees approached me about my story after I'd shared it.

Returning to Scotland

Last year I returned to Scotland and England to search for my birth father, to stay with my birth mother and to meet some of my maternal relations for the first time. When I arrived at my mother's place, we began a process of getting to know each other. I can't say that it was easy: it was strained at times and confronting to discuss issues. My birth mother is from the old school and, in many respects, I was overwhelming her with my eagerness and recovery. I was trying to take her along my path of recovery.

On one occasion I spent 45 minutes on a mobile phone trying to convince my adoptive mother that I had brown skin and that I didn't want her ever to call me "special" again. At the end of the call, she said to me that I *was* special to her and that I looked just like her two natural sons (fair skin and blue eyes). I nearly threw the phone against a wall. I have come to realise that that is her way of loving me. She is in denial and that's OK.

My birth mother and I spent six days together without much of a break and then on the seventh day, she turned and accused me of various "crimes". The stay with her came to an abrupt halt. At the time I felt a very intense feeling of pain, that I was experiencing a second rejection. I said nothing to defend myself. I let her vent her feelings and then quietly left the house. I journeyed to my maternal uncle's place. I connected with him on a very deep level, discovering that we had a lot in common. My uncle was very kind to me and explained that my mother had had issues her whole life. There is a great deal of unresolved rage within her. As I reflect on the experience, I recall that she warned me when I first arrived that she had certain problems.

My mother travelled to Australia a few weeks after my return to stay with a friend. She visited my work and left an unpleasant note for me. Since then, she has emailed me three times. The emails were reasonably innocuous. So what do I make of all this? I see in her behaviour the pain of her own response to the primal wound. I also see the reactive behaviour of someone who grew up in a violent alcoholic home and was a practising alcoholic for most of her life. She and I are very similar.

When we both went to a post-adoption service in the UK, to start the search for my father, the counsellor told her that she could have counselling if she wished. She was amazed and told the counsellor that she would definitely take up the opportunity. I hope she does. She is my birth mother, there is no other than can replace her. She has had a very hard life and perhaps it was the relinquishment that caused much of her pain. Who knows? She hasn't spoken to my half-brother, her oldest son, for 14 years. She has not been in contact with her daughter or other son for a long time. Connecting successfully with them or with me is beyond her current capability. I realise that what happened was not my fault. My relationship with my adoptive mother has improved since my return from that trip, although I wouldn't say that we are the best of friends yet.

Reflection

So, I'm perfect now, right? Far from it. I am much happier than when I wrote, "My own personal Holocaust". I still battle with my addictive nature and am always on the look out for feel-goods. But I take a lot more pride in how I dress and dress to please myself now. Before I stopped drinking, I couldn't even stand to look in the mirror. But I am embracing change. I reject the lies of the past. I am not afraid to be wrong. I am not afraid to say I don't know. I am no longer afraid of the shadow Ron.

Some things that have saved my life

VERONICA DEWAN

Illegitimate, "mixed race", "hard to place", another "adoption fairy tale". London circa 1956 begins "No Coloureds, No Irish, No Dogs". One white Irish Mayo woman is revising for her nursing exams, one Indian law student on a Nehru scholarship arrives from New Delhi. Blue eyes meet brown eyes on the Circle Line; at Holland Park Hotel passion transcends religion (Catholic/Hindu), culture (Celtic/Punjabi), "race" (white/black), class/caste (working/*khatriya*). *Singin' in the Rain*, fish and chips. And then she is pregnant and religion, gender, race and class collide at "digs" in Paddington. He has a friend: 'I was warned about you Irish women snaring unsuspecting foreign students.' At the mother and baby home in Grayshott, the nun says, 'It's a terrible, terrible sin, not only unmarried but sullied by a coloured man.' A.E. Wyeth solicitors of Lincoln's Inn write to Southwark Catholic Rescue Society:

As a matter of courtesy we think we should let you know that our client Mr Dewan consulted us upon the subject matters of your letters of 19th September and 1st October, but paternity is denied.

Enter one benevolent, childless, working-class couple, forty-ish, an Irish Catholic woman and English Protestant man, who receive a letter from the adoption society – 'The father is Indian and she is slightly coloured, she's a dear little baby however' – and perfect promises of a loving home and three "happy ever after" lives. Birth mother swept out of picture, shamed, no place to grieve her loss, "severance is the only way", will marry and move to the US.

First encounter with social services, 1957: six weeks old

My adoptive mother distinctly remembers hearing sobbing that sounded as if it was coming from the next room. She and my adoptive father were collecting me from the Catholic Rescue Society in Southwark to take me home to a charming secluded hamlet in southern England, where they lived in the "tied" cottage owned by my father's employers.

I believe my adoptive mother tried to love me but she still hoped for a child of her own. She was terribly lonely, missed Ireland and soon began to express her unhappiness and grief, sobbing on the kitchen step, recounting how her childhood in Dublin had ended abruptly when her father died. She was 14, the eldest child of five and was immediately removed from school and sent to *Wills* tobacco factory. She earned a good wage, supported her family and had several breakdowns. After 12 years, she rebelled against her mother, left the factory and came to England. Here, she was met with hostility when people heard her Irish accent, the grocer who whispered, 'Here come the IRA,' the baker who sneered 'that stupid Paddy'. My parents were in their thirties when they married; my mother had been engaged once to an Irishman but when he moved to Kerry he promised to send for her but then broke off the engagement. She missed him, she missed city life. My father was from Suffolk, a rose grower who worked long hours in the fields. It was difficult to reconcile the kindness and sensitivity of this man with his refusal to accept that his anti-Irish jokes were deeply hurtful to his wife. 'Why do you get upset? I'm not talking about you.' No one seemed to understand how hard life could be for a working-class Irish Catholic woman in a rural English protestant community.

My mother was unable to deal with my distress in response to playground racial prejudice: 'My dad says you lot should go back to your own country' and 'My mum says you smell of curry.' The more I showed my vulnerability the more she would lash out with words and slaps. In my father's opinion, I was simply making up stories about other children to get attention and it had to stop. 'You're English now. You're my daughter.'

I was seven when she first held a knife to me, 'I'll kill you, then kill myself.' On better days, she would decide 'I'll go home to live in Dublin. Your father can look after you.' She also saw me as English, and maybe it was our combined sense of vulnerability and powerlessness that exacerbated her physical and verbal threats to kill or abandon me. She would invite neighbours' children to tea and tell them that she loved them, but could never love me. Meanwhile my father, exhausted on returning from work, would bury his head in the newspaper, turn the volume up on the TV, accuse me of upsetting my mother, 'Why can't you behave and give me a bit of peace?'

Somehow it felt like we had all been abandoned with no sign of help. I slipped into a wonderful fantasy world. I believed that my real father, a handsome young Indian, turbanned and bejewelled astride a white stallion, was searching the kingdom for me. I believed the migrating birds would guide him to me. I would leave secret notes in the garden for the birds to take to him. When I discovered that planes flew passengers from India to Heathrow, I gave up on horses and created my little hotel in the woods so, when his flight arrived, he would have a place to stay nearby so I could visit him.

And then the fantasy world collapsed. I could no longer sustain being very good and the adopted child who is not very good is suddenly very bad. Being OK and average doesn't often enter the equation. From being "special" and "chosen" I was now "bad blood" and was sure to follow in my birth mother's footsteps. My adoptive mother would curse my birth mother, 'What kind of woman would abandon her own child?'

Everything was unreal; so much so that, when my grandmother in Dublin died of cancer, my mother blamed me for her death.

By the time I was 11, my mother had had a hysterectomy. She was angry when I started my periods and more insults flowed about my origins. We were very poor and my mother would curse me for needing money for sanitary protection. When electricity bills arrived, she said my father would have to go to prison because they could not pay, that I was responsible for our poverty, that it would be my fault when they locked him away.

I was in a state of numbness and confusion, haunted by voices from the radio speaking in a strange monotone, an ache and hollowness in my chest, and my legs would shake so violently I couldn't get downstairs: some physical manifestations of the depression I had sunk into. Also, a sense of guilt enveloped me. I had tarnished the image of the "chosen" child, the "special" child, the "gift from God" for this deserving childless couple. Add constant reminders from nuns, priests, neighbours, teachers and Christian Aid to be especially thankful because I could have been a starving child in India had it not been for my adoptive parents. It seemed relentless.

Suicidal thoughts had accompanied me through childhood. At seven my teacher wrongly accused me in front of the class of cheating in an arithmetic test, telling my classmates that Indians were deceitful and not to be trusted. That's when I started fantasising about different ways to kill myself. My self-esteem was not helped by our neighbour, her son having studied the racist pseudo-science of phrenology. Examining the size of my forehead, she concluded I would never amount to anything. But I recovered and gained confidence because certain teachers recognised my abilities and encouraged me, and I passed the eleven plus.

Yet my mother's resentment festered. As I thrived at school, she would remind me how her childhood had been so cruelly curtailed, and question why I should be given more opportunities than her. I was now at a Catholic convent grammar school. At 12, I took an overdose triggered by my mother storming out of the house because I brought home a tin of curry powder: 'Get that filthy disgusting stuff out of my kitchen.' I was also deeply upset that my PE teacher, who gave me extra tuition and on whom I had a crush, suddenly announced she was pregnant and would be leaving. I soon lost interest in everything.

Several sessions with a child psychiatrist didn't help; I could not articulate my feelings to a middle-aged, middle-class white man in a suit and bow tie. I felt detached from everyone, even my school friends who tried to help, and soon began running away from home, stopped attending school, took weed, acid, barbiturates, speed, barley wine, cough mixture, glue – anything that was offered to me. And that included sex because, suddenly, I was being noticed by men. I was, after all, "the daughter of a whore", a pubescent Indian-looking hippy. Exoticised and eroticised, I liked all the attention. It was 1970.

Second encounter with the official care system: aged 14 sent to an approved school

Police and social workers featured prominently in my life. My delinquency was attributed to my genetic inheritance. Expelled from the convent school, I was found a place at a boarding school near Bristol by my social worker, who felt it would resolve the problems regarding my home life and provide me with an opportunity to get back on track with my education. But I was already pregnant and ran away within the month. I returned home. My GP recommended a termination; he was adamant I was too young to contemplate becoming a mother; that my education should not suffer. But the school refused to take me back and a voluntary arrangement was made with social services to receive me into care. My mother didn't want to go to court, she simply had to sign a form. My father didn't come home that day. My social worker told me that at least now they could understand my behaviour. She had explained to my parents that my promiscuity was attributable to being Indian; that in India I would have been married with children by the age of 12.

It was a traumatic hospital stay, then straight away sent to an approved school in Staines. The school, managed by Mind on behalf of the Home Office, was where I would remain locked up for two years. During this time I met other teenage girls, including those messed up like me after being placed in inappropriate adoptive and foster homes. There were some genuinely caring staff members who provided more safety than I had known at home, but a few staff considered that locking me up was insufficient punishment. One in particular became incensed each time she set eyes on me: 'You should never have been born.' My mother never visited; my father came though. He had to appear in court: my care at the approved school demanded that my parents contribute £4 a week, equivalent to nearly half of his weekly wages. I stopped eating shortly before the case went to appeal. Fortunately, he won the appeal and the amount was reduced.

Once, I escaped from the approved school with another girl. On the run for six weeks, I moved into a squat and worked for a cleaning company. In that time I received much kindness from strangers: the woman at the Samaritans office in Leeds who gave me money from her own purse to buy a coat, a woman who wrote me a reference for a job, another who gave me clothes to attend an interview.

At 16, I was released. I had one 'O' level in English Language that I had sat at 14 but I had no further motivation to study. I had, however, been taught to type – something I hated but was told would help me get a job. Now, it is one of the skills I value as I develop my career as a writer. My transition back into society involved a stay at a working girls' hostel. I was working as an office junior and preparing to leave the hostel when my mother declared she wanted me home, that she had forgiven me. I was naïve, all I wanted was to be loved by her. But it became apparent that it was my income and not me that she welcomed with open arms. She insisted it was my duty and that I owed her. Perhaps she was mirroring the treatment she had received from her own mother.

The third intervention of the official care system: aged 33 a psychiatric in-patient

The first of my several in-patient admissions to an acute psychiatric ward was in 1990. I crashed after my first-year law exams, told I was suicidally depressed. Although I would pass my exams, my consultant considered I was setting my sights too high and advised me to be less ambitious, give up my studies and take medication for the rest of my life. I expressed my belief in the value of talking treatments; he did not agree. In the hospital it was unsafe. Scant regard paid by staff to either the physical or psychological well-being of patients, policies on racial and sexual harassment hardly ever implemented and several admissions increased my feelings of despair and isolation.

Why was it so difficult to get talking treatment? I would not accept as irrefutable the prognosis of the psychiatrist and his other male colleagues, that drug treatment alone would enable me to lead my life. The fourth psychiatrist was a French woman with an Indian partner and children of dual heritage. 'I've seen the harshness in this society towards my own children.' Within minutes she referred me to psychotherapy. Gradually my confidence returned; finally I had someone to help me interpret my experiences, resist psychiatry's peddlers of doom and carry on to complete my law degree in 1993.

During those years, my psychiatric files would construct a paper identity that bore less and less resemblance to me. As each psychiatrist recorded their assessment, the next one would mainly base their opinion on what had already been written, relying on their colleagues' insights. I witnessed many patients being neglected and ignored. I had lost all credibility but still I was shocked to be told by the charge nurse that 'I was too complicated to engage with' and that her staff had been told not to talk to me. The majority of nursing staff at that time were Asian or Irish.

My label of delinquency stuck; it is sometimes hard to accept that no malice was intended. The dictionary definition of delinquency includes failing in or neglectful of duty or obligation. Who then is the delinquent? With staff not allowed to listen to me, in desperation I would ring the Samaritans from the public phone on the psychiatric ward. The Samaritans continued to give me hope while 'being cared for in hospital' had been stripped of its meaning.

On my last admission to a psychiatric unit in 1996, my physical health was deteriorating. It was as though both body and spirit had finally surrendered to the noxious attitudes and oppressive treatment regime. When my legs collapsed beneath me, I was told off by nurses for "attention seeking". I almost believed one psychiatrist's view that the numbness, tingling and weakness in my body were side-effects of medication and that I would soon adapt. But I remained puzzled and decided to stop taking the medication in the hope of getting rid of these so-called side-effects. Within a few weeks I was admitted to a neurological hospital and diagnosed with relapsing remitting multiple sclerosis. My mistrust of psychiatry was complete.

Beyond care

I was being assessed for admission to a psychiatric day unit; my files piled up on the desk. The Head Occupational Therapist assured me he had read them carefully and didn't think it necessary to ask me any questions. He presented me with a programme based on his conclusion that I was incapable of sustaining intimate relationships. That was it. I refused to accept this, asked him to review his assessment. To his credit he was prepared to start again. He listened as I explained that I had in fact sustained too many unsuitable intimate relationships and that the issue was not, in my opinion, one of endurance but, rather, of having the courage to say I had made a mistake and to get out before further damage was done. Here, too, was an opportunity for me to reconsider the benefits of the formal care I had received. I was aware that, in psychiatry, it was not my strengths but my weaknesses that were focused upon, the questions always negatively framed. I felt it was time to conduct a self-assessment.

In terms of formal support I have benefited from psychotherapy. My first therapist, a white European male, helped me through the most difficult times, including recurrent admissions to hospital between 1990 and 1996. He helped me to build my confidence and recognise I had the capacity and would not be punished for pursuing my education. It was with his support that I completed my law degree. Yet we stumbled in our communication about the way that racism had impacted on my life, the misinformation I had internalised about being of mixed heritage and confusion about my sexual orientation. I needed to continue therapy but feared that if I rocked the boat I would lose a lifeline. But I moved home and abruptly ended the sessions. I applied to Nafsiyat, an intercultural therapy service, and received funding through my primary care trust. The service had been recommended by the Post-Adoption Centre where I had briefly attended counselling and undertaken group work with other transracially fostered and adopted adults. Nafsiyat really felt like my last chance and I knew I would have to commit fully. I was matched with a black female psychotherapist of mixed heritage. She understood the effects of the profoundly painful process of assimilation that had distorted my beliefs and identity. I learned that my being had not been erased but that I was fundamentally still intact. I gradually began to value myself and notice the people who loved and cared for me. I would learn to accept why I had made certain choices and my responsibility for taking back control of my life. I was re-emerging stronger and more hopeful.

I have been strengthened by close friendships with other mental health system survivors, people who've been written off as psychiatric patients. Friends have shown me how no longer to be paralysed by my emotional crises, to question the value of the Western model of mental illness. *Mental Health, Race and Culture* by Dr Suman Fernando was particularly important to my understanding of how and why 19th century "race" theories are perpetuated within current psychiatric practice, how myths about the dangerousness of black people are used to justify the most coercive and harmful forms of treatment, why people die in the mental health system.

The discovery of a dynamic community of transracially placed people has contributed to me finding a place in the world. I appreciate everyone who contributed in any way to creating and sustaining ATRAP: even though each of our upbringings has been very different, it remains a powerful connection. I appreciate all the writers who have shared their experience of being adopted or fostered by white parents. At the Edinburgh Festival in 1993 I first heard Jackie Kay and Lemn Sissay reading their poetry. They provided the key for me to enter a world of words that previously had made little sense. I was overwhelmed by Jackie Kay's compassion, generosity and humour when I first read *The Adoption Papers*, the voices of the birth mother, the adoptive mother, and adopted daughter. It was revelatory to hear each of these viewpoints side by side.

In 1999, I attended an Arvon Foundation poetry course "Exciting writing", led by Patience Agbabi and Lemn Sissay. Lemn gave us an exercise to write about a person we really loved or hated. I chose my adoptive mother and automatically thought I would write about hate but ended up writing about my love for her. In this poem I reclaimed my mother's kindness. Patience and Lemn and the course participants were a sustaining gift to me; they gave me confidence and encouragement to develop my writing. Of Patience's amazing poems, 'UFO Woman' (pronounced OOFOE) resonates particularly strongly the alienation of transracial placement: 'So I take a tram, tube, train, taxi trip/hip-hugged, bell-bottomed and thick-lipped, landing/in a crazy crazy cow pat. SUSSEX./Possibly it's my Day-Glo afro, rich/as a child paints a tree in full foliage/that makes them stare with flying saucer eyes.'

A Mind Millennium award in 2001 led me to create "Birthwrites", a poetry project for transracially adopted and fostered poets. Poetry consultants to the project included Patience, Yomi Bazuaye and Valerie Mason-John, the award given for me to learn to facilitate poetry workshops. With the guidance of my mentor, Steve Tasane, and supported by ATRAP and many friends, we created a collective poem that highlighted critical aspects of our transracial placement. The poem was performed to an invited audience at the Diorama Arts Centre in London in November 2001. Valerie Mason-John was our brilliant MC.

Three months after my adoptive mother's death in June 2003, I needed extra support. I referred myself to a crisis house. It was an alternative to a psychiatric ward. I was not forced to take medication and my need to grieve in the way that I chose was respected. I was offered the form of sanctuary I had hoped for when first admitted in 1990 to a psychiatric unit but which had not been forthcoming. While only a few crisis houses exist in different parts of Britain, more are being established; they have different policies about medication and most offer complementary and alternative forms of therapy.

I have a partner. It's going well. A social worker commented recently, 'It's a miracle that you can have a relationship. Thank God for him!' My friendships are closer and deeper. I am fortunate, too, to have friends in my siblings: three siblings from my Indian father's relationship with his German wife, and two siblings from my Irish-American mother's relationship with her Irish husband. My existence has been challenging for each of them at various times. And I am an aunt to my three nieces and four nephews – after being brought up as an only child, a joy I never expected. Reconciliation with my birth mother is difficult, but I have taken steps to get support in place for when I meet her again.

Several years have passed since I sat with the occupational therapist and my bulging files at the psychiatric unit. Those files were full of words, words that had been chosen to mis/represent and mis/understand my distress, written by people who had said they didn't have time or couldn't talk to me. But, unlike his colleagues, this occupational therapist began to show me what he had written about me; we would discuss it and it was mutually respectful and empowering for us both. Perhaps adoption professionals practise in this way. As a transracially adopted person I have often felt I was not in control of my life: other people's often racist interpretations in too many files since birth, research that feels unconnected to my experiences. With the added layer of psychiatry, with its concomitant stigma and discrimination, it gets overwhelming. That is perhaps why writing and reading have become invaluable in helping me to untangle, dismantle and reframe my various experiences. And critical to this process is learning to love and respect myself.

These are some things that have saved my life.

> *Woman,*
> *Punjabi, Irish, Pathan,*
> *brought up/down in England,*
> *institution submerging,*
> *warrior emerging.*

7

Living with transracial adoption

Family

DYLAN CLEMENTS

*(Sandstone) Exhibited in 1999 at the Art Garden,
Bristol, and Woodlands Christian Centre, Bristol*

Transforming destructive anger

DAVID WOODGER

This article explains how challenging my life has enabled me to understand, change and develop my difficult childhood experience where I struggled with being raised within a white family. Negative feelings plagued me through adolescence and early adulthood and I drew on a deep tendency towards destructive anger, which governed the way I lived and viewed the world. Practising Nichiren Buddhism has enabled me to be at ease with my own identity and value my traumatic and confused past. I am now able positively to draw on it in my work and life, to encourage and support others in the field of race equality.

I was born David Kana in 1963 and was separated from my mum at birth. My mother was a first generation Gujarati Hindu Indian living in London and training to be a teacher. I have little information about my father who is not mentioned on my birth certificate.

Just after I was born, I was placed in a care home, then in foster care and then after three months joined the Woodger family who already had two children of their own. I grew up in the idyllic countryside of Shropshire, which was a white community, until I was 19 years old when I left to go to college in London to study social science and community work.

My family was supportive and caring and I have happy memories of my childhood with them. However, growing up in Shropshire did not always feel idyllic as I experienced ongoing racist abuse, bullying and violence from my peers and friends with no acknowledgement of this from my teachers. What was particularly difficult was that I lived in isolation with no one to share my experience, wishing I was white like everyone else around me. I wanted to deny who I was and I lived in fear of attack and rejection. This destroyed my self-confidence and my self-esteem. I didn't understand my place or purpose in the world.

Consequently, my childhood was a mixture of enjoyment at being young with a desire to explore life, as well as playing and eating sweets, contrasted with being worried and scared, not wishing to be seen, and hiding from the world. My consciousness of being black and different meant that I could not be myself and all I could do was to tolerate the abuse I was given on a daily basis. But, mostly, I tried to deny it was happening. Being alone at bedtime was a constant dread, as I could not escape my thoughts, which tormented me. By day I would wear a smile and try my best to fit into the world and, at night, I would cry myself to sleep.

My adoptive family used to foster children and, during my childhood, we had an Indian Hindu baby whose mum had died giving birth to her. I remember that we would visit her family once a week and spend the day with them, eating Indian food and listening to their experiences of life. However, I never felt able to tell my friends about these visits as I wanted to distance myself from anything Indian; I associated it with being attacked and abused and, therefore, felt it was shameful and inferior in some way.

The pain and anguish throughout adolescence turned into an incandescent anger that had few boundaries. My late teens and early twenties were characterised by a crescendo of anger that I directed towards authority, the unequal and unfair system, and the injustices of the world.

This anger attracted more anger from my environment. I recall vividly one particular week when a rumour spread round that I was going to be beaten up as part of "Paki bashing" attacks by local boys. The anxiety and anticipation were unbearable. Eventually I was attacked and beaten up by six boys whilst another six watched. However, my main concern was how to conceal this from my mum and dad. I felt ashamed that this was happening to me.

My relationship with my adoptive dad was difficult; every time we were together we would argue. I felt that he did not understand me or the struggles I was facing. I found his attitude bigoted and a denial of who I was. I had no respect for him and would do anything to antagonise him. At that time, we were unable to share with each other meaningfully. Although my mum knew and understood me better, I could not always fully share with her either what I was going through. I did manage to talk with them both about my point of view and feelings about the importance of "same-race" placements and adoptions. My mum reflected on my thoughts and considered her own identity as a white mum, whilst my dad rejected them completely.

So, even though my family cared about me, I was locked in my own world. My younger adopted sister, who was also Indian but from a different family, experienced the same abuse from her peers yet we were unable to talk or share our problems with each other. I knew she faced difficulties, but at the time I could not really acknowledge my own problems let alone help her.

As I grew older, my anger and frustration hardened and I channelled it into political issues. Everywhere I went I created, led and organised chaos and disruption through school, sixth form, university, and in my work. I would verbally admonish and refute the beliefs of anyone who had a different view to mine. Due to my size I was never physically violent; however, I lashed out with my tongue.

In 1983 I trained to be a community worker, which was a perfect profession for me because it paid me to fight for communities' rights and against injustice. In training I worked with my own community, which was exciting yet uncomfortable because it reinforced my feelings of isolation. Around the same time, I decided to set up the Association of Transracially Adopted People (ATRAP). This is a national organisation for black and racial minority adoptees placed in white families. It is primarily for people growing up in similar circumstances as mine to be able to meet and share experiences.

Meeting and supporting others in this way helped me to further reflect on my experience and I began to promote the importance of placing black and racial minority community children in "same-race" placements to social workers and children's agencies.

My first job was on an estate in west London, working for black and racial minority communities. As a result of this work and my attitude, I soon came into conflict with my superiors leading me on two separate occasions to sue my managers, including the Chief Executive of the council, for racism and racial harassment. I also sued the trade union for failing to represent me. All this ignited huge conflicts amongst staff and the community. It ended up with me being escorted by security guards from my desk in the town hall, with my belongings.

I was not satisfied, even though I achieved a positive outcome from the cases in the courts and gained financial compensation. I felt cynical, frustrated and exhausted, as I could see no real change in my environment despite my great efforts and deep desire for change.

It was at this point in 1993 that I came across Nichiren Daishonin's Buddhism. I was introduced to it by a work colleague who impressed me as he was effectively tackling racism in a sustained way and he was white. From working alongside him I became interested in practising Buddhism. It offers a practical approach to individual empowerment and inner transformation because it allows people to develop themselves to their full potential through taking complete responsibility for their lives.

I did not start practising Buddhism straight away, even though I was unhappy, because at the time I just accepted the way my life was and that I had to make the best of things. On the surface, I did not feel I had any particular difficulties. I was never really religious or spiritual, just political. I found the basic philosophy of Nichiren Buddhism very challenging as I always believed it was the structures and systems that needed changing. I thought the way to make a lasting difference came from external forces not internal human changes. However, what prompted me to start was observing my Buddhist colleague's approach and understanding within a community organisation that he had helped set up which was dedicated to addressing racism and included both black and white people.

I began chanting a little at first then, gradually, I started chanting every day and reading more about Nichiren Buddhism. From chanting the Buddhist phrase *Nam-myoho-renge-kyo* and deepening my understanding of the teachings of Nichiren, I began to make connections with the internal causes of my unhappiness. This had been based on the fact that I had been separated from my birth mother and then placed in a white family rather than an Indian family.

Not long after I began practising Buddhism, I decided to trace my birth mother. I enlisted the help of a third party and engaged in numerous and varied efforts to pursue and make contact with individuals and organisations that may have known her. This led me to India where, despite further enquiries, my quest to find my mother was unsuccessful. However, I reached a point where I felt at ease with my identity and who I was. I realised my happiness was not dependent on meeting my mother and so my need to find her subsided. I continue on a daily basis to include both my birth parents in my Buddhist prayers and I have not abandoned the idea of renewing my efforts to trace my mother; the curiosity is still there.

Through my practice, I also realised that my experience and struggle could become a valuable and powerful means to bring about change. This was based on a new understanding that the power to change my environment came from within my life and was dependent upon deeply respecting myself. I now believed that I was ultimately responsible for changing this sadness and anger. No one else could take away the unhappiness for me and I couldn't keep blaming other people or my environment for how I felt. I came across a quotation from Daisaku Ikeda which clarified this principle better. He said, 'A great revolution of character in just a single individual will help achieve a change in the destiny of a nation and, further, will cause a change in the destiny of humankind.[1]'

From now on, I decided as a starting point to work on my own internal change and then, based on this, to create change in my work and family. I knew that however much justification I had for blaming others, ultimately this wasn't going to resolve my previous experiences or give me the courage to make real changes to my current situation. In fact, blame made me unhappy and took away my power to take action.

This enabled me to gradually re-orient the direction of my life, which had been controlled by anger. Buddhism has taught me that we do not need to change as a person or even eradicate the things we do not like about ourselves. Through my practice, I am able to use all my qualities and tendencies, including anger, in a positive way to help myself and other people.

I now use my anger constructively in my work as a positive source of energy. I have been able to empower black and white people in a range of public sector services including education, health, social services, the police and youth services. I have been able to encourage them to reflect on how their racial identities can impact on the professional services they provide and organisations they work in. This has led to real changes in the types of services provided, with some communities getting an appropriate service for the first time. I now advise senior people within organisations on how to tackle institutional racism and racial conflict. I work as a lecturer at Goldsmiths College, University of London, teaching, amongst other subjects, causes and solutions to institutional racism. I have undertaken research in this field, written articles on the subject and been invited to speak at academic conferences.

My relationship with my adoptive mum and dad for many years now has been open, honest and meaningful. I have been able to share with both of them everything about my life. I was able to embrace my dad and value him for doing his best to be a caring and loving father. As I grew more secure and at ease with my identity, they in turn were able to support me and appreciate the experiences that I had faced. My

[1] Daisaku Ikeda, *The Human Revolution* (Taplow Court Press, 1994) Vol. 1, p 5

sister and I have been able to acknowledge and share our common experiences, opening up and reflecting together on our difficult times.

Undoubtedly, I believe that the racism I was subjected to as a child was exacerbated by the fact that I was placed in a white family. Although they loved and looked after me, my parents were not aware of the need to nurture my self-identity and therefore could not fully relate to my problems. As it was, I became confused, ashamed of being different and had very little self-worth. I was determined that other black and racial minority children put up for fostering and adoption would not suffer as I had.

Up until the point that I met Nichiren Buddhism, I channelled my negative feelings into anger, which I directed at others. I felt the way to bring about lasting change in society was only through external protest, raging against authorities and anyone who challenged my viewpoint. However, I came to realise that this was not a completely effective approach, as it made no lasting change in the field of race equality and it made me suffer even more.

Through my daily Buddhist practice of chanting I have learnt to apply the principle of self-mastery to my work and family life. I am no longer dominated by anger; instead, it motivates my strong desire for social justice, in a direction that will create the maximum change in society and in my life. I am no longer a victim of a pattern of destructive anger.

I have used the experiences of my past to create a positive and strong self-identity. It has taken tremendous courage to face issues and to take responsibility for them. I feel proud and grateful for the journey I have made so far and excited about the challenges I will face in the future.

The road to recovery

KYM COOPER

When you are living in an area where you are in a racial minority, it is inevitable that you will encounter people who express racism either intentionally or without even realising it. They often make a recurring assumption that white people are superior to all the other races. This assumption is so widespread that it can feel like there is a national consensus operating to undermine you. The British Isles has a long history of xenophobia particularly when the racial group is visible by skin colour. Next time you experience this it's worth remembering that white people did not invent everything. Each race has noble heroes, scientists, inventors, historians and political leaders who have contributed towards the advancement of humankind. Without contributions from our ancestors, the world would not be what it is today. Some ideas have been stolen from us only to be claimed by others who have then accepted all the glory for themselves. If you remember this, no one can ever put you down.

Here are some tips to help you on your journey:

1.   If you have access to the internet, look at tourist boards or the world information websites relating to your country of descent or origin. These can be invaluable for finding out about geography, landmarks, climate, national sports, local news, political structure, imports/exports, economy, religion, ethnic make-up and languages.

2.   Order books from a library or the internet or bookshops that give historical accounts of special achievements and events that have taken place in your motherland. Make sure that you include in your search religious and cultural celebrations to mark on your calendar.

3.   Find out if there are any cultural community centres that you can get involved in. You may find that they have international dance classes. Every country has its own unique form(s) of dance and a national instrument that you can learn. The advantage of finding a cultural centre is that they sometimes have regular society meetings that you could join, offering further insights.

4.   Countless areas throughout the UK now have adult education classes. Often,

you can simply learn for fun topics such as international cookery. Why not learn how to cook your national dish and maybe impress people with a few favourite specialities? Alternatively, just buy a relevant recipe book to experiment with at home.

5.   You may find enrolling in an appropriate language class advantageous too, both to speak with other people from your community of origin and, if you are planning to search for them, birth family members who may speak another first language.

6.   Visit city centre newsagents to see if there are any international newspapers or publications you can subscribe to. Some black and minority ethnic communities produce niche market magazines and newspapers that are British based. Many of these newspapers and magazines also have a website.

7.   If you can, try to visit areas that are inhabited by populations representative of your ethnicity. By doing this, you can gradually familiarise yourself with vibrant markets, bookshops, religious venues, traditional dress outlets, authentic foods and community social events. You can also begin to overcome your fear of people who look like you. I strongly recommend purchasing books from these areas as they tend to feature authors who write from a non-Eurocentric point of view, allowing a more authentic and often more balanced perspective.

8.   In some areas of the UK, it may prove more difficult to re-connect with black and minority ethnic communities. The most cosmopolitan city in England is London and if you research thoroughly and plan safely to go with a friend or an adult, you could find travelling down for the day an inspirational experience. The BBC website has a section called United Colours which gives information on multiple minority ethnic groups living in London. The populations I came across after just browsing briefly included Jewish, Turkish, Buddhist and Indian, to name but a few.

9.   Art venues in every city centre play host to a variety of productions such as exhibitions, theatres, film festivals, poetry nights, stand-up comedy, dance shows and musical jams. Inevitably, many of these performances will be of cultural value and will illustrate global customs and folklores. They may also host a range of black and minority ethnic British-based artists.

10. It is well worth getting in touch with an adoption support organisation in the part of the country where you live. They are located throughout the UK. Many of these centres offer counselling, support groups, tracing and intermediary services, and a library on adoption issues. Some run support groups specifically for transracially adopted people.

Food for thought

These ideas are only suggestions, which may not be relevant to everyone. Only attempt activities that you feel comfortable with and do not beat yourself up if you face hurdles along the way. Accept that reclaiming your cultural heritage is a life-long process that takes time and patience. You may not want to embrace your culture of origin fully and some people decide to pick and mix different aspects that appeal to them. Continue your journey when you feel ready, as the benefits will help heal your pain. Once the healing process begins, you'll gain a sense of self, internal love, pride and inner peace. Good luck.

Dear friend

DAVID GILBERT

Dear friend,

I have just finished reading the articles you sent me written by transracially adopted Korean adults in the USA. You were right, I couldn't manage to complete them all in an afternoon, they were too moving. I was left in floods of tears. I have to admit at first, before reading any of them, I wondered how much relevance they might have – how wrong I was. It was interesting to hear about experiences and concerns that, despite the vast differences in ethnic backgrounds, resoundingly echoed some of my own concerns and troubles.

Reading the material has left me with a sense of great sadness about my own father, and a sense of frustration that he has chosen to disown me by refusing to maintain any contact whatsoever. I felt envious of the writers who did meet their birth parents. In one way I suppose I should be glad that my mother, in her own way, has not disowned me. But, as you know, my blackness rests with my father. It is his culture, his language, his religion, his identity that I yearn so much to connect with. Perhaps they are idealistic thoughts that don't really occur in real life. In some ways our distance, emotionally and geographically, is indelible. Things such as culture, religion, language and so on are perhaps so alien, I would never fit in or fully understand. Yet I wish so much that he would at least acknowledge me. Agree to talk, to meet, to do *something*.

I did feel this tremendous need to write to you after reading these pieces. I found them hard to read at an emotional level. When I say I have no one who would understand me (that I know of), what I mean is that friends and relatives could never (and do not) understand the angst and the sadness that runs so very deep. That is why I treasure our friendship. You have been a source of great encouragement and understanding, and *always* sensitive to my worries and sadness. Reading some of the articles was reassuring in some ways and inspirational in others. Some of the writers had clearly found some sense of reconciliation with their situation and emotions surrounding transracial or intercountry adoption. I wish that there were people nearby I could talk to who would help me reconcile what I am, who I am, and who I have become. There seems so much ignorance, so much superficial polarity in views and attitudes about transracial adoption. Perhaps it is only I who can reconcile these feelings. But to do so, one needs to talk about them to people who do understand the complexities, the sadness, the guilt, the frustrations, the hopes.

I am very grateful you sent me the pieces because it helped authenticate some of my own feelings, desires and emotions. It is very easy to feel on the periphery as a transracial adoptee; so easy to be made to feel abnormal psychologically.

Transracial adoptee, you are a true and valued friend.

Take care.

Best wishes,

David x

You are not alone!

KAREN MOIR

When I was growing up in the late 1960s and 70s, I didn't know anyone else who was adopted and my adopted family, who were white English/Australian, had no friends who were from other ethnic backgrounds. As a Chinese child, transracially adopted by a white couple and living in London, I thought I was unique. I believed I was the only one living and trying to make sense of the experience that was my life and my family.

My parents had lived in Hong Kong in the 60s; my father was in the British Army based there for a few years. They returned to England in 1968, having adopted me in Hong Kong before they left. At that time, I had no memory of my country of origin and had to rely on my parents retelling me of their time in Hong Kong. Although mostly positive accounts, their tales were of ex-pats enjoying a privileged life in an Asian country that was still ruled by the British Government.

My parents had no other friends who had adopted and they had no formal support or guidance from adoption agencies in the way that support services exist today. They belonged to a generation which believed that outside agencies had no role to play within the family. Any problems a family experienced were to be kept within the family. I wasn't a particularly troubled or problematic child so they didn't really face many challenges as adopters of a child from abroad. However, as I grew up, I began mixing more at school and started to experience teasing from other pupils about being Chinese. I began to learn that being different meant something negative. In hindsight, I can see that my parents were ill-equipped to deal with such situations, often choosing non-action or advising me to ignore such problems. Thus, I learnt that my ethnicity was a "problem" and that being different was not something to be proud of. I had no sense of my own identity, and no information to give me links to the country I had come from or to help me feel proud of the culture in which my roots lay.

I became shy, introverted and reluctant to acknowledge being Chinese or from Hong Kong. All I wanted was to blend into the background and to be the same as all my school friends who were white and lived without problems with their birth parents and siblings. Fortunately, I channelled my energies into learning. I enjoyed school and formed some good friendships that have lasted for years. I chose to go away to college at 18 to study to become a social worker. I hoped that my own personal experiences would help me assist others during difficult times as I would have liked to have been helped during mine.

It was once I was away from home and at college, during my social work training, that I began to make friends with many people from various ethnic backgrounds. With the support of my friends, and through working with many different people, I was helped to develop a true sense of my own identity and to feel proud of who I am. It is an ongoing process that I continue to work through but now I know my ethnicity is not a problem, in fact it's an asset.

One of the things that has helped me along this road has been meeting others who share my experience of being transracially adopted. Although, while at college, I began to meet many friends and colleagues from different ethnic backgrounds and mixed parentage families, I still had not met anyone in the same situation of being born totally in one race and culture but then raised in a completely different one.

In 1996, an article written by Sue Jardine was spotted by an observant counsellor I had been seeing. It was about a woman who had been adopted from Hong Kong and her experiences of growing up in a white family in the UK. I was so excited by this article and the similarities between this woman's life and mine that I wrote to the magazine and asked them to pass on a letter. Within weeks, Sue and I had arranged to meet up. Although anxious about meeting a stranger, I couldn't wait to meet her and ask her lots of questions about her life, her family and her childhood, to check out if they bore any resemblance to my own. We spent four hours talking non-stop. It was as if I had known this woman all my life. She could've been me and I her. Of course our beginnings and families are not identical, but the sharing of experiences was enough to validate all the things that I had thought and felt over the years. She understood things I wanted to say and explain without me needing to finish the sentence, and I knew exactly how she felt when we spoke about our relationships within our families.

Sue had already been involved in post-adoption groups and so was able to inform me that, in fact, we were not alone. Others had been adopted from Hong Kong in the 1960s and, of course, from other countries around the world too. This news was like a revelation to me. It wasn't just me this had happened to. It was part of a bigger global, social and economic situation and, as I was to discover, not just something that happened in the past. At first, as I began to find a stronger identity, I felt angry that I had been put in this situation and was very anti transracial adoption. However, through my work and my own life experiences as an adult, I have mellowed over the years. But I do still believe that a child should be helped to remain within their own family or a family that represents their ethnicity, as first priority. For me, "Love is not enough[1]!" But if there are to be families who have adopted children from ethnic backgrounds other than their own, I feel they must understand the complexities of identity and belonging in order to help their children feel proud of who they are and comfortable with their differences.

I am still in contact with Sue and consider her one of my good friends. We are both also part of a small group of transracially adopted adults from Hong Kong and India. This group was set up out of a small research project that we all took part in. When we all met up during the research, one of the key things that came out of the work was the importance of support from others in a similar situation. We have since become a social support group which meets a few times a year, with some of the group being involved in the preparation process for prospective adopters. I have always been blessed with good friends who have been supportive of my experiences of being a transracially adopted adult, but now I truly know I am not alone!

---

[1] "Love is not enough" and "Love is enough" are phrases that have often been cited in the debate regarding transracial adoption, each phrase reflecting a different stance. "Love is not enough" is also the title of a UK video on transracial adoption (see Resources for further details).

A journey of discoveries

BELLA FREY

In August 1999 I was sitting in my workspace, a cramped one-metre square cupboard-type office. I was doing some internet research for my employer and, bored with the task in hand, I suddenly found myself typing 'Korea Adoption' into a search engine query form. Maybe it was a general dissatisfaction with my day-to-day existence that led me to key in those words. For most of my life, I had purposely sifted out any information about Korea from my memory. I would take in snippets from the news, from films, but they would somehow filter through me and back out into the English air. Korea was in my face, but not in my heart.

The results of my internet search that day resulted in a life-changing course of events. Within minutes I had stumbled upon the Holt International website and, in front of my eyes, I was reading about an event to be staged in Washington DC, 'The First International Gathering of Korean Adoptees'. The news that other adopted Koreans existed, other than in Korea, hadn't even had time to sink in before my eyes were taking in mind-boggling statistics. There aren't just a few of us. We exist all over the world, in vast quantities. We are practically a small race unto ourselves! I grew up believing I was probably the only one.

My heart raced as I read through the planned itinerary and it sank when I realised that the event was due to take place within the fortnight. I had missed the closing date for registration and had no cash to get to the States or pay for the four star hotel booked for the event. Within one hour of finding this information, I had left a message on the event's website and received replies offering a last minute place, and free lodgings in the home of an American adoptee. I lapsed out of my normally practical and restrained character and impulsively forced myself to dust off my credit card. Within the hour I had booked and confirmed a return flight to Washington DC!

Who would have thought that the USA's capital city would present me with my first Korean experience? I was met at the airport by five smiling Korean faces calling my name. I felt overwhelmed and jet lagged. My welcome party included my host, who had kindly offered me and the rest of the party rooms at his house for the duration of the conference. He was an exceptionally kind but stern ex-army man who had been one of the first generation of babies to be adopted overseas in the 1950s at the end of the Korean War.

I had arrived early afternoon and the first topic of discussion was where to eat. Would we eat Tex-Mex, Fried Chicken, Sushi or Korean? Korean? I had never thought about Korean food before. I had assumed that Korean food would be much like Chinese, but I was in for one big surprise!

After driving for a while, my host pulled in to a large retail park and we all got out of his station wagon. We walked into a giant supermarket. My senses were assaulted by the colours, the noise, the cheesy pop music, but particularly and most disturbingly by the smell. The pungent odour of dried fish, vinegar and garlic filled the store. I found it quite overpowering and the motion sickness I had experienced on the flight was starting to resurface. I could see overly cute ornaments on shelves next to giant bags of rice, and big plastic tubs with red liquid and floating leaves inside. Oversized radishes were sat next to weird little clingfilm-wrapped multicoloured balls. We went through the supermarket and at the rear of the store was a fast food counter, only the pictures I could see weren't burgers and fries, they were of Korean food. I was mesmerised. Most of the dishes were red, and I was advised that these were spicy. Anything not red was not spicy. I was asked what I wanted. I had no idea what to order so I asked one of my new companions to order something for me and, as I enjoy spicy food, I asked for a red dish. I was presented with a tray with some bubbling red soup and three small dishes with a different type of pickle on each. My appetite had suddenly grown and the smell of my spicy soup had suddenly obscured the smell from the main supermarket. I tucked in... WOW, spicy it was! I loved it! The soup contained small pieces of tofu, onion and cabbage and tasted slightly sour. I had never tasted anything like it. I was told that this soup, *kimchi tchigae*, is typical of Korean food flavours. The main ingredient of *kimchi* is used in many ways in the Korean kitchen, but especially as an accompaniment to each meal as a pickle. This was the beginning of my love affair with Korean food. I would eat much more during my stay, as my host's wife was Korean American and her culinary skills were fantastic. I soon became familiar with *kochujang*, the thick spicy red chilli sauce that Koreans mix into anything that isn't spicy enough. I have since made sure I have a tub to hand, in case of emergency food blandness! I find it funny now to think that my first taste of Korean food was in a retail park in Washington. Incidentally, the smell of fermented cabbage and dried fish is one I have since become strangely fond of.

The five days I spent in Washington at 'The Gathering' were life-changing. For most of each day I was in the company of over six hundred Koreans who, like me, had been adopted as children and raised in predominantly Caucasian households. I met American, Swedish, Norwegian, French, Dutch, German, Canadian, Australian and Belgian adoptees. I thought how funny it was that we all seemed to have traits typical of the countries we were raised in. The Americans in particular were very upfront in pointing out how 'totally British' I am, and asking me to 'say anything, because we just love to hear your fabulous accent'. I felt a strange warmth knowing I am such a beacon of Britishness!

The conference consisted of various formal engagements, including canapés at Capitol Hill and a reception at the Korean ambassador's home, with more Korean food. There were discussion groups dealing with various topics from sharing our life experiences, to discussing the latest developments in current adoption policies. I took part in everything with excited enthusiasm. I listened to many people's life stories, including some uplifting accounts of those raised in wonderful close-knit families, but I also heard about adoptees who had been brought up by fanatically religious families who made them say 'thank you' for being adopted every day, families whose only reason for adopting was to 'save a soul'. My tears flowed freely. At one point I found myself telling a room of sixty strangers some of the most painful and intimate details of my own adoption story. I was strangely comfortable sharing my experiences and feelings, as I felt that I was being truly understood for the first time.

It is hard to describe exactly how it feels to meet other adoptees for the first time. At school, I felt awkward and embarrassed about my looks and difference. I shied away from anything Far Eastern, felt self-conscious when eating in a Chinese restaurant, yet there I was walking around Washington DC with hundreds of Koreans. I should have been mortified, but I wasn't. For the first time in my life I had a sense of belonging. Even though onlookers couldn't see it, I felt it. I actually fitted in with these people. We had all shared the strange beginning to our lives, the uprooting and the new start, the loss and displacement. I had found a new community and I felt like I belonged. I felt unbelievably emotional during my stay there, a mixture of joy and sadness swamped me for five days. To think I had worried that the flight ticket would be a waste of money. No amount of money could have bought what I found on that trip. I found a peace that arrived through knowing there were other people who shared my day-to-day struggle, and a deep pride in who I am and where I come from which is a far cry from the shame and embarrassment I had felt whilst growing up. My dream after this was to visit Korea, and start to reclaim the culture of a birth country that had been lost to me.

When I returned to London, I felt strange, yet stronger. For 24 years I hadn't even had a conversation with another Korean, and now I had met so many people that I found I missed being around Korean faces. Whilst in Washington, I had learnt about all the established communities of adopted Koreans that exist around the world. The USA is home to many thousands of adopted Koreans who have developed hundreds of organised groups that meet regularly and have varying levels of interaction, from just socialising, to lobbying governmental organisations on revising adoption laws and post-adoption services. Many European countries also have smaller, more informal groups that meet and organise social activities with their counterparts in other countries. I find it touching how so many people who had been sent away from their country of birth as babies or children eventually felt the need to connect with others from the same beginnings. I felt sad that there wasn't a group in the UK, so I took to my keyboard again and e-mailed a friend I had made in America, putting a call out for anyone who knew if there were any other adopted Koreans living in the UK. Eventually, after my e-mail had been circulated through various web groups, I was put in touch with a Korean adoptee who lived in London! We met, and I discovered that he knew of several other adoptees whom he could try to contact, so letters were written and the ball started rolling…

Now, four years on, I have a close group of adopted Korean friends who live in England. We meet and indulge in Korean food as often as our hectic lives will permit and also have the luxury of being part of the worldwide community of adopted Koreans, who are all within reach of a web chat or phone call.

Being adopted is a complicated life journey. Being a British adopted Korean means wearing a disguise. It means having an exterior mask that doesn't match my identity. Knowing others who are adopted means not having to verbalise every aspect of our daily frustrations or insecurities. Our beginnings may have taken different turns, and we are all such different characters, but we share the distance travelled. We chat a lot, but we don't *have* to speak to *know* or understand. We all lead busy lives, but the time we spend together is truly special to me in ways even I can't fully understand.

Since my trip to Washington, my dream to return to Korea has been realised twice. As difficult, exhausting and emotional as those trips were, I have been privileged enough to have visited some of Korea's most beautiful sites, learnt about her past and present, and eaten some of the best food in the world. I am grateful beyond belief for the opportunities I have had to discover my second culture, and believe that my sudden need to make contact with my past was something that couldn't be ignored. I have gained pride in who I am, as an adopted Korean, and this has only been made possible by meeting so many other people like myself. I have been affected by each person I have met on this journey, from my host in Washington to the friends I have in the UK. They have enriched my life and given me a true and unconditional sense of belonging.

Kamsa hamnida (thank you) to all of them.

8

Contributors

MICHELLE ANDERSON

CHRIS ATKINS

MICHAEL CAINES

VERONICA DEWAN

LAURA FISH

BELLA FREY

DAVID GILBERT

CLARE GORHAM

FAY HALLSWORTH

KATE HOOKINGS

PERLITA HARRIS *with her mother,*
the Chiltern Nursery

357

LUKE HOWARD (centre) with his
brothers

*IMA JACKSON (far left) with her parents, brothers and
sister at her grandparents' golden wedding, 1974. From top left
to right: Des, Neil and Kevin; Ima, Dad (Jim), Mum (Joan),
Michele, John and Ruth*

JACKIE KAY (left) with her dad and brother, Mull

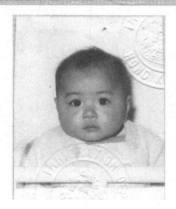

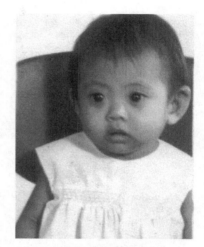

LI-DA KRUGER, *Bangkok*

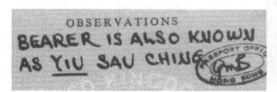

SUE JARDINE

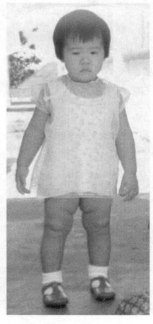

KAGEHA JERUTO MARSHALL, Kenya

JEANNETTE LOAKMAN

JENNY MOHINDRA

MAYA

RON McLAY

KAREN MOIR at her Christening

NICK PENDRY

RACHEL

LIZ SIBTHORPE

MARIE-JAMILA GILLHAM

DEBORAH WEYMONT

MIRANDA WILKINSON *with her parents*

ROS GIHAN WILLIAMS

DAVID WOODGER

A BLACK ADOPTED PERSON This article was first published by BAAF in 1996. Unfortunately, all attempts to identify and trace the author have been unsuccessful.

ANGIE was placed for adoption at birth but did not join a permanent family until she was three-and-a-half. She was fostered up until the age of nine and then adopted by the same family who already had six biological children. Living in predominantly white areas of Liverpool, she often felt out of place. When Angie was 21 she moved to the black community to explore her identity but again struggled to fit in. As she became older she began to fit in to herself rather than the external environment, which demanded that she be a certain way. At the age of 33 Angie went to Lampeter University in Wales to study anthropology; for her dissertation she carried out research on adoption, kinship and identity. Studying anthropology helped Angie to understand the cultural codes of practice that undermine the significance of non-blood relationships. Currently Angie works with adults with learning difficulties but would, at some point, like to carry out more independent research on adoption.

MICHELLE ANDERSON was born in the 1960s in Hackney, London. Her childminder ended up "keeping" her one day when her birth mother failed to pick her up. Her unintended adoptive family were Turkish Cypriot immigrants. Michelle had a unique and somewhat bizarre upbringing being a black child brought up in a Turkish community in London. She graduated with a B.Ed(Hons) first-class degree and holds an MA in English in Education from the Institute of Education, University of London. Michelle has taught in London, Auckland (New Zealand) and Bermuda. In 2005 she moved from Bermuda to New Zealand.

Michelle met her birth mother for the first time around 1990. The need to reconnect with her roots was intensified after she had her own son Jemal. The meetings ended acrimoniously and Michelle has severed that link once and for all. However, she has since met many members of her extended family in New York, Trinidad and Barbados. Some of the meetings were traumatic as the anger she felt against her birth mother resurfaced. With the exception of an aunt, most of the family had not known about her. What Michelle has learnt from this experience is that no one can replace one's real family and that the selfish act of one or two people can have lifetime consequences on many others.

It is the friends along the way who have given her strength, guidance and a shoulder to cry on when the floodgates of emotion became too much: 'Without these very special people who have "held me together" at these vulnerable moments in my life I would be in a different place! So thanks to my angels Verna Drysdale, Seniz Halil, Unun Osman (Yiacoup), Sizen Yiacoup, Sule Yiacoup, Anozie Anywagu, Susan Davis, Rebecca Brand, Taiwo Adeogun, Hazel Scotchbrook, Carla Foggo-Bascome and to all the transracially adopted friends who let me understand I wasn't alone in this, especially Peter Johnson. To the God who has allowed healing to begin after nearly four decades and to the love of my life, George Wales.'

CHRIS ATKINS was born in Hong Kong and raised in the UK with white British parents. A qualified social worker, she now works for a national organisation providing post-adoption support to anyone affected by the impact of adoption. Chris has participated in research projects on intercountry adoption and regularly makes presentations on its impact to groups and organisations. She lives in Hertfordshire with her husband and two daughters.

JULIA AUSTIN was born in Jakarta, Indonesia. Adopted when she was three days old, she lived in Jakarta for one year before coming to London. Currently working as a teaching assistant in an inner London primary school – a job that she adores – she will begin postgraduate work in diaspora studies in the autumn. In time, she hopes to write her own book about searching for belonging.

SHARON BEAZER lives on her own in London and is about to embark on a new business venture in fashion.

MICHAEL CAINES was born in Exeter in 1969. His birth mother is English and his father Jamaican. He joined his adoptive family when he was a few months old. As a young person growing up in a large family, Michael had a passion for cooking. He is one of only ten chefs in Britain to hold two Michelin stars, and has trained in Exeter, Oxfordshire and France. In 1994 he became Head Chef at Gidleigh Park, the prestigious country house hotel on the edge of Dartmoor. Two months into the job, Michael lost his right arm in a car accident. However, he returned to Gidleigh Park even more determined to pursue his dream of reaching the top of his profession. He has since gone on to open his own signature restaurants as well as winning Chef of the Year in 2001 at the prestigious Cateys Awards. Michael Caines at the Bristol Marriott Royal opened in 2003, in the same year as the purchase of the Royal Clarence Hotel in Exeter with his business partner, Andrew Brownsword. Michael lives in mid-Devon with his partner Ruth and their small son, Joseph, and daughter, Hope.

MICHAEL CANDON was born in July 1967 in south London and adopted by Irish parents. At the age of eight he moved to the West of Ireland. He now lives in Meath, Ireland with his partner of ten years. Michael is a counsellor and psychotherapist in private practice and an advocate of best practice in adoption.

AMINA CLARK is of Indian origin and was born in 1976 in London where she still lives. When she was four weeks old, her white family adopted her. Amina has searched for her birth mother and they remain in contact. Over time she has gained five siblings: a sister born to her adoptive mother, two step-siblings who came with her step-mother and two half-siblings who live with her birth mother. Amina currently lives with her Indian partner. She works with homeless people in central London.

DYLAN CLEMENTS was born in Bristol in 1968. His biological mother is white English and his father is of Jamaican origin. Dylan was fostered at three months and at the age of four was placed in a residential nursery. A year later he was adopted. When Dylan was nine, his adoptive parents' marriage broke down. As a result, Dylan was sent away to boarding school and spent the rest of his childhood in various institutions. The selection of writing included in this book has been taken from his autobiography. Dylan is a teacher by profession but his vocation is sculpture; he has been carving stone for the past ten years. Through art and writing Dylan has found a method of self-healing, resolution and closure.

KYM COOPER was born in 1978. Both her birth mother and birth father are African-Caribbean. She lived in a children's home for two years until, when it was being closed down, she was fostered by a young married couple. They connected and the arrangement developed into a long-term foster placement. When Kym was five, her foster carers were given the right to legally adopt her. In 2005, Kym completed a course at the London College of Fashion to become a magazine journalist. She works for a local newspaper in Manchester.

DARSHAN DAVIES was born in 1969 in Birmingham, of Indian Sikh parentage. He joined his adoptive family when he was three months old. Darshan grew up in Birmingham until he was 13 when he went to boarding school in Reading. Now he is living back in Birmingham. He established contact with his birth family a number of years ago.

DAVID was born in 1967 in Nottingham. His birth father is Jamaican and his mother German. David joined his adoptive family at the age of three months and grew up in Leicester. He now lives in Manchester where he is studying counselling.

VERONICA DEWAN was born in 1957, of Punjabi/Irish parentage. She was raised as an only child by an English Protestant father and Irish Catholic mother in rural southern England. She met her birth parents in 1985 within weeks of each other, plus five siblings. Self-employed as a trainer, consultant and writer, Veronica lives with her partner in a cottage near the sea. She is a mental health system survivor.

LAURA FISH is a writer of Caribbean parentage. She was born in England and has over ten years' experience in broadcast television and radio, working for the BBC in news, current affairs, light entertainment and on documentaries. Her first novel, Flight of Black Swans (Duckworth, 1995), is set in Aboriginal Australia and focuses on displacement. Laura has held posts as a tutor in Creative Writing at St Andrews University in Scotland, University of Western Cape in South Africa, and the University of East Anglia in Norwich.

BELLA FREY (CHO, SOON HEE) was found abandoned on a street in Busan City, South Korea, on 17 October 1975. Documents from the children's home report that a piece of paper was attached to Soon Hee's clothes stating her date of birth as 22 April 1975. After spending six months at the Namkwang Children's home in Busan, she eventually joined her new adoptive family in March 1976, when she was immediately quarantined and treated for scabies, head lice and malnutrition. After treatment, Soon Hee was renamed Isabelle Louise, but is known as Bella.

Bella grew up in Southend-on-Sea, Essex with her English mother and Vietnamese adopted brother. She studied in West Yorkshire for three years before moving to London where she now co-runs a female-led painting and decorating company. Bella has regular contact with other British adopted Koreans and has helped to set up and administrate their website. Bella has visited Korea twice since 2000 and plans to return in the near future for an extended trip and to undertake some voluntary work in one of the country's many orphanages.

DAVID GILBERT, aged 43, is "mixed-race" (Yemeni/British) and was transracially adopted nine days after his birth. He first made contact with his biological parents at the age of 30. He has published work on subjects including 'mixed-race' identities, whiteness, institutional racism and meeting the needs of Muslim students within the

British education system. David has wide and varied experiences of working on "race" equality issues. He lives and works in the north west of England.

MARIE-JAMILA GILLHAM is a 31-year-old mother of two young daughters. She lives in Staffordshire and works in education. Since being interviewed for this anthology, with the help of a professional intermediary Marie-Jamila has managed to trace her Nigerian birth mother and is presently building a relationship with her. Although it is still early days, the reunion looks positive. Marie-Jamila hopes to heal some of the issues that have arisen from her experience of adoption and which have inspired her contributions to this book.

CLARE GORHAM was born in 1966 and brought up in Wimbledon, south-west London. Her parentage is Swiss (birth mother) and Nigerian (birth father). She traced her birth mother twelve years go. Although initially successful, the relationship has been challenging, confronting and painful over the years and they have reached an impasse. Clare has recently traced her birth father, Jacob; their evolving relationship is very positive, rewarding and blossoming.

Clare works as a freelance broadcaster and journalist. She has written extensively about and made programmes on transracial adoption, including her own documentary, *The Colour of Love*, for Channel 4 (October Productions). Clare also works as a lecturer at Thames Valley University where she teaches broadcast radio news and journalism.

FAY HALLSWORTH was born in the Welsh Valleys in 1946. Her mother is Welsh and her birth father West Indian. Fay was adopted when her mother married her (white) step-father. She is married with three sons and lives in Cardiff.

PERLITA HARRIS was born in London in 1966. Deemed 'unsuitable for adoption' due to her prematurity, a congenital medical condition and being 'full Indian', she was received into care by the City of Westminster and placed at the Chiltern Nursery in Reading, where her mother continued to visit her. She later moved to an adjacent children's home. In 1969 the prognosis on Perlita's life was revised and in 1971 she joined her foster family (with a view to adoption). She was adopted a year later, growing up with three older siblings in rural Gloucestershire. Perlita has a good relationship with her parents and is close to her sister, Wendy.

In 1983, when she was 17, Perlita's father, Salim Johnson, searched for her. He was now living in Canada. Her mother, Phulwati, had died in 1980. In 1991, Perlita established contact with her younger maternal sister and subsequently her two younger brothers who were living in Southall. She visited her mother's parents and youngest sister in India the same year but did not stay in contact. In 2005, Perlita contacted a maternal aunt in England, becoming close and spending Christmas and New Year with her aunt (her *Khalaji*) and maternal extended family in India. Perlita has a warm relationship with her *Papaji* and a strong sense of belonging in both her paternal and maternal families.

Perlita is a member of the Bristol-based LAFTA (looked after, fostered, transracially adopted) group. She lives in London.

SHARON HARWOOD is 29 years old with two children, a son aged ten and a younger daughter. Sharon was born in South Korea and adopted at the age of two-and-a-half by Welsh parents whom she sees as her "natural" family. She has lived in England ever since and has 'become English'. Her family has supported her through a rollercoaster of emotions which, at times, have been hard to cope with. Sharon's article, 'Eleven hours!' is about her trip back to Korea nearly four years ago. It was difficult writing it as it brought back both good and bad memories. Her poem, 'Who am I?', is about how she feels about her adoption. Sharon hopes that you enjoy her writing and thoughts as much as she has enjoyed sharing them.

KATE HOOKINGS was born in 1981 in Salisbury, Wiltshire. Her mother is English and her father Nigerian. She joined her adoptive family when she was three months old. Her adoptive father was violent towards Kate and her mum, and Kate ended up back in care when she was 12, after which she was in and out of foster care for several years.   Kate has recently met her birth mother and her younger brothers and sisters. She lives with her partner in Swindon.

LUKE HOWARD was born in 1997 in London, England. He joined his large adoptive family when he was a day old. His birth mother was English and his father's parentage is not known. Luke enjoys spelling, reading, computer games and playing football. He lives in south west England.

IMA JACKSON was born in Belfast in 1964 and brought up in Portstewart in Northern Ireland. After leaving school at 18, she had a lot of fun (and stress) travelling round the UK and Europe for a few years with her Danish best friend. In her mid-twenties, Ima decided she needed to settle down a bit and trained as a nurse in Liverpool, then as a midwife in London. She moved to Scotland in 1992 where she married her husband, Michael in 1995. They have lived happily in Glasgow with their two daughters ever since. Ima left the NHS in 1996 to become a lecturer and postgraduate student at Glasgow Caledonian University, where she runs a programme adapting overseas and refugee nurses to UK practice.

JADE was born in 1967 in Plymouth. Her birth mother is English and her birth father Iranian. She was six weeks old when she was adopted. When she was three she moved from Devon to London and, at ten, to the north east of England. Since 1990, Jade has been in contact with her birth mother and is now searching for her birth father. She retains a good relationship with her adoptive parents. Jade lives in Bristol.

SUE JARDINE was born in Hong Kong. She was placed in two orphanages before being fostered and then adopted by her English family. Sue was part of the Hong Kong Adoption Project and joined her adoptive family when she was one-and-a-half. She grew up in Hertfordshire but now lives in London.

Sue was unaware that adoption was an issue for her until her mid-twenties. It did not occur to her to find out about her birth family or to visit Hong Kong. Although Sue knew of other adopted children while she was growing up, she had no contact with other adoptees until she joined the Association for Transracially Adopted and Fostered People (ATRAP). Sue was a co-ordinating member of ATRAP from 1993 to 1999 and ran a workshop on intercountry adoption at the NGO Forum on Women, Beijing 1995. She has worked with a number of adoption agencies including the Catholic Children's Society (Project 16–18, in 1999) and the Post-Adoption Centre (1997). She has also written chapters for two other books published by BAAF (1999 and 2000). Currently Sue works as an Information Manager for the Social Care Institute for Excellence (SCIE).

KATRINA was born in 1963. She has a French Canadian mother and an African-Caribbean father. She was born in Devon at a convent run by nuns for mothers who were pregnant outside of marriage and planning to give up their babies for adoption. Katrina joined her adoptive family when she was three months old, growing up in a small town, Christchurch, on the south coast of England. She still lives on the south coast. Katrina is a qualified counsellor, a trained holistic therapist in Indian head and shoulder massage, and a Reiki practitioner. She would like to work in the adoption and fostering field. In addition to being a counsellor, Katrina works part-time with children with complex health needs. She also co-ordinates workshops in self-esteem/confidence building and works with children who have survived domestic violence. As this book goes to press, she is in the process of setting up supported adoption groups in her area.

JACKIE KAY was born in1961 in Edinburgh and brought up in Glasgow, Scotland. She has published four collections of poetry for adults, including a prize-winning volume titled *The Adoption Papers* (Bloodaxe Books, 1991). Her first novel, *Trumpet* (Picador, 1998), won the Guardian Fiction Prize, a Scottish Arts Council Book Award and the Author's Club First Novel Award. Jackie has written for stage and television, as well as publishing further books, among them *Bessie*, about the blues singer, Bessie Smith, (Absolute Press) and a much acclaimed collection of short stories, *Why Don't You Stop Talking* (Picador, 2002). She is a fellow of the Royal Society of Literature, and the Leading Adviser to the Literature Department at the Arts Council of Great Britain. Jackie lives in Manchester with her son.

LI-DA KRUGER has been working in factual TV programming for six years in the UK's independent sector. It took two years to get support and the generous funding needed to make a feature length documentary called *Belonging*, about her return to Cambodia in search of her roots and biological parents, 26 years after she was airlifted out as an infant. The documentary was short-listed for Grierson Award in 2003, which Nick Broomfield's *Biggie and Tupac* went on to win. Li-da graduated from Strathclyde University in 1998 and began her career by freelancing in South Africa for a year. She is constantly developing her directing, camera and editing skills by making short films and charity promos, and has trained at the New York Film Academy and the National Film & TV School's short course unit in the UK.

LEYTON was born in 1974 in Neath General Hospital and raised in Resolven, South Wales. He is of white Welsh and African-Caribbean parentage and still lives in Wales.

JEANNETTE LOAKMAN was born in 1965 in Singapore, of Chinese parentage, and joined her adoptive family in England when she was three months old, growing up in East Anglia. An award-winning producer and director, Jeannette's career spans nearly ten years in broadcasting and journalism – in front of the camera as well as behind. As Executive Producer in Chocolate Box Entertainment, based in Toronto, Canada, Jeannette currently produces documentaries and factual and lifestyle series. Her film looking for her birth mother, *The Last Seven Days of Annie Ong*, led her birth mother to find her. Jeanette consequently followed up with *Annie Ong: Lost and found*, which delved into the difficult predicament of having two mothers and trying to figure out how to deal with them. She is looking to continue the quest and possibly try and find her birth father too. When not managing her family and business, Jeannette has an obsession with Scrabble, Bridge and real estate.

JENNY MOHINDRA was born in Edinburgh in 1969, given up for adoption at a few days and placed into a white English family at seven months old. She grew up in several different countries, spending the most time in Australia. The discovery of her birth parents when she was 30 also revealed her mixed parentage (Scottish and Indian), as well as the fact that she has two full siblings. Jenny now lives in London and has recently spent some time living with her birth family.

TM is black British and was born in 1974, growing up in south-east London where she is still based. She works in publishing as an editorial assistant. TM is currently travelling and working in Australia for a year where she hopes to write some articles for publication and connect with other transracial adoptees.

KAGEHA JERUTO MARSHALL lives in Wiltshire. She is married and has two daughters, Natasha and Gemma. Kageha has qualifications in Social Work and Early Years Education. The documentary about her search for her birth family won the Bronze Medal Award at the New York Television and Film Festival in 1996. She went on to make a second documentary in 2000. Her interest in adoption issues had led her to be on BBC Radio interview, including 'Home Truths'. She has also featured in Kenya's leading women's magazine in 1997. Kageha has just completed her first children's novel, *Hidden Friend*, which will be published in March/April 2006.

MARIYAM MAULE (15 March 1973–7 May 2005).

Premila Trivedi and Veronica Dewan write:
Our sister, friend and inspiration, Mariyam Maule, died on 7 May 2005. Mariyam was a poet, historian and human rights activist who was brought up in Helensburgh, Scotland. Early photographs show a smiling and happy child, but from a young age Mariyam had an acute awareness of oppression and injustice, and by 14 was a member of Amnesty International. Beautiful, feisty, energetic Mariyam moved to

London to study African History at the School of Oriental and African Studies and continued to pursue her passions for music, football (as a member of the Tottenham Ladies team) and campaigning for social justice.

After graduating in 1994, Mariyam came into contact with psychiatric services. This experience gave her important insights into how people, particularly black people, were treated within the mental health system and it was during this period that Mariyam wrote many very powerful poems about the nature of despair, injustice in the world and neglect and abuse within the psychiatric system. In other, more optimistic poems Mariyam displayed confidence, hope and a truly spiritual take on life, inspired by the Muslim Shi'ai faith she adopted during this period. Yet other poems display tenderness, love and forgiveness as she acknowledges both her love for her adopted family and despair at being separated at birth from her Egyptian cultural roots and a longing for reunion. Her deep respect for the works of Rumi, Frantz Fanon, Malcolm X, Nelson Mandela, Bob Marley and Tracey Chapman, and their influences on her, resonate strongly in her writing.

In 1998, Mariyam co-founded SIMBA, a black survivor group that uses its creativity to campaign for improvement in mental health services. Mariyam inspired and encouraged other less confident members of SIMBA to express themselves through poetry and many proudly performed their work in SIMBA's powerful campaigning readings, both within and outwith mental health services.

Most recently, Mariyam contributed with pride to this anthology. Sadly, she will not see its publication, but her family, friends and colleagues (and others never known to her) are privileged to have access to her thought-provoking work. Mariyam, with her generous spirit, her passion, her energy, her sense of humour, her loyalty and her deep spirituality enriched the lives of so many people in her short life, and has left us all a very special legacy.

MAYA was born in the late 1950s and brought up in the north of England, along with her adoptive parents' own children. Her birth mother is Scottish and her birth father African. As Maya has grown older, her background, and racial and cultural identity have become increasingly important to her. Maya works within the social care profession.

LOUISE McCOY was born in Manchester in 1968. Her mother was Irish and her father Nigerian. She joined her adoptive family when she was two weeks old, growing up in Manchester and then Hertfordshire. In 2003, Louise found her older maternal birth sister and the relationship is developing slowly. In the future she plans to search for other members of her maternal birth family and for her birth father. Louise lives in London with her daughter. She does some teaching.

NICOLE McKENZIE is of mixed parentage – part Jamaican, part English and part Scottish. She was born in London and was adopted as a baby by a white family in the Midlands. Nicky is now in her 30s, married with one daughter and works for a local authority. She has never traced any members of her birth family. Nicky is not interested in finding her birth parents, but would like to meet her siblings at some point in the not too distant future.

RON McLAY was born in Glasgow in 1961. His mother is Scottish and his father is from Pakistani-controlled Kashmir. Ron joined his adoptive family when he was five months old. They moved to Australia when he was eight. In 1991, Ron established contact with his mother in Scotland. He found his father in 2004, living in England, and met him the following year. Ron lives in New South Wales, Australia and has recently married.

KAREN MOIR was born on 2 July 1966 in Hong Kong. She is not sure exactly where but suspects it was Kowloon. Karen was the fifth baby girl born to her family. Her adoption was arranged privately between her birth parents and her adopters for whom they worked. It had been agreed, prior to her birth, that if she was a girl, her adopters would bring her back to England as their daughter. Karen was adopted shortly after her birth and the family arrived in the UK in the spring of 1968. As a child, she moved several times around south-east England but has lived predominately in London.

Karen made contact with her birth family in 1989/90 and made her first trip back to Hong Kong in 1991. She has been back a few times and, although contact is limited due to distance and language, has made good links with family members, especially her sisters. Karen thinks training and working as a social worker has had an impact on her search and contact with her birth family and probably helped her to cope with the different events that have come up along that journey. She now works as a health adviser in a busy London clinic but is still interested in the issues raised by intercountry/interracial adoption. She meets throughout the year with a small group of intercountry adoptees.

CAROL MOY was born in July 1963 in Norwich, Norfolk. Her mother was born in Trinidad, and had a daughter in 1958, and sons in 1960 and 1961, all of whom share the same father. Carol has a different father, whom she believes is also from Trinidad. She was placed with a white UK family (MOY) in August 1963 and was legally adopted in January 1967. Carol was raised in Suffolk and then moved to London in 1984. She married in August 1991 but separated shortly afterwards and is currently single with one son, Tyrone, born in 1992. She has read her adoption records but has not taken any further steps to find her mother. Carol works as an Education Officer for a London local authority, advising parents. She is also a school governor, youth worker, children's advocate at a local church and secretary of her local tenants' association. Carol and Tyrone visited Trinidad for a holiday in 2005.

NICK PENDRY was born in 1972 in London and is of Indian parentage, although some of his birth family migrated to East Africa. He grew up in Morden and then Merton Park in south-west London. He lives in south London and is married to Sue and they have a son called Luke Saleem. Nick qualified as a social worker in 1997 and has practised in child protection and child mental health. He is also a qualified family and systemic psychotherapist.

JOHN PAUL POULSON was born in 1978 in Wigan. He is of English and African-Caribbean (Jamaican) parentage. He was fostered by a family who eventually adopted him at three years old. John Paul traced his mother when he was around 22. He sits on an adoption panel for Barnardo's and is a youth worker working with young offenders. John Paul lives with his partner and their child in Whitley Bay, Tyne and Wear.

RACHEL was born in 1993 in Luton, England. Her birth mother is English and her father is unknown, possibly African-Caribbean or African. She does not know them at all. Rachel went into foster care when she was three-and-a-half years old, and joined her adoptive mother and adoptive sister when she was seven. She enjoys football and taking the dog out for a walk. Rachel lives in south England by the coast.

ANNA JAI LEI RIBKA was born in April 1980 on the island of Java, Indonesia. She was adopted at birth and after living in Indonesia until the age of three, moved with her family to Leicestershire, then down to Surrey in 1990. Anna now lives and works in London. Her interests include dance, reading, writing and a passion for travel. Anna began studying for a Masters degree in October 2005 and hopes to become a successful writer.

SHAKTI is of Indian parentage and lives in London.

SIMON SIBLEY was born in 1975 at St Mary's Hospital, Paddington. His father is Jamaican and his mother English. He was placed with a foster carer before joining his adoptive parents aged six weeks. Simon grew up in Southampton, and now lives and works in Bristol. He has accessed his adoption records and plans to trace his birth parents. Simon is a father of two children.

LIZ SIBTHORPE was born in 1948. Her paternal grandfather was Jamaican, but her birth mother was white. A white single woman adopted Liz at the age of two years. She then went on to adopt five more children from a variety of social and ethnic backgrounds, including black British (African-Caribbean), Anglo-Indian and white British. They were brought up near London. Liz now lives in York, in the north of England.

CARLY STACEY was born in 1987 in El Salvador. She was three months old when she was adopted. Carly has grown up in Preston, Lancashire. She would like to return to El Salvador one day and has recently spent time in Spain learning to speak Spanish. Carly is currently working part time and hopes to study French and Spanish in 2006.

EMMA STANHOPE was born in Eastbourne, on the south coast of England, in 1971 and is of mixed parentage. Her mother is English and her father was originally from Antigua, having settled with his family in Britain in his teens. She joined her adoptive family when she was about three months old and grew up in Surrey with five siblings. Emma thought a lot about her birth family during her upbringing, most intensively from the age of eleven upwards, and when she turned 18 she immediately contacted The Children's Society for information about her birth family. She met her birth father, siblings and extended family at 18 and made contact with her birth mother at age 19. Her birth father has since died.

Emma's poem, 'Fantasy', is about her previously ambiguous feelings about herself, specifically the rootless sense of not belonging and lack of self-love that she fantasised her non-adopted self would not have experienced. The fantasy element of who she would have been if she hadn't been adopted has been a strong theme during her life and this "original model" was everything that she felt she wasn't. The poem was written as a positive self-acknowledgement of where she is now, a celebration of acquiring self-worth, pride in her mixed heritage and laying the fantasy to rest.

Emma has recently returned from teaching in Cambodia and travelling in Asia with her partner for nearly four years. She now lives in London. This is the first time her work has been published under her name.

SUZANNA is of English and Indian parentage. She was adopted in the UK in the early 1970s. She is currently in education and has been living and working outside the UK since 1997. She recently spent several months tracing her birth mother. The search took her from Zambia to Fiji and Australia. At the time of writing 'The sari shop' in 2004, Suzanna believed that her father was Sri Lankan. She has since established contact with both her birth parents.

DEBORAH WEYMONT was born in 1956 and placed in a children's home at six weeks. She was fostered twice before being adopted, aged six, into a large family with four birth children, several other transracial adoptees and a few foster children. Deborah's birth certificate says 'father unknown' because this is what her white English birth mother chose to record. In fact, when she was in her 30s, Deborah discovered in her file that her biological father (who was from Bangladesh) had stayed in touch by sending money to the children's home until she was adopted. Deborah has been unable to meet either of her birth parents but she has been warmly welcomed into her birth father's family (some Bangladeshi cousins living in Tower Hamlets). Deborah considers her real parents (who are sadly both dead) to be the ones who raised her.

Deborah is a teacher and an art therapist. She has worked in special education and on behalf of marginalised children, young people and adults for 25 years. Currently, Deborah works with children and young people who have a range of learning and living difficulties. This includes children looked after and adopted, young offenders, children excluded from school and children bereaved. Deborah is a part-time practising artist and an active member of the LAFTA (looked after, fostered and transracially adopted) "survivors" support group. Deborah lives with her partner and their four children in Bristol.

MIRANDA WILKINSON was born in London in 1971. Her birth mother is white UK and her birth father is from Barbados. She was fostered by an Asian family for four months until her parents took her home to Hoddeston, Hertfordshire on 23 December 1971. Soon afterwards the family moved to Leicestershire and then to Wiltshire. When she was seven they moved again, this time to Reading where Miranda lived until 2002 when she moved, with her own family, to Birmingham where she works as a social worker in a Children and Families Team. She loves her job though emotionally finds it very hard. Miranda accessed her birth records in 2001 but has not, as yet, attempted to trace her birth family. She has two brothers, one 18 months younger who is her parents' own birth child and the other, six years younger, who is also of mixed parentage and adopted. Miranda is a mother to her own teenage son and three younger step-children.

ROS GIHAN WILLIAMS was born in Sri Lanka in 1973 and abandoned on the street a year later. She was subsequently adopted and came to live in England with her adoptive family. In 2004, Ros returned to Sri Lanka for the first time since leaving 30 years earlier. She runs her own production company, InFactuation, through which she directs social issue videos for the voluntary sector and documentaries. Her first video, *Love is Not Enough – Experiences in transracial adoption*, has been shown around the world and sold to over 300 national and international adoption and fostering organisations. In addition, Ros has worked in Channel 4's Multicultural and Night-time departments.

DAVID WOODGER is 41 years old. He is of Hindu Gujarati Indian origin, born in Islington, and joined his white adoptive family in rural Shropshire as a baby of three months. He has a younger sister who is also adopted from a different family and two siblings of his adoptive parents. His parents also fostered other children from black and minority ethnic communities.

David has been active in the field of race and adoption for over 20 years and was responsible for setting up the Association for Transracially Adopted People (ATRAP). He presently lectures in Social Sciences and Community Development at Goldsmiths College, University of London and provides consultancy to private and public sector organisations. David has written and published articles on race equality and, in particular, on transracial adoption. He became a Nichiren Daishonin Buddhist 13 years ago.

WUSHAN is a foundling who was adopted transracially when she was about two years old. Her exact birth details are unknown, as is her identity. Wushan was born in 1965 in Hong Kong where she was found. She assumes her parents are Chinese. She hopes her writing will be of interest to others who are lost and alone in the world. Wushan has previously had her writing published in *MindLink*, National Voices Forum and the Hearing Voices Network. Her piece, 'Foundling', is dedicated to her family whomever they may be.

ELINOR YOUNG was born in 1977 in Bradford and joined her foster family (who later adopted her) when she was two-and-a-half. She is Pakistani and grew up in Sussex. Elinor now lives in Surrey and works as a singing and part-time music teacher. As a classically trained singer, she also performs in concerts and enters competitions.

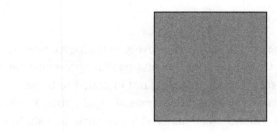

Resources

This resource list brings together published work (novels, anthologies, poetry, articles and book chapters) by transracial and transnational adoptees that touch upon the themes of adoption, race and identity. It is not intended to be an exhaustive list of available literature and resources, instead highlighting key items available in the UK and North America. The material is primarily British, but also includes material from the USA, Canada, Australia and Denmark. This is followed by sections on videos and websites by and for transracial and transnational adoptees; and UK support groups for transracial adoptees. The final two sections detail mainly national adoption support agencies, and other organisations and resources relevant to searching for birth relatives. Only material published in English has been included.

A more extensive list of the above and further resources, including writings by birth relatives, other published material on transracial adoption and adoption in general, children's books on transracial adoption written by transracial adoptees, and fiction and non-fiction about being privately fostered, in residential care or foster care by adults who have been privately fostered or in care, can be accessed via BAAF's website: www.baaf.org.uk/res/pubs/books/book_transadopted.shtml

CREATIVE WRITING, PERSONAL ACCOUNTS AND REFLECTIONS WRITTEN BY TRANSRACIALLY ADOPTED ADULTS

A black adopted person (1996) 'So where are you from?', in Phillips R and McWilliams E (eds) *After Adoption: Working with adoptive families*, London: BAAF

Allen K M (2004) 'Finding my identity as a Vietnamese adoptee', in Duc A (ed) *Hanh Trinh Tuoi Tre/Journey of Youth: Writings for the generations living and growing up overseas*, Montreal: Ngan Thong Publications

Alt J M (2004) 'Please … Don't', in Duc A (ed) as above

Alt J M (2004) 'When voices sing: my story of growing up Vietnamese', in Duc A (ed) as above

Alt J M (2004) 'Identity and transracial adoption', in Duc A (ed) as above

Anderson S W (1990) 'A letter to my daughter', in Anzaldua G (ed) *Making Face, Making Soul: Creative and critical perspectives by feminists of color*, San Francisco CA: Aunt Lute Books

Ando Me-K (1996) 'Living in Half-tones', in Wadia-Ellis S (ed) *The Adoption*

Reader: Birth mothers, adoptive mothers and adopted daughters tell their stories, London: The Women's Press

Austin J (2003) 'Being transracially adopted: what it is really like in the UK', in Douglas A and Philpot T (eds) *Adoption: Changing families, changing times*, London: Routledge

Bruining M O (1995) 'A few thoughts from a Korean, adopted, lesbian, writer/ poet, and social worker', in Hidalgo H (ed) *Lesbians of color: social and human services*, New York: Haworth Press Inc; available online at http://homepage.ntlworld.com/amy.cham/few.htm

Camper C (1994) 'Genetic appropriation: a response to a white liberal fad', in Camper C (ed) *Miscegenation Blues: Voices of mixed race women*, Toronto: Sister Vision Press

Davie S M (1996) 'An adoptee's journal', in Wadia-Ellis S (ed) *The Adoption Reader: Birth mothers, adoptive mothers and adopted daughters tell their stories*, London: The Women's Press

Dewan V (2003) 'A truer image', in Douglas A and Philpot T (eds) *Adoption: Changing families, changing times*, London: Routledge

Dewan V (2001) 'Life support', in *Something Inside So Strong: Strategies for surviving mental distress*, London: The Mental Health Foundation

Dewan V (1996) 'The pressure of being a human chameleon', in Read J and Reynolds J (eds) *Speaking Our Minds: An anthology*, Basingstoke/London: Macmillan

Fish L (1995) *Flight of Black Swans*, London: Duckworth & Co

Harris P (1988) 'In my experience – bridging the gap', *Who Cares?* 4, Summer, p 15

Green H (1994) 'This piece done, I shall be renamed', in Camper C (ed) *Miscegenation Blues: Voices of mixed race women*, Toronto: Sister Vision Press

Hom S G (1999) 'Double lifeline', in Ito S and Cervin T (eds) *A Ghost at Heart's Edge: Stories and poems of adoption*, Berkeley CA: North Atlantic Books

Jackson K and McKinley C (1996) 'Sisters: a reunion story', in Wadia-Ellis S (ed) *The Adoption Reader: Birth mothers, adoptive mothers and adopted daughters tell their stories*, London: The Women's Press

Jardine S (1996) 'A journey to Hong Kong', *Post Adoption Centre Newsletter*, January, pp 9–11

Jardine S (1996) 'Transracial adoption: a personal experience', *Counselling*, May, pp 113–14

Jardine S (1999) 'Transracial placements: an adoptee's perspective', in Barn R (ed) *Working with Black Children and Adolescents in Need*, London: BAAF

Jardine S (2000) 'In whose interests? Reflections on openness, cultural roots and loss', in Selman P (ed) *Intercountry Adoption: Developments, trends and perspectives*, London: BAAF

John J (2002) *Black Baby White Hands: A view from the crib*, Maryland VA: Soul Water Publishing

Kim E (2000) *Ten Thousand Sorrows: The extraordinary journey of a Korean War orphan*, St Helens WA: Doubleday

Lee M G (1999) 'Summer of my Korean soldier', in Ito S and Cervin T (eds), *A Ghost at Heart's Edge: Stories and poems of adoption*, Berkeley CA: North Atlantic Books

McKinley C (2003) *A Book of Sarahs: A family in parts*, Washington DC: Counterpoint Press

McKinley C (1996) 'Afro Jew Fro', in Ruff S S (ed) *Go the Way Your Blood Beats: An anthology of lesbian and gay fiction by African American writers*, New York: Henry Holt & Co.

McKiver B (2001) 'When the heron speaks', in Bensen R (ed) (2001) *Children of the Dragonfly: Native American voices on child custody and education*, Tucson AZ: The University of Arizona Press

Miro A (forthcoming) *The Other Face of the Moon: Finding my Indian family*, Chichester, West Sussex: Summersdale Publishers

Park Clement T (1998) *The Unforgotten War: Dusts of the streets*, Bloomfield IN: Truepeny Publishing Co.

Pool H (2005) *My Father's Daughter*, London: Penguin

Robinson K (2002) *A Single Square Picture: A Korean adoptee's search for her roots*, Berkeley CA: Berkeley Press

Sampson L (2001) 'The long road home', in Bensen R (ed) (2001), see McKiver

Sanwell-Smith K (2000) 'Meeting our needs: some proposals for change', in Selman P (ed) *Intercountry Adoption: Developments, trends and perspectives*, London: BAAF

Shobha and Marylin (1999) '*Tum meri didi hun* (You are my sister)', in Mullender A (ed) *We are Family: Sibling relationships in placement and beyond*, London: BAAF

Sjögren J S (1996) 'A ghost in my country', *Adoption & Fostering* 20:2, pp 32–35

Sjögren J S (1997) 'Dream's end', *Adoption & Fostering* 21:2, pp 16–18

Spears S (2003) 'Strong spirit, fractured identity: an Ojibway adoptee's journey to wholeness', in Anderson K and Lawrence B (eds) *Strong Women Stories: Native vision and community survival*, Toronto: Sumach Press

Stroshane S W (1999) 'Unborn song', in Ito S and Cervin T (eds) *A Ghost at Heart's Edge: Stories and poems of adoption*, Berkeley CA: North Atlantic Books

Sudbury J (1999) 'Hunger', in Ito S and Cervin T (eds) as above

Sunny Jo (2005) *From Morning Calm to Midnight Sun*, Bloomfield, Indiana: Truepeny Publishing Co.; available from www.koreanadoptees.net/MorningCalm.htm)

Sunny Jo (2005) *The KA Directory 2005/6*, Bloomfield IN: Truepeny Publishing Co.; available from www.koreanadoptees.net/KADirectory.htm

Sutherland L (2004) *Venus as a Boy*, London: Bloomsbury

Sutherland L (2004) 'A boy from the islands…', *The Guardian*, 14 March

Tallmountain M (1988) (3rd edition) 'My wild birds flying', in Brant B (ed) *A Gathering of Spirit: A collection by North American Indian women*, Toronto: Women's Press

Trenka J J (2005) *Language of Blood*, St Paul MN: Graywolf Press

Williams I T (2004) 'America's adopted Vietnamese', in Duc A (ed) as above

ANTHOLOGIES OF WRITING BY TRANSRACIALLY ADOPTED ADULTS

Armstrong S and Slaytor P (2001) *The Colour of Difference: Journeys in transracial adoption*, NSW, Australia: The Federation Press

Bishoff T and Rankin J (ed) (1997) *Seeds from a Silent Tree: An anthology by Korean adoptees*, San Diego CA: Pandal Press

Cox Soon-Keum S (ed) (1999) *Voices from Another Place: A collection of works from a generation born in Korea and adopted to other countries*, St Paul MN: Yeung & Yeung Book Co.

IECEF Adoptees' Homecoming (2005) *The Letter Never Sent*, USA: IECEF; available from: www.seoulselection.com

Stolen Generations (2003) *A Book of Voices: Voices of aboriginal adoptees and foster children*, Winnipeg, MB

Trenka J J, Oparah C and Shin S Y (eds) (forthcoming) *Outsiders Within: Racial crossings and adoption politics*, Cambridge MA: South End Press

Wilkinson S and Fox N (eds) (2002) *After the Morning Calm: Reflections of Korean adoptees*, Detroit MI: Sunrise Ventures Publishing.

POETRY BY TRANSRACIALLY ADOPTED ADULTS ON ADOPTION, RACE, LOVE AND LIFE

Bruining M O (1999) 'They said', in Ito S and Cervin T (eds) *A Ghost at Heart's Edge: Stories and poems of adoption*, Berkeley CA: North Atlantic Books

Bruining M O (1990) 'To Omoni, in Korea', in Anzaldua G (ed) *Making Face, Making Soul: Creative and critical perspectives by feminists of color*, San Francisco CA: Aunt Lute Books; available online at: www.akconnection.com/media/miok.asp

Camper C (1991, reprinted 1992) 'Gaia' and 'Untitled', in Silvera M (ed) *Piece of my Heart: A lesbian of colour anthology*, Toronto: Sister Vision Press

Kay J (1991) *The Adoption Papers*, Newcastle Upon Tyne: Bloodaxe Books

Kay J (1998) *Off Colour*, Newcastle Upon Tyne: Bloodaxe Books

Kay J (2005) *Life Mask*, Newcastle Upon Tyne: Bloodaxe Books

Kay J, Burford B, Pearse G and Nichols G (undated) *A Dangerous Knowing: Four black women poets*, London: Sheba Feminist Publishers

Shin SY (forthcoming) *Han*, St Paul MN: Coffee House Press; see www.sunyungshin.com

Tallmountain M (1990) *The Light on the Tent Wall: A bridging*, Los Angeles CA: University of California at Los Angeles

Tallmountain M (1991) *A Quick Brush of Wings*, San Francisco CA: Freedom Voices

Tallmountain M (1995) *Listen to the Night: Poems to the animal spirits of mother earth*, San Francisco CA: Freedom Voices; see http://www.freedomvoices.org

Tallmountain M (1999) 'My Familiar', in Ito S and Cervin T (eds) *A Ghost at Heart's Edge: Stories and poems of adoption*, Berkeley CA: North Atlantic Books

Tallmountain M (2001) 'Five Poems', in Bensen R (ed) (2001) *Children of the Dragonfly: Native American Voices on child custody and education*, Tucson AZ: The University of Arizona Press

Tallmountain M (1999) 'There is no word for goodbye', in Ito S and Cervin T (eds) *A Ghost at Heart's Edge: Stories and poems of adoption*, Berkeley CA: North Atlantic Books

VIDEOS BY TRANSRACIALLY ADOPTED ADULTS

'Love is Not Enough: Experiences in transracial adoption' (30 mins) (2000) Infactuation Productions Limited, Studio 34, The Old Truman Brewery, 91 Brick Lane, London E1 6QL
Contact: Ros Gihan Williams
Tel: +44 (0) 20 7053 2126
Email: admin@infactuation.co.uk
www.infactuation.co.uk

FILMS BY TRANSRACIALLY ADOPTED ADULTS

Belonging by Li-Da Kruger
To purchase a DVD, please contact Tracey Gardiner at the Cambodian Film Company (in association with FulcrumTV)
Bramah House, 65–71 Bermondsey Street, London SE1 3XF
Tel: 020 7939 3160
Email: info@fulcrumtv.com
www.fulcrumtv.com

USEFUL WEBSITES AND FORUMS FOR TRANSRACIAL AND TRANSNATIONAL ADOPTEES

Many of these sites contain links to other related sites and networks of transnational and transracial adoptees, as well as personal accounts and poetry.

Adopted Korean Connection (USA)
www.akconnection.com

Adopted Vietnamese International
www.adoptedvietnamese.org

Also Known As (Korean adoptee group, USA)
www.alsoknownas.org

Association for Transracially Adopted and fostered People (England)
www.atrap.port5.com/

Bastard Nation (USA) page on transnational and transracial adoptees
www.bastards.org/library/inter.htm

Connected Indian Roots
www.people.freenet.de/connectedindianroots/

Filipino Adoptees Network
www.filipino-adoptees-network.org

First Nations Orphans Association (North America)
www.angelfire.com/falcon/fnoa

Global Overseas Adoptees Link (Korea)
www.goal.or.kr/new/

Inter-Country Adoptee Support Network (Australia)
www.icasn.org

Korean Adoptees Worldwide
www.koreanadoptees.net.

Korean American Adoptive Family Network (USA)
www.kaan.com

Korea Club (Denmark)
www.koreaklubben.dk

Motherland Tour to Vietnam
www.motherlandtour.com

Six Nations Adoptees (North America)
www.bodhipines.com/6nations/

South Asian International Adoptees Talk
www.groupsyahoo.com/group/SAIA-T/

The Native Adoptee (Canada)
www.ncf.carleton.ca/~de723/adoptee.html

Transracial Abductees
www.transracialabductees.org

Vietnam Baby Airlift
www.vietnambabyairlift.org

Vietnamese Adoptee Network
www.van-online.org

Personal stories by transracial adoptees (Australia)
www.bensoc.org.au/parc_stories/transracial_fp.html

Personal stories by Korean adoptees (USA)
www.pbs.org/pov/pov2000/firstpersonplural/

UK SUPPORT GROUPS RUN BY AND/OR FOR TRANSRACIAL ADOPTEES

There are very few services that have been developed specifically to meet the needs of transracially adopted children and adults. Here are some that do exist:

LAFTA

An informal and inclusive group for anyone who defines them self as black, brown, mixed-race, or dual-heritage, who has also been looked after/in public care, fostered or adopted.
Contact: Deborah Weymont
Tel: 0117 944 5165 (answer machine)
Email: none available
Location: Bristol

Transnational and Transracial Adoption Group (TTAG)
An informal social support group that meets on a quarterly basis for adult adoptees who have been transnationally and transracially adopted. The group is willing to discuss the possibility of providing specific support to younger adoptees. Some members undertake public speaking at conferences and on training courses for prospective and approved adoptive parents.
Tel: none available
Email: ttag.group@btopenworld.com
Location: London and surrounding areas

The **Association for Transracially Adopted and fostered People (ATRAP)** is a registered charity that is not currently providing any services.

NORCAP is interested in developing services for transracially adopted adults.

The **Post-Adoption Centre** (London) runs fixed-term groups for transracially adopted adults which are also open to adults who have been long-term fostered transracially. The agency provides opportunities for transracially adopted teens to come together.

After Adoption (Manchester) runs a group for transracially adopted adults.

After Adoption Yorkshire has hosted peer-led groups for transracially adopted adults and is interested in establishing a similar group in the future. AAY is able to link transracial adoptees with other transracially adopted people.

REGIONAL ADOPTION SUPPORT SERVICES IN THE UK

Regional adoption support agencies provide a range of services to people who have been affected by adoption: adopted people, birth relatives and adoptive parents Services vary between agencies and many are provided for free. The range of services may include: counselling, tracing, acting as an intermediary, support groups, groups for adopted children, direct work with adopted children, work with adoptive families, training and events for adoptive parents.

Adoption Support
Suite A, 6th Floor, Albany House, Hurst Street, Birmingham B5 4BD
Tel: 0121 666 6014
Fax: 0121 666 6334
Email: adoptionsupport@tiscali.co.uk
www.adoptionsupport.co.uk

After Adoption
Action Line: 0800 0 568 578
Email: information@afteradoption.org.uk
www.afteradoption.org.uk

TALKadoption
Tel: 0808 808 1234 (if you are under 26 years old)
Email: helpline@talkadoption.org.uk

After Adoption (Head Office)
12–14 Chapel Street, Salford, Manchester M3 7NH
Tel: 0161 839 4930 Helpline
Fax: 0161 832 2242
Email: information@afteradoption.org.uk
After Adoption also has regional offices in London, Lancashire, Blackpool, Blackburn and Cumbria, Merseyside, Wirral and North Wales, North East, Greater Manchester, South and West Wales.

After Adoption Yorkshire (AAY)
31 Moor Road, Headingley, Leeds LS6 4BG
Advice line: 0113 230 2100
Fax: 0113 278 6050
Email: info@aay.org.uk
www.afteradoptionyorkshire.org.uk

Family Futures Consortium
35 Britannia Row, Islington, London N1 8QH
Tel: 020 7354 4161
Fax: 020 7704 6200
Email: contact@familyfutures.co.uk
www.familyfutures.org.uk
Offers assessment, support, and treatment programmes.

North East Post-Adoption Service
Royal Quays Community Centre, Prince Consort Way, Royal Quays, North Shields, Tyne and Wear NE29 6XB
Tel: 0191 296 6064
Fax: 0191 296 6064
Email: nepas@nepas.org
www.nepas.org

Post-Adoption Centre
5 Torriano Mews, Torriano Avenue, London NW5 2RZ
Tel: 020 7284 0555
Tel: 0870 777 2197 Advice Line
Email: advice@postadoptioncentre.org.uk
www.postadoptioncentre.org.uk
The Post-Adoption Centre maintains a database of therapists and counsellors who have attended their accredited training on adoption counselling.

South West Adoption Network (SWAN)
Leinster House, Leinster Avenue, Knowle, Bristol BS4 1AL
Tel: 0845 601 2459 Helpline
Email: admin@swan-adoption.org.uk
www.swan-adoption.org.uk

GENERAL REGISTRAR OFFICES

Registrar General (England and Wales)
The General Register Office, Adoption Section, Smedley Hydro, Trafalgar Road, Birkdale, Southport PR8 2HH
Tel: 0151 471 4313
www.gro.gov.uk/gro/content/adoptions/
In England and Wales, adopted people aged 18 and over are entitled to a copy of their original birth certificate. The Registrar General operates the government Adoption Contact Register for adoptees aged 18 and over and birth relatives.

The General Register Office (Scotland)
New Register House, 3 West Register Street, Edinburgh EH1 3YT
Tel: 0131 334 0380
Email: records@gro-scotland.gov.uk
www.gro-scotland.gov.uk
In Scotland, adopted people aged 16 and over are entitled to a copy of their original birth certificate.

The Registrar General (Northern Ireland)
Oxford House, 49-55 Chichester Street, Belfast BT1 4HL
Tel: 02890 252000
www.groni.gov.uk

In Northern Ireland, adopted people aged 18 and over are entitled to a copy of their original birth certificate.

The Registrar General
Joyce House, 8/11 Lombard Street East, Dublin 2, Ireland
Tel: 35 31 6711 863

RECORDS OF BIRTHS, MARRIAGES AND DEATHS: ENGLAND AND WALES

Family Records Centre
1 Myddleton Street, London EC1R 1UW
Tel: 0845 603 7788
Certificate enquiries: certificate.services@ons.gov.uk
Website: www.familyrecords.gov.uk/frc

NATIONAL AND REGIONAL ORGANISATIONS: ENGLAND AND WALES

Adoption UK (providing support for adoptive families)
46 The Green, South Bar Street, Banbury OX16 9AB
Tel: 01295 752240
Fax: 01295 752241
Helpline: 0870 7700 450
Helpdesk email: helpdesk@adoptionuk.org.uk
www.adoptionuk.com

Barnardo's
Tanners Lane, Barkingside, Ilford, Essex IG6 1QG
Tel: 0208 550 8822

Barnardo's Cymru
11–15 Columbus Walk, Brigantine Place, Atlantic Wharf, Cardiff CF10 4BZ
Tel: 0292 049 3387

The Children's Society (formerly the Church of England Waifs and Strays)
Post Adoption and Care: Counselling Research Project, 91 Queen's Road, Peckham, London SE15 2EZ
Tel: 0207 732 9089

Catholic Children's Society (Westminster) (formerly the Catholic Crusade of Rescue Society)
73 St Charles Square, London W10 6EJ
Tel: 0208 969 5305

International Social Service (UK)
Cranmer House (3rd Floor), 39 Brixton Road, London SW9 6DD
Tel: 020 7735 8941
Email: help@issuk.org.uk
www.issuk.org.uk

NCH (formerly National Children's Homes)
NCH Family Placement Adviser, NCH Central Office, Operations Department, 85 Highbury Park, London N5 1UD
Advice line: 0845 3555533
www.nchafc.org.uk

National Organisation for the Counselling of Adoptees and their Parents (NORCAP)
112 Church Road, Wheatley, Oxfordshire 0X33 1LU
Tel: 01865 875000
Fax: 01865 875686
www.norcap.org.uk
Supports adults affected by adoption.

Natural Parents Network (NPN)
Garden Suburb, Oldham, Lancashire OL8 3AY
Tel: 01273 307 597
Email: administrator@n-p-n.fsnet.co.uk
www.n-p-n.fsnet.co.uk

NATIONAL AND REGIONAL ORGANISATIONS: SCOTLAND

Barnardo's Scottish Adoption Advice Service (West Scotland only)
16 Sandyford Place, Glasgow G3 7NB
Advice line: 0141 339 0772

Birth Link
Family Care, 21 Castle Street, Edinburgh EH2 3DN
Tel: 0131 225 6441
Fax: 0131 225 6478

Email: acrform@birthlink.org.uk

www.birthlink.org.uk

Operates the Adoption Contact Register for adoptees aged 16 and over and birth relatives.

Scottish Adoption Association (East Scotland only)

2 Commercial Street, Edinburgh EH6 6JA

Tel: 0131 553 5060

Post Adoption Central Support (PACS)

Rena Phillips, PACS Co-ordinator

Tel: 01259 781 545

Email: renaphillips@hotmail.com

www.postadoptioncentralsupport.org

Group for Adopted People (GAP) (Central Scotland)

Jan Morris, GAP Co-ordinator

Rock Community Project, The Rock Centre, 1st Floor, 61–63 Murray Place, Stirling FK8 1AP

Tel: 01786 850733

Email: gapscotland@yahoo.co.uk

A group run by and for adopted people that is funded by Stirling, Falkirk and Clackmannanshire Councils.

NATIONAL AND REGIONAL ORGANISATIONS: NORTHERN IRELAND AND IRELAND

ADOPT – Northern Ireland

VSB, The Peskett Centre, 2/2a Windsor Road, Belfast BT9 FFQ

Tel: 0289 038 2353

Adopted People's Association

27 Templeview Green, Clare Hill, Dublin 13, Ireland

Tel: (01) 867 4033

Email: info@adoptionireland.com

www.adoptionireland.com

The Adoption Board

Shelbourne House, Shelbourne Road, Ballsbridge, Dublin 4, Ireland

Tel: 00353 1 669 1392

The Adoption Board holds records of all adoptions in Eire.

Barnardo's Adoption Advice Service
Chirstchurch Square, Dublin 8
Tel: 00353 1 453 0355
Confidential advice line: 00353 1454 6388

Church of England Adoption Society
Church of England House, 61–67 Donegall Street, Belfast BT1 2QH
Tel: 0289 023 3885
Email: admin@cofiadopt.org.uk
www.cofiadopt.org.uk

Natural Parents Network (NPN)
PO Box 6714, Dublin 4, Ireland
Tel: Sundays 2–4pm only, (086) 8530 140
Email: naturalparents@indigo.ie

OTHER

Nafsiyat Intercultural Therapy Centre
262 Holloway Road, Holloway, London N7 6NE
Tel: 0207 686 8668
www.nafsiyat.org.uk

Adoption, Search and Reunion
www.adoptionsearchreunion.org.uk

Medicine Management for Nurses

Case Book

Edited by
Paul Barber

Open University Press

Open University Press
McGraw-Hill Education
McGraw-Hill House
Shoppenhangers Road
Maidenhead
Berkshire
England
SL6 2QL

email: enquiries@openup.co.uk
world wide web: www.openup.co.uk

and Two Penn Plaza, New York, NY 10121-2289, USA

First published 2013

A catalogue record of this book is available from the British Library

ISBN-13: 978-0-33-524575-8 (pb)
ISBN-10: 0-33-524575-7 (pb)
eISBN: 978-0-33-524576-5

Library of Congress Cataloging-in-Publication Data
CIP data applied for

Typesetting and e-book compilations by
RefineCatch Limited, Bungay, Suffolk

Praise for this book

"The book offers a unique and engaging approach to an important subject that most students find daunting. Realistic case scenarios are used as a catalyst to introduce information and concepts that underpin practice. The presentation style supports the active participation of the student with the inclusion of questions at the beginning of each topic offering a platform to explore key areas whilst referring to the scenario. I highly recommend it to pre-registered student nurses."

Kris Paget, Senior Lecturer, Faculty of Health,
Social Work and Education, Kingston University

"This collection of case studies provides a unique and user friendly guide to commonly seen pharmacological therapies and treatment options across the lifespan. The case studies have been carefully selected to provide the diverse care needs of complex disease processes in a person centred way. Each case study is relevant to the role of the Nurse and will provide essential and core information whether nurses are working in either a medical or surgical clinical setting.

Government Health Care Directives provide the essential clinical evidence based theory necessary to promote medicine adherence and each chapter provides the relevant patho-physiology which is essential to underpin the safe administration of medication therapies.

The role of the nurse in medicine management with respect to patient education and the professional responsibilities of monitoring and evaluating complex medication therapies is presented in each case study. This provides an holistic approach to the care of patients receiving complex medication therapies."

Barry Ricketts, Senior Lecturer, Adult Nursing,
Oxford Brookes University

Contents

List of figures

List of tables

Contributors

Paul Barber is senior lecturer in nursing at the University of Chester, UK. He teaches both pre- and post-registration nurses. He has over 36 years' nursing experience and before beginning his teaching career previously held numerous nursing positions. He spent his early career in surgery, high dependency and A&E, then progressed to become manager of a small surgical unit. This is his third book for Open University Press. He is the co-author of *Essentials of Pharmacology for Nurses* (2009, 2012), and *Further Essentials of Pharmacology for Nurses* (2012), both published by Open University Press.

Diane Blundell is currently a pre-registration programme leader for the University of Chester. She is also a qualified aromatherapist, reflexologist and Reiki master. She is module leader for the pre-registration applied sciences and also runs the post-registration intensive care and cardiology modules. She is co-author of *Further Essentials of Pharmacology for Nurses* (2012).

Abe Ginourie is a senior lecturer in adult nursing at the University of Chester. He has 37 years of nursing experience and is the leader for the respiratory and diabetic nursing care modules.

Joy Parkes is a senior lecturer in adult nursing at the University of Chester with a particular focus on practice, including complementary therapies, applied anatomy, physiology and pharmacology, and acute pain. She is a co-author of *Further Essentials of Pharmacology for Nurses* (2012).

Ruth Sadik is a senior lecturer at the University of Chester and has been working in child health care and children's nursing for over 40 years.

Pat Talbot began her nursing career in general nursing, followed by a move into learning disability nursing, which has been her main area of interest for 37 years. She has a particular interest in the physical health care needs of people with a learning disability.

Janine Upton is a senior lecturer at the University of Chester. She has an extensive clinical background in orthopaedic nursing, with a special interest in osteoporosis, falls and practice development.

Traci Whitfield is currently a pre-registration programme leader for the University of Chester. She has over 34 years of nursing experience, 21 of those in nurse education. She leads the older person's modules.

Christine Whitney-Cooper is deputy head of acute adult and child care at the University of Chester. She has worked in both adult and children's nursing settings for over 35 years and has a background in medical chronic and complex care.

Debbie Wyatt is a senior lecturer at the University of Chester and Macmillan Lecturer at Clatterbridge Cancer Centre. She has 29 years of nursing experience and has worked in education for 24 years. Her particular areas of interest include cancer and palliative care.

List of useful abbreviations

ACE	angiotensin-converting enzyme
A&E	accident & emergency department
AEDs	anti-epileptic drugs
AMI	anterior myocardial infarction
ARBs	angiotensin receptor blockers
5-ASA	5-aminosalicylic acid
ATP	adenosine triphosphate
B2	beta 2
BMD	bone mineral density
BMI	body mass index
BMR	basal metabolic rate
BNF	British National Formulary
cAMP	cyclic adenosine monophosphate
CD	Crohn's disease
CDS	continuous dopaminergic stimulation
CF	cystic fibrosis
CFTR	cystic fibrosis transmembrane conductance regulator
CHD	coronary heart disease
CNS	central nervous system
CO	cardiac output
CO_2	carbon dioxide
COX	cyclo-oxygenase
COPD	chronic obstructive pulmonary disease
CR	capillary refill
CRF	corticotrophin-releasing factor
CRP	C reactive protein
CSF	cerebrospinal fluid
CT	computerized tomography
CTZ	chemoreceptor trigger zone
CVD	cardiovascular disease
CXR	chest X-ray
D_2	dopamine receptor 2
DMARD	disease-modifying anti-rheumatoid drug
DNA	deoxyribonucleic acid
DXA	dual-energy X-ray absorptiometry
ECG	electrocardiogram
EEG	electroencephalogram

GABA	gamma-aminobutyric acid
GI	gastrointestinal
GP	general practitioner
5HT3	5-hydroxytryptamine 3 receptor
HbA1c	glycosylated haemoglobin
HCLCA1	human calcium-activated chloride channel
HDL	high density lipoprotein
HLA	human leukocyte antigen
HMG CoA	hydroxymethylglutaryl coenzyme A
HPA	hypothalamic-pituitary-adrenal
HR	heart rate
HRT	hormone replacement therapy
HVA	homovanillic acid
IBD	inflammatory bowel disease
ICA	islet cell antigen
IDE	insulin degrading enzyme
IFN-γ	interferon gamma
Ig E	immunoglobulin E
IRT	immunoreactive trypsinogen
IV	intravenous
LABA	longer acting β_2-adrenergic receptor agonists
LDL	low density lipoprotein
LUNSERS	Liverpool University Neuroleptic Side-effect Rating Scale
LVEF	left ventricular ejection fraction
LVF	left ventricular failure
LVSD	left ventricular systolic dysfunction
MAP	mycobacterial species
MDI	metered dose inhaler
MI	myocardial infarction
MIC	minimum inhibitory concentrations
MODY	maturity onset diabetes of the young
6MP	6-mercaptopurine
MRI	magnetic resonance imaging
NADH	nicotinamide adenine dinucleotide
NAG	N-acetylglucosamine
NAM	N-acetylemuramic acid
NG	nasogastric
NMDA	N-methyl-D-aspartate
NSAID	non-steroidal anti-inflammatory drug
NSCLC	non-small-cell lung carcinoma
ONJ	osteonecrosis of the jaw
PD	Parkinson's disease
PEFR	peak expiratory flow rate
PERT	pancreatic enzyme replacement therapy
PHS	Parkinsonism-hyperpyrexia syndrome
pMDI	pressurized metered dose inhaler

PTH	parathyroid hormone
RNA	ribonucleic acid
RR	respiratory rate
SABA	short-acting β_2-adrenergic receptor agonist
SaO$_2$	oxygen saturation
SD	standard deviation
SIADH	syndrome of inappropriate antidiuretic hormone secretion
SRS-A	slow-reacting substances of anaphylaxis
SSNRI	selective serotonin and norepinephrine reuptake inhibitor
SSRI	selective serotonin reuptake inhibitor
SUDEP	sudden unexplained death in epilepsy
SV	stroke volume
TB	tuberculosis
TGFb	transforming growth factor beta
TNFalpha	tumour necrosis factor alpha
TNM	tumour lymph nodes metastases
U&Es	urea and electrolytes
UTI	urinary tract infection

Introduction

The administration of medicines is an important aspect of the professional practice of persons whose names are on the Council's register. It is not solely a mechanistic task to be performed in strict compliance with the written prescription of a medical practitioner (now independent/supplementary prescriber). It requires thought and the exercise of professional judgement . . .

(NMC 2008: 3)

Trends in medical care have been marked by an increased use and complexity of pharmacological therapies, the increased acuity of the general public and the ageing of the population. In this environment, knowledge of drugs, their side-effects and interactions is increasingly important to nurses. Nurses not only administer medication, but they assess both therapeutic and adverse effects, and therefore they *manage* medicines. Media reports of medical errors, specifically medication errors in nursing practice, have focused increased attention on pharmacology in nursing education. Knowledge of clinical pharmacology is therefore an important nursing educational outcome in medicine management.

LEARNING ABOUT MEDICINE MANAGEMENT

The need for learning tools in medicine management is essential because many nursing students struggle with aspects of the topic. Also, because medicine management is often given less importance than behavioural sciences or other subjects within the nursing curricula, supporting resources are important. In contrast to this, government initiatives have identified the need for nurses to undertake multi-skilled professional roles such as supplementary and independent prescribing (V300), and so it is becoming more important that newly qualified nurses have a sound medicine management knowledge base. Furthermore, students at my university regularly suggest they need more confidence and structured education in pharmacology. This is supported by literature regarding nurses' perceptions of their pharmacology educational needs (King 2004). In addition, the importance of pharmacology is being recognized by the nursing profession itself — it is one of the essential skills clusters and the standards for pre-registration education discuss its importance.

THE CASE STUDY APPROACH

The case study approach to teaching and learning is becoming much more widespread in schools of nursing in an attempt to encourage students to integrate their understanding of the

1

link between the underlying normal physiology, the pathophysiology and the pharmacology, and the nursing care required by the patient or service user. This is the approach taken by myself for the teaching of this material and my students appear to find the use of case studies both enjoyable and beneficial. This suggests that there is educational value in the problem-solving approach this book utilizes. It will allow you to contextualize your knowledge and understand its relevance to practice. This is increasingly recognized as an important outcome for most nursing programmes and I hope the structure of this book will promote such an outcome.

The cases used in this book seek to promote:

- recognition of the relationship between normal physiological status, underlying patho-physiology and the presenting clinical features of a condition;
- integration of the student's knowledge of pharmacology in relation to pathophysiology;
- identification of the importance of the nurse's role in assessing the therapeutic and adverse effects of medicines on a patient;
- promotion of the understanding of pharmacology in the nurse's role of educating patients about medications, dosages and possible side-effects.

ABOUT THE CASES

The majority of patients and service users referred to in these case studies are entirely ficti-tious, however the content is drawn from my own experience, in collaboration with clinical colleagues, and therefore represents situations which commonly occur in the clinical area. The case studies based on actual patients have been designed to protect their anonymity. Each case study approaches the aspects of medicine management and nursing care of the patient which the author feels are pertinent to the topic under discussion. This means that although the general principles outlined above will be considered, the case studies are individual and contain variation.

Finally it is my belief that these case studies will allow the reader an opportunity to enhance or consolidate their knowledge of the theory and practice underlying medicine management in nursing. Whether you are a nursing student or a more experienced practitioner, either returning to practice or moving to a new area, this should enhance your confidence and ability to respond appropriately in care situations, and facilitate sound clinical decision-making skills with regard to managing medicines effectively.

REFERENCES

King, R.L. (2004) Nurses' perceptions of their pharmacology educational needs, *Journal of Advanced Nursing*, 45(4): 392–400.
NMC (Nursing and Midwifery Council) (2008) *Standards for Medicines Management*. London: NMC.

The person with Alzheimer's disease
Traci Whitfield

CASE AIMS

After examining this case study the reader should be able to:

- Briefly explain the role of neurotransmitters at a synapse.
- Outline how the brain normally creates, stores and retrieves memories.
- Describe the pathophysiology of Alzheimer's disease.
- Explain the three stages associated with Alzheimer's disease.
- Demonstrate an understanding of the mode of action and side-effects of donepezil and memantine.
- Discuss the role of the nurse in advising relatives regarding the medication.

CASE

Mr B is a 76-year-old man who was diagnosed with Alzheimer's disease, stage one, six years ago and is being cared for at home by his wife. He has a very poor short-term memory and is unable to care for himself without assistance. He wanders around a lot and has been found outside at night several times, which causes his wife great concern. Despite living in the same house for 16 years, Mr B does not recognize his house when he wanders out and so is unable to find his way home.

---

1 **Before Mr B was diagnosed with Alzheimer's disease, how would his neurons have communicated with each other?**

2 **How would Mr B's brain have normally created, stored and retrieved his memories?**

3 **What is thought to be happening in Mr B's brain in order for him to be displaying signs and symptoms of Alzheimer's disease?**

4 **What will be the main effects of the disease on Mr B as it progresses through its stages?**

Mr B is prescribed 10mg donepezil at night, but his wife feels he may be having side-effects. Mrs B has expressed concern that her husband is suffering from lack of appetite, weight loss, diarrhoea and insomnia, and as a result he has been reviewed by a specialist who has suggested Mr B should switch to memantine.

5 How do donepezil and memantine work?

6 What side-effects would you look for in Mr B while he is taking these medicines?

7 What advice would you offer to Mrs B about her husband's medication to assist her understanding of its role in his care?

ANSWERS

1 **Before Mr B was diagnosed with Alzheimer's disease, how would his neurons have communicated with each other?**

A Neurons communicate with each other across gaps or **synapses** that occur between them. In order for the signal to pass from one neuron to another across these synapses, the body would have produced **neurotransmitters** such as **acetylcholine, glutamate** and **dopamine**. Initial impulses would travel along the neurons and at the point where they meet the synapse cause **vesicles** containing neurotransmitters to release their contents. The neurotransmitters would then cross the synapse to the next neuron and attach to receptors on its surface in order to either excite or inhibit it. If enough excitatory neurotransmitter stimulates the receptors then a new impulse is generated and passes down that neuron. Very soon after, the neurotransmitter is removed by being broken down by an enzyme or neuronal **reuptake** taking place. Through this process Mr B's brain would be able to undertake complex functional activity (Krumhardt and Alcamo 2010).

2 **How would Mr B's brain have normally created, stored and retrieved his memories?**

A ## HIPPOCAMPUS

The main area of the brain which processes new memories is located in the temporal lobes. Deep within each lobe is a banana-shaped structure called the hippocampus which is involved in transferring the newly acquired memories into long-term storage in an area of the brain known as the **neocortex**. The neocortex itself forms part of the cortex (or outer layer) of the cerebral hemispheres. The hippocampus communicates with the neocortex by way of other partnership structures, the most important of which is the **enterhinal cortex** (Amaral and Lavanex 2006; Marieb 2010). This communication method is so effective that it means the hippocampus can not only store memories but also retrieve them. Put simply, it acts in the same way as a search engine on the internet, searching quickly and effectively through the memories stored in the neocortex and retrieving those of relevance. These memories can then be used as a basis for other brain functions such as repetition, analysis, interpretation and assimilation. Without this fundamental ability, Mr B will ultimately be unable to carry out forward planning, learn new skills or create new thoughts (Kerr 2007).

TEMPORAL LOBES

The specific function of the hippocampus has been described above and this demonstrates the importance of the temporal lobes in learning. Naturally, the temporal lobes also have other functions which are important. Of particular note is that the right lobe stores visual memory while the left lobe stores verbal memory, whereas both lobes are associated with the sense of smell and taste.

3 **What is thought to be happening in Mr B's brain in order for him to be displaying signs and symptoms of Alzheimer's disease?**

A Evidence of two primary destructive processes is found in the brains of people with Alzheimer's disease. Both processes are involved in the death of neurons, although the exact mechanism and sequence of events is not yet fully understood (Downey 2008). The first process results in the development of beta-amyloid plaques and the second in neurofibrillary tangles.

BETA-AMYLOID PLAQUES

Amyloid plaques are made up of abnormal, fibrous beta-amyloid protein fragments – degenerating neurons which have fused together with aluminium deposits (Lazenby 2011). The sticky amyloid protein material accumulates between the cells, slowing transmission of impulses (Downey 2008), but it is unclear whether the formation of the plaques is the cause of neuron damage or is the body's response to existing damage and is intended to restrict damage by 'walling off' damaged cells (Janicki and Dalton 1999). Since the plaques are found mainly in the hippocampus, they mainly affect the formation of memories, and this results in difficulty in retaining and recalling information, which presents as forgetfulness.

NEUROFIBRILLARY TANGLES

Neurofibrillary tangles are found inside the neurons. The tangles consist of strands of abnormally twisted proteins such as tau, which destroys the neuron from the inside outwards. Tau protein in its normal state is required for growth and development of strong neuronal axons and it is only when it is **hyperphosphorylated** that it forms the tangles. This progressively makes it difficult for signals to travel across the cells in the brain (Parsons et al. 2011). In the earliest stages of Alzheimer's, tangles are found mainly in the enterhinal cortex, and this interferes with the 'search engine' function of the brain described above. Later, the tangles appear in the hippocampus, which affects memory formation, and throughout the whole neocortex of the brain, affecting the function of whichever part of the brain is the host.

The net effect of cell loss is that over time the cerebral cortex atrophies: the brain tissue itself appears shrunken, the ventricles in the brain enlarge and there is vascular degeneration. This is most noticeable in the frontal and temporal lobes (Lazenby 2011). Nerve cell loss due to the two previously outlined processes affects the production and release of neurotransmitters in the brain.

Acetylcholine

The neurotransmitter system most affected is the cholinergic system, which is affected by cell loss, particularly in the frontal lobes and hippocampus. This causes a marked reduction in levels of the neurotransmitter acetylcholine in the brains of sufferers. Acetylcholine is important in the formation and retrieval of memory and so its lack is also thought to lead to the functional deficits of Alzheimer's disease. However, reduced production of other neurotransmitters such as **noradrenaline** and serotonin is also a feature of Alzheimer's disease which may contribute to behavioural and cognitive symptoms (Desai and Grossberg 2005).

Glutamate

Glutamate is the main neurotransmitter in the brain and is involved in all aspects of cognitive function. Glutamate and its receptors are involved in a process called long-term potentiation which is important in learning and memory. The activity of this system is greatly influenced by the activity of the cholinergic system as described above and so is adversely affected in Alzheimer's disease (Francis 2003). One kind of glutamate receptor called N-methyl-D-aspartate (NMDA) is prevalent in the brain and especially found in the same areas as the neurofibrillary tangles and amyloid plaques typical of Alzheimer's disease.

Glutamate and its stimulation of NDMA receptors play an important role in memory formation and learning (Clayton et al. 2002). Therefore, loss of the pyramidal neurons which produce glutamate results in a lack of glutamine and so affects both these functions. Effective functioning of the NDMA receptors at the synapse is also important. In Alzheimer's disease, the presence of small amounts of beta-amyloid protein effectively 'short circuit' the synapse. This is partly because the beta amyloid causes the uptake of glutamate by the synapse to be reduced and the amount outside the synaptic terminal therefore builds up, which then increases the NDMA receptor excitability.

Although lack of glutamate causes features associated with Alzheimer's disease, the progression of the disease itself is actually hastened by the action of glutamate, which is a neurotoxin. In Alzheimer's disease there is an impaired ability to maintain the normal electrical membrane potential of the neuron, which means the membrane potential becomes less negative. This in turn means that NDMA receptors and their associated ion channels become more easily activated and so more excitable. Glutamate causes over-excitation of the neuron in this circumstance and so causes neuronal damage and death.

(**4**)   **What will be the main effects of the disease on Mr B as it progresses through its stages?**

(**A**)   Alzheimer's disease can be described in three stages:

- Stage 1 presents in the first four years and the person is usually forgetful and often has difficulty recalling events from their short-term memory, even when reminded. They often suffer a loss of interest in what is happening around them, their environment and the people they know. They may also find it difficult to make decisions and use their initiative.
- Stage 2 can present anywhere within 2–12 years of onset and the memory loss is more obvious and extends beyond short-term memory. The person may be unable to care for

themselves properly, to follow simple instructions or carry out simple activities. They may wander, especially at night, and become lost even in a familiar environment. The person may show signs of anxiety, anger and paranoia or act in a disinhibited manner. They may lose insight into their disease and may struggle to communicate effectively.

- Stage 3 is the final stage where the person with Alzheimer's disease becomes unable to communicate and fails to recognize close family and friends. They may stop eating and drinking, be unable to maintain their own safety, lack the ability to care for even their basic needs and become incontinent of urine and faeces (Nair and Peate 2009).

5   **How do donepezil and memantine work?**

A   # DONEPEZIL

Donepezil is used to enhance the brain's cholinergic system and so reduce the features of Alzheimer's disease which are associated with deficiency of the neurotransmitter acetylcholine. It is an acetylcholinesterase inhibitor which means that it works at the synaptic junction by blocking the enzyme responsible for breaking down acetylcholine. This means that the action of acetylcholine at the cholinergic nerve synapses is prolonged and is therefore more effective.

MEMANTINE

Memantine is intended primarily to reduce nerve cell death from the adverse effects of glutamine. When glutamate is present at the synapse at normal levels it enhances memory and learning. However, if the level rises excessively then glutamate seems to overstimulate the NMDA receptors, allowing a prolonged influx of calcium ions into the brain cell. The influx leads to over-excitation of the nerve cell (excitotoxicity) which results in the death of that cell. Memantine blocks the NMDA receptors to reduce the excitotoxicity and enables preservation of the physiological functioning of the NMDA receptors, as they can still respond appropriately to glutamate if levels of the neurotransmitter are high enough (NICE 2011).

6   **What side-effects would you look for in Mr B while he is taking these medicines?**

A   # DONEPEZIL

The side-effects of donepezil are related to the cholinergic properties of the drug. Gastrointestinal upset such as nausea, vomiting and diarrhoea resulting in weight loss are the main side-effects. Other significant side-effects include bradycardia, syncope, headache, dizziness, hallucinations and aggression, with some patients reporting difficulties in sleeping or vivid dreams (BNF 2012).

MEMANTINE

Memantine is generally well tolerated but the main side-effects are constipation, dyspnoea, hypertension, dizziness, drowsiness and headache (BNF 2012).

7 **What advice would you offer to Mrs B about her husband's medication to assist her understanding of its role in his care?**

A It is important that Mrs B recognizes that Alzheimer's disease is progressive and that Mr B will continue to deteriorate regardless of whether he is treated or not. She needs to understand that the medication will not cure or arrest the degenerative process as neuronal loss is ongoing, but that the decline in function may be slowed. The aim is therefore to preserve synaptic function to allow Mr B a higher functional level for longer than if he had not received treatment (Downey 2008). This should be conveyed to Mrs B in the way that she herself feels suits her best and, as with all information, it is advisable for the nurse to offer more than one form of giving information in order to allow Mrs B the opportunity to consider it in further depth later.

Mrs B should have realistic expectations of the medication. Donepezil aims to assist the nerve to function and so may slow cognitive decline, and this in turn may delay the emergence of the behavioural features of Alzheimer's disease (Cummings 2004). It is generally used for treatment of mild to moderate Alzheimer's disease which is why it was originally prescribed for Mr B. Memantine aims to protect the nerve against further damage from overstimulation by one particular chemical (glutamate) and therefore may reduce deterioration in the overall condition. It does not appear to have much benefit in mild to moderate Alzheimer's disease (Schneider et al. 2011), therefore Mr B will only be prescribed the medication if he has moderate disease and is not tolerating the donepezil or has more severe disease which is not responding to donepezil. As his carer, Mrs B's opinion on her husband's condition will be sought both before starting new treatment and during the treatment because treatment should only continue if it is felt to have a worthwhile effect on Mr B (DH 2009).

Currently it is not recommended that donepezil and memantine are prescribed together (BNF 2012), so Mr B would stop taking donepezil if prescribed memantine. Mrs B should be aware that if her husband restarts donepezil at any point he will need to start on a lower dose than he currently takes and that the dosage will be titrated back up over a period of weeks (Downey 2008).

If Mr B is prescribed memantine, his wife may notice an initial worsening of his cognitive function due to antagonism at certain (nicotinic) acetylcholine receptors in the brain. Since these receptors soon 'upregulate' in response to the antagonism, long-term memantine treatment should have an overall positive effect (Chen and Lipton 2006). Not all those who take memantine for an extended period of time demonstrate palpable benefits, but those that do may show a moderate decrease in clinical deterioration and a small positive improvement in cognitive and self-care functions, as well mood and behaviour. Mrs B should be made aware that this may happen so that she knows what to expect.

Mrs B will need to know what side-effects may occur so that she can alert Mr B's doctor to them. When discussing donepezil the nurse should advise Mrs B that should vivid dreaming be a problem, the drug can be switched to morning administration which often improves sleep quality. In addition, Mrs B should be advised that due to the potential gastrointestinal side-effects, it is better for Mr B not to take donepezil on an empty stomach, whereas this is not an important consideration when taking memantine. Although the pharmacist will ensure that prescribed drugs are checked for interactions, Mrs B should be advised that she should check with the pharmacist about the suitability of any non-prescribed medications that Mr B might take – for example St John's wort, which can decrease the effect of donepezil (Downey 2008).

KEY POINTS

- Neurons communicate with each other across gaps or synapses that occur between them.
- The hippocampus and temporal lobes are important in memory.
- Alzheimer's disease results in selective loss of neurons and their synapses, especially in areas such as the hippocampus and neocortex.
- The main pathological processes result in the development of beta-amyloid plaques and neurofibrillary tangles.
- Treatment with an acetylcholinesterase inhibitor such as donepezil is recommended in mild to moderate Alzheimer's disease.
- Memantine is recommended for severe Alzheimer's disease or moderate disease where acetylcholinesterase inhibitors are not tolerated.
- It is important that the person's significant family members understand that Alzheimer's disease is progressive and that their relative will continue deteriorating regardless of whether they are treated or not.

REFERENCES

Amaral, D. and Lavenex, P. (2006) Hippocampal neuroanatomy, in P. Andersen, R. Morris, D. Amaral, T. Bliss and J. O'Keefe (eds) *The Hippocampus Book*. Oxford: Oxford University Press.

BNF (British National Formulary) (2012) *BNF 63: March*. London: Pharmaceutical Press.

Chen, H.S. and Lipton, S.A. (2006) The chemical biology of clinically tolerated NMDA receptor antagonists, *Journal of Neurochemistry*, 97(6): 1611–26.

Clayton, D.A., Mesches, M.H., Alvarez, E., Bickford, P.C. and Browning, M.D. (2002) A hippocampal NR2B deficit can mimic age-related changes in long-term potentiation and spatial learning in the Fischer 344 rat, *Journal of Neuroscience*, 22: 3628–37.

Cummings, J. (2004) Alzheimer's disease, *New England Journal of Medicine*, 351: 56–67.

Desai, A. and Grossberg, G. (2005) Diagnosis and treatment of Alzheimer's disease, *Neurology*, 64(Suppl. 3): S34–9.

DH (Department of Health) (2009) *Living Well With Dementia: A National Dementia Strategy*. London: DH.

Downey, D. (2008) Pharmacologic management of Alzheimer's disease, *Journal of Neuroscience Nursing*, 40(1): 55–9.

Francis, P.T. (2003) Glutamatergic systems in Alzheimer's disease, *International Journal of Geriatric Psychiatry*, 18(Suppl. 1): S15–21.

Janicki, M.P. and Dalton, A.J. (eds) (1999) *Dementia, Aging, and Intellectual Disabilities: A Handbook*. Hove: Routledge.

Kerr, D. (2007) *Understanding Learning Disability and Dementia: Developing Effective Interventions*. London: Jessica Kingsley.

Krumhardt, B. and Alcamo, I.E. (2010) *Barrons E-Z Anatomy and Physiology*. New York: Barrons Educational.

Lazenby, R.B. (2011) *Handbook of Pathophysiology*, 4th edn. London: Lippincott Williams & Wilkins.

Marieb, E.N. (2010) *Essentials of Human Anatomy and Physiology*, 10th edn. London: Pearson Education.

Nair, M. and Peate, I. (eds) (2009) *Applied Pathophysiology: An Essential Guide for Nursing Students.* Chichester: Wiley.

NICE (National Institute for Health and Clinical Excellence) (2011) *Technology Appraisal 217: Donepezil, Galantamine, Rivastigmine and Memantine for the Treatment of Alzheimer's Disease (review).* London: NICE.

Parsons, C., Hughes, C., McGuinness, B. and Passmore, P. (2011) Withdrawal or continuation of cholinesterase inhibitors and/or memantine in patients with dementia, *The Cochrane Collaboration.* Oxford: Wiley.

Schneider, S., Insel, P.S. and Weiner, M.W. (2011) Treatment with cholinesterase inhibitors and memantine of patients in the Alzheimer's disease neuroimaging initiative, *Archives of Neurology*, 68(1): 58–66.

The young person with asthma
Ruth Sadik

CASE AIMS

After examining this case study the reader should be able to:

- Briefly explain the pathophysiology of choking and wheezing as symptoms of asthma.
- List the main causes of asthma in childhood.
- Demonstrate an understanding of the mode of action and side-effects of inhaled salbutamol and steroids in asthma.
- Explain why anticholinergics and leukotriene receptor antagonists may also have been considered in the treatment of asthma.
- Describe the role of the nurse in caring for the young person with asthma
- Outline the pharmacological treatment that would be prescribed in the acute phase of asthma.

CASE

Sam was diagnosed with asthma when he was 2 years old. He would awaken choking and wheezy, most nights. His parents were initially told that it was 'teething', but as his symptoms persisted he was investigated more thoroughly by his general practitioner (GP).

1 **With reference to the pathophysiology of asthma, what would lead Sam to experience wheeziness and choking?**

2 **What are the main causes of asthma in childhood?**

Sam was started on pressurized metered-dose inhaled salbutamol (a β_2-adrenergic agonist), one puff as needed, and inhaled corticosteroids on a regular basis. This successfully controlled his symptoms for approximately three years.

3 **Explain the modes of action and possible side-effects that salbutamol and inhaled corticosteroids will have on have on Sam**

4 What other drugs may have been considered for the short- and long-term treatment of Sam's asthma?

5 Outline the role of the nurse in Sam's treatment and care

The family acquired a dog, Pancake, and Sam started school on a full-time basis. Within three weeks of getting Pancake, Sam had been admitted to hospital with an acute exacerbation of his asthma. Initially, his heart rate was 138bpm, his respiratory rate 34, he had dyspnoea with marked recession, a slight wheeze and inability to speak. Sam's temperature was 38.4°C. On attaching an oxygen saturation monitor his saturations were 90%.

---

6 Outline the pharmacological treatment that would be prescribed for Sam in this acute phase of his illness

ANSWERS

1 **With reference to the pathophysiology of asthma, what would lead Sam to experience wheeziness and choking?**

A Asthma is a complex, multifactorial disease. Although airway reactivity, inflammation and increased mucus secretion are agreed on universally as the central components of asthma, the **pathophysiology** of each of these is complex (Lissauer and Clayden 2012).

WHEEZINESS

Following inhalation of a trigger, such as dog hair from Pancake, which is composed of protein alien to Sam's body, a complex system of events are initiated.

- Firstly, **helper T cells** sensitive to the dog hair will bind with it, an action that stimulates **B cells** to produce specific antibodies in the form of immunoglobulin E (Ig E).
- Ig E in turn binds with a specific protein receptor on the surface of mast cells or basophils, which causes the cells to degranulate, releasing histamine, **prostaglandins** and **leukotrienes** (also known as slow-reacting substances of anaphylaxis – SRS-A).
- SRS-A are primarily responsible for the contraction of smooth muscle in the bronchi and bronchioles, which leads to narrowing of the airways and an increase in airway resistance, which would cause Sam to wheeze (Rees et al. 2012).

CHOKING

Excessive mucus production is a universal symptom of asthma and is brought about by the action of histamine, prostaglandins and SRS-A which causes further narrowing of the airways. In 2002 a calcium-activated chloride channel (HCLCA1) was identified as being responsible for regulating excessive mucin production, which is thought to be a critical component of mucus in the airways. Mucus therefore fills the alveoli, inhibiting alveolar respiration and leading to the feeling of choking (Carroll et al. 2002)

2 **What are the main causes of asthma in childhood?**

A
- *Genetics* – there is irrefutable evidence to show that familial and genetic factors play a large part in childhood asthma (Van Bever 2009).
- *Allergy* – approximately 6% of childhood asthma is attributable to allergy to animal dander or foodstuffs, and 90% of these are allergic to dairy products, nuts or shellfish (Sohi and Warner 2008).
- *Viral infections* – infection with rhinovirus in infancy has been linked to future symptomology of asthma in childhood and early adulthood, while **mycoplasma** has been implicated in 20% of children admitted to hospital with asthma (Bizzintino et al. 2011).
- *Obesity and **oesophageal reflux*** – asthma in obese children may be as a result of inactivity rather than the obesity itself. However, there is a link between asthma and abnormal glucose and lipid metabolism that goes beyond the child's basal metabolic rate (BMR) (Cotterell et al. 2011).
- *Hygiene hypothesis* – this is a misleading title, as this notion is actually linked to a presumed *decline* in exposure to dirty environments. This hypothesis has been debated consistently and linked to the current obsession of western civilizations with hygiene and cleanliness. More recent work identified that while exposure in childhood to farmyard living can confer protection from respiratory allergies, the obverse has not yet been identified – i.e. that living in clean cities can actually cause such allergies (Van Mutius 2010).
- *Passive smoking* – smoking around children has been identified as a possible cause of their asthma, although the mechanism is vaguely defined. While there is no specific causal link, the lung development of infants of mothers who smoked during pregnancy has been shown to be affected (NICE 2008; Becker and Kozyrskyj 2010).
- *Emotion and psychological factors* – it has long been identified that there is a link between emotion and asthma development. Establishing what the link is has become the main focus for many researchers (Ritz et al. 2010).

3 **Explain the modes of action and possible side-effects that salbutamol and inhaled corticosteroids will have on have on Sam**

A # B_2-ADRENERGIC RECEPTOR AGONISTS

Short-acting β_2-adrenergic receptor agonists (SABAs) such as salbutamol are commonly known as 'relievers' or 'rescue medications', which act in minutes and last up to four hours. They work by relaxing the smooth muscle of the bronchi and bronchioles (bronchodilation) by potentiating the effect of β_2-adrenergic receptors in the heart and lungs which are activated by the sympathetic nervous system. They also aid in clearing mucus, but do not decrease mucosal swelling (Rees et al. 2012). The impact of their therapeutic mechanism leads patients to complain of tachycardia, tremor, palpitations, nausea and anxiety (Sweetman 2011).

These drugs are frequently supplied as particles in a metered dose inhaler (MDI) or in a liquid form for nebulization for children and young people with difficulty in coordinating a device with breathing (NICE 2002). On occasion, if a child has difficulty with either of the previous modes of administration, an oral formulation may be prescribed, but takes longer to act. This type of drug is normally the first line of treatment (SIGN 2012). Delivery via a pressurized metered dose inhaler (pMDI) and spacer is preferred in mild to moderate asthma as there is less tachycardia and hypoxia compared with delivery via a nebulizer; children aged under 3 years normally require a facemask attached to the spacer. Two to four puffs of β_2 agonists repeated every 20–30 minutes according to clinical response may be sufficient for a mild attack but severe attacks may require up to 10 puffs; drug dosing should be individualized according to severity of attack and response. Those children not improving after receiving up to 10 puffs of β_2 agonists in primary care should be referred to secondary care (DH 2011a).

For a more sustained mode of action, longer-acting β_2-adrenergic receptor agonists (LABAs) such as salmeterol (licensed for children over 4 years) or formoterol (licensed for children over 6 years) are available, which again act in minutes but last for up to 12 hours (BMJ Group 2011).

STEROIDS

Steroids, commonly referred to as 'preventors', are most effective if taken on a regular basis. Their mode of action is to limit the number of SRS-A being released and to interfere with their **cytokine** action, leading to a reduction in mucous membrane inflammation.

Glucocorticoids are the second step in the SIGN 'Stepwise' approach (2012) and are the most effective first-line prophylactic therapy. Inhaled forms are usually used except in the case of severe persistent disease, in which case oral steroids may be needed. Inhaled formulations may be used once or twice daily, depending on the severity of symptoms.

There are a variety of inhaled formulations that include budesonide, which is licensed from 3 months of age and may be mixed with either terbutaline, salbutamol or ipratropium, and fluticasone, which is available for use with young people aged 16 years or older.

Side-effects of inhaled steroids tend to be muted and include impaired growth, adrenal suppression and altered bone metabolism if used in high doses. Oral steroids conversely have major side-effects that include immune-suppression, fluid retention, discolouration or thinning of the skin, hyperglycaemia, redistribution of fat and hypothalamic-pituitary-adrenal suppression. These adverse effects can be mitigated by tapering the lowest effective dose and by alternate-day administration (NICE 2007).

4 **What other drugs may have been considered for the short- and long-term treatment of Sam's asthma?**

A **ANTICHOLINERGICS**

These are a group of drugs that influence the **parasympathetic** nervous system in blocking the effect of the neurotransmitter acetylcholine, leading to an increase in the diameter of bronchi and bronchioles. Ipratropium bromide is the most widely used in childhood and provides additional benefit when used in combination with SABAs in those with moderate or severe symptoms. Anticholinergic bronchodilators can also be used if a person cannot tolerate a

Table 2.1 Stepwise approach to asthma medications

Age	Intermittent asthma	Persistent asthma: daily medication				
	Step 1	Step 2	Step 3	Step 4	Step 5	Step 6
< 5 years	Rapid-acting beta2-agonist prn	Low-dose inhaled corticosteroid (ICS) Alternate regimen: cromolyn or montelukast	Medium-dose ICS	Medium-dose ICS plus either long-acting beta2-agonist (LABA) or montelukast	High-dose ICS plus either LABA or montelukast	High-dose ICS plus either LABA or montelukast; oral systemic corticosteroid
5–11 years	Rapid-acting beta2-agonist prn	Low-dose ICS Alternate regimen: cromolyn, leukotriene receptor antagonist (LTRA), or theophylline	Either low-dose ICS plus either LABA, LTRA, or theophylline or medium-dose ICS	Medium-dose ICS plus LABA Alternate regimen: medium-dose ICS plus either LTRA or theophylline	High-dose ICS plus LABA Alternate regimen: high-dose ICS plus either LABA or theophylline	High-dose ICS plus LABA plus oral systemic corticosteroid Alternate regimen: high-dose ICS plus LRTA or theophylline plus systemic corticosteroid
12 years or older	Rapid-acting beta2-agonist as needed	Low-dose ICS Alternate regimen: cromolyn, LTRA, or theophylline	Low-dose ICS plus LABA or medium-dose ICS Alternate regimen: low-dose ICS plus either LTRA, theophylline, or zileuton	Medium-dose ICS plus LABA Alternate regimen: medium-dose ICS plus either LTRA, theophylline, or zileuton	High-dose ICS plus LABA (and consider omalizumab for patients with allergies	High-dose ICS plus either LABA plus oral corticosteroid (and consider omalizumab for patients with allergies)

SABA and their main side-effects tend to be gastrointestinal upset, dry mouth, anxiety, coughing and headache.

LEUKOTRIENE RECEPTOR ANTAGONISTS

Leukotriene receptor antagonists (also known as leukasts) are one of the newest drugs to be introduced into the arsenal for fighting asthma. Leukotrienes are part of the inflammatory mediators that induce broncho-constriction, so these drugs inhibit their action by blocking the receptor sites in lung tissue. Leukotriene receptor antagonists (such as zafirlukast, montelukast and zileuton) are an alternative to inhaled glucocorticoids, but are not preferred. They may also be used in addition to inhaled glucocorticoids but in this role are second line to LABAs. There are few recognized side-effects, although the *British National Formulary for Children* (BMJ Group 2011) cautions against the development of **eosinophilia**, vasculitic rash, worsening pulmonary symptoms, cardiac complications or peripheral neuropathy.

5   **Outline the role of the nurse in Sam's treatment and care**

A   The nurse has a number of roles in Sam's treatment and care, including the following.

- Assessment of Sam's and his family's lifestyle.
- Involving Sam in decision-making to improve concordance.
- Ascertaining whether the asthma symptoms are affecting Sam's activity during the day or sleeping at night.
- Taking **peak expiratory flow rate** (PEFR) (in children aged over 5 years), using the best of three readings, expressed as a percentage of personal best PEFR.
- Measuring the amount and/or speed of air that can be inspired and expired (spirometry).
- Measuring height and weight annually to monitor correct prescribing dosage and potential drug impact on both.
- Measuring oxygen saturation – low oxygen saturations (<92%) after initial broncho-dilator therapy indicate a more severe subgroup of patients. Children with life-threatening asthma or SpO_2 <92% should receive high flow oxygen via facemask or nasal cannula.
- Giving calm reassurance at all times.
- Assessment of inhaler technique on a six-monthly basis.
- Educating Sam and his parents about asthma and the need for treatment even when no symptoms are present.

6   **Outline the treatment that would be prescribed for Sam in this acute phase of his illness**

A   In the acute phase, Sam's treatment would depend on the severity of his asthma. His treatment would be in line with the British Thoracic Society/Scottish Intercollegiate Guidelines Network (SIGN 2012). He would be commenced on oxygen at a high flow rate of 10–15L via a facemask with a reservoir bag, and given nebulized salbutamol 5mg and ipratropium bromide 250mcg made up to 4ml with normal saline; a flow rate of 6–8L/min of oxygen would be required. This would be repeated every 20–30 minutes as necessary to maintain

Sam's SpO$_2$ above 92%. If he is not responding as well as expected, intravenous (IV) hydrocortisone 4mg/kg four-hourly to a maximum of 200mg/day would be prescribed.

If Sam's lack of improvement continued, the doctor would prescribe IV salbutamol 15mcg/kg followed by IV infusion of 1–5mcg/kg/min as required. To ensure that arrhythmias from this treatment were detected as soon as possible, Sam would be nursed on a cardiac monitor.

KEY POINTS

- Asthma affects 1 in 10 children and is the most common childhood condition in the UK for which GPs are consulted.
- The condition is bi-phasic in nature and mirrors the inflammatory process.
- Current treatment revolves around a 'stepwise' approach that starts with β_2-receptor agonists in addition to inhaled steroids.
- There is an array of both short- and long-term inhaled treatments available.
- The role of the nurse in relation to this condition is wide and includes, for example, assessment of the individual and their lifestyle, involving the child or young person and their family in decision-making to increase concordance, and educating parents and young people about their asthma and the necessity for treatment even when they are not suffering any symptoms.
- Inhaler technique should be assessed six-monthly, in addition to height and weight.
- Nurses should know when to refer to secondary care environments.

REFERENCES

Becker, A.B. and Kozyrskyj, A. (2010) Commentary on asthma and the environment: can asthma be prevented? *Evidence-based Child Health*, 5: 1453–55.

Bizzintino, J., Lee, W.M., Laing, I.A., Vang, F., Pappas, T. and Zhang, G. (2011) Association between human rhinovirus C and severity of acute asthma in children, *European Respiratory Journal*, 37(5): 1037–42.

BMJ Group (2011) *British National Formulary for Children*. London: BMJ Group.

Carroll, N.G., Mutavdzic, S. and James, A.L. (2002) Increased mast cells and neutrophils in submucosal mucous glands and mucus plugging in patients with asthma, *Thorax*, 57: 677–82.

Cotterell, L., Neal, W.A., Perez, M.K. and Piedmonte, G. (2011) Metabolic abnormalities in children with asthma, *American Journal of Respiratory Critical Care Medicine*, 183(4): 441–8.

DH (Department of Health) (2011a) *An Outcomes Strategy for People with Chronic Obstructive Pulmonary Disease (COPD) and Asthma in England*. London: DH.

Lissauer, T. and Clayden, G. (2012) *Illustrated Textbook of Paediatrics*, 4th edn. Maryland Heights, MO: Mosby Elsevier.

NICE (National Institute for Health and Clinical Excellence) (2002) *Technology Appraisal 38: Asthma (Older children) Inhaler Devices*. London: NICE.

NICE (National Institute for Health and Clinical Excellence) (2007) *Technology Appraisal 131: Asthma (in children) – Corticosteroid*. London: NICE.

NICE (National Institute for Health and Clinical Excellence) (2008) *Public Health 14: Preventing the Uptake of Smoking by Children and Young People*. London: NICE.

Rees, J., Kanabar, D., Pattani, S. (2012) *ABC of Asthma*. Oxford: Blackwell.

Ritz, T., Kullowatz, A., Goldman, M.D., Smith, H.J. et al. (2010) Airway response to emotional stimuli in asthma: the role of the cholinergic pathway, *Journal of Applied Physiology*, 108(6): 1542–9.

SIGN (The British Thoracic Society and Scottish Intercollegiate Guidelines Network) (2012) *British Guideline on the Management of Asthma 101: A National Clinical Guidline*. London: British Thoracic Society.

Sohi, D.K. and Warner, J.O. (2008) Understanding allergy, *Paediatrics and Child Health*, 18(7): 301–8.

Sweetman, S. (2011) *Martindale: The Complete Drug Reference*, 37th edn. London: Pharmaceutical Press.

Van Bever, H.P.S. (2009) Determinants in early life for asthma development, *Allergy, Asthma & Clinical Immunology*, 5(6): 1–5.

Von Mutius, E. (2010) 99th Dahlem Conference on Infection, Inflammation and Chronic Inflammatory Disorders: farm lifestyles and the hygiene hypothesis, *Clinical & Experimental Immunology*, 160(1): 130–5.

The person with bipolar disorder
Paul Barber

CASE AIMS

After examining this case study the reader should be able to:

- Describe the pathophysiology of bipolar disorder.
- Demonstrate an understanding of the mode of action of lithium.
- Discuss the role of the nurse in monitoring and caring for a patient taking lithium.
- Briefly explain the role of the nurse in assessing lithium's efficacy.
- Explain the reasons for non-concordance in a service user taking lithium.

CASE

A 29-year-old married mother presented with a past history of concussion at age 18, when she suffered loss of consciousness. She also described a history of mood swings for many years. There was also a history of alcohol abuse when she was a teenager. Prozac had been prescribed initially by her GP but had now been discontinued because it appeared to be worsening the underlying mood swings.

Family history revealed severe mood swings in both her father and paternal grand-mother. Grandmother at times would take to bed for long spells, and she had been hospitalized for 'unknown reasons' that the family refused to talk about. The service user recalled that the secrecy was because of something 'shameful' about her grand-mother's condition and behaviour.

The service user has now been admitted for a period of assessment as an inpatient. She is now displaying aggressive behaviour, insomnia, racing thoughts and pressure of speech (speaking rapidly and frenziedly). She is seen by the consultant psychiatrist and diagnosed with a bipolar disorder.

1 What could have caused the service user's bipolar disorder?

> *The consultant psychiatrist initially prescribed lithium carbonate to be taken in divided doses. Five weeks after the institution of lithium, the service user was feeling 'terrific' and was discharged into the care of the community psychiatric team.*

2 Why would the service user have been prescribed lithium for her bipolar disorder?

3 What would be your role in monitoring and caring for this service user while commencing her lithium in the assessment unit?

4 List the factors you would evaluate as a nurse to ensure the efficacy of lithium

> *After a period of six months the service user was readmitted to the assessment unit as her mental health had deteriorated once again. The community psychiatric team reported that they felt she had not been taking her medication while at home.*

5 What reasons may the service user have for not taking her medicine?

ANSWERS

1 **What could have caused the service user's bipolar disorder?**

A # THE CHOLINERGIC SYSTEM

Lower than normal levels of **choline** have been found in the erythrocytes of bipolar patients, prompting researchers to believe that an imbalance between cholinergic and catecholaminergic activity is important in the pathophysiology of bipolar disorder. Further evidence implicating the cholinergic system in bipolar disorder is the antimanic properties of cholinergic agonists and the modulation of manic symptoms by the **cholinesterase inhibitor** phygostigmine (Manji and Lenox 2000).

THE MONOAMINE SYSTEM

The monoamine hypothesis of depression states that the condition is caused by depleted levels of the monoamine (noradrenaline, serotonin and/or dopamine) in the central nervous system (CNS). While this simplistic model is known not to provide an understanding of the pathoetiology of mood disorders, it continues to have value in providing service users with an explanation of the biochemical basis of mood dysregulation.

Substantial evidence for the role of serotonin in patients with bipolar disorder comes from the study of serotonin receptors. Several studies have shown an increase in the density of serotonin 2 receptors in the platelets and brain of depression patients (Delgado 2000).

Dopamine

One of the most convincing rationales for the role of dopamine in bipolar disorder is the vital role it plays in the reward and/or incentive motivational circuitry. In fact, loss of motivation is one of the key features of depression. The most consistent biochemical finding in depression is the reduced concentration of homovanillic acid (HVA), a major dopamine metabolite, in the cerebrospinal fluid.

A function for dopamine in the aetiology of bipolar disorder is suggested by the role that dopamine agonists have in precipitating mania. It has been postulated that dopamine abnormalities are involved in the hyperactivity associated with the severe stages of mania; whereas noradrenaline is associated with hypomania – as observed in bipolar II disorder (Cousins et al. 2009).

THE HYPOTHALAMIC-PITUITARY-ADRENAL AXIS

The hypothalamic-pituitary-adrenal (HPA) axis is involved in the stress response and abnormalities in the this axis have long been implicated in mood disorders. Increased HPA axis activity has been associated with mixed-maniac states, depression and classic manic episodes (Manji and Lenox 2000). Following neurotransmitter release and binding at the post-synaptic membrane, a secondary messenger signalling cascade occurs that ultimately elicits the cellular response. This is an extremely complex pathway and dysfunction in these second messenger mechanisms have been implicated in the pathoetiology of bipolar disorder. Some agents involved in these responses include cyclic adenosine monophosphate (AMP), protein kinases and phosphoinositol (Rang et al. 2011).

GENETIC FACTORS

There is a well-recognized genetic component to the aetiology of bipolar disorder. Multiple family studies have shown that there is higher prevalence of bipolar disease in family members of service users with bipolar disorder, compared with psychiatrically healthy controls. The lifetime risk of bipolar disorder in first-degree relatives of a patient with this condition is 40–70% for a monozygotic twin and 5–10% for all other first-degree relatives (Muller-Oerlinghausen et al. 2002). In this case study, the service user's father has a tendency to mood swings and there is an assumption that her grandmother was possibly diagnosed with the disease, although the family will not discuss this.

ENVIRONMENTAL FACTORS

Evidence suggests that environmental factors play a significant role in the development and course of bipolar disorder (Serretti and Mandelli 2008). There is fairly consistent evidence from prospective studies that recent life events and interpersonal relationships contribute to the likelihood of onsets and recurrences of bipolar mood episodes. In this case study there is evidence that the service user has been exposed to mood swings from her father that may have complicated her relationship with him.

There have been repeated findings that between a third and a half of adults diagnosed with bipolar disorder report traumatic/abusive experiences in childhood, and this is associated on average with earlier onset, a worse course and more co-occurring disorders such as post-traumatic stress disorder (PTSD) (Leverich and Post 2006). Early experiences of adversity and conflict are likely to make subsequent developmental challenges in adolescence more difficult, and are a potentiating factor in those at risk of developing bipolar disorder (Miklowitz and Chan 2008). We know that our service user has resorted to alcohol, and this may have been an attempt at self-medication or a way of dealing with personal issues within the family unit (Alloy et al. 2005).

2 **Why would the service user have been prescribed lithium for her bipolar disorder?**

A Lithium has been established for more than 50 years as one of the most effective therapies for bipolar mood disorder. However, researchers have never been entirely sure exactly how it operates in the human brain. Lithium stabilizes the neuronal membrane so that it becomes less excitable. It does this by suppressing the production of inositol, which is a simple sugar-like compound present in the normal diet (Ketter 2005).

3 **What would be your role in monitoring and caring for this service user while commencing her lithium in the assessment unit?**

A The nurse's role in monitoring and caring for the service user is as follows.

- Monitoring her mental and emotional status. The nurse should observe her for mania and/or extreme depression (lithium should prevent mood swings). The service user should be requested to keep a symptom log, to document her response to the medication.
- Monitoring her lithium levels. Lithium salts have a narrow therapeutic/toxic ratio and should therefore not be prescribed unless facilities for monitoring plasma concentrations are available. Doses are adjusted to achieve plasma concentrations of 0.8 to 1.00mmol/L (NICE 2006). Overdose usually occurs with plasma concentrations over 1.5mmol/L, and these may prove fatal. Toxic effects include tremor, **ataxia, dysarthria, nystagmus**, renal impairment, confusion and convulsions. If these potentially hazardous signs occur, treatment should be stopped. Lithium levels should be checked 12 hours post-dose and five days following starting therapy. Levels are then checked weekly until they have been stable for four weeks. Once stabilized, levels are checked every three months. The nurse should consider more frequent monitoring (e.g. every two months) if a service user has been prescribed any interacting medication or if they develop renal, thyroid or cardiac disease (Calderdale and Huddersfield and North Kirklees and Wakefield Area Prescribing Committee 2011).
- Monitoring her electrolyte balance. Lithium is a salt affected by dietary intake of other salts such as sodium chloride. Insufficient dietary salt intake causes the kidneys to conserve lithium, increasing serum levels.
- Requesting the service user to monitor dietary salt intake and consume sufficient quantities, especially during illness or physical activity. The service user should be reminded to avoid activities that cause excessive perspiration.
- Checking that she is not receiving any other drugs that can impair renal function or induce **hyponatraemia**, such as diuretics (particularly thiazides) (Kripalani et al. 2009).
- Monitoring her fluid balance. (Lithium causes polyuria by blocking the effects of antidiuretic hormones.) Daily fluid intake should be 1 to 1.5L per day. Caffeine

consumption should be limited or eliminated (caffeine has a diuretic effect, which can cause lithium sparing by the kidneys) (Kripalani et al. 2009).

- Measuring her fluid intake and output. Weight should be measured daily until stabilization and the legs and ankles observed for any signs of oedema (short-term changes in weight are a good indicator of fluctuations in fluid volume). Excess fluid volume increases the risk of heart failure; pitting oedema may signal heart failure (Kripalani et al. 2009).
- Monitoring her renal status by arranging a full blood count and measuring differential, blood urea nitrogen, creatinine and uric acid levels. Urinalysis should be carried out on a regular basis, as lithium can cause degenerative changes in the kidney, which increases drug toxicity. Service users should immediately report anuria, especially when accompanied by lower abdominal tenderness, distension, headache and diaphoresis. Service users should report any nausea, vomiting, diarrhoea, flank pain or tenderness, and any changes in urinary quantity and quality (e.g. sediment) (Kripalani et al. 2009).
- Monitoring her cardiovascular status and vital signs, including apical pulse and status. Lithium toxicity may cause muscular irritability resulting in cardiac dysrhythmias or angina. The drug should be used with caution in service users with any history of coronary artery or heart disease. Service users should be advised to report immediately any palpitations, chest pain or other symptoms suggestive of myocardial infarction (MI) (Shultz and Videbeck 2008).
- Monitoring her GI status (lithium may cause dyspepsia, diarrhoea or a metallic taste in the mouth). Service users should be instructed to take the drug with food to reduce stomach upset and report distressing gastrointestinal (GI) symptoms (Shultz and Videbeck 2008).
- Monitoring her metabolic status. Lithium may cause goitre with prolonged use and false-positive results on thyroid tests. Service users should be instructed to report any symptoms of goitre or hypothyroidism: enlarged mass on neck, fatigue, dry skin or oedema (Shultz and Videbeck 2008).

4 **List the factors you would evaluate as a nurse to ensure the efficacy of lithium**

A
- She should demonstrate stabilization of mood, including absence of mania and suicidal depression.
- She should initiate normal activities of daily living and report an improvement in mood.
- Episodes of harm directed at herself or others should decrease as the drug begins to take effect.
- She should be able to fall and stay asleep.
- She should be able to demonstrate understanding of the drug's action by accurately describing potential side-effects and precautions against them (Shultz and Videbeck 2008).

5 **What reasons may the service user have for not taking her medicine?**

A
- She may miss her high periods. The high periods of bipolar disorder, especially if they are accompanied by euphoria, can be very enjoyable for the service user. When in a manic

phase they will feel more productive, driven, on top of things, cheerful and even invulnerable.

- She said she felt 'terrific' before she left the assessment unit so she may think she no longer needs the medicine on an ongoing basis. Service users do not always see the need for **prophylaxis**.
- She may feel that the medication takes away her creativity. Bipolar disorder has been associated with creativity, goal striving and positive achievements. There is significant evidence to suggest that many people with creative talents have also suffered from some form of bipolar disorder, and it is often proposed that creativity and bipolar disorder are linked (Lam et al. 2004). Therefore it might well be worth this service user discussing lowering the dose with her GP.
- She may have felt that the medication gave her unacceptable side-effects such as fine hand movements that are difficult to control. She should be encouraged to keep a daily record of any side-effects. The dose could be adjusted, taken in different dosing patterns, or extended release formulations could be discussed.
- She may feel that taking medication is a sign of personal weakness, sickness and lack of control. Discussing sleep–wake monitoring, charting of moods, cognitive restructuring and coping with family stress could all help her feel that she has some degree of control rather than none.
- There are widespread problems with social stigma, stereotypes and prejudice against individuals with a diagnosis of bipolar disorder. In this case there is a definite stigma attached to her grandmother's problems. This may be reinforced by taking medication for the disorder (NIMH 2011).
- She may feel that the medication is being used as a form of control by her parents and that she is giving in to her parents or spouse by agreeing to take lithium.
- She may be having problems with her memory and can't remember to take her medication on a regular basis. Using prompts such as alarms or pill boxes can be helpful here (Miklowitz 2011).

KEY POINTS

- Major neurotransmitter systems include the noradrenaline system, the dopamine system, the serotonin system and the cholinergic system. All are important in maintaining a stable mood.
- The exact cause of bipolar disorder is not fully understood. However, experts believe there are a number of different factors that act together to cause the condition. The factors involved are thought to be a complex mix of physical, environmental and social.
- In the UK, lithium carbonate (often referred to as just lithium) is the medication most commonly used to treat bipolar disorder. Lithium is a long-term method of treatment for episodes of mania, hypomania and depression and is usually prescribed for a minimum of six months.

- The role of the nurse in relation to this condition is wide and includes, for example, monitoring lithium levels, monitoring electrolyte and fluid balance, renal, cardiovascular, G I and metabolic status.
- Service users should be informed of the importance of concordance with lithium to prevent relapse and the importance of carrying their lithium record book with them to enable pharmacies to dispense lithium.

REFERENCES

Alloy, L.B., Abramson, L.Y., Urosevic, S., Walshaw, P.D., Nusslock, R. and Neeren, A.M. (2005) The psychosocial context of bipolar disorder: environmental, cognitive, and developmental risk factors, *Clinical Psychology Review*, 25(8): 1043–75.

Calderdale and Huddersfield and North Kirklees and Wakefield Area Prescribing Committee (2011) *Lithium Shared Care Guideline*, available at: www.formulary.cht.nhs.uk.

Cousins, D.A., Butts, K. and Young, A.H. (2009) The role of dopamine in bipolar disorder, *Bipolar Disorders: An International Journal of Psychiatry and Neurosciences*, 11(8): 787–806.

Delgado, P.L. (2000) Depression: the case for a monoamine deficiency, *Journal of Clinical Psychiatry*, 61(Suppl. 6): S7–11.

Ketter, T.A. (ed.) (2005) *Advances in Treatment of Bipolar Disorder*. Arlington, VA: American Psychiatric Press.

Kripalani, M., Shawcross, J., Reilly, J. and Main, J. (2009) Lithium and chronic kidney disease, *British Medical Journal*, 339(7713).

Lam, D., Wright, K. and Smith, N. (2004) Dysfunctional assumptions in bipolar disorder, *Journal of Affective Disorders*, 79(1–3): 193–9.

Leverich, G.S. and Post, R.M. (2006) Course of bipolar illness after history of childhood trauma, *Lancet*, 367(9516): 1040–2.

Manji, H.K. and Lenox, R.H. (2000) The nature of bipolar disorder, *Journal of Clinical Psychiatry*, 61(Suppl. 13): S42–57.

Miklowitz, D.J. (2011) *The Bipolar Disorder Survival Guide: What You and Your Family Need to Know* 2nd edn. London: Guilford Press.

Miklowitz, D.J. and Chan, K.D. (2008) Prevention of bipolar disorder in at-risk children: theoretical assumptions and empirical foundations, *Development and Psychopathology*, 20(3): 881–97.

Muller-Oerlinghausen, B., Berghofer, A. and Bauer, M. (2002) Bipolar disorder, *Lancet*, 359: 241–7.

N I C E (National Institute for Health and Clinical Excellence) (2006) *Clinical Guideline 38: Bipolar Disorder: The Management of Bipolar Disorder in Adults, Children and Adolescents in Primary and Secondary Care*. London: N I C E.

N I M H (National Institute for Mental Health) (2011) *Stigma and Bipolar Disorder*, available at: http://bipolar.about.com/od/stigma.

Rang, H.P., Dale, M.M., Ritter, J.M, Flower, R.J. and Henderson, G. (2011) *Rang and Dale's Pharmacology*, 7th edn. Oxford: Churchill Livingstone.

Serretti, A. and Mandelli, L. (2008) The genetics of bipolar disorder: genome 'hot regions,' genes, new potential candidates and future directions, *Molecular Psychiatry*, 13(8): 742–71.

Schultz, J.M. and Videbeck, S.L (2008) *Lippincott's Manual of Psychiatric Nursing Care Plans*, 8th edn. London: Lippincott Williams & Wilkins.

CASE STUDY 4
The person with lung cancer
Debbie Wyatt

CASE AIMS

After examining this case study the reader should be able to:

- Briefly explain the pathophysiology of dyspnoea on exertion and a cough as symptoms of lung cancer.
- Outline the TNM staging system of cancer.
- Explain why someone with lung cancer would receive cytotoxic therapy.
- Demonstrate an understanding of the mode of action of cisplatin and vinorelbine.
- Explain why the medicines used in cytotoxic chemotherapy are often given in combination.
- Discuss the role of the nurse in monitoring and managing potential side-effects of cisplatin and vinorelbine.
- Demonstrate an understanding of aprepitant, ondansetron and dexamethasone as antiemetic agents used in cytotoxic chemotherapy.

CASE

George is a 62-year-old man who initially presented to his GP two months ago with a six-week history of a cough. He enjoys exercise and walks four to five miles at least four times a week, although he now gets breathless when walking up hills. He has no haemoptysis or pain and until recently has experienced no other ill health. George used to smoke 20 cigarettes a day but has not smoked for 20 years. NICE referral guidelines for suspected lung cancer (2005) prompted the GP to instigate an urgent referral for a chest X-ray which was suggestive of lung cancer. NICE referral guidelines (2011) prompted referral for a bronchoscopy and biopsy which confirmed a diagnosis of non-small-cell lung cancer in the left upper lobe. A CT scan of the lungs staged the cancer at T4, N1, M1 (Stage IV), with evidence of the tumour involving the pulmonary artery and metastatic lung deposits.

1 **Why does George have dyspnoea on exertion and a cough?**

2 **What does T4, N1, M1 (Stage IV) mean in terms of George's cancer?**

George was advised that chemotherapy would aim to improve survival and quality of life as recommended by NICE (2011). George was prescribed four cycles of cisplatin and vinorelbine. The regime consisted of 80mg/m2 iv of cisplatin on day 1 and oral vinorelbine 60mg/m² on days 1 and 8. This was repeated at 21-day intervals for four cycles.

---

3 **Why is George having cytotoxic chemotherapy?**

4 **How do cisplatin and vinorelbine work?**

5 **Why is it better to give George a combination of drugs in his cytotoxic chemotherapy?**

George was worried about the potential side-effects of his chemotherapy as he had heard that the treatment makes you very ill.

---

6 **What is the role of the nurse in monitoring and managing the potential side-effects of George's medicines?**

George managed to complete his treatment with few complications, though he did experience nausea and vomiting and lost 7kg in weight. He was prescribed aprepitant, ondansetron and dexamethasone to prevent and treat nausea and vomiting.

---

7 **How would using aprepitant, ondansetron and dexamethasone help in preventing and controlling George's nausea and vomiting?**

ANSWERS

1 **Why does George have dyspnoea on exertion and a cough?**

A Cancer cells do not follow the same rules of organization as normal cells. Normally, when a cell has divided approximately 40 times, it is programmed to die by a process called apoptosis.

The p53 gene is responsible for this programmed cell death and reduces the risk of old, damaged and worn-out cells producing faulty DNA in subsequent cell divisions. Cancer cells lose this property however, and continue to divide rather than being programmed to die.

As the cancer cells accumulate, tumours form which may press on other structures to produce symptoms. George, for example, has squamous non-small-cell lung carcinoma (NSCLC) which has formed a tumour occupying his left upper lobe. This has reduced the flow of air in and out of his left lung, leading to breathlessness on exertion. It has also caused a local inflammation which has generated sputum production, hence the cough (Merkle and Loescher 2005; King and Robins 2006).

2   **What does T4, N1, M1 (Stage IV) mean in terms of George's cancer?**

A   Investigations help to determine the stage of the cancer which in turn influences the type of treatment. George's NSCLC was staged at T4, N1, M1 (Stage IV) using the American Joint Committee on Cancer (AJCC) TNM staging system. In this system, a combination of letters and numbers communicate information about the tumour (T), presence and location of lymph nodes (N) and the absence or presence of metastases (M). T1, for example, represents a tumour which is confined to the organ of origin compared to T4 which indicates that the cancer has invaded other structures and solid organs. Lymph node status ranges from 1 to 3 with increasing involvement of regional lymph nodes. Metastases is represented by 0 or 1, in other words, there is (1) or is not (0) evidence of metastases. A zero score next to T, N or M indicates that there is no evidence of a tumour, lymph node involvement or metastases (Yarbro et al. 2011).

TNM has different meanings for different tumours and can be found in the TNM atlas (Rubin and Hansen 2008), however the T4, N1, M1 staging of George's NSCLC indicates that his tumour was at the most advanced of the T stages due to extension into the pulmonary artery and that there was evidence of lymph node involvement (N1) and metastases (M1). Once the TNM staging has been completed, this information is used to give the cancer an overall stage, which in George's case is Stage IV. Cancers are normally staged between I and IV, with I representing early stage cancer and IV representing the most advanced. The stage of a cancer is used to assess prognosis and inform the choice of treatment (Gabriel 2004).

3   **Why is George having cytotoxic chemotherapy?**

A   Cytotoxic chemotherapy is a form of treatment which causes cell death, predominantly targeting cells (both normal and cancer) which are in the process of dividing. The treatment interferes with the cells' ability to reproduce. The aim is to maximize damage to the cancer cells while minimizing harm to normal cells.

Cancer cells go through the same phases of the cell cycle (Barber and Robertson 2012) as normal cells and many cancer drugs act by blocking one or more of these phases. Cytotoxic drugs can be classified as cell cycle non-specific or cell cycle specific (Brenner and Stevens 2006). Those which are cell cycle non-specific are effective in damaging cells which are both resting and dividing. Cell cycle specific drugs only damage cells which are in a particular phase of cell reproduction (Barton-Burke and Wilkes 2006).

4 **How do cisplatin and vinorelbine work?**

A # CISPLATIN

Cisplatin is a **platinating agent** which is used for the treatment of lung cancer (BNF 2012). It is a cell cycle non-specific drug which works both in a number of phases of the cell cycle and also in the resting phase (G0). It has a similar action to **alkylating agents** which damage and impede the replication of DNA (Rang et al. 2012). Other cell cycle non-specific drugs include antibiotic agents such as bleomycin and epirubicin which also damage DNA. Cell cycle specific drugs include **antimetabolites** such as methotrexate and mitotic poisons such as vinorelbine. The antimetabolites interfere with DNA replication and tend to be most effective in the S or M phases. The mitotic poisons prevent the formation of mitotic spindles which are essential for cell division in mitosis (Galbraith et al. 2007).

VINORELBINE

Vinorelbine acts in the M phase of the cell cycle by binding to the spindles of the cells, preventing separation of the chromosomes and thus inhibiting mitosis (Simonsen et al. 2006; Chen and Moore 2007).

5 **Why is it better to give George a combination of drugs in his cytotoxic chemotherapy?**

A Cancers which have a greater proportion of cells in the cell cycle (are dividing), and are growing quickly, are likely to respond better to cytotoxic chemotherapy than those dividing less frequently. As cells will all be at different phases of the cell cycle, at any one time, drugs tend to be given in combination to increase the likelihood of killing as many cells as possible. Cisplatin, for example, is most effective in the G0, G1 and S phases, whereas vinorelbine works best in the M phase. Giving combinations of cytotoxic chemotherapy drugs is therefore more effective than giving single agents alone. Unfortunately, cytotoxic chemotherapy targets not only cancer cells, but any cell which is in the process of dividing. As treatment primarily affects cells which are in the process of reproduction, normal cells which reproduce frequently tend to be affected most. These include epithelial cells such as hair and those which line the digestive system, blood cells formed in the bone marrow and the ova and sperm of the reproductive organs (Rang et al. 2012).

6 **What is the role of the nurse in monitoring and managing the potential side-effects of George's medicines?**

A The role of the nurse is varied, and involves monitoring and managing the following aspects of care.

- As cisplatin is highly nephrotoxic, patients need to be advised that their renal function will be monitored prior to, during and after treatment. Intensive hydration with oral, and sometimes IV fluids will be required, so maintaining a record of fluid balance will be essential. Urine output should reach at least 100–150ml per hour (Wilkes and Barton-Burke 2012). If there are signs of kidney dysfunction, cisplatin may be stopped and an alternative regime prescribed.

- As both cisplatin and vinorelbine can cause myelosuppression, patients are at risk of infections, anaemia and bleeding. A full blood count should be undertaken prior to each cycle of treatment and the patient should be advised that treatment will be delayed if they are neutropenic (neutrophil count less than 1000 cells/mm^3). Patients should be monitored carefully for evidence of infection and/or fever and should be advised to protect themselves from infection – for example, by avoiding exposure to people with known infections (Lilley 2006). They should also be advised how to recognize early signs of infection, including monitoring of their temperature. Patients should be asked to take their temperature prior to analgesic medication which may mask infection through its antipyretic activity, and seek immediate medical advice if they have a pyrexia greater than 37.5°C in case antibiotic treatment is needed. Patients may also become anaemic leading to shortness of breath, dizziness or fatigue, and low platelets may lead to unexplained bruising or bleeding. Patients should be advised how to recognize such symptoms and urged to report them promptly.

- As cisplatin is highly **emetogenic**, patients should be advised that prophylactic antiemetics will be prescribed to prevent nausea and vomiting. Advice on the specific antiemetic regimes will be required, emphasizing the need to continue with antiemetic treatment for at least three days after the chemotherapy has been administered. Should prophylaxis not be achieved, patients should be advised to inform the nursing staff so that treatment can be reviewed. Other advice which patients may find helpful includes eating small frequent meals and avoiding spicy food and alcohol. Other GI symptoms which should prompt patients to seek medical advice include diarrhoea and constipation.

- Certain side-effects cannot be prevented, however, patients should be advised to report any hearing loss, buzzing in the ears, pins and needles or altered sensations in fingers or toes. The latter may result in patients being unable to feel extremes of temperature so they should be advised to take care with very hot or cold objects. Assessment of sensory and motor function is therefore important as treatment may need to be stopped if symptoms are severe. Hair may become thinner, though complete hair loss is not usual. Patients may be referred for a wig if desired.

7 **How would using aprepitant, ondansetron and dexamethasone help in preventing and controlling George's nausea and vomiting?**

A Patients at high risk of nausea and vomiting due to cytotoxic drugs should be prescribed a 5-HT$_3$-receptor antagonist in combination with dexamethasone and aprepitant. The 5-HT$_3$ antagonists such as ondansetron block the action of serotonin in the **nucleus tractus solitarius** and **chemoreceptor trigger zone** by binding to the 5-HT$_3$ receptors and blocking transmission of impulses to the vomiting centre. Aprepitant is used to prevent nausea and vomiting by inhibiting the action of substance P in the emetic pathways and dexamethasone in combination with other drugs such as ondansetron is highly effective, though the exact mechanism is unknown (Perwitasari et al. 2011).

As cisplatin is highly emetogenic, anti-nausea treatment is prescribed prior to the administration of chemotherapy in an attempt to prevent the experience of nausea and vomiting. It can also be used to ameliorate symptoms should they occur. It is important to achieve good control during the first cycle of chemotherapy in order to avoid anticipatory nausea and vomiting, though the emetogenic potential of cisplatin may be too powerful to eliminate. Although current emetogenic treatments are 70–80% effective in preventing and treating nausea and vomiting in patients receiving cytotoxic chemotherapy with high emetogenic potential, there are still patients who experience this distressing symptom.

KEY POINTS

- As cancer cells accumulate tumours form which may press on other structures to produce symptoms.
- The staging of cancers guides treatment by communicating information about the tumour, lymph nodes and metastases.
- Cytotoxic chemotherapy causes cell death and works best on cells which are in the process of reproducing. Cytotoxic drugs act by blocking one or more of these phases.
- The aim of cytotoxic chemotherapy is to maximize damage to cancer cells while minimizing harm to normal cells.
- Different cytotoxic drugs act at different stages of the cell cycle and may be cell cycle non-specific or cell cycle specific.
- The role of the nurse in relation to this condition is wide and includes, for example, monitoring of renal function, infections and anaemia as well as advising the patient about antiemetic regimes.
- Antiemetics work at different points of the emetic pathway to prevent and/or treat nausea and vomiting.

REFERENCES

Barber, P. and Robertson, D. (2012) *Essentials of Pharmacology for Nurses*, 2nd edn. Maidenhead: Open University Press.

Barton-Burke, M. and Wilkes, G.M. (2006) *Cancer Therapies*. London: Jones & Bartlett. BNF (British National Formulary) (2012) *BNF 63: March*. London: Pharmaceutical Press.

Brenner, G.M. and Stevens, C.W. (2006) *Pharmacology*. 2nd edn. Philadelphia, PA: Saunders Elsevier.

Chen, E.X. and Moore, M.J. (2007) Antineoplastic drugs, in H. Kalent, D.M. Grant and J. Mitchell (eds) *Principles of Medical Pharmacology*. Toronto: Elsevier.

Gabriel, J. (ed.) (2004) *The Biology of Cancer*. Lodnon: Whurr.

Galbraith, A., Bullock, S., Manias, E., Hunt, B. and Richards, A. (2007) *Fundamentals of Pharmacology: An Applied Approach for Nursing and Health*, 2nd edn. Edinburgh: Pearson Education.

King, R.J.B. and Robins, M.W. (2006) *Cancer Biology*, 3rd edn. London: Pearson Education.

Lilly, E. (2006) *Cancer Chemotherapy*, 6th edn. Eli Lilly & Co. Ltd.

Merkle, C.J. and Loescher, L.J. (2005) Biology of cancer, in C. Henke Yarbro, M. Hansen Frogge and M. Goodman (eds) *Cancer Nursing: Principles and Practice*, 6th edn. London: Jones & Bartlett.

NICE (National Institute for Health and Clinical Excellence) (2005) *Clinical Guideline 27: Referral Guidelines for Suspected Cancer*. London: NICE.

NICE (National Institute for Health and Clinical Excellence) (2011) *Clinical Guideline 121: The Diagnosis and Treatment of Lung Cancer*. London: NICE.

Perwitasari, D.A., Gelderblom, H., Atthobari, J. et al. (2011) Anti-emetic drugs in oncology: pharmacology and individualisation by pharmacogenetics, *International Journal of Clinical Pharmacology*, 33: 33–43.

Rang, H.P., Dale, M.M., Ritter, J.M., Flower, R.J. and Henderson, G. (2012) *Rang and Dale's Pharmacology*, 7th edn. London: Elsevier, Churchill Livingstone.

Rubin, P. and Hansen, J.T. (2008) *TNM Staging Atlas*. London: Lippincott Williams & Wilkins.

Simonsen, T., Aarbakke, J., Kay, I., Coleman, I., Sinnott, P. and Lysaa, R. (2006) *Illustrated Pharmacology for Nurses*. London: Hodder Arnold.

Wilkes, G.M. and Barton-Burke, M. (2012) *Oncology Nursing Drug Handbook*. London: Jones & Bartlett.

Yarbro, C., Wujcik, D., Holmes Gobel, B. et al. (eds) (2011) *Cancer Nursing Principles and Practice*. London: Jones & Bartlett.

CASE STUDY 5
The person with chronic obstructive pulmonary disease
Abe Ginourie

CASE AIMS

After examining this case study the reader should be able to:

- Briefly explain the causes of chronic obstructive pulmonary disease.
- Outline the pathophysiology associated with chronic obstructive pulmonary disease.
- Discuss the role of the nurse in caring and managing a patient with chronic obstructive pulmonary disease.
- Demonstrate an understanding of the mode of action and side-effects of salbutamol and tiotropium.

CASE

John Smith is 60 years old, married and has two grown-up children. Both of them are married but they all live in the same locality. Mr Smith, who works at the local engineering firm, likes going out to his local pub, and enjoys a night out and a beer with his friends. He has been complaining of a cough with 'phlegm' both during the winter and summer. However, these symptoms became worse during the winter after he had suffered a chest infection. His cough has become generally worse in the morning, on waking. John says that cigarettes help him to expectorate. He also claims that the cough is a 'smoker's cough', and not something to worry about. He continues to smoke because he finds that he missed socializing with his friends at work and at the pub when he tried quitting. John has been smoking approximately two packs of cigarettes per day since the age of 17. His wife persuaded him to visit his GP as his cough and daily phlegm production were not going away. He has also recently complained of a sense of increased effort to breathe. After lung function tests, he was diagnosed as suffering from chronic obstructive pulmonary disease (COPD).

One morning, John was having difficulty breathing, and felt hot. He started to have prolonged bouts of coughing which caused him to faint. His wife, who was at home, called the ambulance which took him to the accident & emergency (A&E) department. Following assessment, the doctor explained to Mrs Smith that her husband had experienced an acute exacerbation of his COPD and needed to be admitted to hospital for stabilization.

1 **What could have caused John's COPD?**

2 **What changes have taken place in John's respiratory system?**

3 **How would you care for and manage John's condition?**

> *To manage and treat the exacerbation of the COPD, the doctor prescribes nebulized salbutamol to dilate his bronchioles and establish normal ventilation. The doctor also prescribes controlled oxygen therapy, oral corticosteroids for the inflammation and antibiotics for the infection.*

4 **Why has salbutamol been prescribed?**

5 **What is the normal dose and route of salbutamol?**

6 **What side-effects might John anticipate from salbutamol and what can you do to mitigate these effects?**

> *After three days, John is much improved. He is apyrexial and he is able to breathe more easily. His vital capacity and peak flow readings are being recorded and show irreversible lung disease. John's progress is maintained and the possibility of his discharge is being discussed. The doctor decides to prescribe tiotropium once daily to simplify John's medication regime. He is also on salbutamol to be used as required.*

7 **How does tiotropium work?**

8 **What side-effects might John anticipate from tiotropium and what can you do to mitigate these?**

ANSWERS

1 **What could have caused John's COPD?**

A In COPD there are pathological changes in the main bronchi, the bronchioles, the alveolar ducts, alveolar sacs and the alveoli. The causes of these changes are due to, mainly, cigarette smoke, but not exclusively. So be wary when you encounter patients with COPD, and do not make the assumption that it is self-inflicted by smoking (NICE 2010).

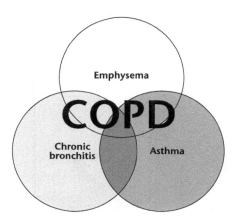

Figure 5.1 Causes of COPD

The other causes of COPD are biomass fuel oxidants, industrial pollution, motor exhaust emissions, mineral dusts and particulates, and genetic factors. There are some patients with COPD who have a severe hereditary deficiency of the alpha 1 anti-trypsin, which is a circulating inhibitor of proteases. People who are deficient of alpha 1 anti-trypsin are at increased risk of developing COPD even if they do not smoke (Stoller and Aboussouan 2005).

2 **What changes have taken place in John's respiratory system?**

A Following chronic exposure to oxidants in cigarette smoke and other inhaled noxious agents, the respiratory system of a patient with COPD responds to these triggers by unleashing the inflammatory system in a very aggressive way. This aggressive response causes tissue destruction and disables the defence and immune system of the body to limit the tissue destruction as compared to a healthy individual. Furthermore, the inflammatory response disrupts the repair system of the body. Consequently, we see massive structural changes in the airways. These changes continue with disease severity, even after a patient stops smoking (Cosio et al. 2009).

In patients with COPD, the pathological changes to the structure of the airways happen because of two main processes. Firstly, there is an imbalance between **proteases** and anti-proteases, and secondly there is an imbalance between **oxidants** and antioxidants in the lungs (MacNee 2007).

Proteases break down connective tissue component and anti-proteases protect the tissue. Proteases are found in inflammatory cells and epithelial cells, and the level is increased in patients with COPD. When the epithelial cells are damaged by cigarette smoke, many inflammatory mediators are released. **Macrophages, neutrophils** and T lymphocytes (CD8) in the lungs release proteases which break down connective tissue in the airways, bronchioles and alveoli.

In emphysema, it is believed that proteases play a major role in its causative factors. **Elastin**, which is a major connective tissue component of the alveoli, is destroyed by proteases

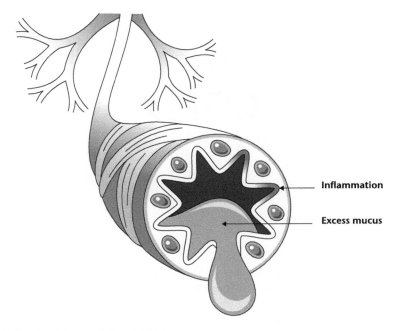

Figure 5.2 Structural changes in bronchial tubes

(Global Strategy for the Diagnosis, Management, and Prevention of Chronic Obstructive Pulmonary Disease 2011). Oxidants are generated by cigarette smoke and other noxious gases, and are also released by macrophages and neutrophils. Antioxidants neutralize the effect of oxidants. There is a reduction in endogenous antioxidant in patients with COPD (Rahman 2005).

3   **How would you care for and manage John's condition?**

A   • You should sit John upright, supported with an adequate number of pillows and provide a bed table for him to lean forward on and rest in the **orthopnoeic position**. Oxygen and a bronchodilator should be administered as prescribed. The bronchodilator acts on the peripheral airways, reduces air and traps and reduces lung volume, which will improve John's breathing and exercise capacity.
   • Because there is a potential risk for John to develop respiratory failure, you must be vigilant to the early warning signs. You must monitor the respiration rate, depth and rhythm and observe whether John is having difficulty breathing, showing signs of confusion or disorientation, or of drowsiness, which may indicate cerebral anoxia (Rodriguez-Roisin et al. 2009).
   • **Pulmonary hypertension** and right **ventricular hypertrophy** are due to the destruction of the pulmonary capillary bed and inflammation of pulmonary arterial vessels. The loss of the pulmonary capillary bed contributes to the increased pressure in the pulmonary

circulation. You need to monitor John's blood pressure closely and administer the prescribed medication. The fluid balance has to be recorded diligently to maintain hydration and electrolyte balance so as to prevent any potential dehydration or circulatory overload.

- Systemic disease and extrapulmonary inflammatory disease occurs in advanced COPD, causing **cachexia** and loss of fat-free mass, with respiratory and peripheral muscle weakness (Barnes and Celli 2009). This would have implications for John's ability to carry on with activities of daily living. People with COPD have a higher energy requirement than average. Increased calorie intake is needed to help John to breathe adequately, which means good nutrition is important. You should liaise with the dietician for advice and support to ensure John has adequate nutrition. You should encourage John to take extra-high calorie drinks and added vitamins. If John is unable to tolerate a normal diet due to his breathlessness, you should offer small, easily digestible meals.

4 **Why has salbutamol been prescribed?**

A Salbutamol is a selective beta$_2$ adrenoceptor agonist that produces bronchodilation. It acts on the beta$_2$ (B$_2$) receptors in the airway smooth muscle by causing an increase in cyclic adenosine monophosphate (cAMP) levels in the cells. An increase in cAMP concentrations prevents the inflammatory and **immunomodulatory** cells from carrying out their harmful effect. The smooth muscles in both the large and small airways to relax, enabling them to dilate. This dilation facilitates easier breathing. It also decreases the airway smooth muscle tone and reduces hyperinflation, thus causing rapid relief of symptoms and improving exercise tolerance.

5 **What is the normal dose and route of salbutamol?**

A Salbutamol has a relatively rapid onset of action, achieving measurable bronchodilation within five minutes and maximal effect in 30 minutes. The effect of the B$_2$ agonist diminishes

Table 5.1 Dosage of salbutamol according to route of administration (BNF 2012)

Route	Dose
By mouth (but use by inhalation preferred)	4mg 3–4 times daily
By subcutaneous or intramuscular injection	500mcg 4 times daily if necessary
By slow IV injection	Dilute to a concentration of 50mcg per ml Then give 250mcg and repeat if necessary
By intravenous infusion	Initially 5mcg per minute, adjusted to a range of 3–20mcg per minute
By aerosol inhalation	100–200mcg (1–2 puffs) 4 times daily
By inhalation of powder	200–400mcg 4 times daily
By inhalation of nebulized solution	2.5–5mg repeated up to 4 times daily 40mg daily is the maximum dose

after two hours and it has a duration of about four to six hours. For regular use, salbutamol must be administered four times daily. It is available in a variety of formulations: pMDIs, nebulized solution, oral and parenteral. Nebulized salbutamol may be appropriate for patients with extremely limited airflows, or in patients who cannot coordinate the use of a pMDI. The actual dose will depend on the route of administration (BNF 2012).

Salbutamol is usually given by the inhaled route for direct effect on bronchial smooth muscle. This is usually achieved through an MDI, nebulizer or other proprietary delivery device (e.g. Rotahaler or Autohaler). In these forms of delivery, the maximal effect of salbutamol can take place within 5 to 20 minutes of dosing, though some relief is immediately seen. It can also be given orally as an inhalant or intravenously.

6 **What side-effects might John anticipate from salbutamol and what can you do to mitigate these effects?**

A
- You should ensure that John is not allergic to any of the constituents of salbutamol (Jordan 2008) before administration. John should be educated to read all labels on medications, whether prescribed or bought over the counter, to ensure there are no drug interactions.
- Salbutamol has positive **inotropic** effects on the heart, so extra care should be taken with patients with myocardial ischaemia and hypokalaemia. The side-effects, within the cardiovascular system are sinus tachycardia, palpitations, susceptibility to prolonged QT interval and vasodilation. It is very rare for a patient to suffer from cardiac arrhythmias, unless there is some susceptibility. The mechanism may be caused by a direct effect on atrial B2 receptors, combined with a reflex effect from increased peripheral vasodilation via B2 receptors. Short-acting inhaled B_2 agonists, such as salbutamol, do not increase the risk of acute MI in patients with COPD.
- You must assess John's vital signs, such as blood pressure, pulse, temperature and respiration to ensure they are within the normal parameters. If the side-effects outweigh the benefits, the doctor may have to consider an alternative bronchodilator (Hansel and Barnes 2004).
- The side-effects of salbutamol on the central nervous system are headache, restlessness, tension, dizziness and nervousness, and disturbances of sleep and behaviour. John should be told about these possible side-effects and given ways to mitigate them. You should monitor blood pressure lying and standing, and dizziness on standing, and record any difference and advise John accordingly. He should be educated about what strategies he can use to manage his sleep, dizziness and postural hypotension. He should also be advised what medication he should take if he suffers from headache.
- The metabolic side-effects are **hypokalaemia**, which is caused by a direct effect on the skeletal muscle uptake of potassium via B_2 receptors, and is usually a small effect, but can be serious. Hypokalaemia can occur especially when treatment is combined with thiazide diuretics, and this may be the case in patients diagnosed with hypertension. John's blood potassium levels should be monitored closely. You should also do a 12-lead electrocardiogram (ECG) to have a baseline, and regularly monitor John's heart rhythm to detect any early signs of hypokalaemia (BNF 2012).
- In patients diagnosed with diabetes mellitus, vigilant monitoring of blood glucose is recommended because salbutamol has a hyperglycaemic effect. There have also been reports of high insulin levels, (hyperinsulinaemia). If John suffers from diabetes mellitus he should be

encouraged to check his blood glucose levels regularly and to have an action plan to deal with hyperglycaemia.

- The possible side-effects on the skeletal muscle are fine tremor, particularly in the hands, and muscle cramps However, in some elderly patients treated with high doses of B_2 agonists, due to a direct effect on skeletal muscle B_2-receptors, the tremors and cramps may be more pronounced. John should be advised to contact a doctor or respiratory specialist nurse if the tremors and muscle cramps appear to be getting worse.

7 **How does tiotropium work?**

A In patients with COPD, the cholinergic pathways may be activated by inflammatory mediators and inhaled irritants such as cigarette smoke. When this happens, vagal cholinergic tone provokes an increase bronchoconstriction and mucus production. This sequence of events causes the patient to become breathless and start coughing up sputum. When the patient is administered an **anticholinergic** drug, such as tiotropium, the bronchioles become dilated and the patient feels an improvement in breathing. There is also a reduction in the amount of sputum produced.

Tiotropium is a long-acting anticholinergic drug. Its long duration of action makes it appropriate for use once a day, which helps compliance and concordance. It is inhaled once a day from the 'HandiHaler', a specialized dry powder inhalation system (Chen et al. 2008).

8 **What side-effects might John anticipate from tiotropium and what can you do to mitigate these?**

A
- The British National Formulary (BNF) reports the following side-effects: constipation, cough, stomatitis, gastro-oesophageal reflux disease, pharyngitis, dysphonia, dysphagia, dysuria, epistaxis and oropharyngeal candidiasis. John should be educated about these side-effects and the strategies to mitigate them.
- The extensive use of the drug in its inhaled form, in a variety of doses and settings, has shown it to be safe. Side-effects include dry mouth and metallic taste. You should advise John to have boiled sweets and drinks readily available, and ice chips to take if his mouth becomes dry.
- Men with prostate disease should be monitored closely for urinary tract effects, because some prostatic symptoms have been reported, however there is no evidence of any causal link. You should monitor John's urine output, by the use of a fluid balance. John should be educated as to the signs and symptoms of urine retention and asked to tell a nurse if he is concerned about his urine output.
- John should be educated and assessed on the right technique for using the inhaler device correctly.
- Tiotropium should be used with caution in patients with glaucoma, since the tiotropium solution with a facemask may precipitate glaucoma, probably due the direct effect of the solution to the eye. Any patients who may be vulnerable to potential systemic anticholinergic side-effects should not be given tiotropium. If John requires tiotropium by the nebulized route, you should stay with him and ensure that a tight-fitting facemask is used to prevent any solution from splashing into his eyes.

KEY POINTS

- COPD is a chronic and progressive disorder which is characterized by inflammation, airflow obstruction and alveolar damage.
- Some response to pharmacological and other therapies can be achieved but they may have limited or no impact on the airflow obstruction.
- Salbutamol causes the smooth muscles in both the large and small airways to relax, enabling them to dilate.
- The side-effects of salbutamol are fine tremor in the hands, muscle cramps, restlessness, tension and dizziness.
- Tiotropium prevents bronchoconstriction and lessens mucus secretion.
- The side-effects of tiotropium include dry mouth, metallic taste, constipation, cough, stomatitis and gastro-oesophageal reflux disease.

REFERENCES

Barnes, P.J. and Celli, B.R. (2009) Systemic manifestations and comorbidities of COPD, *European Respiratory Journal*, 33: 1165–85.

BNF (British National Formulary) (2012) *BNF 63: March*. London: Pharmaceutical Press.

Chen, A.M., Bollmeier, S.G. and Finnegan, P.M. (2008) Long-acting bronchodilator therapy for the treatment of chronic obstructive pulmonary disease, *Annals of Pharmacotherapy*, 42: 1832–42.

Cosio, M., Saetta, M. and Agusti, A. (2009) Immunologic aspects of chronic obstructive pulmonary disease, *New England Journal of Medicine*, 360: 2445–54.

Global Strategy for the Diagnosis, Management, and Prevention of Chronic Obstructive Pulmonary Disease (2011) *Global Initiative for Chronic Obstructive Lung Disease*. London: Global Strategy For the Diagnosis, Management, and Prevention of Chronic Obstructive Pulmonary Disease, available at: www.goldcopd.org/uploads/users/files/GOLD_Report_2011_Feb21.pdf.

Hansel, T.T. and Barnes, P.J. (2004) *An Atlas of Chronic Obstructive Pulmonary Disease*. London: Informa Healthcare.

Jordan, S. (2008) *The Prescription Drug Guide for Nurses*. Maidenhead: Open University Press.

MacNee, W. (2007) Pathology, pathogenesis, and pathophysiology, in G.P. Currie (ed.) *ABC of COPD*. Oxford: Blackwell.

NICE (National Institute for Health and Clinical Excellence) (2010) *Chronic Obstructive Pulmonary Disease (updated) (CG101)*. London: NICE, available at: http://publications.nice.org.uk/chronic-obstructive-pulmonary-disease-cg101/guidance.

Rahman, I. (2005) Oxidative stress in pathogenesis of chronic obstructive pulmonary disease: cellular and molecular mechanisms, *Cell Biochemistry Biophysics*, 43: 167–88.

Rodriguez–Roisin, R., Drakulovic, M., Rodriguez, D.A., Roca, J., Barbera, J.A. and Wagner, P.D. (2009) Ventilation–perfusion imbalance and chronic obstructive pulmonary disease staging severity, *Journal of Applied Physiology*, 1902–8.

Stoller, J.K. and Aboussouan, L.S. (2005) Alpha 1-antitrypsin deficiency, *Lancet*, 362: 2225–36.

The person with acute left ventricular failure following myocardial infarction

Diane Blundell

CASE AIMS

After examining this case study the reader should be able to:

- Outline how the heart normally works as a pump.
- Briefly explain why a patient who has had an anterior MI could have left ventricular failure.
- Outline left ventricular ejection fraction and its significance.
- Demonstrate an understanding of the mode of action and contraindications of cardiac nitrates.
- Demonstrate an understanding of the mode of action and the benefits of giving frusemide in left ventricular failure.
- Demonstrate an understanding of the mode of action and significance of using opiates in left ventricular failure.
- Discuss the role of the nurse in anticipating the side-effects of using opiates in left ventricular failure.

CASE

*Mr D is a 70-year-old man who was admitted to the coronary care unit (CCU) with acute shortness of breath, chest pain, nausea and vomiting. He was diagnosed, with his current history and significant ECG changes, with an acute anterior myocardial infarction (AMI). Previous medical history is of hypertension and angina, and he is a current smoker. He was thrombolyzed according to the CCU protocol for thrombolysis, and appeared to respond well to treatment. Later an echocardiogram was performed which showed he had a poor left ventricular ejection fraction (LVEF) of 40% which showed as left ventricular systolic dysfunction (LVSD) by non-contracting (**akinetic**) or poorly contracting (**hypokinetic**) areas of the left ventricular wall.*

1 **Prior to Mr D's acute AMI, how would his heart have worked as a pump?**

2 **Why has Mr D gone into LVEF following his AMI?**

3 **What is an LVEF?**

4 **What is the significance of determining LVEF following an echocardiogram and potential future events?**

Twenty-four hours post-lysis Mr D developed sudden breathlessness (dyspnoea), tachycardia and confusion, and appeared pale, cold and clammy. His saturations on air were recorded as <80%, blood pressure 126/85mmHg, pulse 120bpm, respirations 25 breaths per minute. He was diagnosed with acute pulmonary oedema with crepitations as a consequence of left ventricular failure upon completion of examination and a portable chest X-ray. He was treated with IV nitrates for the pulmonary oedema, IV frusemide for his left ventricular failure and IV diamorphine.

---

5 **Describe the mode of action of IV nitrates**

6 **Explain the contraindications of giving IV nitrates to a person with acute left ventricular failure**

7 **What is the mode of action of frusemide?**

8 **What are the benefits of giving IV frusemide in left ventricular failure?**

9 **What are opioids?**

10 **What is the significance of using IV diamorphine in acute left ventricular failure?**

11 **What likely side-effects should the nurse anticipate?**

ANSWERS

1 **Prior to Mr D's acute AMI, how would his heart have worked as a pump?**

A Normal cardiac output (CO) is the product of heart rate (HR) and stroke volume (SV). HR is determined by the rate of spontaneous firing at the sinoatrial node but can be modified by the autonomic nervous system. The vagus nerve acts on muscarinic receptors to slow the heart, whereas the cardiac sympathetic fibres stimulate beta adrenergic receptors and increase HR. Stroke volume is determined by three main factors:

- preload;
- afterload;
- contractility.

PRELOAD

Preload is the stretching of the muscle fibres in the ventricles (both right and left). This stretching results from blood volume in the ventricles at end diastole (the relaxation filling period of the cardiac cycle). According to Starling's Law, the more the heart muscle stretches during diastole, the more forcefully it contracts during systole (the contraction phase of the cardiac cycle). Think of preload as being like a balloon stretching as air is blown into it – the more air blown into the balloon the greater the stretch.

AFTERLOAD

This is the resistance to ventricular ejection and is caused by resistance to flow in the systemic circulation, referred to as systemic vascular resistance. This is determined by the diameter of the arterioles and pre-capillary sphincters – the narrower or more constricted, the higher the resistance. The level of systemic vascular resistance is controlled by the sympathetic system which, in turn, controls the tone of the muscle in the wall of the arterioles, and hence the diameter.

CONTRACTILITY

Contractility refers to the inherent ability of the myocardium to contract normally. Contractility is the amount of stretch present in the myocardium muscle fibres at the end of diastole. This is also influenced by preload. So in effect if returned blood flow to the right side of the heart is compromised in any way then ultimately this will have an effect on the amount of blood returning to the left side of the heart. This can affect afterload (Barrett et al. 2009).

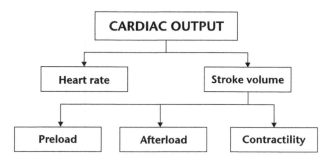

Figure 6.1 Factors affecting cardiac output

BLOOD PRESSURE AND CARDIAC OUTPUT

Blood leaving the left side of the heart (systemic system) is at a greater pressure than blood returning to the right side. This is because the left side of the heart is responsible for delivering oxygenated blood via the aorta into the body and ultimately perfusing all the cells of the body with nutrients and oxygen (a mean arterial pressure of 90–100mmHg is initiated from the left ventricle on systole).

The left ventricle has a thicker myocardium (muscle wall) and consequently has the largest coronary artery that feeds this muscular wall (left ascending coronary artery). The right ventricle has a thinner myocardium and the right side of the heart (pulmonary) is the smaller of the two chambers and functions at a much lower pressure than the left (mean arterial pressure of 12mmHg). This lower pulmonary pressure allows blood to move through the lungs more slowly which is vitally important for gaseous exchange.

As the heart is a closed system it needs to function effectively and requires that both sides pump the same amount of blood over time. If the output of the left heart ventricle were to fall below that of the right, blood would accumulate in the pulmonary circulation. Likewise if the right side were to pump less efficiently than the left then blood would accumulate in the systemic system (Porth 2011).

2 **Why has Mr D gone into LVEF following his AMI?**

A Mr D has been diagnosed and treated for an AMI. Any occlusion of the anterior descending branch of the left coronary artery can lead to an anterior wall infarction (death of muscle tissue). This occurs if the heart muscle is starved of rich oxygenated blood and as a result the portion of the muscle that has been occluded dies (necrosis). This is affecting Mr D's heart's pumping ability.

Because the left ventricle has the largest coronary blood supply, it is the most likely to be involved in MI. Any damage to the left ventricular myocardium through infarction leads to reduced contractility and abnormal movements of the walls of the ventricle (akinetic and hypokinetic contraction); this has had a greater significance as Mr D also has a history of hypertension.

The result is reduced cardiac output or a need for the ventricle to increase its workload to maintain the same cardiac output. This in turn can lead to an increase in muscle bulk (hypertrophy) or an enlargement of the chamber itself (dilation). These physical changes are known as 'remodelling' and although they are a compensatory mechanism the result can be a negative effect as the ventricle becomes overstretched and the fibres lose their elasticity. Further, a dilated heart can also change the shape of the atrioventricular valves, which can in turn lead to **regurgitation** (Nicholson 2007).

Left-sided heart failure associated with elevated pulmonary venous pressure and decreased cardiac output explain Mr D's situation – he is presenting with breathlessness, weakness, pulmonary congestion and associated confusion (Woods et al. 2010).

3 **What is an LVEF?**

A As Mr D has a diagnosis of left ventricular systolic dysfunction (LVSD) the pumping action of his heart is reduced, weakened and/or compromised. This can be quite common following an AMI. A common clinical measurement of the left ventricle, via an echocardiogram, is LVEF.

- The LVEF is a calculation of how much blood is ejected out of the left ventricle (stroke volume), divided by the maximum volume remaining in the left ventricle at the end of diastole (when the heart relaxes).
- A normal LVEF in a healthy person is around 55–75%. Left ventricular systolic heart failure shows as a decreased fraction of <50%.

Table 6.1 Ejection fraction measurements

Ejection fraction measurement	What it means
55–70%	Normal
40–55%	Below normal
Less than 40%	May confirm diagnosis of heart failure
<35%	Patient may be at risk of life-threatening irregular heartbeat

- Mr D has been diagnosed as having an LVEF of 40%. At anything less than 50% his heart can start to have serious problems with its pumping ability, as a direct consequence of his MI (NICE 2010).

4 **What is the significance of determining LVEF following an echocardiogram and potential future events?**

A The significance of establishing ejection fraction is that it estimates the percentage of blood pumped out of the heart each time it contracts. When the heart contracts it ejects blood from the left and right ventricles, and as it relaxes the ventricles refill with blood.

As we have already established, the left ventricle is the heart's main pumping chamber and, as such, ejection fraction is usually only measured in the left ventricle, as it is responsible for sending oxygenated blood via the aorta into the systemic system. A damaged left ventricle has a direct effect on cardiac output, which it compromises (i.e. makes low). This can lead to hypoperfusion of the body's tissues. It also has an effect on the lungs, with an increased pressure in the pulmonary veins. The rise in pressure is due to more and more blood being pumped to the left side of the heart to compensate for its reduced efficiency. The left and right side of the heart must pump the same volume of blood. When this is not possible due to muscle damage, fluid is forced out of the blood vessels in the lungs and into lung tissue, leading to pulmonary oedema (Nicholson 2007).

5 **Describe the mode of action of IV nitrates**

A Nitrates (vasodilators) are recommended as an initial therapy, and are a common choice of drug used in the relief of angina and acute left ventricular failure; they also work by reducing breathlessness in patients with heart failure (BNF 2012). These drugs include isosorbide mononitrate and isosorbide dinitrate, which can be taken orally, sublingually (beneath the tongue) and by IV administration.

They exert their effects in a dose-dependent fashion by a mode of action which sees the release of nitric oxide (an important signalling chemical) into vascular smooth muscle and improves myocardial oxygen supply while reducing the demand of oxygen consumption. In small doses they dilate veins to a greater degree than arteries and this in turn affects preload (left ventricular end diastolic pressure) and right-sided heart filling pressure and volume

(Thompson and Webster 2005). At higher doses nitrates can also act as arterial dilators, which lower peripheral resistance, left ventricular pressures, myocardial work and oxygen demands.

The final action of these drugs is that they dilate the coronary arteries, thereby increasing blood and oxygen supply to the myocardium (Nicholson 2007). For IV administration the starting dose should be low and increased gradually until relief of symptoms is achieved or blood pressure is adversely affected. As IV nitrates are vasodilators it is an important part of nursing care that blood pressure is monitored closely and that IV nitrates are adjusted accordingly. The systolic blood pressure should not drop by >20mmHg and if it does then the dose should be reduced if the systolic blood pressure is <100mmHg. A diastolic blood pressure of >60mmHg is necessary for adequate coronary artery perfusion.

Gardner et al. (2008) clarify that there is evidence that the combination of IV nitrates and frusemide is superior to high-dose diuretic treatment alone in the management of pulmonary oedema.

6 **Explain the contraindications of giving IV nitrates to a person with acute left ventricular failure**

A The contraindications of giving IV nitrates to a person with acute left ventricular failure are that they can cause hypotension (low blood pressure) as a consequence of vasodilation. The supply of blood to the heart is dependent on blood pressure remaining above a critical level; this means that a sufficient pressure to force blood into the coronary arteries is maintained. If it falls below the critical level the heart becomes short of oxygen and this can lead to chest pain. As a person ages a low blood pressure can reduce cerebral blood flow which can ultimately lead to impaired functioning of the brain and confusion (Jordan 2009).

7 **What is the mode of action of frusemide?**

A Frusemide belongs to a group of drugs called diuretics. Their mechanism of action is to work on the kidneys to increase urine volume by reducing salt and water reabsorption from the tubules (BNF 2012). There are several different sodium channels that exist in the renal tubules and, because of this, different diuretic drugs act at different sites along the tubule, providing different molecular actions and clinical side-effects (Dawson et al. 2005). Frusemide is a loop diuretic which acts at the thick ascending segment of the Loop of Henle, which eventually leads into the distal tubule.

Frusemide can cause the excretion of 15–25% of filtered sodium as opposed to the normal 1% or less. This action alone can result in profound diuresis (remember that where sodium goes, water will follow it). The mechanism of action of loop diuretics is that they inhibit the sodium/potassium/chloride co-transporter in the luminal membrane which inevitably increases the amount of sodium reaching the collecting duct. Because of this there is an increase in potassium and proton secretion. Loop diuretics have a venodilatory action which is renowned for bringing relief of clinical symptoms such as acute pulmonary oedema and heart failure in as little as 30 minutes by the IV route (NICE 2010).

8 **What are the benefits of giving IV frusemide in left ventricular failure?**

A The benefit of giving IV frusemide to a patient like Mr D with acute left ventricular failure is that if the patient is showing signs of fluid retention (pulmonary oedema) and is acutely unwell the dose of diuretic can be titrated up quickly to achieve the desired effect (DH 2000). Another benefit is that by removing excess water and by causing vasodilation, the pressure on the heart (preload) is inevitably reduced and consequently the heart is not put under as much strain. This can lead to a marked reduction in breathlessness (Nicholson 2007).

As with any drug there are always some side-effects and the main ones for frusemide are:

- hypotension;
- hypokalaemia;
- hyponatraemia;
- hypovolaemia;
- hyperuricaemia.

9 **What are opioids?**

A • Opioids are drugs that are either naturally occurring (e.g. morphine) or chemically synthesized. They work by interacting with specific opioid receptors to produce the pharmacological effect of analgesia.
- They are also considered to be anxiolytic (reduce anxiety) and are likened to endorphins and encephalins, which are the body's mood changers and analgesics in time of great stress.
- Sometimes, sedation, mental detachment or euphoria are the predominant effects of a dose of diamorphine (BNF 2012).

10 **What is the significance of using IV diamorphine in acute left ventricular failure?**

A As Mr D has gone into acute heart failure, the left ventricle fails and afterload increases. Pressure then rises in the left atrium and left ventricle, while hydrostatic pressure rises and fluid is forced out into the lung tissues, leading to pulmonary oedema. Opioids have a veno-dilatory effect, and because of this they can be used to reduce afterload. They also have the effect of making the patient feel calmer and dissociated from their body.

When a patient goes into acute MI like Mr D they appear very distressed due to their breathlessness, which can make them feel totally out of control. At this time their 'fight and flight' response becomes activated, which makes them feel worse. Administering IV diamorphine calms the patient, allowing time for the nitrates and diuretics to take effect (Nicholson 2007).

11 **What likely side-effects should the nurse anticipate?**

A Some of the adverse side effects of diamorphine include:

- drowsiness and sedation;
- reduction in sensitivity of the respiratory centre to CO_2, which can lead to shallow and slow respirations and should be monitored carefully;
- hypotension and reduced cardiac output;
- activation of the vomiting centre due to stimulation of the chemoreceptor trigger zone (CTZ) – an antiemetic such as cyclizine should also be administered (Dawson et al. 2005).

KEY POINTS

- MI constitutes a mixture of symptoms and signs that are ultimately due to cardiac dysfunction.
- The heart's pumping ability is reliant upon three factors: preload, contractility and afterload.
- Following an acute AMI the left ventricle can become severely damaged.
- LVEF is a common clinical measurement of the left ventricle, via an echocardiogram.
- Ejection fraction is normally around 55–75% in patients without cardiac damage.
- IV nitrates are a common choice of drugs used in the relief of angina and acute left ventricular failure. Their mode of action allows the release of nitric oxide into vascular smooth muscle which improves oxygen supply while reducing the demand for oxygen consumption.
- Frusemide belongs to a group of drugs called diuretics. Their mechanism of action is to work on the kidneys to increase urine volume by reducing salt and water reabsorption from the renal tubules.
- Administering diamorphine to calm the patient allows time for nitrates and diuretics to take effect.
- Some of the adverse side-effects of diamorphine include drowsiness and sedation.

REFERENCES

Barrett, K.E., Barman, S.M., Boitano, S. and Brooks, H.L. (2009) *Ganong's Review of Medical Physiology*, 23rd edn. New York: McGraw-Hill.

BNF (2012) *BNF 63: March*. London: Pharmaceutical Press.

Dawson, J.S., Taylor, M.N.F. and Reide, P.J.W. (2005) *Pharmacology*, 2nd edn. London: Elsevier.

DH (Department of Health) (2000) *National Service Framework: Coronary Heart Disease*. London: DH.

Gardner, R.S., McDonagh, T.A. and Walker, N.L. (2008) *Heart Failure*. Oxford: Oxford University Press.

Jordan, S. (2009) *The Prescription Drug Guide for Nurses*. Maidenhead: Open University Press.

NICE (National Institute for Health and Clinical Excellence) (2010) *Clinical Guideline 108: Chronic Heart Failure: Management of Chronic Heart Failure in Adults in Primary and Secondary Care*. London: NICE.

Nicholson, C. (2007) *Heart Failure – A Clinical Nursing Handbook*. Chichester: Wiley.

Porth, C.M. (2011) *Essentials of Pathophysiology*, 3rd edn. London: Lippincott Williams & Wilkins.

Thompson, D.R. and Webster, R.A. (2005) *Caring for the Coronary Patient*, 2nd edn. London: Butterworth Heinemann.

Watson, R. (2003) *Anatomy and Physiology for Nurses*, 11th edn. London: Bailliere Tindall.

Woods, S.L., Froelicher, E.S.S., Motzer, S.U. and Bridges, E.J. (2010) *Cardiac Nursing*, 6th edn. Philadelphia, PA: Lippincott Williams & Wilkins.

The young person with cystic fibrosis
Christine Whitney-Cooper

CASE AIMS

After examining this case study the reader should be able to:

- Explain the pathophysiology of cystic fibrosis.
- Identify the clinical manifestations of cystic fibrosis.
- Outline the tests used in order to diagnose cystic fibrosis.
- List the indicators that lead to changes in the dietary and enzyme management of patients with cystic fibrosis.
- Discuss the role of the nurse in giving dietary advice to a patient with cystic fibrosis.
- Explain why physiotherapy is important in improving the lung function in a patient with cystic fibrosis.
- Demonstrate an understanding of the mode of action and reasons for prescribing ciprofloxacin to a patient with cystic fibrosis.

CASE

Lauren is 16 years and 3 months and has cystic fibrosis (CF). She attends an out-patient clinic for her CF, which was diagnosed at 3 years after her failing to thrive. The deferential diagnosis was made using a sweat test. Her condition is currently treated with physiotherapy, inhaled salbutamol through an MDI and pancreatic enzyme replacement capsules (creon). Lauren manages her physiotherapy and medications. A respiratory bacterial culture has previously revealed that she has a chronic pseudomonas aeruginosa infection. She was treated with intensive physiotherapy and IV antibiotics and is now receiving inhaled ciprofloxacin. She is 157.5cm tall and weighs 40.4kg. A review of her diet and enzyme intake has led to a prescribed increase in her creon intake.

---

1 **What is CF?**

2 **What are the clinical manifestations of CF?**

3 **What tests can aid the diagnosis of CF?**

4   **What are the indicators that have led to the changes in Lauren's dietary and enzyme management?**

5   **Why does Lauren need her pancreatic enzyme increased?**

6   **What sort of dietary advice would be given to Lauren to optimize her nutrition?**

7   **Why is chest physiotherapy important to improve lung function for Lauren?**

8   **Why has inhaled ciprofloxacin been prescribed and how does it work?**

ANSWERS

1   **What is CF?**

A   CF is a condition with a complex multisystem involvement of the GI and respiratory systems. It is a common **heterogeneous** disorder with more than 1500 mutations and clinical **phenotypes** on chromosome 7 (Montgomery and Howestine 2009). The gene is autosomal recessive, so both parents have to be carriers for the child to inherit the disease. Where both parents are carriers of the faulty gene there is an increased incidence of one in four children being born having CF. Approximately 1 in 25 people in the UK are carriers of the CF gene.

Treatment of CF involves managing the respiratory and GI symptoms caused by the CF transmembrane conductance regulator (CFTR) mutation. Treatments are limited as there are many mutations of chromosome 7 and experimental treatments to reopen the CFTR channel have limited application to a few sufferers (Ledford 2012). The main thrust of research is the development of gene therapy. Where there is chronic respiratory dysfunction some patients are offered lung/heart transplants. CF is a mutation of the CFTR channel which mediates diffusion of chloride through epithelial cell membranes. The CFTR controls the chloride channel that allows the free movement of salt (chloride and sodium) in and out of the cells through diffusion. All cells acquire the molecules and ions they need from their surrounding extracellular fluid and there is an unceasing traffic of molecules and ions in and out of the cell through the plasma membrane. Molecules and ions move spontaneously down their concentration gradient (i.e. from a region of higher to a region of lower concentration) by diffusion (the movement of particles from an area of higher concentration to an area of lower concentration). Water can pass through the cell membrane but ions and charged molecules (e.g. salts dissolved in water) need a **facilitated diffusion**. The transmembrane proteins create a water-filled pore through which ions and some small **hydrophilic** molecules can pass by facilitated diffusion in and out of the cell. The channels can be opened (or closed) according to the needs of the cell. The CFTR provides a chloride channel to facilitate the transport of chloride across the cell membrane. The activity of the CFTR may activate water permeability in healthy individuals but not in CF. In CF the mutation of the CFTR affects diffusion of molecules and ions across the membrane. There is decreased chloride (Cl^-) secretion due to the CFTR mutation. However, there is increased sodium (Na^+) absorption, possibly due to the loss of the inhibitory influence of the CFTR (Goodman and Percy 2005).

In normal tissue, chloride ions enter the lumen from the extracellular space through epithelial cells. This creates an increased negative potential across the epithelial cells, which results in the transport of sodium ions down the potential gradient into the lumen. A higher concentration of ions in the lumen causes water to move from the extracellular space into the lumen. In CF the luminal side of the affected exocrine gland has higher negative ionic potential than normal, due to a marked decrease in the permeability of the cell membrane to chloride ions. This causes an increased uptake of sodium ions, contributing further to the negative ionic potential. The increase in chloride ions and decrease in sodium ions decreases the osmotic movement of water into the airway, thereby increasing the viscosity of the mucus secretions. This movement is found in many epithelial cells, including sweat duct, airway, pancreatic duct, intestine, biliary tree and vas deferens. The result is that the body's secretions, which normally act as a lubricant, have high sodium and low water content and secretions become thick, viscid mucus, causing obstruction of the body's tubes and ducts.

2   **What are the clinical manifestations of CF?**

A   The clinical manifestations of CF are as follows.

* *Pancreatic enzyme deficiency due to blockage of the pancreatic duct.* In approximately 85% of cases the pancreatic exocrine ducts become blocked and cause intestinal malabsorption due to pancreatic insufficiency. The thick viscid secretions in CF affect the digestive tract. Digestive problems may present in infancy as a GI blockage and as a meconium ileus. Infants are unable to pass the first stool that contains meconium. This obstruction means that the pancreatic enzymes are blocked from entering the duodenum, limiting digestion of proteins and fats. Older children may present with failure to thrive due to pancreatic insufficiency, with symptoms of restricted growth in the presence of a voracious appetite and a protuberant belly with decreased subcutaneous tissue on the extremities. Lack of digestive enzymes in the intestinal lumen also causes symptoms including frequent, loose, oily and malodorous stools caused by steatorrhea (fat in stool due to lack of active pancreatic lipases). A faecal elastase evaluation (Turner and McDermott 2006) is a simple and non-invasive test that allows clinicians to estimate pancreatic exocrine function. Elastase is a pancreatic enzyme which helps to break down connective tissue. It is present in the serum, urine and faeces. Pancreatic elastase does not undergo any significant degradation during intestinal transit and, therefore, acts as a useful marker of pancreatic activity.
* *Progressive chronic obstructive lung disease.* Infants with CF often present with respiratory problems. Viral illnesses can progress to bacterial pneumonia as the respiratory cilia cannot clear the thick mucus. Air becomes trapped in the airways leading to bronchospasm, hyperinflation, collapse or closure of alveoli (atelectasis) and secondary infections. Chronic infection and inflammation can lead to a persistent dilation of the bronchi (bronchiectasis). Respiratory problems can present as persistent dry and non-productive coughing or recurrent respiratory infections. Auscultation can demonstrate expiratory wheezing and fine crackles due to bronchospasm. Patients are often infected with *Staphylococcus aureus* and *Pseudomonas aeruginosa*, but also by a number of other organisms, some of which are resistant to many antibiotics. The use of antibiotics is to reduce or prevent a pseudomonas-associated deterioration of respiratory function.

• *Gland dysfunction.* Individuals with CF have changes to the CFTR leading to abnormal concentrations of sodium and chloride in their sweat, leading in turn to salt depletion. In sweat glands, the sweat is normally produced at the base of the gland and then passes through a narrow duct in which reabsorption of salt occurs. In CF, abnormal chloride absorption out of the duct via defective CFTRs leads to excessive sodium and chloride (three to five times normal concentration) in sweat (Goodman and Percy 2005). An inability to conserve salts means increased sweating in hot climates, which can lead to depletion. One sign of CF, often noticed by parents before a diagnosis, is the salty taste of the infant's skin.

3 **What tests can aid diagnosis of CS?**

A A sweat test (*pilocapine iontophoresis*) involves stimulating the production and collection of sweat and measuring the electrolytes, and can be used to identify CF. The quantitative analysis requires a minimum 50mg of sweat. A measurement of sodium chloride of <70mmol/kg in a 100mg sample is indicative of CF. However, in the UK the test for CF is included in the heel-prick test to sample blood, carried out on all children. CF is increasingly being diagnosed through infant screening. The blood test is to detect immunoreactive trypsinogen (IRT) concentrations which are high in newborns with CF. If the IRT reading is high, a chromosomal mutation analysis can be performed on the same or a repeat sample. In addition, there is now a carrier test identified from saliva and an antenatal blood test offered to all mothers who are at high risk as a carrier of CF. However, some infants and older children (and even adults) may not be diagnosed as a newborn through blood tests but later following an unexplained respiratory illness or malnutrition due to pancreatic insufficiency.

4 **What are the indicators that have led to the changes in Lauren's dietary and enzyme management?**

A When plotted on a percentile chart Lauren's height and weight are below the first percentile which suggests she is underweight. As children with CF become adults there is a risk of malnutrition that is strongly linked to the severity of lung disease and body weight. Apart from the general malnutrition associated with more severe disease, many aspects of nutrition that affect bone status, including fat soluble vitamins (A, D, E and K), minerals (calcium and iron in particular) and protein intake, can lead to osteoporosis.

5 **Why does Lauren need her pancreatic enzyme increased?**

A Lauren, as with the majority of patients suffering from CF, is 'pancreatic insufficient'. Unless this is treated with pancreatic enzyme supplements, digestion and absorption of food will be severely impaired. Inadequate absorption of nutrients will lead to unpleasant digestive symptoms such as:

- distended abdomen;
- constipation;
- foul-smelling, greasy stools;
- malnutrition;
- poor growth;
- weight loss;
- specific deficiencies of the fat soluble vitamins and essential fatty acids (Littlewood et al. 2006).

Patients who are well nourished have a better outcome because malnutrition leads to impaired respiratory muscle function, decreased exercise tolerance and immunological impairment resulting in increased susceptibility to infections.

Dietetic management is an integral part of CF care to ensure normal weight gain, growth, body composition, pubertal development and vitamin, mineral and essential fatty acid status. Dietary treatment for CF is achieved by ensuring sufficient pancreatic enzyme through pancreatic enzyme replacement therapy (PERT) which administers the pancreatic enzymes protease, lipase and amylase. The pancreas has both an endocrine and exocrine function that is integral to digestion. The endocrine role is in the production of insulin and glucagon that control carbohydrate metabolism. The exocrine function involves the synthesis and secretion of pancreatic juices into the duodenum via the pancreatic duct. CF can affect both the exocrine and endocrine functions of the pancreas, but most individuals have symptoms associated with the exocrine function, leading to malnutrition due to pancreatic insufficiency.

The pancreatic juices contain:

- sodium bicarbonate, which neutralizes the acidic material from the stomach;
- pancreatic proteases (trypsin and chymotrypsin) that aid digestion by breaking down some proteins (but not all) to amino acids;
- pancreatic lipase, to aid fat digestion by breaking fats down to monoglycerides;
- fatty acids and pancreatic amylase to change starch to maltose.

As Lauren has pancreatic insufficiency she receives PERT. There are various pancreatic enzyme preparations available. All pancreatic insufficient individuals are given enteric-coated, acid-resistant microspheres (small beads in a capsule) pancreatic enzyme preparations (e.g. creon). This is to ensure the enzyme is not destroyed by hydrochloride within the stomach and aids digestion in the duodenum. The capsule therefore should be swallowed whole where possible, but if the capsule is broken open the microsphere beads should be swallowed and not chewed.

There are many factors that affect the efficacy of pancreatic enzymes, including:

- the amount of fat intake;
- the timing of enzyme intake with fatty foods;
- the acidity in the gut;
- GI transit time;
- growth and development.

6   **What sort of dietary advice would be given to Lauren to optimize her nutrition?**

A   The energy requirements of patients with CF vary widely and generally increase with age and disease severity. Lauren, as a 16-year-old adolescent, is growing and requires more enzymes and more calories. Unfortunately, many patients with CF do not manage to eat enough to meet their increased energy requirements. The reasons for this are multifactorial and include chronic poor appetite, infection-related anorexia, gastro-oesophageal reflux, abdominal pain, vomiting and depression (Duff et al. 2003). It is recommended that a detailed dietary assessment and food frequency questionnaire should be performed for all patients every two years, or more often if there are growth problems, in order to identify the factors that may contribute to a reduced energy intake (CF Trust 2009). A review by a dietician experienced in the management of CF will tailor dietary advice to meet to Lauren's needs. There are a number of ways of increasing the energy intake that could be advised, including:

- encouraging frequent meals;
- encouraging high calorie snacks such as crisps and chocolate;
- not restricting dietary fat as this nutrient is essential to achieve a good calorie intake;
- increasing the calorie content of food by frying and roasting;
- increasing the sugar content of diet (drinks, cakes, etc.);
- choosing meat rich in protein;
- choosing dairy foods such as milk, cheese and eggs as good sources of calcium.

   Enzymes should be given with all foods and drinks containing fat. The timing and dose of enzyme administration will be gradually increased until the symptoms of fat malnutrition are controlled (Lowdon et al. 1998).

7   **Why is chest physiotherapy important to improve lung function for Lauren?**

A   Chest physiotherapy is an integral part of the management of CF. Lauren has physiotherapy which she manages herself. There are a wide variety of airway clearance techniques that involve breathing techniques and **postural drainage** and percussion. The aim is to reduce airway obstruction by improving the clearance of the viscid secretions to maintain optimal respiratory function and exercise tolerance. In addition to chest physiotherapy, antibiotics and inhaled medicines that help to open the airways and thin the mucus (*mucolytics*) are also used to help clear mucus from the lungs.

   In normal lung tissue, mucus is secreted from two distinct areas. The epithelium contains mucus-secreting goblet cells and the connective tissue layer beneath the mucosal epithelium serous mucous glands also produces mucus. Continual mucus production is a normal process to keep the airways moist and to trap dust and debris that may enter the lungs. The microscopic hairs (cilia) that line the epithelium aid expectoration of mucus by moving it up to the throat, allowing it to be cleared by coughing.

   Several factors may contribute to respiratory problems in CF. The epithelium lining the airway does not transport salt and water normally, so mucus and other airway secretions are depleted of water. However, there are also chemical changes in the mucus proteins. The mucus becomes so thick that it clogs the airways and provides an environment in which bacteria thrive. In response, white blood cells migrate into the lungs to fight the infection. These white blood cells die and release their genetic material into the mucus that aggravates the already excessive stickiness of the mucus, setting up a vicious cycle of further airway obstruction, inflammation and infection. The bacterial infection results in inflammation and increased mucus production which the cilia are unable to clear effectively. Repeated infections can result in chronic colonization by pseudomonas – infections that lead to chronic lung damage. Lung disease in CF is characterized by endobronchial infection, exaggerated inflammatory response, progressive airway obstruction, bronchiectasis and eventual respiratory failure.

8 **Why has inhaled ciprofloxacin been prescribed and how does it work?**

A Lauren has a new *P. aeruginosa* infection which is a gram-negative bacterium. Patients with *P. aeruginosa* infection have a two- to threefold increased risk of death over an eight-year period (Kosorok et al. 2001). Successful eradication can be achieved in approximately 80% of cases of new infection by various combinations of oral, inhaled and IV antibiotics. There is no consensus on the best combinations, dosage or length of treatment courses. (Li et al. 2009). However, the CF Trust report in 2009 recommended inhaled antibiotics to control infection in patients with *P. aeruginosa*, preserve lung function and decrease the need for additional treatments.

Lauren is treated with ciprofloxacin as an inhaled aerosol. Ciprofloxacin is an antibiotic that belongs to the fluroquinolone class of medications. The fluoroquinolones are a family of synthetic broad-spectrum antibiotics, which eradicate bacteria by interfering with DNA replication. Aerosol antibiotics achieve high local concentrations in the airways, reduce systemic toxicity and have been used successfully for chronic suppressive treatment for established *P. aeruginosa* infections (CF Trust 2009). Antibiotics can be categorized by the pharmacodynamic parameters that best predict **efficacy**. Fluoroquinolones appear to display a 'concentration-dependent' pattern (Geller 2009), that is, the ratio of maximum drug concentration to the minimum inhibitory concentrations (MICs). It is difficult to know how effective the drug is as the therapeutic effect of an inhaled antibiotic depends on the amount of drug deposited in the airways, how well the drug distribution matches the location of the bacteria, and whether the local concentration of antibiotic achieved is adequate to kill the microbes (Geller 2009). Studies have found that, due to a post-antibiotic effect of fluoroquinolones concentrations on *P. aeruginosa*, less frequent doses are required and the medicine may therefore be administered daily or twice daily.

KEY POINTS

- CF is a common heterogeneous disorder with more than 1500 mutations and clinical phenotypes on chromosome 7.
- In CF, the body's secretions, which normally act as a lubricant, have high sodium and low water content and become thick viscid mucus causing obstruction of the body's tubes and ducts.

- The mutation results in a complex multisystem involvement of the GI and respiratory systems.
- CF is diagnosed through a blood test to detect IRT as part of newborn screening.
- The hallmarks of CF include: pancreatic enzyme deficiency due to blockage of the pancreatic duct; progressive chronic obstructive lung disease; gland dysfunction of the CFTR affecting movement of salt and water across the epithelial cell membrane.
- Treatment is through chest physiotherapy and use of antibiotics to control respiratory infections to preserve lung function, dietary management and pancreatic enzyme replacement to optimize nutrition and reduce problems associated with malnutrition.

REFERENCES

CF Trust (2009) *Antibiotic Treatment for Cystic Fibrosis. Report of the UK Cystic Fibrosis Trust Antibiotic Working Group*, 3rd edn. Kent: Cystic Fibrosis Trust.

Duff, A.J.A., Wolfe, S.P., Dickson, C. et al. (2003) Feeding behaviour problems in children with cystic fibrosis in the UK: prevalence and comparison with healthy controls, *Journal of Pediatric Gastroenterology and Nutrition*, 36: 443–7.

Geller, D.E. (2009) Aerosol antibiotics in cystic fibrosis, *Respiratory Care*, 54(5): 658–70.

Goodman, B.E. and Percy W.H. (2005) CFTR in cystic fibrosis and cholera: from membrane transport to clinical practice, *Advanced Physiology Education*, 29: 75–82.

Kosorok, M.R., Zeng, L., West, S.E. et al. (2001) Acceleration of lung disease in children with cystic fibrosis after *Pseudomonas aeruginosa* acquisition, *Pediatric Pulmonology*, 32: 277–87.

Ledford, H. (2012) Drug bests cystic fibrosis, *Nature*, 482: 145.

Li, Z., Kosorok, M.R., Farrell, P.M. et al. (2009) Longitudinal development of mucoid *Pseudomonas aeruginosa* infection and lung disease progression in children with cystic fibrosis, *Journal of the American Medical Association*, 293: 581–8.

Littlewood, J.M., Wolfe, S.P. and Conway, S.P. (2006) Diagnosis and treatment of intestinal malabsorption in cystic fibrosis, *Pediatric Pulmonology*, 41: 35–49.

Lowdon, J., Goodchild, M.C., Ryley, H.C. et al. (1998) Maintenance of growth in cystic fibrosis despite reduction in pancreatic enzyme supplementation, *Archives of Disease in Childhood*, 78: 377–8.

Montgomery, G.S. and Howestine, M. (2009) Cystic fibrosis, *Pediatrics Review*, 30(8): 302–9.

Turner, R.C. and McDermott, R. (2006) Using faecal elastase-1 to screen for chronic pancreatitis in patients admitted with acute pancreatitis, *Journal of the International Hepatic Biliary Association (Oxford)*, 8(3): 223–6.

The person with depression
Paul Barber

CASE AIMS

After examining this case study the reader should be able to:

- Identify the parts of the brain involved in mood regulation.
- Outline the neurotransmitters thought to be involved in pathophysiology of depression.
- Demonstrate an understanding of the reason for prescribing and the mode of action of citalopram.
- Demonstrate an understanding of the reason for prescribing and the mode of action of venlafaxine.
- Discuss the role of the nurse in monitoring and caring for a patient receiving selective serotonin reuptake inhibitors.
- Describe what is meant by serotonin syndrome.
- Discuss the role of the nurse in giving advice about discontinuation syndrome in a service user who suddenly stops their medication.

CASE

Pierre is an extremely successful teacher who is well respected by his peers. Although he has always been thought of as gregarious, outgoing and fun-loving, for the past couple of months he has not been feeling quite himself. He no longer enjoys things they way he used to and he feels a profound sense of sadness on most days; so much so that he feels utterly hopeless about his future. To make matters worse, Pierre's previously healthy appetite has evaporated and he often finds himself waking up very early in the morning and unable to fall asleep again. Although Pierre has always enjoyed hockey and weight training, lately he has found that he just doesn't have the energy to do much of anything. At work, he has been scraping by and cannot seem to concentrate or make quick decisions, both of which have conspired to send his self-esteem and sense of worth into a tailspin.

His friends, co-workers and family are growing increasingly concerned as he is returning phone calls and emails less frequently, and seems very withdrawn and despondent. One evening Pierre finds himself working late and becomes very tearful because he believes he cannot cope with life any more. The next day his wife persuades him to go to the GP who diagnoses depression and prescribes citalopram 20mg once daily. The GP also makes an urgent referral to a psychiatrist and asks him to come back in a week to see her.

1   **What parts of the brain are thought to be involved in regulating Pierre's mood?**

2   **Which neurotransmitters are thought to be involved in the causation of his depression?**

3   **Explain the mode of action of citalopram in helping Pierre become less depressed**

Pierre has now been on citalopram for a number of weeks and reports to the psychiatrist that he has become increasingly anxious and seems unable to relax or rest. He is also complaining of insomnia. The psychiatrist decides that these are side-effects from his current medication and changes his prescription to venlafaxine 75mg daily in two divided doses.

---

4   **Why has Pierre now been prescribed venlafaxine?**

5   **Outline the role of the nurse in monitoring and caring for Pierre while taking his medication**

Pierre is now feeling much better and has returned to work. He visits his GP who has now taken over his care. He says that he does not need the 'tablets' any more and has not taken any for a couple of days.

---

6   **What problems could occur now that Pierre has decided suddenly to stop his venlafaxine because feels he is able to cope without tablets?**

7   **What advice could be given to Pierre in order to prevent or reduce any symptoms of discontinuation of his medicines?**

ANSWERS

1   **What parts of the brain are thought to be involved in regulating Pierre's mood?**

A   Pierre's limbic system is not a structure, but a series of nerve pathways incorporating structures deep within the temporal lobes, such as the **hippocampus** and the **amygdala**. Forming connections with the cerebral cortex, white matter and brainstem, the limbic system is involved in the control and expression of mood and emotion, in the processing and storage of recent memory, and in the control of appetite and emotional responses to food. We can see from the case study that Pierre has lost interest in his food. All these functions are frequently affected in depression and the limbic system has been implicated in the pathogenesis of depression. The limbic system is also linked with parts of the neuroendocrine and autonomic nervous systems, and some neurological disorders, such as anxiety, are associated with both hormonal and autonomic changes (Tortora and Derrickson 2009).

2 **Which neurotransmitters are thought to be involved in the causation of his depression?**

A Evidence now strongly supports the theory that depression has a biologic basis and that certain brain chemicals and neural pathways responsible for regulating mood and associated behaviours are altered. The basic biological causes of depression are strongly linked to abnormalities in the delivery of certain key neurotransmitters (chemical messengers in the brain).

SEROTONIN

Perhaps the most important neurotransmitter in depression is serotonin. Among other functions, it is important for feelings of well-being. Pierre no longer enjoys things the way he used to and feels a profound sense of sadness nearly every day. Indications are that serotonin improves a person's ability to pick up emotional cues from other people, which is important for healthy relationships. People deficient in serotonin are less likely to take risks for high rewards than those with normal levels (Cowen 2002).

OTHER NEUROTRANSMITTERS

Other neurotransmitters possibly involved in depression include acetylcholine and catecholamines, a group of neurotransmitters that consists of dopamine, norepinephrine and epinephrine (also called adrenaline). Corticotrophin-releasing factor (CRF), which is believed to be a stress hormone and a neurotransmitter, is thought to be involved in depression and anxiety. Increased CRF concentrations appear to interact with serotonin and have been detected in patients with either depression or anxiety (Kalia 2005).

3 **Explain the mode of action of citalopram in helping Pierre become less depressed**

A The mechanism of action of citalopram as an antidepressant is presumed to be linked to potentiation of serotonergic activity in the CNS, resulting from its inhibition of CNS neuronal reuptake of serotonin. In vitro and in vivo studies in animals suggest that citalopram is a highly selective serotonin reuptake inhibitor (SSRI) with minimal effects on norepinephrine and dopamine neuronal reuptake. Tolerance to the inhibition of serotonin uptake is not induced by long-term (14-day) treatment of rats with citalopram (Rang et al. 2011).

4 **Why has Pierre now been prescribed venlafaxine?**

A Venlafaxine is an antidepressant in a group of drugs known as selective serotonin and norepinephrine reuptake inhibitors (SSNRIs). Even though its side-effect profile is similar to that of SSRIs, venlafaxine seems to have relative freedom from the side-effects associated with SSRIs (fluoxetine, sertraline, paroxetine, fluvoxamine). It is hypothesized that the action of the venlafaxine molecule on both serotonin and norepinephrine will cause venlafaxine to be a successful antidepressant for some people who have not responded to treatment with SSRIs. As venlafaxine and its active metabolite have relatively short half-lives (4 hours and 11 hours respectively), venlafaxine should be administered in divided doses, two or three times a day (BNF 2012).

5   **Outline the role of the nurse in monitoring and caring for Pierre while taking his medication**

A

- Pierre may feel nauseous, therefore simple advice, such as eating little and often, may be of value. Also, eating simple foods such as dry toast rather than rich foods may be something the service user may wish to contemplate.
- Another common side-effect of these types of medicine is a dry mouth. Therefore, reinforcing the importance of drinking adequate fluids over a 24-hour period will be important (usually 3L). Another tip is to suggest chewing low-sugar gum or sweets in order to promote saliva production.
- You would need to monitor Pierre's vital signs, especially pulse and blood pressure, particularly when initiating treatment. You would need to report any change in Pierre's senses, particularly impending syncope. Syncope is a transient loss of consciousness caused by transient global cerebral hypoperfusion, characterized by rapid onset, short duration and spontaneous complete recovery (European Society of Cardiology 2009). In order to avoid Pierre developing syncope you would avoid abrupt changes in position, monitor vital signs (especially blood pressure) and remind him to report any blood pressure readings (e.g. lower than 80/50mmHg).
- If Pierre suffered from drowsiness then the medicine could be taken at bedtime to aid in sleep and minimize daytime drowsiness. Advise Pierre to ensure he feels his reactions are normal before driving, operating machinery or doing any other jobs which could be dangerous if he were not fully alert. Tell him to avoid alcohol, as this will increase any feelings of drowsiness (BNF 2012). Any sedative effect is likely to be greatest in the first month of treatment, or on increasing the dose. Drugs such as paroxetine have been associated with the highest rate of drowsiness (Greenstein 2009).
- You should monitor Pierre's mental and emotional status. There has been shown to be an increase in suicidal ideation for some time now in children and adolescents who have been prescribed SSRIs/SSNRIs (Hetrick et al. 2007). Although this correlation is rather more unclear in the treatment of adults, you should be risk-assessing, particularly as the therapeutic benefits may be delayed. If severely depressed, and being treated as an outpatient, the service user should have no more than seven days of medication supplied in case of self-harm (DH 2004).
- Part of your role is to observe Pierre for signs and symptoms of improved mood, keeping in mind that it may take two to four weeks to achieve therapeutic effectiveness (the risk of suicide may increase as energy levels rise). The National Institute for Health and Clinical Excellence (NICE) (2009) suggests that advice should be given to the service user with depression about the potential for increased agitation, anxiety and suicidal ideation in the initial stages of treatment. As a result you should be actively seeking out these symptoms and reporting them to the medical staff or GP. Pierre should be advised that it may take

two to four weeks for his mood to improve. He should be reassured that you will always have time to listen and talk to him, especially if he wishes to report any feelings of suicide (Barber and Robertson 2012).

- You should observe Pierre for serotonin syndrome in SSRI use. This is an adverse drug reaction to medicines that increase the amount of serotonin in the CNS. It can occur as a consequence of normal therapeutic drug use, self-poisoning or drug interactions (Boyer and Shannon 2005). Generally you should be looking for three sets of symptoms in Pierre: agitation and **hypervigilance**; increased sweating or heart rate; neuromuscular abnormalities such as temor.

- If serotonin syndrome is suspected, discontinue the drug and initiate supportive care. Respond according to any local emergency department protocols. For example, if the service user has recently ingested or taken a large overdose, then activated charcoal may help to prevent absorption. Supportive measures such as the giving of IV fluids and controlling agitation with benzodiazepines may also be used by the A&E department. One of the problems with serotonin syndrome is that other medicines can cause it to happen. Therefore part of the nurse's role is to educate Pierre to be vigilant about drug combinations and to inform health care workers that he is taking SSRIs (Houlihan 2004).

- According to Rottmann (2007) the use of SSRIs/SSNRIs can also be associated with disruption of the action of the antidiuretic hormone in the body, which affects the individual's homeostasis. This may lead to the syndrome of inappropriate antidiuretic hormone secretion (SIADH), which is characterized by hyponatremia, a potentially fatal condition that is typically asymptomatic until it becomes severe. SIADH is more likely in some populations, including people who are elderly or who take diuretics. Pierre's serum sodium levels may need to be monitored closely, especially if he is at a higher risk.

- Sexual dysfunction could be a real problem for Pierre, so developing an open and honest relationship with him is important. He needs to trust you enough to be able to discuss this type of problem without fear of embarrassment (Rang et al. 2011).

- SSRIs/SSNRIs are associated with an increased risk of bleeding, especially in older people or in people taking other drugs that have the potential to damage the GI mucosa or interfere with clotting. Therefore, Pierre should be educated to avoid taking his SSRI medication with aspirin, warfarin or non-steroidal anti-inflammatory drugs (NSAIDs) such as ibuprofen or naproxen. He should be reassured that if he is already taking medications that may cause GI bleeding, and if no suitable alternative to an SSRI can be found, the doctor may advise him to take another medicine to protect the lining of the gut – for example omeprazole (NICE 2009).

6 **What problems could occur now that Pierre has decided suddenly to stop his venlafaxine because he feels he is able to cope without tablets?**

A Discontinuation symptoms typically arise within days after stopping medication, particularly if it was stopped abruptly. After some people stop taking SSNRIs, they experience a variety of symptoms including:

- a flu-like reaction;
- headache;

- GI distress;
- faintness;
- strange sensations of vision or touch.

This common phenomenon is known as discontinuation syndrome. It may also be known as SSNRI withdrawal syndrome (Michelson et al. 2000). Other symptoms of discontinuation are similar to discontinuing other antidepressants, including:

- irritability;
- restlessness;
- headache;
- nausea;
- fatigue;
- excessive sweating;
- dysphoria;
- tremor;
- vertigo;
- irregularities in blood pressure;
- dizziness;
- visual and auditory hallucinations;
- feelings of abdominal distension and paraesthesia.

Other non-specific mental symptoms may include:

- impaired concentration;
- bizarre dreams;
- delirium;
- agitation;
- hostility;
- worsening of depressive symptoms.

7   **What advice could be given to Pierre in order to prevent or reduce any symptoms of discontinuation of his medicines?**

A
- Pierre should be advised not to suddenly stop taking his medication. People may stop their medicine abruptly for various reasons, including feeling better or experiencing unpleasant side-effects, as well as simply forgetting to renew a prescription. However, as noted above, stopping some medicines abruptly can cause discontinuation or withdrawal symptoms.
- Pierre should be encouraged to talk to his doctor. He should be able to voice any concerns he has so that he does not attempt to stop medicating without help. It should be a collaborative venture between the service user and the doctor. In physical conditions, communication between the service user and the physician within the consultation has also been shown to play an important role in influencing treatment adherence (Hunot et al. 2007).

- One of the best ways to minimize discontinuation syndrome is by reducing the dose slowly. The service user should be advised to work together with their doctor and together decide how to reduce, and then stop, the dose (Haddad and Anderson 2007).
- It is important that the service user be advised not to discontinue if they are under a lot of stress, not sleeping well, not eating nourishing foods, or not sticking to a consistent schedule. Under these conditions stopping their medicine successfully may be unrealistic and could increase anxiety and depression, making stopping even harder.

KEY POINTS

- The limbic system is involved in the control and expression of mood and emotion, in the processing and storage of recent memory, and in the control of appetite and emotional responses to food.
- The basic biological causes of depression are strongly linked to abnormalities in the delivery of certain key neurotransmitters (chemical messengers in the brain).
- The mechanism of action of citalopram as an antidepressant is presumed to be linked to potentiation of serotonergic activity in the CNS.
- Venlafaxine, an SSNRI, affects both serotonin and norepinephrine which is why it is a successful antidepressant for people who have not responded to treatment with SSRIs.
- A person taking SSRIs/SSNRIs requires careful monitoring to avoid dangerous adverse reactions and drug interactions. Some of the more common adverse reactions include anxiety, insomnia, somnolence and palpitations.
- Service users taking citalopram should be carefully monitored for orthostatic hypotension. SSRIs/SSNRIs have also been linked with an increase in suicidal ideation and aggression.
- Many of the drug interactions with SSRIs/SSNRIs are associated with their ability to competitively inhibit one of the liver enzymes that helps metabolize numerous drugs, including antipsychotics, carbamazepine, metoprolol and flecainide.
- Using SSRIs/SSNRIs with other medicines can cause a serious, potentially fatal reaction, called serotonin syndrome.
- One of the most severe adverse reactions of SSRIs/SSNRIs may occur when the patient stops taking the medication.

REFERENCES

Barber, P. and Robertson, D. (2012) *Essentials of Pharmacology for Nurses*, 2nd edn. Maidenhead: Open University Press.

BNF (British National Formulary) (2012) *BNF 63: March*. London: Pharmaceutical Press.

Boyer, E.W. and Shannon, M. (2005) The serotonin syndrome, *New England Journal of Medicine*, 352(11): 1112–20.

Cowen, P.J. (2002) Cortisol, serotonin and depression: all stressed out, *British Journal of Psychiatry*, 180: 99–100.

DH (Department of Health) (2004) *National Service Framework for Mental Health, 5 Years On*. London: DH.

European Society of Cardiology (2009) Guidelines for the diagnosis and management of syncope, *European Heart Journal*, 30: 2631–71.

Greenstein, B. (2009) *Clinical Pharmacology for Nurses*, 18th edn. Edinburgh: Churchill Livingstone.

Haddad, P.M. and Anderson, I. M. (2007) Recognising and managing antidepressant discontinuation symptoms, *Advances in Psychiatric Treatment*, 13(6): 447.

Hetrick, S., Merry, S., McKenzie, J., Sindahl, P. and Proctor, M. (2007) Selective serotonin reuptake inhibitors (SSRIs) for depressive disorders in children and adolescents, *Cochrane Database Systematic Reviews* (3): CD004851, doi:10.1002/14651858.CD004851.pub2.

Houlihan, D.J. (2004) Serotonin syndrome resulting from coadministration of tramadol, venlafaxine, and mirtazapine, *The Annals of Pharmacotherapy*, 38(3): 411–13.

Hunot, V.M., Horne, R., Leese, M.N. and Churchill, R.C. (2007) A cohort study of adherence to anti-depressants in primary care: the influence of antidepressant concerns and treatment preferences, *The Primary Care Companion to the Journal of Clinical Psychiatry*, 9(2): 91–9.

Kalia, M. (2005) Neurobiological basis of depression: an update, *Metabolism*, 54(5): 24–7.

Michelson, D., Fava, M., Amsterdam, J. et al. (2000) Interruption of selective serotonin reuptake inhibitor treatment: double-blind, placebo-controlled trial, *British Journal of Psychiatry*, 176: 363–8.

NICE (National Institute for Health and Clinical Excellence) (2009) *Clinical Guideline 90: Depression in Adults*. London: NICE.

Rang, H.P., Dale, M.M., Ritter, J.M, Flower, R.J. and Henderson, G. (2011) *Rang and Dale's Pharmacology*, 7th edn. Oxford: Churchill Livingstone.

Rottmann, C.N. (2007) SSRIs and the syndrome if inappropriate antidiuretic hormone secretion, *American journal of Nursing*. 107(1), 51–8.

Tortora, G.J. and Derrickson, B.H. (2009) *Essentials of Anatomy and Physiology*, 8th edn. London: Wiley.

The young person with type 1 diabetes mellitus

Ruth Sadik

CASE AIMS

After examining this case study the reader should be able to:

- Briefly explain what is meant by type 1 diabetes.
- Discuss the possible causes of type 1 diabetes.
- Explain why type 1 diabetes can lead to **ketoacidosis** and coma.
- Discuss the normal formation and function of insulin.
- Describe why insulin is prescribed to people with type 1 diabetes.
- Outline why a young person's blood glucose may be difficult to stabilize.
- Discuss the role of the nurse in assisting a patient with type 1 diabetes and their family to maintain their insulin regimen.

CASE

Jamie is a 15-year-old who was diagnosed with type 1 diabetes mellitus at the age of 3 when he was admitted to hospital with diabetic ketoacidosis in a comatose state. At initial diagnosis Jamie's blood pH was 7.18 and his blood glucose (BG) level was 7mmol/L. Although he had shown signs of weight loss and excessive thirst, at the time his parents thought he was 'coming down with something'. They were devastated when they were told that their son had diabetes and were not fully prepared for the impact this would have on their lives.

1 **What is diabetes mellitus?**

2 **Discuss the possible cause of Jamie's type 1 diabetes**

3 **Explain why Jamie's diabetes led to ketoacidosis and coma**

> *Despite his parents' initial distress, by the age of 5 Jamie was helping to give his own insulin and by 9 he was self-managing with limited support from the family, dietician, medical and community nursing services. Jamie is currently prescribed subcutaneous insulin three times a day at 1.3 units/kg per day.*

4 Discuss the normal formation and function of insulin

5 Why has Jamie been prescribed insulin?

> *Over the past six months Jamie's parents have been extremely anxious as he has been experiencing severe nocturnal hypoglycaemic attacks associated with seizures. His mother realizes that he has been drinking alcohol when out with friends and tries to get him to eat toast or cereal when he comes in; however, she is not always around. She is also concerned as Jamie has been eating out but missing his insulin in an attempt to appear 'normal like his mates'.*

6 Why may Jamie's blood glucose be difficult to stabilize at his age?

7 Identify the role of the nurse in assisting Jamie and his family to maintain his insulin regimen

ANSWERS

1 What is diabetes mellitus?

A Type 1 diabetes is a complex and chronic long-term condition in which the child or young person cannot metabolize carbohydrate or sugar due to a lack of insulin production by the β-cells of the Islets of Langerhans in the pancreas and the resultant disturbance of protein and fat metabolism (Hirschorn 2003; McCance and Huether 2010). The incidence of diabetes in childhood has increased over the last 20 years and according to Diabetes UK (2010) now affects almost 3 children per 1000 by the age of 18 years in England, a figure reflected in other parts of the UK (National Centre for Social Research 2008; NHS Scotland 2009). The condition is rare before 9 months old and peaks at 12 years of age (DH 2010).

2 Discuss the possible cause of Jamie's type 1 diabetes

A The interplay of both environmental and genetic factors is implicated in causation, although most authors concur that there is no one, known, cause (King 2003; Meetoo et al. 2007).

GENETIC INHERITANCE

According to the Scottish Intercollegiate Guidelines Network (SIGN 2010), 12–15% of young people under 15 with diabetes have an affected first-degree relative. SIGN also points out that children are three times more likely to develop diabetes if their father has or had the disease than if their mother has or had it. Of patients with CF, 20% will develop secondary diabetes by the age of 20, with the incidence increasing to 80% by 35 years. Genetic factors appear to play a greater part in children who are diagnosed with diabetes under the age of 5, than at any other time (Raine et al. 2011).

Maturity onset diabetes of the young

Maturity onset diabetes of the young (MODY) is the most recently identified cause of diabetes in young people. MODY is a familial **autosomal dominant** condition that affects children of affected parents. All children of an affected parent with MODY have a 50% chance of inheriting the affected gene and developing MODY themselves (Matyka et al. 1998; Kirby 2005).

Autoimmune theory

Heredity appears to be mainly via the human leukocyte antigen (HLA) complex, which is determined by chromosome 6 in humans, resulting in an intolerance of IA-2 (insulinoma-associated tyrosine phosphatase-like protein, or islet cell antigen 512 [ICA512]). This leads to destruction of the β-cells with small islets and subsequent decline in insulin production. There is frequent presence of macrophages, T and B lymphocytes and natural killer cells. However, there is evidence that less than 10% of those children and young people with HLA-conferred diabetes susceptibility do progress to develop the clinical disease, again highlighting the multifactorial nature of diabetes (Knip et al. 2005; Daneman 2006; Marieb et al. 2010).

ENVIRONMENTAL FACTORS

A number of theories have been postulated regarding the aetiology of type 1 diabetes. The most important environmental factors appear to be infectious, dietary, perinatal and psycho-social. **Enteroviruses** (especially *Coxsackie B* virus), breastfeeding, the early presence or lack of certain foods, birth weight, childhood over-nutrition, maternal islet autoimmunity and negative stress events have been shown to be related to the prevalence of type 1 diabetes. There is also an increased risk if the child has autoimmune **co-morbidity** such as rheumatoid arthritis, hypothyroidism, Addison's disease or celiac disease, or if there is a family history (Davendra et al. 2004; Porth 2005; Peng and Hagopian 2006).

3 **Explain why Jamie's diabetes led to ketoacidosis and coma**

A
- In Jamie's circumstances the β-cells of the pancreas have been destroyed and so insulin is not produced, causing the blood glucose level to rise above the normal values of 4–5.9mmol/L (SIGN 2010).
- In an attempt to regain homeostasis, a hyperosmolar diuresis occurs where glucose, sodium and potassium are excreted in the urine, leading to increased fluid loss, hyponatraemia, hypokalaemia and dehydration, which is when Jamie would become thirsty (DH 2010).

- As the cells of the body are unable to uptake glucose from the bloodstream, the counter-regulatory hormone glucagon is secreted from the α-cells of the Islets of Langerhans to convert fat into fatty acids and glycerol which can provide a less efficient, emergency form of energy. The metabolism of fatty acids also creates byproducts of ketone bodies which are mainly acids, and these lower the blood pH as the body buffer system, bicarbonate (HCO_3^-), is used up, with subsequent acidosis (Lewis 2000; McFarlane 2011).
- This is enhanced by dehydration as the acids cannot be secreted into the urine for excretion and so the cycle escalates.
- In an attempt to rid the body of the excessive acids in the form of carbon dioxide and carbonic acid, the respiratory rate increases and deepens (Kussmaul's respirations), and breath may be noted to smell of 'pear drops' or 'plaster remover', but this is not universal.
- The protein carrier GLUT (glucose transporters) 3 cannot convey glucose into the neurons at acidotic pH levels, and so Jamie would experience increasing confusion and eventual loss of consciousness.

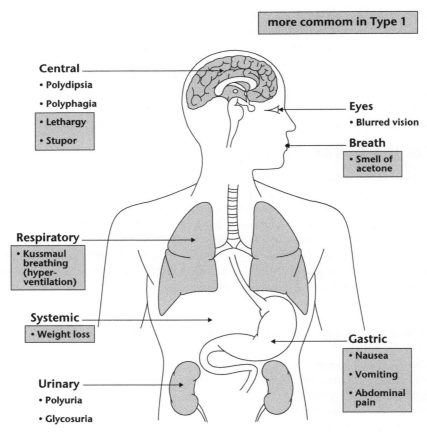

Figure 9.1 Main symptoms of diabetes

4 **Discuss the normal formation and function of insulin**

A # NATURAL INSULIN FORMATION

Insulin is composed of a complex form of amino acid polypeptide which is synthesized in the β-cells as a monomer (single insulin molecule unit) and is stored in a readily available inactive hexamer (6 insulin molecule unit) granule form in the pancreas.

Approximately one to two hours following a meal, insulin is secreted every three to six minutes from the pancreas in pulses into the portal vein, which brings variable amounts of blood into the liver depending on the ingestion of food (Nair 2007a; White and Porterfield 2007). This pulsatile timing is thought to assist the liver in extracting insulin from the blood while maintaining an even blood glucose supply to the cells.

ACTION OF INSULIN

The only mechanism by which cells can take in glucose is via facilitated diffusion (Nair 2007b). A specialized group of proteins known as facilitated GLUT 1–4 transport glucose into specific cell types, across the plasma cell membrane (White and Porterfield 2007). These are:

- GLUT 1, which is responsible for the uptake of glucose and vitamin C by erythrocytes and barrier membranes such as the blood–brain and blood–testicular barriers. The entrance of glucose into erythrocytes generates glycosolated haemoglobin (also known as HbA1c) that is used as the determinant for the stability of diabetes (normal range 4–5.9%).
- GLUT 2, which also carries glucosamine and enables the pancreas and liver to utilize glucose and facilitates renal reabsorption of glucose.
- GLUT 3 is the most important carrier of glucose for sperm, white cells and neurons as it has the highest affinity for glucose and a fivefold greater transport capacity than any of the other transport proteins.
- GLUT 4 is the only insulin-dependent carrier protein and is found in myocytes in striated muscle and adipocytes in fat, which are the main reactor cells to insulin. Where insulin is low, GLUT 4 is locked in an inactive state into intracellular vesicles of fat and muscle. Once in contact with insulin, a protein cascade system is implemented that results in the vesicles being translocated to the cell membrane with which they fuse. GLUT 4 transporters are inserted and become available for transporting glucose across the cell membrane into the cell, resulting in increased glucose absorption (Butler and Kirk 2011).

In order to provide the most efficient energy source for the body, the process of glycolysis is employed. This is the way in which a single molecule of glucose (a 6 carbon sugar) is reconstituted into two three-carbon sugars while generating two molecules of adenosine triphosphate (ATP), two molecules of reduced nicotinamide adenine dinucleotide (NADH), two of pyruvic acid and two of water. This is a process that can occur with or without the presence of oxygen; however, if oxygen is present the process is much more energy efficient (Xuxia and Garvey 2010).

The actions of insulin (indirect and direct) on cells include (Lewis 2000; Kirby 2005; Daneman 2006; Nair 2007a; Holt et al. 2010; Porth 2010; Butler and Kirk 2011):

- *Increased glycogen synthesis* – insulin facilitates the storage of glucose in liver and muscle cells in the form of glycogen. Lowered levels of insulin cause liver cells to convert glycogen to glucose and excrete it into the blood.
- *Decreased gluconeogenesis* – decreases production of glucose from non-sugar substrates, primarily in the liver, as the majority of endogenous insulin arriving at the liver is utilized here. Lack of insulin causes glucose production from assorted substrates in the liver and elsewhere.
- *Increased lipid synthesis* – insulin enables fat cells to take in blood lipids, which are converted to triglycerides; lack of insulin causes the reverse.
- *Decreased lipolysis* – insulin creates a reduction in the conversion of fat cell lipid stores into blood fatty acids. A lack of insulin reverses this process.
- *Increased esterification of fatty acids* – adipose tissue manufactures triglycerides from fatty acid esters. A lack of insulin causes the reverse.
- *Decreased proteolysis* – decreases the breakdown of protein.
- *Increased amino acid uptake* – where circulating amino acids are absorbed by the cells, while a lack of insulin inhibits absorption.
- *Increased potassium uptake* – via the absorption of serum potassium. Lack of insulin inhibits absorption.
- *Arterial muscle tone* – causes arterial wall muscle to relax, increasing blood flow, especially in microarteries. Lack of insulin reduces flow by allowing these muscles to contract.
- *Increased secretion of hydrochloric acid* – by parietal cells in the stomach.
- *Decreased* – renal sodium excretion.

DEGRADATION OF INSULIN

Once the insulin molecule has fused with the receptor in the cell plasma wall and effected its action, it may be released back into the extracellular environment or be degraded by the cell. This is mainly effected in the liver and the kidneys. While the liver clears most insulin during first-pass transit, the kidneys do so in the systemic circulation. Degradation normally involves endocytosis of the insulin-receptor complex, where it is engulfed by the cells, followed by exposure to insulin-degrading enzyme (IDE) which breaks the polypeptide B bond of insulin. An insulin molecule produced endogenously by the pancreatic β-cells is estimated to be degraded within about an hour of its initial release into circulation (Levy 2011).

5 **Why has Jamie been prescribed insulin?**

A Type 1 diabetes is controlled by giving insulin. As we have discussed this helps glucose to be absorbed into the cells and converted into energy, which stops it building up in the person's blood. Insulin injections are the most common form of treatment, where the patient injects insulin under their skin. Jamie will usually inject himself before meals, using either a small needle or a pen-type syringe with replaceable cartridges. There are several different kinds of insulin that work at different rates and act for different lengths of time (see Table 9.1).

Table 9.1 Types of insulin

Insulin type and action

Rapid acting analogue (clear)
Onset: 10–15 minutes
Peak: 60–90 minutes
Duration: 4–5 hours

Fast acting (clear)
Onset: 0.5–1 hour
Peak: 2–4 hours
Duration: 5–8 hours

Intermediate acting (cloudy)
Onset: 1–3 hours
Peak: 5–8 hours
Duration: up to 18 hours

Long acting (cloudy)
Onset: 3–4 hours
Peak: 8–15 hours
Duration: 22–26 hours

Extended long-acting analogue
Onset: 90 minutes
Duration: 24 hours

Premixed (cloudy)
These insulins are presented as a single vial which contains a fixed ratio of insulins (a percentage of rapid/fast-acting to a percentage of intermediate/long-acting)

6 **Why may Jamie's blood glucose be difficult to stabilize at his age?**

A • **Vacillations** in blood glucose levels during adolescence are relatively common. Hyperglycaemia (any blood glucose above 10mmol/L) can be due to the increase in growth hormone secretion associated with a rapid increase in size, which is frequently accompanied by increased appetite. This may call for an increase in insulin dose up to 2 units/kg/day), which the adolescent may not administer in an attempt to prevent hypoglycaemic attacks (SIGN 2010; Wilson 2010; Raine et al. 2011).
  • Hypoglycaemia (blood glucose below 4mmol/L), is most common at this period in life as many young people undertake exercise or dance as part of a healthy lifestyle, which rapidly uses up glucose and hence their insulin supply. In an attempt to avert this, young people prefer to run their 'sugars high' (Wilson 2008, 2010a; Raine et al. 2011).
  • Wilson's research in 2010 highlights the dilemmas that young people can experience when attempting to socialize and fit in with their social peers: 'I find the pressure to drink in order to have a good time difficult when my mates all want to go to the pub at weekends and, even if I have orange juice, it still puts my blood [glucose] up. Once, someone put

vodka in my orange juice and my blood sugar shot down, then up again really high later on. It was a nightmare. You can't give yourself more insulin as you don't know what's working from your evening meal. Eating out and injecting at different times is also difficult. It's easier to just enjoy yourself and not worry about the diabetes' (p. 27).

7   **Identify the role of the nurse in assisting Jamie and his family to maintain his insulin regimen**

A

- The role of the nurse is to perform an exacting assessment of the young person's lifestyle that includes the family. The stress and anxiety that family members can suffer with regard to the child with diabetes has been identified, while young people felt that they matured faster than their peers but that taking responsibility for self could be difficult because of this parental protection and anxiety (Grey 2000; Grey et al. 2000; Huss and Enskar 2007; Streisand et al. 2010).
- Health promotion with regard to healthy eating, exercise, the use and abuse of insulin, injection site maintenance, effects of alcohol consumption on blood glucose levels and its impact in terms of longer-term complications should be undertaken (NICE 2003; Nair 2007b; Butler and Kirk 2011).
- Monitoring blood glucose levels is an important part in the nursing management of children and young people with diabetes. It is recommended (Diabetes UK 2010) that patients with diabetes should aim to maintain their blood glucose levels at 4–6mmol/L before meals (preprandial) and 9mmol/L or less two hours after meals (postprandial). When children are young their blood glucose should be above 10mmol/L prior to bed while older children should have a blood glucose of above 7mmol/L to prevent nocturnal hypoglycaemia (NICE 2004).
- HbA1c should be monitored annually to assess the patient's reporting veracity. This is especially the case with young people, who, like Jamie, may find controlling diet and balancing lifestyle with insulin very difficult.
- If, as with Jamie, hypoglycaemia does occur, then a short-acting carbohydrate such as glucose tablets or drinks, or a snack-sized chocolate bar should be eaten followed by a longer-acting and more complex foodstuff such as bread, cereal or pasta to prevent a reoccurrence.
- Glucose gel rubbed on the inside of the mouth may be necessary if the child or young person is unable or unwilling to eat. If all else fails, intramuscular glucagon (0.5mg if body weight is less than 25kg or 1mg if more than 25kg) (SIGN 2010; Raine et al. 2011).

KEY POINTS

- Diabetes mellitus is one of the most common chronic conditions of childhood.
- The causes remain vague, but genetic, environmental and social factors have been implicated.

- Type 1 diabetes mellitusis treated by the subcutaneous administration of insulin but as many factors such as diet, exercise, emotion, general health and well-being can impact on blood glucose control, both hypo- and hyperglycaemia can occur.
- The role of the nurse is assisting the individual and family to maintain stable blood glucose control in an effort to delay the onset of complications.
- Young people should be informed of the importance of maintaining insulin and carbohydrate balance.

REFERENCES

Butler, G. and Kirk, J. (2011) *Paediatric Endocrinology and Diabetes*. Oxford: Oxford University Press.

Daneman, D. (2006) Type 1 diabetes, *Lancet*, 367(9513): 847–58.

Davendra, D., Liu, E. and Eisenbarth, G.S. (2004) Type 1 diabetes: recent developments, *British Medical Journal*, 328: 750–4.

D H (Department of Health) (2010) *Six Years On: Delivering the Diabetes National Service Framework*. London: D H.

Diabetes U K (2010) *Diabetes in the UK 2010: Key Statistics on Diabetes*. London: Diabetes U K.

Grey, M. (2000) Coping and diabetes, *Diabetes Spectrum*, 13(3): 167.

Grey, M., Boland, E.A., Davidson, M. and Tamborlane, W.V. (2000) Coping skills training for youth with diabetes mellitus has long-lasting effects on metabolic control and quality of life, *Journal of Pediatrics*, 137(1): 107–13.

Hirschhorn, J.N. (2003) Genetic epidemiology of type 1 diabetes, *Pediatric Diabetes*, 4(2): 87–100.

Holt, R.I.G., Goldstein, B.J., Flyvbjerg, A. and Cockram, C. (2010) *Textbook of Diabetes*. Oxford: Wiley-Blackwell.

Huss, K. and Enskar, K. (2007) Adolescents' experiences of living with diabetes, *Paediatric Nursing*, 19(3): 29–31.

King, K.M. (2003) Diabetes: classification and strategies for integrated care, *British Journal of Nursing*, 12(20): 1204–10.

Kirby, M. (2005) Maturity onset of diabetes in the young, *British Journal of Primary Care Nursing*, 2(4): 176–8.

Knip, M., Veijola, R., Virtanen, S.M., Hyöty, H., Vaarala, O. and Åkerblom, H.K. (2005) Environmental triggers and determinants of type 1 diabetes, *Diabetes*, 54(Suppl. 2): S125–36.

Levy, D. (2011) *Practical Diabetes Care*, 3rd edn. Oxford: Wiley Blackwell.

Lewis, R. (2000) Diabetic emergencies, part 2, hyperglycaemia, *Accident and Emergency Nursing*, 8: 24–30.

Marieb, E.N., Hoehn, E. and Hoehn, K. (2010) *Human Anatomy and Physiology*. St Louis, M O: Mosby.

Matyka, K.A., Beards, F., Appleton, M., Ellard, S., Hattersley, A. and Dunger, D.B. (1998) Genetic testing for maturity onset diabetes of the young in childhood hyperglycaemia, *Archives of Disease in Childhood*, 78: 552–4.

McCance, K.L. and Heuther S.L. (2010) *Pathophysiology: The Biological Basis for Disease in Adults and Children*, 5th edn. St Louis, M O: Mosby.

McFarlane, K. (2011) An overview of diabetic ketoacidosis in children, *Paediatric Nursing Journal*, 23(1): 14–19.

Meetoo, D., McGovern, P. and Safadi, R. (2007) An epidemiological overview of diabetes across the world, *British Journal of Nursing*, 16(6): 1002–7.

Nair, M. (2007a) Diabetes mellitus part 1: physiology and complications, *British Journal of Nursing,* 16(3): 184–8.

Nair, M. (2007b) Nursing management of the person with diabetes melitus, part 2, *British Journal of Nursing,* 16(4): 232–5.

National Centre for Social Research (2008) *Welsh Health Survey.* London: National Centre for Social Research.

NHS Scotland (2009) *Scottish Diabetes Survey.* Edinburgh: NHS Scotland.

NICE (National Institute for Health and Clinical Excellence) (2003) *Technical Appraisal 60: Diabetes (Types 1 and 2) – Patient Education Models.* London: NICE.

NICE (National Institute for Health and Clinical Excellence) (2004) *Clinical Guideline 15: Type 1 Diabetes.* London: NICE.

Peng, H. and Hagopian, W. (2006) Environmental factors in the development of type 1 diabetes, *Reviews in Endocrine and Metabolic Disorders,* 7(3): 149–62.

Porth, C.M. (2010) *Pathophysiology Concepts of Altered Health States,* 7th edn. Philadelphia, PA: Lippincott Williams & Wilkins.

Raine, J.E., Donaldson, M., Gregory, J.W. and Savage, M.O. (2011) *Practical Endocrinology and Diabetes in Childhood.* Oxford: Wiley Blackwell.

SIGN (Scottish Intercollegiate Guidelines Network) (2010) *Management of Diabetes: National Clinical Guideline 116.* Edinburgh: SIGN.

Streisand, R., Mackey, E.R. and Herge, W. (2010) Associations of parent coping, stress, and well-being in mothers of children with diabetes: examination of data from a national sample, *Maternal and Child Health Journal,* 14: 612–17.

White, B. and Porterfield, S.M. (2007) *Endocrine Physiology,* 3rd edn. St Louis, MO: Mosby.

Wilson, V. (2008) Experiences of parents of young people with diabetes using insulin pump therapy, *Paediatric Nursing Journal,* 20(2): 14–18.

Wilson, V. (2010) Students' experiences of managing type 1 diabetes, *Paediatric Nursing Journal,* 22(10): 25–8.

Xuxia, W. and Garvey, W.T. (2010) Insulin action, in R.I.G. Holt, B.J. Goldstein, A. Flyvbjerg and C. Cockram (eds) *Textbook of Diabetes.* Oxford: Wiley Blackwell.

The person with diabetes mellitus type 2

Abe Ginourie

CASE AIMS

After examining this case study the reader should be able to:

- Briefly explain what observations and investigations would be carried out in order to diagnose type 2 diabetes.
- Describe the pathophysiology of type 2 diabetes in order to explain the symptoms.
- Discuss the advice the nurse would give regarding diet and exercise in managing type 2 diabetes.
- Outline the key points of the National Institute for Health and Clinical Excellence (NICE) guidelines with regard to oral hypoglycaemics.
- Demonstrate an understanding of the mode of action and side-effects of metformin.

CASE

Deborah Jones, aged 55, has been complaining of feeling tired, generally feeling unwell and being thirsty all the time. She complains that her feet have been feeling 'hot'. She has also been unkind to her children, shouting and arguing with them for no apparent reason. She complains of craving for chocolates and sweet things. She says she knows something is not right. On examination, Mrs Jones explains that she has noticed she has been going to the toilet more than in the past, sometimes getting up at night three to four times. She also complains of itchiness 'down below' (pruritis vulvae) and blurred vision, which she attributes to 'getting old'. Mrs Jones is also overweight with a body mass index (BMI) of 28.

1 **What observations and investigations would the doctor carry out in order to confirm the diagnosis?**

2 **Why has Mrs Jones developed symptoms of feeling thirsty, tired and suffering polyuria, nocturia and itchiness?**

3 **Discuss the role that diet and exercise will have in managing Mrs Jones' type 2 diabetes.**

After three months, Mrs Jones returns to the practice still complaining of feeling tired, thirsty and getting up five to six times a night to go the toilet. Her blood glucose is 15mmol/L. Her HbA1c is 59 mmol/mol (7.5%). On further questioning, it is discovered that Mrs Jones has not been following any specific meal plan as advised by the dietician. Mrs Says that because of her job and children and other commitments, she does not have time to comply with the meal plan. She tends to cook a high-energy food, with a large amount of fried foods. She also says that she cannot fit the suggested exercise plan into her busy lifestyle. The doctor advises her that he must start her on metformin, an oral hypoglycaemic, because the lifestyle advice about diet and exercise has failed to achieve the target blood glucose and HbA1c as recommended by NICE.

4 **What are the key points of the NICE guidelines with regard to oral hypoglycaemics?**

5 **What are the modes of action and side-effects of metformin?**

ANSWERS

1 **What observations and investigations would the doctor carry out in order to confirm the diagnosis?**

(A) HISTORY

The following are key areas when taking this person's history:

- It is important that the doctor considers other illnesses. Malignancy of the liver or pancreas, **hyperparathyroidism** and **Cushing's disease** may produce signs and symptoms similar to diabetes mellitus.
- There are some commonly used medications that may precipitate diabetes mellitus. They are also known as diabetogenic drugs. Some examples are steroids, beta-blockers, such as atenolol, and thiazide diuretics.
- Mrs Jones will be asked about her smoking habits and alcohol intake.
- Her occupational history is also important. Diabetes mellitus, if left uncontrolled and unmanaged, may interfere with judgement and dexterity.
- The doctor will also be asking about any symptoms suggestive of current vascular symptoms – for example, chest pain, breathlessness or orthopnoea (Wass et al. 2011).

EXAMINATION

The doctor will do a complete physical examination, focusing on the cardiovascular assessment. A major complication of diabetes mellitus is macro-vascular complications, such as:

- hypertension;
- heart disease;
- stroke.

Another set of complications is micro-vascular problems, such as:

- diabetic retinopathy;
- neuropathy;
- nephropathy (National Collaborating Centre for Chronic Conditions for NICE 2008).

The doctor will also do a foot examination, including the main pulses in the lower limbs:

- the femoral;
- the popliteal;
- the dorsalis pedis;
- the posterior tibial.

Absence of these pulses may suggest that the artery may be blocked by atheroma, thrombosis or by an embolus. Remember that Mrs Jones complained that her feet were feeling hot. Absence and/or lack of feelings, and 'pins and needles' in her feet and legs may be suggestive of **peripheral neuropathy**.

A complete examination may find that there is some evidence of infection, such as a 'boil', which may have precipitated Mrs Jones into frank diabetes. Mrs Jones is also overweight, which may be a contributing factor.

INVESTIGATIONS

- According to the American Diabetes Association (2012), type 2 diabetes is diagnosed if the 'fasting plasma glucose' level is 6.9mmol/L or greater. In a person who has no symptoms, the investigation must be repeated. If the repeat test is also above 6.9mmol/L, then the person is diagnosed with diabetes mellitus.
- A random plasma glucose level is inexpensive and convenient to obtain, and most people find the test acceptable. However, it has poor sensitivity and specificity compared with the glucose tolerance test. If a random glucose test is used, the findings have to be interpreted with great care, since there may be a risk of a missed diagnosis.
- A fasting plasma glucose level has greater sensitivity and specificity than the random plasma glucose level. However, if the repeat test is normal, the patient would be advised to be monitored regularly by the doctor or nurse. The patient has to fast for at least eight hours prior to the blood test.

- The gold standard for the diagnosis of diabetes is the 75g oral glucose tolerance test. The two-hour plasma glucose level (after a 75g oral glucose load) must be 11.1mmol/L or greater to confirm the diagnosis of diabetes mellitus. However, some clinicians may feel that this option is not feasible for most people because of the demands and costs involved, and they may find a fasting glucose level more acceptable.
- The doctor would ask for a blood test known as HbA1c (glycosylated haemoglobin). This test is also used to monitor the progress of Mrs Jones' diabetes. Glycosylated haemoglobin (HbA1c) is a blood test that measures the average plasma glucose concentration over two to three months. This gives a good indication of the blood glucose level in the previous two to three months. If Mrs Jones' blood glucose is normal, it will produce a normal amount of glycosylated haemoglobin, which is in the range 20–42mmol/mol (4–6%). However, if Mrs Jones' HbA1c is above 48 mmol/mol (6.5%) it may indicate that she has diabetes mellitus. However, to establish a definitive diagnosis, there must be two different criteria – for example, a combination of an elevated HbA1c and elevated fasting plasma glucose.
- A urine test may be carried out to investigate for glucose, **acetone** and albumin. If acetone is found then Mrs Jones' diabetes is in urgent need of control and this will be done before any investigations are undertaken.
- Blood would be taken to test urea and electrolytes (U&Es) and **creatinine**. This is to ensure that Mrs Jones' electrolytes are well within parameters, because a consequence of polyuria is electrolyte loss. Electrolyte imbalance may cause cardiac arrhythmias. Fasting lipids will be carried out, since a high level in people with diabetes predisposes them to acute coronary disease.
- An electrocardiograph may also be done to assess the physiology of the heart and detect any abnormalities early on.

2 **Why has Mrs Jones developed symptoms of feeling thirsty, tired and suffering polyuria, nocturia and itchiness?**

A
- Polyuria is the act of going to the toilet for passing urine more frequently than normal. It is caused by osmotic diuresis caused by a high glucose level in the blood (glycosuria). Getting up at night more than usual to empty the bladder is known as nocturia.
- A pruritis vulva in women is the result of glycosuria and candida infection. Infection is present because hyperglycaemia increases the risk of infection and also because infections stimulate the secretion of stress hormones which weaken the immune system. We know that 50% of women have candida living naturally in their vagina without it causing any problems. However, in diabetes mellitus, the high level of glucose surrounding the vagina affects the balance of acidity and alkalinity, causing an increase in the growth of the yeast-like fungi called candida. Candida causes pruritus vulvae (vaginal thrush) in women, and should be a warning sign for diabetes mellitus.
- Feeling tired is due to the fact that there is a shortage of energy being produced from the carbohydrate ingested, due to either insulin deficiency or resistance to insulin action in the peripheral tissues or both. The energy deficit may be due to glucose being lost through the urine, which may amount to several calories per day.
- Blurred vision is due to glucose-related osmotic changes to the shape of the lens.

- Feeling hot or suffering from 'burning' feet may be due to sensory nerve involvement, or diabetic neuropathy.

Incidentally, the reason why Mrs Jones was so irritable with her children may have been due to mood swings caused by hyperglycaemia (Wass et al. 2011).

3   **Discuss the role that diet and exercise will have in managing Mrs Jones' type 2 diabetes**

A   - The initial management of type 2 diabetes consists of weight loss and exercise which, if substantial, will reverse hyperglycaemia. However, most patients with type 2 diabetes have been making the 'wrong' lifestyle choices all their lives and rarely respond to standard approaches (NICE 2012).

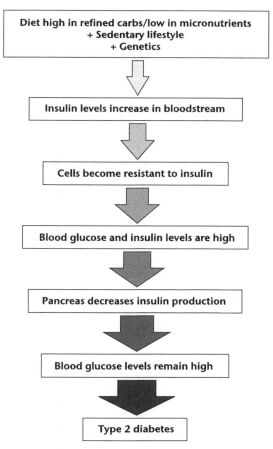

Figure 10.1 How insulin resistance progresses towards type 2 diabetes

- To enable Mrs Jones to manage her diet and exercise regime, she should be offered ongoing and personalized nutritional advice from a diabetic team with specific expertise (DH 2006).
- Advice should be given about the appropriate timing for meals and snacks and the amount of carbohydrate eaten. According to dietary recommendations, people suffering from diabetes should eat starchy foods regularly; eat more fruit and vegetables; reduce animal, saturated and trans-fatty acids; eat low-fat dairy products and oily fish; cut down on sugar; and reduce salt. Mrs Jones should be able to enjoy some foods containing sugar as long as these are part of her overall balanced diet.
- Mrs Jones should be advised about commonly available food marketed specifically for people with diabetes: these tend to be expensive and not necessarily very helpful.
- Advice on alcohol consumption should also be given. Alcohol may compound the effect of diabetes on blood pressure which may have a deleterious effect on the cardiovascular system and specifically the heart. Drinking moderate alcohol (two drinks daily for men, one for women) is acceptable, but drinking alcohol in excess of the recommended level increases the risk of hypoglycaemia as well as other untoward events.
- If Mrs Jones smokes, advice, support and help will be given to help her stop. She should be helped to enrol in a 'smoking cessation' programme.
- Since Mrs Jones is overweight, she will be given advice, help and support to lose some weight. She will be advised that the nearer she gets to a healthy body weight, the better it will be for her long-term health (NICE 2006).
- Mrs Jones will be advised to take regular exercise. This may be used as a complementary tool to caloric restriction for weight reduction and to improve insulin sensitivity in the overweight insulin-resistant person. The objectives for Mrs Jones should be to promote the incentive to incorporate exercise into her daily life – for example, walking. Mrs Jones should also be given advice on how to prevent the complications of exercise – for example, hypoglycaemia. However, if she has any evidence of heart disease, the doctor will have to assess her prior to increasing levels of exercise (Di Loreto et al. 2005).

4   **What are the key points of the NICE guidelines with regard to oral hypoglycaemics?**

A   The NICE guidelines recommend that the management of type 2 diabetes should include:

- patient education;
- advice about diet;
- advice about exercise;
- advice about smoking;
- advice about alcohol;
- advice about lifestyle.

If these initial strategies, as carried out for Mrs Jones above, fail to achieve the blood glucose objectives, blood glucose lowering therapy should then be started. Metformin should be the drug of choice if there is no contraindication.

Table 10.1 Tablets used in type 2 diabetes

Drug group	Product name	Information
Biguanides	Metformin	Helps the cells of the body to use insulin. Does not cause hypoglycaemia as it does not stimulate the pancreas to secrete insulin. Does not cause weight gain. May cause nausea and vomiting
Sulphonureas	Glipizide	These drugs stimulate the pancreas to produce more insulin. They can cause hypoglycaemia and lead to weight gain; therefore they should be prescribed to people of normal weight
Meglitinides	Nateglinide (Starlix)	Increase the amount of insulin produced during a meal. Can be used alongside metformin
Thiazolidinediones	Rosiglitazone	Help insulin sensitivity. May be used with either a sulphonurea or biguanide but not both. At present cannot be used alongside insulin
Alpha-glucosidase inhibitors	Acarbose (Glucobay)	Works by delaying the rate at which sugars are digested. Side-effects include flatulence, a bloated feeling and diarrhoea. Acarbose can be used alongside other hypoglycaemic agents in this table

5 **What are the mode of action and side-effects of metformin?**

A # MODE OF ACTION

Metformin is the treatment of choice when strict dieting has failed to control diabetes. It may also be an option for patients who are not overweight. Metformin works via three mechanisms:

- By reducing hepatic glucose production by inhibiting gluconeogenesis (the formation of glucose from non-carbohydrate carbon) and glycogenolysis (the formation of glucose by converting glycogen) in the liver. This reduces the hepatic glucose output which underpins basal and night-time hyperglycaemia (Warrell et al. 2010).
- By increasing insulin sensitivity in the muscles it improves peripheral glucose uptake and utilization.
- It also delays intestinal glucose absorption.

Metformin only works in the presence of endogenous insulin, therefore it is essential that there is secretion of endogenous insulin. At maximal effective doses, metformin may reduce HbA1c by 1 to 2%. It rarely causes hypoglycaemia when used as monotherapy, because it does not stimulate insulin secretion. It is rarely associated with weight gain. Metformin has favourable effects on lipid metabolism, shown at therapeutic doses. It reduces total cholesterol, low density lipoprotein (LDL), cholesterol and triglyceride levels. Metformin is the only glucose-lowering therapy that has been shown to possibly reduce cardiovascular mortality in type 2 diabetes (UKPDS Group 1998).

SIDE-EFFECTS

Metformin has a short half-life and is therefore a short-acting drug. It needs to be given two or three times a day, which may impact on a patient's compliance and concordance. Some of the side-effects of this drug are:

- nausea;
- vomiting;
- diarrhoea;
- gas;
- abdominal pain;
- taste disturbance;
- anorexia.

These side-effects may discourage Mrs Jones from being concordant with the medication regimen. She must be advised not to give up, since the problems are mild and will subside. The doctor may start the drug regimen with a low dose and increase it slowly to minimize the risk of side-effects (Cramer et al. 1989)

Metformin may impair the absorption of vitamin B12 leading to vitamin B12 deficiency in some patients, causing megaloblastic anaemia. Metformin should be stopped before surgery or contrast dye studies with radiographic dye injection, and not recommence until there is evidence of good renal function. It must be used with caution in patients with impaired renal and liver function and post MI, because there may be a risk of lactic acidosis. Blood lactate levels are slightly raised in patients receiving metformin, and can rise rapidly and cause life-threatening acidosis if lactate accumulates due to renal failure.

Mrs Jones should be advised to contact the doctor and/or the diabetic liaison nurses if she experiences any signs and symptoms associated with renal failure and acidosis. However, it should be emphasized to her not to stop her medications without consultation with the doctor or nurse (UKPDS Group 1998; BNF 2012).

KEY POINTS

- The gold standard for the diagnosis of diabetes is the oral glucose tolerance test.
- The blood test known as HbA1c (glycosylated haemoglobin) would enable the doctor to monitor the development and progress of Mrs Jones' diabetes.
- The aim of treatment is to eliminate symptoms of hyperglycaemia without causing hypoglycaemia and to decrease the risk of long-term damage to organs and tissues.

- The initial management of type 2 diabetes consists of weight loss and exercise which may reverse hyperglycaemia.
- Mrs Jones would be advised about the importance of eating a well-balanced diet, taking her diabetes into consideration.
- Metformin works by reducing hepatic glucose production and increasing insulin sensitivity in the muscles,.
- The side-effects of metformin are mainly GI-related symptoms.

REFERENCES

American Diabetes Association (2012) Standards of medical care in diabetes, *Diabetes Care,* 35(Suppl. 1): S11–63.

BNF (British National Formulary) (2012) *BNF 63: March.* London: Pharmaceutical Press.

Cramer, J., Mattson, R.H., Prevey, M.L., Scheyer, R.D. and Ouellette, V.L. (1989) How often is medication taken as prescribed? A novel assessment technique, *Journal of the American Medical Association,* 261: 3273–7.

DH (Department of Health) (2006) *Care Planning in Diabetes: Report from the Joint Department of Health and Diabetes UK Care Planning Working Group.* London: DH.

Di Loreto, C., Fanelli, C., Lucidi, P. et al. (2005) Make your diabetic patients walk, *Diabetes Care,* 28(6): 1295–302.

National Collaborating Centre for Chronic Conditions (for NICE) (2008) *Type 2 Diabetes: National Clinical Guideline for Management in Primary and Secondary Care (update).* London: NICE, available at: www.nice.org.uk/nicemedia/live/11983/40803/40803.pdf.

NICE (National Institute for Health and Clinical Excellence) (2006) *Clinical Guideline 43: Obesity Guidance on the Prevention, Identification, Assessment and Management of Overweight and Obesity in Adults and Children.* London: NICE, available at: www.nice.org.uk/nicemedia/live/11000/30365/30365.pdf.

NICE (National Institute for Health and Clinical Excellence) (2012) Managing type 2 diabetes, *NICE Pathways,* available at: http://pathways.nice.org.uk/pathways/diabetes/managing-type-2-diabetes#content=view-node%3Anodes-dietary-advice.

UKPDS Group (1998) Effect of intensive blood-glucose control with metformin on complications in overweight patients with type 2 diabetes (UKPDS 34), *Lancet,* 352(9131): 854–65.

Warrell, D.A., Cox, T.M. and Firth, J.D. (eds) (2010) *Oxford Textbook of Medicine,* 5th edn. Oxford: Oxford University Press.

Wass, J.A.H., Stewart, P.M., Amiel, S.A. and Davies, M.J. (eds) (2011) *Oxford Textbook of Endocrinology and Diabetes,* 2nd edn. Oxford: Oxford University Press.

The person with epilepsy
Pat Talbot

CASE AIMS

After examining this case study the reader should be able to:

- Briefly explain the normal mechanism that allows an impulse to be passed along a neuron.
- Define the term epilepsy.
- Identify investigations that are likely to be carried out in order to diagnose epilepsy.
- Highlight why misdiagnosis is a problematic feature in epilepsy.
- Discuss the general management and administration of anti-epileptic drugs.
- Demonstrate an understanding of the mode of action and side-effects of valproate and lamotrigine.
- Explain how epilepsy is monitored to ensure that the medication regime is effective.
- Discuss the role of the nurse in patient concordance.
- Identify the care and medication needed in status epilepticus.
- Describe the information that would be given to carers about sudden unexpected death in epilepsy.

CASE

Mr Ralph is a 45-year-old man who has recently experienced the second of two seizures, in which he fell to the floor with violent jerking of his muscles. He has been admitted to A&E, as his care staff are concerned about his slow recovery from the second attack. It appears that he has experienced a tonic-clonic seizure, but this has yet to be confirmed. He shares a house with two other men and they all receive help with everyday living as they all have learning disabilities. Mr Ralph's learning disability is described as 'moderate'. He is independent in self-care skills and is able to communicate his wishes using a simple vocabulary.

---

1 **What is the normal mechanism that allows an impulse to be passed along a neuron?**

2 **What do you understand by the term 'epilepsy'?**

3 What investigations are likely to be carried out to determine whether Mr Ralph is suffering from epilepsy and, if so, what type(s) of epilepsy he is experiencing?

4 What types of misdiagnosis can occur when a person is thought to have epilepsy?

> *After investigations and an outpatient appointment, Mr Ralph has been diagnosed with epilepsy. He has been prescribed sodium valproate. Over the next few months he continues to experience seizures, resulting in him being prescribed lamotrigine alongside sodium valproate.*

5 Discuss the general management and administration of anti-epileptic drugs (AEDs)

6 Identify the action of valproate and specific issues around its use

7 Identify the action of lamotrigine and specific issues around its use

8 How should Mr Ralph's epilepsy be monitored to ensure that his medication regime is effective?

9 How can Mr Ralph be helped to ensure that he adheres to his medication regime, bearing in mind that he self-medicates when there are no care staff at his house?

10 If Mr Ralph were to develop status epilepticus (often known as 'status'), what changes might be needed to his care and medication?

11 What is **SUDEP**? What information should be given to Mr Ralph and his carers about this condition?

ANSWERS

1 What is the normal mechanism that allows an impulse to be passed along a neuron?

A Neurons differ a great deal in shape but they all consist of dendrites, a cell body and an axon. The dendrites respond to the chemical messengers (neurotransmitters) released from other neurons. The axon carries the impulse from the cell body towards the synaptic terminals, where neurotransmitters transfer the impulse to the next neuron.

Neurons are able to transmit nerve impulses by the following mechanism:

- The exterior of the cell has a greater concentration of positively charged sodium ions and inside the cell there are more positively charged potassium ions. This situation is maintained by special channels within the cell wall called sodium–potassium pumps. The interior of the cell contains negatively charged chloride ions, which gives the interior an overall negative charge, as compared to the exterior. This situation is known as the 'resting potential'.

- When the neuron is stimulated by neurotransmitters released from a nearby neuron, positive sodium ions flow into the cell, causing a change from a negative charge inside the cell to a positive one. This depolarization creates an 'action potential', which moves in a single direction down the axon.
- The resting potential is restored by potassium ions moving outside the axon. The sodium–potassium pumps then pump out the sodium ions that entered the axon and bring the potassium ions back into the cell, restoring the cell to its resting potential.
- The impulse is passed to the next neuron at the synapse. Here there is a tiny gap between the end of the axon of one neuron and the end of the dendrite of the next. As the nerve impulse reaches the synapse it causes vesicles (small spherical packages) to release a chemical neurotransmitter. There are a variety of these within the nervous system.

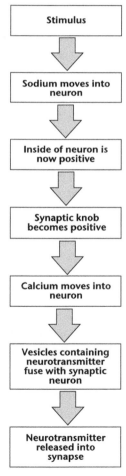

Figure 11.1 Flow chart of a neuron firing

2 What do you understand by the term 'epilepsy'?

A Epileptic seizures have been described as repeated abnormal discharges of a group of neurons. This is caused by a high level of neuronal excitation and a deficit in the mechanism which inhibits this excitation. Put simply, an epileptic seizure is caused by abnormal firing of cerebral neurons, which spreads from a local starting point to other parts of the brain. Epileptic seizures can take many forms, depending on the part of the brain affected and the extent of the spread of abnormal activity. There are more than 40 types of seizure, with some described as unclassifiable (Manford 2003).

3 What investigations are likely to be carried out to determine whether Mr Ralph is suffering from epilepsy and, if so, what type(s) of epilepsy he is experiencing?

A Anyone with newly suspected seizures should be seen urgently (within two weeks) by a specialist. The most important information in the diagnosis of epilepsy is an accurate description of the events. Every piece of information, including the events before and after the seizure, can assist with this process. This will need to be provided by a witness (NICE 2012).

The following information is needed:

- Details of the events, as described by observers and the person. Mr Ralph may be able to describe what happened before the seizure and how he felt afterwards. The duration of the seizures is also important (Kerr 2009).
- The circumstances surrounding the event.
- Any patterns in the seizures such as the time, or any relationship to sleep.
- Any activity the person was undertaking at the time (e.g. exercise, resting, watching TV).
- Any possible circumstances that may have acted as a trigger. This might include stress, sleep deprivation, flickering lights or alcohol intake.
- Personal and family history. However, with people with intellectual disability, there may not always be access to family health information (Panayiotopoulos 2010).

If available, video recordings can be helpful in diagnosis, but clearly consent from Mr Ralph would need to be sought. A complete physical examination will also be carried out in order to identify any neurological abnormalities, any cardiac problems and to assess Mr Ralph's mental status. NICE (2012) recommends an electroencephalogram (EEG) after a second seizure. The most commonly used investigation when epilepsy is suspected is the EEG, which records the electrical activity of the brain. In some cases this investigation will confirm a diagnosis. However, the results can provide a normal reading, and up to 50% of people who have been diagnosed with epilepsy have a normal EEG. Non-specific abnormalities may also be found that cannot be used to confirm a diagnosis (Welsh and Kerley 2009).

Mr Ralph may also be asked to **hyperventilate** while the recording is being made. This will involve him breathing deeply for about three minutes. If he is unable to understand this instruction, he may asked to blow on an item such as a pinwheel (if this approach has to be used it is important to remember to do this in a way that is as age-appropriate as possible). Hyperventilation is the most effective procedure for stimulating absence seizures and abnormal patterns of electrical activity in the brain. The E E G technician may also use intermittent photic stimulation (flashing lights), which can be a trigger for some people. Informed consent is required when photic stimulation and hyperventilation are used.

Brain imaging may also used to assist with diagnosis. This can involve **magnetic resonance imaging** (M R I), which can display structural abnormalities that may be the underlying cause of Mr Ralph's possible epilepsy. X-ray computerized tomography (CT) scans may also be required, but they are less effective than an M R I.

Mr Ralph may also be sent for blood tests to rule out metabolic disorders and for an E C G to rule out heart conditions. On diagnosis, it is important that Mr Ralph and his carers, with his consent, are provided with information on epilepsy, access to counselling, details of an epilepsy specialist nurse and a named individual as a point of contact.

4 **What types of misdiagnosis can occur when a person is thought to have epilepsy?**

A Epilepsy can be difficult to diagnose accurately, with misdiagnosis occurring in up to 25% of people. Conditions that may be misdiagnosed as epilepsy include syncope (a brief loss of consciousness). This can have many causes but among them are some potentially serious conditions such as cardiac arrhythmias. In people with a learning disability, conditions that may be misdiagnosed as epilepsy are also likely to include:

- a variety of repetitive behaviours or apparent unresponsiveness;
- stereotyped movements associated with some syndromes (e.g. **Rett syndrome**);
- side-effects of medication;
- self-stimulation of seizures (Iddon et al. 2010).

This type of misdiagnosis can lead to people receiving medication they do not require, along with the possible side-effects. An underlying condition may remain untreated. They may also experience stress, social stigma and unnecessary lifestyle changes. People with epileptic seizures can also be misdiagnosed as having migraine or even encephalitis, resulting in mismanagement of their condition.

Table 11.1 Differential diagnosis of epilepsy

Syncope
Non-epileptic attack disorder
Migraine
Daydreaming
Vertigo
Panic attacks
Drop attacks
Narcolepsy
Transient global amnesia
Movement disorder

5 **Discuss the general management and administration of AEDs**

A The aim of treatment with AEDs is freedom from seizures without side-effects, or at least minimal reactions. The ability of Mr Ralph to be involved in treatment decisions should always be considered. Some general points include:

- A person-centred approach should be taken, in order to produce a comprehensive care plan, which will include a medication plan.
- Some anti-epileptics act by stabilizing the neuron membrane in order to reduce the excitability of the neuron. Others increase the activity of **gamma-aminobutyric acid** (GABA) (a transmitter which has an inhibiting effect at the synapse), while some appear to combine both actions.
- Polytherapy is best avoided, but Mr Ralph failed to respond to a single drug. This is the case in about 30–50% of patients. Side-effects are more likely in relation to polytherapy.
- It is important that patients and carers are informed regarding the purpose of the medication, the duration of treatment and possible adverse reactions.
- Many AEDs are effective only for certain seizure types and can be contraindicated for others. Others are described as 'broad spectrum', being effective for more than one type of seizure.
- AEDs are particularly prone to drug interactions.
- Side-effects caused by anti-epileptic drugs fall into the following groups: CNS-related (e.g. sedation, poor coordination, tremor and headache); behavioural/mental health-related (e.g. depression) (however, some AEDs have mood-stabilizing properties); cardiovascular and renal effects.
- People with learning disabilities commonly experience weight changes, gait disturbance and altered mood (Sipes et al. 2011).
- People with learning disabilities and epilepsy appear to be more at risk of falls, due either directly to the seizures or to the effects of medication (Willgoss et al. 2010).
- When working with people with limited communication, carers need to be particularly observant to detect adverse drug reactions.
- If drugs need to be changed or withdrawn, this needs to be done slowly, the dose being gradually changed (normally every two weeks).
- It is recommended that the medication dispensed should be obtained from one manufacturer, as there can be differences in the bio-availability of medication obtained from different manufacturers.

Table 11.2 Most commonly used drugs in epilepsy

Primary generalized epilepsies	*Focal epilepsies*
Sodium valproate	Carbamazepine
Lamotrigine	Lamotrigine
Phenytoin (in the developing world)	Sodium valproate
	Phenobarbital and phenytoin (in the developing world)

6 **Identify the action of valproate and specific issues around its use**

A Sodium valproate is effective for virtually all types of seizure. It is believed to have two modes of action. Firstly, it triggers the release of the neurotransmitter GABA. GABA is found throughout the CNS and is considered to be the main inhibitory neurotransmitter. Alongside this it inhibits the sodium channels in the walls of the neuron (Galbraith et al. 2007).

Sodium valproate is eliminated from the body via the liver and one of the major concerns is that it can damage this organ. Mr Ralph may need to have liver function tests before it is prescribed and any impairment of his liver function will prevent him from taking this medication. His liver function might also be monitored for the first six months. Page et al. (2006) identify that toxic effects on the liver are more likely when sodium valproate is used alongside another AED. Liver problems are more likely in people with learning disabilities.

Sodium valproate can also be associated with pancreatitis and **thrombocytopenia**. A full blood count should be carried out before Mr Ralphs starts the medication and prior to any surgery. Mr Ralphs's carers need to be alerted to the symptoms of liver disease and pancreatitis (nausea, vomiting, anorexia, jaundice) and thrombocytopenia (bleeding and bruising). Other possible effects might be increased appetite and weight gain, hair loss and ataxia or tremor. The tremor is usually reversible if the medication is stopped or reduced. He may also experience gastric problems, which can be reduced by the use of an enteric-coated formulation. He should be advised to take his medication with food. Some patients may also experience drowsiness and even confusion, although this is unusual (Bourgeois 2009).

Sodium valproate interacts with other medications. For example, it inhibits the metabolism of drugs such as phenobarbitone, lamotrigine and phenytoin, all of which can be used in the treatment of epilepsy. Sodium valproate is hydroscopic, i.e. it attracts water from the air. For this reason it is packed in foil. If a half tablet is prescribed, the remaining half should be discarded as it will be inactivated by moisture from the air (BNF 2012).

Sodium valproate may have mood stabilizing properties. Lower doses of psychotropic drugs may be used in people receiving sodium valproate. This may be helpful for Mr Ralph if he experiences mood changes (Leunissen et al. 2011).

7 **Identify the action of lamotrigine and specific issues around its use**

A Lamotrigine is used for generalized seizures that are poorly controlled by other medications. The action of lamotrigine involves the inhibition of the passage of sodium through the walls of the neuron. It also reduces the release of glutamate, which is an excitatory neurotransmitter. These actions reduce the uncontrolled repeated firing of the neurons (BNF 2012).

The main advantage of lamotrigine is that it has fewer side-effects, such as cognitive and psychomotor effects, than other medication. However, side-effects can occur and one of the most common is a skin rash. This is more common when the drug is combined with sodium valproate. The rash is often itchy and it can progress to involve the mucous membranes (**Stevens-Johnson syndrome**) or even toxic epidermal necrolysis, which is a potentially life-threatening condition (Matsuo and Riaz 2009).

Other side-effects include insomnia, headache, nausea, dizziness and double vision, particularly when given in combination with other AEDs. Lamotrigine does interact with other medication. When given with sodium valproate it can reduce the rate of elimination of valproate from the body. Mr Ralph and the people caring for him need to be informed regarding the side-effects in general, and in particular the possibility of a rash.

8   **How should Mr Ralph's epilepsy be monitored to ensure that his medication regime is effective?**

A   It is important that this patient's condition is monitored so that medication levels can be adjusted to provide the best possible treatment with minimum side-effects. The monitoring should include:

- Regular reviews. A regular structured review at least annually with a specialist or generalist is important, depending on the success of the treatment regime.
- Regular blood test monitoring, unless there are specific indications. This may be useful if it is suspected that the drug regime is not being adhered to, or if toxicity or drug interactions are suspected.
- The occurrence of any seizures, their duration and any change in their nature.
- Adverse effects observed, such as changes in Mr Ralph's ability to function, his behaviour and anything that he is able to indicate to his carers.
- Possible use of specific screening tools. the Glasgow Epilepsy Outcome Scale (GEOS-C) allows the person with epilepsy to report their concerns about the situation (Watkins et al. 2006).

9   **How can Mr Ralph be helped to ensure that he adheres to his medication regime, bearing in mind that he self-medicates when there are no care staff at his house?**

A   Adherence to medication can be assisted by:

- Education for the person and their carers on their condition and the medication they are prescribed.
- Reducing the stigma of having epilepsy. This may be less of an issue for Mr Ralph, as epilepsy is common among people with learning disabilities – however, you should not make assumptions.
- A simple medication regime. Medication can be dispensed in packaging that simplifies the process.
- A positive relationship between Mr Ralph and his carers and health care professionals. Carers should be aware of the most likely side-effects of his medication, any idiosyncratic effects and sources of help and advice (Welsh and Kerley 2009).

10   **If Mr Ralph were to develop status epilepticus (often known as 'status'), what changes might be needed to his care and medication?**

A   Status epilepticus (often described as 'status') is a condition in which a seizure is prolonged or seizures follow on rapidly from each other. When this occurs in a tonic-clonic seizure, intervention is required as the condition can cause permanent cerebral damage and can be life-threatening. Tonic-clonic status has been defined as prolonged or recurrent seizures lasting for 30 minutes or more (Shorvon 2010). However, some services may use other criteria.

Status requires urgent treatment and the two most commonly used emergency medications are rectal diazepam or buccal midazolam. When a person is known to be prone to status, one of these drugs will often be prescribed and made available for carers to administer. Training will be required in administration. Buccal midazolam is now more often given as it is squirted using a syringe between the lower jaw and the cheek on one side of the mouth, making administration easier and more dignified. For Mr Ralph, his carers will need to be trained in how to identify and treat his status, should it recur, and how to recognize the need to summon emergency help. The service will also need to consider the possibility of this occurring when the house is unstaffed – a careful risk assessment will need to be carried out, along with Mr Ralph, in order to plan his care.

11   **What is SUDEP? What information should be given to Mr Ralph and his carers about this condition?**

A   SUDEP (sudden unexpected death in epilepsy) occurs in about one death per 2500 people with mild epilepsy and about one death per 100 people with those with severe epilepsy. It usually occurs after a seizure of a convulsive type. People with a learning disability are particularly at risk. The condition is poorly understood, but it may be the result of respiratory arrest or cardiac arrhythmias. It occurs most often when people are asleep or alone. Respiration after a seizure can be encouraged by stimulation, which may explain why witnessed seizures are less likely to be followed by SUDEP.

In relation to Mr Ralph, he has the right to know about all the risks posed by his epilepsy. The issue of how much people should be told about SUDEP condition has been debated. Neurologists and epilepsy specialist nurses are more likely to discuss it with patients who are at risk or who have asked about the condition. In general, staff should be guided by how much a patient wants to learn about their condition. Consideration should also be given to the fact that any action to reduce the number of attacks experienced by Mr Ralph will reduce the risk of SUDEP (Lewis 2011).

KEY POINTS

- The axon of a neuron carries the impulse from the cell body towards the synaptic terminals, where neurotransmitters transfer the impulse to the next neuron.
- Epileptic seizures have been described as repeated abnormal discharges of a group of neurons.
- Careful observation is required to ensure an accurate diagnosis of epilepsy.
- AEDs are prone to drug interactions and side-effects. With a person with learning disability, carers need to be observant in order to detect any problems. Regular reviews are important.

- Sodium valproate has two modes of action: it triggers the release of the neurotransmitter GABA and it inhibits the sodium channels in the walls of the neuron.
- The action of lamotrigine involves the inhibition of the passage of sodium and reduces the release of glutamate, which is an excitatory neurotransmitter.
- Any changes to medication need to be carried out gradually, under medical supervision.
- Status epilepticus is more common in people with learning disabilities – care staff need to be able to identify this and know how to respond.
- SUDEP occurs in about one death per 2500 people with mild epilepsy and about one death per 100 people with those with severe epilepsy.

REFERENCES

Bourgeois, B. (2009) Valproate, in S. Shorvon, E. Perucca and J. Engel (eds) *The Treatment of Epilpsy*. Chichester: Wiley/Blackwell.

BNF (British National Formulary) (2012) *BNF 63: March*. London: Pharmaceutical Press.

Galbraith, A., Bullock, S., Manias, E., Hunt, B. and Richards, A. (2007) *Fundamentals of Pharmacology*, 2nd edn. Harlow: Pearson.

Iddon, P., Chapman, M., Parvin, G., Atkinson, K. and Mitchell, D. (2010) The prevalence and implications of a misdiagnosis of epilepsy, *Learning Disability Practice*, 13(7): 26–31.

Kerr, M. (2009) Concensus guidelines into the management of epilepsy in adults with an intellectual disability, *Journal of Intellectual Disability Research*, 53(8): 687–94.

Leunissen, C.L.F., de la Parra, N.M., Tan, I.Y., Rentmeester, Th.W., Vader, C.I., Veendrick-Mekkes, M.J.B.M. and Aldenkamp, A.P. (2011) Antiepilptic drugs with mood stabilising properties and their relation with psychotropic drug use in institutionalised epilepsy patients with intellectual disability, *Research in Developmental Disabilities*, 32: 2660–8.

Lewis, S. (2011) Advances in epilepsy management: the role of the specialist nurse, *Nurses Prescribing*, 9(3): 131–5.

Manford, M. (2003) *Practical Guide to Epilepsy*. Burlington, MA: Elsevier.

Matsuo, F. and Riaz, A. (2009) Lamotrigine, in S. Shorvon, E. Perucca and J. Engel (eds) *The Treatment of Epilepsy*. Chichester: Wiley/Blackwell.

NICE (National Institute for Clinical Excellence) (2012) *Quick Reference Guide: The Epilepsies, Diagnosis and Management of the Epilepsies in Adults in Primary and Secondary Care*. London: NICE.

Page, C., Curtis, M. Walker, M. and Hoffman, B. (2006) *Integrated Pharmacology*, 3rd edn. Philadelphia: Elsevier.

Panayiotopoulos, C.P. (2010) *A Clinical Guide to Epileptic Syndromes and their Treatment*, 2nd edn. London: Springer Healthcare.

Shorvon, S. (2010) *Handbook of Epilepsy Treatment*, 3rd edn. Chichester: Wiley/Blackwell.

Sipes, M., Matson, J.L., Belva, B., Turygin, N., Koslowski, A.M. and Horovitz, M. (2011) The relationship among side effects associated with anti-epileptic medications in those with intellectual disability, *Research in Developmental Disabilities*, 32: 1646–51.

Watkins, J., Espie, C.A., Curtice, L., Mantala, K., Cor, A. and Foley, J. (2006) Development of a measure to assess the impact of epilepsy on people with intellectual disability: the Glasgow Epilepsy Outcome Scale – client version (GEOS-C), *Journal of Intellectual Disability Research*, 50(3): 161–71.

Welsh, R. and Kerley, S. (2009) Nursing patients with epilepsy in secondary care settings, *Nursing Standard*, 23(36): 49–56.

Willgoss, T.G., Yohannes, A.M. and Mitchell, D. (2010) Review of risk factors and preventative strategies for fall related injuries in people with intellectual disabilities, *Journal of Clinical Nursing*, 19: 2100–9.

The person with hypertension
Diana Blundell

CASE AIMS

After examining this case study the reader should be able to:

- Explain why blood pressure is important in the normal circulation of blood.
- Outline how the body normally regulates blood pressure.
- Identify the risk factors involved in the development of hypertension.
- Discuss the importance of waist/hip ratio and lipid profile in the diagnosis of hypertension.
- Demonstrate an understanding of the mode of action and side-effects of angiotensin-converting enzyme inhibitors.
- Discuss the role of the nurse in advising relatives regarding taking angiotensin-converting enzyme inhibitors.
- Demonstrate an understanding of the mode of action and side-effects of statins.
- Discuss the role of the nurse in advising relatives regarding taking statins.

CASE

Mr J is a 55-year-old man who presented to his GP with elevated blood pressure, which had been monitored by the practice nurse for the preceding three months. A mean score of 185/95mmHg had been recorded at varying times of the day.

---

1 **Why is blood pressure important to Mr J's circulatory system?**

2 **How does Mr J's body normally regulate his blood pressure?**

Mr J has a BMI of >32 and is clinically described as obese. He is a type 2 diabetic with elevated low density lipoprotein (LDL) cholesterol levels (4.90mmol/L), reduced high density lipoprotein (HDL) cholesterol (1.034 mmol/L) and triglycerides (5.645mmol/L).

His total cholesterol is 6.19mmol/L. He has a waist circumference of 50in (127cms), is a current smoker of 25 years and drinks above the recommended 21 units per week for a male. He takes no exercise and his diet remains high in fat.

3 What risk factors are involved in the development of hypertension?

4 Why does the doctor want to know Mr J's BMI, waist/hip ratio and lipid profile?

Mr J's GP starts him on the angiotensin-converting enzyme (ACE) inhibitor perindopril 10mg and atorvastatin 10mg (a lipid-lowering drug). He immediately recommends lifestyle changes. Mr J also has bloods taken for liver function tests (LFTs) and U&Es. He is advised to return to the surgery in one week for the results of his blood test and a blood pressure check.

5 Describe the mechanism of action and side-effects of ACE inhibitors

6 What advice would you give to Mr J about his ACE inhibitor?

7 Explain the action of Mr J's lipid-lowering drug

8 What advice would you give Mr J about his lipid-lowering drug?

ANSWERS

1 **Why is blood pressure important to Mr J's circulatory system?**

A Blood circulates due to the heart pump establishing a pressure gradient. Blood pressure is determined largely by the hydrostatic (water) pressure which is exerted by the blood on the walls of blood vessels. The heart is actually two pumps. The left side is responsible for exerting strong pressure within the left ventricle to push blood forward through the aorta into the systemic system. The highest average pressure, created in the left ventricle, is observed in the aortic arch before the coronary branches, and measures approximately 95mmHg.

The right side of the heart, where deoxygenated blood is returning to the lungs, is at a much lower pressure. The average lowest pressure is at the junction of the superior and inferior vena cava as it returns to the right atrium, where it is about 3–5mmHg. Blood circulates in these two systems. The rate of flow is dependent upon arterial blood pressure and the peripheral resistance (opposition to blood flow) provided by blood vessels and blood viscosity (stickiness of blood).

The flow rate of any fluid is proportional to the pressure applied to that fluid, and, as such, fluid flows from high pressure to low pressure regions. The greater the pressure differential, the faster the movement of the fluid. However, flow will only continue if the pressure exceeds the opposing forces of resistance. The rate of flow is inversely proportional to the resistance – since for a given pressure, the higher the resistance, the lower the flow rate (Clancy and McVicar 2009).

The blood vessels are responsible for delivering blood flow from the heart to the cellular level following a direct sequence, as follows.

- The arteries that carry blood away from the heart and towards the tissues, while the heart ventricles pump blood into the aorta (systemic system) and the pulmonary artery (bringing deoxygenated blood back to the lungs for reoxygenation).
- The arterioles, smaller subdivisions of the arteries, carry blood into the capillaries – tiny, thin-walled vessels that allow for gaseous exchanges between the two systems.
- The capillaries then unite the arterioles with the venules – small vessels that receive blood from the capillaries and begin the transportation of deoxygenated blood back to the veins.
- The veins are formed at the merger of the venules. Ultimately their role is to return deoxygenated blood to the right side of the heart (Cohen 2012).

2 **How does Mr J's body normally regulate his blood pressure?**

A Among the factors that affect blood pressure is the total blood volume available. On average, a 70kg healthy man has approximately 5L of blood in his body. This equates to 20% circulating volume for each litre respectfully. Should a loss of volume occur (through haemorrhage, for example), blood pressure will drop. Other considerations are:

- heart rate;
- stroke volume (the volume of blood ejected from the ventricle with each beat of the heart);
- blood vessel compliance;
- blood vessel elasticity;
- resistance to blood flow (Watson 2003).

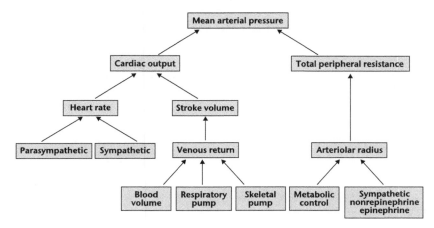

Figure 12.1 Summary of factors that affect mean arterial pressure

The autonomic nervous system plays an important role in the pathophysiology of hypertension and is key in maintaining a normal blood pressure. This is due to the sympathetic nervous system being stimulated which causes both arteriolar constriction and arteriolar dilation, depending on whether the receptors in the autonomic nervous system are excitory or inhibitory (Lip 2003).

THE RENIN–ANGIOTENSIN SYSTEM

The renin–angiotensin system is the most important of the endocrine systems controlling blood pressure, and works in the following way.

- The kidneys' **juxtaglomerular apparatus** secretes renin (an enzyme that is released in response to low serum sodium or low blood pressure).
- Renin activates the inactive plasma protein angiotensinogen to produce angiotensin I (still a physiologically inactive substance).
- This in turn is rapidly converted into angiotensin II in the lungs by ACE.
- Angiotensin II is a potent vasoconstrictor and, as such, causes a rise in blood pressure. It also stimulates the release of aldosterone from the adrenal glomerulosa, which results in both sodium and water retention. These chemical reactions are in a direct response to either reduced glomerular under-perfusion or a reduced salt intake (Thibodeau and Patton 2007).

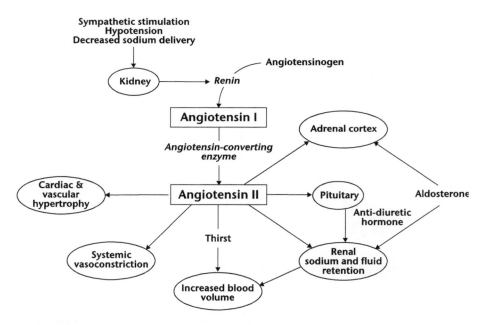

Figure 12.2 The renin–angiotensinogen cycle

3 **What risk factors are involved in the development of hypertension?**

A There are a number of risk factors that can contribute to hypertension. They fall into two categories: modifiable (risks a person can change) and non-modifiable (risks a person cannot change). Factors that are modifiable include smoking, raised cholesterol, diabetes, obesity, stress, lack of exercise, diet (especially consuming larger than average amounts of salt) and alcohol consumption. As we can see from this list, Mr J has seven of the risk factors within his medical profile. Non-modifiable factors include racial background (Afro-American people are more likely to get hypertension in comparison with Caucasians), age, gender (more men get hypertension than women) and inherited genetic factors such as hyperlipidaemia (high cholesterol level) (DH 2000; Noble et al. 2005).

4 **Why does the doctor want to know Mr J's BMI, waist/hip ratio and lipid profile?**

A # BMI

The development of obesity is an independent risk factor for developing diseases such as hypertension, raised blood cholesterol and type 2 diabetes. The management and control of the increase in obese and overweight people is indirectly costing the UK approximately £2 billion per year. To try to control the spiralling costs of caring for obese and overweight patients it has become important to identify individuals who may present as a risk of developing complications of obesity and potential diseases such as hypertension by assessing a person's BMI (kg/m^2) (DH 2000). This has become an internationally accepted numerical range to define degrees of obesity in Caucasians.

WAIST/HIP RATIO

Although widely used and accepted as a risk assessment tool, BMI is not a particularly good indicator of the development of cardiovascular disease and an alternative measure is the waist/hip ratio. As waist size increases in comparison with the hip measurement there is a greater chance of developing hypertension, diabetes, MI and strokes due to the increased laying down of adipose tissue around the abdominal organs as visceral fat. Doctors are claiming that men with a waist size above 40in (102cm) and women with a waist size above 35in (89cm) can quadruple their risk of developing obesity-related diseases (Kaplan and Victor 2010).

LIPID PROFILE

Lipids are a group of naturally occurring organic molecules that do not dissolve in water. Although the term 'lipid' is used interchangeably with the term 'fat', a fat is a lipid but a lipid is not necessarily a fat. The body uses lipids as a source of energy to produce hormones, absorb fat-soluble vitamins and to provide structure to cell membranes. Generally we talk about two main types of lipoproteins: HDLs and LDLs.

HDLs are the smallest of the lipoprotein particles and the densest as they contain the highest proportion of protein to cholesterol. This is why they are regarded as 'good fats'. HDLs are capable of picking up cholesterol from cells by interaction with adenosine triphosphate and delivering it to the liver where it is excreted in bile. Ultimately bile goes to the intestines, either directly or indirectly, after conversion into bile acids. The delivery of HDL cholesterol is an important synthesis for the adrenals, ovaries, testes and for the synthesis of steroid hormones such as glucocorticoids.

HDL cholesterol and its lipid and protein constituents is a vital component in inhibiting oxidation, inflammation, activation of endothelium coagulation and platelet aggregation. HDL cholesterol is therefore to remove cholesterol from the body and thus reduce the risk of the development of atherosclerosis of the arteries (NICE 2011).

LDLs have a similar mechanism. They also transport cholesterol around the body but deliver it to the artery walls, where it is retained and attracts macrophages that engulf the LDL particles and begin the formation of plaque (build up of fatty deposits), which increases the likelihood of developing atherosclerosis over time.

Diabetic patients, like Mr J, have an increased risk of the development of atherosclerosis due to the action of insulin resistance from an increased amount of adipose tissue. If the build-up of plaque over time eventually ruptures this activates the blood clotting process which leads to either arterial stenosis (narrowing of the lumen) or total occlusion of the vessel. Ultimately this can lead to heart attacks, stroke or peripheral vascular disease. With the development of atherosclerosis the walls of the lumen of the arteries become stiff (hardening of the arteries) which in turn forces the heart to pump past this vascular resistance to deliver blood around the body (Jowett and Thompson 2007).

5 **Describe the mechanism of action and side-effects of ACE inhibitors**

A # MECHANISM

These drugs work by preventing the activation of the hormone angiotensin II from its precursors, renin and angiotensin I. As angiotensin II is a powerful vasoconstrictor, ACE inhibitors open up blood vessels resulting in a lowering of blood pressure. Their mechanism of action not only helps to reduce blood pressure but also protects the kidneys of people with diabetes and hypertension.

ACE inhibitors are a first-choice antihypertensive treatment in diabetes, unless contraindicated. They prevent renal absorption of sodium by lowering the production of **aldosterone**, which ultimately has a diuretic effect, causing sodium loss and potassium retention. The ACE inhibitors group includes all the 'prils' – for example, captopril, enalapril, lisinopril and ramipril (NICE 2011; BNF 2012).

SIDE-EFFECTS

Although ACE inhibitors are very effective in their treatment of blood pressure the initial taking of this medication can cause a sudden fall in blood pressure. Therefore patients are advised to monitor their blood pressure initially. ACE inhibitors can cause a dry, irritating cough (especially at night) which can affect sleep. A newer class of ACE inhibitors was introduced in 1995 called angiotensin receptor blockers (ARBs). These drugs work by blocking the angiotensin II receptors, and for this reason they have a more specific effect on blood pressure, and do not cause the irritating dry cough. ARBs are the 'artans' – for example, candesartan, irbesartan, losartan and valsartan.

This group of drugs is often used if there is an intolerance to ACE inhibitors, but may be prescribed in addition to ACE inhibitors in heart failure (Richards 2009; NICE 2011).

6 **What advice would you give to Mr J about his ACE inhibitor?**

A
- You should first ascertain that Mr J does not have an allergy or hypersensitivity to this class of drugs as this carries the risk of **anaphylaxis** (possible with almost any drug).
- You need to know if Mr J has any renal artery stenosis as these drugs reduce the glomerular filtration rate and may cause progressive renal failure.
- It is important for Mr J to be aware of any potential side-effects, most likely to be a persistent dry cough in about 10–20% of users.
- You can advise Mr J that ACE inhibitors can be replaced with ARBs if he suffers from the cough.
- Mr J is drinking over the recommended amount of alcohol each week for a man, so you need to give him information regarding the fact that alcohol also acts as a diuretic. The combination of ACE inhibitor and alcohol can in some cases lead to hypotension (low blood pressure) (Jordan 2009; BNF 2012).

7 **Explain the action of Mr J's lipid-lowering drug**

A
- Lipid-lowering drugs are referred to as 'statins' and include atorvastatin, fluvastatin, pravastatin, rosuvastatin and simvastatin.
- Statins are the first-choice drug for lowering cholesterol levels.
- They act by reducing the formation of lipids or hastening their removal from the body.
- Evidence suggests that taking statins lowers the harmful LDLs and raises the protective HDLs.
- Statins work by inhibiting an important enzyme needed by the liver in the synthesis of cholesterol, known as hydroxymethylglutaryl coenzyme A reductase (HMG CoA reductase). If this enzyme is inhibited, the cells in the liver will reduce their manufacture of cholesterol. This leads to an increase of LDL receptor sites on cell surfaces as there is less cholesterol available to them. This has an added benefit as additional receptor sites further increase the removal of LDLs from the bloodstream.
- Mr J has been prescribed atorvastatin which, apart from lowering blood cholesterol, is also responsible for stabilizing plaque and helping to prevent strokes through anti-inflammatory mechanisms.

8 **What advice would you give Mr J about his lipid-lowering drug?**

A
- Mr J should be advised to refrain from eating grapefruit or drinking grapefruit juice, as there is a chemical in grapefruit that can increase the level of the statin in the bloodstream, thus increasing the risk of side-effects.

- Mr J should be advised to always tell medical professionals such as pharmacists that he is taking a statin. Statins are known to interfere with some antibiotics and can affect their effectiveness; they can also interfere with some over-the-counter medications.
- It is important to advise Mr J that he needs to inform his GP if he develops any sudden shortness of breath or a cough, as, although rare, statins can cause interstitial lung disease.

KEY POINTS

- Blood pressure is determined largely by hydrostatic (water) pressure which is exerted by the blood on the walls of blood vessels.
- The renin–angiotensin system is considered the most important of the endocrine systems controlling blood pressure.
- Risk factors for developing hypertension fall into two categories: modifiable and non-modifiable.
- Although widely used as a risk assessment tool, BMI is now considered a less effective indicator for cardiovascular disease than waist/hip ratio.
- ACE inhibitors work by opening up blood vessels (vasodilation), resulting in the lowering of blood pressure.
- Lipid-lowering drugs (statins) act by reducing the formation of lipids or hastening their removal from the body.

REFERENCES

BNF (British National Formulary) (2012) *BNF 63: March*. London: Pharmaceutical Press.

Clancy, J. and McVicar, A. (2009) *Physiology and Anatomy for Nurses and Healthcare Practitioners – A Homeostatic Approach*, 3rd edn. London: Hodder Arnold.

Cohen, B.J. (2012) *Memmler's The Human Body in Health and Disease*, 12th edn. Philadelphia, PA: Lippincott Williams & Wilkins.

DH (Department of Health) (2000) *National Service Framework: Coronary Heart Disease*. London: DH.

Jordan, S. (2009) *The Prescription Drug Guide for Nurses*. Maidenhead: Open University Press.

Jowett, N.L. and Thompson, D.R. (2007) *Comprehensive Coronary Care*, 4th edn. London: Elsevier.

Kaplan, N.M. and Victor, R.G. (2010) *Kaplan's Clinical Hypertension*, 10th edn. Philadelphia PA: Lippincott Williams & Wilkins.

Lip, G.Y.H. (2003) *Clinical Hypertension in Practice*. London: Royal Society of Medicine Press Limited.

NICE (National Institute for Health and Clinical Excellence) (2011) *Clinical Guideline 127: Hypertension: Clinical Management of Primary Hypertension in Adults*. London: NICE.

Noble, A., Johnson, R., Thomas, A. and Bass, P. (2005) *The Cardiovascular System – Basic Science and Clinical Conditions*. London: Churchill Livingstone.

Richards, A. (2009) *A Nurse's Survival Guide to Drugs in Practice*. London: Churchill Livingstone Elsevier.

Thibodeau, G.A. and Patton, K.T. (2007) *Anatomy & Physiology*, 6th edn. St Louis, MO: Mosby Elsevier.

Watson, R. (2003) *Anatomy and Physiology for Nurses*, 11th edn. London: Baillière Tindall.

CASE STUDY 13
The person with inflammatory bowel disease
Joy Parkes

CASE AIMS

After examining this case study the reader should be able to:

- Briefly explain what diarrhoea is and explain the principles for self-medication.
- Demonstrate an understanding of the mode of action of loperamide.
- Explain why a patient with inflammatory bowel disease would require fluid and electrolyte replacement.
- Describe what is meant by inflammatory bowel disease.
- Identify the causes and symptoms of inflammatory bowel disease.
- Highlight the investigations that would be carried out in order to diagnose inflammatory bowel disease.
- Discuss the range of medicines that are available to help manage Crohn's disease.
- Demonstrate an understanding of the mode of action and side-effects of azathioprine, methotrexate, infliximab and adalimumab.
- Outline the complications of Crohn's disease and how patients adjust their lifestyles to cope.

CASE

Ann, now 37, first became ill aged 28, developing diarrhoea, abdominal pain and bloatedness. These symptoms came and went, and so she tended to self-medicate with loperamide. Despite this, diarrhoea seemed to be a constant feature of her life.

1 What is diarrhoea and what are the principles for self-medication?

2 How does loperamide ease diarrhoea?

After several weeks of diarrhoea, weight loss, pain and bloatedness, Ann visited her GP. A stool specimen for C. difficile was negative. Pale, exhausted and requiring rehydration and electrolyte therapy in hospital, Ann tested positive for Crohn's disease (CD), a type of inflammatory bowel disease (IBD). She was prescribed Asacol orally, and 40mg of prednisolone all week. On discharge this was reduced to 30mg then 20mg over six weeks.

3 Why would Ann require fluid and electrolyte replacement?

4 What is IBD?

5 What could have caused Ann's CD?

6 What symptoms could Ann experience as a result of her CD?

7 What investigations would Ann have in order to diagnose her CD?

Ann has lived with unstable CD for nine years, experiencing regular flare-ups with some remissions. The pain and diarrhoea have continued with bloody stools (always red) containing mucus. She feels exhausted and depressed but is reluctant to have surgery. She has had several courses of steroids, including budesonide and prednisolone. She prefers modified release budesonide (stat doses) to prednisolone which she refuses to take as she has experienced mild psychoses. She has also tried azathioprine which did not suit her and methotrexate which she is no longer allowed as it affected her liver. Since 2009, Ann has had infliximab (with hydrocortisone as she tends to get itchy). She explains that she was well on infliximab but has had an anaphylactic shock to the drug. As a result in December 2010 she started on adalimumab, self-administered by subcutaneous injection.

8 What medicines are available to help manage Ann's CD?

9 Why were azathioprine and methotrexate tried?

10 What are biological therapies and how do they work?

11 What complications might occur in the course of Ann's CD, and what is the role of surgery?

12 How might people like Ann adjust their lifestyle?

ANSWERS

1 **What is diarrhoea and what are the principles for self-medication?**

A Diarrhoea is an increase in the fluidity and frequency of bowel movements. Causes include poor hygiene, stress, drugs, diet, disease and infection (gastroenteritis). Food infected with a virus (norovirus) or bacteria such as campylobacter, *C. difficile*, *E. coli* and salmonella are a common cause (Hogston and Marjoram 2011).

Most attacks of acute uncomplicated diarrhoea are self-limiting and it is recommended that the person abstain from food and that they drink plenty of fluids. Self-medication in otherwise healthy adults may be considered necessary to relieve discomfort and social dysfunction; however, seeking medical advice is important if the diarrhoea does not improve within 48 hours, if the faeces contain blood, or if there is severe abdominal pain and vomiting (BMA 2005).

2   How does loperamide ease diarrhoea?

A   The main types of drugs for non-specific diarrhoea are opioids, bulk-forming and adsorbent agents. Loperamide, a synthetic opioid (bought over the counter), has a direct effect on the large intestine wall, decreasing its activity. This increases the amount of time substances stay in the intestine, allowing more water to be absorbed. Loperamide is taken orally in tablet, capsule or liquid form immediately after each loose bowel movement but should be used with caution when diarrhoea is caused by infection and avoided in those under 12 (Prosser et al. 2000; BNF 2012).

3   Why would Ann require fluid and electrolyte replacement?

A   Chemically, an electrolyte is a substance that, when in fluid, dissociates into electrically charged ions. The positive or negative charge carried by these ions is what allows our body's cells to use electrolytes to carry electrical impulses throughout the body. Electrolytes are crucial in maintaining the body's ability to transmit nerve impulses and contract muscles. Electrolytes also serve other biological functions, including water balance and distribution to working cells as well as acid–base balance.

Prolonged diarrhoea can result in dehydration and electrolyte imbalance and so a priority is the prevention or reversal of fluid and electrolyte depletion. The absorption of water occurs passively in the colon, following the active transport of sodium. As a result there is normally a net secretion of potassium and bicarbonate into the colon, hence the significant hypokalaemia often observed in severe diarrhoea (Long and Scott 2005; Karch 2010).

4   What is IBD?

A   IBD includes ulcerative colitis and CD. Both chronic, non-contagious disorders, these cause inflammation in the GI tract. In ulcerative colitis, inflammation is limited to the superficial layers of the colon. CD, also known as ileitis or regional enteritis, mainly affects the ileum and the colon but any area from the mouth to the anus can be involved. Normal healthy bowel may be present between patches of diseased and inflamed bowel. The whole layer of the GI tract can be involved, starting in the sub-mucosa and spreading to the mucosa and serosa.

5 **What could have caused Ann's CD?**

A • The exact cause of CD is unknown. Genetic susceptibility, an abnormal immune reaction and environmental factors have all been highlighted. CD is more common in developed countries such as the UK and the USA and affects mainly white adults. Men and women are roughly equally affected. Its onset is typically between the ages of 16 and 30, although any age can be affected. CD is characterized by long periods of remission followed by periods where the symptoms flare up. There is no way of predicting when a remission may occur or when symptoms will return, and there is no prevention. Smoking is a significant factor. Smokers are twice as likely to develop CD and experience more severe symptoms compared with non-smokers (NHS Choices 2011).

• CD runs in families, but is genetically complicated and multifactorial. A susceptibility gene at the IBD 1 locus on chromosome 16 has been identified as NOD2/CARD15. Mutations of this gene are associated with CD and a dysfunctional immune response.

• In certain genetically susceptible individuals, a previous infection with the measles virus or bacteria related to the mycobacterial species commonly found in cows, sheep and goats may be implicated in CD.

• There is strong evidence that an abnormal reaction by the body's immune system occurs in CD. The GI mucosa is exposed to abundant antigens in the form of 'friendly bacteria' (commensals) and those derived from ingested food. The immune system has to recognize commensals, allowing them to do their job without attacking them, while eliminating harmful antigens. The intestinal immune system differs from systemic immunity in that the response to foreign antigens is downregulated, resulting in a state of controlled physiological inflammation: harmful antigens are eliminated, helpful ones are not. This is achieved through a balance of T-helper-1 lymphocytes which produce pro-inflammatory cytokines, kept in check with T-helper-2 lymphocytes. These dampen the T1 response by producing anti-inlammatory cytokines such as interleukin 10 and TGFb which promote mucosal healing. In genetically susceptible people, the immune system mistakes 'helpful' microbes and normal flora in the lumen of the intestines for foreign or invading substances, and launches an attack. T-helper-1 lymphocytes are sent to the lining of the intestines. Here they are activated, making increased amounts of a special antibody called tumour necrosis factor alpha (TNFalpha). This cytokine intensifies inflammation by killing all bacteria, friendly or not, ultimately leading to ulceration and injury of the intestines.

• TNFalpha, present in high levels in CD, causes most of the associated inflammation. This is a key point to remember, as will be seen later. CD has a distinct profile of cytokine production. There is a predominant synthesis of type 1 helper T-cell cytokines, including IFN-γ and TNF-α.

6 **What symptoms could Ann experience as a result of her CD?**

A Because CD can affect any part of the intestine its symptoms may vary greatly from patient to patient, making diagnosis a challenge. The most common symptoms are:

• bloating;
• cramping;

- abdominal pain (usually worse after eating);
- persistent diarrhoea (with blood and mucus in the faeces);
- unintentional weight loss;
- fatigue;
- mild fever.

Additional symptoms and complications include:

- anal pain;
- skin lesions;
- uveitis;
- boils;
- anaemia;
- malabsorption;
- rectal abscess;
- fissures;
- arthritis.

The most common complications are fistulas and intestinal blockage caused by thickening of the intestinal wall due to swelling and scar tissue.

7   **What investigations would Ann have in order to diagnose her CD?**

A   There is no single test to establish the diagnosis of CD. Other conditions are ruled out through a combination of information from the patient's history, physical examination (including a range of laboratory tests), X-rays and endoscopy findings. X-ray tests can often confirm or disprove the diagnosis of CD and may include barium studies of the upper and lower GI tract. Barium coats the small intestine, making signs of CD show up more.

Colonoscopy (with biopsy) is commonly used to diagnose CD and determine the extent and location of inflammation, bleeding or ulcers. The wall of the ileum, rectum and the entire colon can be observed through a lighted tube inserted through the anus. Stool specimens are examined for pathogenic organisms to rule out infection and to show if there is bleeding in the intestines (*C. difficile* had been ruled out by Ann's GP).

Blood tests can identify anaemia caused by bleeding, and a high white blood cell count, which is a sign of inflammation or infection somewhere in the body. Raised erythrocyte sedimentation rate and C reactive protein levels may indicate active disease (Talley et al. 2008).

8   **What medicines are available to help manage Ann's CD?**

A   There is currently no cure for CD. The goals of treatment are to suppress the inflammatory response, allowing the intestinal tissue to heal (induce remission), correct nutritional deficiencies, relieve symptoms and prolong (maintain) periods of remission.

Medication, surgery, nutritional supplementation, or a combination of these options together with lifestyle adjustments and coping strategies are required. Women with CD can still become pregnant and have a baby.

Treatment employs several groups of drugs including aminosalicylates (5-ASA) corticosteroids (hydrocortisone, budesonide and prednisolone) and drugs that suppress the immune response. Aminosalicylates and corticosteroids are the backbone of treatment for acute, mild to moderate attacks (BNF 2012). These are now outlined.

AMINOSALICYLATES

Aminosalicylates are aspirin-like compounds known to reduce inflammation in the colon, and may be continued as a maintenance therapy providing long-term relief. The exact mechanism is unknown. A variety of aminosalicylate preparations are available and sulfasalazine is a popular choice. This is a pro-drug activated in the bowel to release 5-aminosalicylic acid and sulapyridine.

As an alternative to steroid medications, sulfasalazine can be used to treat mild cases of CD, and acute, mild to moderate CD affecting the rectum (proctitis) or lower colon can be treated with local application of an aminosalicylate in suppository or retention enema form, together with a local corticosteroid. Disease that is more widespread in the intestine or unresponsive to rectal treatment requires oral treatment. More moderate disease requires corticosteroid tablets.

Asacol is the proprietory name for a prescription-only preparation of the aminosalicylate drug mesalazine. Mesalazine (5-aminosalicylic acid) is a unique compound that releases aspirin in the large intestine for a direct anti-inflammatory effect. It is used when the more commonly used drug sulfasalazine has not worked or cannot be tolerated. Side-effects of mesalazine-containing medications include nausea, vomiting, heartburn, diarrhoea and headache. Particularly troublesome side-effects should be reported as the dose may need adjusting (Ford and Roach 2010).

CORTICOSTEROIDS

Used to treat moderate to severely active CD, corticosteroid (steroid) drugs are a type of hormone medication used to help reduce inflammation. They non-specifically suppress the immune system. Prednisone and methylprednisolone are available orally, intravenously and rectally. During the earliest stages of CD, when symptoms are at their worst, corticosteroids are usually prescribed in large doses. These are gradually lowered once symptoms are controlled and should not be stopped suddenly. Steroids are not used as a maintenance medication as they have significant short- and long-term side-effects. These include greater susceptibility to infection and osteoporosis, acne, weight gain, oedema, mood changes, insomnia, diabetes, muscle cramps and stiffness.

Budesonide is a slow-release steroid used specifically to treat CD. Causing fewer side-effects than prednisolone, it may be less effective. If budesonide is not effective or if symptoms are more severe, prednisolone is used; this has been known to cause mental health problems in an estimated 5% of people.

ANTIBIOTICS

These are used if there is an additional bacterial infection. Ampicillin, sulfonamides, cephalosporin, tetracycline or metronidazole may be prescribed.

9   **Why were azathioprine and methotrexate tried?**

A   Azathioprine (Imuran) is an immunosuppressive (immunomodulator) drug affecting the immune response and is used in the treatment of CD for severe symptoms that have not responded sufficiently to corticosteroids. It helps reduce inflammation on a long-term, maintenance basis, often in combination with corticosteroids when symptoms relapse. It is thought to enhance the action of corticosteroids. Azathioprine is a pro-drug that is metabolized to 6-mercaptopurine (6MP) (both agents are available), effective in treating severe CD and maintaining remissions. The precise action of 6MP is not known but a T-cell suppressant action is thought to be one of the main mechanisms. Depending on the severity of symptoms, azathioprine can be given as a tablet or an injection. Azathioprine may cause nausea, vomiting and diarrhoea, joint pain, bone marrow suppression and occasionally pancreatitis, which resolve on drug withdrawal.

Methotrexate is used in chronically active CD which is resistant to or dependent on steroids. It is given intravenously at a dose of 25mg weekly for 16 weeks, during which time steroids are reduced. Daily folic acid supplementation is recommended. This drug is also used for rheumatoid arthritis and is associated with a range of side-effects including liver damage.

10   **What are biological therapies and how do they work?**

A   A growing range of biological therapies include infliximab (Remicade) and adalimumab (Humera). These are used to treat moderate to severe CD that does not respond to standard therapies, and in the treatment of open, draining fistulas. They work by targeting the tumour necrosis factor alpha (TNFalpha) antibodies responsible for most of the inflammation associated with CD. Some studies suggest that biological therapies may enhance the effectiveness of immunosuppressive medications (NICE 2010).

Infliximab (licensed since 1998) is a chimeric (a blend consisting of 75% human, 25% mouse protein) monoclonal antibody. It is given through an IV infusion over the course of two hours. Depending on how well symptoms respond to treatment, one infusion may suffice, although three infusions given every eight weeks may be necessary.

Around one in four people have an allergic reaction to infliximab so close monitoring is essential. Resuscitation facilities are necessary as anaphylactic shock (as in Ann's case) is not unknown. It is not recommended for people who have previously had tuberculosis (TB), hepatitis or heart disease.

Ann is currently prescribed Humira (adalimumab, licensed in 2007), a synthetic man-made protein. Similar to human protein, it is indicated for adult patients with moderate to severely active CD who have had an inadequate response to conventional therapy, or those intolerant to previous treatment with infliximab (NICE 2010).

Adalimumab is taken by injection every other week, and works by attaching to the tumour necrosis factor and blocking its effects, reducing the inflammation and relieving symptoms associated with CD. It can be administered at home by the patient or family member once instructed by a health care professional. Its common side-effects include pain, swelling, redness and itching at the site of the injection, headache, nausea, vomiting, skin rash, muscle, joint and bone pain, respiratory tract infections such as colds, a runny nose and pneumonia (lung infection).

Corticosteroids, immunsuppressants, infliximab and adalimumab increase vulnerability to infection so people with shingles or chickenpox should not be prescribed these drugs.

11 **What complications might occur in the course of Ann's CD, and what is the role of surgery?**

A The most common complications are fistulas and intestinal blockage caused by thickening of the intestinal wall due to swelling and inflammation. In more advanced or complicated cases of CD, or when symptoms cannot be controlled using medication, surgery may be recommended. An estimated 60–75% of sufferers will require surgery. Because CD often recurs after surgery, those considering surgery should carefully weigh its benefits and risks compared with other treatments. Surgery may be restricted to a resection, or require an ileostomy.

12 **How might people like Ann adjust their lifestyle?**

A It is important that people with CD follow a nutritious diet. Some people find that certain foods make their symptoms worse and decide to try a different diet, although no special diet has been proven effective in the prevention and treatment of CD. In cases where symptoms are severe, a liquid diet (elemental diet) may be recommended. Nutritional and vitamin support may be required during active phases.

While CD is a serious chronic disease with many complications, it is not considered a fatal illness. Most people with the illness may continue to lead useful and productive lives, even though they may be hospitalized from time to time, or need to take medications. In between flare-ups of the disease, many individuals feel well and may be relatively free of symptoms.

KEY POINTS

- CD is a disease that causes inflammation, swelling and irritation of any part of the GI tract.
- It affects both men and women, predominantly aged 16–30.
- Its cause is unknown, but is believed to be the result of an abnormal reaction by the immune system, genetics and environmental factors.
- TNFalpha, present in high levels in CD, causes most of the associated inflammation.
- The most common symptoms of CD are abdominal pain and diarrhoea. Flare-ups and remissions are characteristic.
- Diagnosis is made by performing a physical examination, blood and stool tests, and imaging tests.
- Aminosalicylates and steroids are the main drugs used for mild to moderate CD.
- Biologics and immunosuppressants are used for severe CD.
- The most common complications are fistulas and intestinal blockage.
- No special diet has been proven effective for preventing or treating CD.

REFERENCES

BMA (British Medical Association) (2005) *Concise Guide to Medicines and Drugs*. London: Dorling Kindersley.

BNF (British National Formulary) (2012) *BNF 63: March*. London: Pharmaceutical Press.

Ford, S. and Roach, S. (2010) *Introductory Clinical Pharmacology*, 9th edn. London: Lippincott Williams & Wilkins.

Hogston, R. and Marjoram, B. (2011) *Foundations of Nursing Practice*, 4th edn. Basingstoke: Palgrave Macmillan.

Karch, A. (2010) *Focus on Nursing Pharmacology*. Philadelphia, PA: Lippincott Williams & Wilkins.

Long, R.G. and Scott, B.B. (2005) *Gastroenterology and Liver Disease*. London: Elsevier.

NHS Choices (2011) *Crohn's Disease*, available at: www.nhs.uk/conditions/Chrons-disease.

NICE (National Institute for Health and Clinical Excellence) (2010) *Technology Appraisal 187: Infliximab (Review) and Adalimumab for the Treatment of Crohn's Disease (including a review of technology appraisal guidance 40)*. London: NICE.

Prosser, S., Worster, B., MacGregor, J., Dewar, K., Runyard, P. and Fegan, J. (2000) *Applied Pharmacology*. London: Mosby.

Talley, N.J., Segal, I. and Weltman, M.D. (2008) *Gastroenterology and Hepatology*. London: Elsevier.

The young person with meningitis
Christine Whitney-Cooper

CASE AIMS

After examining this case study the reader should be able to:

- Briefly explain the presenting symptoms of meningitis.
- List the possible causes of meningitis.
- Demonstrate an understanding of the mode of action and reasons for giving penicillin in meningitis.
- With reference to pathophysiology, explain the signs and symptoms of meningococcal meningitis and septicaemia.
- Argue the pros and cons of carrying out a lumbar puncture as an aid to diagnosis.
- Outline the focus of treatment in meningococcal septicaemia in a young person.
- Explain the implications of using intravenous fluids and antibiotics to treat septicaemic shock.
- Explain why meningitis and meningococcal meningitis are notifiable diseases.
- Demonstrate an understanding of why rifampicin would be given to the family of a patient diagnosed as having meningococcal meningitis.

CASE

Fifteen-year-old Mohammed visited his GP at 9 a.m. accompanied by his mother. Mohammed reported that he had been ill since last night; he had vomited his breakfast, but was now drinking water. He felt hot, his head was pounding and he was tired. The GP's observations were: temperature 38°C, pulse 75, blood pressure 110/80, respiratory rate 20 and oxygen saturations of 97% in air. The GP could not find a cause for the febrile illness and advised Mohammed to take ibuprofen every four hours. He arranged to call him at home after surgery. He also advised Mohammed's mother to contact the surgery if Mohammed appeared to get any more agitated or drowsy, or if a rash appeared.

Later that afternoon Mohammed's mother phoned the GP as she was concerned that her son had continued to vomit and was becoming more irritable and had a rash that was spreading. The GP visited and noted his temperature 39°C, pulse 80, blood pressure 100/60 and respiratory rate 20. The patient's oxygen saturation was 95% in air *and there was a capillary refill <2 seconds. Mohammed was becoming drowsier, had a petechial rash, but showed no signs of neck stiffness or photophobia. Bacterial meningitis was suspected. Benzyl penicillin was administered prior to Mohammed being taken to hospital.*

1 **What presenting symptoms have prompted the GP's advice?**

2 **What causes meningitis?**

3 **Why was penicillin administered and how does it work?**

On admission to A&E Mohammed had a non-blanching rash. Meningococcal meningitis was suspected. His observations had deteriorated (temperature 39°C, pulse 85, blood pressure 100/80, respiratory rate 25). His oxygen saturation was 93% in air and capillary refill was sluggish, but still <2 seconds. He was becoming drowsier with no signs of neck stiffness or photophobia. He was complaining that his legs hurt and he felt cold. A lumbar puncture was not performed. Antibiotics and an IV infusion of 0.9% sodium chloride were commenced. Mohammed's close family were given rifampicin.

4 **With reference to pathophysiology, explain the signs and symptoms of meningo-coccal meningitis and septicaemia**

5 **How could a lumbar puncture have aided diagnosis?**

6 **Why was a lumbar puncture not performed?**

7 **What is the focus of treatment in meningococcal septicaemia in a young person?**

8 **Explain the implications of using IV fluids and antibiotics to treat septicaemic shock**

9 **Why are meningitis and meningococcal meningitis notifiable diseases?**

10 **Why was rifampicin given and how does it work?**

ANSWERS

1 **What presenting symptoms have prompted the GP's advice?**

A Mohammed presents with a non-specific febrile illness which may indicate the early stage (**prodromal** phase) of meningitis or **septicaemia**. Young people with bacterial meningitis commonly present with non-specific symptoms and signs such as:

- fever;
- vomiting;
- irritability;
- upper respiratory tract symptoms.

It is often impossible to distinguish a milder self-limiting illness from meningococcal meningitis in the prodromal phase (NICE 2010).

Meningitis is a rapidly evolving illness, requiring urgent treatment. A study found that 50% of young people who presented with early signs can then go on to develop later neurological symptoms of meningitis (neck stiffness and **photophobia**) 12 to 15 hours from onset (Thompson et al. 2006).

Those with more **fulminant** illness will be critically ill within the first 24 hours, leaving a very narrow window of opportunity to deliver life-saving treatment. Early intervention is indicated. Signs of deterioration such as becoming more agitated (meningeal irritation) and a rash that does not blanch when pressed using a glass (petechiae indicating intradermal haemorrhage) can be indications of meningococcal meningitis and/or septicaemia.

2   What causes meningitis?

A   Meningitis can be caused by infection of bacteria, fungus or virus and is classified according to the causative agents. Bacterial meningitis can be caused by:

- pneumococcal species;
- *Haemophilus influenzae*;
- staphylococcal species;
- meningococcal species.

Meningococcal infection is the most common cause of bacterial meningitis in the UK and Ireland. There are several strains of meningococcal bacteria, but with the development of the MenC vaccine, 85% of cases are caused by MenB infection. Meningococcal bacteria (*Neisseria meningitidis*) can cause meningitis or septicaemia (blood poisoning), or a combination of these diseases, known as meningococcal disease.

3   Why was penicillin administered and how does it work?

A   The NICE guidelines (2010) recommend the administration of benzyl penicillin pre-hospital (or ceftriaxone if allergic to penicillin) in the presence of signs of meningococcal septicaemia. Penicillin is the drug of choice to treat meningococcal meningitis. Although it does not normally pass the blood–brain barrier, it can readily penetrate when the meninges are acutely inflamed. There is no clear evidence to indicate that early penicillin treatment improves outcomes, but it is the best current advice. However, early diagnosis and intervention are necessary to reduce mortality (Todar 2006).

Penicillin is bactericidal and has its effect by damaging and penetrating the cell wall of bacteria, thus killing the bacteria cells. A large component of all bacterial walls is a substance known as peptidoglycan. Bacteria are constantly rebuilding their cell walls (peptidoglycan synthesis), which is how they protect themselves and maintain their structure.

Peptidoglycan is principally made from two sugar molecules; N-acetylglucosamine (NAG) and N-acetylemuramic acid (NAM). Bacteria synthesize long, linear chains of these two sugars, alternating between a NAG and a NAM. Attached to each NAM, however, is a chain of a few amino acids (oligopeptide). To complete the structure of peptidoglycan, these oligopeptides are cross-linked to a neighbouring chain's oligopeptides to form a strong mesh.

Penicillins irreversibly bind to the bacterial enzyme transpeptidase (penicillin-binding protein) that cross-links these chains. This binding deactivates the enzyme, and so no cross-linking of the 'amino sugar' chains can take place, thus weakening the cell wall mesh and bacteria structure. Bacteria can build a resistance to the antibiotic by making β-lactamase, which defends the bacterial walls. This defence can be counteracted by combining the penicillin with β-lactamase inhibitors (BNF 2012).

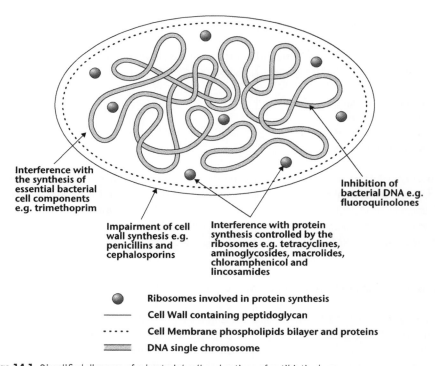

Interference with the synthesis of essential bacterial cell components e.g. trimethoprim

Inhibition of bacterial DNA e.g. fluoroquinolones

Impairment of cell wall synthesis e.g. penicillins and cephalosporins

Interference with protein synthesis controlled by the ribosomes e.g. tetracyclines, aminoglycosides, macrolides, chloramphenicol and lincosamides

●	Ribosomes involved in protein synthesis
——	Cell Wall containing peptidoglycan
· · · · ·	Cell Membrane phospholipids bilayer and proteins
═══	DNA single chromosome

Figure 14.1 Simplified diagram of a bacterial cell and actions of antibiotic drugs

4 **With reference to pathophysiology, explain the signs and symptoms of meningococcal meningitis and septicaemia**

SYSTEMIC PRESENTATION

The clinical features of meningitis are a reflection of the underlying pathophysiology. Early clinical features of bacterial meningitis are non-specific and include:

- fever;
- malaise;
- headache.

The major pathophysiological event in meningococcal septicaemia relates to a change in the functions of the microvasculature. The vascular endothelial surface is a highly specialized organ, regulating vascular permeability and presenting a thrombo-resistant, non-reactive surface to circulating blood cells. The highly specialized properties affected during the inflammatory process result in:

- increased vascular permeability;
- pathological vasoconstriction and vasodilatation;
- loss of intravascular coagulation;
- myocardial dysfunction leading to shock and multi-organ failure as a result of the vascular permeability;
- hypovolemia and shock.

The permeability is caused by bacterial components, such as endotoxins released from the bacterial cell wall, and is indirectly caused by the activation of inflammatory cells and stimulation of the immune system by proinflammatory cytokines. The capillary leak is the most important clinical event, but the underlying pathophysiology is unclear. Some evidence suggests that meningococci and neutrophils cause the loss of negatively charged glycosaminoglycans that are normally present on the endothelium. Albumin is normally confined to the vasculature because of its large size and negative charge, which repels the endothelial negative charge. The repulsive effect of albumin may be reduced in meningococcal infection, which allows the protein leak. The inflammatory process induced by meningococci results in a change in the permeability properties of the endothelium in all vascular beds.

From presentation until two to four days after the onset of illness:

- vascular permeability massively increases;
- albumin and other plasma proteins leak into the intravascular space and urine (proteinuria), causing severe hypovolemia;
- loss of proteins is followed by loss of fluid and electrolytes that leads to hypovolemia;
- loss of circulating plasma is initially compensated for by homoeostatic mechanisms, including vasoconstriction of both arterial and venous vascular beds.

However, as the capillary leak progresses, venous return to the heart is impaired and the cardiac output (heart rate) falls notably.

As compensatory vasoconstriction is an early protective mechanism to maintain tissue and organ perfusion in the face of diminished cardiac output, most patients with meningococcal septic shock have evidence of intense vasoconstriction. This presents as cold peripheries and sluggish blood flows to the tissues.

Although vasoconstriction is primarily protective, the constriction may persist even after resuscitation and measures to improve cardiac output. This can lead to patients developing cold, pale, and ischemic limbs due to disordered coagulation (Pathan et al. 2003).

Examination of the skin may reveal **petechiae** indicating haemorrhage and increased vascular permeability that are suggestive of, but not exclusive to, meningococcal infection (Hoffman and Webber 2009). One of the most dramatic features of severe meningococcal sepsis is the occurrence of widespread **purpura** fulminans, a cutaneous thrombotic disorder usually caused by autoimmune-mediated protein deficiency. This disorder typically presents with petechiae that eventually slowly or rapidly coalesce into extensive, necrotic **eschars** on the extremities. This severe intravascular thrombosis occurs in the presence of thrombocytopenia and prolonged coagulation as meningococcal infection affects the pathways of coagulation. Also, due to endothelial injury, there are platelet-release reactions which, together with the stagnant circulation due to vasoconstriction, cause platelet plugs to form and start the process of intravascular thrombosis.

CENTRAL NERVOUS PRESENTATION

Later on, the following symptoms develop as signs of meningeal irritation (Van de Beek et al. 2004):

- meningismus (neck stiffness);
- photophobia;
- vomiting.

Once the blood–brain barrier is breached, an inflammatory response within the cerebrospinal fluid occurs as follows.

- The inflammation of the meninges causes an activation of the trigeminal sensory nerve fibres and can also elicit a protective reflex to prevent stretching of the inflamed and hypersensitive nerve roots, which is seen clinically as neck stiffness.
- If the inflammatory process progresses to cerebral vasculitis or causes cerebral oedema and elevated intracranial pressure, then alterations in mental status, vomiting, seizures and cranial nerve palsies may be observed. The nerve palsies affect the ability of the pupil of the eye to respond to changes in environmental light and create weakness in the extremities.
- Patients who present with the clinical features of raised intracranial pressure, caused by meningitis, are at risk of cerebral infarction if perfusion is not improved.

5   **How could a lumbar puncture have aided diagnosis?**

A   A lumbar puncture (or spinal tap) is a way to collect CSF and bacteria in the CSF is usually the way to diagnose meningitis. The CSF in bacterial meningitis is characterized by a strongly elevated white blood cell count (<500 cells/µl) with predominant neutrophils and a strongly elevated protein (<1g/L), indicating severe blood-CSF barrier disruption, increased lactate (<0.3g/L) and decreased glucose CSF/blood ratio (>0.4).

6 **Why was a lumbar puncture not performed?**

A
- A lumbar puncture remains controversial where there are contraindications (Pollard et al. 1999). The procedure is contraindicated in the face of widespread purpura, severe coagulopathy, **cerebral herniation** or cardiovascular shock.
- A lumbar puncture is not usually performed where it will add little to the diagnosis, such as in clear-cut cases with fever and generalized purpura, or where it may lead to significant deterioration in those already seriously ill, or may delay treatment.
- Symptoms and signs of cerebral herniation (signs of fluctuating or impaired levels of consciousness) occur in 4–6% of children with bacterial meningitis and this complication accounts for 30% of deaths from the condition (Riordan and Cant 2002). Cerebral herniation can occur when a lumbar puncture has not been performed, but a there is a temporal association between lumbar puncture and herniation. Thus, delaying a lumbar puncture when there are signs and symptoms of herniation may be lifesaving.

Mohammed had no obvious signs of meningeal irritation (neck stiffness or photophobia), but this is not a good indicator of meningitis in young people as they can remain alert and the signs may be non-specific and absent. What was more important was that Mohammed had signs of shock – a sluggish capillary refill time even though it was above the threshold of >2 seconds; cold hands and feet and falling oxygen saturation. He also had some early signs of raised intracranial pressure as he was drowsy, indicating a decreasing conscious level. The purpuric-type rash was also a sign of **coagulopathy**.

7 **What is the focus of treatment in meningococcal septicaemia in a young person?**

A The focus of treatment is to identify signs of raised intracranial pressure or shock and treat the young person based on those findings. Meningococcal meningitis generally has a better prognosis than septicaemia; however, death can occur due to the severity of the inflammatory process within the brain. It is crucial to remember that the underlying meningitis and septicaemia may be very advanced by the time a rash appears. The rapidly evolving haemorrhagic rash can be a very late sign and in some cases it may be too late to save the child's life by the time this rash is seen. Although some of the causes of petechial rashes are self-limiting conditions, many others, including meningococcal disease, are fulminant purpura and life-threatening. So a non-blanching rash should therefore be treated as an emergency.

8 **Explain the implications of using IV fluids and antibiotics to treat septicaemic shock**

A Restoration of circulation volume is the most important component of resuscitation for shock and early treatment with an IV antibiotic such as ceftriaxone, a bactericidal cephalosporin, is essential. Cephalosporins are structurally similar and work in similar ways to penicillins by blocking the construction of the bacterial cell wall (Han et al. 2003). After being absorbed, cephalosporins are widely distributed in the tissues of the body. Some can actually cross over the blood–brain barrier – for example, ceftriaxone. This drug is therefore useful for infections in the CNS, such as bacterial meningitis.

Circulation volume is improved through IV fluids. Mohammed is prescribed **isotonic** fluids initially. The properties of an IV solution are created by the specific materials it contains. Crystalloid solutions are the primary fluids used to correct dehydration and contain electrolytes (e.g. sodium, potassium, calcium, chloride) but lack the large proteins and molecules found in colloids such as plasma albumin. Isotonic crystalloids (*iso* – same; *tonic* – concentration) have an electrolyte tonicity equal to the body plasma. When administered to a normally hydrated patient, isotonic crystalloids do not facilitate osmosis so there is no significant shift of water between the cells and the intravascular space (circulation). However, fluid replacement has to be managed carefully in meningococcal septicaemia due to vascular permeability. There is also a risk of increasing oedema within all tissues and organs as a result of persistent capillary leak. Pulmonary oedema and respiratory failure are direct consequences of the gross increase in vascular permeability.

To improve circulating volumes in shock, colloid solutions may also be prescribed. A colloid solution contains solutes as large proteins or other similarly sized molecules. The proteins and molecules are so large that they cannot pass through the cell walls of the capillaries and can significantly increase the intravascular volume (volume of blood). Colloid solutions facilitate movement of water into the circulation which may be beneficial in the short term, but continual movement can cause dehydration (Corbett and Brodie 2007).

9   **Why are meningitis and meningococcal meningitis notifiable diseases?**

A   Meningococcal disease is contracted through association with infected individuals, as evidenced by the 500- to 800-fold greater attack rate among household contacts than among the general population. Notification to the Health Protection Agency (HPA) is a legal requirement and acts as a trigger for public health actions to be put into place to protect other people from that disease (HPA 2010).

10   **Why was rifampicin given and how does it work?**

A   The risk to contacts is low. Although meningococcal disease is infectious, 97% of cases are isolated, with no links to any other cases. However, people who live in the same household as someone with meningococcal disease, along with intimate kissing contacts (boy/girlfriends) are more at risk than others. For this reason, such people are given rifampicin tablets or syrup. Usually, family members who accompany the patient to hospital will receive antibiotics there. The local public health doctor then has the job of making sure that any other household or intimate contacts receive antibiotics, and usually also tells the nursery or school the patient attends that there has been a case. There is no need to give antibiotics to a wider range of contacts, such as classmates, unless there has been more than one case within a short period of time. The public health doctor follows national guidelines when deciding what needs to be done to protect the community.

Rifampicin works by targeting and inactivating a bacterial enzyme called RNA-polymerase. The bacteria use RNA-polymerase to make essential proteins and to copy their own genetic information (DNA). Without this enzyme the bacteria cannot reproduce. It is important to remember that rifampicin kills the bacteria that live in the nose and throat, but cannot prevent illness in someone who is already incubating the germs. So even if a person is given antibiotics, it is still important they look out for the signs and symptoms of septicaemia and meningitis.

KEY POINTS

- It is often impossible to distinguish someone who has a milder self-limiting illness from someone with the early stages of meningococcal meningitis (prodromal phase).
- Bacterial meningitis is an infection of the surface of the brain (meninges). In young people the most frequent cause is *Neisseria meningitidis* (meningococcus) bacteria.
- Once the blood–brain barrier is breached, the inflammatory response of the meninges causes an activation of the trigeminal sensory nerve fibres, eliciting a protective reflex to prevent stretching of the inflamed and hypersensitive nerve roots. This is seen clinically as neck stiffness.
- Progressive inflammatory processes can lead to cerebral vasculitis, cerebral oedema and elevated intracranial pressure. This presents as alterations in mental status, vomiting and seizures, and causes cranial nerve palsies.
- A raised white cell count in the CSF is usually the way to diagnose bacterial meningitis, but a lumbar puncture is contraindicated when the individual exhibits signs of shock.
- Restoration of circulation volume is the most important component of resuscitation for septicaemic shock.
- Meningitis is a communicable disease so all who have a high risk of contracting it are offered a preventative antibiotic (chemoprophylactic agent).

REFERENCES

BNF (British National Formulary) (2012) *BNF 63: March*. London: Pharmaceutical Press.

Corbett, E. and Brodie, A. (2007) Intravenous fluids: it's more than just 'Fill 'er up!', *Practical Gastroenterology*, available at: www.medicine.virginia.edu/clinical/departments/medicine/divisions/digestive-health/nutrition-support-team/nutrition-articles/CorbettArticle.pdfGY.

Han, Y.Y., Carcillo, J.A., Dragotta, M.A. et al. (2003) Early reversal of pediatric-neonatal septic shock by community physicians is associated with improved outcome, *Pediatrics*, 112(4): 793–9.

Hoffman, O. and Weber, R.J. (2009) Pathophysiology and treatment of bacterial meningitis, *Therapeutic Advances in Neurological Disorders*, 2(6): 1–7.

HPA (Health Protection Agency) (2010) *The Health Protection (Part 2A Orders) Regulations 2010* (SI 2010/658). London: The Stationery Office.

NICE (National Institute for Health and Clinical Excellence) (2010) *CG102 Bacterial Meningitis and Meningococcal Septicaemia*, available at: http://guidance.nice.org.uk/CG102/Guidance.

Pathan, N., Faust, F.N. and Levin, M. (2003) Pathophysiology of meningococcal meningitis and septicaemia, *Archives of Disease in Childhood*, 88(7): 601–7.

Pollard, A.J., Britto, J., Nadel, S., DeMunter, C., Habibi, P. and Levin, M. (1999) Emergency management of meningococcal disease, *Archives of Disease in Childhood*, 80(3): 290–6.

Riordan, F. and Cant, A.J. (2002) When to do a lumbar puncture, *Archives of Disease in Childhood*, 87: 235–7.

Thompson, M.J., Ninis, N., Perera, R. et al. (2006) Clinical recognition of meningococcal disease in children and adolescents, *Lancet*, 367: 397–403.

Todar, K. (2006) Lectures in microbiology, available at: http://textbookofbacteriology.net/themicrobialworld/meningitis.html.

Van de Beek, D., de Gans, J., Spanjaard, L., Weisfelt, M., Reitsma, J.B. and Vermeulen, M. (2004) Clinical features and prognostic factors in adults with bacterial meningitis, *New England Journal of Medicine*, 351(18): 1849–59.

The person with a myocardial infarction

Diane Blundell

CASE AIMS

After examining this case study the reader should be able to:

- Briefly explain the normal anatomy and physiology of blood vessels.
- Describe the pathophysiology of atherosclerosis.
- Outline why the patient's gender is an important factor in diagnosing cardiovascular disease.
- Explain the significance of being post-menopausal in terms of myocardial infarction.
- Identify the importance of checking cholesterol levels in the diagnosis of myocardial infarction.
- Demonstrate an understanding of the mode of action and side-effects of tenecteplase in the treatment of myocardial infarction.
- Articulate how specific biomarkers such as troponin I relate to the confirmation of myocardial infarction.

CASE

A 59-year-old woman presented to the A&E department with a four-hour history of increased shortness of breath (dyspnoea), retrosternal chest pain and sudden extreme fatigue/weakness. She has a strong family history of heart disease, herself suffering from atherosclerosis, angina and hypertension. She is post-menopausal. She takes Imdur 60mg once per day and 5mg of amlodopine. She recently had fasting cholesterol levels checked by her GP and the results were: LDLs 4.9mmol/L, HDLs <1.3mmol/L and triglycerides 5.6mmol/L. This gave her a total cholesterol of 6.2mmol/L. Her BMI is 29 and she has a history of very little exercise before being diagnosed with her angina four years ago. She is a non-smoker and admits to having an occasional glass of wine.

1 **Prior to the patient's cardiovascular disease (CVD), what would have been the normal anatomy and physiology of her blood vessels?**

2 **What is meant by atherosclerosis?**

3 **Why may the patient's gender be an important factor in diagnosing the problem?**

4 **What is significant about the patient being post-menopausal?**

5 **Why has she had her cholesterol levels checked?**

> *The patient is diagnosed via ECG and patient history with an AMI. She is given 300mg of aspirin(stat) tenecteplase (TNK) with IV heparin running alongside as per trust policy. She is also given 2.5mg of diamorphine, an antiemetic and 100% oxygen. Twelve hours after her initial onset of symptoms she is given a troponin I blood test which returns at 16.0ng/ml (which is significant for indication of MI).*

6 **What is the mechanism of action of thrombolytic drugs such as tenecteplase?**

7 **What are the main risks with thrombolytic drugs?**

8 **How do specific biomarkers such as troponin I relate to the confirmation of MI?**

ANSWERS

1 **Prior to the patient's CVD, what would have been the normal anatomy and physiology of her blood vessels?**

A Most blood vessels have a similar construction (with the exception of the capillaries). The walls of all blood vessels, arteries and veins are composed of three layers of tissue called *tunica*. The outer layer, *tunica externa* (adventitia) is composed of connective tissue, collagen and nerve fibres. It surrounds and supports the vessel with sympathetic nerve fibres that transmit nerve impulses to keep the walls of the vessel in a state of *tonus* which stops the vessel from collapsing in on itself. The infiltration of sympathetic nerve fibres is increased (vasoconstriction) and allows for dilation of the vessel walls when nerve impulses are decreased (vasodilation). Generally there is more fibrous tissue found in arteries than in veins.

The middle layer is called the *tunica media* and is made up of vascular smooth muscle supported by a layer of collagen and elastin fibres. The smooth muscle cells that make up this layer produce the vasoconstriction/dilation of the blood vessel by releasing the neurotransmitter norepinephrine which diffuses into the tunica media and acts upon the nearby smooth muscle cells.

The innermost layer is called the *tunica intima* and consists of a single layer of flattened endothelial cells with little sub-endothelial connective tissue. This layer is smooth to prevent turbulent blood flow (Fawcett 2006). Beneath the tissue is an internal elastic lamina (thin layer) that is well developed in muscular arteries. Endothelial cells form a continuous lining throughout the vascular system called the *endothelium*. The endothelium plays a role in vascular resistance, control of platelet adhesion and clotting. Capillaries are composed only of endothelial cells with few or no elastic fibres; this aids the rapid exchange of water and solutes between the tissue fluid and blood plasma (Barber et al. 2012).

2 **What is meant by atherosclerosis?**

A Atherosclerosis is a disease process that affects the large and medium arteries, especially the aorta and the arteries that supply the heart (coronary arteries), brain, kidneys and lower limbs (Woods et al. 2012). As a disease process it is described as a thickening or hardening of the arteries. As it is a progressive disease, and evidence suggests that the disease process starts in childhood, but it may be many years before the effects of poor diet, lack of pertinent exercise, smoking, drinking and lifestyle habits finally show themselves as hypertension, diabetes, obesity and smoking-related disorders which all carry an increased risk of developing coronary heart disease (CHD).

It is under the inner layer of the arteries, the tunica intima, where the progressive disease process of atherosclerosis is most prevalent and where **plaque** formation is accumulated. This build-up of atherosclerotic plaque is the precursor of many forms of angina and ultimately can, and does, lead to the high incidence of MI in both men and women.

In general, atherosclerosis evolves from deposits of lipids, cellular debris, calcium and fibrin (a clotting factor). Together they unite to initiate a progressive inflammatory component. Although not yet completely understood it is hypothesized to be fundamentally initiated by an inflammatory process in the vessel wall in response to retained LDL molecules. Once the molecules are inside the vessel wall they are suspected of becoming susceptible to oxidation by **free radicals** and in essence become toxic in nature to the cells. Because of this toxicity the

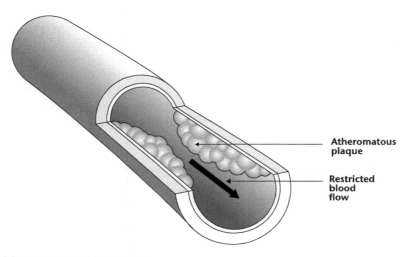

Figure 15.1 The effects of atherosclerosis

molecules trigger a cascade of immune responses which over time produce an atheroma. The body's immune system responds by sending specialized white blood cells such as macrophages and T-lymphocytes to absorb the oxidized-LDL forming specialized foam cells, along with a proliferation of arterial smooth muscle cells in an attempt to heal the lesion. However, in their endeavour to process the oxidized-LDL they grow and then rupture, depositing an even greater amount of oxidized cholesterol into the artery wall. This ultimately triggers more white blood cells which perpetuates the cycle. Eventually, the artery becomes inflamed, and the cholesterol plaque causes the muscle cells to enlarge and form a hard cover over the affected area.

This hard cover is what causes a narrowing of the lumen of the artery, reducing the blood flow, which may lead to angina and increases blood pressure. Advanced plaques, which have a fibrous coating and a lipid-rich core, are known to be unstable. Consequently, thrombi form on the plaque surface, which ultimately restricts the lumen of the artery further and is known to produce the symptoms of acute coronary syndrome (Johnson and Rawlings-Anderson 2007).

3   **Why may the patient's gender be an important factor in diagnosing the problem?**

A
- Heart disease does not discriminate between the sexes and remains a leading killer of both men and women worldwide. The difference lies in the diagnosis and treatment of women with heart disease which seems to have perpetuated a gender gap.
- According to the British Heart Foundation (2011), CVD is the leading cause of death and disability in women in the UK and accounts for more deaths among women than breast cancer. However, despite these findings, many women still do not identify cardiovascular disease as their greatest health risk.
- Rowlands and Clarke (2007) state that, unlike men, women are less likely to seek medical help and are more likely to present themselves late to A&E with symptoms such as breathlessness, abdominal discomfort and fatigue. This late presentation may well result in delays in diagnosis and receiving effective treatment.
- When a hospital assessment is needed, women are less likely to be treated in coronary care units than men, or even to have ECG and cardiac enzymes measured, and this may be due in part to their 'atypical' symptoms.
- In a man, plaque tends to distribute itself in clumps for some reason, whereas women's plaque is distributed more evenly throughout the artery walls. This can result in women's angiographic studies as being misinterpreted as 'normal'. Therefore, women are less likely to receive treatment for their symptoms in line with the evidence-based guidelines for men.

4   **What is significant about the patient being post-menopausal?**

A
- Up until the menopause a woman is thought to be naturally protected by the presence of the hormone oestrogen, which is responsible for the female secondary sexual characteristics and the development and proper functioning of the female genital organs.
- Oestrogen is known to act on the tunica intima and helps to reduce the disease process of atherosclerosis by minimizing the effects of inflammation on the arteries.

- As women move into the menopause, which usually starts around their early fifties, it is thought that the protective effect of oestrogen on the lining of the large arteries is greatly reduced.
- It is around the time of the menopause that researchers find that many doctors see a clustering of obesity, hypertension and dyslipidaemia in their peri/post-menopausal patients, which also increases the risks for developing CHD (Thompson and Webster 2005).
- Recently there has been further discussion by the British Heart Foundation (2011) to confirm that some researchers worldwide are now not totally convinced that it is solely down to the loss of oestrogen that puts women at greater risk of developing CHD.
- Consideration is also being given to other variables such as ageing, diabetes and psychosocial factors such as depression as significant risk factors. Although this research is in its infancy at present there appear to be far too many unanswered questions to conclude a correlation between these variables and the relationship to CHD in women, and, as such, a reduction in the amount of oestrogen still remains a favourable consideration for the development of CHD.

5   **Why has she had her cholesterol levels checked?**

A   Although elevated cholesterol levels are associated with an increased risk of developing CHD in men and women, total cholesterol levels tend to peak approximately 10 years later in women than in men. Due to this factor a low level of HDL appears to be a better predictor of CHD risk in women, especially older women, compared to LDL levels.

This difference in cholesterol levels may well be attributed to the fact that oestrogen keeps the harmful LDL cholesterol levels lower and HDL levels higher. It also plays a role in keeping the blood vessels dilated. This protective effect is believed to be reduced after the menopause (see above).

6   **What is the mechanism of action of thrombolytic drugs such as tenecteplase?**

A   Thrombolytic drugs such as tenecteplase break down the thrombus so that the blood flow to the heart muscle can be re-established to prevent any further damage; this will also assist in the healing process (NICE 2002).

If heart muscle is compromised or occluded from a rich supply of oxygenated blood then the likelihood of death of the heart muscle (necrosis) becomes increasingly high. For our patient in this scenario her clinical symptoms (typically but not exclusively retrosternal chest pain/discomfort) and characteristic changes in her 12-lead ECG (with **ST segment elevation**) have provided the most immediate indication of the diagnosis of AMI which, in the absence of contraindications for this patient, requires thrombolysis as per hospital trust policy.

Tenecteplase is a relatively new type of thrombolytic drug introduced in 2001. It is considered a modified form of **plasminogen** activator and can be given by rapid IV bolus injection rather than by infusion (BNF 2012). Its timing is crucial in determining the extent of beneficial achievement and has a window of opportunity of up to 12 hours from the first onset of symptoms.

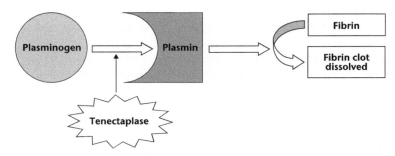

Figure 15.2 The mechanism of action of tenectaplase

Although not completely verified it is thought that tenecteplase binds to fibrin (the insoluble matrix on which a blood clot is formed) and converts plasminogen (a precursor of plasmin) to plasmin, which breaks down fibrin clots when healing is complete. In the presence of fibrin, tenecteplase conversion of plasminogen to plasmin is increased relative to its conversion in the absence of fibrin. Ultimately this decreases systemic activation of plasminogen and the resulting degradation of circulating fibrinogen. In essence its action is to break down the clot by interfering with the body's natural clotting cascade (Khan 2007).

Alongside tenecteplase, heparin (an anticoagulant) is given, usually as an IV bolus injection before thrombolysis, followed by IV infusion. When given alongside tenecteplase the heparin dose is weight-adjusted. It is also recommended that aspirin 300mg (chewable) is given at the same or around the same time as any thrombolytic drug as the benefit of aspirin is that it works on platelet aggregation.

7 **What are the main risks with thrombolytic drugs?**

A Bleeding complications are the main risk that is associated with thrombolytic drugs. The most important of these is the complication due to haemorrhagic stroke which occurs in 0.5–1.0% of patients and carries an associated risk of high mortality and long-term disability in survivors. The risk of a haemorrhagic stroke following the use of thrombolytic drugs increases with a patient's age and blood pressure. Strict guidelines and protocols exist which highlight important contraindications to the giving of this drug in patients with a recent history of any type of:

- haemorrhage;
- trauma;
- surgery;
- acute cerebrovascular events.

As with any drug that has the potential to cause haemorrhage, thrombolytic drugs should be stopped immediately if the patient displays any signs or symptoms of severe bleeding or stroke-type symptoms (BNF 2012).

8 **How do specific biomarkers such as troponin I relate to the confirmation of MI?**

 • Troponin I and T are structural components of cardiac muscle. They are released directly into the bloodstream with a myocardial injury.
  • Troponins will begin to increase following MI within 3 to 12 hours.
  • Troponin I, as a diagnostic marker, is taken at its peak time of 12 hours after initial chest pain/discomfort.
  • Patients that arrive in hospital after the 12-hour window of opportunity can still be given the test but may very well miss out on being given a clot-busting drug such as tenecteplase as these drugs are shown to be most effective in their management of clot busting within the 12-hour window.
  • Troponins will also remain elevated from 5 to 10 days for troponin I and up to two weeks for troponin T. This fact alone makes them a superior marker for diagnosing MI.
  • The disadvantage of this continued elevation is that this particular diagnostic marker makes it more difficult to diagnose re-infarction or extension of infarction in a patient who has already suffered an initial MI (Saenger and Jaffe 2007).

KEY POINTS

  • Heart disease does not discriminate between the sexes and remains a leading killer of both men and women worldwide.
  • CHD accounts for more deaths among women than breast cancer.
  • Women are more likely to present themselves late to A&E with 'atypical' symptoms of a suspected MI.
  • Women are less likely to receive treatment for their symptoms in line with evidence-based guidelines for men.
  • Up until the menopause, women are thought to be naturally protected from CHD by the presence of the hormone oestrogen.
  • Recently new research looked at the links to variables such as age, diabetes, depression and psychosocial factors in the development of MI in women.
  • It is under the inner layer of the tunica intima where the progressive disease process of atherosclerosis is most prevalent and where plaque formation is accumulated.
  • In general, atherosclerosis evolves from deposits of lipids, cellular debris, calcium and fibrin.
  • Plaque in a man tends to distribute itself in clumps whereas women's plaque is distributed more evenly throughout the artery walls.
  • Although elevated cholesterol levels are associated with an increased risk of developing CHD in men and women, total cholesterol levels tend to peak approximately 10 years later in women than in men.
  • Thrombolytic drugs such as tenecteplase break down the thrombus so that the blood flow to heart muscle can be re-established.
  • Bleeding complications are the main risk factors that are associated with thrombolytic drugs.
  • Troponin I and T are highly specific markers for confirmation of myocardial injury.

REFERENCES

Barber, P., Parkes, J. and Blundell, D. (2012) *Further Essentials of Pharmacology for Nurses.* Maidenhead: Open University Press.

BNF (British National Formulary) (2012) *BNF 63: March.* London: Pharmaceutical Press.

British Heart Foundation (2011) *Women and Heart Disease*, available at: www.bhf.org.uk/publications.

Fawcett, J.A.D. (2006) *Hemodynamic Monitoring Made Easy.* London: Elsevier.

Johnson, K. and Rawlings-Anderson, K. (eds) (2007) *Oxford Handbook of Cardiac Nursing.* Oxford: Oxford University Press.

Khan, M.G. (2007) *Cardiac Drug Therapy*, 7th edn. Totowa, NJ: Humana Press.

NICE (National Institute for Health and Clinical Excellence) (2002) *Technology Appraisal Guidance 52: Guidance on the Use of Drugs for Early Thrombolysis in the Treatment of Acute Myocardial Infarction.* London: NICE.

Rowlands, D. and Clarke, B. (eds) (2007) *Recent Advances in Cardiology.* London: Royal Society of Medicine Press.

Saenger, A.K. and Jaffe, A.S. (2007) The use of biomarkers for the evaluation and treatment of patients with acute coronary syndromes, *Medical Clinics of North America*, 91: 657–81.

Thompson, D.R. and Webster, R.A. (2005) *Caring for the Coronary Patient*, 2nd edn. London: Butterworth-Heinemann.

Woods, S.L., Froelicher, E.S.S., Motzer, S.U. and Bridges, E.J. (2012) *Cardiac Nursing*, 6th edn. Philadelphia, PA: Lippincott Williams & Wilkins.

The person with osteoporosis
Janine Upton

CASE AIMS

After examining this case study the reader should be able to:

- Describe the process of normal bone remodelling.
- Briefly explain how bone density changes through a person's lifespan.
- Define osteoporosis and discuss how it affects bone fragility.
- Identify the risk factors for the development of osteoporosis.
- Demonstrate an understanding of the mode of action and side-effects of bisphosphonates.
- Discuss the role of the nurse in advising patients regarding taking bisphosphonates.
- Discuss the role of the nurse in giving lifestyle advice to a patient with osteoporosis.

CASE

Mrs H, a 57-year-old, presented in A&E with a painful right wrist following a fall. She reported slipping on wet grass while walking her dog. Mrs H's wrist was manipulated and immobilized in a below-elbow back slab and she was discharged from the department with plaster instructions and an appointment for a review at the fracture clinic.

Mrs H is a teacher and she works full time at the local high school. She is married with two children and four grandchildren. She has no significant medical or surgical history apart from having had a total hysterectomy and bilateral salpingo-oophorectomy at the age of 39 years. She does not take any regular medication. Mrs H was prescribed hormone replacement therapy (HRT) following her hysterectomy but stopped taking it about 10 years ago after media publicity regarding the increased risks associated with the long-term use of HRT. Mrs H does not smoke; she enjoys an occasional glass of wine when eating out and regularly takes her grandchildren swimming. She is 167cm tall and weighs 64kg.

Mrs H returned to the fracture clinic a few days later and was reviewed by the orthopaedic consultant. She had sustained a fragility fracture and the consultant suspected she might have osteoporosis. He advised her to see her GP for further investigation. The GP referred Mrs H for a dual-energy X-ray absorptiometry (DXA) scan to measure her bone mineral density (BMD).

1 **Describe the process of normal bone remodelling in Mrs H**

2 **How does bone density change through a person's lifespan?**

3 **Define osteoporosis and discuss how it affects bone fragility**

4 **Identify the risk factors for the development of osteoporosis**

Some weeks later the DXA scan was performed and Mrs H returned to her GP for the results. BMD is measured at the hip and the lower spine and the results are recorded as a standard deviation compared against the normal reference range for healthy young adults (T-score) and the normal reference range for a person of the same age (Z-score). NICE (2008) defines osteoporosis as a T-score of −2.5 standard deviations or below on DXA scanning. Mrs H has a T-score of −2.9 at the hip and the diagnosis of osteoporosis was confirmed. The GP outlined the treatment options and, following discussion, Mrs H was prescribed alendronate 70mg once a week.

---

5 **What effect do bisphosphonates have on bone turnover?**

6 **What advice would you give to Mrs H in relation to taking her medication?**

7 **What additional advice would you give to Mrs H?**

ANSWERS

1 **Describe the process of normal bone remodelling in Mrs H**

A The main cells in bone homeostasis are osteoblasts, osteocytes and osteoclasts:

- osteoblasts are bone-building cells that synthesize and secrete collagen and other components that constitute the extracellular matrix of bone tissue;
- osteocytes are mature bone cells that monitor and maintain bone tissue;
- osteoclasts are responsible for the resorption of the extracellular matrix of bone (Rang et al. 2012).

Bone is a complex and dynamic living tissue that is constantly being remodelled. Bone remodelling is a process of bone resorption and bone formation, whereby older, weaker bone is replaced by newer, stronger bone, in response to a variety of factors including exercise, diet, drugs and injury (Tortora and Nielson 2009). The process involves the activity of osteoblasts and osteoclasts, the actions of cytokines, the turnover of the main bone minerals, calcium and phosphate, and the actions of several hormones including, among others, parathyroid hormone (PTH), the vitamin D family and oestrogens.

The cycle begins with osteoclast precursor cells, called into action by cytokines and hormones, which are activated by osteoblasts to develop into osteoclasts. Once released, these

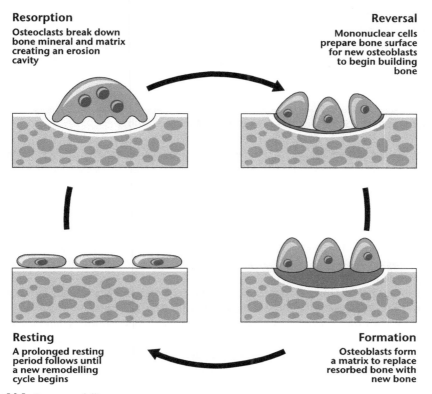

Resorption

Osteoclasts break down
bone mineral and matrix
creating an erosion
cavity

Reversal

Mononuclear cells
prepare bone surface
for new osteoblasts
to begin building
bone

Resting

A prolonged resting
period follows until
a new remodelling
cycle begins

Formation

Osteoblasts form
a matrix to replace
resorbed bone with
new bone

Figure 16.1 Bone remodelling

cytokines activate osteoblasts which take over the freshly dug resorption pit. The osteoblasts synthesize and secrete **osteoid** to refill the pit and, having completed their job, the cytokines are embedded in it again to await their next call to action. The osteoid is then mineralized as calcium phosphate crystals (hydroxyapatite) are laid down. Some of the osteoblasts become trapped in the osteoid and become terminal osteocytes and others go on to activate osteoclast precursors and the cycle begins again (Rang et al. 2012).

2   **How does bone density change through a person's lifespan?**

- In childhood, osteoblast activity is greater than osteoclast activity to enable skeletal development – i.e. growth. At this stage it takes around two years to renew the entire skeleton (compared to 7–10 years in adults).
- Bone stops growing in length at around 16–18 years of age but continues to increase in density until the mid-twenties. At this stage, bone formation and bone resorption are intimately balanced.
- In both men and women, peak bone mass is achieved at around age 35 and after this there is a gradual bone loss of approximately 0.5–1% per year.

- In women, the menopause results in a dramatic acceleration of the rate of bone loss due to increased osteoclast activity, mainly affecting trabecular bone.
- Once this has settled down, bone loss associated with advancing age is seen in both men and women, is due more to decreased osteoblast numbers and affects mainly cortical bone (Tortora and Nielson 2009).

3 Define osteoporosis and discuss how it affects bone fragility

A Osteoporosis is a skeletal disorder characterized by a reduction in bone density and quality as a result of increased bone resorption in relation to bone formation. Bones become progressively porous, brittle and fragile and are at increased risk of fracture. It is often called the 'silent disease' because there are no warning signs or symptoms prior to fracture (see www.iofbonehealth.org).

Osteoporotic fractures are called 'fragility fractures' because they occur in the course of normal daily activity or as a result of minimal trauma such as a fall from standing height or less. The most common sites of fracture are the vertebrae (spine), hip and distal radius (wrist); however, individuals with osteoporosis have an increased risk of all types of skeletal fractures (see www.nos.org.uk).

The incidence of fractures increases with age for both men and women; one in two women and one in five men over the age of 50 in the UK will suffer a fracture.

Vertebral fractures can result in height loss, intense pain and deformity, however it is hip fractures that are associated with the greatest morbidity and mortality. These latter almost always require surgery, which carries an increased risk of complications and long-term disability, resulting in loss of independence or death (see www.nos.org.uk).

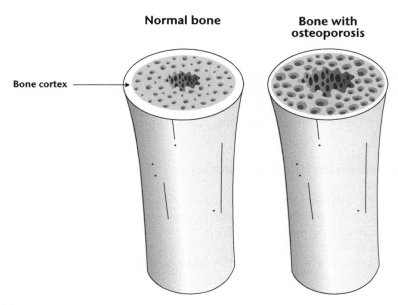

Figure 16.2 Osteoporosis in a bone

While fractures of the distal radius are usually regarded as less severe injuries, they are often seen in middle-aged women who have fallen, like Mrs H, and may be the first indication of osteoporosis. Women who are not diagnosed at this stage may go on to fracture their vertebrae or hips.

Based on current trends, it is predicted that hip fracture rates in the UK will increase from 46,000 in 1985 to 117,000 in 2016. Secondary prevention through early identification and treatment of people at risk of osteoporosis should lead to a reduction in the incidence of major fractures in later life (Dennison et al. 2005; BOA 2007).

4 **Identify the risk factors for the development of osteoporosis**

A The risk factors in the development of osteoporosis can be broadly divided into two categories (see Table 16.1). Although fixed risks are predetermined and cannot be controlled, there are strategies that can minimize their effect and individuals can take action to reduce the modifiable risks through healthy lifestyle choices.

Table 16.1 Risk factors for the development of osteoporosis (www.iofbonehealth.org)

Fixed risks	Modifiable risks
• Age	• Alcohol
• Female gender	• Smoking
• Family history of osteoporosis	• Low BMI
• Previous fracture	• Poor nutrition
• Ethnicity	• Vitamin D deficiency
• Menopause/hysterectomy	• Eating disorders
• Long-term glucocorticoid therapy	• Insufficient exercise
• Rheumatoid arthritis	• Low dietary calcium intake
• Primary/secondary hypogonadism in men	• Frequent falls

In considering the risks in relation to Mrs H, it is evident that her total hysterectomy with bilateral salpingo-oophorectomy resulted in an early menopause (before the age of 45). She was initially prescribed HRT and this would have provided protection for her bones as well as managing the menopausal symptoms, but she stopped taking the HRT after considering the associated risks too great. The recent fragility fracture is also an indicator that she is more likely to sustain another fracture in the future.

5 **What effect do bisphosphonates have on bone turnover?**

A The treatment of osteoporosis aims to reduce the risk of fracture occurring and can be broadly divided into two categories of drug:

- **anti-resorptive agents**, which reduce bone resorption;
- anabolic agents, which stimulate bone formation.

Bisphosphonates are organic pyrophosphate compounds that bind to the hydroxyapatite crystals in the bone. They are only released during the remodelling process and therefore terminal half-life in humans may be greater than 10 years (Brenner and Stephens 2006).

Anti-resorptive agents, such as alendronate, inhibit osteoclast activity, slowing down the rate of bone loss. They do this by preventing the osteoclast precursor cells from attaching to the bone and also affect their ability to resorb bone by reducing their metabolic activity. Initially, bone resorption is reduced without affecting bone formation and this results in significant increases in BMD, but this rapid gain slows down over a period of 12–18 months as the resorption-formation coupling mechanisms catch up. The newly formed bone is of normal quality (McDermott et al. 2004; eMC 2012).

Current guidance on the secondary prevention of fragility fractures in post-menopausal women who have osteoporosis and have sustained an osteoporotic fragility fracture recommends treatment with alendronate as it has been shown to reduce the risk of vertebral and hip fractures (NICE 2008). Alendronate can be taken as 10mg tablets daily or 70mg tablets once weekly. The active ingredient is alendronic acid trihydrate and it is available in generic preparations as alendronic acid or branded as 'Fosamax'. NICE (2008) recommends that the cheapest preparation should be prescribed.

Oral bisphosphonates are very poorly absorbed: less than 5% of the drug is absorbed when taken on an empty stomach and this is further reduced by food, other drugs and liquids (other than water). Of this 5%, about half is deposited in bone and the remainder is rapidly excreted in the urine (Brenner and Stephens 2006).

6   **What advice would you give to Mrs H in relation to taking her medication?**

A

- Alendronate must be taken at least 30 minutes before the first food or drink of the day. It is important to emphasize this because alendronate will only be effective if taken on an empty stomach. The tablet should be taken with a full glass of plain water, as other fluids (including mineral water), food and some medicines reduce the **absorption** of the drug (Brenner and Stephens 2006).
- It is necessary to stay upright (sitting, standing or walking) and patients should not take any food or other medications, vitamins or calcium supplements for at least 30 minutes after taking the tablet. These measures will help to minimize the possibility of oesophageal irritation and maximize intestinal absorption of the medication (Greenstein 2009; eMC 2012).
- The most common side-effect associated with oral preparations is GI upset; however, this is reduced with weekly treatment. Mrs H should be advised to report any symptoms of oesophageal irritation such as dysphagia, pain on swallowing, retrosternal pain or new or worsening heartburn to her GP. She should be given the patient information leaflet for osteoporosis and it should be emphasized that failure to follow the instructions may increase the risk of oesophageal problems. Other side-effects include bone, muscle or joint pain. Stress fractures of the femoral shaft have been reported in patients receiving long-term therapy (eMC 2012).
- Bisphosphonates have been linked with reports of osteonecrosis of the jaw (ONJ); however, these cases were generally associated with high-dose IV administration for neoplastic bone disease and were rarely linked with benign bone disease. Mrs H should be advised

about the importance of good oral and dental hygiene, be encouraged to visit her dentist for routine checkups and to report any oral symptoms (BNF 2012; eMC 2012).

- More recently there have been links reported with atypical fractures, predominantly occurring in the subtrochanteric region of the femur. Mrs H should be encouraged to report any pain in her hip, thigh or groin to her GP who may consider discontinuing the medication pending further investigation (Rizzoli et al. 2011; BNF 2012; eMC 2012).

- Calcium preparations and antacids should not be taken within two hours of bisphosphonates, as they are known to decrease the bioavailability (Brenner and Stephens 2006). Absorption is also reduced by oral iron preparations (BNF 2012).

- It is common for people with long-term conditions such as osteoporosis to find taking the medication challenging, and consequently only half of these patients will still be taking their medication after one year (see www.iofbonehealth.org). To ensure maximum compliance, adherence and concordance, treatment should have a minimal impact on a patient's lifestyle and routine, and patients should be empowered and fully involved in the management of their condition (Barber and Robertson 2012). Mrs H's GP outlined the treatment options and provided her with information on the dosing regimen, the contraindications and the side-effects. Mrs H is an active lady who works full time and following the discussion she opted to take alendronate as a once-weekly tablet. This would allow her to take the tablet at weekends and would not affect her busy morning schedule during the week.

7   What additional advice would you give to Mrs H?

A
- The National Osteoporosis Society is a charity dedicated to the prevention, diagnosis and treatment of osteoporosis and has a network of over 100 support groups across the UK. It runs a helpline staffed by a team of nurses who have specialist knowledge of osteoporosis and bone health. The charity also produces a wide range of booklets and leaflets for both the general public and health professionals (see www.nos.org.uk). Mrs H may find it useful to contact her local patient support group.

- Mrs H should be encouraged to eat a healthy, balanced calcium-rich diet. The recommended daily requirement for most adults is 700mg of calcium, although people with osteoporosis who are taking drug treatments might benefit from 1000 to 1200mg. Excellent sources of calcium include dairy products, tinned fish and green leafy vegetables (National Osteoporosis Society 2011).

- Vitamin D is vital in the role of calcium absorption and 90% of our requirements are produced through exposure of the skin to sunlight. Mrs H should be advised that she needs about 15 to 20 minutes of sun exposure to the face and arms without sunscreen, three or four times a week, between April and October. This should provide enough vitamin D for the year. Dietary sources of vitamin D include margarine, egg yolks, cod liver oil and oily fish (National Osteoporosis Society 2011).

- Mrs H takes her grandchildren swimming and while this is a healthy exercise choice, it is not weight-bearing and this is a key factor in the maintenance of bone density. Weight-bearing exercise, such as walking, dancing, jogging and tennis, stimulates the thickening of bone, strengthening it and reducing the risk of fracture. Lack of exercise reverses these changes leading to lighter, weaker bones (Waugh and Grant 2006). Mrs H should be advised to engage in weight-bearing exercise at least three times a week for a minimum of

20 minutes. However, her swimming will help to strengthen muscle tone which in turn will improve balance and reduce the risk of falls.

KEY POINTS

- Bone is constantly being remodelled in response to a variety of factors.
- Osteoporosis is a skeletal disorder associated with a reduction in bone density and quality.
- The main cells in bone homeostasis are osteoblasts (bone-building cells), osteocytes (mature bone cells) and osteoclasts (bone-resorbing cells).
- Peak bone mass is achieved at around 35 years of age.
- In women there is a dramatic acceleration of bone loss for several years following the menopause.
- One in two women and one in five men over the age of 50 will suffer a fracture.
- Risk factors in the development of osteoporosis include age, gender, smoking, alcohol intake, diet and exercise.
- Bisphosphonates act by reducing bone resorption, preserving bone mineral density.
- People with osteoporosis should be encouraged to eat a healthy, balanced, calcium-rich diet, take regular weight-bearing exercise, give up smoking and drink alcohol in moderation.
- The National Osteoporosis Society is a charity dedicated to the prevention, diagnosis and treatment of osteoporosis.

REFERENCES

Barber, P. and Robertson, D. (2012) *Essentials of Pharmacology for Nurses*. Maidenhead: Open University Press.

BNF (British National Formulary) (2012) *BNF 63: March*. London: Pharmaceutical Press.

BOA (British Orthopaedic Association) (2007) *The Care of Patients with Fragility Fracture*. London: BOA.

Brenner, G.M. and Stephens, C.W. (2006) *Pharmacology*, 2nd edn. Philadelphia, PA: Saunders.

Dennison, E., Cole, Z. and Cooper, C. (2005) Diagnosis and epidemiology of osteoporosis, *Current Opinion in Rheumatology*, 17(4): 456–61.

eMC (electronic Medicines Compendium) (2012) *Summary of Product Characteristics: Alendronic Acid 70mg Tablets*, available at: www.medicines.org.uk/EMC/medicine/23733/SPC/Alendronic+Acid+70+mg+Tablets/.

Greenstein, B. (2009) *Trounce's Clinical Pharmacology for Nurses*, 18th edn. London: Churchill Livingstone.

McDermott, M.T., Zapalowski, C. and Miller, P.D. (2004) *Hot Topics: Osteoporosis*. Philadelphia, PA: Hanley & Belfus.

National Osteoporosis Society (2011) *All About Osteoporosis: A Guide to Bone Health, Fragile Bones and Fractures*. Bath: National Osteoporosis Society.

NICE (National Institute for Health and Clinical Excellence) (2008) *Technology Appraisal Guidance 161: Alendronate, Etidronate, Risedronate, Raloxifene, Strontium Ranelate and Teriparatide for the Secondary Prevention of Fragility Fractures in Postmenopausal Women (amended)*. London: NICE.

Rang, H.P., Dale, M.D., Ritter, J.M., Flower, R.J. and Henderson, G. (2012) *Rang and Dale's Pharmacology*, 7th edn. Oxford: Churchill Livingstone.

Rizzoli, R., Åkesson, K., Bouxsein, M., Kanis, J.A. et al. (2011) Subtrochanteric fractures after long-term treatment with bisphosphonates: a European Society on Clinical and Economic Aspects of Osteoporosis and Osteoarthritis, and International Osteoporosis Foundation Working Group report, *Osteoporosis International*, 22(2): 373–90.

Tortora, G.J. and Nielson, M.T. (2009) *Principles of Human Anatomy*, 11th edn. Chichester: Wiley.

Waugh, A. and Grant, A. (2006) *Ross and Wilson: Anatomy and Physiology in Health and Illness*, 10th edn. Edinburgh: Churchill Livingstone.

The person with pain
Paul Barber

CASE AIMS

After examining this case study the reader should be able to:

- Describe the features of the hip joint.
- Highlight the anatomical structures that would aid in the stability of the hip joint.
- Briefly explain how the sensation of pain is brought about at a neuronal level.
- Demonstrate an understanding of the mode of action of paracetamol.
- Discuss the role of the nurse in advising patients taking paracetamol.
- Describe the pathophysiology of osteoarthritis.
- Demonstrate an understanding of the mode of action and side-effects of arthrotec.
- Explain the mode of action of morphine in relieving post-operative pain
- Outline the role of the nurse in monitoring and caring for a patient receiving morphine post-operatively.

CASE

Emma is a 68-year-old woman who lives in a town outside a large urban centre in the north-west of England. She is a single mother of three grown children and still cares for one of her children who has a disability, at home. She is self-employed so that she can maintain an income and care for her child. A few years ago Emma started feeling pain in her hip and found it increasingly difficult to walk. During an appointment with her GP, she complained of the pain and was prescribed paracetamol. At first, the medication appeared to diminish some of the pain.

1 **Describe the features of Emma's synovial hip joints**

2 **What anatomical structures would aid in the stability of Emma's hip joint?**

3 **How is Emma's sensation of pain brought about at a neuronal level?**

4 **Describe how giving paracetamol to Emma is thought to bring about analgesia**

5 **What advice would you give Emma about her paracetamol?**

Emma's hip became increasingly more painful and made it difficult for her to get around. The pain started having an impact on her ability to work and care for her daughter. With every visit to her GP, Emma complained of increasing pain, stiffness and difficulty getting around. Her GP eventually sent her for X-rays of her hip which showed osteoarthritic changes. As a result, her pain medication was changed to arthrotec for her osteoarthritis.

6 Describe briefly how the condition of osteoarthritis would affect Emma's joints

7 How would arthrotec work in relation to the inflammation caused by Emma's osteoarthritis and what are the side-effects?

After two years of suffering, Emma urged her GP to refer her to a specialist about her hip pain. She also told her doctor about her concerns regarding the side-effects of the medications she had been taking over the past several years. Her GP agreed to refer her to an orthopaedic surgeon. The surgeon has now carried out a total hip replacement and Emma is now being cared for on an orthopaedic ward. She has just returned from the operating theatre and is receiving morphine via a patient-controlled analgesia device. The device contains morphine 50mg in 50ml; she receives a demand dose of 1mg in 1ml with a lockout period of five minutes.

8 Explain the mode of action of morphine in relieving Emma's post-operative pain

9 Outline the role of the nurse in monitoring and caring for Emma as she receives morphine

ANSWERS

1 **Describe the features of Emma's synovial hip joints**

A Emma's synovial joints are her most mobile. They possess the following characteristic features (Marieb 2010).

- The articular surfaces are covered with hyaline cartilage. This cartilage is avascular, non-nervous and elastic. Lubricated with synovial fluid, the cartilage forms slippery surfaces for free movements.
- Between the articular surfaces there is a joint cavity filled with synovial fluid. The cavity may be partially or completely subdivided by an articular disc known as the meniscus.
- The joint is surrounded by an articular capsule which is fibrous in nature and lined with synovial membrane. Because of its rich nerve supply the fibrous capsule is sensitive to stretches imposed by movements.

- The synovial membrane lines the entire joint except the articular surfaces covered by hyaline cartilage. It is this membrane that secretes the slimy fluid called synovial fluid which lubricates the joint and nourishes the articular cartilage.
- Varying degrees of movement are always permitted by the synovial joints.

2 **What anatomical structures would aid in the stability of Emma's hip joint?**

A There are various factors maintaining the stability at Emma's hip joint. These are described below in order of their importance (Tortora and Derrickson 2009).

- *Muscles* – the tone of different groups of muscles acting on the joint is the most important and indispensable factor in maintaining stability. Without muscles, the knee and shoulder would be unstable and the arches of the feet would collapse.
- *Ligaments* – are important in preventing any over-movement and in guarding against sudden accidental stresses. However, they do not help against a continuous strain because once stretched they tend to remain elongated.
- *Bones* – help in maintaining stability only in firm-type of joints such as the hips and ankles. Otherwise in most joints their role is negligible.

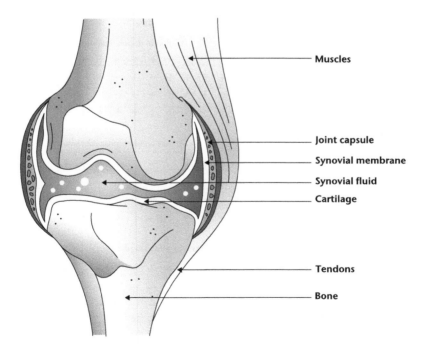

Figure 17.1 Anatomy of a synovial joint

3 **How is Emma's sensation of pain brought about at a neuronal level?**

A At rest, the inside of Emma's nociceptive neuron has a negative charge compared to the outside, which is positive. In order to trigger the sensation of pain in Emma, the inside of the neuron must become positively charged as compared to the outside. Chemicals liberated by damaged tissue bring about a change in the neuronal membrane, allowing sodium to pass into the neuron. This continues until the inside of the neuron is positively charged in relation to the outside. This build-up of positively charged sodium is termed 'depolarization' (Tate et al. 2008). At the synapse, where one neuron meets another, neurotransmitters must be released in order to stimulate the next neuron to continue to pass the message onwards. Once the inside of the neuron has converted to a positive environment, calcium channels in the membrane open, so allowing calcium to enter. The influx of calcium attracts small sacs called synaptic vesicles, which are full of neurotransmitters, towards the synapse. When these vesicles reach the synapse they fuse with the neuron membrane and pour their cargo of neurotransmitter into the synapse itself.

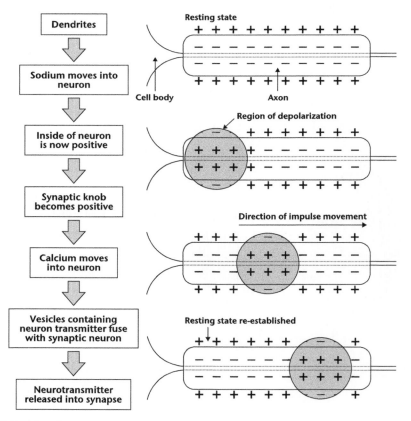

Figure 17.2 Firing of a neuron

The neurotransmitters which are important in Emma's pain pathway are substance P, neurokinin A and B, and glutamate. Once the neurotransmitter attaches itself to receptors on the other side of the synapse, this neuron becomes permeable to sodium and the process continues (Godfrey 2005).

4 **Describe how giving paracetamol to Emma is thought to bring about analgesia**

A Emma's body is producing prostaglandins in response to injury from her osteoarthritis. One of their actions is to sensitize nerve endings, so that when the injury is stimulated it causes pain (presumably to prevent us from causing further harm to the area). As paracetamol reduces the production of these nerve-sensitizing prostaglandins it is thought it may increase our pain threshold, so that although the injury remains, we can feel it less (Hinz et al. 2008).

5 **What advice would you give Emma about her paracetamol?**

A
- You should first ascertain whether Emma has an allergy to paracetamol or similar products. According to Jordan (2008), hypersensitivity or allergic responses are possible with almost any drug.
- Paracetamol should be used with caution in people who have renal or liver disease, so again you should check Emma's medical history. It is possible that regular intake of large doses over a long period may increase the risk of kidney damage (Rang et al. 2011).
- You should inform Emma that she should not take this medicine with any other paracetamol-containing products. This is because other medicines that contain paracetamol in combination with this medicine can easily result in exceeding the maximum recommended daily dose. Many cold and flu remedies and over-the-counter painkillers contain paracetamol so she should be advised to check the ingredients of any other medicines before taking them, or ask the pharmacist for advice (Barber and Robertson 2012).
- Emma should not exceed the dose stated in the information leaflet supplied with her medicine. This is because an overdose of paracetamol is dangerous and capable of causing serious damage to the liver and kidneys. Emma should seek immediate medical advice in the unlikely event of an overdose, even if she feels well, because of the risk of delayed, serious liver damage (Brenner and Stephens 2009).
- If symptoms persist she should consult her doctor, so that more appropriate treatment can be offered.

6 **Describe briefly how the condition of osteoarthritis would affect Emma's joints**

A Osteoarthritis is the most common form of joint disease. It causes pain and stiffness in the joints and affects at least 8 million people in the UK. When Emma's joint becomes affected by osteoarthritis its surfaces become damaged and it doesn't move as well as it should. The following happens:

- the articular cartilage becomes rough and thin;
- the bone at the edge of the joint grows outwards, forming bony spurs called osteophytes;
- the synovium may swell and produce extra fluid, causing the joint to swell;
- the capsule and ligaments slowly thicken and contract.

In severe osteoarthritis the cartilage can become so thin that the bones may start to rub against each other and wear away. The loss of cartilage, the wearing of bone and the osteophyte formation can alter the shape of the joint, forcing the bones out of their normal position (Arthritis Research in the United Kingdom 2011).

7 **How would arthrotec work in relation to the inflammation caused by Emma's osteoarthritis and what are the side-effects?**

A # MODE OF ACTION

- Prostaglandins are very important in triggering the inflammatory response and are formed when a fatty acid called **arachidonic acid** is liberated from a damaged cell membrane by action of an enzyme known as phospholipase.
- The arachidonic acid acts by triggering the **cyclo-oxygenase pathway**. Cyclo-oxygenase pathways in most pharmacological texts are denoted by the prefix COX followed by the number of the pathway (e.g. COX1).
- The prostaglandins derived from COX1 assist in the smooth running of body systems; in particular they help to maintain the protective mucous lining of the stomach and intestine.
- COX2 in comparison produces prostaglandins that facilitate pain and inflammation.
- Arthrotec works by inhibiting the formation of prostaglandins by blocking the cyclo-oxygenase pathways (BNF 2012).

SIDE-EFFECTS

The vast number of current NSAIDs (including diclofenac) blocks both pathways. This is problematic as the drugs reduce the pain and inflammation associated with COX2 but also reduce the homeostatic function of COX1. This leads to a number of GI problems, the most significant of which is peptic ulceration. Often, oral administration of a prostaglandin substitute, such as misoprostol, may be used. This helps to ensure limited damage to the stomach mucosa. Arthrotec is such a drug as it combines in one tablet diclofenac and misoprostol (BNF 2012).

8 **Explain the mode of action of morphine in relieving Emma's post-operative pain**

A
- All opioids exert their effect through binding with specific receptors called opioid receptors, located in the CNS (brain and spinal cord) or peripherally in the GI tract. There are four types of opioid receptor and they are designated by the Greek letters μ (mu), κ (kappa), σ (sigma) and δ (delta).
- Opioid drugs mimic our own endorphins, bringing about a similar analgesic reaction. There are numerous opioid analgesic preparations, some natural (e.g. morphine and codeine) and some synthetic (e.g. diamorphine, methadone, fentanyl and meperidine).

- Opioid drugs are thought to work through a number of mechanisms. Morphine is thought to block calcium channels from opening so that the pain signal breaks down. It is also thought that morphine opens **potassium** channels in neurons, so making the inside more negative, a condition known as 'hyperpolarization'. This makes the firing of a pain neuron more difficult.

ANALGESIA

This term refers to the loss or relief of pain but without the loss of consciousness. Morphine is useful in both acute and chronic types of pain. It not only raises the level at which pain is initiated (higher threshold) but it also alters the brain's perception of pain. The patient is still aware of the pain but does not recognize it as an unpleasant sensation.

9   **Outline the role of the nurse in monitoring and caring for Emma as she receives morphine**

A
- As part of your post-operative care you will be taking Emma's blood pressure. This is an important parameter to monitor when someone is receiving morphine as the drug can cause a drop in blood pressure, as it produces vasodilatation and can increase the release of histamine in an individual (Adams et al. 2008).
- You should monitor Emma's respiratory rate and depth. Respiratory depression is caused by the respiratory centre in the brain stem becoming less sensitive to the respiratory drive of carbon dioxide. It is one of the more troublesome side-effects that you need to be aware of, particularly as it can occur with therapeutic doses. It is also the commonest cause of death in acute opioid poisoning. Medication may be withheld for any difficulty in breathing or respirations below 12 breaths per minute.
- Opioid effects (adverse or otherwise) can be reversed with an opioid antagonist such as naloxone. The elimination half-life of naloxone can be shorter than that of the opioid itself, so repeat dosing or continuous infusion may be required.
- Emma should be assessed regarding the location, quality, intensity and frequency or duration of her pain. Use a nominal scale to determine intensity. Often a numerical score is used and these scales range from a low number usually indicating a low level of pain to a high number indicating worsening or more intense pain (Seers 1988).
- Morphine also affects the smooth muscle of the urinary tract. Therefore it is important that you monitor renal status and urinary output. Morphine may cause urinary retention due to muscle relaxation in the urinary tract.
- Opiates are excreted through the kidneys. Impaired kidney function may result in reduced medication clearance and increased serum drug levels (Aschenbrenner and Venable 2008).
- Nausea and vomiting occurs in up to 40% of people who are prescribed morphine when they first start to take the drug. You should first of all prepare for this by making sure a vomit bowl and tissues are available. You should chart the frequency of the vomiting and often there is an assessment scale for this purpose. Mouth care is important to consider. Emma will have been prescribed an **antiemetic**. It is probably easier to prevent than to treat established nausea and vomiting, so any patient with a risk score for post-operative

nausea and vomiting (PONV) of 2 and above should receive prophylactic antiemetic agents according to that trust's protocol (Gan et al. 2003).

- Monitor Emma for constipation. Opioids have an antispasmodic effect on the GI tract, which decreases peristaltic activity. Therefore you may need to increase dietary fibre or administer **laxatives** (Brunner et al. 2009).
- Immediately report effects such as untoward or rebound pain, restlessness, anxiety, depression, hallucination, nausea, dizziness and itching. Emma's respiratory rate should be maintained at least at 12 breaths per minute.

KEY POINTS

- Synovial joints possess the following characteristic features: articular surfaces covered with hyaline cartilage; a joint cavity filled with synovial fluid; the joint is surrounded by an articular capsule which is fibrous in nature and is lined with synovial membrane; synovial fluid lubricates the joint and nourishes the articular cartilage.
- There are various elements maintaining stability at the hip joint: muscles, ligaments and bones.
- In order to trigger the sensation of pain, the inside of a neuron must become positively charged as compared to the outside.
- Paracetamol reduces the production of nerve-sensitizing prostaglandins and it is thought it may increase our pain threshold, so that although the injury remains, we can feel it less.
- If other medicines containing paracetamol are taken in combination with paracetamol, this can easily result in overdose.
- Osteoarthritis is the most common form of joint disease. It causes pain and stiffness in the joints and affects at least 8 million people in the UK.
- The vast numbers of current NSAIDs block both cyclo-oxygenase pathways. This is problematic because these drugs reduce the pain and inflammation associated with COX2 but also reduce the homeostatic function of COX1. This leads to a number of GI problems such as peptic ulceration.
- All opioids exert their effect through binding with specific receptors called opioid receptors located in the cCNS (brain and spinal cord) or peripherally in the GI tract.
- Different opioid analgesics bind in different ways with a variety of receptors, so explaining why a range of effects and side-effects can occur.

REFERENCES

Adams, M.P., Holland, L.N. and Botwick, P.M. (2008) *Pharmacology for Nurses: A Pathophysiologic Approach*. Upper Saddle River, NJ: Pearson Education.

Arthritis Research in the United Kingdom (2011) *Osteoarthritis*, available at: www.arthritiscare.org.uk.

Aschenbrenner, D.S. and Venable, S.J. (2008) *Drug Therapy in Nursing*, 3rd edn. London: Lippincott Williams & Wilkins.

Barber, P. and Robertson, D. (2012) *Essentials of Pharmacology for Nurses*, 2nd edn. Maidenhead: Open University Press.

BNF (British National Formulary) (2012) *BNF 63: March*. London: Pharmaceutical Press.

Brenner, G.M. and Stevens, C.W. (2009) *Pharmacology*, 3rd edn. Philadelphia, PA: Saunders Elsevier.

Brunner, L.S, Smeltzer, S.C., Bare, B.G., Hinkle, J.L. and Cheever, K.H. (2009) *Brunner and Suddarth's Textbook of Medical-surgical Nursing*, 12th edn. London: Lippincott Williams & Wilkins.

Gan, T.J., Meyer, T., Apfel, C.C. et al. (2003) Consensus guidelines for managing postoperative nausea and vomiting, *Anaesthesia and Analgesia*, 97: 62–71.

Godfrey, H. (2005) Understanding pain, part 1: physiology of pain, *British Journal of Nursing*, 14(16): 846–52.

Hinz, B., Cheremina., O. and Brune, K. (2008) Acetaminophen (paracetamol) is a selective cyclo-oxygenase-2 inhibitor in man, *The FASEB Journal*, 22(2): 383–90.

Jordan, S. (2008) *The Prescription Drug Guide for Nurses*. Maidenhead: Open University Press.

Marieb, E.N. (2010) *Essentials of Human Anatomy and Physiology*, 10th edn. London: Pearson Education.

Rang, H.P., Dale, M.M., Ritter, J.M, Flower, R.J. and Henderson, G. (2011) *Rang and Dale's Pharmacology*, 7th edn. Oxford: Churchill Livingstone.

Seers, K. (1988) Factors affecting pain assessment, *Professional Nurse*, 3(6): 201–5.

Tate, P., Seeley, R.R. and Stephens, T.D. (2008) *Seeley's Principles of Anatomy and Physiology*, 6th edn. Maidenhead: McGraw-Hill.

Tortora, G.J. and Derrickson, B.H. (2009) *Essentials of Anatomy and Physiology*, 8th edn. London: Wiley.

The person with Parkinson's disease
Paul Barber

CASE AIMS

After examining this case study the reader should be able to:

- Briefly explain how movement is normally controlled by the central nervous system.
- Describe the pathophysiology of Parkinson's disease.
- Describe four of the most important motor features of Parkinson's disease.
- Demonstrate an understanding of the mode of action and side-effects of levodopa.
- Discuss the role of the nurse in primary and secondary care with regard to timing of doses, complex regimens of drugs and managing dietary considerations for patients taking anti-Parkinson's medicines.
- Articulate the reasons that ropinirole has been added to levodopa.
- Identify how medicines given for a patient with Parkinson's disease should be managed perioperatively.

CASE

Mr H is a 55-year-old man who has recently been diagnosed with early Parkinson's disease (PD). He has been quite upset and depressed about the diagnosis and has lost interest in his usual activities and hobbies. His wife reports that his tremors, slowness in movement, rigidity and postural instability have worsened over the past 12 months. He has been taking the following medications for six months: carbidopa/levodopa 25mg/100mg four times a day.

---

1 **How is the movement of Mr H's body normally controlled by the CNS?**

2 **What pathophysiology is underlying Mr H's PD?**

3 **Describe the four motor symptoms that Mr H is experiencing**

4 **Outline the mode of action of levodopa and suggest what the main side-effects of this medicine might be for Mr H**

5 **What is the nurse's role in primary and secondary care with regard to helping Mr H manage his timing of doses?**

6 **What is the nurse's role in primary and secondary care with regard to helping Mr H comply with what could be a complex regimen of drugs?**

7 **What is the nurse's role in primary and secondary care with regard to helping Mr H manage his dietary considerations while taking this group of medicines?**

Mr H is now 67, with moderately advanced PD. He has had a fall at home, which has resulted in a humeral fracture. The fall occurred in the morning before he was able to take his medications and was related to his difficulty in initiating movements. On his current regimen, his PD symptoms are controlled. He is able to perform daily living activities independently and ambulates without assistance. He also performs more complex tasks (e.g. cooking and managing his finances). He has not exhibited any symptoms consistent with dementia. He occasionally experiences dyspnoea on exertion and dysphagia, but he has not been evaluated for these complaints. He now takes carbidopa/levodopa 25mg/100mg four times a day and ropinirole 3mg three times a day. He is scheduled for open reduction internal fixation of his fracture. The orthopaedic surgeon has requested a perioperative risk assessment and recommendations concerning medications.

---

8 **What are the reasons that ropinirole has been added to Mr H's prescription and what are the potential side-effects?**

9 **How should his PD medicines be managed perioperatively?**

ANSWERS

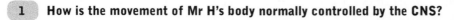

1 **How is the movement of Mr H's body normally controlled by the CNS?**

A
- The pyramidal motor system controls all of our voluntary movements. Pathological processes which damage the pyramidal motor system are extremely important causes of disability and suffering (Marieb 2010).
- The pyramidal system is a major motor system comprising the axons that run through the corticospinal and corticobulbar tracts. Damage to either tract above the level of efferent cranial nerve nuclei will result in problems with the motor activity on the opposite side. For instance, if there is damage to the lateral area of one **precentral gyrus**, the muscle function of the face and oral cavities on the opposite side could be affected (Tate et al. 2008).
- The extrapyramidal system is a neural network that is part of the motor system that causes involuntary reflexes and movement, and modulation of movement (i.e. coordination). The system is called 'extrapyramidal' to distinguish it from the tracts of the motor cortex that reach their targets by travelling through the 'pyramids' of the medulla.

- The extrapyramidal system dampens erratic motions and maintains muscle tone and truncal stability. Extrapyramidal tracts are chiefly found in the **reticular formation** of the pons and medulla, and target neurons in the spinal cord involved in reflexes, locomotion, complex movements and postural control (Barrett et al. 2009).

2 **What pathophysiology is underlying Mr H's PD?**

A PD is a progressive disorder of movement. Certain neurons in part of the brain called the **basal nuclei** degenerate and this leads to a lack of a neurotransmitter called dopamine. PD results from this greatly reduced activity of dopamine-secreting cells caused by cell death in the region of the **substantia nigra**. Typically, this disease occurs in people who are over the age of 50. The reduction in the release of dopamine causes the basal nuclei to become overactive and this overactivity presents itself in a number of ways (Barber and Robertson 2012).

3 **Describe the four motor symptoms that Mr H is experiencing**

A According to Jankovic (2008) there are four motor symptoms which are considered as being cardinal in PD: tremor, rigidity, slowness of movement and postural instability.

Tremor is the most apparent and well-known symptom. It is also the most common, although around 30% of individuals with PD do not have tremor at first but develop it as the disease progresses. A feature of tremor is 'pill-rolling', a term used to describe the tendency of the index finger of the hand to come into contact with the thumb and perform together a circular movement.

Rigidity is stiffness and resistance to limb movement caused by increased muscle tone – an excessive and continuous contraction of the muscles. In PD the rigidity can be uniform (lead-pipe rigidity) or ratchet-like (cogwheel rigidity). With the progression of the disease, rigidity typically affects the whole body and reduces the ability to move.

Slowness of movement (bradykinesia) is is associated with difficulties along the whole course of the movement process, from planning to initiation and finally execution of a movement. Performance of sequential and simultaneous movement is hindered. Bradykinesia is not equal for all movements or times. It is modified by the activity or emotional state of the subject, to the point that some patients are barely able to walk and yet can still ride a bicycle (Samii et al. 2004).

Postural instability is typical in the late stages of the disease, leading to impaired balance and frequent falls, and secondarily to bone fractures. Instability is often absent in the initial stages, especially in younger people. Up to 40% of patients may experience falls and around 10% may have falls weekly, with the number of falls being related to the severity of PD (NICE 2006).

4 **Outline the mode of action of levodopa and suggest what the main side-effects of this medicine might be for Mr H**

A # MODE OF ACTION

Levodopa remains the first-line treatment for PD. It is a drug that can cross the blood–brain barrier and then be converted by the CNS into dopamine. It is nearly always combined with another substance that stops peripheral enzymes breaking down dopamine. Examples of medicines that are combined or given with levodopa are carbidopa and benserazide (Rang et al. 2011). When given levodopa the response rates of patients are good. However, this improvement is often only short-lived and as time goes by the levodopa becomes less effective.

SIDE-EFFECTS

Two major side-effects are associated with giving levodopa. In dyskinesia the individual develops a series of involuntary movements, causing acute embarrassment as they usually affect the face and limbs. If the dose is lowered, the dyskinesia does stop, but is replaced by the rigidity it had improved. This is a fine line that the patient and doctor walk in order to accept the consequences of both illness and treatment (BNF 2012). With the 'on–off' effect, quite suddenly the drug therapy seems to stop working. This can be quite distressing for the patient and can sometimes occur when they are in the middle of doing something. The reason for this fluctuation is not fully understood; however, patients should be made aware of both these side-effects when commencing treatment (Brenner and Stevens 2009).

Short-term side-effects quite often improve over a period of time. The person may feel sick, have no appetite and suffer a slight drop in blood pressure. This decrease in blood pressure could have a more serious effect if the patient is having antihypertensive therapy. A small number of patients may develop delusions and hallucinations as the brain is given extra dopamine which is thought to mimic the high levels found in patients with schizophrenia (Greenstein 2008).

5 **What is the nurse's role in primary and secondary care with regard to helping Mr H manage his timing of doses?**

A
- To get the right balance between benefit and any side-effects, you will need to educate and involve Mr H about which drugs are being used and why drug timing is so important in order to achieve continuous dopaminergic stimulation (CDS) for the optimal control of symptoms and to reduce the incidence of motor complications (Findley et al. 2009).
- When admission to a home or ward occurs, it is important for staff to be aware of why the timing of these drugs is so important and to make sure medication times are accurately documented.
- When going away, Mr H should ensure he has enough medication supplies and have worked out a transient timing regime with his doctor or specialist nurse to deal with different time zones or long-haul flights (Thomas and MacMahon 2002).
- Mr H may exhibit an increase in libido and hypersexuality or pathological gambling associated with dopamine agonist treatment – this is referred to as an impulse control disorder. Its management is complicated and you should be aware of the syndrome in order to provide appropriate management and support (Giovannoni et al. 2000).

6 **What is the nurse's role in primary and secondary care with regard to helping Mr H comply with what could be a complex regimen of drugs?**

A • Nurses have an important role not only in sharing their knowledge with the person with Parkinson's and their carer but also in encouraging patients to take responsibility for their health and well-being (DH 2005).
• Selective information is usually more helpful and the Parkinson's Disease Society has many publications that can help Mr H and his family understand more about PD and the drugs used to treat its symptoms.
• Mr H must be taught to recognize the symptoms of PD and the side-effects of drug treatments in order to become 'expert' in managing his condition, and you, as the nurse, are ideally placed to help with this (DH 2005).
• Compliance with drug regimens will suffer if Mr H does not understand drug side-effects or the different symptoms of the condition and how they respond to the drugs (Parkinson's Disease Society 2007).
• Mr H can be encouraged take part in his local expert patients programme, which may help him to manage his symptoms (DH 2001).

7 **What is the nurse's role in primary and secondary care with regard to helping Mr H manage his dietary considerations while taking this group of medicines?**

A • You should advise Mr H to read the manufacturer and pharmacy information sheets, and that he should take his drugs after food, in order to help alleviate the common early side-effects of nausea and vomiting.
• Some people need to take an antiemetic. Domperidone is the only oral antiemetic recommended for people with Parkinson's, as it does not easily cross the blood–brain barrier and block dopaminergic receptors, causing extrapyramidal symptoms (i.e. symptoms of PD) (Downie et al. 2008).
• It is recommended that the L-dopa be taken not less than 30 minutes before or 60 minutes after meals (Karch 2010).

8 **What are the reasons that ropinirole has been added to Mr H's prescription and what are the potential side-effects?**

A • Dopamine agonists such as ropinirole have shown beneficial effects as adjunctive therapy to reduce 'wearing off'.
• Ropinirole adds clinical benefit in PD patients with motor fluctuations and also permits a reduction in the dosage of levodopa.
• Side-effects of dopamine agonists include ankle oedema, hallucinations, somnolence and impulse control disorders. These effects should be discussed with patients before instituting therapy, and therapy should be discontinued if any of them occur (Clayton 2009).

9 **How should his PD medicines be managed perioperatively?**

A
- Abrupt withdrawal of these medicines can lead to a potentially lethal condition called **Parkinsonism-hyperpyrexia syndrome** (PHS), which is clinically similar to neuroleptic malignant syndrome (Factor and Santiago 2005).
- Even brief interruption of medications can lead to decompensation of Parkinsonian symptoms, which not only delays recovery from surgery but also increases the risk for multisystem complications.
- Traditional anti-Parkinsonian medications can only be delivered orally, presenting significant challenges for nil-by-mouth patients, especially those undergoing enteric surgery requiring bowel rest (Serrano-Dueñas 2003).
- The usual drug regimen should be administered as close to the beginning of anaesthesia as possible. L–dopa can only be administered enterally and its **half-life** is short (1–3 hours). It is absorbed from the proximal small bowel and therefore cannot be given as a suppository (BNF 2012).
- Patients should be able to take L-dopa either with sips of water or by nasogastric tube. Another strategy is to use subcutaneous administration of **apomorphine**. However, this is very emetogenic and patients usually need to take domperidone for several days before an apomorphine challenge. Nevertheless, small doses of apomorphine with sufficient antiemetic cover may be helpful (Nicholson et al. 2002).

KEY POINTS

- The pyramidal motor system controls all of our voluntary movements. Pathological processes which damage this system are extremely important causes of disability and suffering.
- The extrapyramidal system is a neural network that is part of the motor system that causes involuntary reflexes and movement, and modulation of movement (i.e. coordination).
- PD is a progressive disorder of movement. Certain neurons in a part of the brain called the basal nuclei degenerate and this leads to a lack of a neurotransmitter called dopamine.
- There are four motor symptoms which are considered as being cardinal in PD: tremor, rigidity, slowness of movement and postural instability.
- Levodopa remains the first-line treatment for PD. It is nearly always combined with another substance that stops peripheral enzymes breaking down dopamine. Examples of medicines that are combined or given with levodopa are carbidopa and benserazide.
- Two major side-effects are associated with giving levodopa. First, a condition called dyskinesia can develop, and secondly a side-effect known as the 'on–off' effect can develop.
- Allowing patients to control the exact timing of their medication can be empowering. Patients must be taught to recognize the symptoms of PD and the side-effects of drug treatments in order to become 'expert' in managing their condition.

> • Even brief interruption of medications can lead to decompensation of Parkinsonian symptoms, which not only delays recovery from surgery, but also increases the risk for multisystem complications.

REFERENCES

Barber, P. and Robertson, D. (2012) *Essentials of Pharmacology for Nurses*, 2nd edn. Maidenhead: Open University Press.

Barrett, K.E, Barman, S.M., Boitano, S. and Brooks, H.L. (2009) *Ganong's Review of Medical Physiology*, 23rd edn. New York: McGraw-Hill.

BNF (British National Formulary) (2012) *BNF 63: March*. London: Pharmaceutical Press.

Brenner, G.M. and Stevens, C.W. (2009) *Pharmacology*, 3rd edn. Philadelphia, PA: Saunders Elsevier.

Clayton, B.D. (2009) *Basic Pharmacology for Nurses*, 15th edn. St Louis, MO: Mosby Elsevier.

DH (Department of Health) (2001) *The Expert Patient: A New Approach to Chronic Disease Management for the 21st Century*. London: DH.

DH (Department of Health) (2005) *The National Service Framework for Long Term Conditions*. London: DH.

Downie, G., Mackenzie, J. and Williams, A. (2008) *Pharmacology and Medicines Management for Nurses*, 4th edn. Edinburgh: Churchill Livingstone.

Factor, S.A. and Santiago, A. (2005) Parkinson-hyperpyrexia syndrome in Parkinson's disease, in S. Frucht and S. Fahn (eds) *Movement Disorder Emergencies: Diagnosis and Treatment*. New York: Humana Press.

Findley, L.J., Leader, G. and Leader L. (2009) *Parkinson's Disease: Reducing Symptoms with Nutrition and Drugs*. London: Denor Press.

Giovannoni, G., O'Sullivan, J., Turner, K., Manson, A. and Lees, A. (2000) Hedonistic homeostatic dysregulation in patients with Parkinson's disease on dopamine replacement therapies, *Journal of Neurology, Neurosurgery and Psychiatry*, 68(4): 423–8.

Greenstein, B. (2009) *Clinical Pharmacology for Nurses*, 18th edn. Edinburgh: Churchill Livingstone.

Jankovic, J. (2008) Parkinson's disease: clinical features and diagnosis, *Journal of Neurology, Neurosurgery and Psychiatry*, 79: 368–76.

Karch, A.M. (2010) *Focus on Nursing Pharmacology*. London: Lippincott Williams & Wilkins.

Marieb, E.N. (2010) *Essentials of Human Anatomy and Physiology*, 10th edn. London: Pearson Education.

NICE (National Institute for Health and Clinical Excellence) (2006) *Clinical Guideline 35: Parkinson's Disease*. London: NICE.

Nicholson, G., Pereira, A.C. and Hall, G.M. (2002) Parkinson's disease and anesthesia, *British Journal of Anaesthesia*, 89(6): 904–16.

Parkinson's Disease Society (2007) *The Professional's Guide to Parkinson's Disease*. London: Parkinson's Disease Society.

Rang, H.P., Dale, M.M., Ritter, J.M., Flower, R.J. and Henderson, G. (2011) *Rang and Dale's Pharmacology*, 7th edn. Oxford: Churchill Livingstone.

Samii, A., Nutt, J.G. and Ransom, B.R. (2004) Parkinson's disease, *Lancet*, 363(9423): 1783–93.

Serrano-Dueñas, M. (2003) Neuroleptic malignant syndrome-like, or dopaminergic malignant syndrome due to levodopa therapy withdrawal: clinical features in 11 patients, *Parkinsonism Related Disorder*, 9(3): 175–8.

Tate, P., Seeley, R.R. and Stephens, T.D. (2008) *Seeley's Principles of Anatomy and Physiology*, 6th edn. Maidenhead: McGraw-Hill.

Thomas, S. and MacMahon, D. (2002) Continuing professional development: Parkinson's disease – managing Parkinson's disease in long-term care, *Nursing Older People*, 14(9): 23–30.

The person with rheumatoid arthritis
Paul Barber

CASE AIMS

After examining this case study the reader should be able to:

- Suggest reasons why a patient with rheumatoid arthritis should have pain and tenderness in their joints.
- Describe the importance of carrying out blood investigations in a patient with rheumatoid arthritis.
- Demonstrate an understanding of the mode of action and side-effects of ibuprofen with regard to rheumatoid arthritis.
- Discuss the role of the nurse in advising patients taking ibuprofen.
- Demonstrate an understanding of the reason for prescribing, mode of action and side-effects of methotrexate with regard to rheumatoid arthritis.
- Demonstrate an understanding of the reason for prescribing, mode of action and side-effects of steroid medication with regard to rheumatoid arthritis.

CASE

A 37-year-old woman gradually developed painful wrists over three months; she consulted her doctor only when the pain and early morning stiffness stopped her from gardening. On examination, both wrists and the metacarpophalangeal joints of both hands were swollen and tender but not deformed. There were no nodules or vasculitic lesions. On investigation, she was found to have a raised C-reactive protein (CRP) level (27mg/L) (NR<10) but a normal haemoglobin and white-cell count. A latex test for rheumatoid factor was negative and antinuclear antibodies were not detected.

---

1 **Why does this patient have pain and tenderness in her joints?**

2 **Why have the doctors carried out the blood tests that are described above?**

> *The clinical diagnosis was early rheumatoid arthritis and the patient was treated with ibuprofen. Despite some initial symptomatic improvement, the pain, stiffness and swelling of the hands persisted and one month later both knees became similarly affected. The patient was referred to a rheumatologist.*

3 Why has the patient been prescribed ibuprofen?

4 What advice would you give the patient about their ibuprofen?

> *Six months after initial presentation, the patient developed two subcutaneous nodules on the left elbow. These were small, painless, firm and immobile but not tender. A test for rheumatoid factor was now positive (titre 1/64). X-rays of the hands showed bony erosions in the metacarpal heads. The patient still had a raised CRP (43mg/L) but normal serum complement (C3 and C4) levels and had she had a biopsy, pannus would have been demonstrable histologically. This woman now had definite X-ray evidence of rheumatoid arthritis and, in view of the continuing arthropathy, her treatment was changed to weekly low-dose methotrexate.*

5 What is the reasoning behind adding methotrexate to the drug regimen?

6 What side-effects might this patient anticipate as a result of taking methotrexate?

> *Although she receives maintenance methotrexate, periodically the patient has flares of her disease. She has ready access to her rheumatoid arthritis specialist nurse, and when flares occur the rheumatology team manage these, usually by adding prednisolone, an NSAID and proton pump inhibitor, and increasing the dose of her methotrexate and/or adding another disease-modifying anti-rheumatic drug (DMARD). Her DMARD therapy is managed in accordance with a shared-care agreement with the rheumatologists. Recently, the patient has had several flares and this has resulted in several spells of corticosteroid therapy (among other treatments).*

7 How would using a steroid help in controlling the symptoms of this disease?

8 What side-effects would you be monitoring for in a patient taking oral prednisolone?

ANSWERS

1 **Why does this patient have pain and tenderness in her joints?**

A
- Pain is received via specialist receptors called nociceptors, which are free nerve endings that lie in the tissues.
- Nociceptors are stimulated by mechanical, thermal and chemical means. They can become sensitive to a variety of chemicals which are present after local tissue injury (Barrett et al. 2009).
- This patient has a condition that has caused her tissue cells to have become injured and release a number of chemicals that initiate the inflammatory response. Examples of these are kinins, prostaglandin and histamine. These chemicals work collectively to cause increased vasodilation (widening of blood capillaries) and permeability of the capillaries (Tortora and Derrickson 2009). This leads to increased blood flow to the injured site.
- These substances also act as chemical messengers that attract some of the body's natural defence cells – a mechanism known as chemotaxis.
- Although highly beneficial to the body's defence strategies, some chemicals such as **bradykinin** and prostaglandins also increase the sensitivity of the pain fibres in the area so that it becomes painful and tender (Pocock and Richards 2006).

2 **Why have the doctors carried out the blood tests that are described above?**

A ## LATEX TEST

The latex test for rheumatoid factor is used to help diagnose rheumatoid arthritis and to distinguish it from other forms of arthritis and other conditions that cause similar symptoms of joint pain, inflammation and stiffness.

In patients with symptoms and clinical signs of rheumatoid arthritis the presence of significant concentrations of rheumatoid factor indicates that it is likely that they do have the condition – 70–90% of patients with rheumatoid arthritis have a positive rheumatoid factor test. A negative rheumatoid factor test does not exclude rheumatoid arthritis. About 20% of patients with rheumatoid arthritis will be persistently negative or have low levels of rheumatoid factor (Sihvonen et al. 2005).

CRP

CRP is a member of the class of acute-phase reactants, as its levels rise dramatically during inflammatory processes occurring in the body. This increment is due to a rise in the plasma concentration of interleukin-6 and other cytokines that trigger the synthesis of CRP and fibrinogen by the liver. Interleukin-6 is produced predominantly by macrophages that are increased during the inflammatory process. CRP is thought to assist in complement binding to foreign and damaged cells and enhances phagocytosis by macrophages (NICE 2009).

CRP is used mainly as a marker of inflammation. Normal concentration in healthy human serum is usually lower than 10mg/L, slightly increasing with ageing. Higher levels are found in late pregnant women, mild inflammation and viral infections (10–40mg/L), active inflammation, bacterial infection (40–200mg/L), severe bacterial infection and burns (>200mg/L) (Higgins 2007).

FULL BLOOD COUNT

Although a full blood count cannot in itself diagnose rheumatoid arthritis the results can help to support the diagnosis. Platelets – cells used for clotting – are often increased. The white cell count, which reflects immune system response, may be increased. In addition, haemoglobin levels may be low. About 80% of people who develop rheumatoid arthritis have associated anaemia.

3 **Why has the patient been prescribed ibuprofen?**

A Ibuprofen is a common medicine prescribed for rheumatoid arthritis. It and other NSAIDs are thought to work by inhibiting the action of certain hormones that cause inflammation and pain in the body. These hormones are called prostaglandins. By blocking the effects of prostaglandins, ibuprofen can help reduce the pain and joint swelling associated with rheumatoid arthritis (Rang et al. 2011).

4 **What advice would you give the patient about their ibuprofen?**

A
- You should first ascertain if the patient has an allergy to ibuprofen or similar products. Hypersensitivity or allergic responses are possible with almost any drug. Individuals with asthma are more likely to experience allergic reactions to ibuprofen and other NSAIDs.
- Ibuprofen may cause ulceration of the stomach or intestine, and the ulcers may bleed. Sometimes, ulceration can occur without abdominal pain, and black, tarry stools, weakness and dizziness upon standing (postural hypotension), due to bleeding, may be the only signs of an ulcer. Therefore the person should be advised to be aware of these symptoms (Downie et al. 2007).
- Ibuprofen reduces the flow of blood to the kidneys and impairs their function. This impairment is most likely to occur in patients who already have impaired function of the kidney or congestive heart failure, and the use of ibuprofen in these patients should be cautious (BNF 2012).
- The most common side-effects from ibuprofen are rash, ringing in the ears, headaches, dizziness, drowsiness, abdominal pain, nausea, diarrhoea, constipation and heartburn. Therefore the patient should be advised about these potential problems and encouraged to read the information contained in the packaging (Barber and Robertson 2012).
- The drug does have suspected interactions. If taken with lithium (a mood stabilizer) it may lead to increased levels of lithium due to its influence on lithium excretion by the kidneys. Ibuprofen has a similar effect on an antibiotic known as gentamycin. Gentamycin levels may rise, thus increasing the risk of side-effects. Ibuprofen should also be avoided during pregnancy as no adequate studies have been completed on its safety during this period.

5   **What is the reasoning behind adding methotrexate to the drug regimen?**

A   Methotrexate belongs to a group of drugs that go under the umbrella term of DMARDs. The DMARD group includes a variety of drugs with differing chemical structures and, therefore, modes of action, such as sulfasalazine, gold compounds, penicillamine, chloroquine, methotrexate and leflunomide. The anti-rheumatoid actions of the drugs in this category were discovered mostly by accident: we know that they work but have no conclusive evidence to suggest why (NICE 2009).

DMARDs improve patients' lives by reducing the swelling and tenderness in the joints, and while some years ago this class of drugs was usually used as a last resort it is now usual to start a DMARD as soon as possible after the diagnosis has been made, in order to limit the disease as much as possible.

Methotrexate works on DNA, the genetic material within the nucleus of a cell. As with most drugs in this classification, it is not known how exactly methotrexate works in relation to rheumatoid arthritis, however, empirically, it has been shown to reduce the amount of inflammation and slow the progression of the disease process. It is usually the drug of choice as a first-line treatment following diagnosis. The drug has fewer side-effects than others in this group and, because of its favourable results, patients are more likely to be concordant.

Studies have suggested that when methotrexate is given alongside another DMARD, for example leflunomide, disease and, therefore, symptom progression is much less marked than when giving one drug only. Combination therapy may also allow for lower doses of individual drugs to be given.

6   **What side-effects might this patient anticipate as a result of taking methotrexate?**

A   Side-effects include:

- nausea;
- stomatitis;
- diarrhoea;
- fatigue;
- mild inflammation of the liver.

As the drug affects the body's ability to fight infection, the patient should be educated to report signs and symptoms, such as sore throat, shortness of breath and frequency of micturition to a health professional. Low blood cell counts are less likely with this drug than others in this group. Rare side-effects such as liver damage and lung damage may occur (BNF 2012).

7   **How would using a steroid help in controlling the symptoms of this disease?**

A   The important role of glucocorticoids is concerned with their powerful anti-inflammatory and immunosuppressive effects. They not only stop initial redness, pain, heat and swelling but also affect the healing and repair process. They have the ability to stop all types of inflammatory response whether caused by physical stimuli or inappropriate immune responses in the body.

Glucocorticoids have a direct action on the cells involved in the inflammatory response – for example, neutrophils, macrophages and fibroblasts. They also have a direct action on the chemicals responsible for inflammation itself (e.g. COX2 and histamine). If you are wondering why the body would produce such hormones in response to what is a natural part of the healing process, it is thought that the production of glucocorticoid is a homeostatic mechanism aimed at keeping in check the powerful defence systems of the body.

Whatever the reason for their production, glucocorticoids can be harnessed to help treat conditions where hypersensitivity or unwanted inflammatory processes present. This group of drugs can, therefore, be used in a range of conditions, from autoimmune disease and organ rejection following transplantation to hay fever and skin conditions. However, their ability to suppress the normal inflammatory response has consequences due to masking of infections and decreasing the potential healing properties of all tissue.

8   **What side-effects would you be monitoring for in a patient taking oral prednisolone?**

A   Side-effects are a very important issue; however, they are more likely when these drugs are given systemically rather than locally or when they are prescribed in high doses over an extended period of time. Side-effects are not normally seen when these drugs are given as replacement therapy.

- Patients on long continued treatment with glucocorticoids are obviously at risk of developing serious side-effects. As the body's blood sugar is constantly elevated, the body develops a secondary diabetic condition. Also, as sodium is retained by the body, so is water, thereby increasing blood volume and leading to a hypertensive state.
- Glucocorticoid actions of lowering the calcium plasma level lead to the body homeostatically replacing this from the bones. This in turn leads to osteoporosis and potential occurrence of fractures. The Royal College of Physicians (2002) recommends that those aged 65 or over and those with a prior fragility fracture commence bone protective therapy at the time of starting glucocorticoids.
- Glucose being formed by proteins leads to muscular weakness and, in children, can affect growth. However, this is unlikely unless the treatment is extended to six months or beyond.
- As the person's ability to fight infection is compromised, infection can go undetected. Any infection must be treated early with antibiotics and an increased dose of steroids to compensate for the body's natural response.
- A particularly problematic side-effect is the inability of wounds to heal. This can lead to extensive long-term therapies being instigated to treat traumatic injuries.
- The patient must also be educated regarding the risks of suddenly stopping their medication. If the body has stopped stimulating the adrenal cortex, it will lose its ability to make its own corticosteroids. Therefore, any sudden withdrawal will lead to a gross insufficiency and the patient may well enter what is called a steroidal crisis. Patients should be phased off their medication slowly to allow the body to recover its natural abilities. This normally takes about two months, although it may take much longer.
- All patients receiving long-term therapy are advised to carry a card stating that they are receiving steroid treatment, which must not be stopped abruptly. They should also inform their dentist of their treatment (Brunner et al. 2009).

KEY POINTS

- The major signs and symptoms of inflammation are redness, pain, swelling, heat and loss of function.
- The latex blood test is used to detect the presence of rheumatoid factor. The blood test is commonly ordered to diagnose rheumatoid arthritis.
- CRP is used mainly as a marker of inflammation. Normal concentration in healthy human serum is usually lower than 10mg/L, slightly increasing with ageing.
- Ibuprofen blocks the enzyme that makes prostaglandins (cyclo-oxygenase), resulting in lower levels.
- Ibuprofen is generally well tolerated and most people do not experience any side-effects. The most common side-effects are related to stomach irritation and include abdominal pain, indigestion and nausea.
- Methotrexate is a type of drug known as a DMARD. These drugs have the effect of dampening down the underlying disease process, rather than simply treating symptoms.
- In some patients methotrexate can cause nausea, diarrhoea, fatigue, stomatitis and mild inflammation of the liver.
- Prednisolone is a corticosteroid and belongs to the general class of medicines called 'steroids'. Steroids are used to treat a number of conditions, for example inflammation, asthma, arthritis and allergic reactions.
- Steroids lower white cell counts and antibody formation. Immunosuppression with prednisolone occurs at doses in excess of 20mg per day.

REFERENCES

Barber, P. and Robertson, D. (2012) *Essentials of Pharmacology for Nurses*, 2nd edn. Maidenhead: Open University Press.

Barrett, K.E, Barman, S.M., Boitano, S. and Brooks, H.L. (2009) *Ganong's Review of Medical Physiology*, 23rd edn. New York: McGraw-Hill.

BNF (British National Formulary) (2012) *BNF 63: March*. London: Pharmaceutical Press.

Brunner, L.S., Smeltzer, S.C., Bare, B.G., Hinkle, J.L. and Cheever, K.H. (2009) *Brunner and Suddarth's Textbook of Medical-surgical Nursing*, 12th edn. London: Lippincott Williams & Wilkins.

Downie, G., Mackenzie, J., Williams, A. and Hind, C. (2007) *Pharmacology and Medicines Management for Nurses*, 4th edn. London: Churchill Livingstone.

Higgins, C. (2007) *Understanding Laboratory Investigations: For Nurses and Health Professionals*, 2nd edn. Oxford: Blackwell.

NICE (National Institute for Health and Clinical Excellence) (2009) *Clinical Guideline 79: Rheumatoid Arthritis*. London: NICE.

Pocock, G. and Richards, C.D. (2006) *Human Physiology: The Basis of Medicine*, 3rd edn. Maidenhead: Open University Press.

Rang, H.P., Dale, M.M., Ritter, J.M., Flower, R.J. and Henderson, G. (2011) *Rang and Dale's Pharmacology*, 7th edn. Oxford: Churchill Livingstone.

Royal College of Physicians (2002) *Glucocorticoid-induced Osteoporosis: Guidlines for Prevention and Treatment.* London: Royal College of Physicians.

Sihvonen, S., Korpela, M., Mustila, A. and Mustonen, J. (2005) The predictive value of rheumatoid factor isotypes, anti-cyclic citrullinated peptide antibodies, and antineutrophil cytoplasmic antibodies for mortality in patients with rheumatoid arthritis, *Journal of Rheumatology*, 32(11): 2089–94.

Tortora, G.J. and Derrickson, B.H. (2009) *Essentials of Anatomy and Physiology*, 8th edn. Chichester: Wiley.

The person with schizophrenia
Paul Barber

CASE AIMS

After examining this case study the reader should be able to:

- Discuss why a service user's past history is important in the diagnosis of schizophrenia.
- Explain why the diagnosis of schizophrenia in immediate family could be significant.
- Describe the pathophysiological changes that are thought to be occurring in the brain of a service user with schizophrenia.
- Demonstrate an understanding of the mode of action and side-effects of haloperidol in the treatment of schizophrenia.
- Articulate what is meant by dystonic symptoms and explain how haloperidol causes these.
- Outline the role of the nurse in monitoring and caring for a person taking olanzapine.
- Discuss the relationship between weight gain, type 2 diabetes and taking olanzapine.
- Discuss the problems of concordance with medication in a service user with schizophrenia.

CASE

John P is a 25-year-old male with the diagnosis of schizophrenia. He was a healthy child, but his parents report that he was a bed-wetter and seemed slower to develop than his brothers and sisters. A maternal uncle has also been diagnosed with schizophrenia.

---

1 **Discuss why John's past history is important in his diagnosis of schizophrenia**

2 **Explain why the diagnosis of schizophrenia in John's uncle could be significant**

John had two brief hospitalizations in his late teens that were precipitated by anger at his boss, depression and voices in his head. He found the hospital stays unhelpful. He was treated with haloperidol which gave him dystonic symptoms; he was then treated with olanzapine and gained 9kg and developed diabetes mellitus. John smokes marijuana and tobacco frequently to calm himself; he also drinks vodka.

3 **What pathophysiological changes are thought to be occurring in John's brain?**

4 **What type of medicine is haloperidol and what is its mode of action?**

5 **What is meant by dystonic symptoms and why should the haloperidol cause these?**

6 **Outline the role of the nurse in monitoring and caring for a person taking olanzapine**

7 **Why should John have put on weight and developed diabetes while on olanzapine?**

John's parents support him financially. His brothers and sisters are angry with, and frightened of, him and have nothing to do with him. They are particularly upset by his lack of interest in the outside world. John lives in a boarding home and works in a sheltered workshop with difficulty. He sees a psychiatrist for 15 minutes every two months but sometimes misses his appointment. He has a social worker who he sees often. The psychiatrist would like to switch John to long-acting injectable antipsychotic treatment, but John is afraid of injections and isn't sure that he needs this medication. He usually misses his appointments with his primary care physician.

8 **Discuss the problems of concordance with medication in a service user with schizophrenia**

ANSWERS

1 **Discuss why John's past history is important in his diagnosis of schizophrenia**

A
- Information about the medical and psychiatric history of the family, details about pregnancy and early childhood, history of travel, and history of medications and substance abuse are all important. This information is helpful in ruling out other causes of psychotic symptoms. John may have had an unexceptional childhood but began to experience a noticeable change in personality and a decrease in academic, social and interpersonal functioning during mid- to late adolescence.
- In retrospect, family members may describe the person with schizophrenia as a physically clumsy and emotionally aloof child who may have been anxious and preferred to play by

himself or herself. The child may also have been late to learn to walk and may have been a bed wetter (Hyde et al. 2008).

- History-taking is especially important as, usually, one or two years pass between the onset of vague symptoms and the first visit to a psychiatrist (Ho and Andreasen 2001).

2 **Explain why the diagnosis of schizophrenia in John's uncle could be significant**

A The risk of schizophrenia is elevated in biological relatives of patients but not in adopted relatives. The risk of schizophrenia in first-degree relatives of people suffering from schizophrenia is 10%. If both parents have schizophrenia, the risk of the condition in their child is 40%. Concordance for schizophrenia is about 10% for dizygotic twins and 40–50% for monozygotic twins. The gene variants that have been so far implicated are responsible for only a small fraction of schizophrenia, and these findings have not always been replicated in different studies. The genes that have been found mostly change a gene's expression or a protein's function in a small way. Interactions with the rest of the genome and with the environment will doubtless prove to be important (Picchioni and Murray 2007).

3 **What pathophysiological changes are thought to be occurring in John's brain?**

A
- Particular attention has been paid to the function of dopamine in the causation of schizophrenia. This focus largely resulted from the accidental finding that phenothiazine drugs, which block dopamine function, could reduce psychotic symptoms. This is also supported by the fact that amphetamines, which trigger the release of dopamine, may exacerbate the psychotic symptoms in schizophrenia.
- The influential dopamine hypothesis of schizophrenia proposed that excessive activation of D_2 receptors was the cause of (the positive symptoms of) the condition. However, newer antipsychotic medication (atypical antipsychotic medication) can be just as effective, but these drugs also affect serotonin function and may have slightly less of a dopamine blocking effect (Jones and Pilowsky 2002).
- Interest has also focused on the neurotransmitter glutamate and the reduced function of the N-methyl-D-aspartate glutamate receptor in schizophrenia (Rang et al. 2011).

4 **What type of medicine is haloperidol and what is its mode of action?**

A
- Haloperidol is a typical antipsychotic medicine. It is in the butyrophenone class of antipsychotic medications and has pharmacological effects similar to the phenothiazines (BNF 2012).
- The ability of certain drugs to act on dopaminergic transmission and relieve the symptoms of psychosis was the basis of the dopamine hypothesis of schizophrenia first postulated in the 1960s. Most typical antipsychotics act at D_2 receptors (Barber and Robertson 2012).
- It may take several weeks for haloperidol to have its full effect and these drugs are associated with many side-effects.

5   **What is meant by dystonic symptoms and why should the haloperidol cause these?**

A   • Dystonia is a syndrome of spasms and sustained contractions of the muscles. These muscle movements are not under voluntary control and they result in repetitive abnormal movements of parts of the body or persistently abnormal postures.
   • Dystonia can affect virtually any single part of the body or several different areas at once.
   • Although the causes of dystonia are not fully known it is currently thought that the condition results from a malfunction in a part of the brain called the basal ganglia: structures situated deep in the brain that help to regulate voluntary and involuntary movement by controlling muscle contractions in the body. The problem may mainly lie in an area of the basal ganglia called the globus pallidus. The fault in the basal ganglia may be caused by haloperidol as it affects dopaminergic receptors (BNF 2012).

6   **Outline the role of the nurse in monitoring and caring for a person taking olanzapine**

A   The nurse's role in monitoring and caring for a person taking olanzapine should involve the following.

MONITORING WHITE BLOOD CELL COUNT

A condition called agranulocytosis (white blood cell count below 3500) can be a life-threatening side-effect of this medication, which may also suppress bone marrow and lower infection-fighting ability (Tolosa-Vilellaa et al. 2002). Therefore the nurse would advise the service user and caregiver to keep appointments for laboratory testing. They would also instruct the service user to immediately report any sore throat, signs of infection or fatigue without apparent cause.

OBSERVING FOR ADVERSE EFFECTS

Olanzapine may affect:

• blood pressure;
• heart rate;
• other autonomic functions.

Therefore the service user should be instructed to report side-effects (Karch 2008) such as:

• drowsiness;
• dizziness;
• depression;
• anxiety;
• tachycardia;
• hypotension;
• nausea/vomiting;
• excessive salivation;
• urinary frequency or urgency;
• incontinence;
• weight gain;
• muscle pain or weakness;

- rash;
- fever.

The Liverpool University Neuroleptic Side-effect Rating Scale (LUNSERS) has been developed to enable service users to report their experiences of side-effects: the 'LUNSERS may be a useful tool for systematically eliciting side-effect information from patients, and as a brief and cost-effective measure of side-effects in research studies' (Day et al. 1995: 653) (see Figure 20.1).

MONITOR EFFICACY OF THE MEDICATION

The nurse should observe for a decrease of psychotic symptoms. Decreased symptoms indicate an effective dose and type of medication. The nurse should be noticing increases or decreases of symptoms of psychosis, including hallucinations, abnormal sleep patterns, social withdrawal, delusions or paranoia. If symptoms do not decrease over a six-week period then further medical intervention may be considered.

MONITOR ALCOHOL AND ILLEGAL DRUG USE

Used concurrently, these will cause increased CNS depression. The service user may decide to use alcohol or illegal drugs as a means of coping with the symptoms of psychosis, so may stop taking the drug. It may be difficult, but the service user should be encouraged to avoid alcohol or illegal drug use. It might be advantageous to refer the person to a support group as appropriate. The service user should be encouraged to increase dietary fibre, fluids and exercise, to prevent constipation. To relieve the symptoms of a dry mouth it may be useful to suggest sucking sugar-free hard sweets or chewing gum, and taking frequent drinks of water.

The service user should be told to immediately notify the health care provider if urinary retention occurs.

OBSERVE FOR NEUROLEPTIC MALIGNANCY SYNDROME

Neuroleptic malignancy syndrome is a life-threatening neurological disorder most often caused by an adverse reaction to neuroleptic or antipsychotic medication. The nurse should observe for muscle rigidity, fever, autonomic instability and cognitive changes such as delirium, and associated with elevated **creatine phosphokinase**. Generally, removal of the antipsychotic drug treatment, along with supportive medical management, lead to a positive outcome (Strawn et al. 2007).

Figure 20.1 is set out as follows:

Liverpool University Neuroleptic Side Effect Rating Scale

Scoring LUNSERS

The scoring is as follows:

Not at all   0

Very little   1

A little   2

(*Continued overleaf*)

Quite a lot	3
Very much	4

Red herring items (numbers 3, 8, 11, 12, 25, 28, 30, 33, 42 and 45) should be scored separately as this score may indicate individuals who over score generally on the scale (a high score would be over 20 for these items).

The real neuroleptic side-effect score is the sum of the scores for the remaining items (i.e. all items excluding the red herrings).

Hence, LUNSER side-effect scores fall between:

0 – 164 female
0 – 156 male

Level of distress

There is also a column to determine the distress which a side-effect causes the individual and is scored out of 10. A score of below 3 is considered as not very distressing and a score of above 7 as being very distressing.

Patient's name	
Rater's name	
Assessment number	
Assessment date	

		NOT AT ALL	VERY LITTLE	A LITTLE	QUITE A LOT	VERY MUCH
1	Rash	☐	☐	☐	☐	☐
2	Difficulty staying awake during the day	☐	☐	☐	☐	☐
3	Runny nose	☐	☐	☐	☐	☐
4	Increased dreaming	☐	☐	☐	☐	☐
5	Headaches	☐	☐	☐	☐	☐
6	Dry mouth	☐	☐	☐	☐	☐
7	Swollen or tender chest	☐	☐	☐	☐	☐
8	Chilblains	☐	☐	☐	☐	☐
9	Difficulty in concentrating	☐	☐	☐	☐	☐
10	Constipation	☐	☐	☐	☐	☐
11	Hair loss	☐	☐	☐	☐	☐
12	Urine darker than usual	☐	☐	☐	☐	☐
13	Period pains	☐	☐	☐	☐	☐
14	Tension	☐	☐	☐	☐	☐
15	Dizziness	☐	☐	☐	☐	☐
16	Feeling sick	☐	☐	☐	☐	☐
17	Increased sex drive	☐	☐	☐	☐	☐

18	Tiredness	☐	☐	☐	☐	☐
19	Muscle stiffness	☐	☐	☐	☐	☐
20	Palpitations	☐	☐	☐	☐	☐
21	Difficulty in remembering things	☐	☐	☐	☐	☐
22	Losing weight	☐	☐	☐	☐	☐
23	Lack of emotions	☐	☐	☐	☐	☐
24	Difficulty in achieving climax	☐	☐	☐	☐	☐
25	Weak fingernails	☐	☐	☐	☐	☐
26	Depression	☐	☐	☐	☐	☐
27	Increased sweating	☐	☐	☐	☐	☐
28	Mouth ulcers	☐	☐	☐	☐	☐
29	Slowing of movements	☐	☐	☐	☐	☐
30	Greasy skin	☐	☐	☐	☐	☐
31	Sleeping too much	☐	☐	☐	☐	☐
32	Difficulty passing water	☐	☐	☐	☐	☐
33	Flushing of face	☐	☐	☐	☐	☐
34	Muscle spasms	☐	☐	☐	☐	☐
35	Sensitivity of sun	☐	☐	☐	☐	☐
36	Diarrhoea	☐	☐	☐	☐	☐
37	Over-wet or drooling mouth	☐	☐	☐	☐	☐
38	Blurred vision	☐	☐	☐	☐	☐
39	Putting on weight	☐	☐	☐	☐	☐
40	Restlessness	☐	☐	☐	☐	☐
41	Difficulty getting to sleep	☐	☐	☐	☐	☐
42	Neck muscles aching	☐	☐	☐	☐	☐
43	Shakiness	☐	☐	☐	☐	☐
44	Pins and needles	☐	☐	☐	☐	☐
45	Painful joints	☐	☐	☐	☐	☐
46	Reduced sex drive	☐	☐	☐	☐	☐
47	New or unusual skin marks	☐	☐	☐	☐	☐
48	Parts of body moving of their own accord (e.g. foot moving up and down)	☐	☐	☐	☐	☐
49	Itchy skin	☐	☐	☐	☐	☐
50	Periods less frequent	☐	☐	☐	☐	☐
51	Passing a lot of water	☐	☐	☐	☐	☐

(*Continued overleaf*)

LUNSERS SCORE SHEET

Patient's name	
Assessor's name	
Date of test	

Total LUNSERS score (all 51 questions)		**Score 0–4**
		'Not at all' 0
		'Very little' 1
		'A little' 2
		'Quite a lot' 3
		'Very much' 4
'Red herring' item score: (questions 3, 8, 11, 12, 25, 28, 30, 32, 42, 45)		Score as above (>20 high)
Total minus 'red herring' score		
(0–40 = low, 41–80 = medium, 81–100 = high, >101 = very high)		

Neuroleptics and doses (including PRNs) at the time of assessment:

1

2

3

4

Other relevant drugs and doses (e.g. anticholinergics, antidepressants, etc.):

Figure 20.1 LUNSERS

7   **Why should John have put on weight and developed diabetes while on olanzapine?**

A   Service users taking either olanzapine or risperidone show significant weight gain as compared to those taking typical phenothiazines. Several explanations have been proposed for gaining weight while taking atypical antipsychotic drugs. These medications may have an affinity for dopamine, serotonin and histamine receptors that could lead to increased eating and weight gain (Farwell et al. 2004). Weight gain is not the cause of diabetes mellitus among patients taking atypical antipsychotics but suggests that the development of diabetes is due to an independent effect of atypical antipsychotic drugs on metabolism.

In the UK, guidelines published by NICE for the treatment of schizophrenia in secondary and primary care (2009) recommend that primary and secondary care practitioners provide routine physical checks for people with schizophrenia unless the service user does not want contact with or has no GP.

8   **Discuss the problems of concordance with medication in a service user with schizophrenia**

A   One of the major clinical problems in the treatment of people with schizophrenia is partial or complete non-concordance with medication and this limits the clinical effectiveness of the prescribed drugs. Antipsychotic medication can only be effective if it is taken continuously over a sustained period of time (Kikkert et al. 2006).

LACK OF INSIGHT

The problem of non-concordance may be more prevalent among those with schizophrenia due to the nature of the condition – for example, due to a lack of insight. Non-concordance with medication is often linked to the person's level of insight into their illness and lack of insight is a frequent concomitant of psychosis. In schizophrenia, insight has been defined as an awareness of illness – an ability to recognize the symptoms as part of the illness and the need for treatment. Patients diagnosed with schizophrenia have been shown to be partially or totally lacking insight into the presence of their mental disorder and these individuals are often difficult to engage with treatment (Urquhart 2005).

HEALTH BELIEF SYSTEMS

Some patients may have their own explanations of their illnesses, such as religious or cultural beliefs which may not coincide with the western medical model of mental disorders, and this can be even more complicated if one tries directly to impose the models of insight on patients from non-western cultures. Gamble and Brennan (2006) suggest that different cultures in the UK perceive mental illness in different ways and that this can have an impact on treatment as some cultures prefer to seek help from religious leaders rather than mental health services. Alternatively, religion or spiritual beliefs in western culture can have a positive impact on concordance with medication, as religious individuals with schizophrenia have better social support compared to non-religious individuals.

STIGMA

Patients can have different levels of awareness into their illness and they may consciously or unconsciously avoid acknowledging that they are suffering from mental health problems because of their reluctance to bear the stigma of being mentally ill. The power and influence of the media with respect to mental illness has been a key issue of debate over many years as people with schizophrenia are frequently portrayed as violent and dangerous. Gamble and Brennan (2006) emphasize this point by stating that when the boxing champion Frank Bruno was admitted to hospital in 2003, one of the newspaper headlines was 'Bonkers Bruno Locked Up'. Stigma has the grave potential to cause reluctance to seek treatment and can be detrimental to the person's health as a result of stereotyping (DH 1999).

SELF-MEDICATION WITH ALCOHOL AND ILLICIT DRUGS

There is evidence that patients with schizophrenia who misuse illicit drugs and alcohol have an increased rate of re-hospitalization. The higher relapse rate in people with established schizophrenia who use substances may be partially explained by non-concordance to the medication regimen. Evidence suggests that the substance used most frequently by people with schizophrenia is cannabis (Gamble and Brennan 2006).

NEWER MEDICINES LEAD TO GREATER CONCORDANCE

It has been widely assumed that the introduction of atypical (second-generation) antipsychotics has revolutionized the management of schizophrenia and will lead to improved concordance with medication regimes for patients with this condition. However, there is an argument that despite the introduction of so-called second-generation antipsychotics, there is no significant difference in the rates of concordance.

DOCTOR–SERVICE USER RELATIONSHIP

Concordance with prescribed antipsychotics will be difficult to achieve in people with schizophrenia who are not well engaged with mental health services and who are not experiencing good therapeutic relationships with psychiatric professionals. NICE (2009) recommends that prescribing antipsychotic medications should be a joint decision by the clinician and the service user, and this discussion should be documented in the service user's notes.

KEY POINTS

- History-taking is especially important as usually one to two years pass between the onset of vague symptoms and the first visit to a psychiatrist.
- The risk of schizophrenia is elevated in biological relatives of patients but not in adopted relatives.
- Particular attention has been paid to the function of dopamine in the causation of schizophrenia.
- Antipsychotic drugs in general interfere with the functioning of several neurotransmitters and receptors, notably dopamine.

- Haloperidol is a typical antipsychotic medicine. It is in the butyrophenone class of antipsychotic medications and has pharmacological effects similar to the phenothiazines.
- Dystonia is a syndrome of spasms and sustained contractions of the muscles.
- The nurse should monitor for a range of side-effects in a patient taking clozapine and track white blood cell count, blood pressure, heart rate and other autonomic functions along with looking for signs of neuroleptic malignancy syndrome.
- Although it is difficult to know for sure, studies suggest that people taking olanzapine may be at a higher risk of developing diabetes.
- One of the major clinical problems in the treatment of people with schizophrenia is partial or complete non-concordance with medication and this limits the clinical effectiveness of the prescribed medication.

REFERENCES

Barber, P. and Robertson, D. (2012) *Essentials of Pharmacology for Nurses*, 2nd edn. Maidenhead: Open University Press.

BNF (British National Formulary) (2012) *BNF 63: March*. London: Pharmaceutical Press.

Day, J.C., Wood, G., Dewey, M. and Bentall, R. (1995) A self-rating scale for measuring neuroleptic side-effects: validation in a group of schizophrenic patients, *British Journal of Psychiatry*, 166: 650–3.

DH (Department of Health) (1999) *National Service Framework for Mental Health: Modern Standards and Service Models*. London: DH.

Farwell, W.R., Stump, T.E., Wang, J., Tafesse, E., L'Italien, G. and, Tierney, W.M. (2004) Weight gain and new onset diabetes associated with olanzapine and risperidone, *Journal of General Internal Medicine*, 19(12): 1200–5.

Gamble, C. and Brennan, G. (2006) *Working With Serious Mental Illness: A Manual for Clinical Practice*, 2nd edn. London: Baillière Tindall.

Ho, B.C. and Andreasen, N.C. (2001) Long delays in seeking treatment for schizophrenia, *Lancet*, 357(9260): 898–900.

Hyde, T.M., Deep-Soboslay, A., Iglesias, B. et al. (2008) Enuresis as a premorbid developmental marker of schizophrenia, *Brain*, 131: 2489–98.

Jones, H.M. and Pilowsky, L.S. (2002) Dopamine and antipsychotic drug action revisited, *British journal of Psychiatry*, 181: 271–5.

Karch, A.M. (2008) *Focus on Nursing Pharmacology*, 4th edn. Philadelphia, PA: Lippincott Williams & Wilkins.

Kikkert, M.J., Schene, A.H., Koeter, M.W.J. et al. (2006) Medication adherence in schizophrenia: exploring patients', carers' and professionals' views, *Schizophrenia Bulletin*, 32(4): 786–94.

NICE (National Institute for Health and Clinical Excellence) (2009) *Clinical Guideline 82: Schizophrenia Core Interventions in the Treatment and Management of Schizophrenia in Adults in Primary and Secondary Care*. London: NICE.

Picchioni, M.M. and Murray, R.M. (2007) Schizophrenia, *British Medical Journal*, 335(7610): 91–5.

Rang, H.P., Dale, M.M., Ritter, J.M., Flower, R.J. and Henderson, G. (2011) *Rang and Dale's Pharmacology*, 7th edn. Oxford: Churchill Livingstone.

Strawn, J.R., Keck, P.E. and Caroff, S.N. (2007) Neuroleptic malignant syndrome, *American Journal of Psychiatry*, 164: 870–6.

Tolosa-Vilellaa, C., Ruiz-Ripollb, A., Mari-Alfonsoa, B. and Naval-Sendraa, E. (2002) Olanzapine-induced agranulocytosis: a case report and review of the literature, *Progress in Neuro-Psychopharmacology & Biological Psychiatry*, 26: 411–14.

Urquhart, E. (2005) Challenging perceptions of long-acting injectable antipsychotic medications, *Mental Health Practice*, 8(10): 14–19.

The woman with a urinary tract infection

Joy Parkes

CASE AIMS

After examining this case study the reader should be able to:

- Briefly outline the structure and function of the urinary system.
- Describe normal urine and explain how the urinary tract is kept healthy.
- Explain what is meant by the term lower urinary tract infection and suggest the most likely cause.
- Identify the causes of recurrent urinary tract infection.
- Describe the pathophysiology leading to the common signs and symptoms of lower urinary tract infection.
- List the investigations used in the diagnosis of lower urinary tract infection.
- Articulate the usual treatment of uncomplicated lower urinary tract infection.
- Demonstrate an understanding of the mode of action and side-effects of trimethoprim and nitrofurantoin.
- Outline the health promotion activities that would help in preventing reoccurrence of lower urinary tract infection.

CASE

Bella has a history of urinary tract infection (UTI) since she was at primary school aged about 7. She recalls having feelings of pressure 'down below' and wanting to pass urine all the time, but when she tried she couldn't pass much, and it hurt. Her mother remembers taking her to the doctor who tested her urine, diagnosing a lower UTI and prescribing an antibiotic (she can't remember which one). Her symptoms disappeared quickly and she was back to normal within 24 hours.

---

1 **What is the structure and function of the urinary system?**

2 **Describe normal urine and explain how the urinary tract is kept healthy**

3 **What do you understand by a lower UTI? What is the most likely cause?**

> *Since reaching the age of 18, Bella, now sexually active although not pregnant, has had three more severe UTIs. She always experiences the same sudden symptoms described earlier. Her urine is cloudy, sometimes offensive, contains blood and tests positive for leukocytes and nitrites. On microscopy it is shown to contain bacteria. Following her last and most severe UTI, she had a cystoscopy which revealed no abnormality.*

4 What might be causing Bella's recurrent UTIs?

5 How would you account for the signs and symptoms?

6 What investigations might be considered?

> *For her recurrent severe infections Bella was prescribed trimethoprim for three days. Analgesia was also required. Episodes lasted until the antibiotics took effect, usually by the second day, when the symptoms calmed down. Bella feels that the UTI is usually gone by the fourth day. Low-dose, long-term nitrofurantoin was also considered.*

7 What is the usual treatment for uncomplicated lower UTIs?

8 Describe the mode of action of trimethoprim and nitrofurantoin

> *Bella had lapsed from adhering to the health promotion activities as a child. She drank little, preferring cola or tea to water. She also tended to hold on to her urine, only going to the toilet on waking and perhaps once or twice in the evening. Bella has now made some significant lifestyle changes and has been symptom free for a year.*

9 What health promotion activities might Bella have chosen?

ANSWERS

1 **What is the structure and function of the urinary system?**

A • The urinary (sometimes called renal) system helps maintain homeostasis by keeping normal blood constituents, including water and salts, at healthy levels.
   • It includes two kidneys (located on the posterior abdominal wall) and the urinary tract, comprising the ureters, bladder and urethra (Karch 2010). The kidneys and ureters generally refer to the *upper urinary tract*, the bladder and urethra to the *lower urinary tract*.

- The kidneys form urine by removing waste products, salts and excess fluid from the blood.
- Once formed, urine passes from each kidney into a thin tube, a ureter. Each ureter continuously squirts small amounts of urine into the bladder, for temporary storage.
- When 300 to 400ml of urine accumulate in the adult bladder, sensitive nerve fibres in the stretched bladder wall are stimulated. These send a message to the brain, telling the person the bladder needs emptying.
- The muscles in the bladder wall contract, 'pumping' urine into a single slit-shaped tube called the urethra from where it is expelled outside the body. The urethra is longer in men (18–20cm, running the extra length of the penis) than in women (4cm).
- The process of expelling urine, called micturition, usually occurs voluntarily, when convenient and in private.
- In babies and small children, a simple spinal reflex controls the passage of urine. By school age, the urinary system has reached maturity. Children normally have bladder control at age 5 (Hogston and Marjoram 2011).

2 **Describe normal urine and explain how the urinary tract is kept healthy**

A # NORMAL URINE

- Normal urine is pale (when dilute) to deep amber (when concentrated) in colour, clear, slightly aromatic and acidic (pH 6 with a range of 4.5–8). The pH can change as a result of metabolic processes or diet. Changes in colour (red) may occur after eating beetroot or rhubarb.
- The daily amount of urine produced (1000–1500ml in a healthy adult) and the amount of waste it contains is tailored to the body's needs at the time it is formed.
- The **specific gravity** varies from 1.001–1.035. Urine is more concentrated in the morning; with reduced fluid intake during sleep, hot weather and muscular exercise urine production is decreased.
- Normal urine contains little or no protein, no glucose, ketones or blood.

HEALTHY URINARY TRACT

Several physiological and immunological mechanisms keep the urinary tract healthy.

- The bladder has a thick muscular wall, lined with specialized mucus-producing cells (transitional epithelium). This allows it to stretch, recoil and form a protective coat from the acidic urine.
- Antibacterial substances in the mucous lining of the bladder eliminate many organisms, protecting against potential invading bacteria. Surviving micro-organisms tend to be washed out of the urethra.
- Reflux of urine is prevented by the one-way valve effect at the junction between the ureters and the bladder. A further sphincter is located where the bladder meets the urethra (Mulryan 2011).
- A child's elimination pattern is similar to an adult's, occurring six to eight times a day. Adequate intake of fluids (preferably water) and regular micturition 'flush' the urinary tract, keeping it healthy. This is aided by the bactericidal effect of acid urine and the presence of urea (Prosser et al. 2000).

3   What do you understand by a lower UTI? What is the most likely cause?

A   The distinction between a lower UTI and an upper UTI can often be made on the basis of the patient's symptoms; there is no specific laboratory test for the differentiation of a lower and an upper UTI (Finch et al. 2003). Typically, in a lower uncomplicated UTI there will be dysuria (pain on micturition), frequency, urgency, pain and discomfort in the lower abdomen but no fever. The urine may appear cloudy and offensive. Lower UTIs can be symptomatic, asymptomatic, sporadic or recurrent. They can present silently or with symptoms. Many cases of urethritis have no known cause – i.e. non-specific urethritis (Thomas et al. 2007).

A more complicated upper UTI may involve **loin pain**, fever, rigors (shivering similar to the shaking associated with feeling cold) and possibly confusion. Hospital treatment may be required (Ford and Roach 2010).

The most common cause of a UTI is gram negative *E. coli* bacteria from the patient's own faecal flora (Thomas et al. 2007). These originate from the bowel and settle around the urethra. They then ascend into the bladder, infecting the normally sterile urine. The 'opening' (meatus) of the urethra, the anus, and the vagina in females, are in close proximity, separated only by a moist, small, skin-covered structure called the perineum. This is often heavily colonized with *E. coli*, commensal bacteria, which, living happily in our intestines, break down foodstuffs and allow us to absorb vitamin K. They can, however, cause a UTI if they gain entry to the bladder, and cause over 80% of childhood UTIs in the community (Polnay 2003). Females are particularly susceptible to the development of UTIs due to the shortness of the urethra and the relative ease with which micro-organisms may enter the bladder via an ascending infection. Urinary stasis (when the bladder isn't emptied often enough or residual volumes of urine are left in the bladder after micturition) is a major contributory factor.

4   What might be causing Bella's recurrent UTIs?

A   The cause could be the same bacteria that caused Bella's previous episode or it could be different. *E. coli* is responsible for 85% of recurrent uncomplicated lower UTIs but other bacteria become increasingly frequent. Less commonly the cause is bacteria such as Staphylococcus (Saprophyticus in sexually active women), Proteus, Klebsiella and Enterobacteria especially in older women. Recurrent UTIs are more likely to be caused by a resistant strain of bacteria (Royal College of Physicians 2008).

Recurrent, uncomplicated lower UTIs are common in healthy, young, sexually active women. During sexual intercourse there may be trauma to the urethra which is easily irritated. Bacteria may be inoculated into the urinary tract, possibly made worse by the use of contraceptive devices such as diaphragms or spermicides.

5   How would you account for the signs and symptoms?

A   • It is not uncommon for a UTI to be asymptomatic when bacteria are present in the urine without any symptoms, but this has few consequences apart from in pregnant women.
   • **Hypersensitivity** and stimulation of the sensory nerves in the bladder mucosa occurs. This produces an urge to micturate as soon as urine enters the bladder but before it has filled,

resulting in urinary frequency with very small amounts of urine being produced (Prosser et al. 2000).

- Urine becomes more acid than normal so that even small amounts irritate the bladder's sensitive lining and urethra, producing dysuria (burning sensation on micturition).
- The urine may be cloudy because it contains pus or blood, and smell unpleasant.
- Lower abdominal pain often accompanies cystitis.
- Inflammation of the protective mucosa may also lead to blood in the urine (haematuria) which further worsens the irritability of the bladder.
- The person would have a raised white cell count as the bone marrow increases production of certain types of white blood cells (neutrophils and monocytes).

6   **What investigations might be considered?**

A Recurrent, uncomplicated lower UTIs in otherwise healthy, young, sexually active women require investigation and screening for *Chlamydia trachomatis* (HPA 2011). When a lower UTI is suspected in primary care, a dipstick urine test is carried out to guide treatment. Bella's urine contained leukocytes (pyuria, present in order to fight infection), nitrites and blood (haematuria) indicating a UTI.

Bella's urine also contained bacteria (bacteriuria). This would have been determined from a midstream specimen of urine (MSU), examined in a microbiology lab to determine the nature and sensitivity of the infection for treatment. Occasionally, it may be necessary to image the urinary tract (ultrasound) as this can eliminate abnormalities. Bella was referred to a urologist (a doctor specializing in urinary disorders) who performed a cystoscopy. Here, a rigid or flexible cystoscope is inserted through the urethra to inspect the interior surface of the lower urinary tract, a procedure also used to identify stones and fistulae and take a tissue biopsy.

7   **What is the usual treatment for uncomplicated lower UTIs?**

A The treatment for UTIs mostly consists of antimicrobials to remove bacteria from the urinary tract. Any antimicrobial therapy should be consistent with local antibiotic therapy, guided by the microbiology laboratory. Uncomplicated lower UTIs often respond to trimethoprim and nitrofurantoin, with amoxicillin or cefalexin as an alternative (BNF 2012). Drugs are also available to stop urinary tract muscle spasm, decrease urinary pain and protect the cells of the bladder from irritation. Bella is likely to have taken paracetamol for pain relief but, if this wasn't strong enough, may have been prescribed diclofenac or mefanamic (Karch 2010).

8   **Describe the mode of action of trimethoprim and nitrofurantoin**

A Although Bella can't remember which antibiotic she had when younger, it is likely to have been trimethoprim. This was first used in 1980 and is currently the first choice for lower UTIs. Amoxicillin was previously the antibiotic of choice for lower UTIs in children, however, increased rates of *E. coli* resistance have made this less acceptable.

TRIMETHOPRIM

Trimethoprim, a synthetic (man-made) antibiotic similar to the sulphonamides, is used to treat many forms of bacterial infection, but particularly infections of the urinary and respiratory tracts. It is cost effective, works well and is generally well tolerated. Trimethoprim interferes with the production of tetrahydrofolic acid, a chemical that is needed to produce proteins in bacteria and human cells.

Trimethoprim does not achieve significant levels in the bloodstream because it is primarily excreted by the kidneys, exerting its effect on bacteria in the urinary tract. Because of the ease with which the kidneys concentrate antibiotics in the urine, lower UTIs may be effectively treated using single doses of trimethoprim (600mg). More persistent infections, particularly those affecting the upper urinary tract (ureters and renal pelvis) are treated with 7–10 day courses of trimethoprim, 100mg at night or 200mg twice daily according to severity.

Trimethoprim is well absorbed by the GI system and administration may be as tablets, in suspension or by injection. Unwanted side-effects may be nausea, vomiting and GI disturbances. Itchy rashes may break out, and there may be effects on blood constituents, causing certain blood disorders. The drug can also lead to a type of anaemia due to its effects on folate. This is usually counteracted by giving the patient folic acid (Barber and Robertson 2012). Had Bella been pregnant, or had severely impaired kidney function, trimethoprim would not have been prescribed.

NITROFURANTOIN

Nitrofurantoin is a synthetic antimicrobial, available for oral use only. It is thought to damage the DNA of the bacteria. Used specifically for UTIs, it is absorbed from the gut and excreted through the kidneys very quickly. It is not as effective against as many gram negative bacteria as newer drugs but is reserved as a second-line drug (HPA 2011). Nitrofurantoin should be taken with caution as side-effects include anorexia, nausea, vomiting, diarrhoea and acute and chronic pulmonary reactions. Bella discussed taking a low dose of nitrofurantoin long term (a year), but declined and decided to examine her lifestyle instead.

9 **What health promotion activities might Bella have chosen?**

- Drink 2L (4 pints) or 8–10 glasses of plain water a day including a glass of water before sexual intercourse to allow for urinary output afterwards.
- Avoid bladder irritants such as caffeine products, alcohol, artificial sweeteners, spicy foods and carbonated drinks (remember, urine contains all the waste products filtered from the kidneys – the more these are ingested, the more waste from them there will be in the urine).
- Be aware that vigorous or frequent intercourse may contribute to UTIs.
- Make a point of going to the toilet often, and always before and after sexual intercourse to cleanse the urethra and empty the bladder. The maintenance of good personal and perineal hygiene is a must.
- Make sure she visits the toilet to pass urine as soon as she feels the urge rather than putting it off, or at least every two to three hours and always before and after sex to ensure

the bladder is empty. This prevents urinary stasis and will help maintain the sterility of the urinary tract.

- Avoid constipation.
- Ensure good hygiene and wiping techniques (from front to back), avoiding introduction of pathogens from the bowel.
- Avoid irritating soaps and bubble baths.
- Wear cotton underwear which is not too tight, allowing ventilation.
- Keep taking the medication as directed, even if the symptoms appear to have cleared up (very important) (adapted from Polnay 2003; Edelman and Mandle 2010).

Having followed the advice above, Bella also learned that drinking cranberry (or blueberry) juice might help. The use of cranberry juice for individuals with recurrent UTIs may relieve some of the symptoms. There is evidence that adherence to the urinary tract by *E. coli* can be impaired by cranberry juice (Lavender 2000; Edelman and Mandle 2010).

KEY POINTS

- UTIs are very common, particularly in females due to the shorter urethra.
- A UTI can be upper, which is more serious and even life threatening, or lower, which is restricted to the urethra and bladder.
- UTIs are usually caused by the bacteria E. coli which is a commensal of the gut but can enter the urethra via the perineum and travel upwards into the bladder where is multiplies in the urine causing a lower UTI.
- The normal flow of urine washes out micro-organisms that enter the urinary tract.
- Leukocytes and nitrites and possibly blood and protein will be present in the urine when a UTI is present.
- Recurrent infections require further investigation.
- The standard treatment for a UTI is antimicrobials. When treated promptly a lower UTI does not cause permanent damage.
- There are a range of health promotion activities which prevent the recurrence of a UTI.

REFERENCES

Barber, P. and Robertson, D. (2012) *Essentials of Pharmacology for Nurses,* 2nd edn. Maidenhead: Open University Press.

BNF (British National Formulary) (2012) *BNF 63: March.* London: Pharmaceutical Press.

Edelman, C.L. and Mandle, C.L. (2010) *Health Promotion Throughout the Life Span,* 7th edn. Oxford: Mosby Elsevier.

Finch, R., Greenwood, D., Norrby, S. and Whitley, R. (2003) *Antibiotic and Chemotherapy,* 8th edn. Oxford: Churchill Livingstone.

Ford, S. and Roach, S. (2010) *Clinical Pharmacology,* 9th edn. London: Lippincott Williams & Wilkins.

Hogston, R. and Marjoram, B. (eds) (2011) *Foundations of Nursing Practice,* 4th edn. Basingstoke: Palgrave Macmillan.

HPA (Health Protection Agency) (2011) *Diagnosis of UTI, Quick Reference Guide for Primary Care.* London: HPA.

Karch, A.M. (2010) *Focus on Nursing Pharmacology.* London: Lippincott Williams & Wilkins.

Lavender, R. (2000) Cranberry juice for UTIs, *Nursing Standard,* 96(40): 5.

Mulryan, C. (2011) Urinary tract infections, causes and management, *British Journal of Healthcare Assistants,* 5(8): 392–6.

Polnay, L. (ed.) (2003) *Community Paediatrics,* 3rd edn. Oxford: Elseiver.

Prosser, S., Worster, B., MacGregor, J., Dewar, K., Runyard, P. and Fegan, J. (2000) *Applied Pharmacology.* Oxford: Mosby Elsevier.

Royal College of Physicians (2008) *Medical Masterclass: Nephrology.* London: Royal College of Physicians.

Thomas, R., Stanley, B. and Datta, T.S. (2007) *Renal and Urinary Systems, Crash Course,* 3rd edn. Oxford: Mosby Elsevier.

Glossary

A

absorption: process by which a drug reaches the general circulation and becomes biologically available.

acetone: a type of ketone, which is a substance released when the body uses fat for energy instead of carbohydrates.

acetylcholine: chemical transmitter released by certain nerve endings.

adrenaline: hormone produced by adrenal medulla to prepare the body for fight or flight.

akinetic: loss of normal motor function, resulting in impaired muscle movement.

aldosterone: a steroid hormone. Its main role is to regulate salt and water in the body, thus having an effect on blood pressure.

alkylating agents: used in cancer treatment. They attache an alkyl group (CnH2n+1) to DNA.

amygdala: part of the limbic system, plays a key role in the processing of emotions.

anaphylaxis: a severe, potentially life-threatening, allergic reaction that can affect many of the systems of the body.

anticholinergic: a substance that blocks the neurotransmitter acetylcholine in the central and the peripheral nervous system.

antiemetic: a drug given to stop nausea and vomiting.

antimetabolites: chemicals that inhibit the use of a metabolite, which is another chemical that is part of normal metabolism.

anti-resorptive agents: reduce further bone loss and slow down disease progression.

apomorphine: a medicine which is used in treating motor fluctuations in Parkinson's disease.

arachidonic acid: substance liberated from the cell enabling the cyclo-oxygenase pathway.

ataxia: a neurological sign consisting of lack of voluntary coordination of muscle movements.

autosomal dominant: you only need to get the abnormal gene from one parent in order for you to inherit the disease.

B

B cells: one the main types of lymphocytes. B cells work chiefly by secreting substances called antibodies into the body's fluids.

basal nuclei: a collection of masses of grey matter situated within each cerebral hemisphere.

bradykinin: a potent endothelium-dependent vasodilator, causes contraction of non-vascular smooth muscle, increases vascular permeability and also is involved in the mechanism of pain.

C

cachexia: loss of weight, muscle atrophy, fatigue, weakness and significant loss of appetite in someone who is not actively trying to lose weight.

cerebral herniation: a deadly side-effect of very high intracranial pressure that occurs when a part of the brain is squeezed across structures within the skull.

chemoreceptor trigger zone: an area of the medulla that receives inputs from blood-borne drugs or hormones, and communicates with the vomiting centre.

choline: a water-soluble essential nutrient. It is usually grouped within the B-complex vitamins.

cholinesterase inhibitor: developed to improve the effectiveness of acetylcholine either by increasing the levels in the brain or by strengthening the way nerve cells respond to it.

coagulopathy: a condition in which the blood's ability to clot is impaired.

co-morbidity: a disease or condition that coexists with a primary disease but also stands on its own as a specific disease.

creatine phosphokinase: an enzyme found mainly in the heart, brain and skeletal muscle.

creatinine: a breakdown product of creatine phosphate in muscle, usually produced at a fairly constant rate by the body.

creon: a standard strength, acid-resistant pancreatic enzyme preparation.

Cushing's disease: a condition in which the pituitary gland releases too much adrenocorticotropic hormone.

cyclo-oxygenase pathway: a metabolic pathway which results in the formation of prostoglandins.

cytokines: proteins that serve as messengers between cells.

D

dopamine: neurotransmitter implicated in movement.

dysarthria: a condition that occurs when problems with the muscles that assist speech make it difficult to pronounce words.

E

efficacy: the capacity to produce an effect.

elastin: a protein in connective tissue that is elastic and allows many tissues in the body to resume their shape after stretching or contracting.

emetogenic: a substance that causes vomiting.

enterhinal cortex: part of the medial temporal lobe or hippocampal memory system.

enterovirus: a virus that enters the body through the gastrointestinal tract and thrives there, often moving on to attack the nervous system.

eosinophilia: an increase in peripheral blood eosinophilic leukocytes.

eschar: a slough or piece of dead tissue that is cast off from the surface of the skin.

F

facilitated diffusion: transportation of molecules that does not require adenosine triphosphate but does require cell membrane channel proteins, also called carrier proteins, to bring molecules across the cell membrane.

fistula: an abnormal connection between two parts inside of the body.

free radicals: atoms or groups of atoms that can cause damage when they react with important cellular components such as DNA or the cell membrane.

fulminant: any event or process that occurs suddenly and quickly, and is intense and severe to the point of lethality.

G

gamma-aminobutyric acid: neurotransmitter associated with a dampening effect on brain activity.

glutamate: the major excitatory neurotransmitter in the mammalian central nervous system.

H

half-life: time taken for a drug to lose 50% of its plasma concentration in the body.

helper T cell: a type of white blood cell that plays an important role in the immune system.

heterogeneous: consisting of dissimilar or diverse ingredients or constituents.

hippocampus: part of the limbic system. Plays an important role in long-term memory and spatial navigation.

hydrophilic: compounds that have an affinity to water and are usually charged or have polar side groups to their structure that will attract water.

hyperparathyroidism: a disorder in which the parathyroid glands in the neck produce too much parathyroid hormone.

hyperphosphorylated: occurs when a biochemical with multiple phosphorylation sites is fully saturated.

hypersensitivity: excessive, undesirable (damaging, discomfort-producing and sometimes fatal) reaction produced by the normal immune system.

hyperventilate: the state of breathing faster or deeper than normal, causing excessive expulsion of circulating carbon dioxide.

hypervigilance: an enhanced state of sensory sensitivity accompanied by an exaggerated intensity of behaviours whose purpose is to detect threats.

hypokalaemia: a lower than normal amount of potassium in the blood.

hypokinetic: pertaining to a diminished power of movement.

hyponatraemia: a metabolic condition in which there is not enough sodium (salt) in the body fluids outside the cells.

I

immunomodulatory: an agent that augments or diminishes immune responses.

inotropic: commonly used in reference to various drugs that affect the strength of contraction of the heart muscle.

isotonic: a solution that has the same tonicity as another solution with which it is compared.

J

juxtaglomerular apparatus: a microscopic structure in the kidney, which regulates the function of each nephron.

K

ketoacidosis: a potentially life-threatening complication in patients with diabetes mellitus.

L

laxative: drug given to promote defecation.

leukotrienes: a class of small molecules produced by cells in response to allergen exposure; they contribute to allergy and asthma symptoms.

loin pain: a pain commonly originating from the kidney.

M

macrophages: cells that engulf and then digest cellular debris and pathogens, either as stationary or as mobile cells.

magnetic resonance imaging: an imaging test that uses powerful magnets and radio waves to create pictures of the body.

mycoplasma: a genus of bacteria that lacks a cell wall.

N

neocortex: the top layer of the cerebral hemispheres, 2–4mm thick, made up of six layers.

neuron: a cell specialized to transmit electrical nerve impulses and so carry information from one part of the body to another.

neurotransmitters: endogenous chemicals that transmit signals from a neuron to a target cell across a synapse.

neutrophils: the most abundant type of white blood cell in mammals; they form an essential part of the innate immune system.

nucleus tractus solitarius: a brainstem nucleus on each side of the upper medulla.

nystagmus: an uncontrolled movement of the eyes.

O

oesophageal reflux: a condition in which the stomach contents (food or liquid) leak backwards from the stomach into the oesophagus.

orthopnoeic position: a body position that enables a patient to breath effectively. This is often sitting up, or bent forward with the arms supported on a table or chair arms.

osteoid: the unmineralized, organic portion of the bone matrix that forms prior to the maturation of bone tissue.

oxidants: occur naturally as part of the normal body process; however, harmful oxidants, or 'free radicals', which are forms of oxygen, can cause damage to cells.

P

parasympathetic nervous system: part of the autonomic nervous system that tends to act in opposition to the sympathetic nervous system.

Parkinsonism-hyperpyrexia syndrome: a rare but potentially fatal complication seen in Parkinson's disease.

pathophysiology: the changes of normal mechanical, physiological and biochemical functions, either caused by a disease, or resulting from an abnormal syndrome.

peak expiratory flow rate: a person's maximum speed of expiration, as measured with a peak flow meter.

peripheral neuropathy: damage to the peripheral nervous system.

petechiae: a small (1–2mm) red or purple spot on the body, caused by a minor haemorrhage (broken capillary blood vessels).

phenotype: a person's observable trait.

photophobia: a symptom of abnormal intolerance to visual perception of light.

plaque: waxy substance that builds up inside the blood vessels.

plasminogen: inactive plasma protein.

platinating agents: agents are used in the treatment of many cancers, yet can induce toxicities and resistance that limit their utility.

postural drainage: where gravity is used to help move mucus from the lungs up to the throat.

potassium: major intra-cellular cation.

precentral gyrus: the convolution of the frontal lobe of the brain that is bounded by the central sulcus and contains the motor area.

prodromal symptom: an early symptom indicating the onset of an attack or a disease.

prophylaxis: prevention of or protective treatment for disease.

prostaglandin: any member of a group of lipid compounds that are derived enzymatically from fatty acids and have important functions in the body.

proteases: a group of enzymes whose catalytic function is to hydrolyse (break down) the peptide bonds of proteins.

pulmonary hypertension: an increase in blood pressure in the pulmonary artery, pulmonary vein or pulmonary capillaries.

purpura: the appearance of red or purple discolorations on the skin that do not blanch on applying pressure.

R

regurgitation: a disorder of the heart in which the valves do not close properly when the heart pumps out blood.

reticular formation: a region in the brainstem that is involved in multiple tasks such as regulating the sleep–wake cycle and filtering incoming stimuli to discriminate irrelevant background stimuli.

Rett syndrome: a genetic disorder that affects approximately 1 in 12,000 females (it is rarely seen in boys). It causes severe physical and mental disability that begins in early childhood.

reuptake: a process by which chemicals in the brain (called neurotransmitters) are absorbed back into a transmitting neuron (brain cell).

S

septicaemia: overwhelming infection of the blood.

serosa: a smooth membrane consisting of a thin layer of cells, which secrete serous fluid, and a thin connective tissue layer.

specific gravity: a laboratory test that measures the concentration of all chemical particles in the urine.

ST segment elevation: occurs when a thrombus forms on a ruptured atheromatous plaque and occludes an epicardial coronary artery.

Stevens–Johnson syndrome: an immune-complex-mediated hypersensitivity disorder. It ranges from mild skin and mucous membrane lesions to a severe, sometimes fatal, systemic illness.

substantia nigra: a brain structure located in the mesencephalon (midbrain) that plays an important role in reward, addiction and movement.

synapse: a small gap separating neurons.

T

thrombocytopenia: reduced platelet (thrombocyte) count.

V

vacillations: movements from one side to the other; oscillations.

ventricular hypertrophy: the thickening of the ventricular walls (lower chambers) in the heart.

vesicle: small bubble within a cell.

Index

Locators shown in *italics* refer to tables and figures.